About This Book

Why This Book Is Important

Communication and Implementation: Sustaining the Practice, book six in the M&E series, discusses the importance of reporting results and sustaining the ROI Methodology within an organization. The worst situation is having program results and other data in hand and doing nothing with them. If the results are not communicated, decision makers will have no idea whether the programs have added value or whether the ROI Methodology is worth supporting.

Managers or others within an organization sometimes resist implementation of the ROI Methodology. To overcome resistance, concerns must be addressed, myths must be eliminated, and obstacles must be removed. This book examines the many ways in which these goals can be achieved.

What This Book Achieves

This book explains why and how to report ROI results and clarifies which audiences should be targeted for communication. It also explores ways to successfully implement the ROI process, gain support, and remove resistance.

How This Book Is Organized

This book describes how to report results and sustain the ROI Methodology. It begins with a brief introduction to the ROI process model and the Twelve Guiding Principles. Chapter One discusses why communication of ROI results is needed, the important principles of such communication, and how to plan the communication. How to develop the report and select the media for the report is detailed in this chapter as well. Finally, handling and analyzing the reactions to the communication are examined. Chapter Two explains how to implement the ROI Methodology; resistance to implementation must be mitigated, and the transition must be planned.

Chapter Three discusses the fundamental issues involved in gaining support for the ROI Methodology. The steps necessary to prepare the staff and remove obstacles are detailed. This chapter also covers how to select the programs for ROI evaluations, prepare the management team, and monitor progress. Chapter Four explores specific actions and best practices that can be used to ensure success with the ROI Methodology.

The Measurement and Evaluation Series

Editors

Patricia Pulliam Phillips, Ph.D.

Jack J. Phillips, Ph.D.

Introduction to the Measurement and Evaluation Series

The ROI Six Pack provides detailed information on developing ROI evaluations, implementing the ROI Methodology, and showing the value of a variety of functions and processes. With detailed examples, tools, templates, shortcuts, and checklists, this series will be a valuable reference for individuals interested in using the ROI Methodology to show the impact of their projects, programs, and processes.

The Need

Although financial ROI has been measured for over one hundred years to quantify the value of plants, equipment, and companies, the concept has only recently been applied to evaluate the impact of learning and development, human resources, technology, quality, marketing, and other support functions. In the learning and development field alone, the use of ROI has become routine in many organizations. In the past decade, hundreds of organizations have embraced the ROI process to show the impact of many different projects and programs.

Along the way, professionals and practitioners need help. They need tools, templates, and tips, along with explanations, examples, and details, to make this process work. Without this help, using the ROI Methodology to show the value of projects and

programs is difficult. In short, practitioners need shortcuts and proven techniques to minimize the resources required to use this process. Practitioners' needs have created the need for this series. This series will provide the detail necessary to make the ROI Methodology successful within an organization. For easy reference and use, the books are logically arranged to align with the steps of the ROI Methodology.

Audience

The principal audience for these books is individuals who plan to use the ROI Methodology to show the value of their projects and programs. Such individuals are specialists or managers charged with proving the value of their particular project or program. They need detailed information, know-how, and confidence.

A second audience is those who have used the ROI Methodology for some time but want a quick reference with tips and techniques to make ROI implementation more successful within their organization. This series, which explains the evaluation process in detail, will be a valuable reference set for these individuals, regardless of other ROI publications owned.

A third audience is consultants and researchers who want to know how to address specific evaluation issues. Three important challenges face individuals as they measure ROI and conduct ROI evaluations: (1) collecting post-program data, (2) isolating the effects of the program, and (3) converting data to monetary values. A book is devoted to each of these critical issues, allowing researchers and consultants to easily find details on each issue.

A fourth audience is those who are curious about the ROI Methodology and its use. The first book in this series focuses specifically on ROI, its use, and how to determine whether it is appropriate for an organization. When interest is piqued, the remaining books provide more detail.

Flow of the Books

The six books are presented in a logical sequence, mirroring the ROI process model. Book one, *ROI Fundamentals: Why and When to Measure ROI,* presents the basic ROI Methodology and makes the business case for measuring ROI as it explores the benefits and barriers to implementation. It also examines the type of organization best suited for the ROI Methodology and the best time to implement it. Planning for an ROI evaluation is also explored in this book.

Book two, *Data Collection: Planning For and Collecting All Types of Data,* details data collection by examining the different techniques, methods, and issues involved in this process, with an emphasis on collecting post-program data. It examines the different data collection methods: questionnaires, interviews, focus groups, observation, action plans, performance contracts, and monitoring records.

Book three, *Isolation of Results: Defining the Impact of the Program,* focuses on the most valuable part of the ROI Methodology and the essential step for ensuring credibility. Recognizing that factors other than the program being measured can influence results, this book shows a variety of ways in which the effects of a program can be isolated from other influences. Techniques include comparison analysis using a control group, trend line analysis and forecasting methods, and expert input from a variety of sources.

Book four, *Data Conversion: Calculating the Monetary Benefits,* covers perhaps the second toughest challenge of ROI evaluation: placing monetary value on program benefits. To calculate the ROI, data must be converted to money, and *Data Conversion* shows how this conversion has been accomplished in a variety of organizations. The good news is that standard values are available for many items. When they are not, the book shows different techniques for converting them, ranging from calculating the value from records to seeking experts and searching databases. When data cannot be

converted to money credibly and with minimum resources, they are considered intangible. This book explores the range of intangible benefits and the necessary techniques for collecting, analyzing, and recording them.

Book five, *Costs and ROI: Evaluating at the Ultimate Level*, focuses on costs and ROI. This book shows that all costs must be captured in order to create a fully loaded cost profile. All the costs must be included in order to be conservative and to give the analysis additional credibility. Next, the actual ROI calculation is presented, showing the various assumptions and issues that must be addressed when calculating the ROI. Three different calculations are presented: the benefit-cost ratio, the ROI percentage, and the payback period. The book concludes with several cautions and concerns about the use of ROI and its meaning.

Book six, *Communication and Implementation: Sustaining the Practice*, explores two important issues. The first issue is reporting the results of an evaluation. This is the final part of the ROI Methodology and is necessary to ensure that audiences have the information they need so that improvement processes can be implemented. A range of techniques is available, including face-to-face meetings, brief reports, one-page summaries, routine communications, mass-audience techniques, and electronic media. All are available for reporting evaluation results. The final part of the book focuses on how to sustain the ROI evaluation process: how to use it, keep it going, and make it work in the long term to add value to the organization and, often, to show the value of all the programs and projects within a function or department.

Terminology: Programs, Projects, Solutions

In this series the terms *program* and *project* are used to describe many processes that can be evaluated using the ROI Methodology. This is an important issue because readers may vary widely in their perspectives. Individuals involved in technology applications may

Table I.1. Terms and Applications

Term	Example
Program	Leadership development skills enhancement for senior executives
Project	A reengineering scheme for a plastics division
System	A fully interconnected network for all branches of a bank
Initiative	A faith-based effort to reduce recidivism
Policy	A new preschool plan for disadvantaged citizens
Procedure	A new scheduling arrangement for truck drivers
Event	A golf outing for customers
Meeting	A U.S. Coast Guard conference on innovations
Process	Quality sampling
People	Staff additions in the customer care center
Tool	A new means of selecting hotel staff

use the terms *system* and *technology* rather than *program* or *project*. In public policy, in contrast, the word *program* is prominent. For a professional meetings and events planner, the word *program* may not be pertinent, but in human resources, *program* is often used. Finding one term for all these situations would be difficult. Consequently, the terms *program* and *project* are used interchangeably. Table I.1 lists these and other terms that may be used in other contexts.

Features

Each book in the series takes a straightforward approach to make it understandable, practical, and useful. Checklists are provided, charts are included, templates are presented, and examples are explored. All are intended to show how the ROI Methodology works. The focus of these books is implementing the process and making it successful within an organization. The methodology is based on the work of hundreds of individuals who have made the ROI Methodology a successful evaluation process within their organizations.

About Pfeiffer

Pfeiffer serves the professional development and hands-on resource needs of training and human resource practitioners and gives them products to do their jobs better. We deliver proven ideas and solutions from experts in HR development and HR management, and we offer effective and customizable tools to improve workplace performance. From novice to seasoned professional, Pfeiffer is the source you can trust to make yourself and your organization more successful.

Essential Knowledge Pfeiffer produces insightful, practical, and comprehensive materials on topics that matter the most to training and HR professionals. Our Essential Knowledge resources translate the expertise of seasoned professionals into practical, how-to guidance on critical workplace issues and problems. These resources are supported by case studies, worksheets, and job aids and are frequently supplemented with CD-ROMs, websites, and other means of making the content easier to read, understand, and use.

Essential Tools Pfeiffer's Essential Tools resources save time and expense by offering proven, ready-to-use materials–including exercises, activities, games, instruments, and assessments–for use during a training or team-learning event. These resources are frequently offered in looseleaf or CD-ROM format to facilitate copying and customization of the material.

Pfeiffer also recognizes the remarkable power of new technologies in expanding the reach and effectiveness of training. While e-hype has often created whizbang solutions in search of a problem, we are dedicated to bringing convenience and enhancements to proven training solutions. All our e-tools comply with rigorous functionality standards. The most appropriate technology wrapped around essential content yields the perfect solution for today's on-the-go trainers and human resource professionals.

Pfeiffer
www.pfeiffer.com   *Essential resources for training and HR professionals*

Communication and Implementation

Sustaining the Practice

Jack J. Phillips, Ph.D.
Wendi Friedman Tush, M.B.A.

Pfeiffer
A Wiley Imprint
www.pfeiffer.com

Copyright © 2008 by John Wiley & Sons, Inc. All rights reserved.

Published by Pfeiffer
An Imprint of Wiley
989 Market Street, San Francisco, CA 94103-1741
www.pfeiffer.com

No part of this publication may be reproduced, stored in a retrieval system, or transmitted in any form or by any means, electronic, mechanical, photocopying, recording, scanning, or otherwise, except as permitted under Section 107 or 108 of the 1976 United States Copyright Act, without either the prior written permission of the Publisher, or authorization through payment of the appropriate per-copy fee to the Copyright Clearance Center, Inc., 222 Rosewood Drive, Danvers, MA 01923, 978-750-8400, fax 978-646-8600, or on the web at www.copyright.com. Requests to the Publisher for permission should be addressed to the Permissions Department, John Wiley & Sons, Inc., 111 River Street, Hoboken, NJ 07030, 201-748-6011, fax 201-748-6008, or online at http://www.wiley.com/go/permissions.

Limit of Liability/Disclaimer of Warranty: While the publisher and author have used their best efforts in preparing this book, they make no representations or warranties with respect to the accuracy or completeness of the contents of this book and specifically disclaim any implied warranties of merchantability or fitness for a particular purpose. No warranty may be created or extended by sales representatives or written sales materials. The advice and strategies contained herein may not be suitable for your situation. You should consult with a professional where appropriate. Neither the publisher nor author shall be liable for any loss of profit or any other commercial damages, including but not limited to special, incidental, consequential, or other damages.

Readers should be aware that Internet websites offered as citations and/or sources for further information may have changed or disappeared between the time this book was written and when it is read.

For additional copies/bulk purchases of this book in the U.S. please contact 800-274-4434.

Pfeiffer books and products are available through most bookstores. To contact Pfeiffer directly call our Customer Care Department within the U.S. at 800-274-4434, outside the U.S. at 317-572-3985, fax 317-572-4002, or visit www.pfeiffer.com.

Pfeiffer also publishes its books in a variety of electronic formats. Some content that appears in print may not be available in electronic books.

Library of Congress Cataloging-in-Publication Data

Phillips, Jack J., date.
  Communication and implementation: sustaining the
practice/Jack J. Phillips, Wendi Friedman Tush.
    p. cm.
  Includes bibliographical references and index.
  ISBN: 978-0-7879-8722-0 (pbk.)
  1. Communication in personnel management. 2. Employees—Training of.
3. Communication in management. I. Tush, Wendi Friedman, date. II. Title.
  HF5549.5.C6P53 2008
  658.3—dc22

2007046924

Production Editor: Michael Kay   Editorial Assistant: Julie Rodriguez
Editor: Matthew Davis   Manufacturing Supervisor: Becky Morgan

Printed in the United States of America

PB Printing 10 9 8 7 6 5 4 3 2 1

Contents

Acknowledgments from the Editors ... xix

Principles of the ROI Methodology ... xxi

Chapter 1: Reporting Results ... 1

The Importance of Communication ... 1
Principles of Communicating Results ... 3
    Timely Communication ... 4
    Targeted Communication ... 4
    Effective Media Selection ... 5
    Unbiased Communication ... 5
    Consistent Communication ... 5
    Testimonials from Respected Individuals ... 5
    Communication Strategy Shaped by the Audience's Opinion of the Program Team ... 6
Analysis of the Need for Communication ... 6
Communication Planning ... 9
    Communication Policies ... 9
    Communication Plan for the Entire Program ... 10
    Communication Plan for the Impact Study ... 11
Audience Selection ... 13
    Preliminary Issues ... 13
    Basis for Selecting the Audience ... 14
Development of the Information: The Impact Study ... 17
    Executive Summary ... 17

Background Information	18
Objectives	18
Evaluation Strategy or Methodology	18
Data Collection and Analysis	18
Program Costs	19
Reaction and Planned Action	19
Learning and Confidence	19
Application and Implementation	19
Business Impact	20
Return on Investment	20
Intangible Measures	20
Barriers and Enablers	20
Conclusions and Recommendations	20
Report Development	21

Selection of Communication Media — 21
- Meetings — 21
  - Staff Meetings — 23
  - Manager Meetings — 23
  - Best-Practice Meetings — 23
  - Business Update Meetings — 24
- Progress Reports — 24
- Organizational Publications and Standard Communication Tools — 25
- E-Mail and Electronic Media — 27
- Brochures — 27
- Case Studies — 28
- A Case Example — 29

Process of Communication — 30
- Providing Continual Feedback — 30
- Presenting Impact Study Data to Senior Management — 34
- Communicating with Executives and Sponsors — 38
  - Strengthen the Relationship with Executives — 38
  - Distribute Program Results — 38
  - Ask Executives to Participate in Program Review — 39

Analysis of Reactions to Communication — 39

Creating a Macro-Level Scorecard — 40
- Advantages of a Macro-Level Scorecard — 42
- Example — 42

Final Thoughts — 45

Chapter 2: Making the Transition to the ROI Methodology **47**

Overcoming Resistance to the ROI Methodology 47
   Resistance Is Always Present 49
   Implementation Is Key 49
   Consistency Is Necessary 50
   Efficiency Is Always an Issue 50
Transition Issues 50
Transition-Planning Steps 52
   Step 1: Assess Readiness 52
   Step 2: Overcome Resistance 56
   Step 3: Communicate a Vision 57
   Step 4: Manage the Transition 66
   Step 5: Establish Management Infrastructure to Support the Process 66
      Prepare Policy, Procedures, and Guidelines 75
      Structure ROI as a Learning Tool, Not a Performance Evaluation Tool 90
      Develop a Project Plan 90
      Integrate Cost-Saving Methods 93
Final Thoughts 93

Chapter 3: Building Capability and Support **101**

Fundamental Issues in Implementing the ROI Methodology 102
   Identifying a Champion 103
   Developing the ROI Leader 104
   Assigning Responsibilities 106
   Tapping into a Network 110
      The ROI Network 111
      Local Networks 111
      Internal Networks 111
   Developing Evaluation Targets for the Staff 112
   Preparing the Program Staff 114
      Involving the Staff 114
      Using ROI as a Learning Tool 115
      Addressing Objections to Implementation 116
      Teaching the Staff 117

ROI Evaluations	118
Selecting Programs for ROI Evaluation	118
Reporting Progress	121
Preparing the Management Team	121
Building an Effective Partnership Between Program Staff and Senior Management	122
Training Managers	122
Target Audience	122
Timing	123
Enlisting Support from Top Management	123
Content	124
Monitoring Progress and Communicating Results	128
Final Thoughts	128

Chapter 4: Sustaining the Use of the ROI Methodology: Keeping the Process on Track — 129

The Challenges of Sustainability	130
Stages of Implementation	131
Stage 1: Recognition	131
Stage 2: Reservation	137
Stage 3: Renewal	141
Stage 4: Integration	143
Actions That Sustain the ROI Methodology	147
Publishing Case Studies	147
Holding Annual Progress Reviews	149
Calculating the ROI on Implementation of the ROI Methodology	150
Reviewing Staff Roles	151
Establishing Mechanisms for Continuous Improvement	152
Development of Best Practices	153
Best Practice 1	161
Best Practice 2	161
Best Practice 3	162
Best Practice 4	162
Best Practice 5	163

Best Practice 6	163
Best Practice 7	163
Best Practice 8	163
Best Practice 9	164
Best Practice 10	164
Best Practice 11	165
Summary	165
Final Thoughts	167
Index	171
About the Authors	177

Acknowledgments from the Editors

From Patti

No project, regardless of its size or scope, is completed without the help and support of others. My sincere thanks go to the staff at Pfeiffer. Their support for this project has been relentless. Matt Davis has been the greatest! It is our pleasure and privilege to work with such a professional and creative group of people.

Thanks also go to my husband, Jack. His unwavering support of my work is always evident. His idea for the series was to provide readers with a practical understanding of the various components of a comprehensive measurement and evaluation process. Thank you, Jack, for another fun opportunity!

From Jack

Many thanks go to the staff who helped make this series a reality. Lori Ditoro did an excellent job of meeting a very tight deadline and delivering a quality manuscript.

Much admiration and thanks go to Patti. She is an astute observer of the ROI Methodology, having observed and learned from hundreds of presentations, consulting assignments, and engagements. In addition, she is an excellent researcher and student of the process, studying how it is developed and how it works. She has become an ROI expert in her own right. Thanks, Patti, for your many contributions. You are a great partner, friend, and spouse.

Principles of the ROI Methodology

The ROI Methodology is a step-by-step tool for evaluating any program, project, or initiative in any organization. Figure P.1 illustrates the ROI process model, which makes a potentially complicated process simple by breaking it into sequential steps. The ROI process model provides a systematic, step-by-step approach to ROI evaluations that helps keep the process manageable, allowing users to address one issue at a time. The model also emphasizes that the ROI Methodology is a logical, systematic process that flows from one step to another and provides a way for evaluators to collect and analyze six types of data.

Applying the model consistently from one program to another is essential for successful evaluation. To aid consistent application of the model, the ROI Methodology is based on twelve Guiding Principles. These principles are necessary for a credible, conservative approach to evaluation through the different levels.

1. When conducting a higher-level evaluation, collect data at lower levels.
2. When planning a higher-level evaluation, the previous level of evaluation is not required to be comprehensive.
3. When collecting and analyzing data, use only the most credible sources.

Figure P.1. The ROI Process Model

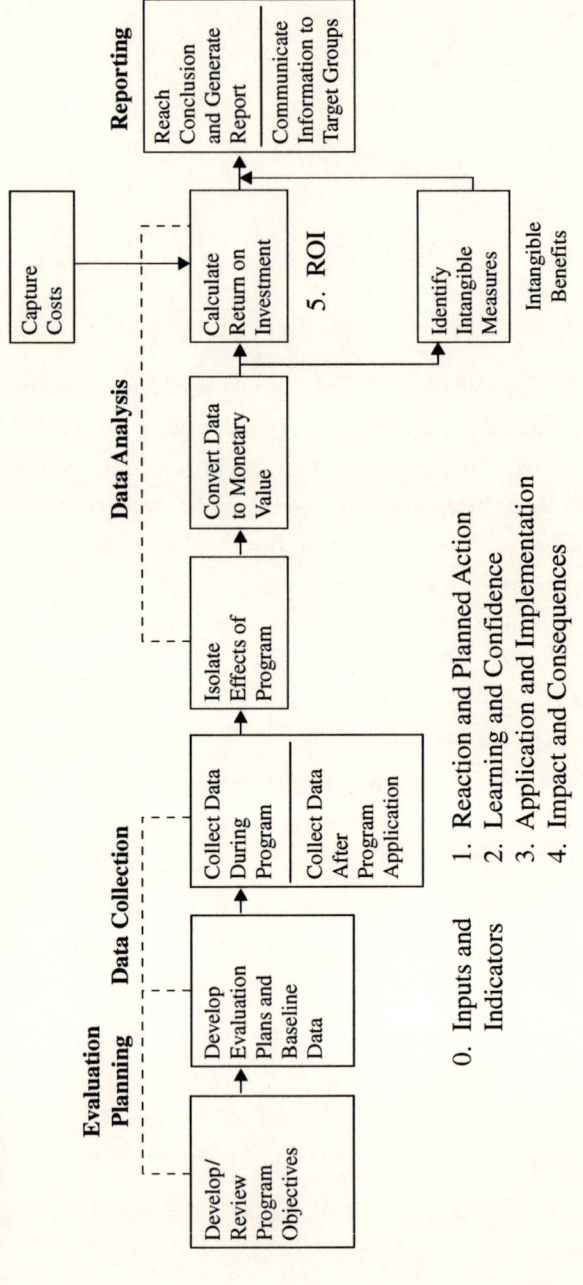

Evaluation Planning — Develop/Review Program Objectives → Develop Evaluation Plans and Baseline Data

Data Collection — Collect Data During Program / Collect Data After Program Application

→ Isolate Effects of Program

Data Analysis — Convert Data to Monetary Value → Calculate Return on Investment (5. ROI)

Capture Costs → Calculate Return on Investment

Identify Intangible Measures → Intangible Benefits

Reporting — Reach Conclusion and Generate Report / Communicate Information to Target Groups

0. Inputs and Indicators
1. Reaction and Planned Action
2. Learning and Confidence
3. Application and Implementation
4. Impact and Consequences

4. When analyzing data, select the most conservative alternative for calculations.
5. Use at least one method to isolate the effects of a project.
6. If no improvement data are available for a population or from a specific source, assume that little or no improvement has occurred.
7. Adjust estimates of improvement for potential errors of estimation.
8. Avoid use of extreme data items and unsupported claims when calculating ROI.
9. Use only the first year of annual benefits in ROI analysis of short-term solutions.
10. Fully load all costs of a solution, project, or program when analyzing ROI.
11. Intangible measures are defined as measures that are purposely not converted to monetary values.
12. Communicate the results of the ROI Methodology to all key stakeholders.

1

Reporting Results

Once the data collection and the ROI analysis are completed, the real fun begins. All the results need to be organized into a report and communicated to appropriate parties. Preparing for this final stage of the ROI process requires some thought on the following questions. Should the data be used to modify the program, change the process, show the contribution, justify new programs, gain additional support, or build goodwill? How should the data be presented, and who should present them? Where should the presentation take place? Who should hear the presentation, and who should receive a report? These and other questions are examined in this chapter. The worst course of action is to do nothing with the data. Communicating the results is as important as achieving them. This chapter explains how to present evaluation data to different audiences in both oral and written formats.

The Importance of Communication

Communicating results is a critical issue in the ROI Methodology. While it is important to communicate results to interested stakeholders after a program is complete, communication throughout the program is important as well. A regular flow of information ensures that necessary adjustments can be made and that all stakeholders are aware of the successes and issues of the program. There are at least five key reasons to be concerned about communicating results:

1. *Measurement and evaluation mean nothing without communication.* Measuring success and collecting evaluation data mean nothing unless the findings are promptly communicated to the appropriate audiences, making them aware of what is occurring and allowing them to take action if necessary. Communication is necessary so that program results can be put to use quickly and aggressively.
2. *Communication is necessary in order to make improvements.* Information is collected at different points during the program process. This allows adjustments to be made to the process along the way; however, this can happen only when the information is communicated to the appropriate audience. Therefore, the quality and timeliness of communication become critical issues when adjustments or improvements are required. Even after a program is completed, communication is necessary to make sure that the target audience fully understands the results and how the results could be used to enhance current or future programs. Communication is the key to making important adjustments at all phases of a program.
3. *Communication is needed in order to explain the contributions of a program.* Explaining the contribution of a program by means of six major types of measures can be complex. Target audiences need a thorough explanation of the results—especially business impact and ROI. The quality of a well-executed communication strategy—including the techniques, the media, and the overall process used—will determine the extent to which the audiences understand the contribution of a program. Communication must be planned and implemented with the goal of ensuring that the audiences understand the full impact of the program.

4. *Communication can be a sensitive issue.* Communication is a critical function that can cause major problems if it is mishandled. Especially when the results of a program are closely linked to the performance of others or to political issues within an organization, the communication may upset some individuals and please others. If certain individuals do not receive the information or if it is delivered inconsistently from one group to another, problems may quickly surface. It is important that the communication is properly constructed and effectively delivered to all the individuals who need the information.
5. *Different audiences need different information.* Communication must be tailored directly to the needs of different stakeholders. Planning and effort must be employed to make sure that each audience receives all the information it needs, in the proper format and at the proper time. A single report for all audiences may not be appropriate. The scope and size of the report, the media used, and even the types and levels of information included will vary significantly from one group to another. In other words, the makeup of the target audience determines which communication process is appropriate.

The preceding reasons indicate why communication is a critical issue, although its role in a program is often overlooked or underestimated. This chapter further explores this important issue and provides a variety of techniques for effective communication to any target audience.

Principles of Communicating Results

The skills required to successfully communicate program results are almost as intricate and sophisticated as those needed to obtain the results. The style is as important as the substance. Regardless of the message, audience, or medium, a few general principles apply. These general principles are important to the overall success of the communication effort and should be used as a checklist for the program team as it disseminates program results.

Timely Communication

As a rule, results should be communicated as soon as they are known. From a practical standpoint, it may be best to delay the communication until a convenient time, such as the next general management meeting or publication of the next newsletter. The timing of the communication should be consciously addressed. Is the audience ready for the results in light of other things that have happened or are currently happening? Does the audience expect the results? When is the best time to communicate in order to achieve the maximum effect on the audience? Do circumstances dictate a change in the timing of the communication?

Targeted Communication

Communication will be more effective if it is designed for a particular group. The message should be specifically tailored to the interests, needs, and expectations of the target audience.

The program results described in this chapter reflect outcomes at all levels, including the six types of data discussed in this series. Some of the data are collected early in a program and are communicated during the program. Other data are collected after implementation and communicated in a follow-up study. Thus, the program results range from early feedback in qualitative terms to ROI values in varying degrees of quantitative terms. Choices should be made up front about who needs to see the results and in how much detail.

Effective Media Selection

For particular groups, some media may be more effective than others. Face-to-face meetings may be better than special bulletins. A memo distributed exclusively to top management may be more effective than the company newsletter. The proper method of communication can help improve the effectiveness of the process.

Unbiased Communication

It is important to make sure that the communication is accurate, credible, and objective, both in fact and in appearance. Some audiences view these results with great skepticism, anticipating biased opinions. Boastful statements may turn off recipients, and as a result, most of the content is lost on them. Observable, believable facts carry far more weight than extreme or sensational claims. Although such claims may get the audience's attention, they often detract from the credibility of the results.

Consistent Communication

The timing and content of the communication should be consistent with past practices. A special communication at an unusual time may provoke suspicion. Also, if a particular group, such as top management, regularly receives communication on outcomes, it should continue receiving that communication—even if the results are not positive. If some results are omitted, it will leave the impression that only positive results are being reported.

Testimonials from Respected Individuals

Individuals' opinions are strongly influenced by other people, particularly those who are respected and trusted. Testimonials about program results from individuals who are respected by others in the organization (particularly the target audience for the communication) can positively influence the effectiveness of the message. The credibility of the individual may be related to his or her leadership ability, position, special skills, or knowledge. In contrast, a testimonial from an individual who commands little respect and has little credibility may have a negative impact on the message.

Communication Strategy Shaped by the Audience's Opinion of the Program Team

Opinions are difficult to change, and a pre-existing negative opinion of the program team may not change with a simple presentation of facts. However, communicating the facts may help strengthen the opinions held by existing supporters. It helps reinforce their position and provides a defense when they discuss the program with others. A team with a high level of credibility and respect may have an easy time communicating results. Low credibility can create problems when trying to be persuasive. Thus, the reputation of the program team should be a consideration when the overall communication strategy is being developed.

Analysis of the Need for Communication

The specific reasons for communicating program results depend on the program, the setting, and the unique needs of the sponsor. Following are the most common reasons:

- *To secure approval for a program and allocation of time and money.* The initial communication about a program presents a proposal, a projected ROI, or other data that are intended to secure approval for the program. This communication may not have much data but anticipates the data to come.

- *To gain support for a program and its objectives.* Support from a variety of groups within an organization is important to the success of a program. Often, communication is intended to build this support to allow a program to work successfully.

- *To secure agreement on issues, solutions, and resources.* As a program begins, all who are directly involved must agree on and understand the important elements and requirements of the program.

- *To build the credibility of a program or a program team.* Early in the process of developing a program, the audience should understand the approach and reputation of the program team, the techniques that it will use, and its expected products. The audience should understand the commitments that must be made by all parties as a result of the approach that has been chosen.

- *To reinforce program processes.* Key managers must support a program and reinforce the processes used in its design, development, and delivery. Some communication is designed to facilitate those processes.

- *To drive action for program improvements.* Sometimes, communication early in the process of creating a program is designed as a process improvement tool, in order to effect changes and improvements as needs are uncovered and as individuals make suggestions.

- *To prepare participants for a program.* Those most directly involved in a program, the participants, must be prepared for the learning, the application of that learning, and the responsibilities that will be required of them in order to make the program a success.

- *To improve results and obtain quality feedback in the future.* Some communication is designed to update stakeholders on the status of a program and to influence decisions, seek support, or communicate events and expectations to key stakeholders. In addition, it will enhance both the quality and quantity of information provided in the future as stakeholders see the feedback cycle in action.

- *To show the complete results of a program.* The most important communication of the program cycle occurs after data on the results of a program have been collected and analyzed. At this time, the results from all six types of measures are communicated to the appropriate individuals so that they have a full understanding of the success or shortcomings of the program.

- *To underscore the importance of measuring results.* Some individuals need to understand or be convinced of the importance of measurement and evaluation. They must be made to see the need for having important data on the measures that matter to the organization.

- *To explain the techniques used to measure results.* The program sponsor and support staff need to understand the techniques used in measuring the results; they need to know that a sound theoretical framework has been used. In some cases, the techniques may be transferred internally and used to measure the results of other programs.

- *To stimulate participants to become involved in a program.* Ideally, participants will want to be involved in the program that is being offered. Communication is designed to pique their interest in the program and inform them of its importance.

- *To stimulate interest in the department or function that produced a program.* Some communications are designed to create interest in all the products and services offered by a unit or department, based on the results of current programs.

- *To demonstrate accountability for expenditures.* All individuals involved must understand the need for accountability and the approach that the program team uses to address that need. Communicating these points helps to ensure accountability for program expenditures.

- *To market future programs.* Building a database of successful programs is important. Past successes can be used to convince others that programs can add value.

Although the preceding list is quite comprehensive, there may be other reasons for communicating program results. The specifics of each situation should be considered when the program team is developing reports to communicate program results.

Communication Planning

Planning is also a critical part of communicating the results of major programs. Planning the communication is important in order to ensure that each audience receives the proper information at the right time and that appropriate actions are taken. Three elements are important in planning the communication of program results: general communication policies, the communication plan for the entire program, and the communication plan for the impact study.

Communication Policies

Some general policies need to be developed when planning the communication of program results. Seven questions require attention as the policies are developed.

1. *What will be communicated?* The types of information that will be communicated should be detailed. The six types of data from the ROI model should be included, and the overall progress of the program should be described.
2. *When will the data be communicated?* In all communication, timing is critical. If adjustments need to be made to the program,

the information should be communicated quickly so that swift action can be taken.

3. *How will the information be communicated?* Different audiences and different organizations prefer different communication media. For example, some managers prefer written reports, others prefer face-to-face meetings, and still others want their employees to use electronic communications whenever possible.

4. *Where will the communication take place?* Some stakeholder groups prefer that communication take place close to the program sponsor; others prefer the central offices. The location can be an important issue in terms of convenience and perception.

5. *Who will communicate the information?* Will the program team, an independent consultant, or an individual from the sponsor's office communicate the information? The person communicating must have credibility so that the information will be believed and accepted.

6. *Who is the target audience?* Target audiences that should always receive information should be identified as well as others who will receive information when appropriate.

7. *What specific actions are required or desired?* In some cases, when information is presented no action is needed. In other situations, changes are desired and sometimes required.

These seven issues should frame the policy that governs communication as a whole.

Communication Plan for the Entire Program

The communication plan for a major program is usually developed when the program is approved. This plan details how specific information will be developed and communicated to various groups, and it identifies the expected actions that will be taken on the basis of the information. In addition, the plan details how the overall results will be communicated, the time frames for communication, and the appropriate groups to receive the information. The program team and the sponsor need to agree on the extent of the detail required in the communication plan. Additional information on communication planning for an entire program is provided later in this chapter.

Communication Plan for the Impact Study

A third element in communicating program results is the plan to present the results of the specific impact study. This communication occurs when a major program is completed and the detailed results are known. Two important issues to address are who should receive the results and in what form. The communication plan for the final impact study is more specialized than the plan for the entire program. Table 1.1 shows the communication plan for the impact study of a major stress reduction program. Teams had been experiencing high levels of stress; through numerous activities and behavior changes brought about by the program, stress began to diminish among the teams.

In this case, five communication pieces were developed, each for a different audience. The complete seventy-five-page report on the ROI impact study, which served as the historical document for the program, went to the sponsor, the program team, and the manager of each of the participant teams involved in the studies. The executive summary, a much smaller document, went to high-level executives. A general interest overview and summary, without the ROI calculation, went to the participants. A general interest article was developed for company publications, and a brochure was developed to highlight the success of the program. The brochure was used to market the same program internally to other teams and served as additional marketing material for the program team. The detailed communication plan for the impact study may be

Table 1.1. Communication Plan for the Impact of a Major Program

Communication Document	Communication Targets	Distribution Method
Complete report with appendixes (75 pages)	• Program sponsor • Program team • Participants' managers	Distribute and discuss in a special meeting
Executive summary (8 pages)	• Senior management in the business units • Senior corporate management	Distribute and discuss in a routine meeting
General interest overview and summary without the ROI calculation (10 pages)	• Participants	Mail with a letter
General interest article (1 page)	• All employees	Publish in a company publication
Brochure highlighting the program, objectives, and specific results	• Team leaders with an interest in the program • Prospective sponsors of future programs	Include with other marketing materials

part of the overall communication plan for the project but may be fine-tuned as the impact study develops.

These plans underscore the importance of organizing the communication strategy for a program.

Audience Selection

Not everyone in an organization needs to see or hear the results of a program. Early in the process, the audiences should be chosen and a decision made about how much information each group should receive. This section details the selection process and the criteria for selecting each audience.

Preliminary Issues

When considering an audience, ask the following questions about the members of each group:

- Are they interested in the program?
- Do they want to receive the information?
- Has someone already made a commitment to them about receiving the communication?
- Is the timing right for communicating with this audience?
- Are they familiar with the program?
- How would they prefer to receive the results?
- Do they know the program team members?
- Are they likely to find the results threatening?
- Which medium will be most convincing to this group?

For each potential target audience, three actions are needed:

1. To the greatest extent possible, the program team should know and understand the target audience.
2. The program team should find out what information is needed and why. Each group will have its own needs in relation to the information desired. Some will want detailed information, while others will want brief information. Input from others should be used to help determine what the audience needs and wants.
3. The program team should try to understand audience biases. Some audiences will tend toward a particular bias or opinion, while other audiences will represent a variety of different opinions. Some will quickly support the results, whereas others may be against them or be neutral. The staff should be empathetic and try to understand differing views. With this understanding, communications can be tailored to each group. Understanding the biases of an audience is especially critical when an audience may react negatively to the results.

Basis for Selecting the Audience

The audiences targeted to receive information on results are likely to be varied in terms of job levels and responsibilities. Determining which groups will receive a particular communication piece deserves careful thought, for problems can arise when a group receives inappropriate information or when a group is omitted altogether. A sound basis for audience selection is analysis of the reason for the communication. Table 1.2 shows common target audiences and the basis for selecting them.

Perhaps the most important audience is the sponsor—the individual or team supporting the ROI study. This individual (or group) initiates the program, reviews data, and weighs the final assessment of the effectiveness of the program.

Table 1.2. Common Target Audiences for Communication of Program Results

Reason for Communication	Target Audiences
To secure approval for a program	Sponsor, top executives
To gain support for a program	Immediate managers, team leaders
To secure agreement on the issues	Participants, team leaders
To build the credibility of a program	Top executives
To reinforce program processes	Immediate managers
To drive action for improvement	Sponsor, program team
To prepare participants for a program	Team leaders
To improve results and the quality of future feedback	Participants
To show the complete results of a program	Sponsor
To underscore the importance of measuring results	Sponsor, program team
To explain the techniques used to measure results	Sponsor, support staff
To stimulate participant involvement	Participants' team leaders
To stimulate interest in the functional unit that produced a program	Top executives
To demonstrate accountability for expenditures	All employees
To market future programs	Prospective sponsors

Another important target audience is the senior management group. This group is responsible for allocating resources to the program and needs information to help justify expenditures and gauge the effectiveness of the efforts.

Selected groups of managers (or all managers) are also important target audiences. Management's support and involvement in the process and the department's credibility are important to success. Effectively communicating program results to management can increase both support and credibility.

Communicating with the participants' team leaders or immediate managers is essential. In many cases, they must encourage the participants to implement the program. Also, they often support and reinforce the objectives of the program.

Occasionally, results are communicated in order to encourage participation in a program, especially if participation is voluntary. In such cases, potential participants are important targets for communication.

Participants need feedback on the overall success of the program effort. Some individuals may not have been as successful as others in achieving the desired results. Communicating the results puts additional pressure on participants to effectively implement the program and improve future results. For those who are already achieving excellent results, the communication will serve as a reinforcement of the program. Communicating results to participants is often overlooked; it is sometimes assumed that once the program is complete, there is no point in informing them of its success.

The program team must receive information about program results. Those who have designed, developed, facilitated, or implemented a program must be given information on its effectiveness, whether it is a small program on which the program team receives a brief update or a large program on which a complete program team needs detailed feedback. Evaluation information is necessary so that adjustments can be made if a program is not as effective as it could be.

An organization's support staff should receive detailed information about the measurement and evaluation process. This group provides support services to the program team, usually as part of the same department.

Company employees and stockholders may be less likely targets. General interest news stories may increase employee respect for a program. Goodwill and positive attitudes toward an organization may also be by-products of communicating program results. Stockholders, on the other hand, are more interested in the return on their investment.

While Table 1.2 shows the most common target audiences, there may be others within an organization. For instance, management or employees could be subdivided into different departments, divisions, or even subsidiaries of the organization that may have different reasons to be interested in program results. In a complex organization, the number of audiences can be large. At a minimum, we recommend that program results be communicated to four target audiences: the senior management group, the participants' immediate manager or team leader, the participants, and the program team.

Development of the Information: The Impact Study

The decision on the type of formal evaluation report to be prepared will depend on how much detail should be presented to the target audiences. Brief summaries of results with appropriate charts may be sufficient for some communication efforts. In other situations, particularly when significant programs with extensive funding are involved, the amount of detail in the evaluation report is more crucial. A complete and comprehensive report on the impact study may be necessary. This report can then be abridged and tailored for specific audiences and for different media. The full impact study should include the major components discussed in this section.

Executive Summary

The executive summary is a brief overview of the entire report, explaining the basis for the evaluation and the significant conclusions and recommendations. It is designed for individuals who are too busy to read a detailed report. It is usually written last but appears first in the report for easy access.

Background Information

The background information provides a general description of the program. If applicable, the needs assessment that led to implementation of the program is summarized. The program is fully described, including the events that led to the intervention. Other specific items necessary to provide a full description of the program are included. The extent of detailed information depends on the amount of information that the audience needs.

Objectives

The objectives for both the impact study and the program are outlined. Sometimes, they are the same, but they may be different. The report details the objectives of the study itself so that the reader can clearly understand the rationale for the study and how the data will be used. In addition, specific program objectives are detailed because they form the basis for collecting the different levels of data.

Evaluation Strategy or Methodology

The evaluation strategy outlines all the components that make up the total evaluation process. The specific purposes of evaluation are outlined, and the evaluation design and methodology are explained. The instruments used in data collection are described and presented as exhibits. Any unusual issues or other useful information related to the design, timing, and execution of the evaluation are also included.

Data Collection and Analysis

This section explains the methods used to collect the data. Such methods were detailed in *Data Collection,* book two of this series. The data collected are usually summarized in the report, and then the methods used to analyze the data are presented, along with any interpretations that have been made. Among other issues covered, isolation and data conversion techniques are presented in this section.

Program Costs

Program costs are presented in this section of the report. A summary of the costs, by category, is included. For example, analysis, development, implementation, and evaluation costs are recommended categories for cost presentation. The assumptions made in developing and classifying the costs are also discussed in this section.

Reaction and Planned Action

This section details the data collected from key stakeholders, particularly the participants of the program, to measure their reaction to the program and to determine what actions they planned to take following the program. Other input from the sponsor or managers may be included in order to show their reactions and their satisfaction with the program.

Learning and Confidence

This section contains a brief summary of the formal and informal methods that were used to measure learning. The results of those measurements explain how participants have learned the new processes, skills, tasks, procedures, and practices presented in the program and describe participants' confidence in their ability to use or apply this new knowledge.

Application and Implementation

This section details how the program was implemented and the success that the participants experienced in applying their new skills and knowledge. Implementation issues are addressed, including any major success or lack of success.

Business Impact

This section explains the business impact measures that were used, which represent the business needs that initially drove the program. The data from these measures show the extent to which performance changed during implementation of the program.

Return on Investment

This section shows the ROI calculation, along with the benefit-cost ratio. It compares the value to what was expected and provides an interpretation of the calculation.

Intangible Measures

This section describes the intangible measures that are directly linked to the program. Intangible measures are measures that are not converted to monetary values or included in the ROI calculation.

Barriers and Enablers

Barriers to implementation—the problems and obstacles that affect the success of the program—are detailed. In addition, enablers—factors or influences that positively affect the program—are described. Barriers and enablers provide insight into what might hinder or enhance programs in the future.

Conclusions and Recommendations

This section presents conclusions based on all the results. If appropriate, brief explanations of how each conclusion was reached are presented. A list of recommendations or changes in the program, if appropriate, is provided, along with brief explanations of each recommendation. The conclusions and recommendations must be consistent with one another and with the findings described in the previous sections of the report.

Report Development

Exhibit 1.1 shows the table of contents of a typical report on an ROI evaluation. This format represents an effective, professional way to present ROI data.

Potential trouble spots need to be observed. This document reports on the success of a group of employees; therefore, credit for the success must actually be given to the participants and their immediate managers. Their performance generated the success, and that should be made clear in the report.

Another important caution: avoid boasting about the results. Although the ROI Methodology may be an accurate and credible process, it still has some subjective issues. Huge claims of success may quickly turn off an audience and interfere with the delivery of the desired message.

A final issue concerns the structure of the report. The methodology should be clearly explained, along with any assumptions made in the analysis. The reader should be able to readily see how the values were developed and how specific steps were followed to make the process more conservative, credible, and accurate. Detailed statistical analyses should be placed in the appendixes.

Selection of Communication Media

Many options are available to communicate program results. In addition to the impact study report and macro-level scorecard (discussed later in this chapter), the most frequently used media are meetings, interim and progress reports, the organization's publications, e-mail, brochures, and case studies. Exhibit 1.2 provides a summary of the various media used to communicate results.

Meetings

Meetings are fertile ground for communicating program results. All organizations have meetings. But it is important to choose the

Exhibit 1.1. Format of an Impact Study Report

- I. Executive Summary
- II. General Information
  - Background
  - Objectives of the Study
- III. Methodology for the Impact Study
  - Evaluation Framework
  - The ROI Methodology
  - Data Collection Strategy
  - ROI Analysis Strategy
    - Isolating the Effects of the Program
    - Converting Data to Monetary Values
    - Program Costs

  This section builds credibility for the process.

- IV. Results: General Information
  - Response Profile
  - Success with Objectives
- V. Results: Reaction and Planned
  - Data Sources
  - Data Summary
  - Key Issues
- VI. Results: Learning and Confidence
  - Data Sources
  - Data Summary
  - Key Issues
- VII. Results: Application and Implementation
  - Data Sources
  - Data Summary
  - Barriers to Application
  - Enablers of Application
  - Key Issues
- VIII. Results: Business Impact
  - General Comments
  - Linkage with Business Measures
  - Key Issues
- IX. Results: ROI and Its Meaning
- X. Results: Intangible Measures

  The results from six measures: Levels 1, 2, 3, 4, 5, and intangibles tell the complete story of program success.

- XI. Conclusions and Recommendations
  - Conclusions
  - Recommendations
- XII. Appendixes

Exhibit 1.2. Options for Communicating Program Results

Meetings	Detailed Reports	Brief Reports	Electronic Reporting	Mass Publications
Executives	Impact study	Executive summary	Web site	Announcements
Managers	Case study (internal)	Slide overview	E-mail	Bulletins
Stakeholders	Case study (external)	One-page summary	Blog	Newsletters
Staff	Major articles	Brochure	Video	Brief articles

proper context for reporting results. A few examples illustrate the variety of meetings, including some that are listed in Exhibit 1.2, and indicate how program results can be worked into the format of each.

Staff Meetings

Throughout the chain of command, staff meetings are held to review progress, discuss current problems, and distribute information. These meetings can be an excellent forum for discussing the results achieved in a major program when it relates to the group's activities. Program results can be sent to executives for use in staff meetings, or a member of the program team can attend the meeting to make the presentation.

Manager Meetings

Regular meetings of frontline managers are quite common. Typically, ways to help their work units are discussed. Thus, discussion of a program and its results can be integrated into the regular meeting format.

Best-Practice Meetings

Some organizations have best-practice meetings or videoconferences in order to discuss recent successes and best practices. These present excellent opportunities to learn about methodologies (such as those addressed in programs) and to share results.

Business Update Meetings

Some organizations hold a periodic meeting for all members of management in which the CEO reviews progress and discusses plans for the coming year. A few highlights of major program results can be integrated into the CEO's speech, indicating top executive interest, commitment, and support. Results are mentioned along with operating profit, new facilities and equipment, new company acquisitions, and the coming year's sales forecast.

Progress Reports

A highly visible way to communicate results is through routine memos and progress reports. This method is usually used only for large programs. Published or disseminated via the intranet on a periodic basis, they usually have several purposes:

- To inform management about the status of a program
- To communicate periodic results achieved in a program
- To activate needed changes and improvements

A more subtle reason for progress reports may be to gain additional support and commitment from the management group and thus keep a program intact. Progress reports are produced by the program team and distributed to a select group of managers in the organization. Format and scope vary considerably. Common topics include the following:

- *Schedule of activities*. A schedule of planned steps or activities should be an integral part of this report. A brief description of the activities should also be presented.

- *Reactions from participants.* A brief summary of reaction evaluations in order to report initial success may be appropriate. Also, brief interviews with participants might be included.

- *Results.* A key focus of a progress report is the results achieved from the program. Significant results that can be documented should be presented in an easy-to-understand format. The method (or methods) of evaluation should be briefly outlined, along with the measurement data.

- *Changes in responsibilities.* Occasionally, people involved in planning, developing, implementing, or evaluating a program are reassigned, transferred, or promoted. How these changes affect responsibilities and the program must be communicated.

- *Participant spotlight.* A section that highlights a participant can focus additional attention on results. This section provides an opportunity to recognize outstanding participants who are responsible for excellent results and bring attention to unusual achievements.

While the items on the preceding list may not be suitable for every report, they represent topics that should be presented to the management group. When produced in a professional manner, progress reports can improve management support and commitment to the effort.

Organizational Publications and Standard Communication Tools

To reach a wide audience, the program team can use in-house publications. Whether a newsletter, magazine, newspaper, or electronic file, these media usually reach all employees. The information can be quite effective if communicated appropriately. The scope should be limited to general interest articles, announcements, and interviews. Following are the types of issues that should be covered in these publications.

- *Program results.* Results communicated through these media must be significant enough to arouse general interest. For example, a story with the headline "Safety Training Program Helps Produce One Million Hours Without a Lost-Time Accident" will catch the attention of many people because they may have participated in the program and can appreciate the significance of the results. Reports on the accomplishments of a small group of participants may not create interest unless the audience can relate to the accomplishments.

For many program implementations, results are achieved weeks or even months after the program is completed. Participants need reinforcement from many sources. If results are communicated to a general audience, including a participant's subordinates or peers, additional pressure to continue with the program or similar ones in the future occurs.

- *Participant recognition.* General audience communication can bring recognition to participants, particularly those who excel in some aspect of a program. When participants deliver unusual performance, public recognition can enhance their self-esteem.
- *Human interest stories.* Many human interest stories can come out of major programs. A rigorous program with

difficult requirements can provide the basis for an interesting story on participants who implement the program. In one organization, the editor of the company newsletter participated in a demanding program and wrote a stimulating article about what being a participant was like. The article gave the reader a tour of the entire program and its effectiveness in terms of the results achieved. It was an interesting and effective way to provide information about a challenging activity.

The benefits are many and the opportunities endless for a program team to use in-house publications and company-wide intranets to let others know about successful programs.

E-Mail and Electronic Media

Internal and external Web pages on the Internet, company-wide intranets, and e-mail are excellent vehicles for releasing results, promoting ideas, and informing employees and other target groups about results. E-mail, in particular, provides a virtually instantaneous method of communicating with and soliciting responses from large numbers of people.

Brochures

A brochure might be appropriate for programs that are conducted on a continuing basis and in which participants have produced excellent results. A brochure should be attractive and should present a complete description of a program, with a major section devoted to results obtained by previous participants, if available. Measurable results, reactions from participants, or direct quotes from other individuals can add spice.

Case Studies

Case studies are an effective way to communicate the results of a program; thus, it may be useful to develop a few program evaluations in a case study format. A typical case study provides background information (including the situation or events that led to the intervention), presents the techniques and strategies used to develop the study, and highlights the key issues in the program. Case studies tell an interesting story of how an evaluation was developed and the problems and concerns identified along the way.

Case studies have many additional useful applications within an organization. First, they can be used in group discussions, during which interested individuals can react to the material, offer different perspectives, and draw conclusions about approaches or techniques. Second, the case study can serve as a self-teaching guide for individuals who are trying to understand how evaluations are developed and used within the organization. Finally, case studies provide appropriate recognition for those who were involved in the evaluation. They recognize the participants who achieved the results, as well as the managers who allowed the participants to be involved in the program. The case study format has become one of the most effective ways to learn about program evaluation. Exhibit 1.3 shows the ways in which case studies can be used.

Exhibit 1.3. Uses of Case Studies

Internal Uses of Case Studies	External Publication of Case Studies
Communicate results	Provide recognition to participants
Teach others	Improve image of functional unit
Build a history	Enhance brand of department
Serve as a template	Enhance image of organization
Make an impression	

A Case Example

Methods for communicating program results can be creatively combined to fit any situation. Here is an example that uses three approaches: case study, management meeting, and brochure.

The production unit of a major manufacturing company had achieved outstanding results through the efforts of a team of two supervisors. The results consisted of improvements in key measures such as absenteeism, turnover, lost-time accidents, grievances, scrap rate, and unit hour. The unit hour was a basic measure of individual productivity.

These results had been achieved through the efforts of the supervisors in applying the basic skills that they had been taught in a supervisor program—a fact that was mentioned at the beginning of a presentation made by the supervisors at a monthly meeting for all supervisors. In a panel discussion format with a moderator, the two supervisors outlined how they had achieved their results and answered questions. The comments were published in a brochure and distributed to all supervisors through their department managers. The title of the publication was "Getting Results: A Success Story." On the inside cover, specific results were detailed, along with additional information on the supervisors. A close-up photograph of each supervisor, taken during the panel discussion, was included on this page. The next two pages presented a summary of the techniques used to secure the results. The brochure was used in staff meetings as a discussion guide in order to cover the points from the panel discussion. Top executives were also sent copies of the brochure. In addition, the discussion was videotaped and used in subsequent programs as a model of how to apply skills. The brochure was used as a handout in those sessions.

The communication effort was a success. Favorable responses were received from all levels of management. Top executives asked the human resources development department to prepare and conduct similar meetings. Other supervisors began to use more of the skills and techniques presented by the two supervisors.

Process of Communication

Perhaps the greatest challenge of communication is the actual delivery of the message. Information can be communicated in a variety of ways and in many settings, depending on the target audience and the media selected for the message. Three practices deserve additional coverage. The first is relaying feedback data throughout a program so that necessary changes can be made. The second is presenting an impact study to a senior management team, which is one of the most challenging tasks for evaluators. The third is communicating regularly with the executive management group.

Providing Continual Feedback

One of the most important reasons for collecting reaction and learning data is to provide feedback so that adjustments or changes can be made throughout a program. In most programs, data are routinely collected and quickly communicated to the groups who need to know. Table 1.3 shows a feedback action plan designed to provide information to several feedback audiences, using a variety of media.

As the plan shows, data are collected during the program at four specific time intervals and communicated to at least four audiences: participants, team leaders, program team members, and the program sponsor. Some of these feedback sessions result in identification of specific actions that need to be taken. This process becomes wide-ranging and needs to be managed in a proactive way. We recommend the following guidelines for providing feedback and managing the feedback process (Block, 2000).

- *Communicate quickly.* Whether the news is good or bad, letting individuals involved in the program have the

Table 1.3. Feedback Action Plan

Data Collection Item	Timing	Feedback Audience	Media	Timing of Feedback	Action Required
1. Pre-program survey	Beginning of the program	Participants	Meeting	1 week	None
• Climate, environment		Team leaders	Survey summary	2 weeks	None
• Issue identification		Program team	Survey summary	2 weeks	Communicate feedback
		Sponsor	Meeting	1 week	Adjust approach
2. Implementation survey	Beginning of implementation	Participants	Meeting	1 week	None
• Reaction to plans		Team leaders	Study summary	2 weeks	None
• Issue identification		Program team	Study summary	2 weeks	Communicate feedback
		Sponsor	Meeting	1 week	Adjust approach
3. Implementation reaction survey or interviews	1 month into implementation	Participants	Meeting	1 week	Comments
		Support staff	Survey summary	2 weeks	None
• Reaction to solution		Team leaders	Survey summary	2 weeks	None
• Suggested changes		Immediate managers	Study summary	2 weeks	Support changes
		Program team	Study summary	3 weeks	Support changes
		Sponsor	Meeting	3 days	Adjust approach
4. Implementation feedback questionnaire	End of implementation	Participants	Meeting	1 week	Comments
		Support staff	Study summary	2 weeks	None
• Reaction (planned action)		Team leaders	Study summary	2 weeks	None
• Barriers		Immediate managers	Study summary	2 weeks	Support changes
• Projected success		Program team	Study summary	3 weeks	Support changes
		Sponsor	Meeting	3 days	Adjust approach

information as soon as possible is important. The recommended time for providing feedback is usually a matter of days, certainly no longer than a week or two after the results are known.

- *Simplify the data.* Condense the data into a concise, understandable presentation. This is not the time for detailed explanations and analysis.

- *Examine the role of the program team and the sponsor in the feedback situation.* On the one hand, sometimes the program team is the judge, jury, prosecutor, defendant, or witness. On the other hand, sometimes the sponsor is the judge, jury, prosecutor, defendant, or witness. The respective roles of the team and sponsor, in terms of their likely reactions to the data and the actions that need to be taken, should be examined.

- *Use negative data in a constructive way.* Some of the data will show that things are not going well, and the fault may rest with the program team or the sponsor. In either case, the story basically changes from "Let's look at the success we've had" to "Now we know which areas to change."

- *Use positive data in a conservative way.* Positive data can be misleading, and if they are communicated too enthusiastically, they may create expectations beyond what may materialize later. Positive data should be presented conservatively—with constraints and qualifiers outlined in detail.

- *Choose the language of the communication carefully.* Use language that is descriptive, focused, specific, short, and simple. Avoid language that is too judgmental, general, stereotypical, lengthy, or complex.

- *Ask the sponsor for reactions to the data.* After all, the sponsor is the customer, and the sponsor's reaction is critical.

- *Ask the sponsor for recommendations.* The sponsor may have some good recommendations about what needs to be changed to keep a program on track or to get it back on track if it has derailed.

- *Use support and confrontation carefully.* These two elements are not mutually exclusive. At times, support and confrontation may be needed for the same group. The sponsor may be confronted about lack of improvement or lack of active sponsorship yet may need support on those issues. Similarly, the program team may be confronted about problem areas but may require support as well.

- *React and act on the data.* Different alternatives and possibilities should be considered in order to arrive at the adjustments and changes to be made.

- *Secure agreement from all key stakeholders.* It is essential to ensure that everyone is willing to make the adjustments and changes that seem necessary.

- *Keep the feedback process short.* Don't let it become bogged down in long, drawn-out meetings or lengthy documents. If this occurs, stakeholders will avoid the process instead of being willing to participate in the future.

Following these guidelines will help you move your program forward and provide important feedback, often ensuring that adjustments are supported and made.

Presenting Impact Study Data to Senior Management

Perhaps one of the most challenging and stressful types of communication is the presentation of an impact study to the senior management team, which often is the sponsor of a program. The challenge is convincing this highly skeptical and critical group that outstanding results have been achieved (assuming that they have). The presenter needs to address the salient points and make sure the managers understand the evaluation process. Figure 1.1 shows our approach to presenting an impact study.

Two issues in particular can create challenges. First, if the results are impressive, convincing the managers to believe the data may be difficult. At the other extreme, if the data are negative, ensuring

Figure 1.1. Presenting an Impact Study to Executive Sponsors

Purpose of the Meeting
- Create awareness and understanding of ROI.
- Build support for the ROI Methodology.
- Communicate results of the ROI study.
- Drive improvement from results.
- Cultivate effective use of the ROI Methodology.

Guidelines for Conducting the Meeting
- Do not distribute the impact study until the end of the meeting.
- Be precise and to the point.
- Avoid jargon and unfamiliar terms.
- Spend less time on the lower levels of evaluation data.
- Present the data with a strategy in mind.

Presentation Sequence
1. Describe the program and explain why it is being evaluated.
2. Present the methodology.
3. Present the input and indicators.
4. Present the reaction and learning data.
5. Present the application data.
6. List the barriers to and enablers of success.
7. Present the business impact.
8. Show the monetary value of benefits.
9. Show the costs.
10. Present the ROI.
11. Show the intangibles.
12. Review the credibility of the data.
13. Summarize the conclusions.
14. Present the recommendations.

Figure 1.2. Streamlining Communication with Executives

First 2 ROI Studies	Detailed Study	Meeting
3–5 ROI Studies	Executive Summary	No Meeting
6 ROI Studies or More	One-Page Summary	No Meeting

that the managers don't overreact to the negative results and look for someone to blame can be a challenge.

The following guidelines can help you ensure that your presentation is planned and executed properly.

- Plan a face-to-face meeting with senior team members for the first one or two major impact studies, as shown in Figure 1.2. If the audience is unfamiliar with the ROI Methodology, a face-to-face meeting is necessary to make sure that they understand the process. The good news is that they will probably attend the meeting because they have not seen ROI data developed for programs or projects before. The bad news is that it takes a lot of time, usually an hour, for this presentation.

- After a group has had a face-to-face meeting for a couple of presentations, an executive summary may be all that is necessary for the next three to five studies. At this point, they understand the process, so a shortened version may be appropriate.

- After the target audience is familiar with the process, an even briefer version may be all that is needed; perhaps you can use a one- to two-page summary with charts or graphs showing all six types of measures. Exhibit 1.4 shows a one-page summary.

- During the initial face-to-face presentation, the results of the evaluation should not be distributed until the end of the session. This will allow the presenter to explain the evaluation process and obtain reactions to it before the target audience sees the actual ROI number.

- Present the process step by step, showing how the data were collected, when they were collected, who provided the data, how the data were isolated from other influences, and how they were converted to monetary values. Any assumptions, adjustments, and conservative approaches should be presented. Fully loaded costs should be presented so that the target audience will begin to buy into the process of developing the ROI.

- When the data are presented, the results should be presented step by step, beginning with Level 1, moving through Level 5, and ending with the intangibles. This sequence allows the audience to see the chain of impact from reaction and planned action to learning and confidence, application and implementation, business impact, and ROI. After some discussion of the meaning of the ROI, the intangible measures should be presented. Allocate time to each level as appropriate for the audience. This progression will help overcome potential negative reactions to a very positive or negative ROI.

- Show the consequences of additional accuracy, if it is an issue. The trade-off for more accuracy and validity is often more expense. Address this issue whenever necessary, agreeing to add more data if required.

Exhibit 1.4. Sample Streamlined Report

ROI Impact Study

Program Title: Preventing Sexual Harassment at Healthcare, Inc.
Target Audience: First- and second-level managers (655); secondary audience: all employees, through group meetings (6,844)
Duration: 1 day; 17 sessions
Techniques for Isolating the Effects of the Program: Trend line analysis; participant estimation
Techniques for Converting Data to Monetary Values: Historical costs; internal experts
Fully Loaded Program Costs: $277,987

Results

Level 1: Reaction	Level 2: Learning	Level 3: Application	Level 4: Impact	Level 5: ROI	Intangible Benefits
• 93% provided action items	• 65% increase in scores from pretest to posttest • Skill practice demonstration	• 96% conducted meetings and completed meeting record • 4.1 out of 5 overall average on behavior change survey • 68% report all action items complete • 92% report some action items complete	• Turnover reduction: $2,840,632 • Complaint reduction: $360,276 • Total improvement: $3,200,908	• 1,051%	• Job satisfaction • Reduced absenteeism • Stress reduction • Better recruiting

- Collect concerns, reactions, and issues with the process, and then make appropriate adjustments for the next presentation.

These steps will help you prepare and present your impact study, which is a critical step in the ROI Methodology.

Communicating with Executives and Sponsors

When you are communicating results, no group is more important than the top executives. In many situations, this group is also the sponsor. Improving communication with them requires developing an overall strategy, which may include some or all of the actions outlined in this section.

Strengthen the Relationship with Executives

An informal and productive relationship should be established between the manager responsible for the program evaluation and the top executive at the location where the program is being implemented. Each should feel comfortable with discussing needs and program results. One approach is to hold frequent informal meetings with the executive in order to review problems with current programs and discuss other performance problems or opportunities within the organization. Frank and open discussions may provide the executive with insight that is not available from any other source. Such discussions may also be very helpful to the program manager in determining the direction of the program.

Distribute Program Results

When a program has achieved significant results, inform the appropriate top executives by sending them a brief memo or summary outlining what the program was supposed to accomplish, when it was implemented, who was involved, and the results that were achieved. Use a for-your-information format that consists of facts rather than opinions. Keep it brief; a full report may be presented later. All significant communications on evaluation programs, plans, activities, and results should include the executive group. Frequent information on programs, as long as it is not boastful, can reinforce credibility and highlight accomplishments.

Ask Executives to Participate in Program Review

An effective way to increase commitment from top executives is to ask one or more of them to serve on a program review committee. A review committee provides input and advice to the program staff on a variety of issues, including needs, problems with current programs, and program evaluation issues. A program committee can be helpful in letting executives know about what programs are achieving.

Analysis of Reactions to Communication

The best indicator of how effectively the results of a program have been communicated is the level of commitment and support from the management group. Allocation of requested resources and strong commitment from top management are tangible evidence that management's perception of the results is positive. In addition to observing this macro-level reaction, the program team can use a few techniques to measure the effectiveness of its communication efforts.

Whenever results are communicated, the target audiences' reactions can be monitored. Their reactions may include nonverbal gestures, oral remarks, written comments, or indirect actions that reveal how the communication was received. Usually, when results are presented during a meeting, the presenter will have some indication of how the results were received by the group. The interest and attitudes of the audience can usually be quickly evaluated.

During the presentation, questions may be asked or, in some cases, the information may be challenged. A tabulation of these challenges and questions can be useful when the program team is evaluating the type of information to include in future communications. When positive comments about the results are made, formally or informally, they should also be noted and tabulated.

Staff meetings are an excellent arena for discussing the reaction to communications of results. Comments can come from many sources, depending on the target audience. Input from different members of the staff can be summarized to help judge the overall effectiveness of communications.

When major program results are communicated, a feedback questionnaire may be distributed to the audience or a sample of the audience. The purpose of this questionnaire is to determine the extent to which the audience understood or believed the information presented. Such a survey is practical only when the effectiveness of the communication will have a significant impact on future programs or actions.

Another approach is to survey the management group in order to determine its perceptions of the program results. Specific questions should be asked about the results. What does the management group know about the results? How believable are the results? What additional information is desired about the program? This type of survey can provide guidance for tailoring future communications.

The purpose of analyzing reactions is to make adjustments in the communication process—if adjustments are necessary. Although analyzing the reactions may involve intuitive assessments, a more sophisticated analysis will provide more accurate information, so that better adjustments can be made. The net result should be a more effective communication process.

Creating a Macro-Level Scorecard

In the last decade, organizations have shown growing interest in building a scorecard of the contributions of all programs within a function or organization. Sometimes, this is referred to as the *balanced scorecard* (Kaplan and Norton, 1996). A balanced scorecard includes data that represent a macro view and are balanced between qualitative and quantitative, customer and noncustomer, and financial and nonfinancial. Essentially, a scorecard is a group of measures that are important to the management team, and the management team takes action when the measures indicate a problem. Scorecards are a way to report the overall results of all programs within a function or all programs directed at a particular audience of executives and senior management.

Using the ROI Methodology, evaluations can be taken all the way to Level 5 (ROI), generating a scorecard of performance with seven types of data (including intangibles) for a program or project. A program scorecard is a micro-level scorecard (see Figure 1.3). To create a macro-level scorecard, micro-level scorecards are developed for all programs within a function or organization; every program usually has Level 0 (Inputs and Indicators) data and Level 1 (Reaction and Planned Action) data. Then, the micro-level evaluation data that were collected for each program are integrated into a macro-level scorecard, as illustrated in Figure 1.3. However, to keep the process effective and meaningful, only a few measures collected at Levels 0, 1, and 2 and data important to the management

Figure 1.3. Creating a Macro-Level Scorecard

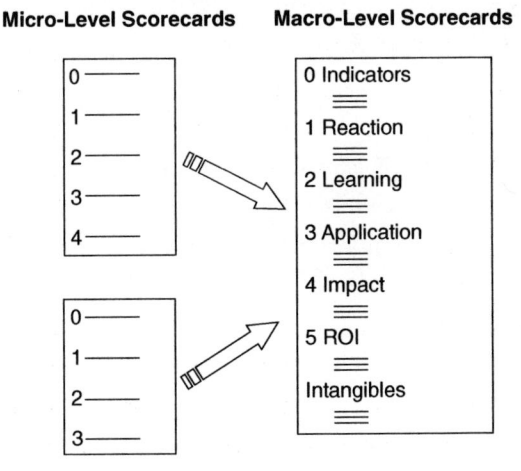

Micro-Level Scorecards → Macro-Level Scorecards

Micro-Level Scorecards contain levels 0, 1, 2, 3, 4 and separately 0, 1, 2, 3.

Macro-Level Scorecards:
- 0 Indicators
- 1 Reaction
- 2 Learning
- 3 Application
- 4 Impact
- 5 ROI
- Intangibles

team are used at the macro level. For example, if a typical reaction questionnaire contains fifteen or twenty items, only four or five critical measures that are meaningful to the management group are chosen for each program. These critical measures are integrated into the macro-level scorecard. As each program is evaluated, measures are added to the overall scorecard.

Advantages of a Macro-Level Scorecard

A macro-level scorecard has several advantages. First, it provides a high-level view of a process or organizational function. For example, a macro-level scorecard for learning and development offers an overview of the activities, results, and contributions of the whole functional unit. Second, a macro-level scorecard provides a brief report on how the department is performing without the audience having to review detailed studies. Most executives prefer this type of report so they can have a bird's-eye view of how things are going overall. It is important to remember, however, that reviews of impact studies—or summaries of impact studies—of major programs and projects are also important. A simple scorecard won't do the trick in those cases.

Because some of the macro-level measures are linked to the business, a macro-level scorecard shows how programs connect to business objectives. A macro-level scorecard also provides a balanced perspective, offering activity, perception, qualitative, quantitative, application, and financial contribution measures. When used properly, this type of scorecard can indicate the alignment between an organization and a function. Thus, the macro-level scorecard can be an important tool for reporting results.

Example

Exhibit 1.5 shows a macro-level scorecard for a corporate university. In this example, thirty measures were collected, reflecting seven

Exhibit 1.5. An Example of a Corporate University Scorecard

First University
- 0. Indicators
    1. Number of Employees Involved
    2. Total Hours of Involvement
    3. Hours per Employee
    4. Training Investment as a Percentage of Payroll
    5. Cost per Participant
- I. Reaction and Planned Action
    1. Percentage of Programs Evaluated at This Level
    2. Ratings on Seven Items Versus Targets
    3. Percentage with Action Plans
    4. Percentage with ROI Forecast
- II. Learning
    1. Percentage of Programs Evaluated at This Level
    2. Types of Measurements
    3. Self-Assessment Ratings on Three Items Versus Targets
    4. Average Differences Between Pretest and Posttest Scores
- III. Application
    1. Percentage of Programs Evaluated at This Level
    2. Ratings on Three Items Versus Targets
    3. Percentage of Action Plans Completed
    4. Barriers (List of Top Ten)
    5. Enablers (List of Top Ten)
    6. Management Support Profile
- IV. Business Impact
    1. Percentage of Programs Evaluated at This Level
    2. Linkage with Measures (List of Top Ten)
    3. Types of Measurement Techniques
    4. Types of Methods to Isolate the Effects of Programs
    5. Investment Perception
- V. ROI
    1. Percentage of Programs Evaluated at This Level
    2. ROI Summary for Each Study
    3. Methods of Converting Data to Monetary Values
    4. Fully Loaded Cost per Participant

    Intangibles
    1. List of Intangibles (Top Ten)
    2. How Intangibles Were Captured

levels of data: the six levels described in this series of books plus intangibles. Some of these measures need additional explanation. For example, at Level 1 (Reaction and Planned Action), for item 2, Ratings on Seven Items Versus Targets, seven specific measures were collected in every program. In practice, this firm used several Level 1 instruments (consisting of seven to twenty-one items). However, the seven measures on the macro scorecard were collected for every program. The seven measures included items such as relevance, importance, usefulness, and the amount of new material.

At Level 2 (Learning), self-assessments were administered to determine the participants' assessment of the learning that had taken place. The three metrics in item 3, Self-Assessment Ratings, involved the following items: "the extent to which I have learned the objectives of the program," "the extent to which I have learned all the materials presented during the program," and "the extent to which I have learned the skills and knowledge taught in the program." These measures can be taken for each program and integrated into the macro-level scorecard. When these data were collected each time, Level 2 measures were captured 100 percent of the time (item 1). In practice, some Level 2 measurements were much more detailed. There were objective tests, simulations, skill practices, and a variety of other measurement processes. The data from these detailed measurements were used to make adjustments in each program's design, development, and delivery; however, it would be difficult to integrate such detailed data into a macro-level scorecard. Therefore, some measurements were taken only for use in making adjustments in the program at the micro level, while other measurements were integrated into the macro-level scorecard.

Level 3 (Application) represents a rich source of data. Item 2, Ratings on Three Items Versus Targets, reflects the extent to which participants used the material, their success in the use of the material, and the frequency of use of the material. These three items can be collected in any type of program and therefore were collected as part of the follow-up process for all programs at this corporate university, then integrated into the macro-level scorecard. The top ten barriers and the top ten enablers were taken directly from participants' forced-choice responses, providing evaluators with important information about which overall factors are helping and which are inhibiting success.

At Level 4 (Business Impact), item 2 requires explanation. As part of the follow-up evaluation for each program, the measures that matter to the organization were listed, and participants were given an opportunity to indicate the extent to which the program influenced each measure. Some integration rules were used on the data in order to determine the top ten measures that were influenced by the programs during a particular time frame. When these data were compared with the management team's priorities for the measures, the relationship between the programs and the overall business objectives was revealed.

At Level 5 (ROI) the data integration into the scorecard is relatively straightforward. ROIs on those programs evaluated to this level are reported. Methods for data conversion are listed and the fully loaded costs per participant. To complete the scorecard, intangible benefits are also listed. Additional information on developing a macro-level scorecard can be found at www.roiinstitute.net.

Final Thoughts

This chapter presents the final step in the ROI Methodology: communicating program results. Communicating results is a crucial step in the evaluation process. If this step is not taken seriously, the full impact of the results will not be realized.

This chapter covers some general principles for communicating program results and provides a framework of seven issues that should be addressed in any significant communication effort. Target audiences are discussed; the executive group is emphasized because it is the most important audience. A recommended format for a detailed evaluation report is provided. The chapter also presents details on the most commonly used media for communicating program results, including meetings, publications, electronic media, and macro-level scorecards.

References

Block, P. *Flawless Consulting.* (2nd ed.) San Francisco: Pfeiffer, 2000.

Kaplan, R., and Norton, D. *The Balanced Scorecard: Translating Strategy into Action.* Boston: Harvard Business School Press, 1996.

2

Making the Transition to the ROI Methodology

The best-designed methodology is still worthless if it is not integrated efficiently and effectively within an organization for which it was intended. Although the ROI Methodology presented in this series of books is a step-by-step, methodical, and simple procedure, in order for it to be applied successfully, it must be broadly incorporated and fully accepted and supported by those who must make it work. This chapter focuses on the critical issues involved in making the transition from an activity-based approach to a results-based approach through a comprehensive measurement and evaluation process.

Overcoming Resistance to the ROI Methodology

Any new process or change engenders resistance. Resistance appears in many ways: negative comments, inappropriate actions, or dysfunctional behaviors. Exhibit 2.1 lists some comments that might reflect open resistance to the ROI Methodology among staff members. Each comment represents an issue that must be resolved or addressed. A few of the comments are based on real barriers, while others are based on myths that must be dispelled. Sometimes, resistance to ROI reflects underlying concerns. The individuals involved may fear losing control. Others may feel that they could be vulnerable to actions that might be taken in response to unsuccessful

Exhibit 2.1. Typical Objections to the ROI Methodology

- This costs too much.
- This takes too much time.
- Who is asking for this?
- This is not listed in my job duties.
- I did not have input on this.
- I do not understand this.
- Is this a credible process?
- What happens when the results are negative?
- How will the data be used?
- How can we be consistent with this?
- The ROI process seems too subjective.
- Our managers will not support this.
- ROI is too narrowly focused.
- This is not practical.
- Who is responsible for this?

programs. Still others may be concerned about any process that requires additional learning and actions.

Members of all the major target audiences addressed in this book may resist the use of the ROI Methodology. Resistance may appear among the program staff, and they may make comments similar to those listed in Exhibit 2.1. Heavy persuasion and evidence of tangible benefits may be needed to convince individuals that the ROI Methodology should be implemented because it is in their best interest.

Another key player, the sponsor, may also resist. Although most sponsors want to see the results of an ROI evaluation, they may have concerns about the quality or accuracy of data. In addition, they may be concerned about the time commitments and the costs involved in conducting an ROI study.

The managers of participants in programs make up another group that may develop resistance. Managers may have concerns about the information they will be asked to provide and about how their performance will be judged along with that of the participants. They may express some of the fears listed in Exhibit 2.1.

The challenge is implementing the ROI Methodology methodically and consistently so that it becomes a routine and standard process that is built into the programs of an organization. Implementation of the ROI Methodology needs to include a detailed plan for overcoming the resistance to the process, for several reasons.

Resistance Is Always Present

There is always resistance to change. Sometimes there are good reasons for resistance, but often it exists for the wrong reasons. The important point is to sort out both types of resistance. When legitimate barriers are the basis for resistance, try to minimize them or remove them altogether.

Implementation Is Key

In any process, effective implementation is the key to its success. Implementation is successful when the new technique or tool is integrated into the routine framework of the function or organization. Without effective implementation, even the best process will fail. A process that is never removed from the shelf will never be understood, supported, or improved. A comprehensive implementation process with clear steps for overcoming resistance must be developed.

Consistency Is Necessary

As the ROI Methodology is implemented, consistency from one program evaluation to another is a critical consideration. With consistency come accuracy and reliability. The only way to ensure consistency is to follow clearly defined processes and procedures each time an ROI evaluation is conducted. Proper implementation will ensure that consistency occurs. Consistency can melt resistance.

Efficiency Is Always an Issue

Cost control and efficiency will always be an issue in any major undertaking, and using the ROI Methodology is no exception. The implementation process must ensure that tasks are completed efficiently as well as effectively, so that the costs associated with the process are kept to a minimum, time is used appropriately, and the process remains affordable.

The implementation process that is necessary to overcome resistance covers many areas. Figure 2.1 shows the actions outlined in this book that are the building blocks in overcoming resistance. They are all necessary, and together they form the base or framework for dispelling myths and removing or minimizing barriers. The remainder of this chapter presents specific strategies and techniques for performing each of the actions identified in Figure 2.1.

Transition Issues

After a decision has been made to introduce the ROI Methodology, it is important to review the resource issues that may arise from the changes and consider how to address them. Individuals frequently have different views on whether a change is needed, what drives it, and how much impact it will have. No one in an organization will support a results-based change effort without some understanding of

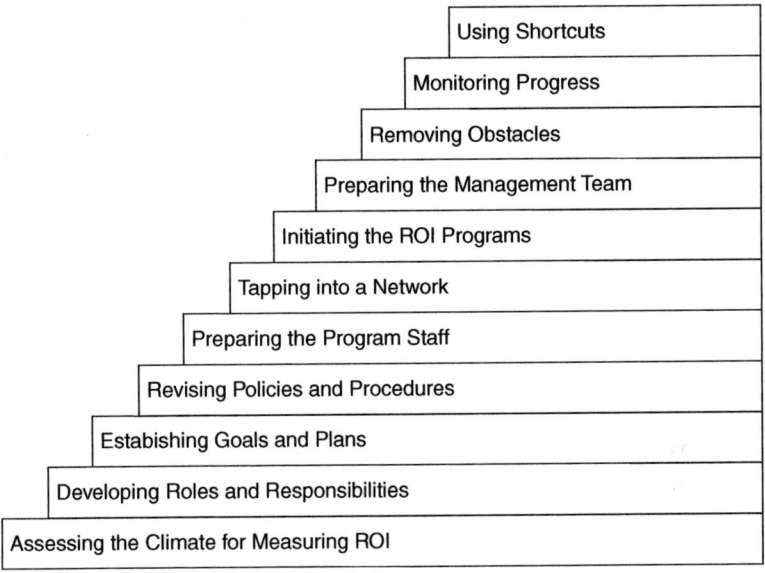

Figure 2.1. A Transition Plan: Building Blocks for Overcoming Resistance

- Using Shortcuts
- Monitoring Progress
- Removing Obstacles
- Preparing the Management Team
- Initiating the ROI Programs
- Tapping into a Network
- Preparing the Program Staff
- Revising Policies and Procedures
- Estabishing Goals and Plans
- Developing Roles and Responsibilities
- Assessing the Climate for Measuring ROI

why the change is needed and what benefits it may produce. Implementing the ROI Methodology requires significant commitment, knowledge, and support across *all* organizational levels. Unless the purposes and desired outcomes are clear, it is unrealistic to expect others to invest time and effort in the process.

Recognizing long-term implementation of the ROI Methodology as a change effort is critical to addressing the transition challenges. Most executives, managers, or employees think of major organizational change in terms of reengineering, restructuring, or culture change. For the purposes of this book, change is the fundamental shift from an old state (activity-based measurement and evaluation) to another, transformed state (results-based measurement and evaluation). This shift will encompass reengineering the function or organization; restructuring policy, procedures, and practices; and influencing organizational culture in regard to the value of the organizational function and the role that executives,

Figure 2.2. Steps in Planning a Transition

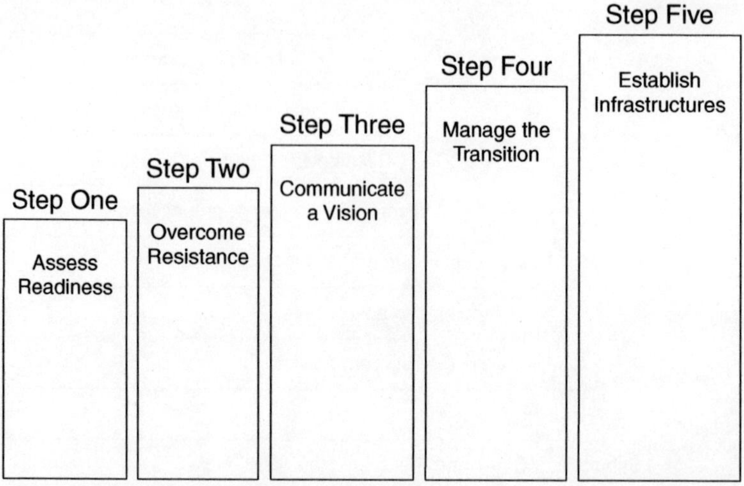

- Step One: Assess Readiness
- Step Two: Overcome Resistance
- Step Three: Communicate a Vision
- Step Four: Manage the Transition
- Step Five: Establish Infrastructures

managers, and employees play in achieving performance results. Most change efforts involve more than one type of change. Given that context and scope, moving from an old to a new state is likely to be more successful when incremental transition-planning steps are applied.

Transition-Planning Steps

Proven steps in transition planning are illustrated in Figure 2.2. Each step comprises specific activities that reveal potential barriers to ROI readiness and help the organization identify areas of strength and opportunity in the implementation process.

Step 1: Assess Readiness

By some estimates, 70 to 75 percent of major organizational change efforts fail. Imagine the wasted time, money, and human effort that are represented by that dismal figure. If implementing organizational change is truly that difficult, then it is clear that planning, resource, and management needs have to be addressed from the very beginning. Time must be spent up front to assess the kinds of planning, resource, and management activities needed to support

ROI implementation efforts. Proper planning on the front end will save time and other resources on the back end.

Prior to undertaking a time-consuming, labor-intensive ROI evaluation, it would be prudent to assess perceptions and mindsets about evaluation within your organization, along with its readiness for the robust ROI Methodology. Completing the readiness assessment, "Is Your Organization a Candidate for Implementation of the ROI Methodology?" from *ROI Fundamentals*, book one in this series, will help you determine how best to focus organizational readiness activities. This assessment, along with the scale for determining if your organization is ready for the ROI Methodology, is shown in Exhibit 2.2.

Before implementation, the response to each of the fifteen statements in the assessment should be examined or reexamined in light of its potential effect on the effort to implement results-based measurement. For example, strong agreement with item 11 indicates an immediate need or opportunity to position implementation of the ROI Methodology as a compelling part of organizational strategy and then define the readiness conditions required to support it.

Using the responses from the readiness assessment, identify and prioritize key focus areas for readiness activities. In particular, consider the following:

- What programs, processes, or persons in your organization support the desired future state of measurement focus? (*Strengths*)

- Where are there gaps between where your organization is and where it should be with respect to results-based measurement? (*Weaknesses*)

- What processes or programs may have to be changed or reconfigured?

- To what extent do managers and program staff perceive current programs to be effective? (*Opportunities*)

Exhibit 2.2. Is Your Organization a Candidate for Implementation of the ROI Methodology?

Read each question and check the box that corresponds to the most appropriate level of agreement:

1 = Disagree; 5 = Agree

	DISAGREE 1	2	3	4	AGREE 5
1. My organization is considered a large organization with a variety of projects and programs.					
2. My function has a large budget that attracts the interest of senior management.					
3. My organization has a culture of measurement and is focused on establishing a variety of measures for all functions.					
4. My organization is undergoing significant change.					
5. There is pressure from senior management to measure the results of our programs.					
6. My function has a low investment in measurement and evaluation.					
7. My organization has experienced more than one program disaster in the past.					
8. My function has a new leader.					
9. My team would like to be the leader in evaluating programs and processes.					
10. The image of my function is less than satisfactory.					
11. My clients are demanding that programs and processes show bottom-line results.					

Exhibit 2.2. Is Your Organization a Candidate for Implementation of the ROI Methodology? (*Continued*)

12. My function competes with other functions in our organization for resources.					
13. Increased focus has been placed on linking programs and processes to the strategic direction of the organization.					
14. My function is a key player in change initiatives currently taking place in our organization.					
15. Our function's overall budget is growing, and we are required to prove the bottom-line value of our processes.					

Scoring
Add your score based on the level of agreement to each question. A score of "1" equals 1 point; a score of "5" equals 5 points.

If you scored:

15–30	Your organization is not yet a candidate for the ROI Methodology.
31–45	Your organization is not a strong candidate for the ROI Methodology. However, you should start pursuing some type of measurement process.
46–60	Your organization is a candidate for building skills to implement the ROI Methodology. At this point there is no real pressure to show ROI, which means that you have the perfect opportunity to put the ROI Methodology in place within your organization and perfect the process before it becomes a requirement.
61–75	Your organization should already be implementing a comprehensive measurement and evaluation process, including ROI calculations.

- What resource constraints may impede implementation? (*Threats*)

- What processes may have to be created from scratch?

- What particular areas need immediate support in order for implementation to proceed?

- What metrics, milestones, or status reports are needed to track and monitor progress on implementation?

Exhibit 2.3. SWOT Analysis of Organizational Readiness for Implementation of the ROI Methodology

Strengths	Weaknesses
✓	✓
✓	✓
✓	✓
✓	✓
Opportunities	**Threats**
✓	✓
✓	✓
✓	✓
✓	✓

Based on your review of the readiness assessment and deliberation on the preceding questions, complete a strengths, weaknesses, opportunities, and threats (SWOT) analysis of your organization's readiness for implementation of the ROI Methodology (see Exhibit 2.3).

When the SWOT analysis is completed, identify and prioritize key focus areas. Once this is complete, developing a readiness plan to address specific areas that will need attention or action during implementation should be much easier to do.

Step 2: Overcome Resistance

With any new process or change, resistance is typical, as we discussed earlier. The group that most often resists the ROI Methodology is the program staff, who are tasked with the design, development, delivery, and coordination of programs and with their evaluation. These individuals may perceive the implementation of ROI measurement as threatening or time-consuming or as an unwelcome intrusion on an already overloaded schedule of looming deadlines, multiple requests for service, and never-ending client demands. Many practitioners are also deterred from pursuing systematic evaluation efforts because of false assumptions about the cost and complexity of evaluating at the ROI level. Compounding these issues is the occasional misuse of measurement data as a corrective or fault-finding tool rather than a source of continuous improvement. Furthermore, environmental barriers are typically present in that most functions have not established the infrastructure and success criteria to support a results focus.

ROI Fundamentals, the first book in this series, discusses the many common myths, fears, and false assumptions about implementing the ROI Methodology. Some of the more prevalent myths, fears, and assumptions are listed in Table 2.1, along with approaches for eliminating resistance associated with these preconceived notions. Each approach for eliminating resistance is detailed in this book.

Exhibit 2.4 provides a checklist of common myths, fears, or false assumptions associated with implementing the ROI Methodology. Complete this exercise to determine how you can overcome resistance in your organization. First, identify the preconceived notions in your organization.

Step 3: Communicate a Vision

Organizational readiness can be enhanced by actively communicating the vision, mission, and desired outcomes of a results-focused evaluation and measurement strategy. The vision highlights the difference between the current reality of where the organization is with its measurement focus and where its leaders want it to be. Through communication forums or briefings with senior, mid-level, and line managers, the value of moving from an activity-based measurement focus to a results-based focus can be described and input can be gathered about how others view the change. These initial communications should be designed to help organizational leaders

Table 2.1. How to Overcome Myths, Fears, and False Assumptions About the ROI Methodology

Myth, Fear, or Assumption	Specific Approaches
1. Measurement and evaluation are too expensive.	• A comprehensive measurement and evaluation system can typically be implemented for less than 5 percent of a function unit's budget. • Benchmark with other organizations to determine a reasonable range for evaluation costs. For most programs, it is sufficient to collect learning and application data, so the cost of a detailed impact study is infrequent.
2. Evaluation takes too much time.	Take advantage of these proven shortcuts and cost-saving approaches: • Use automated techniques and templates. • Build evaluation into the performance improvement process. • Develop criteria for selecting program measurement levels. • Plan for evaluation early in the process. • Share the responsibilities for evaluation. • Require participants to conduct major steps. • Use shortcut methods for major steps. • Use estimates in the data collection and analysis. • Develop internal capability in the ROI Methodology. • Streamline the reporting process. • Use Web-based technology.

Table 2.1. How to Overcome Myths, Fears, and False Assumptions About the ROI Methodology (*Continued*)

Myth, Fear, or Assumption	Specific Approaches
3. If senior management does not require additional measurement, there is no need to pursue it.	• Leaders are demanding more and more accountability. • A unit that produces no evidence of results becomes an easy target for staff reductions. • When senior leaders suddenly ask for results, they expect a quick response. • Having results available and not needing them is better than needing results and not having them. • Developing ROI information is one of the best ways to garner the respect of senior management and show the business value of a function.
4. Measurement and evaluation is a passing fad.	• Increased accountability and measurement are among the most critical issues today. • Although the status of ROI practice among professionals is mixed, there is a persistent trend toward showing the bottom-line value of program investments.
5. Evaluation generates only one or two types of data.	• The ROI Methodology can generate up to seven different types of qualitative and quantitative data, including intangible benefits.
6. Evaluation cannot be easily replicated.	• Follow the Twelve Guiding Principles and adopt operating standards in order to ensure consistency in using the ROI Methodology.

(*Continued*)

Table 2.1. How to Overcome Myths, Fears, and False Assumptions About the ROI Methodology (*Continued*)

Myth, Fear, or Assumption	Specific Approaches
7. Evaluation is too subjective.	• The use of estimates is extremely reliable when sound operating standards are followed. • Accounting, engineering, and technology fields routinely use estimates.
8. Impact evaluation is not possible for programs involving soft skills; it is only possible for programs involving technical and hard skills.	• Hundreds of case studies document successful application of the ROI Methodology to soft-skill programs. • Link needs, objectives, and impact measures to identify performance improvement at Levels 3, 4, and 5.
9. Evaluation is more appropriate for certain types of organizations.	• The ROI Methodology has been successfully used by organizations of multiple sizes in diverse fields around the globe. • Impact measures that can be used to measure program success exist in any organizational setting.
10. Isolating the effects of a program is not always possible.	• Several methods for isolating the effects of a program are available; the challenge lies in selecting the appropriate method for a given situation. • Ignoring the isolation issue decreases the credibility of the function and makes linking the program to key business measures difficult.

Table 2.1. How to Overcome Myths, Fears, and False Assumptions About the ROI Methodology (*Continued*)

Myth, Fear, or Assumption	Specific Approaches
11. Because program staff have no control over participants after they complete a program, evaluating on-the-job improvement is not appropriate.	• Although the program staff may not have direct control over what happens to participants in the workplace, they do have influence on the process of transferring skills that participants will use in the workplace. • Objectives must be developed that focus on application of learning and expected outcomes. • Partnerships between key managers and program staff help ensure that learning transfer takes place.
12. A participant is rarely responsible for the failure of a program.	• Participants need to be held accountable for their own learning and are a credible source of information about the consequences of learning. • Programs need to be positioned with results-based expectations for participants. • Participants have the ultimate responsibility for learning and applying new skills and knowledge and for identifying enablers and barriers to their success in doing so.
13. Evaluation is the evaluator's responsibility.	Evaluation must be a shared responsibility: • Managers and performers provide input on performance and skill deficits. • Program team members design, develop, and deliver the program.

(*Continued*)

Table 2.1. How to Overcome Myths, Fears, and False Assumptions About the ROI Methodology (*Continued*)

Myth, Fear, or Assumption	Specific Approaches
	• Managers and stakeholders review and approve the evaluation plan. • Participants and key stakeholders provide data about success after the program.
14. Successful evaluation implementation requires a degree in statistics or evaluation.	• An effective, credible evaluation process can be implemented by means of a simple step-by-step process and without a complicated set of formulas. • Many evaluation studies do not require the use of statistics. • Statistical software packages can be purchased as a resource for evaluation staff, or statistical expertise can be hired for specific ROI impact studies.
15. Negative data are always bad news.	• Communicate a vision of the ROI Methodology as a continual learning tool that will help assess program priorities and areas of impact. • Develop staff capability in the ROI Methodology and share ownership of evaluation results.

understand the following points:

- Why the paradigm shift to a results-based measurement focus is needed
- What the desired outcomes are
- Who the targets for change are, and who is needed to make it work

Exhibit 2.4. Overcoming Resistance in the Form of Myths, Fears, and False Assumptions

A. For each item in the following list of common myths, fears, or false assumptions associated with implementing the ROI Methodology, check the box that reflects the mindset in your organization.		
Myth, Fear, or False Assumption	Yes	No
1. Measurement and evaluation are too expensive.	☐	☐
2. Evaluation takes too much time.	☐	☐
3. If senior management does not require additional measurement, there is no need to pursue it.	☐	☐
4. Measurement and evaluation is a passing fad.	☐	☐
5. Evaluation generates only one or two types of data.	☐	☐
6. Evaluation cannot be easily replicated.	☐	☐
7. Evaluation is too subjective.	☐	☐
8. Impact evaluation is not possible for programs involving soft skills; it is only possible for programs involving technical and hard skills.	☐	☐
9. Evaluation is more appropriate for certain types of organizations.	☐	☐
10. Isolating the effects of a program is not always possible.	☐	☐
11. Because program staff have no control over participants after they complete a program, evaluating the on-the-job improvement is not appropriate.	☐	☐

(Continued)

Exhibit 2.4. Overcoming Resistance in the Form of Myths, Fears, and False Assumptions (*Continued*)

12. A participant is rarely responsible for the failure of a program.	☐	☐
13. Evaluation is the evaluator's responsibility.	☐	☐
14. Successful evaluation implementation requires a degree in statistics or evaluation.	☐	☐
15. Negative data are always bad news.	☐	☐

B. Review the preceding list of objections associated with the ROI Methodology, and identify the three that *most* reflect your organization's current mindset about measurement and evaluation.
  1. _____
  2. _____
  3. _____

C. Referring to the approaches listed in Table 2.1 for ideas, identify an action, strategy, or approach that you will use to counter each assumption listed in item B as your team completes an ROI impact study.
  1. _____
  2. _____
  3. _____

D. Indicate the date by which you will complete each action listed in item C.
  1. _____
  2. _____
  3. _____

E. Identify a person with whom you will share progress on each item.
  1. _____
  2. _____
  3. _____

- When the impact will occur

- How a results-based function will align with the company's performance goals, vision, mission, and values

- How the organization, its internal processes, and its key people will be developed in order to manage the change effort

- Where the checkpoints will be and what process documents and project plans will detail the scope of the effort and its impact on the business

Communication should also include education about the components of a results-based measurement strategy, including the following:

- How evaluation data can be used to uncover barriers to successful application of skills or knowledge

- How the data can be used to manage and correct barriers

- The role of management in ensuring a program's success

- The role of top management in supporting data collection

- How a focus on results can save money and enhance business performance

The next chapter discusses management's role in implementing the ROI Methodology in more detail and provides additional tools for developing and strengthening partnerships with management groups. In communicating the vision for a results-based effort, however, it should be emphasized that results-based evaluation is not a quick fix and that successful implementation will require sustained support and participation across all organizational levels.

Communication with stakeholders typically acknowledges that implementation of a results-based evaluation framework is a gradual process.

Developing and maintaining a communication plan to promote awareness of and commitment to results-based evaluation is critical, not only for your current impact study but for future ROI efforts. Table 2.2 is an example of a communication plan. Exhibit 2.5 helps identify areas of strength and opportunities for improvement in existing communication work.

Step 4: Manage the Transition

As happens in many change efforts, people may underestimate the time, energy, and resources required to achieve evaluation goals. In fact, one of the most common errors made in any change effort is inaccurately defining the scope; typically, planners define the scope of the change effort too narrowly, overlooking the internal dynamics of day-to-day communications and working relationships. Imagine the losses of time and productivity that occur when those who must support and participate in a new evaluation strategy are unclear about their roles and the resources needed to support their roles. That's why defining roles and responsibilities is such an important part of transition planning and change management in the ROI Methodology. This essential step is discussed in more detail in Chapter Three.

Step 5: Establish Management Infrastructure to Support the Process

Systems, policies, and procedures ensure consistency in application of the ROI Methodology across an organization. They also keep the process focused, consistent, and credible by communicating how new approaches for measuring performance will be aligned with existing business processes and structures. Developing the proper infrastructure to support the ROI Methodology requires the following actions.

Table 2.2. Sample Communication Plan

Process: Results-Based Measurement and Evaluation

Key Message	Stakeholder	Objective	Approach	Frequency	Responsibility	Delivery	Considerations
What is the primary message to be conveyed or issue to be addressed?	*Target audience*	*Info only, seeking support, requesting review, or action?*	*Web, newsletter, e-mail, face to face, hard copy, town hall, intranet, and so on*	*Timing or milestone date*	*Who will develop content?*	*Who will deliver the communication?*	*Potential obstacles, time availability, stakeholder concerns or issues with message*
Stage 1: Initial Rollout							
Value proposition of ROI and results-based measurement processes. Why, what, who, when, and how evaluation data will be used. Communicate best practices within the industry and the profession.	Senior leadership	Solicit support, resources for initial impact study.	Face-to-face PowerPoint presentation, including benchmarking data	One time, by [date]; ongoing, as needed	Process sponsor or program leader	Process sponsor or program leader	Why ROI? Why now? How to manage with limited resources? Should we do ROI for all programs? What will we do with the results? What about negative results? How can results of soft-skill programs be measured? How can we know whether it was the training that got the result?

(*Continued*)

Table 2.2. Sample Communication Plan (*Continued*)

Key Message	Stakeholder	Objective	Approach	Frequency	Responsibility	Delivery	Considerations
Emphasize focus on process, not project. Not a one-time-only initiative.	Senior leadership	Request technical review of revised policies and procedures as part of infrastructure needed to support results-based process.	Face-to-face PowerPoint presentation, including benchmarking data	One time, then ongoing as needed	Program leader	Process sponsor or program leader and initial evaluation team	Any conflict with existing critical business issues? Compatibility, synergies? Accountability measures.
Summary of current impact study. Show how ROI can be used to solve real business problems.	Senior leadership	Seek support for implementation plan. Generate accountability for mid-level managers', line supervisors', and employees' participation. Request documented support, with sign-off on data collection plan.	Face-to-face PowerPoint presentation, including benchmarking data; data collection plan	One time, then ongoing as needed	Process sponsor or program leader	Process sponsor or advisor	Amount of resources needed. Confidentiality of results. What will happen if results are negative or less than desirable?

Value proposition: how results-based measurement processes can solve real business problems.	Line supervisors	Seek support for implementation plan. Request line supervisors' involvement in task force. Request documented support, with sign-off on data collection plan.	Face-to-face PowerPoint presentation, including benchmarking data; data collection plan; transfer strategy matrix	One time, then ongoing as needed	Process sponsor or program leader	Process sponsor or advisor	Resource constraints? How will performance tracking be conducted? What impact will this have on performance management processes? What's in it for me? How will organizational or management barriers be addressed?
Value proposition: how results-based measurement processes can solve real business problems.	Employees, program participants	Seek support for implementation plan. Request documented support, with sign-off on data collection plan.	Face-to-face PowerPoint presentation, including benchmarking data; data collection plan; transfer strategy matrix	One time, then ongoing as needed	Process sponsor or program leader	Process sponsor or advisor	Resource constraints? How will performance tracking be conducted? What impact will this have on performance management processes? What's in it for me? How will organizational or management barriers be addressed?

(Continued)

Table 2.2. Sample Communication Plan (*Continued*)

Key Message	Stakeholder	Objective	Approach	Frequency	Responsibility	Delivery	Considerations
Stage 2: Evaluation Planning							
Explain business needs or gaps that are being addressed, in terms of current and desired performance levels. Discussion of performance measures available to track progress on objectives.	Line supervisors	Review extant baseline data; collect input for cause analysis, proposed performance improvement solution; establish evaluation targets with corresponding measures.	Face-to-face PowerPoint presentation, including benchmarking data; data collection plan; transfer strategy matrix	Weekly, as needed. Evaluation plan to be completed, with senior management input, by [date].	Evaluation lead, task force members, instructional design team rep, subject matter experts, participants	Evaluation lead, task force members, instructional design team rep, subject matter experts, participants	What about conflicting priorities? Moving targets?
Stage 3: Data Collection							
Solicit feedback about success on reaction, planned action, learning, performance, and impact objectives. Collect application and business measures of program impact.	Line supervisors	Request feedback during and after program implementation. Instruct participants on how to provide feedback. Gather input in order to convert data to monetary values and calculate ROI.		Per data collection plan, by [date]	Evaluation lead, task force members, instructional design team rep, subject matter experts, participants	Evaluation lead, task force members, instructional design team rep, subject matter experts, participants	What about extreme data? What about missing data? Standards for converting data and ensuring credibility? Confidentiality? Annualized data?

Solicit feedback about success on reaction, planned action, learning, performance, and impact objectives. Collect application and business measures of program impact.	Program participants	Request feedback during and after program implementation. Instruct participants on how to provide feedback. Gather input in order to convert data to monetary values and calculate ROI.	Level 1 feedback survey. Pre-program and post-program assessments. Action plan and impact survey sixty days after program.	Per data collection plan, by [date]	Evaluation lead, task force members, instructional design team rep, subject matter experts, participants	Evaluation lead, task force members, instructional design team rep, subject matter experts, participants	What about extreme data? What about missing data? Standards for converting data and ensuring credibility? Confidentiality? How can barriers in management support be reported? Annualized data?

Stage 4: Reporting Results

Report on degree of success in achieving program objectives. List enablers and barriers.	Senior and mid-level managers	Communicate results. Seek support for action planning, program revisions, or other improvements, as needed.	Town hall meetings. Impact study report. Lessons learned report.	Selected senior and mid-level management briefings. Two town hall forums by [date].	Sponsor, evaluation lead, task force members, subject matter experts, participants	Sponsor, evaluation lead, task force members, subject matter experts, participants	How will results be used for continuous improvement and action planning? How will issues of management support (or lack thereof) be addressed?

(Continued)

Table 2.2. Sample Communication Plan (*Continued*)

Key Message	Stakeholder	Objective	Approach	Frequency	Responsibility	Delivery	Considerations
Report on degree of success in achieving program objectives. List enablers and barriers.	Line supervisors	Communicate results. Seek support for future participation in impact studies and involvement in task force. Generate enthusiasm for process.	Briefings. Intranet communications. Poster boards. Lessons learned report.	Ongoing, as needed	Sponsor, evaluation lead, task force members, subject matter experts, participants	Sponsor, evaluation lead, task force members, subject matter experts, participants	How will results be used for continuous improvement and action planning? How will issues of management support (or lack thereof) be addressed?

Exhibit 2.5. Communication Planning

1. Using Table 2.2 as a guide, complete a communication plan for your current impact study. Next, use the checklist below to identify areas of strength and opportunities for improvement in your existing communication plan.		
Communication Planning Checklist	Yes	No
Have I checked with members of my target audience to assess communication needs, concerns, or questions?	☐	☐
Have I considered the organizational impact of a results-based focus?	☐	☐
Have I engaged the support of a credible sponsor at the senior leadership level?	☐	☐
Have I clarified the purpose of the results-based evaluation, what outcomes are desired, and what decisions will be made based on the results?	☐	☐
Have I used baseline data to support my case?	☐	☐
Have I positioned this effort as a compelling piece of company strategy?	☐	☐
Have I assessed external factors that may be out of the program staff's or individual client's control?	☐	☐
Have I developed an evaluation plan with program objectives at multiple levels?	☐	☐
Have I included communication about timelines and resource requirements?	☐	☐
Have I included communication about evaluation roles and responsibilities across all organization levels?	☐	☐
Have I included communication about how a results-based evaluation process will be integrated with existing policy and purpose statements?	☐	☐
Have I included a transition plan with realistic milestones?	☐	☐

(Continued)

Exhibit 2.5. Communication Planning (*Continued*)

Have I included communication about the data collection instruments to be used for measuring results in targeted areas?	☐	☐
Have I included clear communication about the resource requirements for stakeholders who participate in the evaluation process?	☐	☐
Have I included communication about accountability measures for stakeholders who commit to participation in the evaluation process?	☐	☐
Have I provided adequate communication about how participants will be trained to provide data?	☐	☐
Have I included communication about how results will be used for continuous improvement and action planning?	☐	☐

Areas of strength:
_____
_____
_____

Opportunities for improvement:
_____
_____
_____

2. Identify planned actions you will take to maintain and enhance communication efforts in the areas needing improvement.
Sustaining actions:
_____
_____
_____

Enhancing actions:
_____
_____
_____

Prepare Policy, Procedures, and Guidelines

As part of the integration process, operating policies, procedures, or standards concerning measurement and evaluation should be established or revised. For example, one organization used the following policy statement to frame the purpose of its results-based initiatives: "The purpose of workplace learning programs is to increase organizational, operational, and individual effectiveness. Programs will offer tangible and intangible returns to customers and will assist the company in addressing all factors influencing organizational, operational, and individual performance."

Policy statements should also address critical issues that will influence the effectiveness of the measurement and evaluation process. Policy statements are best developed with input from the program staff and key stakeholders or clients of programs and services. Typical topics include these:

- Adoption of an evaluation framework (such as the five-level model presented in this series)
- Requirements that some or all programs set performance or business impact objectives
- Definition of roles and responsibilities

Policy statements provide an excellent opportunity to communicate basic evaluation requirements, including accountability requirements for those responsible for carrying out the evaluation process. Exhibit 2.6 provides a list of topics to include when you are updating organizational policy statements to better reflect a results-based strategy.

Guidelines tend to be more technical and detailed than policy statements and are meant to show how aspects of a results-based policy are undertaken and put into practice. They often include specific forms, instruments, and tools that are necessary to facilitate the process.

Exhibit 2.6. Checklist of Topics for Policy Statements

Policy Statement	Yes	No
Purpose of results-based measurement and evaluation strategy stated?	☐	☐
Purpose aligned with compelling business strategy?	☐	☐
Evaluation framework stated?	☐	☐
Evaluation process clearly linked with the entire performance improvement cycle, beginning with needs analysis and ending with communicating results?	☐	☐
Evaluation targets stated (that is, percentage of programs to be evaluated at Level 3 and above)?	☐	☐
Evaluation responsibilities stated for participants, managers, program staff, and stakeholders?	☐	☐
Standards for developing, applying, and ensuring the credibility of data collection instruments addressed?	☐	☐
Required capabilities for internal and external measurement staff stated?	☐	☐
Administrative and database issues addressed?	☐	☐
Criteria for communicating evaluation results stated?	☐	☐
Process of reviewing evaluation data for purposes of continuous improvement explained?	☐	☐

Exhibit 2.7 shows how one learning and development department applied a corporate template for business process development to its efforts to standardize results-based processes as credible business practices throughout the organization. In this example, policy statements are referenced as supporting documentation.

Exhibit 2.7. Learning and Development Standardization Process

Contents

1.0 Process Overview

2.0 Procedures

3.0 Resources, Roles, and Responsibilities

4.0 Measurement and Verification

5.0 Continual Improvement

6.0 Document Control Information

7.0 Document List

1.0 Process Overview

1.1 Purpose and Objective

Develop, approve, and deploy standardized learning and development (L&D) processes that are capable of enhancing and improving operational performance.

1.2 Scope

These L&D standardization processes will establish specific, mandatory requirements related to learning throughout the organization and will also contain additional guidelines to help business units meet the intent of the L&D standardization expectations. The process includes

- Governance
- Process development
- Training for governance team members and key L&D process implementers

Exhibit 2.7. Learning and Development Standardization Process (*Continued*)

1.3 Link to Operational Goals

This process facilitates meeting operational goals of excellence throughout the organization.

1.4 Process Requirements

1. All L&D processes will be consistent with
   - The company's way
   - The company's mission, vision, and values
2. A development team will manage the creation of the initial set of L&D standardized processes.
3. L&D standardized processes will be developed using a team approach, with membership that includes subject matter experts and representatives from select business units.
4. L&D standardized processes will be benchmarked against recognized best practices and industry leaders in L&D to ensure that the company processes are capable of delivering the intended objectives.
5. L&D standardized processes will be reviewed and approved by critical stakeholders before finalization.
6. A review council will examine final L&D standardized processes for business alignment and fitness for purpose.
7. An approval board will ensure that L&D standardized processes align with the company's strategic plan and that significant implementation issues and business impact have been accounted for.
8. Each L&D standardized process will be deployed with an implementation plan that identifies and gives guidance on significant implementation issues, such as communication, resource planning, and alignment with operational excellence (OE) strategies.

Exhibit 2.7. Learning and Development Standardization Process (*Continued*)

9. An exception procedure will be available for use by business units and departments in cases in which they feel that they cannot comply with a specific L&D process requirement or that compliance would not make business sense.

1.5 Links to Other Operational Processes

L&D standardization supports all other appropriate business processes, such as annual business planning, performance appraisal cycles, and individual development planning processes.

2.0 Procedures

2.1 Overview

A governance model will be used to develop, review, and approve L&D processes. The governance model has four representative components, including the following:

- Process sponsor to provide executive leadership and allocate resources for process implementation.
- Process champion to provide L&D technical expertise, mentoring, and training for process development team members and organizational stakeholders.
- Process development team to revise, write, and implement L&D processes. This plan will identify significant implementation issues and give guidance on approaches and timing.
- Process review council to examine processes to ensure fitness for purpose and alignment with business plans and give final approval.

Exhibit 2.7. Learning and Development Standardization Process (*Continued*)

2.2 Details of Governance

2.2.1 Governance—Process Sponsor Charter

Description: This charter describes process sponsorship roles, responsibilities, and procedures used for scheduling, resourcing, and soliciting stakeholder engagement in L&D standardized process development.

2.2.2 Governance—Process Champion Charter

Description: This charter describes process champion roles, responsibilities, and procedures used for advising, resourcing, and training process development team members and organizational stakeholders.

2.2.3 Governance—Process Development Team Charter

Description: This charter describes team membership, roles, responsibilities, and procedures used for scheduling, resourcing, writing, and soliciting input and approval for L&D standardized processes.

2.2.4 Governance—Review Council Charter

Description: This charter describes team membership, roles, responsibilities, and procedures used for advising on overall priorities and reviewing and approving the L&D standardized processes.

2.3 Components of Process Development

2.3.1 L&D Processes—Terms and Definitions

2.3.2 Purpose and Scope Statements

Exhibit 2.7. Learning and Development Standardization Process (*Continued*)

  2.3.3 Process Development Procedures

  2.3.4 Process Development Flowchart

  2.3.5 Process Approval Procedure

3.0 Resources, Roles, and Responsibilities

L&D standardization process sponsor:	Name(s), Title
L&D standardization process champion:	Name(s), Title
L&D standardization process development team:	Name(s), Title
L&D standardization process review council:	Name(s), Title

The following table outlines the roles and responsibilities associated with this process.

Role	Responsibilities	Competencies
L&D standardization process sponsor	• Provides executive leadership for the L&D standardization process integration • Ensures that this process is kept current • Allocates personnel, funding, and other resources to support process execution • Reviews standardization process documentation and records • Participates in an annual review of process effectiveness and efficiency	• Fluency in operational excellence • Comprehensive knowledge of all elements of a results-based L&D focus, including understanding of the five-level measurement and evaluation framework • Ability to provide vision and strategic direction

(*Continued*)

Exhibit 2.7. Learning and Development Standardization Process (*Continued*)

Role	Responsibilities	Competencies
L&D standardization process champion	• Provides subject matter expertise and technical assistance for process development and execution • Ensures that processes adhere to operating standards, policies, and guidelines • Conducts performance reporting and trend analysis company-wide • Facilitates organization-wide changes in L&D process methodology • Mentors, trains, and manages the internal L&D and/or ROI community of practice	• Extensive experience and comprehensive knowledge of best-practice L&D processes, including results-based learning and ROI process models • Facilitative skills • Ability to evaluate results against organizational goals • Data analysis/interpretation skills • Strong business acumen, including understanding of operational excellence (OE) components • Demonstrated performance-consulting skills • Influencing skills
L&D standardization process development team members	• Described in the development team charter	• Influencing skills • Technical subject matter expertise • Understanding of internal business unit networks

Exhibit 2.7. Learning and Development Standardization Process (*Continued*)

Role	Responsibilities	Competencies
		• Understanding of continual improvement • Understanding of OE components • Strong communication skills
Review council members	• Described in the review council charter	• Fluency in OE components • Ability to provide vision and strategic direction • Understanding of the L&D standardization process • Understanding of business impact of deploying L&D standardization processes

4.0 Measurement and Verification

4.1 Measurement of L&D Effectiveness

Phillips's five-level framework and ROI process model will be used to measure L&D effectiveness across multiple levels of results. The following metrics will be tracked to determine that the L&D standardization process is effective in meeting its stated purpose. Measures will include:

Exhibit 2.7. Learning and Development Standardization Process (*Continued*)

4.1.1 Leading Measures

4.1.2 Lagging Measures

4.2 Verification

The following steps will be conducted to measure and verify that L&D processes, services, and products operate within defined standards of performance.

4.2.1 Review of Process Effectiveness

The L&D standardization process sponsor and process champion will review and verify that all parts of the L&D process are effective in fulfilling the OE expectations and results-based process purpose. The review will be performed annually, at a minimum.

4.2.2 Audit of Performance

The L&D standardization process sponsor and process champion will verify adherence and identify non-conformance to the L&D processes as designed and documented. A documented audit of the processes will occur at least annually and will be based on the following:

- Documents and records
- Demonstrated competence across five levels of L&D performance measures
- Process leading and lagging metrics
- Benchmarking data, if applicable

Exhibit 2.7. Learning and Development Standardization Process (*Continued*)

4.2.3 Governance Body Reviews

Governance bodies will perform the following reviews:

- Under the direction and guidance of the L&D standardization process sponsor and the process champion, the review council will evaluate the performance of the process development team annually.

5.0 Continual Improvement

The following steps will be conducted to assess and improve process performance.

5.1 Review of Process Effectiveness

The L&D standardization process sponsor and process champion will review and verify that all parts of the L&D processes are effective in fulfilling the operational expectations and results-based process purpose. The review will be performed at least annually.

5.2 Audit of Performance

The L&D standardization process sponsor and process champion will verify adherence and identify non-conformance to L&D processes as designed and documented. A documented audit of these processes will occur at least annually and will be based on the following:

- Documents and records
- Adherence to documented operating standards, policies, and guidelines

Exhibit 2.7. Learning and Development Standardization Process (*Continued*)

- Demonstrated competence across five levels of L&D performance measures
- Process leading and lagging metrics
- Benchmarking data, if applicable

5.3 Governance Body Reviews

Governance bodies will perform the following reviews:

- The review council will perform annual reviews to ensure appropriate progress toward implementation of the L&D processes throughout the organization.
- The review council will evaluate the performance of the process development team annually.
- The process sponsor will evaluate the performance of the review council annually.

5.4 Gap Analysis

The L&D standardization process sponsor, process champion, and development team will prioritize performance gaps and non-conformities that are identified as part of the process improvement step. Considerations will include operational directives, deviations from standard operating procedures, risk issues, and resource enablers/barriers.

5.5 Continual Improvement Plans

Process gaps, non-conformance, and improvement opportunities identified from 5.4 will be summarized and used to assist in building continual improvement plans.

Exhibit 2.7. Learning and Development Standardization Process (*Continued*)

5.6 Link to Annual Business Plan

The L&D standardization process champion and development team will use the prioritized performance gaps and nonconformities to develop a continual improvement plan that is linked with annual business plans. In some circumstances, improvement activities may extend over several years.

5.7 Contents

The continual improvement plan for OE processes will identify the following:

- Improvement opportunities and gaps to be closed
- Resources required
- Responsible person(s)
- Timing and milestones for improvements

6.0 Document Control Information

Revision dates, frequency of revisions, and control numbers should be recorded to ensure that only the most recently updated documents are used.

Description	Policy and Procedure Statement
Revision Date	
Revision Frequency	Every 3 years
Control Number	

Exhibit 2.7. Learning and Development Standardization Process (*Continued*)

7.0 Document List

This is a complete list of the documents referenced in this process.

- Five-Level Framework for Measuring L&D Results
- ROI Process Model
    Selection matrix
    Sample data collection plan
    Sample ROI analysis plan
- Sample Client Engagement and Service Level Agreement
- L&D Policy, Procedures, and Guidelines, including Operating Standards for L&D Measurement and Evaluation
- L&D Standardization Process Sponsor Charter
- L&D Standardization Process Champion Charter
- L&D Standardization Process Development Team Charter
- L&D Standardization Process Review Council Charter
- Glossary of Terms and Definitions

Defining operating standards for the ROI Methodology that will stand up under scrutiny is important. Again, operating standards are needed to ensure that practice is consistent and conservative from one staff member to the next and from one evaluation to the next. When you are developing and communicating operating standards for the ROI Methodology, follow these guidelines:

- *Report the complete story.* ROI is a critical measure, but it is only one of many types of data generated by the ROI Methodology. When a program is implemented, evaluate participant reaction, the extent to which participants improved their knowledge, how well participants applied the skills, and the business impact. If measurements are not taken at all levels, concluding that the results are due to the program is difficult.

- *Enhance credibility.* Using the most credible source (often the participants) will enhance stakeholders' perception of the quality and accuracy of the data analysis and results.

- *Be conservative.* If multiple options are available, select the most conservative data. This choice lowers the ROI but builds credibility.

- *Account for other factors.* Because the ROI Methodology is implemented as a systems approach, you must account for other factors in the environment that may have helped or hindered the results. At least one method should be used to isolate a program's effects. These methods are detailed in *Isolation of Results,* book three of this series. Without some method of isolation, the evaluation results will be inaccurate and overstated. Isolation strategies include comparing a pilot group that participated in a program to a control group that did not participate in the program; forecasting results without the program and then comparing the forecast to post-program results; and using participants' estimates of the influence of a program on key measures.

- *Account for missing data.* Sometimes, program participants leave the organization or change job functions. If participants cannot provide post-program improvement data, assume that little or no improvement has occurred. Making assumptions about improvements without data to back them up damages the credibility of the evaluation.

- *Adjust estimates for error*. Using estimates in reporting financial and benefit-cost information is common. To enhance the credibility of estimated data, the estimates should be adjusted according to the level of confidence in the data.

- *Omit the extremes*. Extreme data items can skew results, so omit them.

- *Capture annual benefits*. Use only the first year of benefits of short-term programs. If benefits are not quickly realized, they are probably not worth the cost. Reserve multiple-year ROI analyses for more extensive programs.

- *Tabulate all program costs*. The ROI must include all costs associated with a program. Omitting or understating costs will destroy the credibility of ROI results.

Collectively, these guidelines will do much to overcome resistance and convince stakeholders that the ROI Methodology is credible and that it produces accurate values and consistent outcomes.

Structure ROI as a Learning Tool, Not a Performance Evaluation Tool

A common reason program staff may resist the ROI Methodology is that they fear evaluation results will be used to highlight personal or program failures. For this reason, policies and guidelines should be used as a framework in order to position the ROI Methodology as a continuous process improvement tool that can help assess whether programs are meeting their objectives and proving their worth.

Develop a Project Plan

An important part of transition planning is establishing a project plan, as shown in Exhibit 2.8. Having a project plan is helpful for tracking progress toward goals and for identifying specific

Exhibit 2.8. Project Plan

| Program: _____ |
| Description: _____ |
| Duration: _____ No. Participants: _____ Begin Date: _____ End Date: _____ |

	J	F	M	A	M	J	J	A	S	O	N	D
Formation of Evaluation Team												
Team member 1												
Team member 2												
Evaluation Planning												
Develop data collection plan												
Develop data collection instruments												
Design												
Test												
Revise												
Data collection administration plan												
Data Collection												
Implement data collection plan												
Collect responses												
Distribute incentives (see data collection administration plan)												

(*Continued*)

Exhibit 2.8. Project Plan (Continued)

Program: _____
Description: _____
Duration: _____ No. Participants: _____ Begin Date: _____ End Date: _____

	J	F	M	A	M	J	J	A	S	O	N	D
Data Analysis												
Develop ROI analysis plan												
Develop cost profile												
Analyze data												
Communication of Results												
Develop communication report												
Report results to Stakeholder Group 1												
Report results to Stakeholder Group 2												
Report results to Stakeholder Group 3												
Evaluation Follow-Up												
Develop steps to be taken to improve program												
Respond to questions from stakeholders												

individuals, timetables, milestones, and deliverables required to initiate and implement the evaluation process. The project plan is a fluid document, yet it serves as the master plan for the completion of the action items necessary to implement the evaluation process. Exhibit 2.9 presents a results-based transition plan.

Integrate Cost-Saving Methods

Some of the more common organizational concerns about implementing the ROI Methodology focus on the costs, time, and human resources required for the process. A department with limited time and resources can use proven shortcut methods to economize on major steps in the evaluation process. This provides a practical way to make the transition to the ROI Methodology and addresses resistance that may arise because of concerns about resource requirements. Figure 2.3 shows how these cost-saving approaches can be used in implementation of the ROI Methodology.

Final Thoughts

Making the transition to the ROI Methodology typically includes these challenges:

- False assumptions, myths, or fears about the process
- Resistance to change
- Real or imagined resource constraints
- Limited infrastructure to support a results-based focus

Concerns about the cost, time, and resources required to show results certainly have merit. In business climates that increasingly demand more results from fewer resources, many leaders may have to leverage existing resources and compete for the additional resources needed to demonstrate a program's bottom-line value. Exhibit 2.10 provides a summary of some cost-saving approaches.

Exhibit 2.9. Results-Based Transition Plan

Key Tasks	Milestone	1st Quarter										
		Jan 9	Jan 16	Jan 23	Jan 30	Feb 6	Feb 13	Feb 20	Feb 27	Mar 6	Mar 13	Mar 20	Mar 27
Form measurement team													
Assess stakeholder engagement opportunities													
Recruit process sponsor													
Deliver internal awareness presentations													
Develop measurement policy, guidelines													
Define operating standards													
Conduct internal readiness assessment													
Set evaluation targets, with stakeholder input													
Define roles and responsibilities													

Identify business critical priorities and "quick wins"								
• Identify ROI Project 1								
• Identify ROI Project 2								
Develop scorecard framework								
Develop communication plan								
Provide professional development training for internal staff								
Train supplier partners								
Revise RFP guidelines								
Provide management, executive briefings								
Acquire or develop support tools								
Develop sustaining mechanisms (that is, standardization processes)								
Present impact study results (internally and externally)								

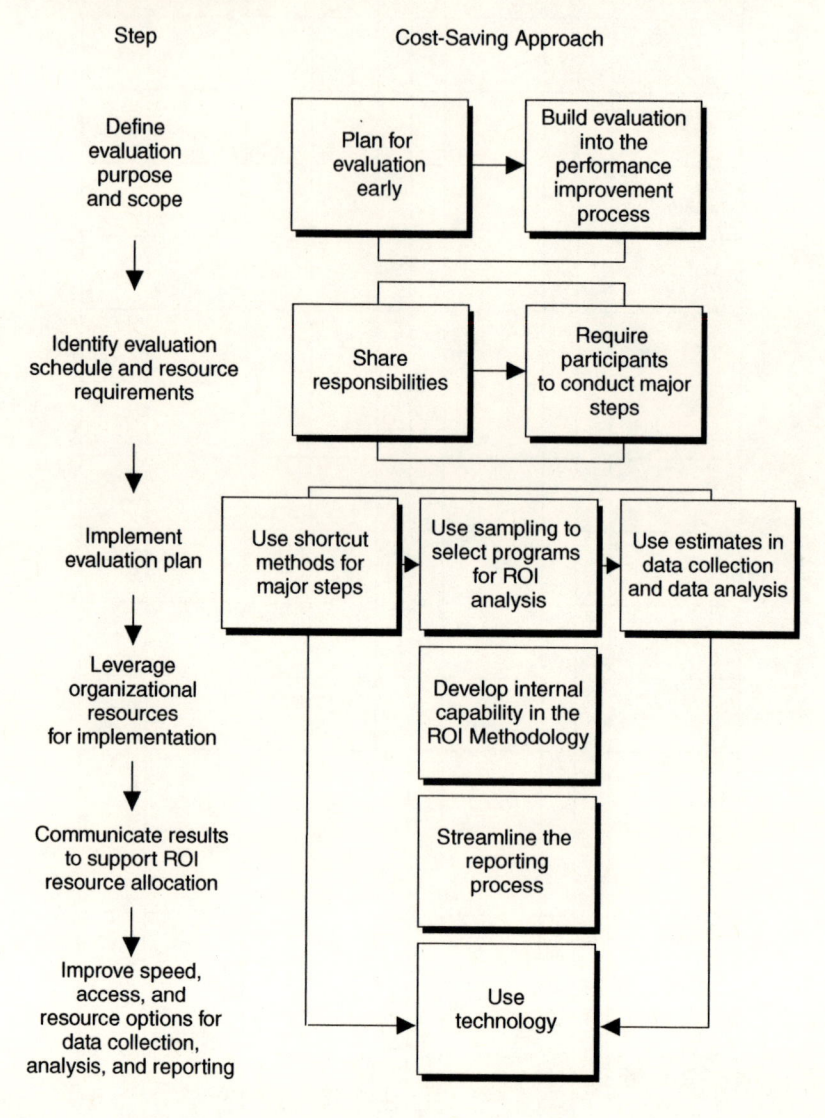

Figure 2.3. Cost-Saving Approaches to Implementation of the ROI Methodology

Step	Cost-Saving Approach
Define evaluation purpose and scope	Plan for evaluation early → Build evaluation into the performance improvement process
Identify evaluation schedule and resource requirements	Share responsibilities → Require participants to conduct major steps
Implement evaluation plan	Use shortcut methods for major steps / Use sampling to select programs for ROI analysis / Use estimates in data collection and data analysis
Leverage organizational resources for implementation	Develop internal capability in the ROI Methodology
Communicate results to support ROI resource allocation	Streamline the reporting process
Improve speed, access, and resource options for data collection, analysis, and reporting	Use technology

Exhibit 2.10. Cost-Saving Approaches to Implementation of the ROI Methodology

Approach 1: Plan for evaluation early in the process.

Guidelines: Define business needs, establish evaluation purposes, determine evaluation levels, develop project objectives, and determine evaluation timing.

Tools: Data collection plan, ROI analysis plan

Approach 2: Build evaluation into the process.

Guidelines: Link business needs, program objectives, and evaluation targets throughout the entire cycle of the needs assessment, instructional design, program delivery, and evaluation. Establish an infrastructure of evaluation policies, procedures, guidelines, and operating standards.

Tools: Linking needs to objectives and evaluation, policies, and procedures

Approach 3: Share responsibilities for evaluation.

Guidelines: Invite managers and employees to provide input on performance and skill deficits; ask stakeholders to review and approve evaluation plans; collect feedback data from participants and key stakeholders after the program.

Tools: Transfer approach matrix, management involvement checklist

Approach 4: Require participants to conduct major steps.

Guideline: Hold participants accountable for learning, applying new skills and knowledge, and identifying enablers and barriers to planned application of learning.

Tool: Action plan

Approach 5: Use shortcut methods for major steps.

Guidelines: Use just-in-time solutions for gap analysis, solution design, and data collection. Caution against an overreliance on shortcut methods and a quick-fix mentality.

Tool: Impact questionnaire

(Continued)

Exhibit 2.10. Cost-Saving Approaches to Implementation of the ROI Methodology (*Continued*)

Approach 6: Use sampling to select the most appropriate programs for ROI analysis.

Guidelines: Specific types of programs should be selected for a comprehensive, detailed analysis. Set targets for the number of programs to be evaluated at each level.

Tool: Matrix of selection criteria

Approach 7: Use estimates in data collection and data analysis.

Guidelines: Using estimates can save a great deal of time and money in the isolation and data conversion steps. Use the most credible and reliable sources for estimates, take a conservative approach, and develop a culture that accepts the estimation process.

Tools: Reaction and impact questionnaires, action plans

Approach 8: Develop internal capability in the ROI Methodology.

Guidelines: Communicate the purpose and scope of the ROI Methodology as a continuous improvement tool that will help assess program priorities and areas of impact. Develop staff capability and shared ownership through education and training and targeted development plans.

Tools: Management briefing outline, individual development plan

Approach 9: Streamline the reporting process.

Guideline: Once management is comfortable with ROI evaluations and a results-based measurement focus has been integrated into the organization, a streamlined approach to reporting results may be more appropriate and cost-effective.

Tool: Streamlined impact study template

Approach 10: Use technology.

Guidelines: Use suitable software packages to speed up various aspects of ROI analysis, design, evaluation, and reporting. Use technology to increase internal capability by offering online needs assessments, self-assessments, or evaluation templates for key stakeholders.

Tools: KnowledgeAdvisors' Metrics that Matter, Apian's SurveyPro, Gaelstorm's SenseiROI, iDNA's Audience Response System, Meeting Metrics Survey Tool, nTag Electronic Name Tags and Survey Tool, eePulse Assessment

Achieving a results-based evaluation strategy can be time-consuming and labor-intensive; in addition, it can be perceived as threatening. Yet with proper transitional planning and clearly defined, shared responsibilities, the ROI Methodology can be implemented in a proactive, systematic manner. Transition planning should allow for the fact that business alignment is still a new process for most managers and that the implementation of a results-based culture evolves over time. Assessing and creating individual and organizational readiness for implementation of the ROI Methodology is a vital step toward establishing business partnerships that will increase commitment to performance improvement programs going forward.

In this chapter, we see implementation of the ROI Methodology as an iterative change process and emphasize the importance of transition planning as a way of moving toward long-term integration of the process into the mainstream of the organization. Transition-planning steps, guidelines, and tools are provided in order to facilitate this effort.

The best-designed tools and techniques for implementation of the ROI Methodology are meaningless unless they are integrated into the fabric of an organization and accepted by those responsible for making it work. An evaluation champion and change agent is necessary for successful implementation. Organizational readiness and resistance to change should be routinely assessed. Objections should be addressed, responsibilities for results assigned, and a transition plan for measuring progress developed. The evaluation champion must commit to teaching others. The next chapter focuses on the role of the evaluation champion and on building capability and support for implementing the ROI Methodology.

3

Building Capability and Support

The preceding chapter discusses implementation of the ROI Methodology as a transitional change process and emphasizes the importance of addressing objections as part of effective transition planning. In this chapter we will focus on assigning responsibilities for results and on teaching others in order to build capability in the ROI Methodology. Implementing results-based evaluation strategies requires support from an infrastructure of diverse stakeholders whose complex interactions are structured by an array of reporting relationships. Because many individuals assume multiple or shifting roles in an evaluation effort, a major implementation challenge is identifying the right people, getting them involved, gaining their commitment, and keeping them well informed at all stages of the process.

Engaging the participation and commitment of different management groups is also a critical component of building internal capability and support for the ROI Methodology. Because managers must approve the time and resource allocations for all phases of implementation—including planning, data collection and analysis, and communication of results—addressing their unique needs and concerns poses special challenges.

Few initiatives are successful without the support and commitment of those involved in making them happen, and implementation of the ROI Methodology is no different. This chapter outlines approaches for creating shared ownership of implementation of the ROI Methodology for both the short term and the long term.

Fundamental Issues in Implementing the ROI Methodology

Educating stakeholders, managers, and responsible internal parties will provide them with a thorough understanding of evaluation using the ROI Methodology, promote consistency in its use, and ensure a common organizational language in regard to its application. Consistency is required, for with consistency come accuracy and credibility from one impact study to another and from one practitioner to the next. Staff members must be provided with consistent preparation for each step of the ROI Methodology.

Preparation of internal staff is a critical issue that must be addressed as part of implementation planning for the following reasons:

- Effective and consistent implementation requires capable and knowledgeable practitioners who can deliver on the promise of the ROI Methodology.
- Skill development in measurement and evaluation is not always a formal part of becoming a facilitator, instructional designer, performance improvement specialist, organizational effectiveness consultant, or manager.
- Effective development is key to increasing internal capability in the ROI Methodology.

Given the need to support implementation across all organizational levels, it may be helpful to identify key gaps as well as engagement opportunities as a first step toward developing internal capability in the ROI Methodology. This assessment of gaps and opportunities will help you pinpoint critical business partners with whom to apply the engagement and skill-building tactics described in this chapter. It can also help program teams identify where to leverage internal resources in order to

- Promote results-based measurement objectives
- Develop organizational understanding about the business value of a results-based process
- Create support for resource allocation
- Build organizational commitment to ensure implementation success

Identifying a Champion

Early in the implementation process, one or more individuals should be designated as the internal leader (or leaders) of the ROI Methodology implementation. As in most change efforts, someone must take the responsibility for ensuring that implementation is successful. This leader will champion the ROI Methodology; he or she should be the individual who understands the process best and has a vision of its potential contribution to the organization. More important, this leader should be willing to show and teach the methodology and its benefits to others.

Being the ROI leader is usually a full-time responsibility for a staff member in a large organization or a part-time one for someone in a small organization. The typical job title for a full-time ROI leader is manager of measurement and evaluation. Some organizations assign this responsibility to a team and empower this group to lead the implementation effort. In essence, team members are the champions for the ROI Methodology in their respective areas. For example, at Wachovia, one of the largest U.S. financial institutions, a task force of twenty-six professionals was selected, and each member became certified in the ROI Methodology and acted as a champion in his or her specific business unit. The vice president of assessment, measurement, and evaluation served as the chair of the team—the ROI leader.

Developing the ROI Leader

In preparation for the assignment of the ROI leader, an individual usually receives special training to build specific skills and knowledge in the ROI process. The role of the ROI leader is broad and fulfills a variety of specialized duties. The leader can take on many roles, as shown in Exhibit 3.1.

At times, the ROI leader serves as a technical expert, providing advice and making decisions about some of the issues involved in evaluation design, data analysis, and presentation. As an initiator, the leader identifies programs for ROI analysis and takes the lead in conducting the ROI studies. When needed, the leader is a cheerleader, bringing attention to the ROI Methodology, encouraging others to become involved, and showing how the methodology can add value to the organization. Finally, the ROI leader is a communicator, letting others know about the process and communicating results to a variety of target audiences. All the roles can come into play at one time or another as the leader implements the ROI Methodology within an organization.

The role of the ROI leader is a difficult and challenging one that will need special preparation and skill building. In the past,

Exhibit 3.1. Roles of the ROI Leader

• Technical expert	• Cheerleader
• Consultant	• Communicator
• Problem solver	• Process monitor
• Initiator	• Planner
• Designer	• Analyst
• Developer	• Interpreter
• Coordinator	• Teacher

Exhibit 3.2. Skill Set for ROI Certification

- Planning for ROI calculations
- Collecting evaluation data
- Isolating the effects of programs
- Converting data to monetary values
- Monitoring program costs
- Analyzing data, including calculating the ROI
- Presenting evaluation data
- Implementing the ROI Methodology
- Providing internal consulting on the ROI Methodology
- Teaching others about the ROI Methodology

only a few programs to build these skills have been available. Now, many are available, and some are comprehensive. For example, the ROI Institute has developed a program to certify individuals who are assuming a leadership role in the implementation of the ROI Methodology. The process involves preliminary work and preparation prior to attending a one-week workshop. The weeklong comprehensive workshop is the shortest of three ways to become certified in the ROI Methodology. All certification programs are designed to build essential skills needed to apply and implement the ROI process. Exhibit 3.2 lists the skills that are covered.

During the workshop, each participant plans a project for ROI evaluation, develops the data collection and ROI analysis plans for the project, and presents it to the other workshop participants for feedback. In addition, the participants develop and present plans to show how they will help implement the ROI Methodology in their organization, addressing the issues under their control. The typical participant is charged with implementing the ROI Methodology (or a part of it) in his or her division or organization. Sometimes, participants are part of an entire team that attends the certification workshop.

A public version of this certification workshop was first offered in 1995, when it became apparent that many organizations did not have the resources to send an entire team to an internal certification workshop but wanted instead to send one or two individuals to this type of session to develop the skills to lead the implementation of the ROI Methodology.

To date, more than 5,000 individuals, representing 3,000 organizations in fifty countries, have attended a certification workshop. Exhibit 3.3 shows a small sample of the private sector organizations that have participated in certification. Almost one-third of this group had an internal team certified. Others sent one or more individuals to a public workshop. Adoption of this strategy has been widespread; certification workshops have been conducted on every continent except Antarctica. No other process is available to satisfy this critical need; thus both internal and public certification are still very popular and successful. For more information on certification in the ROI Methodology, visit www.roiinstitute.net.

Apart from private sector organizations, many public sector organizations, including universities, nonprofit organizations, and health care providers, have participated in ROI certification. The organizations listed in Exhibit 3.4 represent a small sample of the many public sector organizations that have attended certification workshops.

Assigning Responsibilities

Determining specific responsibilities for implementation is a critical issue, because confusion arises when individuals are unclear about their specific assignments when implementing the ROI Methodology. Responsibilities apply to two broad groups. The first assignment is the entire program staff's responsibility for measurement and evaluation. All who are involved in designing, developing, delivering, coordinating, and supporting programs have some responsibility for measurement and evaluation. These responsibilities may include providing input on the design of instruments, planning a specific

Exhibit 3.3. Private Sector Organizations That Have Participated in Certification Workshops in the ROI Methodology

- Accenture
- Aetna
- Allstate Insurance Company
- Amazon.com
- AmSouth Bank
- Apple Computer
- Asia Pacific Breweries
- AT&T
- Bank of America
- BlueCross BlueShield
- Boston Scientific
- BP Amoco
- Bristol-Myers Squibb
- British Telecom
- Caltex Pacific
- Canadian Imperial Bank of Commerce
- Canadian Tire
- Chevron/Texaco
- CIGNA
- Cisco
- Comcast
- Commonwealth Edison
- CVS
- Delta Airlines
- Deloitte & Touche
- DHL Worldwide Express
- Discover Card
- Duke Energy
- Eli Lilly
- Eskom (South Africa)
- Federal Express
- First American Bank
- Ford Motor Company
- Genentech
- General Mills
- Georgia Pacific
- GlaxoSmithKline
- Harley Davidson
- Hewlett-Packard
- Hilton Hotels
- Hong Kong Bank
- HSBC
- IBM
- Intel
- Illinois Power
- KPMG
- Lockheed Martin
- M&M Mars
- MasterCard
- Mead
- Merck
- Meridian Hotels
- Microsoft
- Molson Coors
- Motorola
- NCR
- Nortel Networks
- Novus Services
- Olive Garden Restaurants
- Oversea-Chinese Banking Corporation
- Pfizer
- PriceWaterhouseCoopers
- Raytheon
- Rolls Royce
- SABMiller
- Scotia Bank

(*Continued*)

Exhibit 3.3. Private Sector Organizations That Have Participated in Certification Workshops in the ROI Methodology (*Continued*)

• Singapore Airlines	• Vodafone
• Singapore Technologies	• Volvo of North America
• Sprint/Nextel	• Wachovia Bank
• TD Canada Trust	• Wal-Mart
• Time Warner	• Waste Management Company
• United Parcel Service	• Wells Fargo
• UNOCAL	• Whirlpool
• Verizon Communications	• Xerox

evaluation, collecting data, or interpreting the results of a program. Typical responsibilities include these:

- Ensuring that the needs assessment addresses specific business impact measures targeted for improvement

- Developing application objectives (Level 3) and business impact objectives (Level 4) for each program

- Focusing the content of the program on performance improvement, ensuring that exercises, tests, case studies, and skill practices relate to the desired objectives

- Keeping participants focused on application and impact objectives

- Communicating the rationale and reasons for evaluation

- Assisting with follow-up activities to capture application and business impact data

- Providing assistance with data collection, data analysis, and reporting

- Developing plans for data collection and analysis

Exhibit 3.4. Public Sector Organizations That Have Participated in Certification Workshops in the ROI Methodology

Federal Government

Department of Defense, Department of Homeland Security, Department of Labor, Department of the Treasury, Department of Veterans Affairs, Office of Personnel Management

State Government

California, Colorado, Mississippi, Washington

Higher Education

Harvard University, Indiana University, Lansing Community College, Penn State University, University of Southern Mississippi

Healthcare

Banner Healthcare, Baptist Health Systems, Children's Hospitals, Covenant Healthcare System, Guthrie Healthcare, Los Angeles Hospital

- Presenting evaluation data to target audiences
- Assisting with the design of instruments

While having each member of the staff involved in all of these activities may be appropriate, each individual should have one or more of these responsibilities as part of their routine job duties. This assignment of responsibility keeps the implementation of the ROI Methodology from being disjointed and separate from major organizational activities. More important, it allocates accountability to those who develop, deliver, and implement the programs.

The second assignment of responsibility involves technical support. Those responsible for technical support are usually the ROI champions and ROI leaders. If the department and its staff are large, it may be helpful to establish a group of technical experts to assist in implementing the ROI Methodology. When this group is established, everyone must understand that these experts are provided not to relieve others of evaluation responsibilities but to supplement their technical expertise. For example, at one time, Accenture had a full-time measurement and evaluation staff of thirty-two individuals to provide technical support for the evaluation of internal professional education. Today, because program staff capabilities have been developed so that individuals can share evaluation responsibilities, full-time staff number less than ten, even though there are now more programs and more employees.

When technical support is developed, responsibilities center on eight key areas:

1. Designing data collection instruments
2. Assisting with development of an evaluation strategy
3. Coordinating a major evaluation project
4. Analyzing data, including specialized statistical analyses
5. Interpreting results and making specific recommendations
6. Developing an evaluation report or case study to communicate overall results
7. Presenting results to critical audiences
8. Providing technical support in any phase of the ROI Methodology

Assignment of responsibilities for evaluation is an issue that may require attention throughout the process. Although the entire staff must have specific responsibilities, others in support functions may need to be responsible for data collection. These responsibilities are defined when a particular evaluation strategy plan is developed and approved.

Tapping into a Network

Because the ROI Methodology is new to many individuals, having a peer group of individuals who are experiencing similar issues and frustrations can be helpful. Tapping into an international network that is already developed, joining or creating a local network, or building an internal network are all ways to access the resources, ideas, and support of others.

The ROI Network

In 1996, the ROI Network was created to facilitate the exchange of information among the graduates of the ROI Certification™ workshop. During the certification process, the participants bond and freely exchange information with each other. The ROI Network provides a permanent vehicle for information and support.

The ROI Network, which claims about 4,000 members, is supported by the ROI Institute, Inc. The network operates through a variety of committees and communicates with members through newsletters, Web sites, list serves, and annual meetings. The ROI Network represents an opportunity to build a community of practice around the ROI Methodology. To learn more about the ROI Network, visit www.roiinstitute.net.

Local Networks

In some situations, establishing a group of local individuals who share similar interests in and concerns about the ROI Methodology may be feasible. A local network can be set up in a country (for example, the Irish ROI Network) or in a more confined entity (for example, the Puerto Rico ROI Network). In Puerto Rico, a group of one hundred individuals who participated in the certification process challenged each other to remain together as a group in order to discuss issues and report progress. Members come from a wide variety of backgrounds, and they meet routinely to report progress; discuss problems, barriers, and issues; and plan next steps. This active group is typical of what can develop if individuals are willing to share information and support each other. Sometimes, a statewide network, such as the California ROI Network, is created. In a few cases, a citywide network, such as the Toronto ROI Network, has been created.

Internal Networks

One way to integrate the needs of practitioners for an effective ROI evaluation process is through an internal ROI network.

Organizations in which networks have been created report that they are powerful tools for accelerating skill development in evaluation, as well as for cultivating a new culture of accountability.

The concept of an internal network is simple. The idea is to bring together people from throughout an organization who are interested in ROI evaluations to work under the guidance of trained ROI evaluators. Typically, advocates for the network within a function or department see both the need for beginning a network and the potential of ROI evaluation to change how the function does its work. Interested network members learn by designing and executing real evaluation plans. This process generates commitment for accountability as a new way of doing business.

Developing Evaluation Targets for the Staff

ROI Fundamentals, the first book in this series, explains that establishing targets for evaluation levels is an important way to make progress in measurement and evaluation. Targets enable the staff to focus on improvements at specific evaluation levels. The percentage of programs to be evaluated at each level must be targeted.

The first step in developing targets is to assess the current situation. The number of programs, including repeated sessions of a program, is tabulated, along with the level (or levels) of evaluation conducted for each program. Next, the percentage of programs collecting Level 1 (Reaction) data is calculated or estimated. This process is repeated for each level of evaluation. The initial percentages for evaluations at Levels 3, 4, and 5 are usually low.

After determining the current situation, the next step is to establish a realistic target for each level within a specific time frame. Many organizations set annual targets for the percentages. This process should involve input from the entire program team to ensure that the targets are realistic and that the staff is committed to the process and the targets. If the staff does not develop ownership of this process, the targets will not be met. The targets must be achievable yet challenging and motivating. Table 3.1 shows the

Table 3.1. Evaluation Targets for a Large Pharmaceutical Company

Level of Evaluation	Percentage of Programs Evaluated at this Level
Level 0: Inputs and Indicators	100%
Level 1: Reaction	100
Level 2: Learning	70
Level 3: Application	30
Level 4: Business Impact	10
Level 5: ROI	5

targets for a large pharmaceutical company with hundreds of programs.

In the pharmaceutical company described in Table 3.1, 100 percent of the programs are to be measured at Levels 0 and 1, which is consistent with many other organizations. Seventy percent of the programs will be measured at Level 2, using a formal method of measurement. At Level 3, 30 percent of the programs will collect application data. This means that almost one-third of the programs will have some type of follow-up method, at least for a small sample of participants. Ten percent of programs are planned for business impact evaluations, and half of those will have ROI evaluations. These percentages are typical and are often recommended, although the Level 2 percentage may increase significantly if formal testing or informal measures (such as self-assessments) are used to evaluate learning. In many companies, there is no need to go beyond 10 percent and 5 percent at Level 4 and Level 5, respectively.

Table 3.2 shows the current percentages (year 0) and the targets for four years in a large Eastern European multinational company. This table reflects the gradual improvement of increasing evaluation activity at Levels 3, 4, and 5. In this firm, several issues involving infrastructure and organizational culture had to be addressed before major performance improvement could be expected.

Table 3.2. Percentage Targets for Four Years in a Large Eastern European Company

	Percentage of Programs Evaluated				
	Year 0	Year 1	Year 2	Year 3	Year 4
Level 0: Inputs and Indicators	85%	90%	95%	100%	100%
Level 1: Reaction and Planned Action	74	85	95	100	100
Level 2: Learning	32	40	50	60	65
Level 3: Application	0	10	15	20	25
Level 4: Business Impact	0	2	4	6	10
Level 5: ROI	0	1	2	4	5

Target setting is a critical implementation issue. It should be completed early in the process, with the full support of the entire program staff. Also, if it is practical and feasible, the targets should have the approval of key managers, particularly the senior management team.

Preparing the Program Staff

One group that will often resist implementation of the ROI Methodology is the staff that must design, develop, deliver, and coordinate the programs. These staff members often see evaluation as an unnecessary intrusion on their responsibilities that will absorb precious time and stifle their freedom to be creative. This section outlines some important issues that must be addressed when preparing staff for implementing the ROI Methodology.

Involving the Staff

The program staff should be involved in the process whenever a key issue is being resolved or a major decision is being made. As policy statements are prepared and evaluation guidelines are developed, staff input is essential. It is difficult for staff members to be critical of something that they helped design, develop, and plan. Using meetings, brainstorming sessions, and task forces, staff should be involved in every phase of developing the framework and the supporting documents for implementing the ROI Methodology. Ideally, staff would learn the process in a two-day workshop and, at the same time, develop guidelines, policies, and application targets. This approach is efficient, allowing participants to complete several key tasks at the same time.

Using ROI as a Learning Tool

Many reasons for staff resistance to implementation of the ROI Methodology have been discussed in this book. One of those reasons is that the effectiveness of their programs that are being evaluated will be fully exposed, placing their reputation on the line. Some participants may have a fear of failure. To overcome this fear, the ROI Methodology should be clearly positioned as a tool for process improvement and not a tool to evaluate staff performance, at least during the early years of its implementation. Staff members will not be interested in developing a tool that will be used to expose their shortcomings and failures.

Evaluators can actually learn more from failures than from successes. If a program is not working, it is best to find out quickly and to gain insight into critical issues firsthand rather than to find out from others. If a program is ineffective and not producing the desired results, that fact will eventually be known to clients or the management team, if they are not already aware of it. A lack of results will cause managers to become less supportive of programs. Dwindling support takes many forms, ranging from budget reductions to refusing to let individuals participate in programs. If the weaknesses of programs are identified and adjustments are made quickly, not only will more effective programs be developed and promoted but the credibility of the function or department and the respect for its staff will increase.

Addressing Objections to Implementation

Several objections to the implementation of the ROI Methodology will usually be encountered. Some of these reflect real barriers, while others are based on misconceptions. Most of these were presented and analyzed in the preceding chapter. However, the most common objections from the staff and ways to address them are reviewed here.

- *ROI is a complex process.* Many members of the program staff will perceive the ROI Methodology as too complex to implement. To counter this perception, the staff must be shown how the process can be simplified by breaking it into manageable components and steps. Many tools, templates, and software programs that simplify the use of the ROI Methodology are available. (The Appendix of *ROI Fundamentals*, the first book in this series, lists many of these tools.)

- *We have no time for evaluation.* Staff members need to understand that evaluation can save time in the future. An ROI impact study may show that a program should be slightly modified, radically changed, or even eliminated, thereby improving their processes, which results in efficiency gains. Thoroughly planning the evaluation strategy can save additional follow-up time.

- *Management does not require evaluation.* Most staff members know when top managers are pushing the accountability issue. If they do not see that push, they may be reluctant to take the time to make the ROI Methodology work. They must be helped to see the benefits of pursuing the process, even if it is not required or encouraged from the top. The staff should see the ROI Methodology as a preventive strategy or leading-edge strategy. The payoff of implementation should be underscored.

- *Results will lead to criticism.* Many staff members will be concerned about how the results of ROI impact studies will be used. If the results are used to criticize or evaluate the performance of program designers or facilitators, they will be reluctant to embrace the concept. The ROI Methodology should be considered a learning process.

These and other objections can thwart an otherwise successful implementation. Each must be addressed or reduced to a manageable issue.

Teaching the Staff

The program staff may have inadequate skills in measurement and evaluation in general and in the ROI Methodology specifically and thus may need to develop some expertise. Measurement and evaluation is not always a formal part of preparing to become a facilitator, designer, performance analyst, or program leader. Therefore, each staff member must be provided with training on how to implement the ROI Methodology step by step. In addition, staff members must learn how to develop plans for collecting and analyzing data and how to interpret the results of data analysis. A one- or two-day workshop can be used to build their skills and knowledge and can enable them to understand the ROI Methodology, appreciate what it can accomplish for the organization, understand its necessity, and participate in a successful implementation. (A list of public two-day workshops is available at www.roiintitute.net. Teaching materials, outlines, slides, workbooks, and other support materials for workshops are also available through the ROI Institute.) Each staff member should understand the ROI Methodology and should know how to utilize and support it.

ROI Evaluations

The first tangible evidence of success with the ROI Methodology may be initiation of the first program for which the ROI is calculated. This section outlines some key issues involved in identifying the programs that are appropriate for ROI evaluations and keeping them on track.

Selecting Programs for ROI Evaluation

Selecting a program for ROI analysis is an important issue. Under most circumstances, certain types of programs are more suitable for comprehensive, detailed analyses. *ROI Fundamentals*, the first book of this series, briefly explains that typically, the programs identified as appropriate for ROI evaluation are expensive, strategic, and highly visible. Exhibit 3.5 lists six common criteria used to select programs for this level of evaluation. The process for selection is simple. Using a list like the one in Exhibit 3.5 or a more detailed one, each program is rated on each criterion. A typical scale uses ratings of 1 to 5. All programs are rated, and the program with the highest number is the best candidate for ROI evaluation. This process only identifies the best candidates. Which programs are actually evaluated may depend on other factors, such as the resources available to conduct the studies.

Additional criteria should be considered when selecting the first programs for ROI evaluations. For example, the first program should be as simple as possible. Complex programs should be evaluated later, after ROI evaluation skills have been mastered. Also, the initial program should be one that is currently considered successful. (For example, all the current feedback data suggest that the program adds significant value.) This criterion helps avoid a negative ROI on the first use of the ROI Methodology. Still another criterion is that the program be free of strong political issues or biases. While such programs can be effectively evaluated with the ROI Methodology, it is better to avoid the complexity that may be added by controversy in early applications.

Exhibit 3.5. Selection Tool for ROI Evaluations

Criteria	Programs				
	#1	#2	#3	#4	#5
1. Life cycle					
2. Company objectives					
3. Costs					
4. Audience size					
5. Visibility					
6. Management interest					
Total					

	Rating Scale
1. Life cycle	1 = short life cycle
	5 = long life cycle
2. Company objectives	1 = not directly related to company objectives
	5 = closely related to company objectives
3. Costs	1 = inexpensive
	5 = expensive
4. Audience size	1 = small audience
	5 = large audience
5. Visibility	1 = low visibility
	5 = high visibility
6. Management interest	1 = low level of interest in evaluation
	5 = high level of interest in evaluation

We have touched on only the basic criteria; criteria can be added as needed to bring the organization's evaluation issues into focus. Some large organizations with hundreds of programs in a corporate university use as many as fifteen criteria to determine which programs should be targeted for ROI evaluation. The most important point is to select the programs that are designed to make a difference and represent tremendous investments by the organization. Also, programs that command much attention from senior management are ideal candidates for an ROI evaluation. Almost any senior management group will have a perception about the effectiveness of a particular program. Senior managers may definitely want to know the impact of some programs but be less concerned about others. Therefore, management interest may drive the selection of programs to be evaluated at Level 5 (ROI).

The next major step is to determine how many programs to evaluate initially and in which areas. Evaluating a small number of programs is recommended at first, perhaps two or three. The selected programs may represent the functional areas of the business, such as operations, sales, finance, engineering, and information systems. A similar approach is to select programs that represent different areas within a function; for example, within the organizational function of learning and development, programs such as sales training, management and supervisor training, computer-based training, and technical training might represent a sample of the various areas. It is important to select a manageable number so that the process will be implemented.

Ultimately, the number of programs selected will depend on the resources available to conduct the studies, as well as the internal need for higher levels of accountability. Evaluation of programs at the percentages indicated in Table 3.1 can be accomplished within 3 to 5 percent of the total learning and development budget. For a learning and development organization with two hundred programs, this would mean that in a given year, 5 percent (ten) of the programs would receive ROI evaluations and at least 30 percent (sixty programs) would receive some type of follow-up (Level 3) evaluation. The entire program can be accomplished for less than 5 percent of the total learning and development budget. The costs of the ROI Methodology need not drain the resources of an organization; nonetheless, the programs selected for Level 5 analysis should be limited and should be carefully selected.

Reporting Progress

When programs are developed and implementation of the ROI Methodology gets under way, status meetings should be conducted in order to report progress and discuss critical issues with appropriate team members. For example, if a leadership program is selected as one of the programs for ROI evaluation, all the key staff members involved in the program (design, development, and delivery) should meet regularly to discuss its status. This keeps the program team focused on the critical issues, generates the best ideas for addressing problems and barriers, and builds a knowledge base for evaluating future programs. Sometimes, this group is facilitated by an external consultant who is an expert in the ROI Methodology. In other cases, the internal ROI leader may facilitate the group.

These meetings serve three major purposes: reporting progress, learning, and planning. The meeting usually begins with a status report on each ROI program, describing what has been accomplished since the previous meeting. Next, specific barriers and problems are discussed. During the discussions, new issues may be interjected as the group considers possible tactics, techniques, or tools that can be used to remove barriers or solve problems. Finally, the group focuses on suggestions and recommendations for next steps, developing specific plans.

Preparing the Management Team

Perhaps no group is more important to successful implementation of the ROI Methodology than the management team responsible for allocating resources for programs and providing other kinds of support for them. In addition, the management team often provides valuable input and assistance for the implementation. Specific actions to train and develop the management team should be carefully planned and executed.

Building an Effective Partnership Between Program Staff and Senior Management

A critical issue that must be addressed in preparing the managers is the relationship between the program staff and key managers. A productive partnership is needed; each party must understand the concerns, problems, and opportunities of the other. Developing this type of relationship is a long-term process that must be deliberately planned and initiated by key staff members. The decision to commit resources and support for a program is often based on the effectiveness of this relationship.

Training Managers

One effective way to prepare managers for implementation of the ROI Methodology is to conduct a workshop on the "Manager's Role in Learning and Performance." Varying in duration from one-half to two days, this practical workshop shapes critical skills and changes perceptions to enhance the support of the ROI methodology. Managers leave the workshop with an improved perception of the impact of programs and a clearer understanding of their role in the implementation process. More important, managers often renew their commitment to making programs within their organization successful.

Target Audience

While the target audience for this workshop is usually middle-level managers, this may vary. In some organizations, the target may be senior managers, and in others, the target may be middle-level managers. Three important questions will help determine the proper audience:

- Which group has the most direct influence on the programs being implemented?
- Which management group is causing serious problems through a lack of support?
- Which group needs to understand the ROI Methodology so that group members can influence the implementation of programs and the methodology?

The answer to these questions is often "middle-level managers."

Timing

This workshop should be conducted early in the management development process, before nonsupportive habits are developed. When the ROI Methodology is implemented throughout the organization, it is best to educate high-level managers first and then work down the organization. If possible, a version of the workshop should become part of the traditional management development program required for supervisors when they are promoted into managerial positions.

Enlisting Support from Top Management

Convincing top management to require this workshop may be difficult; at least three approaches can be taken:

1. Discuss and illustrate the consequences of inadequate management support for programs and evaluation. For example, the statistics on wasted time and money when the programming process does not work are staggering.

2. Show how current support is lacking. An evaluation of a program will often reveal the barriers to successful application and implementation. Lack of management support is often the main reason, a fact that brings the issue close to home and illustrates the importance of this support.

3. Demonstrate how money can be saved and how results can be achieved by using the ROI Methodology.

Endorsement of the top management group is important. In some organizations, top managers actually attend the workshop in order to explore firsthand what is involved and what they must do to make the process work. At a minimum, top management should support the program by signing memos describing the program or by approving policy statements about the content of the workshop. They should also ask provocative questions about evaluation in their staff meetings from time to time. This will not happen by chance; executives may need tactful coaching.

Content

The program will usually cover the topics outlined in this section. The program can be developed in separate modules, and managers can be exempted from some modules based on their previous knowledge or experience with the topic. Using the module concept is recommended.

The Overall Importance of Programs. Managers need to be convinced that programs are a mainstream responsibility that is gaining importance and influence in many organizations. They need to understand the results-based approach of progressive functions or departments. After completing this module, managers should perceive programs and projects as critical processes in their organization and should be able to describe how programs contribute to strategic and operational objectives. Data from the organization should be presented to show the full scope of the function's impact within the organization. Tangible evidence of top management commitment to the ROI Methodology should be presented in the form of memos, directives, or policies signed by the CEO or another appropriate top executive. In some organizations, the invitation to attend the workshop comes from the CEO, a gesture that shows strong commitment from top management. Also, external data should be included to illustrate the growth of the unit's budget and the increasing importance of the unit's programs within the organization. Presenting a case study that shows the link between specific programs and the organization's overall strategy might be helpful.

The Impact of Programs. Too often, managers are unsure whether programs have been successful or useful. After completing this module, managers will be able to identify the steps for measuring the impact of specific types of programs on important output measures. Reports and studies that show the impact of programs, using measures such as productivity, quality, cost, response times, and customer satisfaction, should be presented. Internal evaluation reports, if available, should be presented to managers, showing convincing evidence that a variety of programs make a significant difference within the organization. If internal reports are not available, other success stories or case studies from other organizations can be used. Managers need to be convinced that their unit's programs, whatever the function or department, are successful and results-based, not only to help effect change but also to meet critical organizational goals and objectives.

The Process of Program Development and Evaluation. Managers usually will not support activities or processes that they do not fully understand. After completing this module, managers should be able to describe how the program development and evaluation process works within the organization and understand each critical step, from needs assessment to ROI calculation. Managers need to be aware of the effort that goes into developing and evaluating a program and their role in each step of the process. Presenting a short case study that illustrates all the steps is helpful. This discussion also reveals different areas of the potential impact of programs.

Responsibilities During the Process. Defining who is responsible for programs is important to their success. After completing this module, managers should be able to list their specific responsibilities for successful programs. Managers must see how they can influence programs and the degree of responsibility they must assume in the future. Multilevel responsibility for programs is advocated—that is, managers, participants, participants' managers, trainers, developers, and facilitators should share the responsibility. Case studies should be presented that illustrate the consequences when responsibilities are neglected or when managers fail to follow up. In some organizations, job descriptions are revised to reflect these responsibilities. In other organizations, major job-related goals are established in order to highlight management responsibility for programs. Overall, this module should leave the participants with a clear understanding of how their responsibilities are linked to the success of any program within the organization.

Active Involvement. One of the most important ways to increase manager support is to get managers actively involved in a process. After completing this module, managers will often commit to one or more avenues of active involvement in the future. Exhibit 3.6 shows twelve avenues for management involvement that were identified in one company. The information in the exhibit was presented to managers during the workshop with a request for them to commit to at least one area of involvement. After these areas were fully explained and discussed, each manager was asked to select one or more ways in which he or she would become involved in program development and evaluation in the future.

Exhibit 3.6. Management Involvement in Learning and Development

Following are twelve areas for present and future involvement in the learning and development process. Please check your areas of planned involvement.

	Within Your Area	Outside Your Area
• Attend a program designed for your staff	☐	☐
• Provide input on a needs analysis	☐	☐
• Serve on an advisory committee	☐	☐
• Provide input on program design	☐	☐
• Serve as a subject matter expert	☐	☐
• Serve on a task force to develop a program	☐	☐
• Volunteer to evaluate an external learning and development program	☐	☐
• Assist in the selection of a vendor-supplied learning and development program	☐	☐
• Provide reinforcement to your employees after they attend a program	☐	☐
• Coordinate a program	☐	☐
• Assist in program evaluation or follow-up	☐	☐
• Conduct a portion of the program as a facilitator	☐	☐

A commitment to sign up for at least one involvement role was required.

If used properly, these commitments can be a rich source of input and assistance from the management group. There will be many offers for involvement, and the function or department must follow through. A quick follow-up on all offers is recommended.

Monitoring Progress and Communicating Results

The final part of the implementation process is to monitor the overall progress made and communicate the results of programs selected for ROI evaluations. Although it is often an overlooked part of the process, an effective communication plan can help keep implementation on target and let others know how the use of the ROI Methodology is affecting an organization.

Communication must be an ongoing part of the process in order to ensure that all stakeholders know their responsibilities, understand the progress made and barriers confronted, and develop insight into the results and successes achieved. Because communication is so important in the ROI Methodology, this topic was explored in Chapter One, which provides comprehensive coverage of all the issues involved in communicating the results of programs and providing routine feedback for decision making and process improvement. Detailed information on how to develop and present an impact study is also included in that chapter.

Final Thoughts

Building capability in the ROI Methodology and support for its use is a critical part of implementation. If it is not approached in a systematic, logical way, the ROI Methodology will not become an integral part of the development and evaluation of programs and projects, and accountability for programs will be lacking. This chapter presents the elements that must be considered and the issues that must be addressed in order to ensure that capability and support are established and that implementation is as smooth as possible. The result should be full integration of the ROI Methodology as a mainstream activity in the program evaluation process.

4

Sustaining the Use of the ROI Methodology
Keeping the Process on Track

Keeping the process on track is one of the biggest challenges of ROI Methodology implementation. Staying on track in the face of continual change and maintaining the health and integrity of the process over time typically pose formidable challenges to an organization's efforts to create enduring, systemwide results-based measurement and evaluation.

This chapter explores the stages of implementation and identifies the inhibitors and enablers of successful integration of the ROI Methodology and outlines the strategies for facilitating integration of the ROI Methodology over time.

As in any change effort, consistent attention and focus must be maintained in order to build and sustain the evaluation process. Chapter Three examined the importance of building internal capabilities and skill sets in order to help develop and maintain a results-based measurement and evaluation process. Without this attention, the organization's commitment to the ROI Methodology might wane and the process might be labeled another "flavor of the month." Long-term, effective evaluation solutions must stand the test of time. Emphasizing the ROI Methodology as a long-term process improvement tool adds value and keeps it from becoming a passing fad or a short-term phenomenon.

Motivation for long-term implementation could come initially from the results of a current impact study. Motivation may also be maintained as programs continue to be adjusted, modified, enhanced, or eliminated to add value. To ensure complete integration of the ROI Methodology as a mainstream approach, critical stages in implementation must be addressed. This final chapter will help you to anticipate the predictable stages of implementation, identify signs and symptoms of implementation trouble spots that may require action, and move past trouble spots by taking actions to remain on track.

The Challenges of Sustainability

Why might implementation of the ROI Methodology fail to be sustained in an organization? Here are the top reasons, which occur in all types of business environments.

- Lack of a clear vision or goal
- Changing directions in midstream
- Conflicting priorities
- Inadequate communication
- Unmet customer expectations
- No buy-in or support from key stakeholders
- Ineffective leadership
- Inadequate planning or no planning
- No clear understanding of what needs to be done (who is going to do what by when)
- Change in scope
- Not enough resources
- Unrealistic expectations

Each of these issues must be addressed in both short-term and long-term implementation. In the short term, applying tips, tools, and strategies from Chapter Two will help mitigate many of these issues. High-level strategies for addressing each challenge are shown in Table 4.1.

It may be helpful to identify which implementation issues have posed or may pose the greatest threat to the success of the impact study. The tactics and tools to address the issues should then be identified, and action plans should be put in place to prevent problems. To add context in regard to the appropriate time and place for use of these methods for addressing implementation issues, it is important to understand the typical stages in implementation of the ROI Methodology.

Stages of Implementation

As the ROI Methodology is introduced and integrated into a workplace, predictable obstacles to progress often arise. Large or small, public or private, most organizations undergo distinct stages on their journey toward increased accountability. As Figure 4.1 shows, these stages are part of a naturally evolving process.

Stage 1: Recognition

In the recognition stage, an organization realizes that accountability for evaluation is an issue, and preliminary action is taken. This stage is usually initiated by a single person or a small group, and at this point, implementation of the ROI Methodology is not viewed as a strategic imperative by senior management. For these reasons, commitment may be limited or marginal, and long-lasting evaluation processes are not yet in place. Indicators of the recognition stage are noted as readiness issues in the assessment "Is Your Organization a Candidate for Implementation of the

Table 4.1. Causes of Ineffective Implementation

If Your Organization Is Experiencing . . .	Then . . .	Support Tools
Lack of a clear vision or goal	Initiate goal setting, stakeholder communication, and action planning based on the value of a results-based measurement focus.	Communication briefings Communication plan
Changing directions midstream	Integrate change efforts into existing management systems and cycles such as • Business planning • Budget development • Corporate and departmental measurement plans • Compensation planning • Succession planning	Implementation issues to address with your sponsor
Conflicting priorities	Balance organizational priorities to protect resources dedicated to ROI implementation efforts. Make necessary compromises or adjustments in the implementation schedule in order to meet organizational needs.	Transition plan Project plan

Inadequate communication	Commit to regular review meetings to assess progress. Make performance data available to implementation team members or stakeholders.	Communication plan Transfer strategy matrix Action planning
Unmet customer expectations	Develop metrics and communication methods in order to routinely track progress and productivity.	Stakeholder identification
No buy-in or support from key stakeholders	Meet with key stakeholders from client organizations to define the value proposition of a results-based measurement focus.	Stakeholder identification Stakeholder engagement Management involvement checklist Communication briefings
Ineffective leadership	Solicit a credible sponsor. Use a credible, competent evaluation lead. Follow up on established consequences if desired performance levels are not being achieved. Identify tactics to build program team strengths and minimize weaknesses.	Professional development, training, or ROI certification for internal staff Senior or mid-level management briefings Best-practice benchmarking Professional networking
Inadequate planning or no planning	Work from an implementation plan. Initiate a task force to address and remove inhibitors.	Project plan Transition plan Data collection plan Roles and responsibilities matrix Evaluation team charter Transfer strategy matrix

(Continued)

Table 4.1. Causes of Ineffective Implementation (*Continued*)

If Your Organization Is Experiencing ...	Then ...	Support Tools
No clear understanding of what needs to be done (who is going to do what by when)	Plan and deploy well. Break down implementation tasks into manageable, meaningful activities. Ensure adequate staffing and funding to support the implementation plan.	Project plan Transition plan Data collection plan Roles and responsibilities matrix Evaluation team charter Transfer strategy matrix
Change in scope	Communicate implementation plan, scope, schedule, and resource requirements to appropriate executives or stakeholders.	Project plan Transition plan Data collection plan Roles and responsibilities matrix Transfer strategy matrix
Not enough resources	Acknowledge legitimate organizational issues of capacity and resource constraints. Use cost-saving approaches to consolidate steps and conserve resources. Conduct ROI impact studies on a selective basis.	Ten cost-saving approaches Selection criteria matrix
Unrealistic expectations	Continually ensure that results are related to business and strategic goals. Address organizational myths, fears, and concerns.	Matching objectives with needs Stakeholder identification Communication plan Myths, fears, and countermeasures worksheet

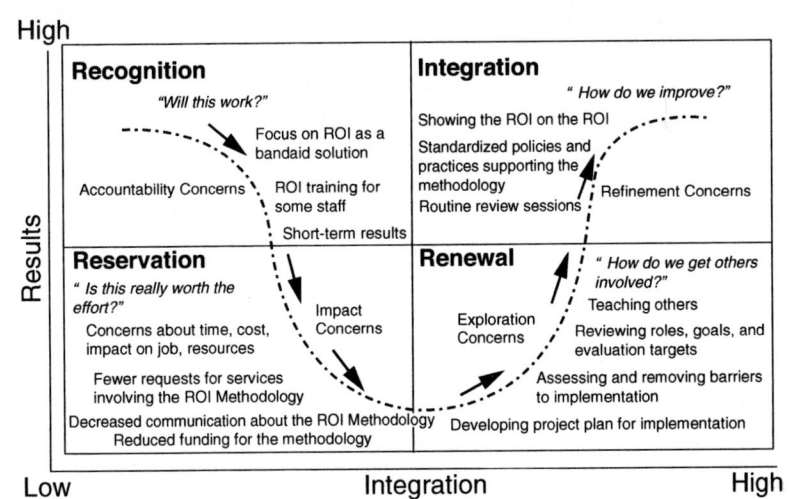

Figure 4.1. Stages in Implementation of the ROI Methodology

Results (vertical axis: Low to High)
Integration (horizontal axis: Low to High)

Recognition
"Will this work?"
- Focus on ROI as a bandaid solution
- Accountability Concerns
- ROI training for some staff
- Short-term results

Integration
"How do we improve?"
- Showing the ROI on the ROI
- Standardized policies and practices supporting the methodology
- Routine review sessions
- Refinement Concerns

Reservation
"Is this really worth the effort?"
- Concerns about time, cost, impact on job, resources
- Impact Concerns
- Fewer requests for services involving the ROI Methodology
- Decreased communication about the ROI Methodology
- Reduced funding for the methodology

Renewal
- Exploration Concerns
- "How do we get others involved?"
- Teaching others
- Reviewing roles, goals, and evaluation targets
- Assessing and removing barriers to implementation
- Developing project plan for implementation

Source: Adapted from Scott and Jaffe, 1999.

ROI Methodology?" in Chapter Two. These issues include such factors as:

- Expenditures of a department or function are identified as significant.
- An organization is undergoing important change.
- Complaints or concerns from clients about the value of programs and services have been noted.
- A department or function has a history of more than one program disaster.
- Clients or decision makers are demanding that the department or function show bottom-line results.
- The focus on linking the department or function to strategic directions of the organization has increased.

- The department or function has a low investment in measurement and evaluation.

- The department or function is a key player in current change initiatives.

- The unit competes with other departments or functions for resources.

- The department's or function's image is less than satisfactory.

The responsibility of a program team at this stage is finding solutions. Some of the necessary tasks at the recognition stage are as follows:

1. Remove barriers to implementation and facilitate problem solving by taking some of the following actions:
   - Make sure that the program team or ROI champion is an effective change agent.
   - Assess the needs of the organization.
   - Establish partnerships between the program team and key stakeholders.
   - Obtain executive input.
   - Prepare your organization for the changes that will occur as it shifts to a results-based focus.
2. Initiate goal setting, stakeholder communication, and action planning to show the value of a results-based measurement focus. Complete these actions:
   - Relate the change effort to organizational strategies.
   - Identify and research the factors that will affect change strategies within your organization.
   - Plan, communicate, and deploy all programs effectively.

- Consistently educate executives and senior management on the requirements for implementing the ROI Methodology so that funding and staffing will be adequate.
- Ensure that time and resources are available for the evaluation team to develop the skills required for proper implementation.
- Make sure that the program team is aware of any resource constraints within the organization.

3. Initiate short-term solutions:
   - Select, orient, and educate program team members about what is required for implementation of the ROI Methodology.
   - Institute a reward system that is linked to desired program outcomes, and communicate it to all parties prior to implementation.
   - Identify one to three "quick hit" opportunities, and use them to show the value of the ROI Methodology.
4. Evaluate solutions in order to determine whether they meet organizational goals. Use these methods to:
   - Hold weekly review meetings in order to assess implementation progress.
   - Assign responsibilities for deliverables.
   - Define metrics for tracking progress and productivity.

Stage 2: Reservation

In the reservation stage, symptoms that the ROI Methodology is no longer achieving its intended objectives may begin to emerge. For example, renewed objections may arise about the impact of the process on time and resources, or an organization may become preoccupied with new business demands that compete for time and resources. Stakeholders may become impatient and may voice the concern that the investment of time and effort needed to move toward a results-based focus is not worth it. The initial support and goodwill resulting from preliminary successes with the process may have waned. It is not uncommon at this stage for an organization to abandon the effort or to significantly decrease support from what was originally committed.

Indicators that an organization is in the reservation stage include these:

- Reduced funding for the process of ROI evaluation
- Fewer communications about the programs and processes
- Lack of participation and involvement of the management team
- Constant shuffling of people involved in the process
- Fewer requests for products and services related to the accountability process
- Postponing or eliminating review sessions aimed at keeping the process on track
- Complaints about the time or cost required for evaluation activities
- A change of direction toward some other process that appears to be competing with or eliminating the need for the accountability
- Reduction in the dissemination of information and communication on the progress of the ROI Methodology and ROI studies, even in a streamlined fashion

Several key tasks are required at the reservation stage.

1. The program leader or ROI champion must jump-start individuals and groups and eliminate inertia by doing the following:
   - Break implementation and program tasks into manageable, meaningful activities.
   - Develop contingency plans to bolster participants in the implementation (including program team members) who may have become worn down by the process.
   - An implementation plan should have been developed prior to implementation. Rigorously adhere to this plan, and make sure all participants have a copy of it.
   - Encourage program team members to contribute information and insights on how to revive the implementation effort.
   - Ensure that the results sought from implementation are manageable in the time frame allowed.
2. Initial goal setting and action planning should be reactivated by doing the following:
   - Translate the details of the change effort into job-level details and tasks, then assign them to implementation team members, who will be responsible and accountable for carrying them out.
   - Ask participants' managers to link performance appraisals with individual accomplishments related to implementation of the ROI Methodology, if appropriate.
   - Identify the budget impacts of implementation efforts.
   - Hold regular meetings in order to inform executives and stakeholders about the status of implementation and to gather input.
   - Get financial experts involved in estimating the financial impact of the change on your organization.

3. Enthusiasm about the desired future state should be rejuvenated through performing these tasks:
   - Share with all the success of those who have implemented the ROI Methodology.
   - If some metrics are not improving as projected, identify more appropriate metrics with which to measure progress.
   - Try holding a contest in order to address an issue involved in the results-based change effort.
   - Continually assess the implementation process and conditions, and change them as necessary to ensure success.
   - Publicize and celebrate successes and progress toward goals.
   - Avoid bragging and boasting about success, even if some progress is being made.
4. Objections to the process should be openly addressed with these actions:
   - Initiate a task force to address and remove inhibitors to the process, and use the influence of management or other stakeholders to neutralize problems or remove obstacles.
   - Discount any negative rumors, and reconfigure systems or dynamics that could foster negativity.
   - Have the implementation team follow up relentlessly with stakeholders.
   - Report apprehensions about the implementation plan, scope, or schedule to executives or stakeholders.
   - Establish clear milestones for the implementation plan.
5. Consistent messages about the vision and purpose of the implementation and the value of change should be repeated to the stakeholders. Try these ideas:

- Leverage personal alliances to communicate business drivers for the change effort.
- Assign the executive sponsor and key stakeholders specific accountabilities and responsibilities.
- Set an example by seizing learning opportunities, and communicate about them on a regular basis.
- Develop a communication plan and follow it.

Stage 3: Renewal

In the renewal stage, an organization starts to move past its inhibitors and explores how to renew its initial commitment to invest in expanded evaluation solutions. The need for integrated evaluation processes and solutions achieves increased visibility and attention from internal staff, including senior management. Some of the indicators that an organization or function is in the renewal stage include the following:

- Adjustments in the evaluation process and organizational course corrections toward the desired state are initiated.
- The ROI Methodology, its concepts, and its value are embraced.
- Mechanisms for monitoring and addressing mindsets, behaviors, and practices in regard to evaluation are renewed.
- Energy and potential chaos increase as team members identify where further support is needed and consider how to get it.
- Some conflict arises as multiple solutions are explored.

Several key tasks need to be performed at the renewal stage.

1. Recognize and define needs within the change process at each leverage point by doing the following:
   - Continue to monitor milestone achievements, needs, and gaps.
   - Scale back plans, if necessary.
   - Integrate change efforts into existing management systems and cycles, such as
     - Business planning
     - Budget development
     - Corporate and departmental measurement planning
     - Compensation planning
     - Succession planning
     - Employee orientation and training
   - Link accomplishments in ROI evaluation to individual performance appraisals, include accomplishment of goals as a criterion in team bonus plans, and give informal rewards—such as congratulatory notes or special luncheons—to participants in the implementation.
   - Have the implementation team continually ensure that results are related to business and strategic goals.
   - Tailor targets and metrics to the appropriate organizational life cycles.
2. Encourage teamwork and interdependence with these actions:
   - Incorporate action-oriented program members into the implementation effort.
   - Continually monitor the effectiveness of the implementation team.
   - Identify the program team's strengths, and minimize its weaknesses.
   - Close any skill gaps in special ROI training.

- Develop a charter for the team that is implementing the ROI Methodology.
- Avoid changes in the implementation team.
- Address issues involving the implementation team immediately; do not let issues fester unchecked.

3. Keep the implementation team focused on priorities and short-term goals with these actions:
   - Keep the program and metrics simple.
   - Agree on data sources; clearly define the source of each metric, who should obtain the information, and how the information will be reported.
   - Incorporate a review of performance data into routine implementation meetings, and make it available to stakeholders prior to the meetings.

4. Recognize and reward small wins by doing the following:
   - Identify and communicate any examples of success that signify that the ROI Methodology and its implementation are taking hold within your organization. Routinely report this information to management.
   - Establish communication vehicles for informing all stakeholders of achievements in implementation. Address all milestones outlined in the communication plan, and communicate their status.
   - Present formal and informal rewards for efforts made in implementing the ROI Methodology; participants achieve the things for which they are rewarded.

Stage 4: Integration

In the integration stage, enabling strategies and infrastructures should be in place to ensure that the ROI Methodology is firmly integrated into programs. These elements may range from technology-based support processes to standardized guidelines, policies, and procedures. (Chapter Two covers policies in more detail.) In the integration stage, the ROI Methodology is universally and mutually understood by all stakeholders.

Some of the indicators that an organization or function is in the integration stage are the following:

- The organization or function has increased its focus on linking programs to the strategic directions of the organization.

- The organization or function displays a spirit of continuous improvement, innovation, and "out of the box" thinking about evaluation.

- The department or function is a key player in organizational change initiatives.

- The function's budget is growing.

- The function has strengthened collaborations with other key functional areas.

- The function is viewed as the internal expert on evaluation.

- The implementation team is able to routinely perform evaluation at best-of-class levels.

- Mentoring in evaluation practices is occurring, and there is management support for increased internal capabilities in evaluation.

- Best practices are identified and shared.

Several key tasks need attention at the integration stage.

1. Build and maintain stable links for integration of the change effort within other organizational systems through the following actions:
   - Build organizational self-reliance by reinforcing new behaviors and systems.
   - Position implementation of the ROI Methodology at the forefront of the unit's strategic plan.
   - Establish accountability everywhere, particularly away from senior leadership.
   - Enforce the consequences if desired performance levels are not being met.
   - Evaluate all environmental factors that are contributing to lack of progress.
2. Build and maintain cohesiveness and interdependence on all sides of the change effort by performing the following tasks:
   - Maintain strategic alliances with key stakeholder groups and individuals, and hold all stakeholders accountable for their commitments.
   - Emphasize the fact that comprehensive integration and implementation of the ROI Methodology may take several years; secure commitments for long-term support.
   - Plan informal rewards and recognition to support the achievement of milestones.
   - Keep in mind that many implementation team members must carry out their implementation assignments without relief from their daily job duties.
3. Ensure that the pace of organizational change does not compromise the integrity of the ROI Methodology by means of the following actions:
   - Challenge the implementation team to develop appropriate measures. Evaluate these measures

continually to ensure that they are measuring desired change outcomes at appropriate intervals.
- Balance organizational priorities to protect the resources dedicated to implementation efforts. Examine the allocation of resources for implementation in order to discover any negative impacts on your organization's critical business issues.
- Recognize, analyze, and respond to all threats to the implementation of the ROI Methodology.
- Make the implementation team aware that senior management may not be close enough to the implementation to properly appraise its value to the organization and its level of accomplishment.
- Make compromises or adjustments in the implementation schedule as necessary to meet your organization's needs.

4. Share excitement about the ROI Methodology and its value to your organization through the following actions:

- Schedule and conduct periodic enthusiastic progress reviews, presented by the implementation team to senior management. These reviews should include the benefits of the process, including intangible benefits.
- Publicize success stories and best practices.
- Tailor statements of benefits to reinforce the business payoffs from the perspectives of multiple stakeholders.

Figure 4.2 illustrates key roles during each of the stages identified in this section. These stages of implementation do not necessarily occur in a linear fashion, one after another. However, the concerns and indicators of each stage are typical, to varying degrees, of most organizations as they begin to implement the ROI Methodology

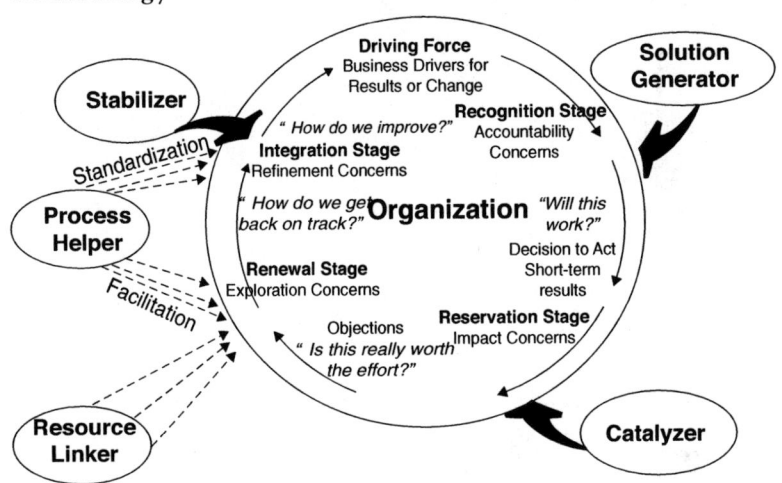

Figure 4.2. Roles During Stages in Implementation of the ROI Methodology

```
                    Driving Force
                    Business Drivers for          Solution
                    Results or Change             Generator
   Stabilizer       Recognition Stage
              "How do we improve?"  Accountability
   Standardization  Integration Stage  Concerns
              ↘    Refinement Concerns
   Process      "How do we get  Organization  "Will this
   Helper       back on track?"                work?"
                                          Decision to Act
          Facilitation  Renewal Stage       Short-term
                        Exploration Concerns   results
                        Objections  Reservation Stage
                        "Is this really worth  Impact Concerns
                         the effort?"
   Resource                                   Catalyzer
   Linker
```

Source: Copyright © by Evaluation Works.

as standard practice. By understanding these stages, an evaluator or consultant can identify critical leverage points and assume roles that will accelerate organizational movement from one stage to the next. The key is to keep moving toward integration and avoid prolonged inertia.

Actions That Sustain the ROI Methodology

A few powerful actions that help sustain the ROI Methodology are covered in this section. They represent proven techniques for keeping the ROI Methodology vital for many years.

Publishing Case Studies

Targeted case studies foster internal capabilities in the ROI Methodology and build acceptance for its integration. Regular attention to selected impact studies is also important in order to show the following:

- Which programs have achieved success
- What organizational enablers or barriers occurred during the process of achieving desired results
- What new program expenditures are justified

Some organizations take the extra step of publishing case studies. Case studies can be published internally or externally. Internally, a printed case study becomes a useful document. It serves as a history of how the evaluation was conducted and serves as an excellent learning tool for others who wish to understand the methodology. In that situation, a case study can become the impetus for workshops for the staff.

Perhaps most important is the value that internally published case studies offer to prospective and current clients. It shows tangible evidence that an organizational function or program does make a difference. A case study in which the impact and the ROI are calculated may be one of the most effective ways of changing senior executives' perception of a function or department. A few larger organizations prepare case studies and publish them as a combined book. For example, SAP, Nokia, and the Department of Veterans Affairs published their own softcover casebooks, which served as excellent reference and learning tools and impressive documents to show others the influence and impact of their organizations.

Externally published case studies validate the success of an organizational function or unit. These studies are routinely published in books, journals, and the trade press. Having members of the staff write up and publish a case study provides recognition not only for the individual but for the unit and the organization as well. Sometimes, externally published case studies win awards from professional associations. For additional information on how case studies can be used, contact the ROI Institute, Inc., through its Web site at www.roiinstitute.net.

Holding Annual Progress Reviews

It is helpful to hold regular reviews for the senior executive team in order to show how well the ROI process is working. Such reviews are designed to show how the process is working, what success has been enjoyed, what is planned for the near future, and what is needed to keep it going. A typical agenda for an annual review includes the following topics:

- Review of previous year's programs
- Methods and levels of evaluation
- Results achieved from programs
- Significant deviations from expected results
- Basis for determining needs for the coming year
- Scheduled initiatives, programs, or services
- Proposed methods of evaluation
- Potential payoffs
- Problem areas or barriers to success
- Concerns from management (all levels)

These sessions should be framed as part of a continuous improvement process that will systematically do the following:

- Show the value derived from specific actions recommended in impact studies
- Track targeted improvements

- Track suggestions for continuous improvement
- Establish and review policy and practice in regard to mechanisms for communication
- Reinforce the role of management in building and sustaining a results-based culture

Calculating the ROI on Implementation of the ROI Methodology

Understanding the payoff from implementation of the ROI Methodology is important. No management team will support a process if they don't see its value. Individually, an impact study will show the value of a program; however, managers will quickly realize that conducting these studies requires significant resources. Does the entire process have a payoff? Some managers will ask for the ROI on implementation. The major positive impact associated with using the ROI Methodology over time includes the following:

- It can transform the role of a department or function within an organization.
- It increases alignment of programs with business needs.
- It improves the efficiency of solution design, development, and delivery by allowing program teams to

    Reduce costs

    Prevent a program from being implemented after the pilot process shows that it delivers no value

    Expand programs when other areas need the benefits of these programs

    Discontinue programs when they add no value

- It enhances the value of learning and development in an organization.

- It builds respect, support, and commitment from internal groups, including senior executives and major program sponsors.

Identifying potential payoffs early is important. Evaluating the preceding propositions to ensure that the evaluation process delivers on its promised value should be the role of the task force created during transition planning.

Reviewing Staff Roles

Program staff must continue to ensure that policies are implemented, that practices are followed, and that data are delivered in a timely manner. If the team members lose enthusiasm for implementation of the ROI Methodology or fail to complete each of the tasks, their actions will be perceived as a lack of commitment. Lack of commitment can be contagious and may cause others to lose support and commitment as well.

The importance of staff members' roles as advocates and champions who sustain the ROI Methodology over time can be illustrated by the experience of one health care organization. In this example, eleven employees involved in the original ROI Certification workshop, along with the senior executive team, were committed to adopting the ROI Methodology as a standard policy practice. However, members of the group described initial frustration with their own inexperience with the process and the difficulty of incorporating ROI programs into their already busy schedules. To deal with these challenges and continue moving forward, group members learned to find support in each other and in their shared beliefs about the value of the ROI Methodology to the business.

As the team continued to develop expertise in the ROI Methodology and began to successfully measure the results of programs, their confidence and enthusiasm galvanized partnerships with managers and the senior executive team, which in turn helped sustain the implementation throughout the organization.

To ensure continued organizational understanding, acceptance, and adoption of the methodology as routine, the team worked closely with senior executives across all functions to establish the ROI Methodology as a systemwide philosophy in which accountability for adding value was seen as the responsibility of everyone in the organization. In addition, the team assisted functional managers in conducting front-end needs assessments, provided learning opportunities on the ROI Methodology, and partnered with managers on subsequent ROI programs, with the goal of making all managers comfortable with the ROI Methodology. The program team catalyzed the successful implementation of the ROI Methodology throughout the organization.

In almost any situation, periodic reviews of staff roles and how they translate into day-to-day job descriptions will be helpful to ensure that

- Team members understand their responsibilities in making the process work as a systemwide approach
- Team members understand what they are supposed to accomplish and how and when they should do it
- Specific responsibilities are incorporated into job descriptions so that they become a routine part of work

This process can be integrated into midyear or annual performance appraisal processes or incorporated into individual developmental planning checkpoints and review dates. Any issues in managing evaluation outputs or work products associated with revised roles or the broader scope of the unit's results should also be a factor in annual budget planning.

Establishing Mechanisms for Continuous Improvement

Implementing the ROI Methodology and monitoring its progress within the realm of a single organizational function may be a relatively simple task. However, as the process becomes more visible and integrated within an organization, it becomes increasingly critical to build continuous improvement mechanisms into the process so that it remains credible and flexible over time. Some improvement mechanisms include the following:

- Progress reports that include recommendations from annual progress reviews
- Published success stories that document recommendations for improvement that were implemented
- Routine meetings in which lessons learned and solutions implemented are reviewed and tracked

Many organizations use a postmortem forum to review lessons learned from programs that involved considerable time or expense. Exhibit 4.1 provides an example of a lessons learned report that was used in a public sector organization. In this case, the report mirrored an organizational template and was used (a) as a supplement to impact study reports with programs that did not achieve desired results or (b) in lieu of an impact study report when the resources for an impact study were diverted and the impact study program was postponed or discontinued.

Finally, use the best practices described in the next section as a framework for continuous improvement.

Development of Best Practices

More than 3,000 organizations have taken the initiative to implement the ROI Methodology, based on the number of organizations that have participated in a comprehensive certification process designed to help individuals and teams implement the ROI

Exhibit 4.1. Lessons Learned Report

Version: Draft v0.2
Date:
Author:
Owner:

Table of Contents

About This Document
Related Documents
Summary of Changes
Reviews and Approvals
Distribution
Document Control Information

Chapter 1: Lessons Learned Report

1.1 Purpose of Document
1.2 Program Summary
    1.2.1 Program Background
    1.2.2 Program Milestones and Metrics
    1.2.3 Program Deliverables
1.3 Lessons Learned
    1.3.1 What Went Well
    1.3.2 What Didn't
    1.3.3 Enablers
    1.3.4 Barriers
    1.3.5 Suggestions for Improvement
1.4 Methodologies
    1.4.1 Program Management
    1.4.2 Resource Management

Exhibit 4.1. Lessons Learned Report (*Continued*)

    1.4.3 System Design

    1.4.4 Evaluation Management

  1.5 Summary of Findings

  1.6 Appendix: Tables, Figures, Exhibits

About This Document

Related Documents

This document should be used in conjunction with

Evaluation Policy and Procedures

Impact Study "X" Communication Plan

Impact Study "X" Data Collection Plan

Summary of Changes

This section records the history of changes to this document. Only the most significant changes are described here.

Version	Date	Author	Description of Change

When significant changes are made to this document, the version number will be increased by 1.0. When changes are made for clarity and reading ease only and no change is made to the meaning or intention of this document, the version number will be increased by 0.1.

(Continued)

Exhibit 4.1. Lessons Learned Report (*Continued*)

Reviews and Approvals

This document requires review and approval.

This document was approved by

Name	Role	Date

This document was reviewed by

Name	Role	Date

Distribution

This section lists all the persons or areas that will receive a copy of this document after it has been finalized.

Name	Area	Date

Document Control Information

At the end of this document is a labeled box indicating the end of text. _____

<Program Name> Lessons Learned Report
END OF DOCUMENT

Exhibit 4.1. Lessons Learned Report (Continued)

Chapter 1: Lessons Learned Report

1.1 Purpose of Document

Summarize the purpose of the Lessons Learned Report (that is, to pass on lessons learned that can be practically applied to other results-based evaluation programs).

1.2 Program Summary

1.2.1 Program Background

Summarize the business case for this results-based program and identify its key objectives in terms of needs/gaps in the following areas:

- Reaction to the program, including planned actions if appropriate
- Learning goals for program participants—desired knowledge and skills, as well as changes in perceptions
- Performance objectives—desired application and implementation of program learning
- Targeted business impact—metrics such as cost savings, productivity improvements, time reductions, increased sales, and so on
- As indicated, return on investment target—desired monetary benefits versus costs of the program
- Desired intangible benefits, such as employee satisfaction and customer satisfaction

Include summary information about the program sponsor, key stakeholders or client groups, and expected deliverables from the program.

(Continued)

Exhibit 4.1. Lessons Learned Report (*Continued*)

1.2.2 Program Milestones and Metrics

Summarize the relevant milestones and metrics of this program. These may include the following components in the chart below:

Program Components	Milestone or Metric
Estimated start date	
Estimated end date	
Actual start date	
Actual end date	
Schedule variance (days)	
Team size at start date	
Team size at end date	
Team size variance or attrition (individuals)	
Estimated program costs	
Actual program costs	
Cost variance (dollars)	
Estimated program monetary benefits	
Actual program monetary benefits	
Benefits variance (dollars)	
Program's return on investment	
Number of quality assurance reviews	
Number of incidents	

1.2.3 Program Deliverables

Deliverable	Due Date	Status/Comments

Exhibit 4.1. Lessons Learned Report (*Continued*)

1.3 Lessons Learned

Summarize what went well or did not and what can be improved as it applies to this results-based program.

1.3.1 *What Went Well*

1.3.2 *What Didn't*

1.3.3 *Enablers*

1.3.4 *Barriers*

1.3.5 *Suggestions for Improvement*

1.4 Methodologies

1.4.1 *Program Management*

Include recommendations for enhancement/modification to the program management methodology in this section. Include the following: program sponsorship; overall program planning; work plan; estimates; managing the work plan; managing resources; managing scope; managing communications, stakeholder expectations; managing quality; managing risk; and team characteristics.

Consider any recommendations related to the program management tools used during the program.

1.4.2 *Resource Management*

Include recommendations for enhancement/modification to the resource management (people, material, money) with regard to this program. Include how resources were approved, allocated, diverted, constrained, and/or used during the program life cycle. Also, include recommendations for improving resource use for future results-based programs.

(*Continued*)

Exhibit 4.1. Lessons Learned Report (*Continued*)

1.4.3 *System Design*

Include recommendations for enhancement/modification to the methodology used, including the assessment and design phase; the develop, build, and test phase; and the implementation and evaluation phase. Also include recommendations related to any tools used during the program.

1.4.4 *Evaluation Management*

Include recommendations for enhancement/modification to the evaluation management methodology used by the Workplace Learning function to achieve desired results. Include recommendations related to any of the following phases of evaluation management: evaluation planning, data collection, data analysis, and communication of results, including communication strengths/opportunities for improvement with key stakeholders. Include recommendations related to any data collection, survey, or testing tools or sampling groups used during the program.

1.5 Summary of Findings

Provide a high-level summary of your overall observation of this program, and state how these lessons can be used for continuous improvement and action planning with future results-based programs.

1.6 Appendix: Tables, Figures, Exhibits

Lessons Learned Report
END OF DOCUMENT

Methodology. Now that the ROI Methodology enjoys wide acceptance, the focus of many practitioners has turned to best practices for its implementation. The eleven best practices in this section represent the state of the art in organizations that have successfully implemented the ROI Methodology.

Best Practice 1

The ROI Methodology is implemented as a process improvement tool and not a performance evaluation tool. Staff acceptance is critical for successful implementation of the ROI Methodology. Few individuals or groups will want to use a tool that might ultimately be used to evaluate their performance. As a result, many organizations accept the notion of the ROI Methodology as a process improvement tool and communicate this posture early.

Best Practice 2

The ROI Methodology generates a micro-level scorecard with seven types of data. Each type of data reflects a distinct measure with a specific focus:

- *Level 0 (Inputs and Indicators)*: Measures the inputs into the program (people, resources, and so on)
- *Level 1 (Reaction and Planned Action)*: Measures participant satisfaction with the program and captures planned actions
- *Level 2 (Learning)*: Measures changes in knowledge, skills, and attitudes
- *Level 3 (Application)*: Measures changes in on-the-job behavior
- *Level 4 (Business Impact)*: Measures changes in business impact variables

- *Level 5 (ROI):* Compares program benefits with program costs
- *Intangible Benefits:* Data that are purposely not converted to monetary values

The types of data shown in the preceding list constitute a scorecard of a program's performance, representing both qualitative and quantitative data, often taken at different time frames and from different sources.

Best Practice 3

ROI Methodology data collected at the program level are integrated to create a macro-level scorecard for an entire department or function. As more studies are conducted, their data are also incorporated. This concept was covered in more detail in Chapter One and illustrated in Figure 1.3. This approach requires that a few similar questions be asked each time data are gathered, so that consistent measures can be shown. Data from the responses are integrated, using technology, to create the macro-level scorecard.

Best Practice 4

ROI impact studies are conducted selectively, usually involving 5 to 10 percent of all programs and solutions. Programs that are usually targeted for Level 4 and 5 evaluations are those that are strategically focused, expensive, high-profile, controversial, or have management's interest. This does not mean that other programs are not evaluated. All programs should be evaluated at Level 1, the vast majority at Level 2, and many at Level 3, but only a few select programs are taken to Levels 4 and 5. More important, programs targeted for a Level 5 evaluation with an ROI calculation are, as best practice, evaluated at all five levels, up to and including ROI.

Best Practice 5

Setting ROI evaluation targets—the percentage of programs to be evaluated at each level—is another best practice. Considerations in developing target levels are the resources available and the feasibility of evaluation at each level. The target is usually 100 percent of programs at Level 1 and 5 to 10 percent of programs at Level 5.

Best Practice 6

Using a variety of data collection methods is a best practice in ROI analysis. Robust ROI evaluation is not restricted to a particular type of data collection method, such as monitoring business data. Instead, questionnaires, action plans, focus groups, and observations (among others) are used to develop the complete profile of seven types of data in the ROI Methodology.

Best Practice 7

For a specific ROI evaluation, the effects of programs and projects should be isolated from other factors. Although isolation of program effects is difficult, best-practice organizations realize that some method must be in place to show the direct contribution of a program to business impact. Many best-practice organizations use a variety of techniques, ranging from control group analysis to expert estimation, to address this issue in each evaluation. Some argue that this is too difficult. In reality, it must be done in order for executives to understand the relative contribution of a department or function. Otherwise, a temptation to slash the budgets of major programs may arise because executives see no clear connection between the programs and their business impact.

Best Practice 8

Business impact data are converted to monetary values. These days, simply reporting program outcomes—expressed in units of quality improvement, cycle-time reduction, turnover reduction, or percentage points of increased customer loyalty or job satisfaction—is not enough. The value in monetary terms is essential in calculating the ROI because an ROI calculation compares the benefits of a program with its costs. To allow this comparison, benefits must be valued in monetary terms, just as the costs are. Best-practice organizations use a full array of approaches to convert impact data to monetary values.

Best Practice 9

The ROI Methodology can be implemented for about 3 to 5 percent of a function's budget. One of the common fears about implementing the ROI Methodology is excessive cost in both time and funds. Best-practice organizations report that they can implement the ROI Methodology for roughly 3 to 5 percent of the total budget when they use evaluation targets as discussed in Best Practice 5.

When implementing the ROI Methodology, many organizations have migrated from a low level of investment (1 percent or less) to a higher level (3 to 5 percent) through a process of gradual budget increases. These increases sometimes come directly from the cost savings generated through the use of the ROI Methodology. In addition, cost-saving approaches can be used in resource-constrained environments.

Best Practice 10

Best practice organizations implement ROI forecasting routinely to improve the decision-making process. Senior executives sometimes ask for an ROI forecast before a program is launched. The credibility of the process is greatly increased by the use of conservative adjustments and built-in steps to secure input from the best experts. Forecasting is discussed in *Costs and ROI*, the fifth book in this series.

Best Practice 11

The ROI Methodology is used by best practice enterprises as a tool to strengthen and improve an organizational function or a department. A significant payoff for using the ROI Methodology over time is that it transforms the role of a function or department within an organization. Application of the process increases alignment with business needs; improves the efficiency of program design, development, and delivery; and increases the value of a function or department within an organization. Furthermore, it builds respect, support, and commitment from other internal groups, including senior executives and major program sponsors.

These best practices are evolving as hundreds of organizations use the ROI Methodology each year. Best practices underscore the progress that has been made in the methodology's implementation and use.

Summary

As in any change effort, constant attention and focus must be maintained in order to build and sustain the ROI Methodology over time. Without such attention, the methodology will ultimately fade out in an organization and be labeled as a passing fad. Paying regular attention to the ultimate business purposes of the evaluation process while maintaining its integrity is often one of the most challenging aspects of being an evaluation leader.

After the initial changes in measurement methods are implemented, the program team members may lose their sense of urgency and drift back to old cultures, mindsets, behaviors, and systems. Ultimately, the task of sustaining the ROI Methodology is not the sole responsibility of the implementation team; support must be generated from all stakeholders. A key challenge is securing and fostering ongoing support, cooperation, interaction, and dedication from all stakeholders in the evaluation process. Focusing on the following actions will help with these challenges.

- Remember that organizations migrate through predictable growth stages in the move from episodic implementation to long-term integration of the ROI Methodology.
- Look for specific indicators that implementation may be off track.
- Identify key roles and actions that will help your organization move successfully from one stage to the next.
- Continually renew and refresh commitment for the methodology across individual, process, and organizational levels so that it remains consistent, reliable, and credible in the eyes of stakeholders.
- Develop best practices for capturing organizational responses and lessons learned during the entire cycle of accountability.
- Continually seek best-practice examples from professional associations, training literature, journals, case studies, colleagues, and the ROI Network.

Exhibit 4.2 presents a checklist that can help leaders sustain momentum for implementation of the ROI Methodology within an organization.

Now that the typical stages of ROI Methodology implementation have been identified, roles in the implementation process have been defined, and specific enabling strategies to assist in this effort have been outlined, it's time to commit to action. Exhibit 4.3 will help you plan your action steps.

Exhibit 4.2. Checklist for Implementation of the ROI Methodology

Enabling Strategies	Yes	No
Have stages of ROI implementation been identified?	☐	☐
Have roles been assigned to facilitate organizational movement toward the integration stage?	☐	☐
Are case studies developed on a regular basis?	☐	☐
Has the ROI on the ROI Methodology been effectively and routinely communicated to stakeholders?	☐	☐
Are staff roles in implementation of the ROI Methodology regularly reviewed, revised, and updated?	☐	☐
Are continuous improvement mechanisms in place for the ROI Methodology?	☐	☐
Are lessons learned captured and reported?	☐	☐
Are best practices routinely identified?	☐	☐
Are best practices routinely applied?	☐	☐
Are best practices routinely shared?	☐	☐

Final Thoughts

This chapter focuses on the actions needed to build and sustain the ROI Methodology over time. Emphasizing the ROI Methodology as a long-term process improvement tool adds value and keeps it from becoming a passing fad or short-term phenomenon. If ROI evaluation is not an integral part of the way a functional unit does business, then the accountability for programs and projects will ultimately suffer. Specifically, this chapter helps to

- Identify organizational stages of ROI Methodology implementation
- Define roles in facilitating movement from one stage to the next

Exhibit 4.3 Action Planning for Enabling Strategies

1. Commit to take action on one or more of the following enabling strategies defined in this chapter:

    a. Implement specific impact or case studies.
    b. Schedule and enthusiastically conduct periodic review sessions.
    c. Calculate the payoff of the ROI Methodology in order to show that it is worthwhile.
    d. Build continuous improvement mechanisms to ensure that enhancements to the process are routinely explored.
    e. Routinely review roles.
    f. Publicize success stories and identify best practices.

2. Identify one enabling strategy or continuous improvement action on which you are willing to focus for the next thirty days. It can be an action that you will continue to do or an action to attempt in the future. Write down this strategy or continuous improvement action and the date by which you will act:
   _____
   _____

3. Identify a person with whom you will share your plan, and select a date when you both will review your progress (for example, thirty days from initiation).
   Action plan partner: _____
   Review date: _____

- Identify inhibitors and enablers to successful implementation of the ROI Methodology
- Apply enabling strategies and specific actions to sustain the implementation of the ROI Methodology over time

All the tips and tools in this book will support implementation of the ROI Methodology as a mainstream, value-added activity.

Reference

Scott, C., and Jaffe, D. *Getting Your Organization to Change*. Menlo Park, CA.: Crisp, 1999.

Index

A
Annual progress reviews, 149–150
Audience. *See* Target audience

B
Balanced scorecard. *See* Macro-level scorecard
Barriers to implementation, 20
Best-practice meetings, 23–24
Block, P., 30
Brochures, 27
Business impact, 20
Business update meetings, 24

C
California ROI Network, 111
Case studies
  example of, 29–30
  ROI sustainability using, 147–149
  uses of, 28
Communication
  analysis of the need for, 6–9
  analysis of reactions to, 39–40
  five key reasons to be concerned with, 1–5
  and monitoring ROI evaluation progress, 128
  planning, 9–13
  principles of results and, 3–6
  selecting the audience for, 13–17

Communication media
  brochures, 27
  case studies, 28–30
  e-mail and electronic media, 27
  meetings, 21, 23–24
  organizational publications and communication tools, 25–27
  progress reports, 24–25
Communication plan
  for entire program, 10–11
  establishing policies for, 9–10
  for feedback, 31
  for impact study, 11–13
Communication process
  communicating with executives and sponsors, 38–39
  continual feedback provided during, 30–33
  impact study presented to senior management, 34–38
Consistent communication, 5
Cost-saving implementation
  importance of developing, 90
  recommended approaches to, 95, 97–98

D
Data collection/analysis (impact study), 18–19

171

E

E-mail communication, 27
Effective media selection, 5
Electronic media, 27
Executive summary, 17
Executives. *See* Senior management

F

Feedback
  action plan for, 31
  providing continual, 30, 32–33

I

Impact study
  communication used for, 11–13
  format of, 22
  presented to senior management, 34–38
  sample streamlined, 37
  sections and information included in, 17–21
Implementation. *See* ROI Methodology implementation
Infrastructure support. *See* Organization infrastructure
Intangible measures, 20

J

Jaffe, D., 135

K

Kaplan, R., 40

L

Learning and development
  management involvement in, 127
  organizational standardization of, 77–90
  reporting on, 19
  ROI Methodology as tool for, 90, 115
Learning/development standardization
  1: overview of process, 77–79
  2: procedures for, 79–81
  3: resources, roles, and responsibilities, 81–83
  4: measurement and verification of, 83–85
  5: review of process effectiveness, 85–87
  6: document control information, 87
  7: document list, 87
Lessons Learned Report, 153, 154–161

M

Macro-level scorecard
  advantages of, 42
  creating, 41–42
  description of, 40–41
  example of, 42–45
Manager meetings, 23
  See also Senior management
Managers
  developing ROI leaders among, 104–106
  identifying ROI champions among, 103–104
  learning and development involvement by, 127
  preparing and training, 121–127
  as target audience, 122–123
  See also Senior management
Media selection, 5
Meetings, 21, 23–24
Monitoring ROI evaluation, 128

N

Norton, D., 40

O

Opinions, 6
Organization infrastructure
  checklist of policy statement topics, 76
  cost-saving methods implementation as, 93, 96, 97–98

learning/development
  standardization process, 76–90
  project plan as, 90, 91–95
  structuring ROI as learning tool,
    90
  transition step establishing, 66,
    75–76
Organizational readiness
  SWOT analysis of, 56
  worksheet for assessing, 54–55
Organizations
  assessing for ROI Methodology
    readiness, 53–56
  certification workshop
    participation by private sector,
    107–108
  certification workshop
    participation by public sector,
    109
  establishing infrastructure
    supporting ROI Methodology,
    66, 75–94
  reporting results through
    publications of, 25–27
  tapping into ROI network by,
    110–112
Overcoming resistance
  addressing implementation
    resistance, 116–117
  importance and focus of, 47–49
  process and steps for, 56–57
  to ROI Methodology myths and
    fears, 56–64
  transition plan for, 51–52
  for typical ROI Methodology
    objections, 48

P
Programs
  creating macro-level scorecard of,
    40–45
  reporting costs of, 19
  selected for ROI evaluation,
    118–121
Progress reports, 24–25

Project plan
  example of, 91–92
  as part of transition, 90, 93
  results-based transition, 93–95

R
Reporting results
  common target audiences of,
    13–17
  communication media used for,
    21, 23–30
  communication role in, 1–13
  impact study used for, 11–21,
    22
  monitoring process and
    communicating and, 128
  of ROI evaluations, 121
Resistance. *See* Overcoming
  resistance
ROI certification, 105–108
ROI evaluations
  monitoring progress/
    communicating results of, 128
  reporting progress on, 121
  selecting programs for, 118–121
  selection tool for, 119
ROI Institute, Inc., 105, 111, 149
ROI leaders, 104–106
ROI Methodology
  best practices for, 161–165
  as learning tool, 90, 115
  macro-level scorecards created
    using, 41–45
  myths, fears, and false assumptions
    about, 57–64
  overcoming resistance to, 47–52,
    56–64, 116–117
  transition issues of, 50–52
  transition-planning steps for,
    52–94
  typical objectives to, 48
ROI Methodology implementation
  assessing organizational readiness
    for, 54–56
  barriers to, 20

ROI Methodology implementation (*Continued*)
  calculating ROI of, 150–151
  causes of ineffective, 132–134
  checklist for, 167
  consistency and efficiency issues of, 50
  cost-saving approaches to, 96, 97–98
  impact study reporting on, 19
  as key to success, 49
  stages of, 131, 135–147
ROI Methodology implementation issues
  assignment responsibilities, 106, 108, 109–110
  developing evaluation targets for staff, 112–114
  developing the ROI leader, 104–106
  identifying a champion, 103–104
  monitoring progress and communicating results, 128
  overview of, 102–103
  preparing the management team, 121–127
  preparing the program staff, 114–117
  ROI certification, 105–109
  selecting programs for ROI evaluation, 118–121
  tapping into a network, 110–112
ROI Methodology implementation stages
  1: recognition, 131, 135–137
  2: reservation, 135, 137–141
  3: renewal, 135, 141–143
  4: integration, 135, 143–147
ROI Methodology sustainability
  action planning for, 168
  best practices developed for, 153, 161–165
  calculating ROI on implementation, 150–151
  challenges of, 130–131
  establishing mechanisms for continuous improvements for, 152–153
  holding annual progress reviews for, 149–150
  importance of, 129–130
  Lessons Learned Report to facilitate, 153, 154–161
  publishing case studies for, 147–149
  reviewing staff roles for, 151–152
  stages of implementation and, 131–147
ROI Methodology transition
  issues related to, 50–52
  overcoming resistance during, 51, 58–62, 63–64
  step 1: assess readiness, 52–56
  step 2: overcome resistance, 56–57
  step 3: communicate a vision, 57, 62, 65–66, 67–74
  step 4: manage the transition, 66
  step 5: establish infrastructure to support process, 66, 75–98
ROI networks
  description of, 110–111
  internal, 111–112
  local, 111
ROI (return on investment)
  calculated on ROI Methodology, 150–151
  reporting on the, 20

S

Scott, C., 135
Senior management
  building partnership between staff and, 122
  communicating with sponsors and, 38–39

developing ROI leaders among, 104–106
identifying ROI champions among, 103–104
learning and development involvement by, 127
presenting impact study to, 34–38
See also Manager meetings; Managers

Staff
developing evaluation targets for, 112–114
preparing partnership between senior management and, 122
preparing the program, 114–117
reviewing roles for ROI sustainability, 151–152

Staff meetings, 23

T

Target audience
analysis of communication reactions by, 39–40
communication shaped by program team opinion by, 6
managements as, 122–123
selection of common program results, 13–17

Targeted communication, 4

Testimonials, 5–6

Timely communication, 4

Toronto ROI Network, 111

U

Unbiased communication, 5

W

Wachovia, 103–104

About the Authors

Jack J. Phillips, Ph.D., a world-renowned expert on accountability, measurement, and evaluation, provides consulting services for Fortune 500 companies and major global organizations. The author or editor of more than fifty books, Phillips conducts workshops and makes conference presentations throughout the world.

His expertise in measurement and evaluation is based on more than twenty-seven years of corporate experience in the aerospace, textile, metals, construction materials, and banking industries. Phillips has served as training and development manager at two Fortune 500 firms, as senior human resources officer at two firms, as president of a regional bank, and as management professor at a major state university. This background led Phillips to develop the ROI Methodology, a revolutionary process that provides bottom-line figures and accountability for all types of learning, performance improvement, human resources, technology, and public policy programs.

Phillips regularly consults with clients in manufacturing, service, and government organizations in forty-four countries in North and South America, Europe, Africa, Australia, and Asia.

Books most recently authored by Phillips include *Show Me the Money: How to Determine ROI in People, Projects, and Programs* (Berrett-Koehler, 2007); *The Value of Learning* (Pfeiffer, 2007); *How to Build a Successful Consulting Practice* (McGraw-Hill, 2006);

Investing in Your Company's Human Capital: Strategies to Avoid Spending Too Much or Too Little (Amacom, 2005); *Proving the Value of HR: How and Why to Measure ROI* (Society for Human Resource Management, 2005); *The Leadership Scorecard* (Butterworth-Heinemann, 2004); *Managing Employee Retention* (Butterworth-Heinemann, 2003); *Return on Investment in Training and Performance Improvement Programs*, 2nd edition (Butterworth-Heinemann, 2003); *The Project Management Scorecard* (Butterworth-Heinemann, 2002); *How to Measure Training Results* (McGraw-Hill, 2002); *The Human Resources Scorecard: Measuring the Return on Investment* (Butterworth-Heinemann, 2001); *The Consultant's Scorecard* (McGraw-Hill, 2000); and *Performance Analysis and Consulting* (ASTD, 2000). Phillips served as series editor for the In Action casebook series of the American Society for Training and Development (ASTD), an ambitious publishing project featuring thirty titles. He currently serves as series editor for Butterworth-Heinemann's Improving Human Performance series and for Pfeiffer's new Measurement and Evaluation series.

Phillips has received several awards for his books and his work. The Society for Human Resource Management presented him with an award for one of his books and honored a Phillips ROI study with its highest award for creativity. ASTD gave him its highest award, Distinguished Contribution to Workplace Learning and Development. *Meeting News* named Phillips one of the twenty-five most influential people in the meetings and events industry, based on his work on ROI within the industry.

Phillips holds undergraduate degrees in electrical engineering, physics, and mathematics; a master's degree in decision sciences from Georgia State University; and a Ph.D. degree in human resources management from the University of Alabama.

Jack Phillips has served on the boards of several private businesses—including two NASDAQ companies—and several associations, including ASTD, and nonprofit organizations. He is

chairman of the ROI Institute, Inc., and can be reached at (205) 678-8101, or by e-mail at jack@roiinstitute.net.

Wendi Friedman Tush, M.B.A., is president of the Lexicomm Group, a strategic communications consulting company. The Lexicomm Group specializes in "thought leadership" marketing. The company raises executive profiles, revitalizes corporate identities, changes hearts and minds, and provides crisis management for companies and their key executives.

Tush has rebranded, repositioned, and created strategic communications and public relations campaigns for many CEOs and companies, including DuPont, Samsung, Malcolm Bricklin and Visionary Vehicles, David Silverstein and Breakthrough Management Group, Jeff Johnson and Cano Petroleum, Cybersettle, Anvil Knitwear, Gottaplay, iDNA, and US Luggage.

Prior to her career in communications consulting, Tush was a broadcast journalist for CNN, FNN, CNBC, and VH1. She holds a bachelor of arts degree in psychology from Cornell University and a master's degree in business administration from Columbia University.

Pfeiffer Publications Guide

This guide is designed to familiarize you with the various types of Pfeiffer publications. The formats section describes the various types of products that we publish; the methodologies section describes the many different ways that content might be provided within a product. We also provide a list of the topic areas in which we publish.

FORMATS

In addition to its extensive book-publishing program, Pfeiffer offers content in an array of formats, from fieldbooks for the practitioner to complete, ready-to-use training packages that support group learning.

FIELDBOOK Designed to provide information and guidance to practitioners in the midst of action. Most fieldbooks are companions to another, sometimes earlier, work, from which its ideas are derived; the fieldbook makes practical what was theoretical in the original text. Fieldbooks can certainly be read from cover to cover. More likely, though, you'll find yourself bouncing around following a particular theme, or dipping in as the mood, and the situation, dictate.

HANDBOOK A contributed volume of work on a single topic, comprising an eclectic mix of ideas, case studies, and best practices sourced by practitioners and experts in the field.

An editor or team of editors usually is appointed to seek out contributors and to evaluate content for relevance to the topic. Think of a handbook not as a ready-to-eat meal, but as a cookbook of ingredients that enables you to create the most fitting experience for the occasion.

RESOURCE Materials designed to support group learning. They come in many forms: a complete, ready-to-use exercise (such as a game); a comprehensive resource on one topic (such as conflict management) containing a variety of methods and approaches; or a collection of like-minded activities (such as icebreakers) on multiple subjects and situations.

TRAINING PACKAGE An entire, ready-to-use learning program that focuses on a particular topic or skill. All packages comprise a guide for the facilitator/trainer and a workbook for the participants. Some packages are supported with additional media—such as video—or learning aids, instruments, or other devices to help participants understand concepts or practice and develop skills.

- *Facilitator/trainer's guide* Contains an introduction to the program, advice on how to organize and facilitate the learning event, and step-by-step instructor notes. The guide also contains copies of presentation materials—handouts, presentations, and overhead designs, for example—used in the program.
- *Participant's workbook* Contains exercises and reading materials that support the learning goal and serves as a valuable reference and support guide for participants in the weeks and months that follow the learning event. Typically, each participant will require his or her own workbook.

ELECTRONIC CD-ROMs and web-based products transform static Pfeiffer content into dynamic, interactive experiences. Designed to take advantage of the searchability, automation, and ease-of-use that technology provides, our e-products bring convenience and immediate accessibility to your workspace.

METHODOLOGIES

CASE STUDY A presentation, in narrative form, of an actual event that has occurred inside an organization. Case studies are not prescriptive, nor are they used to prove a point; they are designed to develop critical analysis and decision-making skills. A case study has a specific time frame, specifies a sequence of events, is narrative in structure, and contains a plot structure—an issue (what should be/have been done?). Use case studies when the goal is to enable participants to apply previously learned theories to the circumstances in the case, decide what is pertinent, identify the real issues, decide what should have been done, and develop a plan of action.

ENERGIZER A short activity that develops readiness for the next session or learning event. Energizers are most commonly used after a break or lunch to

stimulate or refocus the group. Many involve some form of physical activity, so they are a useful way to counter post-lunch lethargy. Other uses include transitioning from one topic to another, where "mental" distancing is important.

EXPERIENTIAL LEARNING ACTIVITY (ELA) A facilitator-led intervention that moves participants through the learning cycle from experience to application (also known as a Structured Experience). ELAs are carefully thought-out designs in which there is a definite learning purpose and intended outcome. Each step—everything that participants do during the activity—facilitates the accomplishment of the stated goal. Each ELA includes complete instructions for facilitating the intervention and a clear statement of goals, suggested group size and timing, materials required, an explanation of the process, and, where appropriate, possible variations to the activity. (For more detail on Experiential Learning Activities, see the Introduction to the *Reference Guide to Handbooks and Annuals*, 1999 edition, Pfeiffer, San Francisco.)

GAME A group activity that has the purpose of fostering team spirit and togetherness in addition to the achievement of a pre-stated goal. Usually contrived—undertaking a desert expedition, for example—this type of learning method offers an engaging means for participants to demonstrate and practice business and interpersonal skills. Games are effective for team building and personal development mainly because the goal is subordinate to the process—the means through which participants reach decisions, collaborate, communicate, and generate trust and understanding. Games often engage teams in "friendly" competition.

ICEBREAKER A (usually) short activity designed to help participants overcome initial anxiety in a training session and/or to acquaint the participants with one another. An icebreaker can be a fun activity or can be tied to specific topics or training goals. While a useful tool in itself, the icebreaker comes into its own in situations where tension or resistance exists within a group.

INSTRUMENT A device used to assess, appraise, evaluate, describe, classify, and summarize various aspects of human behavior. The term used to describe an instrument depends primarily on its format and purpose. These terms include survey, questionnaire, inventory, diagnostic, survey, and poll. Some uses of instruments include providing instrumental feedback to group

members, studying here-and-now processes or functioning within a group, manipulating group composition, and evaluating outcomes of training and other interventions.

Instruments are popular in the training and HR field because, in general, more growth can occur if an individual is provided with a method for focusing specifically on his or her own behavior. Instruments also are used to obtain information that will serve as a basis for change and to assist in workforce planning efforts.

Paper-and-pencil tests still dominate the instrument landscape with a typical package comprising a facilitator's guide, which offers advice on administering the instrument and interpreting the collected data, and an initial set of instruments. Additional instruments are available separately. Pfeiffer, though, is investing heavily in e-instruments. Electronic instrumentation provides effortless distribution and, for larger groups particularly, offers advantages over paper-and-pencil tests in the time it takes to analyze data and provide feedback.

LECTURETTE A short talk that provides an explanation of a principle, model, or process that is pertinent to the participants' current learning needs. A lecturette is intended to establish a common language bond between the trainer and the participants by providing a mutual frame of reference. Use a lecturette as an introduction to a group activity or event, as an interjection during an event, or as a handout.

MODEL A graphic depiction of a system or process and the relationship among its elements. Models provide a frame of reference and something more tangible, and more easily remembered, than a verbal explanation. They also give participants something to "go on," enabling them to track their own progress as they experience the dynamics, processes, and relationships being depicted in the model.

ROLE PLAY A technique in which people assume a role in a situation/scenario: a customer service rep in an angry-customer exchange, for example. The way in which the role is approached is then discussed and feedback is offered. The role play is often repeated using a different approach and/or incorporating changes made based on feedback received. In other words, role playing is a spontaneous interaction involving realistic behavior under artificial (and safe) conditions.

SIMULATION A methodology for understanding the interrelationships among components of a system or process. Simulations differ from games in that they test or use a model that depicts or mirrors some aspect of reality in form, if not necessarily in content. Learning occurs by studying the effects of change on one or more factors of the model. Simulations are commonly used to test hypotheses about what happens in a system—often referred to as "what if?" analysis—or to examine best-case/worst-case scenarios.

THEORY A presentation of an idea from a conjectural perspective. Theories are useful because they encourage us to examine behavior and phenomena through a different lens.

TOPICS

The twin goals of providing effective and practical solutions for workforce training and organization development and meeting the educational needs of training and human resource professionals shape Pfeiffer's publishing program. Core topics include the following:

Leadership & Management

Communication & Presentation

Coaching & Mentoring

Training & Development

E-Learning

Teams & Collaboration

OD & Strategic Planning

Human Resources

Consulting

What will you find on pfeiffer.com?

- The best in workplace performance solutions for training and HR professionals
- Downloadable training tools, exercises, and content
- Web-exclusive offers
- Training tips, articles, and news
- Seamless on-line ordering
- Author guidelines, information on becoming a Pfeiffer Affiliate, and much more

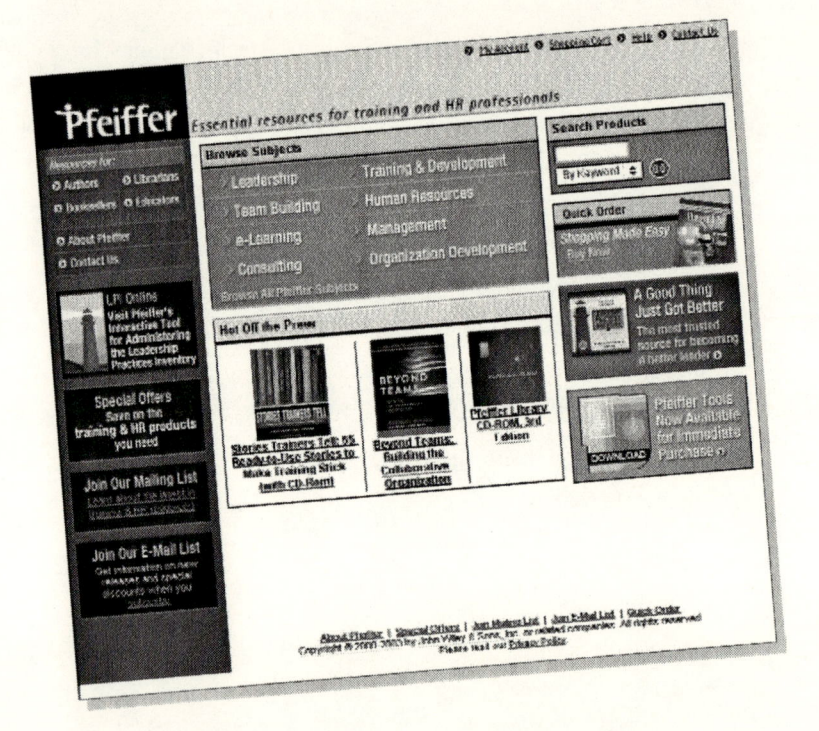

Discover more at www.pfeiffer.com

Measurement and Evaluation Series

Series Editors
Patricia Pulliam Phillips, Ph.D., and Jack J. Phillips, Ph.D.

A six-book set that provides a step-by-step system for planning, measuring, calculating, and communicating evaluation and Return-on-Investment for training and development, featuring:

- Detailed templates
- Complete plans
- Ready-to-use tools
- Real-world case examples

The M&E Series features:

1. *ROI Fundamentals: Why and When to Measure ROI*
   (978-0-7879-8716-9)
2. *Data Collection: Planning For and Collecting All Types of Data*
   (978-0-7879-8718-3)
3. *Isolation of Results: Defining the Impact of the Program*
   (978-0-7879-8719-0)
4. *Data Conversion: Calculating the Monetary Benefits*
   (978-0-7879-8720-6)
5. *Costs and ROI: Evaluating at the Ultimate Level*
   (978-0-7879-8721-3)
6. *Communication and Implementation: Sustaining the Practice*
   (978-0-7879-8722-0)

Plus, the *ROI in Action Casebook* (978-0-7879-8717-6) covers all the major workplace learning and performance applications, including Leadership Development, Sales Training, Performance Improvement, Technical Skills Training, Information Technology Training, Orientation and OJT, and Supervisor Training.

The **ROI Methodology** is a comprehensive measurement and evaluation process that collects six types of measures: Reaction, Satisfaction, and Planned Action; Learning; Application and Implementation; Business Impact; Return on Investment; and Intangible Measures. The process provides a step-by-step system for evaluation and planning, data collection, data analysis, and reporting. It is appropriate for the measurement and evaluation of *all* kinds of performance improvement programs and activities, including training and development, learning, human resources, coaching, meetings and events, consulting, and project management.

Special Offer from the ROI Institute

Send for your own ROI Process Model, an indispensable tool for implementing and presenting ROI in your organization. The ROI Institute is offering an exclusive gift to readers of The Measurement and Evaluation Series. This 11" x 25" multicolor foldout shows the ROI Methodology flow model and the key issues surrounding the implementation of the ROI Methodology. This easy-to-understand overview of the ROI Methodology has proven invaluable to countless professionals when implementing the ROI Methodology. Please return this page or e-mail your information to the address below to receive your free foldout (a $6.00 value). Please check your area(s) of interest in ROI.

Please send me the ROI Process Model described in the book. I am interested in learning more about the following ROI materials and services:

- ☐ Workshops and briefing on ROI
- ☐ Books and support materials on ROI
- ☐ Certification in the ROI Methodology
- ☐ ROI software
- ☐ ROI consulting services
- ☐ ROI Network information
- ☐ ROI benchmarking
- ☐ ROI research

Name _____
Title _____
Organization _____
Address _____
Phone _____
E-mail Address _____

Functional area of interest:

- ☐ Learning and Development/Performance Improvement
- ☐ Human Resources/Human Capital
- ☐ Public Relations/Community Affairs/Government Relations
- ☐ Consulting
- ☐ Sales/Marketing
- ☐ Technology/IT Systems
- ☐ Project Management Solutions
- ☐ Quality/Six Sigma
- ☐ Operations/Methods/Engineering
- ☐ Research and Development/Innovations
- ☐ Finance/Compliance
- ☐ Logistics/Distribution/Supply Chain
- ☐ Public Policy Initiatives
- ☐ Social Programs
- ☐ Other (Please Specify) _____

Organizational Level

- ☐ executive   ☐ management   ☐ consultant   ☐ specialist
- ☐ student   ☐ evaluator   ☐ researcher

Return this form or contact The ROI Institute
P.O. Box 380637
Birmingham, AL 35238-0637

Or e-mail information to info@roiinstitute.net
Please allow four to six weeks for delivery.

About This Book

Why This Book Is Important

ROI Fundamentals, the first book in the Measurement and Evaluation Series, introduces the ROI Methodology, a methodical approach to evaluation that can be replicated throughout an organization, enabling comparisons of results between one program and another. The process described in this book is the most documented method in the world, and its application has been phenomenal, with over five thousand individuals participating in five-day certification programs designed for implementation. Although other books may delve into accountability in certain types of programs or data, this book introduces a method that works across all types of programs, ranging from leadership development to basic skills training for new employees. With this approach, every program is evaluated at some level. With executives asking for more accountability from program leaders and teams, the information in this book—and series—is critical.

Evaluating Program Value

This book introduces a results-based approach to program implementation, focusing on a variety of measures, categorized into seven data types:

1. Inputs and indicators
2. Reaction and planned action
3. Learning and confidence
4. Application and implementation

5. Impact and consequences
6. Return on investment
7. Intangible benefits

ROI Fundamentals describes a process that will help those challenged with implementing and evaluating programs to identify, collect, analyze, and report all seven types of data in a consistent manner that ensures credible results.

How This Book Is Organized

This book introduces and follows the value chain of program evaluation throughout the program cycle. Chapter One, "A Brief Description of the ROI Methodology," introduces the ROI Methodology discussed throughout the remainder of this series. Chapter Two, "Why ROI? Key Issues and Trends," discusses why program evaluation and measurement (up to and including ROI) and the move toward results-based measurement are currently so critical. It also discusses the barriers to the ROI Methodology and the benefits of the process. Chapter Three, "Who Should Use the ROI Methodology?" helps determine if an organization is a candidate for implementing the ROI Methodology.

Chapter Four, "How to Build a Credible Process," describes the ROI Methodology framework and the ROI process model, along with the operating standards and the implementation of the methodology. Chapter Five, "Inhibitors of Implementation," explains the many barriers to the implementation of the ROI Methodology. It lists these barriers and discusses ways to avoid or neutralize them. Many myths about the methodology, and also its realities, are included.

Finally, Chapter Six, "Planning for Evaluation," begins by discussing how to establish the purpose and feasibility of a program. Then it details the steps for developing program objectives and planning documents. The chapter ends by discussing how to conduct a planning meeting and how to identify data sources.

The Measurement and Evaluation Series

Editors

Patricia Pulliam Phillips, Ph.D.

Jack J. Phillips, Ph.D.

Introduction to the Measurement and Evaluation Series

The ROI Six Pack provides detailed information on developing ROI evaluations, implementing the ROI Methodology, and showing the value of a variety of functions and processes. With detailed examples, tools, templates, shortcuts, and checklists, this series will be a valuable reference for individuals interested in using the ROI Methodology to show the impact of their projects, programs, and processes.

The Need

Although financial ROI has been measured for over one hundred years to quantify the value of plants, equipment, and companies, the concept has only recently been applied to evaluate the impact of learning and development, human resources, technology, quality, marketing, and other support functions. In the learning and development field alone, the use of ROI has become routine in many organizations. In the past decade, hundreds of organizations have embraced the ROI process to show the impact of many different projects and programs.

Along the way, professionals and practitioners need help. They need tools, templates, and tips, along with explanations, examples, and details, to make this process work. Without this help, using the ROI Methodology to show the value of projects and

programs is difficult. In short, practitioners need shortcuts and proven techniques to minimize the resources required to use this process. Practitioners' needs have created the need for this series. This series will provide the detail necessary to make the ROI Methodology successful within an organization. For easy reference and use, the books are logically arranged to align with the steps of the ROI Methodology.

Audience

The principal audience for these books is individuals who plan to use the ROI Methodology to show the value of their projects and programs. Such individuals are specialists or managers charged with proving the value of their particular project or program. They need detailed information, know-how, and confidence.

A second audience is those who have used the ROI Methodology for some time but want a quick reference with tips and techniques to make ROI implementation more successful within their organization. This series, which explains the evaluation process in detail, will be a valuable reference set for these individuals, regardless of other ROI publications owned.

A third audience is consultants and researchers who want to know how to address specific evaluation issues. Three important challenges face individuals as they measure ROI and conduct ROI evaluations: (1) collecting post-program data, (2) isolating the effects of the program, and (3) converting data to monetary values. A book is devoted to each of these critical issues, allowing researchers and consultants to easily find details on each issue.

A fourth audience is those who are curious about the ROI Methodology and its use. The first book in this series focuses specifically on ROI, its use, and how to determine whether it is appropriate for an organization. When interest is piqued, the remaining books provide more detail.

Flow of the Books

The six books are presented in a logical sequence, mirroring the ROI process model. Book one, *ROI Fundamentals: Why and When to Measure ROI*, presents the basic ROI Methodology and makes the business case for measuring ROI as it explores the benefits and barriers to implementation. It also examines the type of organization best suited for the ROI Methodology and the best time to implement it. Planning for an ROI evaluation is also explored in this book.

Book two, *Data Collection: Planning For and Collecting All Types of Data*, details data collection by examining the different techniques, methods, and issues involved in this process, with an emphasis on collecting post-program data. It examines the different data collection methods: questionnaires, interviews, focus groups, observation, action plans, performance contracts, and monitoring records.

Book three, *Isolation of Results: Defining the Impact of the Program*, focuses on the most valuable part of the ROI Methodology and the essential step for ensuring credibility. Recognizing that factors other than the program being measured can influence results, this book shows a variety of ways in which the effects of a program can be isolated from other influences. Techniques include comparison analysis using a control group, trend line analysis and forecasting methods, and expert input from a variety of sources.

Book four, *Data Conversion: Calculating the Monetary Benefits*, covers perhaps the second toughest challenge of ROI evaluation: placing monetary value on program benefits. To calculate the ROI, data must be converted to money, and *Data Conversion* shows how this conversion has been accomplished in a variety of organizations. The good news is that standard values are available for many items. When they are not, the book shows different techniques for converting them, ranging from calculating the value from records to seeking experts and searching databases. When data cannot be

converted to money credibly and with minimum resources, they are considered intangible. This book explores the range of intangible benefits and the necessary techniques for collecting, analyzing, and recording them.

Book five, *Costs and ROI: Evaluating at the Ultimate Level*, focuses on costs and ROI. This book shows that all costs must be captured in order to create a fully loaded cost profile. All the costs must be included in order to be conservative and to give the analysis additional credibility. Next, the actual ROI calculation is presented, showing the various assumptions and issues that must be addressed when calculating the ROI. Three different calculations are presented: the benefit-cost ratio, the ROI percentage, and the payback period. The book concludes with several cautions and concerns about the use of ROI and its meaning.

Book six, *Communication and Implementation: Sustaining the Practice*, explores two important issues. The first issue is reporting the results of an evaluation. This is the final part of the ROI Methodology and is necessary to ensure that audiences have the information they need so that improvement processes can be implemented. A range of techniques is available, including face-to-face meetings, brief reports, one-page summaries, routine communications, mass-audience techniques, and electronic media. All are available for reporting evaluation results. The final part of the book focuses on how to sustain the ROI evaluation process: how to use it, keep it going, and make it work in the long term to add value to the organization and, often, to show the value of all the programs and projects within a function or department.

Terminology: Programs, Projects, Solutions

In this series the terms *program* and *project* are used to describe many processes that can be evaluated using the ROI Methodology. This is an important issue because readers may vary widely in their perspectives. Individuals involved in technology applications may

Table I.1. Terms and Applications

Term	Example
Program	Leadership development skills enhancement for senior executives
Project	A reengineering scheme for a plastics division
System	A fully interconnected network for all branches of a bank
Initiative	A faith-based effort to reduce recidivism
Policy	A new preschool plan for disadvantaged citizens
Procedure	A new scheduling arrangement for truck drivers
Event	A golf outing for customers
Meeting	A U.S. Coast Guard conference on innovations
Process	Quality sampling
People	Staff additions in the customer care center
Tool	A new means of selecting hotel staff

use the terms *system* and *technology* rather than *program* or *project*. In public policy, in contrast, the word *program* is prominent. For a professional meetings and events planner, the word *program* may not be pertinent, but in human resources, *program* is often used. Finding one term for all these situations would be difficult. Consequently, the terms *program* and *project* are used interchangeably. Table I.1 lists these and other terms that may be used in other contexts.

Features

Each book in the series takes a straightforward approach to make it understandable, practical, and useful. Checklists are provided, charts are included, templates are presented, and examples are explored. All are intended to show how the ROI Methodology works. The focus of these books is implementing the process and making it successful within an organization. The methodology is based on the work of hundreds of individuals who have made the ROI Methodology a successful evaluation process within their organizations.

About Pfeiffer

Pfeiffer serves the professional development and hands-on resource needs of training and human resource practitioners and gives them products to do their jobs better. We deliver proven ideas and solutions from experts in HR development and HR management, and we offer effective and customizable tools to improve workplace performance. From novice to seasoned professional, Pfeiffer is the source you can trust to make yourself and your organization more successful.

Essential Knowledge Pfeiffer produces insightful, practical, and comprehensive materials on topics that matter the most to training and HR professionals. Our Essential Knowledge resources translate the expertise of seasoned professionals into practical, how-to guidance on critical workplace issues and problems. These resources are supported by case studies, worksheets, and job aids and are frequently supplemented with CD-ROMs, Web sites, and other means of making the content easier to read, understand, and use.

Essential Tools Pfeiffer's Essential Tools resources save time and expense by offering proven, ready-to-use materials—including exercises, activities, games, instruments, and assessments—for use during a training or team-learning event. These resources are frequently offered in looseleaf or CD-ROM format to facilitate copying and customization of the material.

Pfeiffer also recognizes the remarkable power of new technologies in expanding the reach and effectiveness of training. While e-hype has often created whizbang solutions in search of a problem, we are dedicated to bringing convenience and enhancements to proven training solutions. All our e-tools comply with rigorous functionality standards. The most appropriate technology wrapped around essential content yields the perfect solution for today's on-the-go trainers and human resource professionals.

Pfeiffer *Essential resources for training and HR professionals*
www.pfeiffer.com

ROI Fundamentals

Why and When to Measure ROI

Patricia Pulliam Phillips, Ph.D.
Jack J. Phillips, Ph.D.

Pfeiffer
A Wiley Imprint
www.pfeiffer.com

Copyright © 2008 by John Wiley & Sons, Inc. All rights reserved.

Published by Pfeiffer
An Imprint of Wiley
989 Market Street, San Francisco, CA 94103-1741
www.pfeiffer.com

No part of this publication may be reproduced, stored in a retrieval system, or transmitted in any form or by any means, electronic, mechanical, photocopying, recording, scanning, or otherwise, except as permitted under Section 107 or 108 of the 1976 United States Copyright Act, without either the prior written permission of the publisher, or authorization through payment of the appropriate per-copy fee to the Copyright Clearance Center, Inc., 222 Rosewood Drive, Danvers, MA 01923, 978-750-8400, fax 978-646-8600, or on the web at www.copyright.com. Requests to the publisher for permission should be addressed to the Permissions Department, John Wiley & Sons, Inc., 111 River Street, Hoboken, NJ 07030, 201-748-6011, fax 201-748-6008, or online at http://www.wiley.com/go/permissions.

Limit of Liability/Disclaimer of Warranty: While the publisher and author have used their best efforts in preparing this book, they make no representations or warranties with respect to the accuracy or completeness of the contents of this book and specifically disclaim any implied warranties of merchantability or fitness for a particular purpose. No warranty may be created or extended by sales representatives or written sales materials. The advice and strategies contained herein may not be suitable for your situation. You should consult with a professional where appropriate. Neither the publisher nor author shall be liable for any loss of profit or any other commercial damages, including but not limited to special, incidental, consequential, or other damages.

Readers should be aware that Internet Web sites offered as citations and/or sources for further information may have changed or disappeared between the time this book was written and when it is read.

For additional copies/bulk purchases of this book in the U.S. please contact 800-274-4434.

Pfeiffer books and products are available through most bookstores. To contact Pfeiffer directly call our Customer Care Department within the U.S. at 800-274-4434, outside the U.S. at 317-572-3985, fax 317-572-4002, or visit www.pfeiffer.com.

Pfeiffer also publishes its books in a variety of electronic formats. Some content that appears in print may not be available in electronic books.

Library of Congress Cataloging-in-Publication Data

Phillips, Patricia Pulliam.
  ROI fundamentals: why and when to measure ROI/ Patricia Pulliam Phillips, Jack J. Phillips.
    p. cm.—(Measurement and evaluation series)
  Includes bibliographical references and index.
  ISBN: 978-0-7879-8716-9 (pbk.)
  1. Employees—Training of—Cost effectiveness. 2. Rate of return.
3. Project management—Evaluation.
I. Phillips, Jack J., date. II. Title. III. Title: Return on investments fundamentals.
HF5549.5.T7P437 2008
658.15′52—dc22

                                    2007028787

Production Editor: Michael Kay	Editorial Assistant: Julie Rodriguez
Editor: Matthew Davis	Manufacturing Supervisor: Becky Morgan

Printed in the United States of America

PB Printing 10 9 8 7 6 5 4 3 2 1

Contents

Acknowledgments from the Editors	xix
Preface: The Realities of ROI	xxi

Chapter 1: A Brief Description of the ROI Methodology — 1

Evaluation Levels: A Beginning Point	1
Evaluation Planning	9
Data Collection	14
Isolation of Program Effects	17
Data Conversion	19
Intangible Benefits	22
Program Costs	22
Return on Investment Calculation	23
Reporting	24
Case Study	24
Final Thoughts	26

Chapter 2: Why ROI? — 27

Progress and Status of ROI	28
Global Trends in Measurement	29
ROI Applications Across Fields and Sectors	30
Growth of ROI as a Conference Topic	32

Global Expansion of ROI Applications	32
The Move from Activity to Results	33
ROI Is Here to Stay	34
Why ROI?	**34**
Increased Budgets	35
The Ultimate Level of Evaluation	36
Change, Quality, and Reengineering	36
Business Mindset of Support Managers	37
The Trend Toward Accountability	38
Top Executive Requirements	39
Concerns About Using ROI	**39**
Practitioners	40
Senior Managers, Sponsors, and Clients	40
Researchers	41
Criteria for an Effective ROI Process	41
Barriers to ROI Implementation	**43**
Financial and Time Costs	44
Lack of Staff Skills and Orientation	44
Faulty Needs Assessment	44
Fear	44
Lack of Discipline or Planning	45
False Assumptions	45
Benefits of Using ROI	**46**
Measurement of a Program's Contribution	46
Clear Priorities	46
Focus on Results	46
Respect from Senior Executives and Program Sponsors	47
Positive Changes in Management Perceptions	47
ROI Best Practices	**47**
Evaluation Targets	48
Microlevel Evaluation	48
A Variety of Data Collection Methods	49
Isolation of the Program	49
Sampling for ROI Calculations	49
Conversion of Program Results to Monetary Values	51
Final Thoughts	**51**

Chapter 3: Who Should Use the ROI Methodology? — 53

The Typical Organization — 54
The Typical Program — 55
Signs That an Organization Is Ready for the ROI Methodology — 57
Taking a Reactive Versus a Proactive Approach — 61
   Reactive Approach — 62
   Proactive Approach — 62
Final Thoughts — 63

Chapter 4: How to Build a Credible Process — 65

The Evaluation Framework — 67
The Process Model — 72
The Operating Standards: Guiding Principles — 72
   1. Report the Complete Story — 73
   2. Conserve Important Resources — 73
   3. Enhance Credibility — 73
   4. Be Conservative — 73
   5. Account for Other Factors — 74
   6. Account for Missing Data — 74
   7. Adjust Estimates for Error — 74
   8. Omit the Extremes — 74
   9. Capture Annual Benefits for Short-Term Programs — 75
   10. Account for All Program Costs — 75
   11. Report Intangible Benefits — 75
   12. Communicate Results — 75
Case Applications and Practice — 76
Implementation — 77
   Assign Responsibilities — 77
   Develop Skills — 77
   Develop an Implementation Plan — 78
   Prepare or Revise Evaluation Guidelines — 81
   Brief Managers on the Evaluation Process — 81
Final Thoughts — 81

Chapter 5: Inhibitors of Implementation — 83

- Barriers to Implementation — 83
  - Costs and Time — 83
  - Lack of Skills — 84
  - Faulty or Inadequate Initial Analysis — 85
  - Fear — 85
  - Discipline and Planning — 86
- ROI Myths — 86
  - ROI Is Too Complex for Most Users — 87
  - ROI Is Expensive, Consuming Too Many Critical Resources — 87
  - If Senior Management Does Not Require ROI, There Is No Need to Pursue It — 87
  - ROI Is a Passing Fad — 88
  - ROI Is Only One Type of Data — 88
  - ROI Is Not Future-Oriented; It Reflects Only Past Performance — 89
  - ROI Is Rarely Used by Organizations — 89
  - The ROI Methodology Cannot Be Easily Replicated — 89
  - ROI Is Not a Credible Process; It Is Too Subjective — 90
  - ROI Is Not Credible When Evaluating Soft-Skill Programs — 90
  - ROI Is Only for Manufacturing and Service Organizations — 90
  - Isolation of the Influence of Factors Other Than the Program Is Not Always Possible — 91
  - Measurement of On-the-Job Activities Is Impossible Because Post-Program Control of Application Is Impossible — 91
  - ROI Is Appropriate Only for Large Organizations — 92
  - The ROI Methodology Has No Standards — 92
- It's All About Change Management — 92
- Next Steps — 94
- Final Thoughts — 95
- ROI Quiz — 96
- Quiz Answers — 98

Chapter 6: Planning for Evaluation — 99

- Establishing Purpose and Feasibility — 99

Purpose	99
Make Decisions About Programs	100
Improve Programs and Processes	100
Demonstrate Program Value	101
Feasibility	103
Validation of Program Objectives	103
Availability of Data	104
Appropriateness for ROI Measurement	104
Defining Program Objectives	**104**
Reaction Objectives	105
Learning Objectives	108
Application Objectives	111
Impact Objectives	112
ROI Objectives	115
Developing the Planning Documents	**117**
Data Collection Plan	117
What Do You Ask?	117
How Do You Ask?	117
Whom Do You Ask?	121
When Do You Ask?	121
Who Asks?	121
ROI Analysis Plan	121
Methods for Isolating the Effects of the Program	121
Methods for Converting Data to Monetary Values	123
Cost Categories	123
Intangible Benefits	123
Communication Targets for the Final Report	123
Other Application Influences and Issues	123
Comments	124
Project Plan	124
Conducting the Planning Meeting	**125**
Who Should Be Involved	125
Agenda	126
Factors for Success	126
Identifying Data Sources	**127**
Organizational Performance Records	127

Participants	127
Participants' Managers	128
Participants' Direct Reports	128
Team or Peer Group	128
Internal and External Groups	129
Final Thoughts	129
Appendix	131
Index	133
About the Authors	143

Acknowledgments from the Editors

From Patti

No project, regardless of its size or scope, is completed without the help and support of others. My sincere thanks go to the staff at Pfeiffer. Their support for this project has been relentless. Matt Davis has been the greatest! It is our pleasure and privilege to work with such a professional and creative group of people.

Thanks also go to my husband, Jack. His unwavering support of my work is always evident. His idea for the series was to provide readers with a practical understanding of the various components of a comprehensive measurement and evaluation process. This first book sets the stage for that understanding. Thank you, Jack, for another fun opportunity!

From Jack

Many thanks go to the staff who helped make this series a reality. Lori Ditoro did an excellent job of meeting a very tight deadline and delivering a quality manuscript.

Much admiration and thanks go to Patti. She is an astute observer of the ROI Methodology, having observed and learned from hundreds of presentations, consulting assignments, and engagements. In addition, she is an excellent researcher and student of the process, studying how it is developed and how it works. She has become an ROI expert in her own right. Thanks, Patti, for your many contributions. You are a great partner, friend, and spouse.

Preface: The Realities of ROI

We are pleased to introduce to you the first book in the ROI Six Pack, which is part of the Measurement and Evaluation Series at Pfeiffer. These six books provide the latest tools, practical research, and how-to advice on measuring return on investment (ROI) in a variety of programs. This book offers an overview of the ROI Methodology.

The term *return on investment* summons a variety of images, ideas, concerns, and even fears. Some professionals are frightened by the idea of evaluating ROI for learning and development, performance improvement, human resources, technology, quality, and marketing. They become anxious about how ROI may be interpreted and used. Professionals who are open to learning about the ROI Methodology and its benefits, however, view it as an opportunity, a challenge, and a tool for improving programs and solutions. Although some debate its appropriateness, others quietly and deliberately pursue ROI in a variety of settings—and achieve impressive results.

The ROI Methodology is not for everyone or for every organization. Some organizations lack the trust and support that ROI requires. The successful champion of the ROI Methodology must be willing to learn, change, and try new things, using ROI as a process improvement tool. Without this attitude and approach, it may be best not to try. *ROI Fundamentals* provides the information necessary for individuals to use ROI to their advantage and become an advocate for the ROI Methodology.

ROI is growing in prominence and popularity; many professionals, managers, and senior leaders are trying to decide whether it is right for their organization, particularly for nontraditional applications. They need information about ROI, so that they can make decisions based on fact. Barriers to the implementation of ROI do exist; many of them are real, others perceived. Either way, these barriers can be eliminated—and success achieved—with the ROI Methodology. In the last decade, through our work with ROI, we have observed some realities about ROI; knowing about these realities may help individuals decide whether the pursuit of the ROI Methodology is worth the effort. The realities presented here reflect the drivers behind these six books and illustrate some of the challenges that an advocate will face. The stage is set for training and performance improvement executives who can accept the realities and challenges of ROI and use it to reach their goals.

ROI Reality #1

> Although the ROI Methodology can be implemented in many situations, several perceived issues inhibit its use. Although real barriers exist, most of the inhibitors are myths based on misunderstandings of the process and what it can achieve.

The ROI Methodology is a tool that currently enjoys widespread application; however, many individuals involved in ROI implementation attend ROI certification workshops with built-in resistance. Their participation is driven by senior management or by ultimatums from the top executive group. Their hesitancy is due, in part, to fear of the unknown and fear of what the results of an ROI evaluation will do, particularly if the resulting ROI is negative. Individuals are concerned that a negative ROI might bring an end to their programs or, worse, their job. This concern is often based on misunderstanding and lack of knowledge. A comment from the audience at a keynote presentation at the International Conference of the American Society for Training and Development underscores this concern: "I [a store manager] transferred to the training and development function to escape numbers and, ultimately, the accountability that goes along with them. Now, it looks like I have to face the same type of numbers here." The comment drew a round of applause and also illustrates another fear—the fear of anything to do with numbers. The reality is that numbers are involved, but it is not necessary to be a statistician to apply or benefit from ROI. The perception that one needs a graduate degree in program evaluation is not at all correct and presents one of many unwarranted claims against the use of ROI.

ROI Fundamentals, the first book in the ROI Six Pack, explores and dispels many of the myths about ROI that challenge its use. Misconceptions act as barriers, deterring application and implementation of the ROI Methodology. Although very real barriers do exist—for example, barriers of time, cost, and skill—the benefits of the methodology far outweigh the investment.

ROI Reality #2

> Lack of information about ROI or, worse, misinformation about ROI can send clients on a misdirected course. Prospective clients need more information on the benefits of and barriers to implementing ROI.

The ROI Six Pack was developed in response to clients' needs. Organizations pursuing ROI have asked for more detail on the business realities of ROI. They want to know up front the actual benefits and the expected payoff of using the ROI Methodology.

An understanding of what the ROI Methodology can achieve requires clarification of the issues, terms, and concepts that are basic to understanding the process. *ROI Fundamentals* addresses this need by providing information that will help readers

- Increase their understanding of the ROI Methodology, its concept, and its assumptions.

- Identify who is using the ROI Methodology, why they are using it, and for what types of applications they are using it. It is important to see who is—and who is not—embracing this process improvement tool.

- Make a decision about ROI. This is a critical issue! Most people explore the ROI Methodology with these questions: "Is this right for us? Is this needed in our organization at this time?" *ROI Fundamentals* provides the information needed to answer these questions.

- Increase their understanding of how the ROI Methodology can add value to an organization.

- Dispel the inhibiting myths about ROI that can prevent successful implementation.

- Plot their next steps.

This first book in the Six Pack is not a detailed reference for the ROI Methodology; the other five books in this series detail each step in the process, providing resources for application and implementation. Instead, *ROI Fundamentals* is about understanding and making sense of the ROI Methodology from a business perspective.

ROI Reality #3

Using ROI effectively will require individuals and organizations to build new skills and learn processes.

Unfortunately, preparation for most of today's professionals in learning and development, human resources, quality, technology, and marketing has not involved learning how to conduct measurement and evaluations. Few courses in college degree programs cover appropriate analytical techniques, and measurement and evaluation is rarely required. Therefore, individuals may be unprepared to conduct ROI analyses. The ROI Six Pack is designed specifically to address this need, using simple, straightforward language. The steps, tasks, processes, and issues involved in calculating ROI are fully explored in these six books.

ROI Reality #4

> The ROI Methodology is being implemented globally in all types of organizations and for all types of programs. Many training and development, organizational development, performance improvement, and human resources professionals are using the ROI Methodology to radically change the way they design, develop, and deliver programs and solutions.

The number of applications of the ROI Methodology has grown significantly; hundreds of organizations in different settings across the globe now use it. The ROI Methodology has been used in practically every country. Through our international associates, we have been involved in its implementation in organizations in almost fifty countries. The ROI Methodology is proving to be a valuable performance tool, and the number of converts is rapidly growing.

Growth in the application of the ROI Methodology cuts across all types of organizations and industries. When one major organization in an industry begins using it, others become interested. For example, the three largest package delivery companies in the world have implemented the ROI Methodology, partly because their peers were using it. For the same reason, almost all major telecommunications companies in the United States have implemented this methodology.

The ROI Methodology has also moved into different organizational sectors. At first, it was used almost exclusively in the manufacturing sector—the logical birthplace of any process improvement. It quickly moved to the service sector, then to nonprofit organizations, and on to government organizations. Now, it is being applied in the education sector, where schools and universities are using ROI to show the value of their programs.

Whereas initially the ROI Methodology was employed to show the impact of training in cooperative education programs, it quickly spread to all types of programs, from highly technical programs to long-term executive development. The ROI Methodology has been successfully applied in coaching and management development programs—for example, business coaching, mentoring, and career development. Human resources programs—such as orientation, compensation systems, recruiting strategies, employee relation initiatives, and retention solutions—have also been successfully evaluated using the ROI Methodology. Applications have moved beyond the human resources and learning and performance improvement arena to include systems, technology, change, quality, meetings and events, marketing, and a variety of public sector and social programs.

Finally, the number of individuals who have attended formal training in the ROI Methodology continues to grow rapidly. Over 20,000 specialists and managers have attended almost 1,000 ROI two-day workshops conducted in major cities throughout the world. Over 5,000 individuals have been prepared to implement the methodology internally through an ROI certification process.

ROI Reality #5

A new breed of performance improvement executive is achieving success with the ROI Methodology. Operating with a business mindset, such executives are using the methodology to prove the value of their programs. They are becoming business partners in the organization.

The good news is that changes are being made and success achieved. A new breed of performance improvement executive is managing training and development, performance improvement, and human resources functions. The new executives bring a business mindset to the table. They want to operate their function as an important business enterprise, as a major contributor that adds value to the business, and they use the ROI Methodology to support their cause.

In implementing the ROI Methodology, the new executives are choosing to be proactive instead of reactive. They realize that they must take the lead and initiate change or it will not happen. ROI is being recognized as a necessary tool. In any functional part of a business, performance must be validated in order to be recognized as a contributor.

Finally, the new breed of performance improvement executive accepts the challenging aspects of implementing the ROI Methodology. It is difficult to apply the process to all the different situations, scenarios, and environments in which it must work in order to be a useful tool. The new executives understand that it will take time to change their practices and implement the methodology.

ROI Reality #6

> Sooner or later, every function will face a need for increased accountability and will have to address ROI. For some, the time is now. For others, the time may come later, but the need will eventually surface.

Let's face it, even in organizations in which tradition offers plentiful financial endowment, stakeholder questions arise, such as

- Did the program make a difference?
- Was it worth the investment?

- Did we make or save more than we spent on the project?
- Could another program or even another department achieve better results at less cost?

Resources are limited. A tool is needed that allows decision makers to base their decisions about investments on a single common measure. That measure is ROI, and although it is not new, in many organizations its use is expanding across functions. Ultimately, the use of ROI across an organization will allow decision makers to compare functional as well as programmatic contributions, based on a common metric and using a standard process.

ROI Fundamentals details the important influences responsible for the growth of the ROI Methodology. These influences include the following:

- Global economic forces that make it necessary for all segments of an organization to show the payoff of all types of solutions and programs. Every function must make a contribution.

- ROI's position as the ultimate level of evaluation, in which the cost of the solution is compared with the monetary benefits of the solution. Even though other levels of evaluation are important, nothing tells the story quite like ROI, particularly for sponsors and clients who require a monetary payback.

- ROI's familiarity among managers, particularly those who have a business degree. They see ROI as an important accountability tool. They have seen it applied in the evaluation of capital expenditures and welcome its use in evaluation of performance initiatives. They realize that ROI is not a fad; it is a proven technique that will be here for years to come.

- Top executives' requirement that the ROI of new (and existing) programs be measured. Previously, executives hesitated to ask for ROI because they didn't realize it could be done. In some situations, they were told that it is impossible to measure ROI for certain projects or programs. Now, they are learning that this level of evaluation can be done, so they are requiring it.

Some people still believe that ROI is an unrealistic approach to measuring value for learning and development, performance improvement, human resources, quality, and other programs. In reality, the ROI Methodology presented in this book provides data that are important to all stakeholders and dispels the myths and mysteries about measuring value for program investments.

1

A Brief Description of the ROI Methodology

The ROI Methodology is represented by the basic model shown in Figure 1.1. This process model provides a systematic approach to ROI calculations; a potentially complicated process is simplified by breaking it into sequential steps. This step-by-step approach keeps the process manageable so that users can tackle one issue at a time. Applying the model also provides consistency from one ROI calculation to another. This chapter provides a brief description of the ROI Methodology and how it fits into a comprehensive process.

Evaluation Levels: A Beginning Point

The ROI Methodology collects and processes up to five levels of evaluation results. The process also considers what is referred to as Level 0, the initial data or inputs, which represent activities and investment associated with a program or project. Each level represents a different category of data; each category of data answers questions asked by various stakeholders.

For example, Level 0, Inputs and Indicators, represents the various inputs of the project or program. These data are collected for all programs; they include costs, efficiencies, duration (in hours or days), participants, and topics. These data are input only and do not necessarily correspond to the results; they merely represent

Figure 1.1. The ROI Process Model

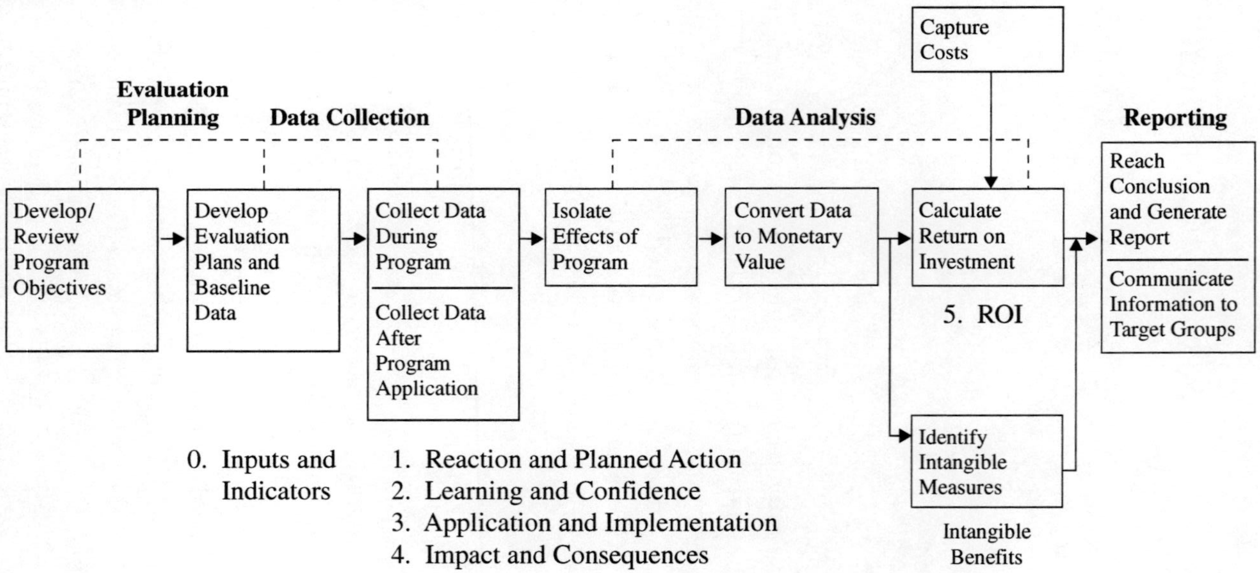

Evaluation Planning | **Data Collection** | **Data Analysis** | **Reporting**

- Develop/Review Program Objectives
- Develop Evaluation Plans and Baseline Data
- Collect Data During Program
- Collect Data After Program Application
- Isolate Effects of Program
- Convert Data to Monetary Value
- Capture Costs
- Calculate Return on Investment — **5. ROI**
- Identify Intangible Measures → Intangible Benefits
- Reach Conclusion and Generate Report
- Communicate Information to Target Groups

0. Inputs and Indicators
1. Reaction and Planned Action
2. Learning and Confidence
3. Application and Implementation
4. Impact and Consequences

activity. Specific questions answered by data categorized at Level 0 include

- What steps have been taken to implement the program?
- How many people are involved in the program?
- Who was involved in the program?
- How much time has been spent on the program?
- What did the program cost the organization?

Level 1, Reaction and Planned Action, represents reaction from participants as well as actions planned as a result of the program. This level of evaluation is the first level that represents results—results from the perspective of participants. Almost all organizations evaluate at Level 1, usually with a generic end-of-program questionnaire. Specific questions answered by data collected at this level include

- Was the program delivered successfully?
- Was the content relevant to participants' current work?
- Was the content important to participants' current jobs?
- Do the participants intend to apply what they learned?
- Did the content represent new information?
- Will participants recommend the program to others?

While this level of evaluation is important as a customer satisfaction measure, a favorable reaction does not ensure that participants have learned new skills or knowledge.

At Level 2, Learning and Confidence, measurements focus on what participants learned during the program; learning is assessed through self-assessments, checklists, role plays, simulations, group evaluations, or other tools. A learning check is helpful to ensure that participants have absorbed the desired content and messages and know how to use or apply them properly. This level may also measure the number of new professional contacts made and the extent to which existing contacts were strengthened through networking that occurred during program implementation. Specific questions that are answered with Level 2 data include

- Do the participants "get it"?
- Do participants know what to do?
- Do participants know how to do it?
- Have participants' attitudes changed so that they are prepared to change behaviors or processes?
- Are participants confident in applying their newly acquired skills, knowledge, or information?

It is important to remember, however, that a positive learning measure is no guarantee that the learning or contacts acquired will actually be used.

At Level 3, Application and Implementation, a variety of follow-up methods are used to determine whether participants have applied what they learned. Completion of action items, behavior change, use of skills, and follow-up with contacts are important measures at Level 3. Questions answered by Level 3 data include

- Are participants applying their newly acquired knowledge, skills, or information?
- Are participants applying their newly acquired knowledge, skills, or information at the level of frequency expected?

- If participants are applying their newly acquired knowledge, skills, or information, what is supporting them?
- If they are not, why not?

While Level 3 evaluations are important to gauge the success of the application, they still do not guarantee that a positive impact will occur in the individual or the organization.

Level 4, Impact and Consequences, represents the actual results, or outcomes, achieved by participants as they successfully apply the content, messages, or contacts. Typical Level 4 measures include output, sales, quality, costs, time, and customer satisfaction. An important step taken during Level 4 data collection and analysis is isolating the impact of the program on these measures. Specific questions answered with Level 4 data include

- How does the application of newly acquired knowledge, skills, or information affect output, quality, cost, time, job satisfaction, employee satisfaction, or work habits?
- How does an organization know whether the program caused the impact?

Although the program may produce a measurable business impact, a concern may still exist that the program costs too much.

At Level 5, Return on Investment—the ultimate level of evaluation—the program's monetary benefits are compared with the program's costs. Although ROI can be expressed in several ways, it is usually presented as a percentage or benefit-cost ratio. The evaluation chain is not complete until the Level 5 evaluation is conducted. Here, the analysis should answer the most fundamental question: Do program benefits exceed program costs?

Table 1.1 summarizes the evaluation levels and the measures developed at each level. Readers should consider each level and

Table 1.1. Measurement at Each Level of Evaluation

Level	Measurement Category	Current Status in Your Organization	Evaluation Target for Most Organizations	Comments
0	**Inputs and Indicators** Measures inputs into programs, including the number of programs, participants, audience, costs, and efficiencies	100%	100%	This is being accomplished now.
1	**Reaction and Planned Action** Measures reaction to and satisfaction with the experience, ambience, content, and value of the program, as well as planned action after the program		100%	Most organizations evaluate 100% of programs at this level but need to focus more on content and planned action.
2	**Learning and Confidence** Measures what participants have learned in the program—information, knowledge, skills, or contacts (take-aways from the program)		80–90%	Simple learning measures can be integrated into the data collection process at Level 1.

3	**Application and Implementation** Measures progress after the program—the use of information, knowledge, skills, or contacts	15–30%	Progress has been made, but more follow-up measures are needed.
4	**Impact and Consequences** Measures changes in business impact variables (such as output, quality, time, or cost) linked to the program	10%	The link between the program and business impact is analyzed for select programs.
5	**Return on Investment** Compares the monetary benefits of the business impact measures to the costs of the program	5%	The ultimate evaluation.

note the percentage of programs within their organization that are evaluated at each level. They should compare the current status of their evaluations with the targeted percentages in the table. These targets were developed on the basis of the evaluation practices of organizations currently implementing the ROI Methodology. As shown, not all programs should be evaluated at each level. Selecting programs to be evaluated at the higher levels depends on a variety of factors, including

- Purpose of evaluation
- Need for the program
- Program profile
- Stakeholders' needs

Selecting Programs for ROI Evaluation

Evaluation at Levels 4 and 5 is reserved for programs that are
- Expensive
- High-profile
- Offered to a large audience
- Linked to business objectives and strategy
- Of interest to senior management

Even though data at the lower levels of evaluation do not necessarily predict success at the higher levels, data must be collected at the lower levels when evaluating at the higher levels. As participants take part in a program and react positively to it, acquiring knowledge, then applying that knowledge, business impact will occur as long as what was presented was needed and the right audience was targeted. If the business impact is as planned and program costs are less than the monetary benefits of program results, a positive

ROI will occur. This chain of impact provides the complete story of program success. Data important to all stakeholders are developed; together, these data can explain why the ROI is what it is and how it can be improved for future program implementations.

From the client's perspective, the value of information increases as evaluation moves up the chain of impact. The ROI Methodology is a client-centered process, meeting the data needs of the individuals who initiate, approve, and sponsor programs. Placing the client at the center of the evaluation process is consistent with the practices of benchmarking forum members of the American Society for Training and Development (ASTD) (Van Buren, 2002) and the best practices of corporate universities as identified in a study conducted by the American Productivity and Quality Center (Phillips, 2000).

Evaluation Planning

Planning is a critical phase in the ROI Methodology. A solid evaluation plan will foster successful execution as well as capture client buy-in before results are rendered. Several issues must be addressed when developing the evaluation plan for an ROI impact study. Five specific elements are important to evaluation success:

1. The evaluation purpose should be considered prior to developing the evaluation plan because the purpose will determine the scope of the evaluation, the types of instruments used, and the types of data collected.
2. The feasibility of a Level 4 or 5 evaluation should be examined. Feasibility is determined not only by the type of program undergoing evaluation but also by resources and time constraints.
3. It is imperative that objectives for different levels of evaluation be developed. Program objectives position the program for success as well as give direction to the evaluation.

4. Sources of data are an important consideration. While program participants will be the primary source of data in most cases, including other sources is also important to provide a balanced perspective and add credibility.
5. The timing of data collection is another consideration. In some cases, pre-program measurements are taken to compare with post-program measures. In other cases, measures are taken at intervals throughout the program. Sometimes, pre-program measurements are not available but post-program follow-up measures are still taken.

To complete the planning process, three simple planning documents are developed: the data collection plan, the ROI analysis plan, and the project plan. These documents should be completed before the evaluation project is implemented (ideally, before the program is designed or developed). Appropriate up-front attention will save much time later when data are actually collected.

The data collection plan outlines the major elements and issues involved in collecting data for evaluation at Levels 1 through 4. A target ROI (Level 5) is also established during planning. Table 1.2 shows a completed data collection plan for a program on interactive sales skills. The three-day training program was designed for retail sales associates in the electronics department of a major store chain (Phillips and Phillips, 2001). An ROI calculation was planned for a pilot of three groups.

The ROI analysis plan is a continuation of the data collection plan. It captures information on several key items that are necessary to develop the actual ROI calculation, including techniques to isolate the effects of the program as well as convert Level 4 measures to units of money. Along with these elements, cost categories, intangible benefits, and communication targets are identified. Table 1.3 shows a completed ROI analysis plan for the interactive selling skills program.

Table 1.2. Sample Data Collection Plan

Program: Interactive Sales Training   **Responsibility:** P. Phillips   **Date:** _____

Level	Broad Program Objectives	Measures	Data Collection Method and Instruments	Data Sources	Timing	Responsibility
1	**REACTION AND PERCEIVED VALUE** • Positive reaction— 4 out of 5 • Action items	• A 1–5 rating on a composite of five measures • Yes or No	• Questionnaire	• Participant	• End of program (third day)	• Facilitator
2	**LEARNING** • Learn to use five simple skills	• Pass or fail on skill practice	• Observation of skill practice by facilitator	• Facilitator	• Second day of program	• Facilitator

(Continued)

Table 1.2. Sample Data Collection Plan (*Continued*)

Level	Broad Program Objectives	Measures	Data Collection Method and Instruments	Data Sources	Timing	Responsibility
3	**APPLICATION AND IMPLEMENTATION**					
	• Initial use of five simple skills	• Verbal feedback	• Follow-up session	• Participant	• Three weeks after second day	• Facilitator
	• At least 50% of participants use all skills with every customer	• Fifth item checked on a 1–5 scale	• Follow-up questionnaire	• Participant	• Three months after program	• Store training coordinator
4	**BUSINESS IMPACT**					
	• Increase in sales	• Weekly average sales per sales associate	• Business performance monitoring	• Company records	• Three months after program	• Store training coordinator
5	**ROI**					
	• 50%					

Comments: The ROI objective was set at a high value because of the store sample size; the executives wanted convincing data.

Table 1.3. Sample ROI Analysis Plan

Program: Interactive Sales Training   **Responsibility:** P. Phillips   **Date:** _____

Data Items	Methods of Isolating the Effects of the Program	Methods of Converting Data	Cost Categories	Intangible Benefits	Communication Targets	Other Influences and Issues
• Weekly sales per associate	• Control group analysis • Participant estimate	• Direct conversion using profit contribution	• Facilitation fees • Program materials • Meals and refreshments • Facilities • Participant salaries and benefits • Cost of coordination • Evaluation	• Customer satisfaction • Employee satisfaction	• Program participants • Electronics department managers at targeted stores • Store managers at targeted stores • Senior store executives in district, region, headquarters • Training staff: instructors, coordinators, designers, and managers	• Must have job coverage during training • No communication with control group • Seasonal fluctuations should be avoided

The third plan that is developed in the evaluation planning phase is a project plan, which provides a description of the program and a timeline for the project, from planning of the evaluation to communication of the results. Exhibit 1.1 shows a sample project plan.

Collectively, these three planning documents provide the necessary direction for the ROI evaluation. Because most of the decisions about the evaluation process are made as these planning tools are developed, the remainder of the project becomes a systematic process of implementing the plan. Time allocated to this process will save precious time later.

Data Collection

Data collection is central to the ROI Methodology. Deciding how to collect the data, from whom to collect the data, and when to collect the data is fundamental to a successful ROI study. Both hard data (for example, output, quality, cost, and time data) and soft data (for example, job satisfaction and customer satisfaction) are collected, using a variety of methods:

- *Surveys* are administered to determine whether participants are satisfied with the program and to what degree, whether they have learned the desired skills and knowledge, and whether they have used various aspects of the program. Survey responses usually consist of perception or attitudinal data, often represented on a scale. Surveys are used to collect data at Levels 1, 2, and 3.

- *Questionnaires* are more detailed than surveys and can be used to uncover a variety of quantitative and qualitative data. Participants provide responses to

Exhibit 1.1. Project Plan

	FEB	MAR	APR	MAY	JUN	JUL	AUG	SEP
Decision to conduct ROI study	■							
Evaluation planning complete	■							
Instruments designed	■							
Instruments pilot-tested		■						
Data collected from Group A		■	■					
Data collected from Group B				■				
Data collected from Group C					■			
Data tabulation, preliminary summary					■			
Analysis conducted						■		
Report written						■		
Report printed						■		
Results communicated							■	
Improvements initiated							■	
Implementation complete								■

several types of open-ended and forced-response questions. Questionnaires can be used to capture data at Levels 1, 2, 3, and 4.

- *Tests* are conducted to measure changes in knowledge and skills (Level 2). A wide variety of methods are used, ranging from formal (criterion-referenced tests, norm-referenced tests, performance tests, simulations, and skill practices) to informal (facilitator assessment, self-assessment, and team assessment).

- On-the-job *observation* captures actual skill application and use. Observations are particularly useful in customer service training and are most effective when the observer is unnoticeable to the participant being observed. Observations are appropriate for collecting Level 3 data.

- *Interviews* are conducted with participants to determine the extent to which learning has been used on the job. Interviewers can probe to uncover specific applications. Interviews are most often used for collecting Level 3 data but can also be used to collect Level 1 and Level 2 data. Occasionally, interviews are used to collect Level 4 data.

- *Focus groups* are conducted to determine the degree to which a group of participants has applied the program to job situations. Focus groups are usually appropriate for collecting Level 3 data, but are also used in making the link between business impact and the program.

- *Action plans and program assignments* are developed by participants during the program and are implemented on the job after the program is completed. Follow-up on action plans and program assignments provides evidence of program success. Level 3 and Level 4 data can be collected using action plans.

- *Performance contracts* are developed by the participant, the participant's supervisor, and the facilitator. They all agree on job performance outcomes from the program. Performance contracts are appropriate for collecting both Level 3 and Level 4 data.

- *Business performance monitoring* is useful when performance records and operational data can be examined for improvement. This method is particularly useful for collecting Level 4 data.

Along with selecting the appropriate data collection method, consideration must be given to the source of data, which is primarily (but not always exclusively) the participant. Timing is a third consideration. Fundamental timing considerations include the time at which data are needed, the availability of data, and the availability of resources. These issues are covered in more detail in *Data Collection*, the second book of this series.

Isolation of Program Effects

An issue that is overlooked in most evaluations is how to isolate the effects of the program. In this step of the process, evaluation planners explore specific techniques for determining the amount of impact directly related to the program. Because many factors will affect performance data, this step is essential for increasing the accuracy and credibility of ROI calculations. The following techniques have been used by organizations to address this important issue.

- A *control group* arrangement is often used to isolate the impact of a specific program. One group participates in the program, while another similar group (the control group) does not participate. The difference in the performance of the two groups is attributed to the program. When properly set up and implemented, the control group arrangement is the most effective way to isolate the effects of a program or project.

- *Trend lines* are used to project the values of specific impact measures before the program is undertaken. The projection is compared with the actual data after the program is conducted, and the difference represents an estimate of the impact of the program. Under certain conditions, this technique can accurately isolate the program impact.

- When mathematical relationships between input and output measures are known, a *forecasting model* can be used to isolate the effects of a program. The impact measure is predicted by using the forecasting model with pre-program data. The actual performance of the measure, weeks or months after the program, is compared with the forecasted value. The results are an estimate of the impact.

- *Participants* estimate the amount of improvement that is related to the program. Participants are provided with the total amount of improvement, based on a comparison of pre- and post-program measurements, and are asked to indicate the percentage of the improvement that is related to the program.

- *Participants' supervisors* estimate the effect of the program on the impact measures. The supervisors are given the total amount of improvement and are asked to indicate the percentage that can be directly attributed to the program.

- *Senior management* estimates the impact of the program. In such cases, managers provide an estimate of how much of the improvement is related to the program. Although it may be inaccurate, having senior management involved in the process has some advantages.

- *Experts* provide estimates of the program's impact on the performance measure. Because the estimates are based on previous experience, the experts must be familiar with the type of program and the specific situation.

- When feasible, all *other influencing factors* are identified and their impact is estimated or calculated; the remaining unexplained improvement is attributed to the program.

- In some situations, *customers* provide input on the extent to which the program has influenced their decisions to use a product or service. Although this strategy has limited applications, it can be quite useful for isolating the effects of customer service and sales programs.

Collectively, these techniques provide a comprehensive set of tools to address the critical issue of isolating the effects of a program. The third book in this series, *Isolation of Results*, is devoted to this important step in the ROI Methodology.

Data Conversion

To calculate the return on investment, Level 4 impact data are converted to monetary values and compared with program costs. This step requires that a value be placed on each unit of data connected with the program. Many techniques for converting data to monetary values are available; which technique is appropriate depends on the type of data and the situation.

- *Output data* are converted to profit contribution or cost savings. When using this technique, output increases are converted to monetary values based on their unit contribution to profit or the unit of cost reduction. Standard values for these items are readily available in most organizations.

- The *cost of quality* is calculated, and quality improvements are converted directly to cost savings. Standard values for these items are available in many organizations.

- For programs in which employee time is saved, the *participants' wages and employee benefits* are used to develop a value for the time saved. Because a variety of programs focus on improving the time required to complete projects, processes, or daily activities, the value of time is an important issue. This is a standard formula in most organizations.

- *Historical costs*, developed from cost statements, are used when they are available for a specific measure. Organizational cost data thus establish the specific monetary costs saved or avoided by an improvement.

- When available, *internal and external experts* may be used to estimate the value of an improvement. In this situation, the credibility of the estimate hinges on the expertise and reputation of the experts themselves.

- *External databases* are sometimes available to estimate the value or cost of data items. Research, government, and industry databases can provide important information on these values. Although data are plentiful, the difficulty of this technique lies in finding a specific database related to the program or situation.

- *Participants* estimate the value of the data item. For this approach to be effective, participants must be capable of providing a value for the improvement.

- *Supervisors or managers* can provide estimates if they are both willing and able to assign values to the improvement. This approach is especially useful when the participants are not fully capable of providing this input or in situations in which supervisors need to confirm or adjust the participants' estimates. This approach is particularly helpful in establishing values for performance measures that are important to senior management.

- *Soft measures are linked mathematically to other measures* that are easier to measure and value. This approach is particularly helpful in establishing values for measures that are very difficult to convert to monetary values—for example, data related to intangibles such as customer satisfaction, employee satisfaction, conflict, or employee complaints.

- *Staff estimates* may be used to determine a value for an output data item. The estimates must be provided on an unbiased basis.

The data conversion step is absolutely necessary in order to determine the monetary benefits of a program. The process is challenging, particularly when soft data are involved, but it can be accomplished by methodically using one or more of the listed techniques. Because of the importance of assigning monetary values to impact data, the fourth book in this series, *Data Conversion*, is devoted to this step in the ROI Methodology, along with identifying intangible benefits.

Intangible Benefits

In addition to their tangible monetary benefits, most programs will have intangible nonmonetary benefits. The ROI calculation is based on converting both hard and soft data to monetary values. Intangible benefits are program benefits that individuals choose not to convert to monetary values. Intangible benefits often include such measures as

- Increased job satisfaction
- Increased employee engagement
- Improved teamwork
- Improved creativity
- Reduced complaints
- Reduced conflicts

During data analysis, every attempt is made to convert all data to monetary values. All hard data, such as those related to output, quality, and time, are converted to monetary values. The conversion of soft data is attempted for each data item. However, if the process used for conversion is too subjective or inaccurate, the resulting values lose credibility; in such cases, the data are listed as an intangible benefit, with an appropriate explanation. For some programs, intangible nonmonetary benefits are extremely valuable, carrying as much influence as the hard data items.

Program Costs

The second part of a benefit-cost analysis is the program costs. Tabulating costs involves monitoring or developing all the related costs of the program targeted for ROI evaluation. Among the cost components that should be included are

- The cost of the needs assessment (when conducted) prorated over the program's expected life
- The cost of designing and developing the program, possibly prorated over the program's expected life
- The cost of all program materials provided to each participant
- The cost of the instructor or facilitator, including preparation time as well as delivery time
- The cost of the facilities
- Travel, lodging, and meal costs of the participants, if applicable
- Salaries and employee benefits of the participants for the time that they are involved in the program
- Administrative and overhead costs of the functional unit, allocated in some convenient way

In addition, specific costs related to the needs assessment and evaluation should be included. The conservative approach is to include all these costs so that the total is fully loaded. Because of the importance of ascertaining program costs, the fifth book in the series, *Costs and ROI*, is devoted to this step, along with ROI calculation.

Return on Investment Calculation

The benefit-cost ratio (BCR) is calculated from the program benefits and costs. The benefit-cost ratio is the program benefits divided by the program costs. In formula form, it is written like this:

$$BCR = \frac{\text{Program Benefits}}{\text{Program Costs}}$$

The ROI for a program is the program's net benefits divided by the program's costs. (Net benefits are the program's benefits minus the program's costs.) Thus, in formula form, ROI is as follows:

$$\text{ROI (\%)} = \frac{\text{Net Program Benefits}}{\text{Program Costs}} \times 100$$

This is the same basic formula that is used in evaluating other investments, in which ROI is traditionally reported as earnings divided by investment. The fifth book in our series, *Costs and ROI*, provides more detail on ROI calculations.

Reporting

The final step in the ROI Methodology is reporting. Reporting often does not receive the attention and planning that is needed to ensure its success. This step involves developing appropriate information in impact studies and other brief reports. The heart of the step is the different techniques used to communicate to a wide variety of target audiences. In most ROI studies, several audiences are interested in and need the information. Careful planning in order to match the communication method with the audience is essential, to ensure that the message is understood and that appropriate actions follow. The sixth book in the ROI Six Pack, *Communication and Implementation*, is devoted to this critical step.

Case Study

Table 1.4 shows the results from a sample case study. The table includes all the elements described in this chapter. The All-Inclusive Workforce Program explored diversity issues and targeted both

Table 1.4. Case Study of Program Evaluation Using ROI Methodology

Sprint/Nextel

Program Title: Diversity

Target Group: Managers and employees

Solution: All-Inclusive Workforce Program (AIW)

Results:

Level 1: Reaction and Planned Action	Level 2: Learning and Confidence	Level 3: Application and Implementation	Level 4: Impact	Level 5: ROI	Intangible Benefits
Composite rating: 4.39 out of 5 (for six items)	Averaged 4.28 out of 5 (for learning on six objectives)	*Managers:* Support AIW (87%) Address problems (81%) Encourage staff (78%) *Employees:* Support AIW (65%) Identify differences (63%) Encourage staff (60%) 91% of managers successfully completed action plans	Attrition rate improvement = 9.77%	BCR: 2.6 ROI: 163%	Employee satisfaction Communication Cooperation Diversity mix Teamwork

Technique for Isolating the Effects of the Program: Manager's estimate, adjusted for error
Technique for Converting Data to Monetary Values: Standard cost item ($89,000 per turnover)
Fully Loaded Program Costs: $1,216,836

Source: Schmidt, 2003.

managers and employees. All six types of data were collected, including the actual ROI. This summary shows all the types of data and also addresses the issues of isolating the effects of the program, converting the data to monetary values, and monitoring the program costs.

Final Thoughts

This chapter presents the basic process for calculating the return on investment for programs or projects. The step-by-step process breaks the complicated problem of calculating ROI into simple, manageable tasks and steps. When the process is thoroughly planned, taking into consideration all potential strategies and techniques, it becomes manageable and achievable. The remaining chapters focus on the major elements of this model and on ways to implement it.

References

Phillips, J. J. *The Corporate University: Measuring the Impact of Learning*. Houston, Tex.: American Productivity and Quality Center, 2000.

Phillips, P. P., and Phillips, J. J. *In Action: Measuring Return on Investment*. Vol. 3. Alexandria, Va.: ASTD, 2001. (See the chapter titled "Measuring Return on Investment in Interactive Sales Training.")

Schmidt, L. *In Action: Implementing Training Scorecards*. Alexandria, Va.: ASTD, 2003.

Van Buren, M. E. *State of the Industry*. Alexandria, Va.: ASTD, 2002.

2

Why ROI?

Measuring ROI has earned a place among the critical issues in the fields of learning and development, human resources, technology, quality, and marketing. The topic appears routinely on the agendas of conferences and professional meetings. Journals and newsletters have been devoting increasing print space to articles about ROI. A professional organization has been developed to exchange information on ROI. At least a dozen books provide detailed coverage of the topic. Even top executives have increased their appetite for ROI information.

Measurement of ROI is a much-debated topic. Few business topics stir up emotions to the degree that the ROI issue does. Measuring ROI is characterized as flawed and inappropriate by some, while others describe it as the only answer to their accountability concerns. The truth lies somewhere in the middle. Understanding the drivers of the ROI Methodology and its inherent weaknesses and advantages makes it possible to take a rational approach to the issue and implement an appropriate mix of evaluation strategies that include measuring ROI. This chapter presents the basic issues and trends in ROI measurement.

Although interest in the topic has grown and much progress has been made, ROI is still an issue that challenges even the most sophisticated and progressive organizations. While some professionals argue that calculating ROI is too difficult, others quietly and deliberately develop measures and routinely calculate ROI. The latter group is gaining support from senior management teams. Regardless of the position one takes on the issue, the reasons for measuring ROI are clear. Almost all professionals in the fields mentioned earlier share a concern that they must eventually show a return on investments made in their major programs. If they do not, funds may be reduced or their department or functional unit may not be able to maintain or enhance its present status and influence within the organization.

The measurement dilemma at the heart of the ROI process is a source of frustration for many senior executives. Executives realize that major processes such as learning, human resources, technology, and marketing are necessary when organizations experience significant growth or increased competition. These processes are also important during business restructuring and rapid change. Executives intuitively feel that these processes add value and logically conclude that they pay off in terms of important bottom-line measures such as productivity improvement, quality enhancement, cost reduction, and time saved, as well as enhanced customer satisfaction, improved morale, and improved teamwork. Yet executives become frustrated with the lack of evidence that shows the actual contributions of initiatives in the fields in which ROI measurement is difficult. The ROI Methodology represents the most promising way to achieve such accountability through a logical, rational approach; and this methodology is fully described in the Measurement and Evaluation Series.

Progress and Status of ROI

This chapter begins with a review of global trends in the use of ROI, a look at the overall progress that has been made in ROI evaluations, and the current status of ROI Methodology use. The status varies from field to field. In determining the economic benefit of public projects, cost-benefit analysis has been used for centuries.

The same is true for the use of ROI in accounting and finance. In learning and development, ROI evaluations are becoming routine in most organizations. In other fields, such as meetings and events, ROI evaluations are just starting to become frequently used tools for professionals.

Global Trends in Measurement

A few trends in measurement and evaluation in organizations in both the private and public sectors have been observed on a global basis. The following measurement trends have been identified in our research and are slowly evolving across organizations and cultures in nearly fifty countries. Collectively, these trends have an important impact on the way accountability issues are being addressed.

- No longer thought of as an add-on activity, evaluation is an integral part of the design, development, delivery, and implementation of programs.

- Organizations are shifting from a reactive approach to a more proactive approach, addressing evaluation early in the cycle.

- Measurement and evaluation processes are systematic and methodical, and they are often built into the delivery process, such as by the use of action plans.

- Technology is significantly enhancing the measurement and evaluation process, enabling large amounts of data to be collected, processed, analyzed, and integrated across programs.

- Evaluation planning is becoming a critical part of the measurement and evaluation cycle because only a carefully planned implementation will be successful.

- The implementation of a comprehensive measurement and evaluation process usually leads to increased emphasis on the initial needs analysis.

- Organizations without a comprehensive measurement and evaluation process have often reduced or eliminated their program budgets.

- Organizations with comprehensive measurement and evaluation have increased their program budgets.

- Use of ROI is emerging as an essential part of the measurement and evaluation process. *ROI* is a familiar term and concept for most executives; therefore they understand ROI and appreciate its usefulness.

- Many examples of successful ROI applications are available.

- A comprehensive measurement and evaluation process, including measurement of ROI, can be implemented for about 3 or 5 percent of the direct program budget.

ROI Applications Across Fields and Sectors

The ROI Methodology described in this book had its beginnings in the 1970s when it was applied to a cooperative education program. Since then, it has been developed, modified, and refined into the process described here, and it has been applied in many types of situations and sectors.

Exhibit 2.1 shows how the process has evolved in different applications and fields. Manufacturing and service sectors were early adopters of the ROI Methodology. In the health care arena, applications evolved as the industry sought ways to improve educational services, human resources, quality, risk management, and case management. Nonprofit applications emerged as nonprofit organizations pursued ways to reduce costs and generate efficiencies. Finally, applications appeared in a variety of government organizations. Public sector implementation has increased in recent years. An outgrowth of public sector applications is the use of the ROI Methodology in academia, where it is now being applied not only to internal processes but to continuing education and graduate programs as well. The ROI Methodology is spreading to all types of organizations, settings, and professional fields. The specific types of program applications vary; current applications represent a full range of programs from learning and development, education, human resources, quality, marketing, change, and technology. Cases have been published in all of these areas. The process is flexible, versatile, and adaptable to almost any type of setting and environment.

Exhibit 2.1. ROI Applications

- Human resources, human capital
- Learning and development, performance improvement
- Technology, information technology systems
- Meetings and events
- Sales, marketing
- Public relations, community affairs, government relations
- Project management solutions
- Quality, Six Sigma
- Operations, methods, engineering
- Research and development, innovation
- Finance, compliance
- Logistics, distribution, supply chain
- Public policy initiatives
- Social programs
- Charitable projects
- Community and faith-based initiatives

Growth of ROI as a Conference Topic

Sometimes, the best way to judge interest in a topic or trend is to observe the conferences offered on the subject. The International Quality and Productivity Center routinely offers conferences on ROI—sometimes as many as four or five per year—not only in the United States but also in Europe, Southeast Asia, and Australia. These conferences are designed to explore issues involving ROI, particularly its implementation and use.

The ROI Network has offered conferences each year for a decade. The American Productivity and Quality Center has also offered conferences on ROI. The Institute for Industrial Relations, based in Europe, has offered conferences that included topics on ROI in Europe, Canada, and the United States.

Training magazine's annual conference, the Training Director's Forum; ASTD; and the International Society for Performance Improvement (ISPI), and other associations routinely feature ROI as an important agenda topic.

Global Expansion of ROI Applications

Measuring ROI is becoming a truly global issue. Organizations from all over the world are concerned about accountability and are exploring techniques to measure the results of various programs. In a survey of thirty-five members of the International Federation of Training and Development Organizations, measuring ROI was consistently rated the hottest topic. Whether an economy is mature or developing, accountability remains a critical issue.

Many professional associations in different countries have offered workshops, seminars, and dedicated conferences on issues of measurement, including measurement of ROI. Some associations have sponsored individual workshops on ROI. Formal presentations on ROI have been made in over fifty countries and implementation organized and coordinated in at least forty countries.

Table 2.1. Paradigm Shift Toward Accountability in Programs and Projects

Characteristics of an Activity-Based Process	Characteristics of a Results-Based Process
• No business need for the program	• Program linked to specific business needs
• No assessment of performance issues	• Assessment of performance effectiveness
• No specific measurable objectives for application and impact	• Specific objectives defined for application and impact
• No effort to prepare program participants to achieve results	• Results expectations communicated to participants
• No effort to prepare the work environment to support application	• Environment prepared to support application of the program
• No efforts to build partnerships with key managers	• Partnerships established with key managers and clients
• No measurement of results or cost-benefit analysis	• Measurement of results and cost-benefit analysis
• Input-focused planning and reporting	• Output-focused planning and reporting

The Move from Activity to Results

The widespread growth of interest in ROI applications underscores the need for programs to shift from an activity-based process to a results-based process. Table 2.1 depicts the paradigm shift that has occurred in recent years, dramatically affecting accountability in all types of programs. Organizations have moved from activity to a focus on bottom-line results. The shift has often occurred because of the trends described earlier in this chapter. In some cases, the shift has occurred because progressive departments have recognized the need to measure ROI and have been persistent in making progress on the issue.

ROI Is Here to Stay

One thing in the ROI debate is certain: ROI measurement is not a fad. As long as investment payoff and accountability for program expenditures are required, ROI will be used to evaluate major investments.

A fad is a new idea or approach or a new spin on an old approach. ROI has been used for centuries. The seventy-fifth anniversary issue of the *Harvard Business Review* (HBR) traced the tools used to measure results in organizations (Sibbet, 1997). In the early issues of HBR, during the 1920s, ROI was reported as an emerging tool for assigning a value to the payoff of investments.

Today, hundreds of organizations are routinely developing ROI calculations for their programs. Given this increased adoption and use, it appears that the ROI Methodology as an accountability tool is here to stay.

Its status and implementation have grown at a high rate. The number of organizations and individuals involved with the process underscores the magnitude of ROI implementation. Exhibit 2.2 presents a summary of the ROI Methodology's current status. With this much evidence of growing interest, the ROI Methodology appears well on its way to becoming a standard tool for program evaluation.

Why ROI?

There are good reasons why ROI has gained acceptance as a business tool. Although the viewpoints and explanations may vary, some things are very clear. The key reasons are outlined in this section.

Exhibit 2.2. ROI by the Numbers: A Summary of the Current Status of the ROI Methodology

- The ROI Methodology has been refined over twenty-five years.
- The ROI Methodology has been adopted by hundreds of organizations in manufacturing, service, nonprofit, and government settings.
- Thousands of studies using the ROI Methodology are developed each year.
- Over one hundred case studies have been published on the ROI Methodology.
- Almost five thousand individuals have been certified to implement the ROI Methodology in their organizations.
- Organizations in forty countries have implemented the ROI Methodology.
- Two dozen books have been developed to support the process of implementing the ROI Methodology.
- A professional network has been formed to share information on the ROI Methodology.
- The ROI Methodology can be implemented for 3 to 5 percent of a program or project budget.

Increased Budgets

Most program budgets have continued to grow year after year. In almost any of the functional areas of human resources, quality, technology, and marketing, the cumulative average growth rate of expenditures in the last decade is greater than the changes in the producer price index.

As organizations recognize the importance and necessity of these functional areas, budgets continue to increase annually in organizations, industries, and even entire countries. Many organizations and countries see these expenditures as investments instead of costs. Consequently, senior managers are willing to invest because they anticipate a payoff for their investments. As expenditures grow, accountability becomes more critical. A growing budget creates a larger target for internal critics, often prompting the development of an ROI evaluation process. The function, department, or process showing the most value will likely receive the largest budget increase.

The Ultimate Level of Evaluation

Table 1.1, in Chapter One, shows the five-level framework used in this book. The framework categorizes program results as follows:

- Level 1, Reaction and Planned Action
- Level 2, Learning and Confidence
- Level 3, Application and Implementation
- Level 4, Impact and Consequences
- Level 5, ROI

While data at all levels are important, Level 5, ROI, is the ultimate level. It is ROI that allows projects and programs across the organization to be compared according to common criteria. It is the ROI calculation that reports not only the benefits of a program but also how those benefits compare with the investment that was made to achieve them.

Change, Quality, and Reengineering

ROI applications have increased because of the growing interest in a variety of organizational improvement, quality, and change programs, which have dominated organizations, particularly in North America, Europe, and Asia. In their zeal for improvement, organizations have embraced almost any trend that appeared on the horizon. Unfortunately, many of these change efforts have not been successful and have turned out to be passing fads. Implementation of the ROI Methodology requires a thorough needs assessment and significant planning before a program is implemented. If these two elements are in place, passing fads, which are usually doomed to failure, can be avoided. With the ROI Methodology in place, a new change program that does not produce results will soon be exposed. Management will be aware of it early, and as a result, adjustments can be made.

Total quality management, continuous process improvement, and Six Sigma have brought increased attention to measurement issues. Today, organizations measure processes and outputs that were not previously measured, monitored, or reported. This focus has placed increased pressure on all functions to develop measures of program success.

Restructuring and reengineering initiatives and the threat of outsourcing have caused executives to focus more directly on bottom-line issues. Many processes have been reengineered to align programs more closely with business needs and to obtain maximum efficiencies in the project cycle. These change processes have brought increased attention to evaluation issues and have resulted in measurements of the contribution of specific programs, including ROI.

Business Mindset of Support Managers

The business management mindset of many staff and support managers causes them to place more emphasis on economic issues within their function. Today's managers are more aware of bottom-line issues in their organization and more knowledgeable about operational and financial concerns. These new, more enlightened managers often take a business approach to programs and measure ROI as part of their strategy.

ROI is a familiar concept for business managers, especially those with business administration and management degrees. They have studied ROI applications in their academic courses, using ROI to evaluate the decision to purchase equipment, build a new facility, or buy a new company. Consequently, they understand ROI and appreciate the benefits of applying the ROI Methodology to the evaluation of programs and projects.

The Trend Toward Accountability

A persistent trend toward accountability has occurred in organizations everywhere. Every support function now tries to show its worth by documenting the value that it adds to the organization. Given the emphasis on accountability, all functions must provide evidence of their contributions to their organization.

The trend toward accountability has resulted in a variety of measurement processes (shown in Figure 2.1), sometimes leaving potential users of the processes extremely confused. Amid the confusion, many organizations have migrated to the proven acceptance of ROI. Used for hundreds of years, ROI has, for

Figure 2.1. A Variety of Measurement Possibilities

Balanced Scorecard
Profitability
PROGRAM IMPACT
ROI
Value-Based Evaluation
Strategic Accountability
Vital Signs
BOTTOM-LINE CONTRIBUTION
PERFORMANCE STANDARDS
Effectiveness
ECONOMIC VALUE ADDED
Shareholder Value
Benefits vs. Costs

the reasons outlined here, become a preferred choice for practitioners who need to demonstrate the monetary payoff of their programs.

Top Executive Requirements

ROI is drawing increased interest in the executive suite. Top executives who have watched their budgets continue to grow without appropriate accountability measures have become frustrated. In response, they have turned to ROI. Consequently, top executives are now demanding ROI calculations from departments and functions that previously were not required to provide them. For years, support managers convinced top executives that the monetary contribution of their functions couldn't be measured. Now, however, many executives are aware that it can be and is being measured in other organizations, and therefore they are demanding the same accountability from their own support managers.

The topic of ROI has been covered in a wide range of publications, including *Fortune*, *USA Today*, *Business Week*, *Harvard Business Review*, *The Wall Street Journal*, and the *Financial Times*. Executives seem to have a never-ending desire to explore applications of ROI. Even in Europe, Africa, and Asia, it is not unusual for the majority of participants in an ROI workshop to attend because their top executives require it.

Concerns About Using ROI

Although much progress has been made, many professionals and their managers still have concerns about the use of ROI. The mere presence of the process can create a dilemma for many organizations. When an organization embraces the ROI concept and implements the methodology, the management team usually anxiously waits for results, only to be disappointed when they are not readily available. For an ROI process to be useful, many issues—such as feasibility, simplicity, credibility, and soundness—must be balanced.

In addition, in order for the ROI process to be successfully used and accepted, it must satisfy three major audiences:

- Practitioners who design, develop, and deliver programs
- Senior managers, sponsors, and clients who initiate and support programs
- Researchers who need a credible process

Practitioners

For years, many practitioners and professionals have assumed that ROI for their particular unit could not be measured. When they examined a typical ROI measurement process, they found long formulas, complicated equations, and complex models that made the process appear too confusing. Given this perceived complexity, managers envisioned that huge efforts would be required for data collection and analysis and, more important, that high costs would be necessary to make the process successful. In light of these concerns, practitioners seek an ROI measurement process that is simple and easy to understand so that they can easily implement its steps and strategies. They also need a process that will not take an excessive period of time to implement and will not consume too much precious staff time. Finally, practitioners need a process that is affordable. Because they are competing for financial resources, they need a process that will require only a small portion of their budgets. In summary, the ROI measurement process, from the practitioner's perspective, must be user-friendly, time-saving, and cost-efficient.

Senior Managers, Sponsors, and Clients

Managers who must approve budgets, request programs, or live with the results of programs have a strong interest in developing ROI measurements. They want a process that provides quantifiable results, using a measure similar to the ROI formula applied to other types of investments. Senior managers have a never-ending desire to boil results down to an ROI calculation, reflected as a percentage.

And like practitioners, they want a process that is simple and easy to understand. The assumptions made in the calculations and the methodology used should reflect their point of reference, background, and level of understanding. They do not want or need a string of formulas, charts, and complicated models. Instead, they need a process that they can explain to others, if necessary. More important, they need a process with which they can identify, one that is sound and realistic and that earns their confidence.

Researchers

Finally, researchers will support only a process that measures up to close examination. Researchers usually insist that models, formulas, assumptions, and theories be sound and based on commonly accepted practices. The process must also produce accurate values and consistent outcomes. If estimates are necessary, researchers want the most accuracy possible within the constraints of the situation, realizing that adjustments must be made when there is uncertainty in the process.

Thus, the challenge is to develop a process of ROI measurement that will satisfy researchers and please practitioners and senior managers at the same time.

Criteria for an Effective ROI Process

To satisfy the needs of the three critical groups—practitioners, senior managers, and researchers—the process of measuring ROI must meet several requirements. Eleven essential criteria for an effective ROI process are described in this section.

1. The ROI process must be *simple*—void of complex formulas, lengthy equations, and complicated methodologies. Most ROI evaluation attempts fail to meet this requirement. Some ROI models have become too complex to understand and use because they attempt to obtain statistical perfection and use too many theories. Consequently, they have not been implemented.

2. The ROI process must be *economical* and easy to implement. The process should become a routine part of project development without requiring significant additional resources. Selecting sample program groups for ROI evaluations and early planning for ROI measurement are often necessary in order to make progress without adding staff.

3. The assumptions, methodology, and techniques must be *credible*. Logical, methodical steps are needed in order to earn the respect of practitioners, senior managers, and researchers. This requires a practical approach to the process.

4. From a researcher's perspective, the ROI process must be *theoretically sound* and based on generally accepted practices. Unfortunately, this requirement can lead to an extensive, complicated process. Ideally, the process will strike a balance between a practical, sensible approach and a sound theoretical basis. This may be one of the toughest challenges for those who wish to develop a model for measuring ROI.

5. The ROI process must *account for factors other than the program being evaluated* that may also have influenced output variables. Isolating the influence of the program or project, an issue that is often overlooked, is necessary to build the credibility and accuracy of the process. The ROI process should pinpoint the contribution of the program as opposed to other influences.

6. The ROI process must be *appropriate for a variety of programs*. Some models apply to only a small number of programs, such as sales or productivity training. Ideally, the process should be applicable to all types of programs.

7. The ROI process must have the *flexibility* to be applied on a pre-program basis as well as a post-program basis. In some situations, an estimate of the ROI is required before the program is developed. Ideally, practitioners should be able to adjust the process for a range of potential time frames.

8. The ROI process must be *applicable to all types of data*—hard data, which typically represent output, quality, costs, and time, as well as soft data, which represent less tangible concepts, such as job satisfaction and customer satisfaction.
9. The ROI process must *include the costs of the program*. The ultimate level of evaluation involves comparing benefits with costs. Although the term *ROI* has been loosely used to express any benefit of a program or project, an acceptable ROI formula must include costs. Omitting or underestimating the costs will destroy the credibility of the ROI values.
10. The actual calculation must use an *acceptable ROI formula*. This formula is often the benefit-cost ratio or the ROI calculation, expressed as a percentage. These formulas compare the actual expenditures for a project with the monetary benefits driven by the project. Although other financial terms may be substituted, using a standard financial calculation in the ROI process is important.
11. Finally, the ROI process must have a *successful track record* in a variety of applications. In far too many situations, models are created but never successfully applied. An effective ROI process should withstand the wear and tear of implementation and get the expected results.

We consider these criteria to be essential; thus, an ROI methodology should meet most if not all of these criteria. Unfortunately, most ROI processes do not. The good news is that the ROI Methodology presented in this book meets all of them.

Barriers to ROI Implementation

Although progress has been made in implementation of the ROI Methodology, barriers may inhibit its implementation. Some of these barriers are real, and others are myths based on misperceptions. Each barrier is briefly described in this section.

Financial and Time Costs

The ROI Methodology will add some cost and time to program evaluations, although the added amount will not be excessive. This barrier alone may stop many ROI implementations early in the process. However, a comprehensive ROI process can be implemented for only 3 to 5 percent of a unit's overall budget, and the additional investment in ROI could be offset by the positive results achieved from the programs or the elimination of unproductive or unprofitable programs.

Lack of Staff Skills and Orientation

Many professional staff members do not understand ROI, nor do they have the basic skills necessary to apply the methodology within the scope of their responsibilities. Measurement and evaluation are not usually part of the preparation for staff jobs. Also, programs typically focus on learning outcomes rather than financial results. Staff members often assess results by measuring reaction or learning. Consequently, a major barrier to ROI implementation is the need to orient the staff, change their attitudes, and teach them the necessary skills.

Faulty Needs Assessment

Many programs have been undertaken without an adequate needs assessment. Some of these programs were implemented for the wrong reasons, based on management requests or efforts to chase a popular fad or trend within the industry. If the program is not needed, its benefits will be minimal. An ROI calculation for an unnecessary program will likely yield a negative value. This likelihood deters practitioners from implementing ROI, because they fear facing such a negative reality.

Fear

Some departments and functions do not pursue evaluation of ROI because of fear of failure or fear of the unknown. Fear of failure can manifest in different ways. Designers, developers, facilitators, or program owners may be concerned about the consequence of a negative ROI. They may fear that ROI evaluations will be used as performance evaluation tools instead of process improvement tools. Use of the ROI Methodology may be feared due to a dislike of change. This fear of change, often based on unrealistic assumptions and a lack of knowledge, is a real barrier for many ROI implementations.

Lack of Discipline or Planning

Successfully implementing the ROI Methodology requires planning and a disciplined approach in order to keep the process on track. Implementation schedules, evaluation targets, ROI analysis plans, measurement and evaluation policies, and follow-up schedules are required. Staff members may not have enough discipline and determination to stay on course. This lack of staying power can become a barrier, particularly if measuring the ROI is not an immediate requirement. If the current senior management group does not require an ROI evaluation, the staff may not allocate time for the necessary planning and coordination. Only a carefully planned implementation will be successful.

False Assumptions

Many staff members have false assumptions about the ROI process that keep them from attempting ROI implementation. Some typical assumptions are the following:

- The impact of a program cannot be accurately calculated.

- Managers do not want to see the results of projects and programs expressed in monetary values.

- If the CEO does not ask for the ROI, he or she does not expect it.

- "I have a professional, competent staff; therefore, I do not have to justify the effectiveness of our programs."

- "Our programs are complex but necessary; therefore, they should not be subjected to an accountability process."

These false assumptions can become real barriers that impede the progress of ROI implementation.

Benefits of Using ROI

This section outlines several important benefits that can be derived from the implementation of the ROI Methodology within an organization.

Measurement of a Program's Contribution

Measuring ROI is the most accurate, credible, and widely used process to show the impact of a program. The staff will know the specific contribution from a select number of programs. The ROI will determine whether the benefits of a program, expressed in monetary values, have outweighed the costs. It will determine whether the program made a positive contribution to the organization and whether it was a good investment.

Clear Priorities

Calculating ROI in different areas will determine which programs contribute the most to an organization, allowing priorities to be established for high-impact programs. Successful programs can then be expanded into other areas (if those areas have similar needs) ahead of other programs. Inefficient programs can be redesigned and redeployed. Ineffective programs can be discontinued.

Focus on Results

The ROI Methodology is a results-based process that requires instructional designers, facilitators, participants, and support groups to concentrate on measurable objectives. This process tends to bring a focus on results to all programs, even those not targeted for an ROI evaluation. Thus, ROI implementation has the added benefit of improving the effectiveness of all programs.

Respect from Senior Executives and Program Sponsors

Measuring the ROI of programs is one of the best ways to earn the respect of your senior management team and your program sponsor. Senior executives always want to see ROI figures. They will appreciate efforts to connect programs with business impact and to show programs' monetary value. The sponsors who support, approve, or initiate programs will view ROI measurement as a breath of fresh air. They will be able to see an actual value for a program, building confidence in the decision to use the ROI process.

Positive Changes in Management Perceptions

The ROI Methodology, when applied consistently and comprehensively, can convince top management that projects and programs are investments, not expenses. Managers will see that programs make viable contributions to their objectives, thus increasing their respect for the function or department that produces those programs. Changing perceptions is an important step in building a partnership with management and increasing management support.

ROI Best Practices

Continuing progress with ROI implementation has provided an opportunity to determine specific strategies that are common among organizations pursuing the ROI Methodology. Several common strategies that are considered the best practices in measurement and evaluation have emerged. Although the following strategies are presented as a comprehensive framework, few organizations have adopted them all. However, parts of the strategy are practiced in each of the several hundred organizations involved in ROI certification, which is described in the sixth book of the ROI Six Pack, *Communication and Implementation*.

Evaluation Targets

Evaluations targets were discussed in Chapter One. The targets for evaluation at each level are

Level 0, Inputs and Indicators	100 percent
Level 1, Reaction and Planned Action	100 percent
Level 2, Learning and Confidence	80–90 percent
Level 3, Application and Implementation	15–30 percent
Level 4, Impact and Consequences	10 percent
Level 5, ROI	5 percent

Establishing evaluation targets has two major advantages. First, the process provides benchmarks that the staff can use to clearly measure the accountability of all programs or any segment of a function. Second, adopting targets focuses more attention on the accountability process, communicating a strong message about the extent of commitment to measurement and evaluation.

Microlevel Evaluation

Evaluating an entire functional area—such as human resources, management development, technology, or quality—is difficult. The ROI Methodology is more effective when applied to one program that can be linked to a direct payoff. For this reason, ROI evaluation should be considered a microlevel activity that usually focuses on a single program or a few tightly integrated programs. The decision whether to evaluate several programs or just one program should involve consideration of the objectives of the programs, the timing of the programs, and the cohesiveness of the programs. Attempting to evaluate a group of programs conducted over a long period can be difficult, partly because the cause-and-effect relationship becomes more confusing and complex.

A Variety of Data Collection Methods

Best-practice companies use a variety of approaches to collect evaluation data. They avoid becoming aligned with one or two methods for data collection, recognizing that each program, setting, and situation is different and that, consequently, different techniques are needed to collect the data. Interviews, focus groups, and questionnaires work well in some situations. In others, action plans, performance contracts, and performance monitoring are needed to determine the specific impact of the program. Best-practice organizations deliberately match the data collection method with the program, following a set of criteria developed internally.

Isolation of the Program

One of the most critical elements of the ROI Methodology is attempting to isolate the impact of the program from other influences that may have occurred during the same period. Best-practice organizations recognize that many influences affect business impact measures. Although programs are implemented in harmony with other systems and processes, it is often necessary to determine the contribution of a single program, particularly when the owners or sponsors of separate programs or processes are different parties. Consequently, after a program is conducted, it usually can take only part of the credit for improved performance. When an ROI evaluation is planned, best-practice organizations attempt to use one or more methods to isolate the effects of the program. They go beyond the typical use of a control group arrangement, which has set the standard for this process for many years, exploring a variety of other techniques in order to arrive at a realistic estimate of the program's impact on output measures.

Sampling for ROI Calculations

Because of the resources required for the process, most programs cannot include ROI calculations. Therefore, organizations must determine how many ROI evaluations are appropriate. There is no prescribed formula, and the number of ROI evaluations depends on many variables, including

- Staff expertise in evaluation
- The nature and type of programs
- Resources that can be allocated to the process
- The level of management support for the department
- The organization's commitment to measurement and evaluation
- Pressure from others to show ROI calculations

Other variables specific to an organization may affect how many evaluations are performed. It is rare for organizations to use statistical sampling to select programs for ROI evaluation. For most, a statistical sampling approach requires far too many calculations and too much analysis. Using a practical approach, most organizations settle on evaluating one or two sessions of each of their most significant programs.

While statistically sound sampling is important, it is more important to consider the trade-off between resources available and the level of activity that management needs in order to feel confident in the ROI calculations. The primary objective of an ROI evaluation is not only to convince the staff that the process being evaluated works but also to show others (usually senior management) that the function or department being evaluated makes a difference. Therefore, the sampling plan must be developed with the input and approval of senior management. In the final analysis, the selection process should yield a level of sampling that allows senior management to feel comfortable in its assessment of the function or unit.

Conversion of Program Results to Monetary Values

Because ROI is needed for some programs, business impact data must be converted to monetary values. Best-practice organizations are not content to show that a program improved productivity, enhanced quality, reduced employee turnover, decreased absenteeism, or increased customer satisfaction. Going further, the organizations convert such data items to monetary units so that the benefits can be compared with the costs, leading, in turn, to an ROI calculation. Best-practice organizations take an extra step to develop a realistic value for their data items. For hard data items such as productivity, quality, or time, the conversion is relatively easy. However, for soft data items such as customer satisfaction, employee turnover, employee absenteeism, or job satisfaction, the conversion process is more difficult. Still, techniques are available and are used to make these conversions reasonably accurate.

Final Thoughts

Most professionals agree that more attention to measuring ROI is needed, and its use is expanding. The payoff for using ROI can be huge, and the ROI Methodology is not very difficult. The approaches, strategies, and techniques are not overly complex and can be used in a variety of settings. The combined and persistent efforts of practitioners and researchers will continue to refine the techniques and create successful applications.

Reference

Sibbet, D. "75 Years of Management Ideas and Practice, 1922–1997." *Harvard Business Review*, 1997, Supplement.

3

Who Should Use the ROI Methodology?

The ROI Methodology is not intended for just one type of organization. Bringing accountability to programs or processes is a concern for all organizations, regardless of their product, service, mission, or scope. Organizations have accountability issues, whether economic conditions are favorable or unfavorable. During positive economic times, expenditures increase, and organizational leaders have concerns about whether those investments are being properly allocated. During tough economic times, programs and projects that produce the best results are more likely to survive reorganization and restructuring efforts. A comprehensive evaluation system helps pinpoint the areas that will receive available funding.

The ROI Methodology grew quickly in private sector organizations. The growth has been slower in public sector organizations due to their culture and their reliance on cost-benefit analysis. For decades, the public sector has used cost-benefit analysis to support resource allocation. While cost-benefit analysis uses measures similar to those used for ROI calculation, it falls short of the balanced approach of a complete ROI evaluation. Today, therefore, public sector organizations are also moving toward use of the ROI Methodology so that all measures that explain the impact of a program can be taken into consideration.

The Typical Organization

The ROI Methodology is suitable for any organization, but some organizations that are currently implementing ROI as part of their evaluation process share similar characteristics. Typical characteristics include the following:

- *Large size.* Typically, organizations that implement the ROI Methodology are large. Whether in the public or private sector, large organizations have many different programs that are delivered to a diverse target audience, usually over a vast geographical area. Large organizations also have the budget to develop comprehensive evaluation processes. Nonetheless, measurement of ROI should be built into the accountability process in smaller organizations as well. Small organizations have an even greater reason to conserve resources and ensure that they are getting the most out of their dollars. Using several cost-saving approaches described in book four, *Data Conversion,* small organizations (and larger organizations with limited budgets) can implement the ROI Methodology and achieve credible results.

- *Large, highly visible budget.* Whether the function is human resources, learning and development, quality, technology, or marketing, budgets have a way of escalating. The budgets for those functions almost always grow at a faster rate than the producer price index, which means that these processes are becoming much more expensive. Regardless of how it is benchmarked—whether as a total dollar amount, expenditure per employee, percentage of operating costs, or percentage of revenue—a large budget brings the need for additional measurement and evaluation.

Executives demand increased accountability for large expenditures.

- *Focus on measurement.* Organizations that implement the ROI Methodology focus on establishing a variety of measures throughout the organization. Organizations that use the Balanced Scorecard or other approaches at the strategic level are ideal candidates for the ROI Methodology because they already have a measurement-focused environment.

- *Key drivers requiring additional accountability.* In organizations that implement ROI measurement, one or more key drivers are in place, resulting in an increased focus on accountability. These issues and trends, presented in Chapter Two, drive the need to change current practices. In most situations, multiple drivers create interest in ROI accountability.

- *High level of change.* Organizations that use the ROI Methodology are usually undergoing significant change. As they adjust to competitive pressures, they are transforming, restructuring, and reorganizing. Such change often increases interest in bottom-line issues, resulting in a need for greater accountability.

The Typical Program

The ROI Methodology is used in all types of programs, ranging from technical training to child care for the disadvantaged. Exhibit 3.1 provides a sample of the various programs in which ROI has been used. The methodology can be applied to these types of programs and many more.

Exhibit 3.1. Typical Programs That Use the ROI Methodology

- Absenteeism control or reduction
- Business coaching
- Career development, career management
- Communications
- Compensation plans
- Compliance
- Diversity
- E-learning
- Employee benefits plans
- Employee relations
- Gainsharing plans
- Labor-management cooperation
- Leadership development
- Marketing and advertising
- Meeting planning
- Orientation, on-boarding
- Personal productivity and time management
- Procurement
- Project management
- Public policy
- Public relations
- Recruiting source (new)
- Retention management
- Safety incentive plans
- Selection tool (new)
- Self-directed teams
- Sexual harassment prevention
- Six Sigma
- Skill-based pay
- Strategy, policy
- Stress management
- Technical training
- Technology implementation
- Wellness, fitness

Although the ROI Methodology is being applied to a wide variety of programs, specific characteristics define the type of programs that should be considered. These characteristics include

- *Needs assessment.* Most programs evaluated by means of the ROI Methodology are the result of a comprehensive needs assessment that identified the program as an appropriate solution to a problem or an opportunity.

- *Major investment.* Programs to which the ROI Methodology is applied are usually expensive, representing a major investment of resources.

- *Long life cycle.* The programs are usually offered multiple times, rather than being one-time offerings.

- *Broad reach.* Programs evaluated with the ROI Methodology reach a large target audience, affecting more than just a single functional unit or work team.

- *High profile.* Programs have a great deal of visibility within their organization, raising interest, curiosity, and in some cases, skepticism.

- *Executive interest.* Often, a program that uses the ROI Methodology has piqued the interest of senior management, driving their interest in quantifying the economic contribution of the program.

Signs That an Organization Is Ready for the ROI Methodology

An organization that is ready to implement the ROI Methodology in its programs displays several revealing characteristics. Many of the signs in the following list reflect the key drivers discussed in

Chapter Two, which can cause pressure to pursue ROI measurement.

- *Pressure from senior management to measure results.* Such pressure can range from a direct requirement that program effectiveness be measured to a very subtle expression of concern about the accountability of a functional unit, department, or program.
- *Extremely low investment in measurement and evaluation.* Most organizations spend about 1 percent of their direct budget on measurement and evaluation processes. Investment significantly lower than this amount may indicate that little or no measurement and evaluation is taking place, suggesting a need for greater accountability. Expenditures in the 3 to 5 percent range indicate that programs and functions are already undergoing serious evaluation.
- *Recent disastrous results from programs.* Every organization has had one or more situations in which a major program was implemented with no success. When multiple occurrences of a program fail, the originating function or department often bears the blame. Such failures may force the implementation of measurement and evaluation processes in order to quickly determine the impact of programs or, more appropriately, to forecast ROI prior to implementation.
- *A new director or leader of a function.* A new leader is often a catalyst for change and may initiate a review of previous programs. New leaders do not carry the stigma of ownership, nor do they have any attachment to old programs; therefore, they are often more objective than

the previous leaders. New leaders are often good for an organization, perhaps partly because they increase the need for accountability. They want to know which programs are effective and which are not and thus may demand that evaluation processes be put in place if they do not already exist.

- *Some managers want to create leading-edge programs and functions.* Some managers strive to build leading-edge processes and functions. In order to do so, they build comprehensive measurement and evaluation processes into the strategy. These managers often set the pace for measurement and evaluation, highlighting the fact that they are serious about bringing accountability to their functions. These functions' measurement and evaluation systems have formal guidelines, and evaluation is built into the program development function from the beginning. Measurement and evaluation often begin with a thorough needs assessment to determine the best solution, then they monitor the progress of the program and determine the business impact.

- *Lack of management support for a department's efforts.* In some cases, the image of a department or function is so poor that management does not support its efforts. While the unsatisfactory image may be caused by a number of factors, increasing accountability within the department or function and focusing on improving systems and processes may shore up the unit's image.

Exhibit 3.2 provides a self-assessment to help an organization determine whether it is ready to implement the ROI Methodology.

Exhibit 3.2. Self-Check: Is Your Organization a Candidate for Implementation of the ROI Methodology?

Read each question and check the box that corresponds to the most appropriate level of agreement:

1 = Disagree; 5 = Agree

	DISAGREE 1	2	3	4	AGREE 5
1. My organization is considered a large organization with a variety of projects and programs.					
2. My function has a large budget that attracts the interest of senior management.					
3. My organization has a culture of measurement and is focused on establishing a variety of measures for all functions.					
4. My organization is undergoing significant change.					
5. There is pressure from senior management to measure the results of our programs.					
6. My function has a low investment in measurement and evaluation.					
7. My organization has experienced more than one program disaster in the past.					
8. My function has a new leader.					
9. My team would like to be the leader in evaluating programs and processes.					
10. The image of my function is less than satisfactory.					

	DISAGREE 1	2	3	4	AGREE 5
11. My clients are demanding that programs and processes show bottom-line results.					
12. My function competes with other functions in our organization for resources.					
13. Increased focus has been placed on linking programs and processes to the strategic direction of the organization.					
14. My function is a key player in change initiatives currently taking place in our organization.					
15. Our function's overall budget is growing, and we are required to prove the bottom-line value of our processes.					

Scoring

If you scored:

- 15–30 Your organization is not yet a candidate for the ROI Methodology.
- 31–45 Your organization is not a strong candidate for the ROI Methodology. However, you should start pursuing some type of measurement process.
- 46–60 Your organization is a candidate for building skills to implement the ROI Methodology. At this point there is no real pressure to show ROI, which means that you have the perfect opportunity to put the ROI Methodology in place within your organization and perfect the process before it becomes a requirement.
- 61–75 Your organization should already be implementing a comprehensive measurement and evaluation process, including ROI calculations.

Taking a Reactive Versus a Proactive Approach

Probably one of the most telling issues in regard to who experiences success using the ROI Methodology and who does not is the rationale for pursuing it. Collectively, we've had the pleasure of working with thousands of people who have made the decision to implement the ROI Methodology. We've watched some succeed at their efforts and some fail. One of the most important determinants of success or failure is taking a proactive approach instead of a reactive approach.

Reactive Approach

If individuals pursue measurement of ROI in reaction to a pressure point, a request, or an urgent need, implementation may be difficult. If an individual is attempting to justify a budget or an expenditure, gain support for a program, or defend a particular standpoint, that individual is pursuing ROI measurement from a difficult position, often in reaction to a request. Unfortunately, a request often comes with a short time frame and tremendous pressure to show a positive value. When this is the case, there is often not enough time to properly collect program data, which may be inadequate in both quality and quantity. Also, since there has been no opportunity to appropriately plan the program from the beginning, the results may be diminished, perhaps even negative. This is not the desired scenario. When this occurs, the chance of a failed ROI measurement process greatly increases.

Proactive Approach

The ideal scenario is proactive implementation of the ROI Methodology. In this situation, the interested individuals see the value of measuring ROI. They understand that they may need to show the value of their budget to executives in the future, but they are under no immediate pressure to do so. Or if there is pressure, it is in the form of encouragement or support, not an ultimate requirement. These individuals see that they must show the value of their budget just as other departments or functions often do. They know that to be a business partner and an ally in making their organization effective, they must be accountable for their resources and take steps to demonstrate the contribution of their department or function to the overall success of the organization. They realize that process improvement is essential and that ROI measurement is a process improvement method. It can make things better—make the program work when it is not working or make it work better when it is. Proactive individuals also use the ROI Methodology to change the entire image of their department or function so that it will be involved in important decisions and ultimately earn a seat at the table. This proactive approach forms the rationale for pursuing the ROI Methodology. When a proactive approach is used, success is almost guaranteed.

Final Thoughts

This chapter discussed who is best suited to use the ROI Methodology and to which programs ROI is best applied. In reality, any organization can evaluate any program using this process. However, the organization must be ready and willing to take on the task of measuring ROI. The individuals involved in the process must have the right mindset; they should be taking a proactive approach to measuring ROI and not reacting to a request or demand for data and results. This process takes time and money and should be reserved for programs that are perceived as large investments—ones that are being considered for expansion, elimination, or improvement. Most of all, programs from which value is needed but whose value is unknown are candidates for the ROI Methodology.

4

How to Build a Credible Process

Developing a credible and comprehensive measurement and evaluation process is much like putting together the pieces of a puzzle. Figure 4.1 shows the major elements of this evaluation puzzle.

The first piece of the puzzle is the evaluation framework. This framework defines the levels at which programs are evaluated and how data are captured at different times and from different sources. Basically, these levels represent the categories of data collected and analyzed for the various stakeholders in the program.

The second piece of the puzzle is the process model for the ROI Methodology. The process model is critical because it depicts systematic steps that ensure consistent application of the evaluation methodology. The model shows step by step how and when to collect and analyze the data categorized by the five levels.

The third piece of the evaluation puzzle is operating standards and philosophy. These standards build credibility into the process by supporting a systematic methodology and a conservative approach to ROI evaluation. The standards, presented as the Twelve Guiding Principles in this book, also support consistency in the evaluation process.

Case studies showing real-world applications of the process are the fourth piece of the puzzle. Case studies describe the practical applications of the process as well as the use of the standards. It

Figure 4.1. The Evaluation Puzzle

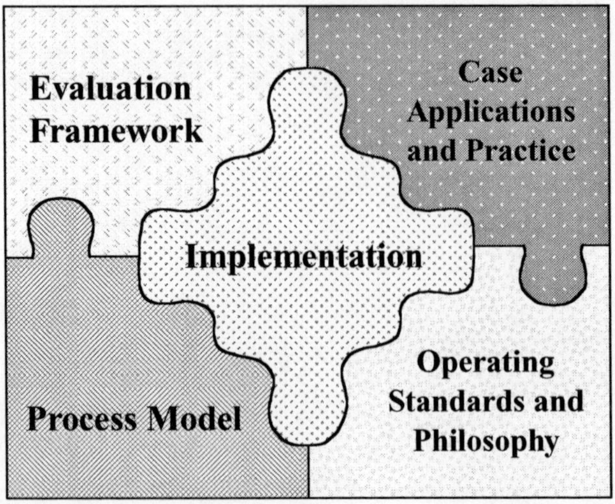

[Puzzle diagram with five pieces: Evaluation Framework, Case Applications and Practice, Implementation, Process Model, Operating Standards and Philosophy]

Source: Phillips, 2001.

is real-life applications that move the first three puzzle pieces from theory to practice. Case studies provide the initial step for the fifth piece of the evaluation puzzle.

The final piece of the puzzle, implementation, brings together the other four pieces to implement the ROI Methodology. Critical elements of implementation, which will be discussed later in this chapter, ensure that the evaluation process is fully integrated into the organization; that the organization develops the skills, procedures, and guidelines necessary for success; and that a comprehensive communication strategy is in place to ensure that the process is used to its fullest extent and that credibility with key stakeholders is maintained.

Together, the five pieces of the evaluation puzzle form a comprehensive measurement and evaluation system that contains a balanced set of measures, has credibility, and can be replicated from one group to another.

The Evaluation Framework

The evaluation framework, described briefly in Chapter One, is the first piece of the evaluation puzzle.

The concept of levels of evaluation evolved from work by Donald Kirkpatrick, which he began publishing in 1959 (Kirkpatrick, 1959). At that time, Kirkpatrick suggested four specific steps of program evaluation:

1. Reaction
2. Learning
3. Job behavior
4. Results

During the next three decades, although the concept of steps morphed into the concept of levels, no effort was made to refine the fundamental premise or develop a system of standards to support the collection and analysis of data that would be gathered through the steps. It was in the 1970s and 1980s that others began to make some improvements on the concept of evaluation levels. Table 4.1 shows the five-level framework introduced in the 1980s by Jack Phillips (1983). The levels shown represent important adjustments and refinements of Kirkpatrick's initial steps.

Kirkpatrick's work provided the initial steps for evaluation of training programs. However, the need to take evaluation further has intensified in the past two decades. Executives are increasingly requiring the training and performance improvement function to demonstrate the value it brings to an organization. Other support functions need a process through which to demonstrate value too. The most common measure of value-added benefits is return on investment (Horngren, 1982; Anthony and Reece, 1983). ROI is the ratio of earnings (net benefits) to investment (costs) (Kearsley, 1982).

Table 4.1. Phillips's Five Levels of Evaluation

Level	Description	Focus	Frequency of Use	Comments	Challenges
1. Reaction and Planned Action	Measures participants' reaction to the program, stakeholders' satisfaction with the program, and the actions planned as a result of the program, if feasible	Consumer	Very high	Data at this level are very easy to measure. Level 1 data are usually measured in 100% of evaluations but have very little value from the client's perspective.	Data collection is frequently automated, and data must be used appropriately.
2. Learning	Measures skills, knowledge, or attitude changes resulting from the program	Consumer	High	Data are more difficult to measure than in Level 1. This level of evaluation is very important in learning and development functions but less important in other functions.	Data collection is sometimes automated and data must be used appropriately.

Level	Description	Focus	Frequency of Use	Comments	Challenges
3. Application and Implementation	Measures changes in behavior on the job and specific application and implementation of the program	Consumer and client	Moderate	Data collected at this level are critical for most programs in assessing whether any behavior or process change related to the program has occurred.	An organization or unit must work hard to get good data and keep costs and disruption low.
4. Business Impact	Captures changes in business impact related to the program	Client	Occasional	Data are easy to measure but are perceived as difficult to analyze.	Isolating the effects of the program on the data is difficult but necessary to determine a valid relationship between the program and reported results.
5. Return on Investment	Compares the monetary values of the impact with the costs of the program	Client	Rare	Data at this level are more difficult to analyze but constitute the most valuable data set available.	This analysis is pursued for only a limited number of projects.

Table 4.1 not only reemphasizes the definitions of each level provided in Chapter One but shows some of the characteristics of the different levels. The focus moves from the consumer at the lower levels to the client at the higher levels. In other words, key clients who pay for projects and programs are more interested in the higher levels of evaluation, particularly Levels 4 and 5. The consumers involved in the programs and projects may have more interest in their own reaction and what they are learning from the program than in the higher levels of data. Ironically, the frequency of data collection is higher at the lower levels than it is at the higher levels, partly because collecting data at the lower levels is easier, even though Level 4 data are not difficult to capture in most organizations. The daunting problem, however, is connecting Level 4 measures to the program. The challenges of data collection and analysis increase as measurement is pursued at the higher levels. Nonetheless, the measurement landscape has essentially changed so that it now includes a requirement for higher levels of data, up to and including ROI.

Whereas Kirkpatrick's fourth step stops with identifying the results of the program (Level 4, Results), the ROI Methodology refines Level 4 and then creates a fifth level. First, at Level 4, the results of the program need to be isolated. Ignoring the other factors that could have contributed to the improvement in Level 4 measures would be inappropriate; isolation must occur in order to answer the question, "How does the organization know that the program caused the reported results?"

Next, to move from Level 4 to Level 5, the steps of cost-benefit analysis are employed. Level 4 measures (the ones that have been connected to the program through isolation) are converted to monetary values and then compared with the fully loaded cost of the program. The steps for moving from Level 4 to Level 5 are not new (cost-benefit analysis has been around for centuries); however, the economic indicator resulting from cost-benefit analysis alone

Table 4.2. Phillips's Five-Level Evaluation Framework Compared with Cost-Benefit Analysis

	Phillips's Five-Level Framework (ROI Methodology)	Cost-benefit analysis
Measures participant reaction to program	✓	
Measures learning resulting from program	✓	
Measures applications and behavior resulting from program	✓	
Measures impact and benefits of program	✓	✓
Measures ROI	✓	✓
Isolates effects of program	✓	
Determines cost of program	✓	✓
Converts program benefits to monetary values	✓	✓
Identifies intangible benefits of program	✓	✓

provides an insufficient story of program success. By using the first four levels of program evaluation, adding the step to isolate the impact of the program, and bringing in benefit-cost analysis, the ROI Methodology tells a complete story of program success. In addition, improvement data are developed that can enhance future program implementations. Table 4.2 provides a comparison of the Phillips framework and the cost-benefit analysis.

Although the distinction between the Phillips framework and cost-benefit analysis is important, not all programs are evaluated at all five levels. Perhaps the best explanation for this is that as the level of evaluation increases, so does its difficulty and expense.

A comprehensive ROI evaluation takes time and resources, so conducting one for every program is not feasible. Only a limited number of programs should be targeted for evaluation at the ROI level, as discussed in Chapter Two.

It is important to note that when programs are evaluated at a higher level, they must be evaluated at the lower levels as well. A chain of impact should occur as participants react and plan action (Level 1) based on the skills and knowledge acquired during the program (Level 2) that will be applied on the job (Level 3) to produce business impact (Level 4). If success is achieved with business impact and the cost of the program was appropriate, a positive ROI (Level 5) will occur. If measurements are not taken at each of these levels, it is difficult to conclude that the results achieved are a result of the program and to understand how the results, including ROI, evolved.

The Process Model

The second piece of the evaluation puzzle is the process model for the ROI Methodology, which was briefly explored in Chapter One. The process model shows a systematic, step-by-step process that will ensure that the methodology is implemented consistently. The process model consists of four stages: evaluation planning, data collection, data analysis, and reporting of results.

The Operating Standards: Guiding Principles

Operating standards, the third piece of the evaluation puzzle, help ensure that the evaluation process is consistent and that a conservative approach is taken. Standards and guiding principles keep the evaluation credible and allow the process to be replicated. Twelve Guiding Principles are used as operating standards in implementing the ROI Methodology (Phillips, 1997).

1. Report the Complete Story

When conducting a higher-level evaluation, collect data at lower levels. ROI is a critical measure, but it is only one of six measures necessary to explain the full impact of the program. Therefore, lower levels of data must be included in the analysis. Data at the lower levels also provide important information that may be helpful in making adjustments for future program implementation.

2. Conserve Important Resources

When planning a higher-level evaluation, the previous level of evaluation is not required to be comprehensive. Lower-level measures are critical in telling the complete story, and they cannot be omitted. However, shortcuts can be taken in order to conserve resources. For example, when the client is interested in business impact, shortcuts can be taken at Levels 1, 2, and 3.

3. Enhance Credibility

When collecting and analyzing data, use only the most credible sources. Credibility is the most important factor in the measurement and evaluation process. Without it, the results are meaningless. Using the most credible source, which is often the participants, will enhance the perception that the data analysis and results are accurate and of high quality.

4. Be Conservative

When analyzing data, select the most conservative alternative for calculations. This principle is at the heart of the evaluation process. A conservative approach lowers the ROI and helps build the needed credibility with the target audience. Being conservative is better than providing a generous estimate and having results that are not believable.

5. Account for Other Factors

Use at least one method to isolate the effects of a program. This step is imperative. Without some method of isolating the effects of the program, the evaluation results will be considered inaccurate and overstated.

6. Account for Missing Data

If no improvement data are available for a population or from a specific source, assume that little or no improvement has occurred. If participants do not provide data—for example, if they are no longer part of the organization or they now perform a different function—it should be assumed that little or no improvement has occurred. To assume otherwise would damage the credibility of the evaluation. This ultraconservative approach will further enhance the credibility of the results.

7. Adjust Estimates for Error

Adjust estimates of improvement for potential errors of estimation. This principle contributes to a conservative approach. Using estimates is a common process in reporting financial and benefit-cost information. To enhance the credibility of estimated data used in ROI evaluation, estimates are weighted with a level of confidence in the estimate by the respondent, adjusting the estimate for potential error.

8. Omit the Extremes

Avoid using extreme data items and unsupported claims when calculating ROI. Again, to maintain the credibility of results, steps should be taken to be conservative in the analysis. Extreme data items can skew results toward the low side or the high side. To eliminate the influence of extreme data items, they should be omitted from the analysis. Also, when benefits are presented with no explanation of how they were derived, they should be omitted from the analysis.

9. Capture Annual Benefits for Short-Term Programs

Use only the first year of annual benefits in ROI analysis of short-term solutions. For most programs, if benefits are not quickly realized, the program is probably not worth the cost. Therefore, for short-term programs, only first-year benefits should be considered. For longer-term programs in which implementation spans a year or more, multiple-year benefits can be captured.

10. Account for All Program Costs

Fully load all costs of a solution, project, or program when analyzing ROI. All costs of the program should be tabulated, beginning with the cost of the needs analysis and ending with the cost of the evaluation. In a conservative approach, the costs are loaded into the analysis, reducing the ROI.

11. Report Intangible Benefits

Intangible measures are defined as measures that are purposely not converted to monetary values. Understanding the significance of intangible measures and how to work with them properly is important. Specific rules must be developed for deciding when to leave data in the form of intangible benefits. If data can be credibly converted to monetary values with minimum resources, they should become tangible. Otherwise, they can be reported as intangible benefits.

12. Communicate Results

Communicate the results of the ROI Methodology to all key stakeholders. Many stakeholders may need to receive the data from an ROI evaluation. Four key groups will always need the information: the participants, the participants' immediate managers, the key sponsor or client, and the function's or department's staff.

Collectively, these twelve principles will ensure that a conservative approach is taken to ROI measurement, that the evaluation can be replicated, and that the ROI for programs and projects can be compared with the ROI of other operational processes and initiatives.

Case Applications and Practice

A critical piece of the evaluation puzzle is the development of case studies to show success, to promote programs, or to justify new programs. Case studies from other organizations can also be used for benchmarking or as examples of success. Today, almost three hundred case studies have been published about this methodology, and more are being published each year. Cases have been published about the use of the ROI Methodology in a variety of settings and also in different countries, cultures, and languages. Go to www.roiinstitute.net for more details on published case studies.

Case studies within specific industries may indicate the status of ROI measurement in organizations similar to your own—organizations that may be addressing issues and targeting concerns similar to those in your organization. Case studies from a global perspective provide evidence of progress in ROI measurement in a variety of organizations and industries. Case studies provide support to practitioners, managers, and executives who are interested in learning how to apply the ROI Methodology.

While the use of case studies from other organizations is helpful in understanding the merits of ROI measurement and the success of specific programs, studies within an organization are more powerful and persuasive for individuals in that organization, displaying evidence of success through use of the ROI Methodology in internal programs.

Implementation

The final piece of the evaluation puzzle is implementation. The best tool, technique, or model will not be successful unless it is properly used and becomes a routine part of operations. As with any change, the people affected by the implementation of a comprehensive measurement and evaluation process may resist it. Some of the resistance will be based on real barriers. Part of it, however, may be based on misunderstandings and perceived problems. In both cases, the organization must work to overcome the resistance by carefully and methodically implementing the ROI Methodology, using a few critical steps:

1. Assign responsibilities.
2. Develop skills.
3. Develop an implementation plan.
4. Prepare or revise evaluation guidelines.
5. Brief managers on the evaluation process.

Assign Responsibilities

To ensure successful implementation of the ROI Methodology, responsibilities are assigned up front—before implementation begins. Who will lead the evaluation effort? Will evaluation be integrated into the department or function, or will it report to the CFO? Is it more appropriate to contract with a third-party evaluation provider and have only an internal coordinator? These questions and others must be considered when implementing any evaluation strategy.

Develop Skills

Another key step in successful implementation is the development of skills and capabilities. Skills in evaluation planning, data collection design and analysis, and communication are important to successful implementation. A complete understanding of each step in the evaluation process simplifies implementation, reducing the stress and frustration often associated with jumping from one process to another.

Develop an Implementation Plan

Planning for implementation will save time and money. By using a basic set of criteria to review existing programs as well as proposed new programs, a department or function can develop an implementation plan. This plan will assist in determining which programs will be evaluated and at which levels (by using the criteria discussed in Chapters Two and Three) as well as how the necessary resources will be allocated.

Along with an implementation plan for selecting programs for different levels of evaluation, a project plan should be developed to help manage the overall evaluation process. From a practical standpoint, this project plan supports the transition from the present situation to a desired future situation. Exhibit 4.1 shows a sample project plan. This particular evaluation project includes skill development as well as implementation of ROI for several programs. The project plan is a summary of the evaluation. The ten key tasks in the following list should be addressed in each project plan. Other tasks should be considered for specific projects.

1. *Review of existing programs, processes, reports, and data.* This step is essential in order to understand past practices and how to incorporate the new methodology most effectively.
2. *Skill development.* Developing the skills necessary to implement the ROI Methodology is essential for its complete integration into the function or department.
3. *Finalization of evaluation planning documents.* Completing the planning documents that are necessary to implement the ROI Methodology is critical in order to ensure that every step of the process is taken and that key stakeholders are in agreement with those steps.

4. *Collection of data for evaluation.* This step represents the data collection process. This process includes selecting the appropriate instrument, identifying the most credible sources of data, and determining the most appropriate timing of data collection.
5. *Analysis of the data.* This step represents the time necessary to analyze the data after it is collected.
6. *Development of reports.* Developing a variety of reports helps address the needs of specific audiences. A complete impact study should be developed for the department's records. After the executive management group understands the evaluation process, it will be necessary to prepare a brief (in some cases only one page) summary to give executives key results without overwhelming them with details.
7. *Presentation of evaluation results.* Different audiences need different information. In the initial implementation of the ROI Methodology, the results should be presented in a formal setting to ensure clear communication about the process itself. Presentation of the results to the staff members may take place in a less formal setting, such as a weekly staff meeting.
8. *Development of scorecard framework.* In the Exhibit 4.1 example, the client requested a summary scorecard that would report the results for all the function's projects and programs.
9. *Development of guidelines.* As the ROI Methodology is implemented and integrated into a function, guidelines are developed to ensure consistent long-term implementation.
10. *Manager briefings.* Management understanding of the ROI evaluation process is critical. Managers who are not involved in a particular evaluation project might still be interested in the process. Manager briefings are a way to communicate not only the results of the evaluation but also about the process in general.

Exhibit 4.1. Project Plan

	OCT	NOV	DEC	JAN	FEB	MAR	APR	MAY	JUN	JUL	AUG	SEP
Review existing programs, processes, reports, and data	▓	▓										
Develop skills			▓									
Finalize evaluation planning documents			▓	▓								
Collect data for evaluation						▓	▓	▓				
Analyze data								▓	▓	▓	▓	
Develop reports									▓	▓	▓	
Present evaluation results											▓	▓
Develop scorecard framework										▓	▓	
Develop guidelines								▓	▓			
Brief managers									▓			

Each individual program evaluation will have individual project plans that detail the steps necessary to complete the project as well as keep the evaluation project on track. Planning is the key to successful implementation of the ROI Methodology.

Prepare or Revise Evaluation Guidelines

Guidelines keep the implementation process on track. A clear set of guidelines will help ensure that the process continues as designed when changes in staff or management occur. Guidelines also establish the evaluation process as an integral part of the overall strategy of a unit or department. Guidelines should be updated or revised as implementation progresses, incorporating what is learned during the process.

Brief Managers on the Evaluation Process

Communicating to managers about the evaluation process as it proceeds will help enlist their support during the implementation process. The unknown can often become a barrier, so if the organization makes the effort to explain each step, managers will generally be more likely to understand and support the evaluation efforts.

Final Thoughts

Implementing an evaluation method begins with planning. Setting up an evaluation framework that supports and sustains the process is critical. The ROI Methodology is a step-by-step process that collects six types of data, including ROI, through its five-level framework. When implemented properly, it is a credible and comprehensive measurement and evaluation system. It must also be supported by the Twelve Guiding Principles, which add credibility and consistency by ensuring a conservative process.

References

Anthony, R. N., and Reece, J. S. *Accounting Text and Cases.* New York: Irwin, 1983.

Horngren, C. T. *Cost Accounting.* Upper Saddle River, N. J.: Prentice Hall, 1982.

Kearsley, G. *Costs, Benefits, and Productivity in Training Systems.* Reading, Mass.: Addison-Wesley, 1982.

Kirkpatrick, D. L. "Techniques for Evaluating Programs." *Journal of the American Society of Training Directors,* Nov. 1959.

Phillips, J. J. *Handbook of Training and Evaluation Methods.* (1st ed.) Houston, Tex.: Gulf, 1983.

Phillips, J. J. *Return on Investment in Training and Performance Improvement Programs.* Boston: Butterworth-Heinemann, 1997.

Phillips, J. *The Consultant's Scorecard: Tracking Results and Bottom-Line Impact of Consulting Projects.* New York: McGraw-Hill, 2001.

5

Inhibitors of Implementation

Although progress is being made in the implementation of the ROI Methodology on many fronts, a variety of factors can inhibit implementation of the concept. Some factors are real barriers; others are perceptions based on myths. The key to overcoming barriers is distinguishing reality from myth and taking steps to overcome the barriers.

Barriers to Implementation

A variety of barriers can deter or prevent successful implementation of the ROI Methodology. While the barriers may be real, steps can be taken to overcome them.

Costs and Time

A comprehensive measurement and evaluation process that includes ROI will add additional costs and time to programs, although the added amount should not be excessive. The additional costs should be no more than 3 to 5 percent of the total budget. The additional investment in ROI should be offset by the results achieved from implementation (for example, elimination or prevention of unproductive or unprofitable programs). Barriers of cost and time stop many ROI implementations early in the process. However, there are a few shortcuts and cost-saving approaches that

Exhibit 5.1. Tips and Techniques for Reducing the Cost of Implementing the ROI Methodology

- Build evaluation into the process.
- Develop criteria for selecting program measurement levels.
- Plan for evaluation early.
- Share the responsibilities involved in evaluation.
- Require participants to conduct major steps, such as providing impact data or converting measures to monetary values.
- Use shortcut methods of performing major steps, such as using questionnaires.
- Use estimates.
- Develop internal capability in developing data collection instruments and analyzing data.
- Streamline the reporting process.
- Use technology.

Source: Phillips and Burkett, 2001.

can be taken to help reduce the cost of the actual implementation. Exhibit 5.1 presents ten ways to save time and money.

Lack of Skills

Many staff members do not understand ROI or do not have the basic skills necessary to apply the process. Also, many programs focus more on qualitative feedback data (Level 1) than quantitative results (Levels 4 and 5). Therefore, a possible barrier to implementation is the need for overall orientation and for a change in the attitude and skills of staff members. Suggestions for building ROI evaluation skills include

- Attending public workshops
- Becoming certified in the ROI Methodology
- Conducting internal workshops

- Starting with less comprehensive evaluations and building skills toward a more comprehensive evaluation
- Participating in evaluation networking forums

Faulty or Inadequate Initial Analysis

Many projects and programs do not include an adequate initial analysis and assessment of their evaluation process. Some functions implement programs for the wrong reasons, such as management requests or efforts to chase a popular fad or trend in the industry. If a program is not necessary or not based on business needs, it may not produce enough benefits to overcome the costs. An ROI calculation for an unnecessary program will likely yield a negative value. This is a real barrier for evaluating many programs, because many individuals do not want to acknowledge that their program is not working as expected. To overcome this barrier, develop or enhance the initial analysis process. Become engaged with the client to gain a deeper understanding of the needs from which a project arises. This helps to ensure that an appropriate program is implemented, yielding a greater ROI.

Fear

Some staff members do not pursue ROI because of a fear of failure or a fear of the unknown. Fear of failure appears in several forms. Some people are concerned about the consequences of a negative ROI. They perceive the evaluation process as an individual performance evaluation rather than a process improvement tool. For others, a comprehensive measurement process can stir up the traditional fear of change and the unknown. Although often based on unrealistic assumptions and a lack of knowledge about the process, the fear can be so strong that it becomes a real barrier to many ROI implementations. Ensuring that staff members understand the process and its intent is the key to removing this fear.

Discipline and Planning

A successful ROI implementation requires planning and a disciplined approach. Implementation schedules, transition plans, evaluation targets, ROI analysis plans, measurement and evaluation policies, and follow-up schedules are required. The practitioner may not have enough discipline and determination to stay the course. This lack of will can become a barrier, particularly when no immediate pressures to measure ROI exist. If clients or other executives are not demanding ROI, staff members may not allocate time for planning and coordination. Also, other pressures and priorities often take precedence over ROI implementation. Planning the work and working the plan are key to successful implementation.

ROI Myths

Although most practitioners recognize the ROI Methodology as an important addition to measurement and evaluation, they often struggle with how to address the issue. Many professionals see it as a ticket to increased funding and prosperity for their programs. They believe that without it they may be lost in the shuffle and that with it they may gain the respect they need to continue moving their department or function forward. Regardless of their motivation, the key questions are, "Is the ROI Methodology a feasible process that can be implemented with reasonable resources?" and, "Will implementation of ROI measurement provide the benefits necessary to make it a useful, routine tool?" The answers to these questions may lead to debate and even to controversy.

The controversy surrounding the ROI Methodology stems from misunderstandings about the process, what it can and cannot do, and how it should be implemented within an organization. These misunderstandings are summarized in this section as fifteen myths about the ROI Methodology. The myths have been revealed during years of experience with ROI and from perceptions observed during hundreds of projects and workshops. Along with each myth, we present an appropriate explanation.

ROI Is Too Complex for Most Users

This myth is a problem because of a few highly complex ROI models that have been publicly presented. Unfortunately, these models have done little to help users and have caused confusion about ROI. The ROI Methodology is a basic financial formula for accountability that is simple and understandable: earnings are divided by investment; earnings are the net benefits from the program, and the investment equals the actual cost of the program. Straying from this basic formula can add confusion and create misunderstanding. The ROI model provides a step-by-step, systematic process that allows users to collect and analyze data important to overall program improvement. These data also help users explain why the ROI is what it is and how to improve it in the future. Each step is taken separately, and issues are addressed for that particular step. The decisions are made incrementally throughout the process. This method helps make a complex process simpler and more manageable.

ROI Is Expensive, Consuming Too Many Critical Resources

The ROI Methodology can become expensive if it is not carefully organized, precisely controlled, and properly implemented. While the cost of an external ROI impact study can be significant, many actions can be taken to lower costs, as shown earlier in Exhibit 5.1.

If Senior Management Does Not Require ROI, There Is No Need to Pursue It

This myth affects the most innocent bystanders. It is easy to be lulled into providing evaluation and measurement that simply preserves the status quo, believing that no pressure or request means no requirement. The truth is that if senior executives have seen only

Level 1 reaction data, they may not ask for higher-level data because they think those data are not available. In some cases, leaders have convinced top management that programs cannot be evaluated at the ROI level or that the specific impact of a program cannot be determined. Given these conditions, it comes as no surprise that some top managers are not asking for Level 5 (ROI) data.

This kind of thinking may cause another problem later. Changes in corporate leadership sometimes initiate important paradigm shifts. New leaders often require proof of accountability. The process of implementing the ROI Methodology in an organization takes time—about twelve to eighteen months for many organizations; it is not a quick fix. When senior executives suddenly ask for data that show the value of a function or program, they may expect quick results. Because this type of short-term request can happen unexpectedly, departments or functions should initiate ROI evaluation long before they are asked for ROI data.

ROI Is a Passing Fad

Unfortunately, this perception applies to many processes being introduced in organizations today. However, the need to account for expenditures will always be present, and the ROI Methodology provides the ultimate level of accountability. ROI has a rich history of use as an accountability tool. In the past, ROI was used mostly to measure investment in equipment and new plants. Today, its use is being extended to many other areas. In the future, its flexibility and broad applicability will ensure that ROI continues to be used as a tool for measurement and evaluation.

ROI Is Only One Type of Data

This is a common misunderstanding. The ROI calculation represents one type of data that shows the benefits versus the costs for a program. However, when the complete five-level evaluation framework is used, six types of data are generated, representing both qualitative and quantitative data and often involving data from different sources, making the ROI Methodology a rich source for a variety of data.

ROI Is Not Future-Oriented; It Reflects Only Past Performance

Unfortunately, many evaluation processes are past-oriented and reflect only what has already happened in a program. This is the only way to have an accurate assessment of impact. However, the ROI Methodology can easily be adapted to forecast ROI for a program.

ROI Is Rarely Used by Organizations

This myth is easily dispelled when the evidence is fully examined. More than 3,000 organizations use the ROI Methodology, and at least one hundred case studies on its implementation have been published. Leading organizations throughout the world, including businesses of all sizes and from all sectors, use the ROI Methodology to increase accountability and improve programs. This process is also being used in the nonprofit, educational, and government sectors. There is no doubt that it is a widely used process that is growing in use.

The ROI Methodology Cannot Be Easily Replicated

This is an understandable concern. In theory, any process worthy of implementation is one that can be replicated from one study to another. For example, if two people conducted an ROI evaluation on the same program, would they obtain the same results? Fortunately, the ROI Methodology is a systematic process with specific standards and guiding principles, so the likelihood of two evaluators obtaining the same results is high. And because it is a process that involves step-by-step procedures, the ROI Methodology can be replicated from one program to another.

ROI Is Not a Credible Process; It Is Too Subjective

This myth has evolved because some ROI evaluations involving estimates have been promoted in the literature and at conferences. Many ROI studies have been conducted without the use of estimates. The issue of estimates often surfaces during attempts to isolate the effects of a program from other influences. Using estimates from the participants is only one of several techniques used to isolate the effects of a program. Other techniques involve analytical approaches such as the use of control groups and trend line analysis. Sometimes, estimating is used in other steps of the ROI process, such as converting data to monetary values or estimating output in the data collection phase. In each of these situations, other options are often available, but for reasons of convenience or economics, estimation is often used. While the use of estimates may be the least ideal situation when evaluating ROI, estimates can be extremely reliable when they are obtained carefully, adjusted for error, and reported appropriately. The accounting, engineering, and technology fields routinely require the use of estimates, often without question or concern.

ROI Is Not Credible When Evaluating Soft-Skill Programs

ROI is often most effective in soft-skill programs. Soft skills such as training and learning often influence hard data items such as output, quality, cost, or time. Case after case shows successful application of the ROI Methodology to programs in areas such as team building, leadership, communications, and empowerment. Additional examples of successful ROI implementation can be found in compliance programs in areas such as diversity, sexual harassment prevention, and policy implementation.

ROI Is Only for Manufacturing and Service Organizations

Although initial studies on ROI appeared in the manufacturing sector, the service sector quickly picked up the process as a useful tool.

After that, use of the ROI Methodology migrated to the nonprofit sector, and organizations such as hospitals and health care firms began endorsing and using the process. Next, ROI evaluation moved around the world through the government sector, and now, educational institutions are using the ROI Methodology. Several educational institutions use ROI to measure the impact of their formal degree programs and less-structured continuing education programs.

Isolation of the Influence of Factors Other Than the Program Is Not Always Possible

Isolating the effects of influences external to a program is always achievable when using the ROI Methodology. At least nine ways to isolate the influence of other factors are available, and at least one method will work in any given situation. The challenge is selecting the appropriate isolation method for the resources and accuracy needed in each situation. This myth probably stems from unsuccessful attempts at using a control group arrangement—a classic way of isolating the effect of a program. In practice, a control group does not work in a majority of situations, causing some researchers to abandon the issue of isolating other factors. In reality, many other techniques provide accurate, reliable, and valid methods for isolating the effects of a program.

Measurement of On-the-Job Activities Is Impossible Because Post-Program Control of Application Is Impossible

This myth is fading as organizations face the reality that knowledge transfer is critical if change is to occur as a result of a program or process, and as leaders within organizations realize the importance of measuring on-the-job results. Although the program staff does not have direct control over what happens in the workplace, it does have influence on the learning transfer process. A program must be considered within the context of the workplace; the program is owned by the organization. Many individuals and groups may be involved with objectives that push expectations beyond the classroom or keyboard. Objectives focus on application and impact data used in the ROI analysis. Also, the partnership that is often needed between key managers produces objectives that drive the program. In effect, a process with partnerships and a common framework to drive the results—not just classroom activity—is necessary to ensure that application of new knowledge is transferred to improved job performance.

ROI Is Appropriate Only for Large Organizations

While large organizations with enormous budgets have the most interest in ROI, smaller organizations can also use the process, particularly when it is simplified and built into their programs. Organizations with as few as fifty employees have successfully applied the ROI Methodology, using it as a tool for increasing accountability and involvement in their programs.

The ROI Methodology Has No Standards

An important problem facing measurement and evaluation is a lack of standardization or consistency. Questions that are often asked include, "What is a good ROI?" "What should be included in the costs so that I can compare my data with other data?" and, "When should specific data be included in the ROI value instead of left as an intangible benefit?" While these questions are not easily answered, some help can be found in this book. The ROI Methodology has Twelve Guiding Principles, which are discussed in Chapter Four. These principles give consistency and rigor to the ROI measurement process. In addition, some of the more specific questions posed in this section will be answered in subsequent books in this series.

It's All About Change Management

The material in this chapter illustrates that implementing the ROI Methodology is about more than simply putting a measurement system in place. Effective use of the process requires a change in the way organizations implement programs and projects. Evaluation data must be acted upon; in knowledge roles, transfer must be recognized and put into action. Previous processes must be unlearned and new knowledge acquired and ultimately applied. It is about change management.

Any book about the steps of change management would apply to this process. Implementing the ROI Methodology brings change to the following individuals:

- Clients, who request or initiate projects or programs
- Program designers and analysts, who link projects to business results
- Program designers and developers, who build or create projects or programs to focus on results
- Participants and other stakeholders actively involved in the process, who must change their perception of their role in program success (specifically, what they have to do to ensure that success)
- Senior executives, who provide the funding for projects or programs and who expect results
- Organizers, project managers, and facilitators, who administer and teach programs
- Evaluators, who must change the way they evaluate programs

Because so much change is involved, much effort is required to ensure that it is properly implemented. The sixth book in this series, *Communication and Implementation*, will focus on some of the issues involved in implementing this method.

Exhibit 5.2. Checklist for ROI Implementation

- Assess progress with evaluation and readiness for ROI implementation.
- Organize a task force or network to initiate the process.
- Develop and publish a philosophy or mission statement concerning accountability and ROI of all programs.
- Clarify roles and responsibilities of task force members.
- Develop a transition plan, detailing the steps necessary to successfully implement ROI.
- Set targets for evaluating programs at the various levels of evaluation.
- Develop guidelines to ensure that ROI is implemented completely and consistently.
- Build staff skills in using the ROI Methodology.
- Establish a management support system or champions of ROI.
- Through communication, enhance management support, commitment, and participation in the implementation of ROI.
- Achieve short-term results by evaluating one program at a time.
- Communicate results to stakeholders.
- Teach the process to others in order to enhance their understanding of ROI.
- Establish a quality review process to ensure that the evaluation process remains consistent and credible.

Next Steps

Now that the ROI Methodology has been explained, assess your knowledge by taking the ROI Quiz at the end of this chapter. Then, to help you get started with ROI implementation, Exhibit 5.2 provides a checklist of steps. As you make progress and issues surface, numerous resources will be available to assist in implementing ROI. The Appendix at the end of this book lists some of these resources.

Final Thoughts

So what is the bottom line on ROI? ROI has been used for generations to show the value of programs, projects, and processes within organizations. The ROI calculation is the financial ratio used by accountants, chief financial officers, and executives to measure the return on all investments. The term *ROI* is familiar to all executives and operational managers. It is not a fly-by-night new catchphrase with an unknown meaning that can only be explained through elaborate presentations and is only understood in a very small area of the organization.

The ROI Methodology described in this book goes beyond a benefit-cost comparison. Rather, it provides a balanced viewpoint of projects and programs by taking into consideration participant reactions, learning, application of new skills and knowledge, and business impact achieved as a result of the program. The process presents a complete picture of program success. Further, by including the critical step of isolating the effects of the program, the impact on business can be further linked to programs. The process presented in this book is based on sound research and conservative guidelines. Although not all programs should be evaluated at the ROI level, for those meeting specific criteria, ROI is a credible approach to providing evidence of a program's financial impact on the organization. A thorough and complete understanding of the ROI Methodology can help eliminate fears and overcome barriers to its implementation.

Reference

Phillips, P., and Burkett, H. *ROI on a Shoestring*. Alexandria, Va.: ASTD, 2001.

ROI Quiz

True or false? Please choose the answer you feel is correct.

	True	False
1. The ROI Methodology generates just one data item, expressed as a percentage.	☐	☐
2. A program with monetary benefits of $200,000 and costs of $100,000 translates into a 200% ROI.	☐	☐
3. The ROI Methodology is a tool to strengthen organizations and improve processes.	☐	☐
4. After reviewing a detailed ROI impact study, senior executives will usually require ROI studies on all programs.	☐	☐
5. ROI studies should be conducted very selectively, usually involving 5–10% of programs.	☐	☐
6. While it may be a rough estimate, it is always possible to isolate the effects of a program on impact data.	☐	☐
7. A program costing $100 per participant, designed to teach basic skills on job-related software, is an ideal program for an ROI impact study.	☐	☐
8. Data can always be credibly converted to monetary value.	☐	☐
9. The ROI Methodology contains too many complicated formulas.	☐	☐
10. The ROI Methodology can be implemented for about 3–5% of my budget.	☐	☐

	True	False
11. ROI is not future-oriented; it reflects only past performance.	☐	☐
12. It is not possible to measure ROI for soft-skills programs.	☐	☐
13. When an ROI impact study conducted on an existing program shows a negative ROI, the client is usually already aware of the program's weaknesses.	☐	☐
14. The best time to consider an ROI evaluation is three months after the program is completed.	☐	☐
15. In the early stages of implementation, the ROI Methodology is a process improvement tool and not a performance evaluation tool for the staff.	☐	☐
16. If senior executives are not asking for ROI, there is no need to pursue the ROI Methodology.	☐	☐

Quiz Answers

1. False
2. False
3. True
4. False
5. True
6. True
7. False
8. False
9. False
10. True
11. False
12. False
13. True
14. False
15. True
16. False

So, how did you do?

Now that the answers to the quiz have been given, see how you fared. Tally your score. Look at the interpretations that follow. What is your ROI acumen?

Number of Correct Responses	
14–16	You could be an ROI consultant!
10–13	You could be a speaker at the next ROI conference.
7–9	You need a copy of a thick ROI book.
4–6	You need to attend a two-day ROI workshop.
1–3	You need to attend the ROI certification.

6

Planning for Evaluation

The first part of this book presented the fundamentals of the ROI Methodology. Understanding the theoretical basis of the process is important, for it is the foundation of a successful, sustainable practice. This book now concludes by introducing the first step in the process. This step, evaluation planning, is the foundation of a successful ROI evaluation study.

Establishing Purpose and Feasibility

The first step in planning an evaluation is identifying the purpose and feasibility of conducting a comprehensive evaluation, including ROI.

Purpose

A clear evaluation purpose helps keep the evaluator and the team on track, preventing the project from becoming too overwhelming. Purpose keeps the evaluation focused on the "why," providing a basis for using the data once they are generated. All too often, an evaluation is conducted without understanding the reason for the process. Therefore, the raw data sit for days and months before the evaluator analyzes them to obtain the results. Defining the purpose of the evaluation helps determine the scope of the evaluation project. It drives the type of data to be collected as well as the type of data collection instruments used. Evaluation purposes range from demonstrating the value of a particular program to boosting the credibility of an entire function or department.

Make Decisions About Programs

Decisions are made every day, with and without evaluation data. But with evaluation data, departments can better influence those decisions. Evaluation data can aid decision making about a program prior to the launch of the program, for example, when ROI is forecast for a pilot program. Once the results of the evaluation are known, department leaders can decide whether to pursue the program further.

Evaluation data can help the staff make decisions about internal development issues. For example, reaction (Level 1) data provide information that helps determine the extent to which facilitators need additional skill building. Learning (Level 2) data can help the project leader decide whether an additional learning activity will better emphasize a skill that has been left undeveloped. Application (Level 3) data reveal the extent to which barriers are preventing employees from applying knowledge and skills on the job. Impact (Level 4) and ROI (Level 5) data help senior managers and executives decide whether they will continue investing in certain programs. The five levels of evaluation provide different types of data that influence different decisions.

Improve Programs and Processes

One of the most important purposes for generating comprehensive data with the ROI Methodology is improvement of programs and processes. As data are generated, the programs under evaluation can be adjusted so that future programs will be more effective than those that did not fare well according to the data. Reviewing evaluation data during early stages of the program or initiative allows the staff to apply additional tools and processes to support the program.

Evaluation data can help a function improve its accountability processes. By consistently evaluating programs, the function will find ways to collect and analyze data more efficiently through technology or through the use of experts within the organization. Evaluation will also cause the staff to view its programs and processes in a different light, asking such questions as, "Will this prove valuable to the organization?" "Can the organization get the same results for less cost?" and, "How can the staff influence the manager to better support this program?"

Demonstrate Program Value

The ultimate purpose of conducting comprehensive evaluation is to show the value of programs—specifically their economic value. However, when individual programs are considered for evaluation, the question is often "the value to whom?"

Value usually does not have one definition within an organization. Similar to the way learning occurs at the societal, community, team, and individual levels, value is defined from the perspectives of different stakeholders:

- Is a program valuable to those involved?

- Is a program valuable to the system that supports it?

- Is a program economically valuable?

The different definitions of value come from three perspectives. These perspectives are put into context by comparing them to the five-level ROI framework. Figure 6.1 presents these perspectives. The consumer perspective represents the extent to which those directly involved in the program react positively and acquire some level of knowledge or skills from their participation. The system perspective represents the supporting elements within the organization that make the program work. The economic perspective represents the extent to which the knowledge or skills that are transferred to the job positively affect key business measures. When appropriate,

Figure 6.1. Value Perspectives

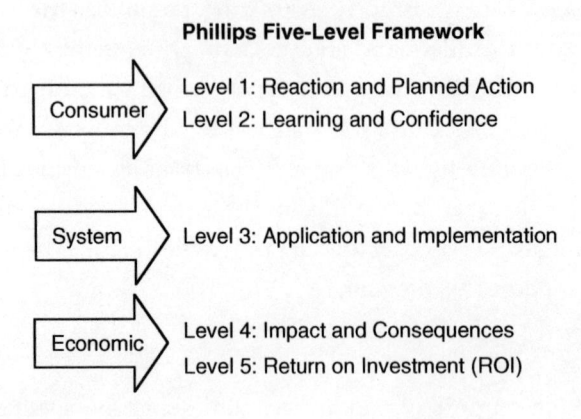

Phillips Five-Level Framework

Consumer → Level 1: Reaction and Planned Action
Level 2: Learning and Confidence

System → Level 3: Application and Implementation

Economic → Level 4: Impact and Consequences
Level 5: Return on Investment (ROI)

these benefits are converted to monetary values and compared to the costs of the program to calculate an economic value, ROI.

Consumer Perspective. Consumers are those who have an immediate connection with a program. Facilitators, designers, developers, and participants represent consumers. Value to this group is represented at Levels 1 and 2. Data from those levels provide feedback so that the staff can make immediate changes to a program as well as decide where developmental needs exist. The data also provide the participants with information on what the group thought about the program as well as how much success they had in learning the knowledge and skills taught in the program. Specific measures—those representing use of knowledge gained—are often used to predict the application of knowledge and skills that will occur when participants return to their jobs.

System Perspective. The system represents the people and functions that support programs within an organization. This group includes participants' managers, participants' peers, program team members, executives, and other support functions. While Level 3 data provide evidence of participants' application of their newly acquired knowledge and skills, the greatest value in evaluating at this level is determining the extent to which the system supported learning transfer and application of the program. This is determined by the barriers and enablers identified through the Level 3 evaluation.

Economic Perspective. The economic perspective is important for the client—the person or group funding the program. While certainly the participants' managers are interested in whether the program influenced business outcomes and may be interested in the ROI, the client—usually senior management—makes the financial investment in the program. Levels 4 and 5 provide data that show the economic value of the investment.

Feasibility

Program evaluations have multiple purposes. Even when a program is being evaluated at Level 5 in order to aid funding decisions, Level 1 data are still needed to improve delivery and design of the program. This is one reason that lower-level evaluations are conducted more often than higher-level ones. Other drivers that determine the feasibility of evaluating programs include validation of program objectives, availability of data, and appropriateness of the ROI Methodology for the organization.

Validation of Program Objectives

Program objectives are the fundamental basis for evaluation. Program objectives drive the design and development of a program and define how to measure success. Program objectives define what the program is intended to do, how to measure participant achievement, and a support system for application of the learning on the job. Evaluation provides data to determine whether these objectives have been met. Too often, however, too little emphasis is placed on developing objectives and defining their measures.

Availability of Data

Is information available that will determine whether the objectives have been met? The availability of Level 1 and Level 2 data is rarely a concern. Simply ask program participants for their opinion, test them, or facilitate role-playing or exercises to assess their overall understanding, and the data are there. Level 3 data are often obtained through follow-ups with participants or their managers, peers, or direct reports. The challenge is availability of Level 4 data. Are measures being monitored on a routine basis? If not, who or where is the best source of this information and how can it be collected?

Appropriateness for ROI Measurement

Program objectives and data availability are key drivers in determining the feasibility of evaluating a program's ROI. However, it is good to keep in mind that some programs are just not appropriate for an ROI evaluation.

The issue to consider in assessing the appropriateness of a program for ROI is whether it meets specific criteria. An inexpensive program offered on a one-time basis is usually not suitable for ROI. Why invest resources in conducting such a comprehensive evaluation on a program for which the data will serve no valuable or ongoing purpose? Basic skill building—for example, instruction in basic computer skills—is not always suitable for ROI. Sometimes, you just want to know that participants know how to do something rather than what impact their doing it has on the organization. Orientation or on-boarding programs are not always suitable for a full ROI evaluation—especially entry-level programs in which participants are just beginning their professional career.

Defining Program Objectives

Before evaluation begins, program objectives must be developed. Program objectives are linked to needs assessment. When a problem or opportunity is identified, needs assessment begins. Assessments are conducted to determine exactly what the problem is, how on-the-job performance change can resolve the problem, what knowledge or skills need to be acquired to change on-the-job performance, and how best to present the solution so that those involved, the consumers, can acquire the knowledge and skills to change performance and solve the business problem. From this point, program objectives are developed to guide program designers and developers, provide guidance to facilitators, establish goals for participants, and set up a framework for evaluators.

Program objectives reflect the same five-level ROI framework used in categorizing evaluation data (see Chapter One). When you are writing program objectives, the key is to be specific in identifying measures of success. All too often, very broad program objectives are stated. While broad objectives are acceptable in the initial phases of program design, it is specific measures of success that drive results and serve as the basis for evaluation.

Reaction Objectives

Level 1 objectives are critical because they describe expected immediate and long-term satisfaction with a program. They describe issues that are important to the success of the program, including facilitation, relevance and importance of content, logistics, and intended use of knowledge and skills. But there has been criticism of the use of Level 1 overall satisfaction as a measure of success. The overuse of the overall satisfaction measure has led many organizations to make funding decisions based on whether participants like a program; but later such organizations may find that the data were misleading.

Level 1 objectives should identify important, measurable issues rather than esoteric indicators that provide limited useful information. Level 1 objectives should be attitude-based, clearly worded, and specific. Level 1 objectives specify that the participants have changed their thinking or perceptions as a result of the program and underscore the link between attitude and the success of the program. While Level 1 objectives represent a satisfaction index from the consumer's perspective, these objectives should also be capable of predicting program success. Given these criteria, Level 1 objectives must be represented by specific measures of success.

A good predictor of the application of knowledge and skills is participants' perception of the relevance of a program's content. Thus, an example of a Level 1 objective might be

- At the end of the program, participants indicate that the program content is relevant to their job.

A question remains, however: "How will evaluators know that they have achieved this objective?" A more specific objective is

- At the end of the program, 80 percent of participants rate the program's relevance at 4.5 out of 5 on a Likert scale.

Those who are research-oriented might want to take the objective a step further by defining *relevance*. Relevance may be defined as

- Knowledge and skills that participants can immediately apply in their work

- Knowledge and skills reflective of participants' day-to-day work activities

If this is the case, the measures of success (the objectives) can be even more detailed:

- At the end of the program, 80 percent of the participants indicate that they can *immediately apply the knowledge and skills in their work* and indicate this by rating this measure at 4.5 out of 5 on a Likert scale.

- At the end of the program, 80 percent of the participants view the knowledge and skills as *reflective of their day-to-day work activities* and indicate this by rating this measure 4.5 out of 5 on a Likert scale.

The ratings on these two measures can be reported individually or combined to create a relevance index.

Overall satisfaction is often referred to as a measure of how much participants liked the cookies offered during a program or the shrimp at a conference. For example, recent analysis of a comprehensive Level 1 end-of-course questionnaire showed that participants viewed the program as less than relevant and not useful and that they had little intention of applying what they had learned. Mean scores were as follows:

- Knowledge and skills presented are relevant to my job. (2.8 out of 5)

- Knowledge and skills presented will be useful to my work. (2.6 out of 5)

- I intend to use what I learned in this course. (2.2 out of 5)

Surprisingly, however, respondents scored the overall satisfaction measure, "I am satisfied with the program," 4.6 out of 5. Perhaps they were rating the cookies.

Breaking down objectives to specific measures provides a clearer picture of success. However, it also lengthens your Level 1 data collection instrument and requires more analysis. The question to ask is, "Is this detail in my measures really needed?" For a program planned for an ROI evaluation, no. Simple but specific Level 1 objectives and measures are sufficient when evaluating a program to the ROI level. Conserve your resources for the more challenging tasks of Level 4 and Level 5 evaluation. Exhibit 6.1 summarizes the guidelines for Level 1 objectives.

Learning Objectives

Organizations are increasingly interested in evaluating the acquisition of knowledge and skills. Drivers of the heightened interest include an increase in the number of learning organizations, emphasis on intellectual capital, and more use of certification as a discriminator in the employee selection process. Given this, Level 2 objectives should be well defined.

Learning objectives communicate the expected outcomes of the program; they describe competent performance that should result from the program. The best learning objectives describe behaviors that are observable and measurable. Like reaction objectives, learning objectives are outcome-based. Clearly worded and specific, they spell out what the participant must do as a result of the skills and knowledge learned during the program.

A typical learning objective might be

- At the end of the program, participants will be able to implement Microsoft Word.

Sounds reasonable, but what does successful implementation look like? How will you know the objective has been achieved? Measures are needed to evaluate the success of learning, such as:

- At the end of the program, participants will be able to demonstrate to the facilitator the following applications of Microsoft Word within a ten-minute time period and with zero errors:
  - File, Save As, Save As Web Page

Exhibit 6.1. Guidelines for Reaction and Satisfaction Objectives

Reaction objectives are critical in this measurement chain because they

- Describe expected immediate and long-term satisfaction.
- Describe issues that are important to the success of the program.
- Provide a basis for evaluating the beginning of the measurement chain of impact.
- Place emphasis on planned action, if feasible.

The best reaction objectives

- Identify issues that are important and measurable.
- Are attitude-based, clearly worded, and specific.
- Specify that the participant has changed in thinking or perception as a result of the program.
- Underscore the link between attitude and the success of the program.
- Represent a satisfaction index from key stakeholders.
- Predict program success.

Key questions:

- How relevant is this program?
- How important is this program?
- Are the facilitators effective?
- How appropriate is this program?
- Is this new information?
- Is this program rewarding?
- Will you implement this program?
- Will you use the concepts or advice?
- What would keep you from implementing the objectives of this program?
- Would you recommend this program to others?

- Formatting, including font, paragraph, background, and themes
- Insert tables, add columns and rows, and delete columns and rows

Exhibit 6.2 summarizes the guidelines for Level 2 objectives.

Exhibit 6.2. Guidelines for Learning Objectives

Learning objectives are critical to measuring learning because they
- Communicate expected outcomes from instruction.
- Describe competent performance that should be the result of learning.
- Provide a basis for evaluating learning.
- Focus on learning for participants.

The best learning objectives
- Describe behaviors that are observable and measurable.
- Are outcome-based, clearly worded, and specific.
- Specify what the learner must do as a result of the learning.
- Have three components:
    1. *Performance:* what the learner will be able to do at the end of the program
    2. *Conditions:* circumstances under which the learner will perform the task
    3. *Criteria:* degree or level of proficiency that is necessary to perform the job

Three types of learning objectives are

1. *Awareness:* familiarity with terms, concepts, and processes
2. *Knowledge:* general understanding of concepts and processes
3. *Performance:* ability to demonstrate the skill (at least at a basic level)

Application Objectives

Whereas learning objectives describe what participants can do, Level 3 objectives describe what participants are expected to do to implement the program. Application objectives describe the expected intermediate outcomes of the program. They describe competent performance that should occur as a result of the program and provide the basis for evaluating on-the-job performance changes. The emphasis is on applying what was learned.

The best Level 3 objectives identify behaviors that are observable and measurable; in addition, they are outcome-based, clearly worded, specific, and spell out what the participant has changed as a result of the program.

A typical application objective might read like this:

- Participants will use effective meeting behaviors.

Again, specifics may be needed in order to define success. What are effective meeting behaviors, and to what degree should participants use those skills? Here are some examples of more specific objectives:

- Returning to their job, participants will develop a detailed agenda outlining the specific topics to be covered for 100 percent of their meetings.

- Participants will establish meeting ground rules at the beginning of 100 percent of their meetings.

- Participants will follow up on meeting action items within three days following 100 percent of their meetings.

Two important elements of Level 3 evaluation are barriers and enablers. Does the system support learning? Barriers to application as well as supporting elements (enablers) need to be examined. It is important to collect data about these issues so that corrective action can be taken when evidence of a problem exists. How can issues outside the program be controlled? For example, what should be done if participants indicate that their manager prevents them from applying newly acquired knowledge? Through the evaluation process, data are collected that prepare evaluators to engage in dialogue with managers. Bringing managers into the fold and asking them for help gets them involved in the process and helps gain their support. One example might be informing a group of managers that there is evidence that some managers do not support the project and that the group's advice on how to remedy the situation is needed. Initiating such a dialogue gives some control to evaluators.

Comprehensive assessment at Level 3 provides the tools to begin a dialogue with all stakeholders. Through such dialogue, managers and colleagues in other departments may admit, for example, that they do not understand the role of the program. Exhibit 6.3 summarizes the guidelines for Level 3 objectives.

Impact Objectives

Success in achieving Level 4 objectives is critical when a positive ROI is desired. Impact objectives provide the basis for measuring the application of skills and knowledge while placing emphasis on bottom-line results. The best impact objectives contain measures that are linked to the skills and knowledge in the program and are easily collected. Impact objectives are results-based, clearly worded, and specific. They spell out what a participant has accomplished in their business unit as a result of the program.

Impact objectives involving hard data are output, quality, cost, and time. Impact measures involving soft data are customer service, work climate, and attitudes.

Exhibit 6.3. Guidelines for Application Objectives

Application objectives are critical to measuring application of skills and knowledge because they

- Describe expected intermediate outcomes.
- Describe competent performance that should be the result of the program.
- Provide a basis for evaluation of on-the-job performance changes.
- Place emphasis on applying what was learned.

The best application objectives

- Identify behaviors that are observable and measurable.
- Are outcome-based, clearly worded, and specific.
- Specify what the participant has changed or will change as a result of the training.
- May have three components:
  1. *Performance:* what the participant has changed or accomplished at a specified follow-up time after the program
  2. *Conditions:* circumstances under which the participant performed the task
  3. *Criteria:* degree or level of proficiency at which the task or job was performed

Two types of application objectives are

- *Knowledge-based:* general use of concepts and processes
- *Behavior-based:* demonstration of the skill (at least at a basic level)

Key questions:

- What new or improved knowledge will be applied on the job?
- What new or improved skill will be applied on the job?
- What will be the frequency of skill application?
- What new tasks will be performed?
- What new steps will be implemented?
- What new action items will be implemented?
- What new procedures will be implemented or changed?
- What new guidelines will be implemented or changed?
- What new processes will be implemented or changed?

For example, the beer industry is losing market share to high-end spirits. Coors implements a marketing strategy that includes new ads showing a sleek, silver Love Train delivering Coors to upscale partygoers (Howard, 2005). The impact objective and measure of success might look like this:

- Increase market share of young professionals by 10 percent within nine months of new ad launch

In another example, a large multinational computer manufacturer prides itself on the quality of the computer systems it sells and the service provided when problems arise. The company makes it easy for purchasers to secure assistance by selling lucrative warranties on all of its products. One particular system, the X-1350, comes with a three-year warranty that includes "gold standard" technical support for only an additional $105.

In the past year, the number of calls to repair contractors has increased, particularly in regard to the X-1350. This increase is costing the company not only money but also customer satisfaction. A new program is implemented to improve the quality of the computer. The impact objective and specific measures of success are

- Reduce the number of warranty claims on the X-1350 by 10 percent within six months after the start of the program

- Improve by 10 percent the overall customer satisfaction with the quality of the X-1350 as indicated by a customer satisfaction survey taken six months after the start of the program

- Achieve top box scores on product quality measures included in an industry quality survey

Exhibit 6.4. Guidelines for Impact Objectives

Impact objectives are critical to measuring business performance because they

- Describe expected outcomes.
- Describe business unit performance that should be the result of a program.
- Provide a basis for measuring the consequences of application of skills and knowledge.
- Place emphasis on achieving bottom-line results.

The best impact objectives

- Contain measures that are linked to the skills and knowledge of the program.
- Describe measures that are easily collected.
- Are results-based, clearly worded, and specific.
- Specify what the participants have accomplished in their business unit as a result of the program.

Four types of impact objectives involving hard data are

- Output-focused
- Quality-focused
- Cost-focused
- Time-focused

Three common types of impact objectives involving soft data are

- Customer service–focused
- Work climate–focused
- Work habit–focused

Exhibit 6.4 summarizes the guidelines for Level 4 objectives.

ROI Objectives

Level 5 objectives target the specific economic return anticipated when an investment is made in a program. This objective defines *good* when someone asks, "What is a good ROI?" When you are setting a target ROI, there are four options. The first is to set the target ROI at the same level as the desired ROI for capital investments in plant, equipment, and buildings. Targeting the same ROI for programs and capital investments is not uncommon. Many groups use this approach to ensure a link with operations. To establish this target, finance and accounting should be asked what the average return is for other investments.

Another option for establishing ROI objectives is to raise the bar for the program, setting the target ROI at a higher level than for other investments. Because programs affect so many and contribute so much to an organization, expecting a higher-than-normal ROI is not unreasonable.

Some organizations are satisfied with another option: a 0 percent ROI—that is, breaking even. Breaking even means that the organization got its investment back; for example, if an organization spent $50,000 on a program and the benefits were $50,000, there was no gain, but the investment was returned. Many organizations—such as public sector, nonprofit, community, and faith-based organizations—value the break-even ROI.

A fourth way to set an ROI objective is to ask the client. The client is the person or group that is funding the program. This person or group may be willing to invest in a program for a specific return on investment. Exhibit 6.5 summarizes the guidelines for establishing a Level 5 target.

Exhibit 6.5. Guidelines for ROI Objectives

Level 5 objectives are established by considering the following:

- Current level of return on capital investments
- A percentage return higher than typical for investment returns on capital equipment
- Break-even
- Client needs and expectations

Developing the Planning Documents

Three basic documents must be created when you are planning an ROI evaluation: a data collection plan, an ROI analysis plan, and a project plan. If you are thorough in completing these documents, your ROI evaluation plan will be well under way. Once they are completed, the client should sign off on the plan for evaluation. By taking this important step, the client buys into and shows confidence in the approach.

Data Collection Plan

The data collection plan lays the initial groundwork for the ROI study. Table 6.1 presents an example of a completed data collection plan. The columns of this plan hold the answers to several questions.

What Do You Ask?

The answers to this question lie in the program objectives and their respective measures. Specific measurable objectives and measures of success are the basis of the questions you will ask. When broad objectives are developed, the measures must be clearly described so that you will know when success is achieved.

How Do You Ask?

How you will ask for the information depends on a variety of issues, including the resources available for data collection. Level 1 data are typically collected by means of an end-of-course questionnaire. To collect Level 2 data, tests, role-playing, self-assessments, and facilitator assessments are used. Obtaining application data (Level 3) and impact data (Level 4) is the most challenging. However, a variety of options are available, including questionnaires, focus groups, interviews, action plans, and performance monitoring. These options provide flexibility and ensure that a lack of data collection methods is not a barrier to assessing the application and impact of a program.

Table 6.1. Completed Data Collection Plan

Data Collection Plan—Metro Transit Authority
Program: Absenteeism Reduction
Evaluation Purpose: Responsibility: Jack Phillips
Date: January 15

Level	Broad Program Objective(s)	Measures	Data Collection Method and Instruments	Data Sources	Timing	Responsibility
1	**REACTION AND PLANNED ACTION** • Positive employee reaction to the no fault policy	• Positive reaction from employees	• Feedback questionnaire	• Employees	• At the end of employee meetings	• Supervisors
2	**LEARNING** • Employee understanding of the policy	• Score of at least 70 on posttest	• True/false test	• Employees	• At the end of employee meetings	• Supervisors

3 **APPLICATION AND IMPLEMENTATION**

1. Effective and consistent implementation and enforcement of the program

2. Little or no adverse reaction from current employees toward no fault policy

3. Use the new screening process

1. Supervisors' response on program's influence	1. & 2. Follow-up questionnaire to supervisors (two sample groups)	1. & 2. Supervisors
2. Employee complaints and union cooperation		
	3. Sample review of interview and selection records	3. Company records

1. & 2. Following employee meetings, sample one group at three months and another group at six months

2. Three months and six months after implementation

1., 2., & 3. HR program coordinator

(*Continued*)

Table 6.1. Completed Data Collection Plan (*Continued*)

Level	Broad Program Objective(s)	Measures	Data Collection Method and Instruments	Data Sources	Timing	Responsibility
4	**IMPACT**					
	1. Reduce driver absenteeism at least 2% during first year	1. Absenteeism	1. Monitor absenteeism	1. Company records	1. Monitor monthly; analyze one year before and one year after implementation	1., 2., & 3. HR program coordinator
	2. Maintain present level of job satisfaction as new policy is implemented	2. Employee satisfaction	2. Follow-up questionnaire to supervisors	2. Supervisors	2. Three months and six months after employee meetings	
	3. Improved customer service and satisfaction with reduction in schedule delays	3. Impact of delays on customer service	3. Monitor bus schedule delays	3. Dispatch records	3. Monthly	
5	**ROI**					
	Target ROI 25%					

Comments:

Whom Do You Ask?

Data sources are critical. Only the most credible sources should be used, and sometimes, maximizing credibility means using multiple sources to corroborate the data. The more credible the sources of the data, the more reliable the data are. The only constraint is the expense of going to multiple sources.

When Do You Ask?

The timing of data collection is critical, and getting it right is sometimes a challenge. Enough time must pass to allow new behaviors to become routine, but not so long that participants might forget how they developed the new behavior. Also, enough time must pass to allow results to occur, yet most executives are not willing to wait a year. Therefore, a time must be chosen with which all stakeholders are comfortable.

Who Asks?

Who will be responsible for each step in the data collection process? Typically, the facilitator or project leader collects data at Levels 1 and 2. For the higher levels of evaluation, representatives of the evaluation team are assigned specific roles, including data collection. A person or team is assigned the task of developing the data collection instrument and administering it. This task includes developing a strategy to ensure an adequate response rate.

ROI Analysis Plan

The second evaluation planning document is the ROI analysis plan (see Table 6.2 for an example). The ROI analysis plan identifies several elements.

Methods for Isolating the Effects of the Program

The technique that will be used to isolate the effects of the program must be chosen. Typically, the method of isolation is the same for all measures. Sometimes, some measures can be isolated through

Table 6.2. Completed ROI Analysis Plan

ROI Analysis Plan—Metro Transit Authority
Program: Absenteeism Reduction   **Responsibility:** Jack Phillips   **Date:** January 15

Data Items (Usually Level 4)	Methods for Isolating the Effects of the Program or Process	Methods for Converting Data to Monetary Values	Cost Categories	Intangible Benefits	Communication Targets for Final Report	Other Influences and Issues	Comments
1. Absenteeism 2. Employee job satisfaction 3. Bus schedule delays (influence on customer satisfaction)	1. Trend line analysis and supervisor estimates 2. Supervisor estimates 3. Management estimates	1. Wages and benefits and standard values N/A N/A	**Screening Process** • Development • Interviewer preparation • Administration • Materials **No Fault Policy** • Development • • Implementation • Materials **Evaluation**	• Sustain employee satisfaction • Improve employee morale • Improve customer satisfaction • Fewer disruptive bottlenecks in transportation grid • Ease of implementation by supervisors	• Senior management • Managers and supervisors • Union representatives • HR staff	• Concern about whether supervisors are providing consistent administration • Partner with union reps on how to communicate results of study to employees	

the use of a control group, but other measures have to use another technique.

Methods for Converting Data to Monetary Values

The ROI analysis plan identifies the methods for converting impact measures to monetary values. In some cases, a measure will purposely not be converted to a monetary value.

Cost Categories

This section includes all the costs of the program. These costs include needs assessment, program design and development, program delivery, evaluation costs, and some amount for overhead and administrative costs for the people and processes that support the program. Each cost category is listed on the ROI analysis plan.

Intangible Benefits

Not all measures will be converted to monetary values. The measures that are not converted to monetary values are considered intangible benefits. Any Level 4 measures that are not converted to monetary values should be moved to this column. Also, this column includes any anticipated intangible benefits that might occur as a result of the program.

Communication Targets for the Final Report

In many cases, organizations plan their communication targets in detail. During the evaluation planning phase, the audiences to whom the final report will be submitted should be identified. Four key audiences always get a copy or summary of the report: participants, staff, participants' supervisors, and client.

Other Application Influences and Issues

This section provides an opportunity to anticipate any issues that might occur during the program that might have a negative effect (as well as ones that might have no effect) on the identified measures. This column can also be used to list issues that might have a negative effect on the evaluation process.

Comments

The final section of the ROI analysis plan is for comments. Notes can be included to remind the evaluation team of key issues. Comments about the potential success or failure of the program can be listed in this column as well as reminders of specific tasks to be conducted by the evaluation team.

The importance of planning the data collection for an ROI analysis cannot be stressed enough. Carefully planning, in detail, what will be asked, how it will be asked, who will be asked, when to ask, and who will do the asking, along with the key steps in the ROI analysis, will ensure successful implementation. In addition, having clients sign off on the plans will ensure support when the evaluation results are presented.

Project Plan

After the data collection plan and the ROI analysis plan have been developed, the next step is to develop a simple project plan. This plan is essentially a timeline of the major steps, activities, and milestones in implementing the program and conducting an ROI evaluation. It should be simple, perhaps using whatever project management tool is typically used in any organization. It begins with the planning stage and ends when all the steps are completed and the data are communicated to the appropriate audiences. Some add another step and track adjustments and changes that are made after the results have been communicated. Exhibit 6.6 shows a simple, completed project plan.

Exhibit 6.6. Project Plan

	FEB	MAR	APR	MAY	JUN	JUL	AUG	SEP
Decision to conduct ROI study	■							
Evaluation planning complete	■							
Instruments designed	■							
Instruments pilot-tested		■						
Data collected from Group A		■	■					
Data collected from Group B				■				
Data collected from Group C					■			
Data tabulation preliminary summary					■			
Analysis conducted						■		
Report written						■		
Report printed						■		
Results communicated							■	
Improvements initiated							■	
Implementation complete								■

Conducting the Planning Meeting

The evaluation planning meeting is crucial to developing the plans described in this chapter. In most situations, it is a formal meeting with specific individuals involved, an agenda, and a strategy for success.

Who Should Be Involved

Essentially, the people who know the program or project best should be involved: the person who owns the program, the individual who will design it, the person who analyzed the initial need for the program, the facilitator, and a person in the business unit who understands the business data. Perhaps one of the most important individuals is the subject matter expert who understands the content of the program. If it's appropriate and feasible, having these typical participants at the meeting may be useful. Each may uncover issues not seen by the others.

Agenda

The agenda should be simple and basic, and it should include the following items:

- Explanation of the purpose of the program
- Finalized or adjusted objectives
- Completed data collection plan
- Completed ROI analysis plan
- Completed project plan

The meeting can usually be accomplished (1) in a day for individuals who are just beginning to use the ROI Methodology, (2) in about a half day as confidence builds and comfort and expertise increases, or (3) with help from some technology to support data entry, in two hours.

Factors for Success

The evaluation planning meeting must be successful because it is the beginning point of the process, and all the key decisions about the evaluation, methodology, and approach are defined within it. Several factors can contribute to success. First, the most credible sources must either attend the meeting or be available to the group. Full access to data must be available, and in some cases, the data should be brought to the meeting. All the issues that might affect the program's success must be covered completely during this meeting. It should move quickly to save the precious time of the group. The output of the meeting should be considered a draft, not final; the planning documents may go through several iterations before they are finalized. At the end of the meeting, the key sponsor of the project or program should sign the planning documents, stating that he or she approves and understands the approaches that are being taken. This can avoid confusion, frustration, and disappointment later in the project or, even worse, when the results are presented.

Identifying Data Sources

When considering the possible sources for data collection, six categories are easily defined. Each source will have its advantages and disadvantages.

Organizational Performance Records

The most useful and credible data source for an ROI analysis is the records and reports of the organization. Whether individualized or group-based, the records reflect performance in a work unit, department, division, region, or the entire organization. Organizational records can include all types of measures, which are usually available in abundance throughout the organization. Collecting data from performance records is preferred for Level 4 evaluation because the data usually reflect business impact data and are relatively easy to obtain. However, sloppy record keeping by some organizations may make locating some data difficult.

Participants

The most widely used data source for an ROI analysis is program participants. Participants are frequently asked about their reactions and planned actions, the extent of their learning, and how they have applied the skills and knowledge on the job. Sometimes, they are asked to explain the impact of those actions. Participants are a rich source of data at Levels 1, 2, 3, and 4. They are credible because they are the individuals who were involved in the program and who achieved the performance. Also, they are often the most knowledgeable about the processes and other influencing factors. The challenge is finding an effective and efficient method of capturing data consistently.

Participants' Managers

Another important source of data is the immediate managers of the program participants. This group will often have a vested interest in the evaluation process because they approved the participants' involvement in the program. In many situations, they observe the participants as they attempt to apply the knowledge and skills acquired through the program. Consequently, they can report on the successes linked to the program as well as the difficulties and problems associated with application. Although manager input is usually best for Level 3 data, it can be useful for Level 4. However, the managers must maintain objectivity and give an unbiased assessment of the program participants.

Participants' Direct Reports

In situations in which supervisors and managers are involved in a program, their direct reports can provide information about perceived changes in observable behavior that have occurred since the program. Input from direct reports is appropriate for Level 3 data (behavior) but not necessarily Level 4 (impact). Collecting data from a manager's direct reports can be very helpful and instructive; however, it is often avoided because of potential biases that can enter into the feedback process.

Team or Peer Group

Individuals who are teammates of the participant or who occupy peer-level positions within the organization are another potential source of data for a few types of programs. In these situations, peers provide input on perceived behavioral changes of participants (Level 3). This source of data is more appropriate when all team members participate in the program and, consequently, when they report on the collective efforts of the group or behavioral changes of specific individuals. Because of the subjective nature of this process and the lack of opportunity to fully evaluate the application of skills, this source of data is somewhat limited.

Internal and External Groups

In some situations, internal or external groups, such as project staff, program facilitators, expert observers, or external consultants, may provide input on the success of individuals when they learn and apply the skills and knowledge involved in a program. Sometimes, expert observers or assessors may be used to measure learning (Level 2). This source may also be useful for on-the-job observation (Level 3) after the program has been completed. Collecting data from internal or external groups has limited uses. Because internal groups may have a vested interest in the outcome of evaluation, their input may not be very credible.

Final Thoughts

This chapter detailed the entire ROI evaluation planning process. From establishing the purpose of the program to identifying data sources, evaluation planning is the critical first step for successful programs. Each step of the planning process must be completed so that essential data are collected at the right time, analyzed, and reported to the right people. Without this evaluation framework in place—from the beginning—the program is likely doomed to fail. Once the planning process has been established and a data collection plan, ROI analysis plan, and project plan have been signed by all stakeholders, the program and the data collection can begin.

Reference

Howard, T. "Brewers Get into the Spirits of Marketing." USA *Today*, May 16, 2005, p. 18.

Appendix: Resources

The Bottomline on ROI, by Patricia Pulliam Phillips. Atlanta, Ga.: Center for Effective Performance, 2002.

The Chief Learning Officer, by Tamar Elkeles and Jack J. Phillips. Woburn, Mass. Butterworth-Heinemann, 2006.

The Consultant's Scorecard, by Jack J. Phillips. New York: McGraw-Hill, 2000.

Handbook of Training Evaluation and Measurement Methods, by Jack J. Phillips. (3rd ed.) Woburn, Mass.: Butterworth-Heinemann, 1997.

How to Measure Training Results, by Jack J. Phillips and Ron Drew Stone. New York: McGraw-Hill, 2002.

The Human Resources Scorecard, by Jack J. Phillips, Patricia Pulliam Phillips, and Ron Drew Stone. Woburn, Mass.: Butterworth-Heinemann, 2001.

The Leadership Scorecard, by Jack J. Phillips and Lynn Schmidt. Woburn, Mass.: Butterworth-Heinemann, 2004.

Make Training Evaluation Work, by Jack J. Phillips, Patricia Pulliam Phillips, and Tony Krucky Hodges. Alexandria, Va.: ASTD, 2004.

The Project Management Scorecard, by Jack J. Phillips, Timothy W. Bothell, and G. Lynne Snead. Woburn, Mass.: Butterworth-Heinemann, 2002.

Proving the Value of HR: How and Why to Measure ROI, by Jack J. Phillips and Patricia Pulliam Phillips. Alexandria, Va.: Society for Human Resource Management, 2005.

Proving the Value of Meetings and Events, by Jack J. Phillips, Monica Myhill, and James B. McDonough. Birmingham, Ala.: ROI Institute and MPI, 2007.

Return on Investment in Training and Performance Improvement Programs, by Jack J. Phillips. (2nd ed.) Woburn, Mass.: Butterworth-Heinemann, 2003.

Return on Investment (ROI) Basics, by Patricia Pulliam Phillips and Jack J. Phillips. Alexandria, Va.: ASTD, 2005.

ROI at Work: Best-Practice Case Studies from the Real World, by Jack J. Phillips and Patricia Pulliam Phillips. Alexandria, Va.: ASTD, 2005.

The ROI Field Book, by Patricia Pulliam Phillips, Jack J. Phillips, Ron D. Stone, and Holly Burkett. Woburn, Mass.: Butterworth-Heinemann, 2006.

Show Me the Money: How to Determine ROI in People, Projects, and Programs, by Jack J. Phillips and Patricia Pulliam Phillips. San Francisco: Berrett-Koehler, 2007.

The Value of Learning, by Patricia Pulliam Phillips and Jack J. Phillips. San Francisco: Pfeiffer, 2007.

Index

A

Accountability
  organizational drivers requiring additional, 55
  paradigm shift toward, 33
  ROI applications and trend toward, 38–39
  ROI used to evaluate, 34
Action plans, 16–17
American Productivity and Quality Center, 9, 32
American Society for Training and Development (ASTD), 9, 32
Anthony, R. N., 67
Application and implementation. *See* Level 3 (Application and Implementation)
Application objectives, 111–112, 113

B

Benefit-cost analysis
  calculating benefit-cost ratio (BCR), 23–24
  comparing Phillips's five-level evaluation with, 71–72
  of intangible benefits, 22, 25, 75
  of program costs, 22–23
  See also Costs

Benefit-cost ratio (BCR)
  as acceptable ROI formula, 43
  calculating, 23–24
Best practices. *See* ROI best practices
Burkett, H., 84
Business impact. *See* Level 5 (Return on Investment)
Business performance monitoring, 17
Business Week, 39

C

Case studies
  on calculating intangible benefits, 25
  on calculating program costs, 25
  as data conversion technique, 25
  on impact objectives (Coors and X-1350 system), 114
  on isolating program effects, 25
  on ROI Methodology for evaluations, 24–26
  on using each individual level of evaluation, 25
  value of development of, 76
Change
  new leaders as catalyst for, 58–59
  organizational use of ROI during, 55
  possible through good change management, 92–93
  ROI for facilitating, 36–37

Clients
　as ROI audience, 40–41
　ROI Methodology changes for, 93
Comments (ROI analysis plan), 124
Communication
　on evaluation process to management, 81
　of ROI result to key stakeholders, 75–76
　See also Reporting
Consumer value perspective, 102
Control group, 17–18
Coors impact objectives, 114
Cost of quality, 20
Costs
　as barrier to implementation, 83–84
　historical, 20
　program, 23, 25, 75
　of quality, 20
　ROI analysis plan on categories of, 123
　of ROI Methodology, 44
　tips for reducing implementation, 84
　See also Benefit-cost analysis
Credibility
　Guiding Principle on enhancing, 73
　ROI myth on ROI's, 90
Customer program effects input, 19

D

Data
　accounting for missing, 74
　availability of, 104
　avoiding extreme, 74–75
　conversion of, 19–21, 25
　ROI myth of ROI being only one type of, 88–89
　sources of, 11–12, 73
Data analysis
　benefit-cost, 23
　conservative approach to, 73
　converting data into monetary value for, 19–21
　credibility issue of, 73
　intangible benefits assessed during, 22, 25, 75
　ROI process model phase of, 2
Data collection
　credibility issue of, 73
　at the lower levels, 73
　methods available for, 14, 16–17
　planning timing of the, 10
　responsibility for, 121
　ROI best practice on, 49
　ROI process model phase of, 2
Data collection plans
　questions to ask when developing, 117, 121
　sample examples of, 10–12, 118–120
Data conversion
　case study technique for, 25
　described, 19–21
　ROI analysis plan on, 123
　techniques used for, 20–21
Data sources
　credibility of, 73
　internal and external groups as, 129
　organizational performance records as, 127
　participants and managers as, 127–128
　planning for, 10, 121
　sample data collection plan on, 11–12
　team or peer group as, 128–129

E

Economic value perspective, 103
Errors of estimation, 74
Evaluation framework
　comparing Phillips's with cost-benefit analysis, 71–72
　Kirkpatrick's, 67, 70–71
　as part of the evaluation puzzle, 67–72
　Phillips's five levels of evaluation, 6–7, 68–69

Evaluation levels
  comparing cost-benefit analysis and Phillips's five, 71–72
  evaluating at both higher and lower, 72
  overview of Phillips's five, 6–7, 68–69
  See also specific levels
Evaluation planning
  conducting meeting for, 125–127
  consequences of lack of, 45
  defining program objectives, 9, 11–12, 104–116
  on degree of comprehensive evaluation, 73
  developing planning documents, 117–125
  establishing feasibility, 103–104
  establishing purpose, 99–103
  five specific elements of, 9–10
  identifying data sources, 127–129
  implementation barrier of inadequate, 86
  ROI analysis plan, 10, 13
  ROI process model phase of, 2
  sample project plan, 11–12
Evaluation puzzle
  development of case studies element of, 76
  evaluation framework element of the, 67–72
  implementation element of, 77–81
  major elements of the, 65–66
  operating standards/guiding principles element of, 72
  ROI process model element of, 2, 72
Evaluations
  case study on using ROI Methodology for, 24–26
  four specific steps of, 67
  isolation of program effects problem in, 17–19, 25, 49, 74
  linking program objectives to, 104–105
  overview of each level of, 6–7, 68–69
  planning, 9–13, 45
  ROI process model of, 2, 72
  ultimate level of, 6–7, 36
  See also Programs; ROI Methodology
Evaluators
  checklist for ROI implementation for, 94
  ROI Methodology changes for, 93
Experts
  program effects estimates by, 19
  value of improvement estimated by, 20
External databases, 20–21
External group data, 129
Extreme data, 74–75

F

Fear of failure, 44–45, 85
Feasibility drivers
  appropriateness for ROI measurement, 104
  availability of data, 104
  determining, 103
  validation of program objectives, 103
Financial Times, 39
Focus groups, 16
Forecasting model, 18
Fortune (magazine), 39

G

Guiding Principles. *See* ROI Guiding Principles

H

Harvard Business Review (HBR), 34, 39
Historical costs, 20
Horngren, C. T., 67
Howard, T., 114

I

Impact objectives, 112, 114–115
Implementation
  checklist for ROI, 94
  inhibitors to, 83–93
  ROI Quiz for assessing readiness for, 96–98
  steps for, 77–81
  tips for reducing cost of, 84
Implementation barriers
  costs and time as, 83–84
  faulty or inadequate initial analysis, 85
  fear, 85
  lack of discipline and planning, 86
  lack of skills, 84–85
Implementation inhibitors
  barriers to implementation as, 83–86
  change management as possible, 92–93
  ROI myths as, 86–92
Implementation steps
  1: assign responsibilities, 77
  2: develop skills, 77–78
  3: develop an implementation plan, 78–81
  4: prepare or revise evaluation guidelines, 81
  5: brief managers on the evaluation process, 81
Intangible benefits
  calculating measures of, 22
  case study on calculating, 25
  reporting, 75
  ROI data analysis on, 123
Internal group data, 129
International Federation of Training and Development Organizations, 32
International Society for Performance Improvement (ISPI), 32
Interviews, 16

Isolating program effects
  case study techniques for, 25
  importance of, 74
  ROI analysis plan on, 121, 123
  as ROI best practice, 49
  techniques for solving problem of, 17–19

K

Kearsley, G., 67
Kirkpatrick, D., 67

L

Learning
  barriers and enablers of, 111–112
  objectives of, 11, 108–110
Learning objectives
  described, 108, 110
  guidelines for, 110
  sample data collection plan, 11
Level 0 (Inputs and Indicators), 1, 3, 6
Level 1 (Reaction and Planned Action)
  availability of data in, 104
  case study on using, 25
  consumer value perspective represented in, 102
  data sources during, 127
  decision making using data from, 100
  interviews used during, 16
  Phillips's framework on, 3, 6, 68
  questionnaires used during, 16
  reaction and satisfaction objectives, 105–108, 109
  sample data collection plan on, 11
  surveys used during, 14
Level 2 (Learning and Confidence)
  availability of data in, 104
  case study on using, 25
  consumer value perspective represented in, 102
  data sources during, 127, 129

decision making using data from, 100
interviews used during, 16
Phillips's framework on, 3–4, 6, 68
questionnaires used during, 16
sample data collection plan on, 11
surveys used during, 14
tests used during, 16
Level 3 (Application and Implementation)
action plans and program assignments used during, 16–17
application objectives of, 111–112, 113
availability of data in, 104
case study on using, 25
data sources during, 127–129
decision making using data from, 100
focus groups used during, 16
interviews used during, 16
on-the-job observation used during, 16
performance contracts used during, 17
Phillips's framework on, 4–5, 7, 68
questionnaires used during, 16
sample data collection on, 12
surveys used during, 14
system value perspective represented in, 102–103
Level 4 (Impact and Consequences)
action plans and program assignments used during, 16–17
availability of data in, 104
business performance monitoring used during, 17
case study on using, 25
data conversion during, 19–22
data sources during, 127–128
decision making using data from, 100
economic value perspective represented in, 103
examining feasibility of, 9

impact objectives of, 112, 114–115
performance contracts used during, 17
Phillips's framework on, 5, 7, 68
questionnaires used during, 16
sample data collection on, 12
selecting programs for, 8
Level 5 (Return on Investment)
case study on using, 25
decision making using data from, 100
economic value perspective represented in, 103
establishing target ROI, 10
examining feasibility of, 9
Phillips's framework on, 5, 7, 8, 68
ROI objectives of, 115–116
sample data collection on, 12
selecting programs for, 8
See also ROI (return on investment)

M

Managers
as data source, 128
program effects estimated by, 18
See also Participants; Senior management
Measures
at each level of evaluation, 6–7
intangible benefits, 22, 25, 75
organizational focus on, 55
organizational investment in, 58
sample data collection plan on, 11–12
of value, 21
See also ROI (return on investment)
Monetary values
data conversion to, 19–21, 25
ROI analysis plan on converting data to, 123
ROI best practice of converting program results to, 51

N

Needs assessment
  ROI Methodology used for, 57
  ROI results in case of faulty, 44, 85

O

Objectives
  defining program, 104–115
  developing evaluation, 9
  ROI, 115–116
  sample data collection plan, 11–12
  validation of program, 103
Observation, 16
On-the-job observation, 16
Organizational performance records, 127
Organizations
  characteristics of those using ROI, 54–55
  self-checking readiness of your, 60–61
  signs of readiness for ROI Methodology, 57–61
  taking a reactive versus proactive approach, 61–62
  typical programs using ROI Methodology in, 55–57
Output data conversion, 20

P

Participants
  as data course, 127
  data on wages and benefits, 20
  isolating from program effects, 18
  ROI Methodology changes for, 93
  See also Managers
Peer group data, 128–129
Performance contracts, 17
Phillips, J. J., 10, 67
Phillips, P. P., 9, 10, 84
Phillips's five-level framework
  comparison of cost-benefit analysis and, 71–72
  overview of, 6–7, 68–69
  value perspectives in, 102–103

Planning documents
  data collection plans, 10–12, 117–121
  project plan, 15, 78–80, 124–125
  ROI analysis plan, 10, 13, 121–124
  See also Sample plans
Planning meeting
  agenda for, 126
  factors for success, 126–127
  who should be involved in, 125
Practitioners
  as ROI audience, 40
  ROI process criteria for satisfying, 41–43
Program assignments, 16–17
Program costs
  benefit-cost analysis of, 22–23
  case study on calculating, 25
  Guiding Principles on accounting for, 75
Program objectives
  application, 111–112, 113
  impact, 112, 114–115
  learning, 108, 110
  linking assessment to, 104–105
  reaction and satisfaction, 105–108, 109
  validation of, 103
Program value
  consumer perspective on, 102
  economic perspective on, 103
  Phillips's five-level framework on, 101–102
  ROI for measuring, 46, 101–103
  system perspective on, 102–103
Programs
  costs of, 22–23, 25, 75
  isolating effects of, 17–19, 25, 49, 74, 121, 123
  paradigm shift toward accountability in, 33
  ROI for making decision about/improving, 100–101
  ROI for measuring contributions of, 46, 101–103

types using ROI Methodology, 55–57
See also Evaluations
Project plan
  description and purpose of, 124
  samples of, 15, 80, 125
  steps in developing, 78–79
Purpose
  improving programs and processes, 100–101
  making decision about program, 100
  need for establishing, 99–100

Q
Questionnaires, 14, 16

R
Reaction/satisfaction objectives, 105–107, 109
Reece, J. S., 67
Reporting
  communicating ROI results to key stakeholders, 75–76
  intangible benefits, 75
  ROI data analysis on communication targets for, 123
  ROI process model phase of, 2, 24
  See also Communication
Researchers
  as ROI audience, 41
  ROI process criteria for satisfying, 41–43
Responsibilities
  for data collection process, 121
  implementation step of assigning, 77
  sample data collection plan on, 11–12
ROI analysis plan, 10, 13, 121–124
ROI applications
  across fields and sectors, 30–31
  business mindset of support managers facilitating, 37–38
  change, quality, and reengineering facilitating, 36–37, 55

false assumptions about, 45–46
global expansion of, 32
increased budgets facilitating, 35–36
trend toward accountability increasing, 38–39
ROI audiences
  practitioners as, 40
  researchers as, 41
  senior managers, sponsors, and clients as, 40–41, 47, 57
  See also Stakeholders
ROI best practices
  conversion of program results to monetary values as, 51
  development of, 47–48
  establishing evaluation targets, 48
  isolation of the program as, 17–19, 25, 49, 74
  microlevel evaluation as, 48
  sampling for ROI calculations as, 49–50
  using variety of data collection methods, 49
ROI Guiding Principles
  1: report the complete story, 73
  2: conserve important resources, 73
  3: enhance credibility, 73
  4: be conservative, 73
  5: account for other factors, 74
  6: account for missing data, 74
  7: adjust estimates for error, 74
  8: omit the extremes, 74–75
  9: capture annual benefits for short-term programs, 75
  10: account for all program costs, 75
  11: report intangible benefits, 75
  12: communicate results, 75–76
ROI Methodology
  applications of, 30–31
  barriers to, 43–46
  benefit-cost analysis using, 22–24
  case study on use of, 24–26
  data collection phase of, 2, 14–17

ROI Methodology (*Cont.*)
  data conversion phase of, 19–21
  described, 1
  evaluation planning phase of, 9–14
  Guiding Principles of, 72–76
  illustrated diagram of, 2
  implementation of, 77–97
  isolating of program effects, 17–19, 25, 49, 74
  organizational use of, 54–63
  origins and development of, 53
  reactive versus proactive approach to, 61–62
  reporting phase of, 24
  as results-based process, 46–47
  self-checking your organization's readiness for, 60–61
  summary of the current status of the, 35
  See also Evaluations; Sample plans; *specific levels*
ROI myths
  controversy over, 86–87
  isolating effects of external influences as not possible, 91
  on measuring on-the-job activities, 91–92
  ROI is a passing fad, 88
  ROI is appropriate only for large organizations, 92
  ROI is not a credible process, 90
  ROI is not future-oriented, 89
  ROI is only for manufacturing/service organizations, 90–91
  ROI is only one type of data, 88–89
  ROI is rarely used by organizations, 89
  ROI is too complex for most users, 87
  ROI is too expensive, 87
  ROI Methodology cannot be easily replicated, 89
ROI Methodology has no standards, 92
ROI not needed without senior management demand, 87–88
ROI Network, 32
ROI objectives, 115–116
ROI Quiz, 96–98
ROI (return on investment)
  as accepted business tool, 34–39
  applications across fields and sectors, 30–31
  barriers to implementation of, 43–46
  benefits of using, 46–47, 75
  best practices for, 47–51
  concerns about using, 39–43
  global expansion of applications of, 32
  growth as conference topic, 32
  increasing focus on measuring, 27–28
  reviewing global trends in use of, 29–30
  shift from activity to results like, 33–34
  See also Level 5 (Return on Investment); Measures

S
Sample plans
  data collection plan, 11–12
  project plan, 15, 80, 125
  ROI analysis plan, 13, 122
  See also Planning documents; ROI Methodology
Senior management
  communicating about the evaluation process to, 81
  estimating impact of program, 19
  ROI applications demanded by, 39, 58
  as ROI audience, 40–41, 47, 57
  ROI Methodology changes for, 93
  ROI myth regarding lack of demand by, 87–88

ROI process criteria for satisfying, 41–43
See also Managers
Sibbet, D., 34
Skills/capabilities
  development of, 77–78
  implementation barrier due to lack of, 84–85
Sponsors, 40–41
Staff value estimates, 21
Stakeholders
  communicating ROI results to key, 75–76
  practitioners, 40
  researchers, 41
  ROI Methodology changes for, 93
  senior management, 19, 39–43, 47, 57, 58
  sponsors and clients, 40–41, 47, 57
  See also ROI audiences
Supervisors. *See* Managers
Surveys, 14
System value perspective, 102–103

T
Team group data, 128–129
Tests, 16
Timing
  as implementation barrier, 83–84
  planning data collection, 10, 121
  as ROI Methodology cost, 44
  sample data collection plan on, 11–12
Training Director's Forum, 32
Training (magazine), 32
Trend lines, 18

U
USA Today, 39

V
Van Buren, M. E., 9

W
Wall Street Journal, 39

X
X-1350 system impact objectives, 114

About the Authors

Patricia Pulliam Phillips, Ph.D., is president of the ROI Institute, Inc., the leading source of ROI competency building, implementation support, networking, and research. She supports organizations in their efforts to build accountability into their training, human resources, and performance improvement programs with a primary focus on building accountability in public sector organizations. She helps organizations implement the ROI Methodology in countries around the world, including South Africa, Singapore, Japan, New Zealand, Australia, Italy, Turkey, France, Germany, Canada, and the United States.

In 1997, after a thirteen-year career in the electrical utility industry, she embraced the ROI Methodology by committing herself to ongoing research and practice. To this end, Phillips has implemented the ROI Methodology in private sector and public sector organizations. She has conducted ROI impact studies of programs in leadership development, sales, new-hire orientation, human performance improvement, K–12 educator development, National Board Certification mentoring for educators, and faculty fellowship. Phillips is currently expanding her interest in public sector accountability by applying the ROI Methodology in community- and faith-based initiatives.

Phillips teaches others to implement the ROI Methodology through the ROI certification process, as a facilitator for ASTD's

ROI and Measuring and Evaluating Learning workshops, and as an adjunct professor for graduate-level evaluation courses. She speaks on the topic of ROI at conferences such as ASTD's International Conference and Exposition and the International Society for Performance Improvement's International Conference.

Phillips's academic accomplishments include a master's degree in public and private management and a Ph.D. degree in international development. She is certified in ROI evaluation and has earned the designation of certified performance technologist (CPT) and certified professional in learning and performance (CPLP). She has authored a number of publications on the subject of accountability and ROI, including *Show Me the Money: How to Determine ROI in People, Projects, and Programs* (Berrett-Koehler, 2007); *The Value of Learning* (Pfeiffer, 2007); *Return on Investment (ROI) Basics* (ASTD, 2005); *Proving the Value of HR: How and Why to Measure ROI* (Society for Human Resource Management, 2005); *Make Training Evaluation Work* (ASTD, 2004); *The Bottomline on ROI* (Center for Effective Performance, 2002), which won the 2003 ISPI Award of Excellence; *ROI at Work* (ASTD, 2005); the ASTD In Action casebooks *Measuring Return on Investment*, Volume 3 (2001), *Measuring ROI in the Public Sector* (2002), and *Retaining Your Best Employees* (2002); the ASTD Infoline series, including *Planning and Using Evaluation Data* (2003), *Mastering ROI* (1998), and *Managing Evaluation Shortcuts* (2001); and *The Human Resources Scorecard: Measuring Return on Investment* (Butterworth-Heinemann, 2001). Phillips's work has been published in a variety of journals. She can be reached at patti@roiinstitute.net.

Jack J. Phillips, Ph.D., a world-renowned expert on accountability, measurement, and evaluation, provides consulting services for Fortune 500 companies and major global organizations. The author or editor of more than fifty books, Phillips conducts workshops and makes conference presentations throughout the world.

His expertise in measurement and evaluation is based on more than twenty-seven years of corporate experience in the aerospace, textile, metals, construction materials, and banking industries. Phillips has served as training and development manager at two Fortune 500 firms, as senior human resources officer at two firms, as president of a regional bank, and as management professor at a major state university. This background led Phillips to develop the ROI Methodology, a revolutionary process that provides bottom-line figures and accountability for all types of learning, performance improvement, human resources, technology, and public policy programs.

Phillips regularly consults with clients in manufacturing, service, and government organizations in forty-four countries in North and South America, Europe, Africa, Australia, and Asia.

Books most recently authored by Phillips include *Show Me the Money: How to Determine ROI in People, Projects, and Programs* (Berrett-Koehler, 2007); *The Value of Learning* (Pfeiffer, 2007); *How to Build a Successful Consulting Practice* (McGraw-Hill, 2006); *Investing in Your Company's Human Capital: Strategies to Avoid Spending Too Much or Too Little* (Amacom, 2005); *Proving the Value of HR: How and Why to Measure ROI* (Society for Human Resource Management, 2005); *The Leadership Scorecard* (Butterworth-Heinemann, 2004); *Managing Employee Retention* (Butterworth-Heinemann, 2003); *Return on Investment in Training and Performance Improvement Programs*, 2nd edition (Butterworth-Heinemann, 2003); *The Project Management Scorecard* (Butterworth-Heinemann, 2002); *How to Measure Training Results* (McGraw-Hill, 2002); *The Human Resources Scorecard: Measuring the Return on Investment* (Butterworth-Heinemann, 2001); *The Consultant's Scorecard* (McGraw-Hill, 2000); and *Performance Analysis and Consulting* (ASTD, 2000). Phillips served as series editor for the In Action casebook series of the American Society for Training and Development (ASTD), an ambitious publishing project featuring thirty titles. He currently serves as series editor for Butterworth-Heinemann's Improving Human Performance series and for Pfeiffer's new Measurement and Evaluation series.

Phillips has received several awards for his books and his work. The Society for Human Resource Management presented him with an award for one of his books and honored a Phillips ROI study with its highest award for creativity. ASTD gave him its highest award, Distinguished Contribution to Workplace Learning and Development. *Meeting News* named Phillips one of the twenty-five most influential people in the meetings and events industry, based on his work on ROI within the industry.

Phillips holds undergraduate degrees in electrical engineering, physics, and mathematics; a master's degree in decision sciences from Georgia State University; and a Ph.D. degree in human resources management from the University of Alabama.

Jack Phillips has served on the boards of several private businesses—including two NASDAQ companies—and several associations, including ASTD, and nonprofit organizations. He is chairman of the ROI Institute, Inc., and can be reached at (205) 678-8101, or by e-mail at jack@roiinstitute.net.

Pfeiffer Publications Guide

This guide is designed to familiarize you with the various types of Pfeiffer publications. The formats section describes the various types of products that we publish; the methodologies section describes the many different ways that content might be provided within a product. We also provide a list of the topic areas in which we publish.

FORMATS

In addition to its extensive book-publishing program, Pfeiffer offers content in an array of formats, from fieldbooks for the practitioner to complete, ready-to-use training packages that support group learning.

FIELDBOOK Designed to provide information and guidance to practitioners in the midst of action. Most fieldbooks are companions to another, sometimes earlier, work, from which its ideas are derived; the fieldbook makes practical what was theoretical in the original text. Fieldbooks can certainly be read from cover to cover. More likely, though, you'll find yourself bouncing around following a particular theme, or dipping in as the mood, and the situation, dictate.

HANDBOOK A contributed volume of work on a single topic, comprising an eclectic mix of ideas, case studies, and best practices sourced by practitioners and experts in the field.

An editor or team of editors usually is appointed to seek out contributors and to evaluate content for relevance to the topic. Think of a handbook not as a ready-to-eat meal, but as a cookbook of ingredients that enables you to create the most fitting experience for the occasion.

RESOURCE Materials designed to support group learning. They come in many forms: a complete, ready-to-use exercise (such as a game); a comprehensive resource on one topic (such as conflict management) containing a variety of methods and approaches; or a collection of like-minded activities (such as icebreakers) on multiple subjects and situations.

TRAINING PACKAGE An entire, ready-to-use learning program that focuses on a particular topic or skill. All packages comprise a guide for the facilitator/trainer and a workbook for the participants. Some packages are supported with additional media—such as video—or learning aids, instruments, or other devices to help participants understand concepts or practice and develop skills.

- *Facilitator/trainer's guide* Contains an introduction to the program, advice on how to organize and facilitate the learning event, and step-by-step instructor notes. The guide also contains copies of presentation materials—handouts, presentations, and overhead designs, for example—used in the program.

- *Participant's workbook* Contains exercises and reading materials that support the learning goal and serves as a valuable reference and support guide for participants in the weeks and months that follow the learning event. Typically, each participant will require his or her own workbook.

ELECTRONIC CD-ROMs and web-based products transform static Pfeiffer content into dynamic, interactive experiences. Designed to take advantage of the searchability, automation, and ease-of-use that technology provides, our e-products bring convenience and immediate accessibility to your workspace.

METHODOLOGIES

CASE STUDY A presentation, in narrative form, of an actual event that has occurred inside an organization. Case studies are not prescriptive, nor are they used to prove a point; they are designed to develop critical analysis and decision-making skills. A case study has a specific time frame, specifies a sequence of events, is narrative in structure, and contains a plot structure—an issue (what should be/have been done?). Use case studies when the goal is to enable participants to apply previously learned theories to the circumstances in the case, decide what is pertinent, identify the real issues, decide what should have been done, and develop a plan of action.

ENERGIZER A short activity that develops readiness for the next session or learning event. Energizers are most commonly used after a break or lunch to

stimulate or refocus the group. Many involve some form of physical activity, so they are a useful way to counter post-lunch lethargy. Other uses include transitioning from one topic to another, where "mental" distancing is important.

EXPERIENTIAL LEARNING ACTIVITY (ELA) A facilitator-led intervention that moves participants through the learning cycle from experience to application (also known as a Structured Experience). ELAs are carefully thought-out designs in which there is a definite learning purpose and intended outcome. Each step—everything that participants do during the activity—facilitates the accomplishment of the stated goal. Each ELA includes complete instructions for facilitating the intervention and a clear statement of goals, suggested group size and timing, materials required, an explanation of the process, and, where appropriate, possible variations to the activity. (For more detail on Experiential Learning Activities, see the Introduction to the *Reference Guide to Handbooks and Annuals*, 1999 edition, Pfeiffer, San Francisco.)

GAME A group activity that has the purpose of fostering team spirit and togetherness in addition to the achievement of a pre-stated goal. Usually contrived—undertaking a desert expedition, for example—this type of learning method offers an engaging means for participants to demonstrate and practice business and interpersonal skills. Games are effective for team building and personal development mainly because the goal is subordinate to the process—the means through which participants reach decisions, collaborate, communicate, and generate trust and understanding. Games often engage teams in "friendly" competition.

ICEBREAKER A (usually) short activity designed to help participants overcome initial anxiety in a training session and/or to acquaint the participants with one another. An icebreaker can be a fun activity or can be tied to specific topics or training goals. While a useful tool in itself, the icebreaker comes into its own in situations where tension or resistance exists within a group.

INSTRUMENT A device used to assess, appraise, evaluate, describe, classify, and summarize various aspects of human behavior. The term used to describe an instrument depends primarily on its format and purpose. These terms include survey, questionnaire, inventory, diagnostic, survey, and poll. Some uses of instruments include providing instrumental feedback to group

members, studying here-and-now processes or functioning within a group, manipulating group composition, and evaluating outcomes of training and other interventions.

Instruments are popular in the training and HR field because, in general, more growth can occur if an individual is provided with a method for focusing specifically on his or her own behavior. Instruments also are used to obtain information that will serve as a basis for change and to assist in workforce planning efforts.

Paper-and-pencil tests still dominate the instrument landscape with a typical package comprising a facilitator's guide, which offers advice on administering the instrument and interpreting the collected data, and an initial set of instruments. Additional instruments are available separately. Pfeiffer, though, is investing heavily in e-instruments. Electronic instrumentation provides effortless distribution and, for larger groups particularly, offers advantages over paper-and-pencil tests in the time it takes to analyze data and provide feedback.

LECTURETTE A short talk that provides an explanation of a principle, model, or process that is pertinent to the participants' current learning needs. A lecturette is intended to establish a common language bond between the trainer and the participants by providing a mutual frame of reference. Use a lecturette as an introduction to a group activity or event, as an interjection during an event, or as a handout.

MODEL A graphic depiction of a system or process and the relationship among its elements. Models provide a frame of reference and something more tangible, and more easily remembered, than a verbal explanation. They also give participants something to "go on," enabling them to track their own progress as they experience the dynamics, processes, and relationships being depicted in the model.

ROLE PLAY A technique in which people assume a role in a situation/scenario: a customer service rep in an angry-customer exchange, for example. The way in which the role is approached is then discussed and feedback is offered. The role play is often repeated using a different approach and/or incorporating changes made based on feedback received. In other words, role playing is a spontaneous interaction involving realistic behavior under artificial (and safe) conditions.

SIMULATION A methodology for understanding the interrelationships among components of a system or process. Simulations differ from games in that they test or use a model that depicts or mirrors some aspect of reality in form, if not necessarily in content. Learning occurs by studying the effects of change on one or more factors of the model. Simulations are commonly used to test hypotheses about what happens in a system—often referred to as "what if?" analysis—or to examine best-case/worst-case scenarios.

THEORY A presentation of an idea from a conjectural perspective. Theories are useful because they encourage us to examine behavior and phenomena through a different lens.

TOPICS

The twin goals of providing effective and practical solutions for workforce training and organization development and meeting the educational needs of training and human resource professionals shape Pfeiffer's publishing program. Core topics include the following:

- Leadership & Management
- Communication & Presentation
- Coaching & Mentoring
- Training & Development
- E-Learning
- Teams & Collaboration
- OD & Strategic Planning
- Human Resources
- Consulting

What will you find on pfeiffer.com?

- The best in workplace performance solutions for training and HR professionals
- Downloadable training tools, exercises, and content
- Web-exclusive offers
- Training tips, articles, and news
- Seamless on-line ordering
- Author guidelines, information on becoming a Pfeiffer Affiliate, and much more

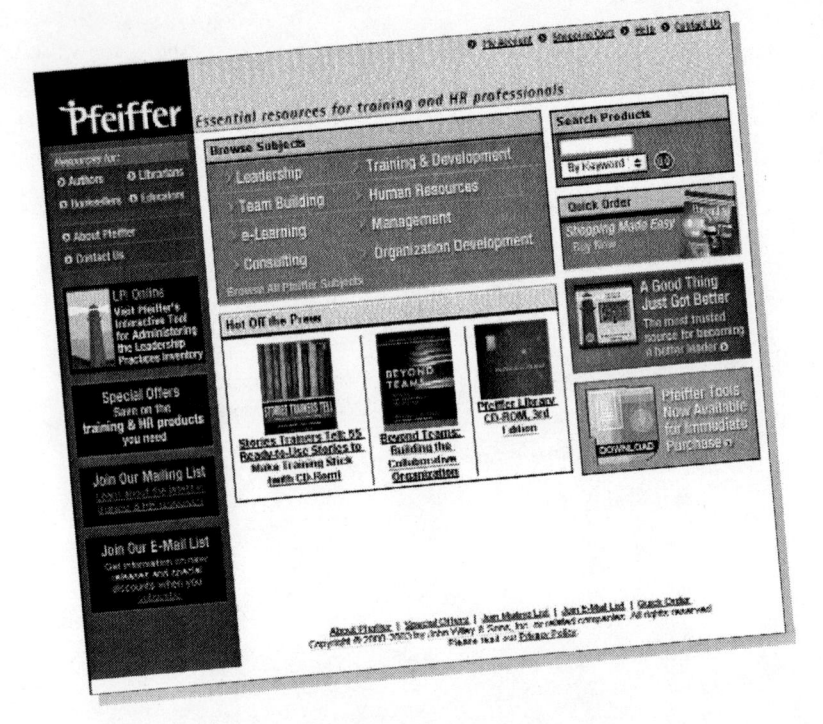

Discover more at www.pfeiffer.com

Measurement and Evaluation Series

Series Editors
Patricia Pulliam Phillips, Ph.D., and Jack J. Phillips, Ph.D.

A six-book set that provides a step-by-step system for planning, measuring, calculating, and communicating evaluation and Return-on-Investment for training and development, featuring:

- Detailed templates
- Complete plans
- Ready-to-use tools
- Real-world case examples

The M&E Series features:

1. *ROI Fundamentals: Why and When to Measure ROI*
   (978-0-7879-8716-9)
2. *Data Collection: Planning For and Collecting All Types of Data*
   (978-0-7879-8718-3)
3. *Isolation of Results: Defining the Impact of the Program*
   (978-0-7879-8719-0)
4. *Data Conversion: Calculating the Monetary Benefits*
   (978-0-7879-8720-6)
5. *Costs and ROI: Evaluating at the Ultimate Level*
   (978-0-7879-8721-3)
6. *Communication and Implementation: Sustaining the Practice*
   (978-0-7879-8722-0)

Plus, the *ROI in Action Casebook* (978-0-7879-8717-6) covers all the major workplace learning and performance applications, including Leadership Development, Sales Training, Performance Improvement, Technical Skills Training, Information Technology Training, Orientation and OJT, and Supervisor Training.

The **ROI Methodology** is a comprehensive measurement and evaluation process that collects six types of measures: Reaction, Satisfaction, and Planned Action; Learning; Application and Implementation; Business Impact; Return on Investment; and Intangible Measures. The process provides a step-by-step system for evaluation and planning, data collection, data analysis, and reporting. It is appropriate for the measurement and evaluation of *all* kinds of performance improvement programs and activities, including training and development, learning, human resources, coaching, meetings and events, consulting, and project management.

Special Offer from the ROI Institute

Send for your own ROI Process Model, an indispensable tool for implementing and presenting ROI in your organization. The ROI Institute is offering an exclusive gift to readers of The Measurement and Evaluation Series. This 11"×25" multicolor foldout shows the ROI Methodology flow model and the key issues surrounding the implementation of the ROI Methodology. This easy-to-understand overview of the ROI Methodology has proven invaluable to countless professionals when implementing the ROI Methodology. Please return this page or e-mail your information to the address below to receive your free foldout (a $6.00 value). Please check your area(s) of interest in ROI.

Please send me the ROI Process Model described in the book. I am interested in learning more about the following ROI materials and services:

- ☐ Workshops and briefing on ROI
- ☐ Books and support materials on ROI
- ☐ Certification in the ROI Methodology
- ☐ ROI software
- ☐ ROI consulting services
- ☐ ROI Network information
- ☐ ROI benchmarking
- ☐ ROI research

Name _____

Title _____

Organization _____

Address _____

Phone _____

E-mail Address _____

Functional area of interest:

- ☐ Learning and Development/Performance Improvement
- ☐ Human Resources/Human Capital
- ☐ Public Relations/Community Affairs/Government Relations
- ☐ Consulting
- ☐ Sales/Marketing
- ☐ Technology/IT Systems
- ☐ Project Management Solutions
- ☐ Quality/Six Sigma
- ☐ Operations/Methods/Engineering
- ☐ Research and Development/Innovations
- ☐ Finance/Compliance
- ☐ Logistics/Distribution/Supply Chain
- ☐ Public Policy Initiatives
- ☐ Social Programs
- ☐ Other (Please Specify) _____

Organizational Level

☐ executive   ☐ management   ☐ consultant   ☐ specialist
☐ student   ☐ evaluator   ☐ researcher

Return this form or contact   The ROI Institute
                              P.O. Box 380637
                              Birmingham, AL 35238-0637

Or e-mail information to info@roiinstitute.net
Please allow four to six weeks for delivery.

About This Book

Why This Book Is Important

This second book in the M&E Series begins with a brief introduction to the ROI process model and the Twelve Guiding Principles. It goes on to explain, in detail, one of the most critical activities in the evaluation process: data collection. Data are collected during every step of the ROI Methodology, and how and when these data are collected are crucial to successful program evaluation. This book provides detailed information about data collection methods and how and when to collect data at each evaluation level.

What This Book Achieves

This guide details how to develop or use each of the following data collection tools:

- Surveys
- Questionnaires
- Tests
- Simulations
- Interviews
- Focus groups
- Direct observation
- Performance monitoring

- Action plans
- Performance contracts

In addition, this book explains how to select the appropriate data collection method for any situation and any level of evaluation.

How This Book Is Organized

This book begins by introducing and describing each data collection method and ends by discussing the methods that are best for each evaluation level. Chapter One details how to design effective questionnaires and surveys in order to maximize response rates. It also provides tips for presenting questionnaires to participants in ways that will encourage them to provide valuable data. Chapter Two discusses the major types of tests, including how to develop and administer them. When and how to use simulations to collect data are also explained.

Chapter Three explores how to conduct interviews and focus groups for optimal results, including question development and interview techniques. Guidelines for effective observation are also provided. Chapter Four explains how to use business performance monitoring, action planning, and performance contracts to collect data.

Chapter Five focuses on measuring reaction and planned action and the importance of gathering participant feedback. Chapter Six discusses the reasons for measuring learning data and then describes how to use the data. Measurement and administrative issues involved in data collection at this level are also explored.

Chapter Seven explains the importance of collecting application and implementation data. The challenges and issues of collecting application data are explored, and appropriate data collection methods are also discussed. Chapter Eight explores the critical reasons for collecting impact data. Effective impact measures, appropriate data collection measures, and linking the measures to business needs are all discussed in this chapter.

Finally, Chapter Nine illustrates how to select the appropriate data collection method for each program and each level of evaluation.

The Measurement and Evaluation Series

Editors

Patricia Pulliam Phillips, Ph.D.

Jack J. Phillips, Ph.D.

Introduction to the Measurement and Evaluation Series

The ROI Six Pack provides detailed information on developing ROI evaluations, implementing the ROI Methodology, and showing the value of a variety of functions and processes. With detailed examples, tools, templates, shortcuts, and checklists, this series will be a valuable reference for individuals interested in using the ROI Methodology to show the impact of their projects, programs, and processes.

The Need

Although financial ROI has been measured for over one hundred years to quantify the value of plants, equipment, and companies, the concept has only recently been applied to evaluate the impact of learning and development, human resources, technology, quality, marketing, and other support functions. In the learning and development field alone, the use of ROI has become routine in many organizations. In the past decade, hundreds of organizations have embraced the ROI process to show the impact of many different projects and programs.

Along the way, professionals and practitioners need help. They need tools, templates, and tips, along with explanations, examples, and details, to make this process work. Without this help, using the ROI Methodology to show the value of projects and

programs is difficult. In short, practitioners need shortcuts and proven techniques to minimize the resources required to use this process. Practitioners' needs have created the need for this series. This series will provide the detail necessary to make the ROI Methodology successful within an organization. For easy reference and use, the books are logically arranged to align with the steps of the ROI Methodology.

Audience

The principal audience for these books is individuals who plan to use the ROI Methodology to show the value of their projects and programs. Such individuals are specialists or managers charged with proving the value of their particular project or program. They need detailed information, know-how, and confidence.

A second audience is those who have used the ROI Methodology for some time but want a quick reference with tips and techniques to make ROI implementation more successful within their organization. This series, which explains the evaluation process in detail, will be a valuable reference set for these individuals, regardless of other ROI publications owned.

A third audience is consultants and re-searchers who want to know how to address specific evaluation issues. Three important challenges face individuals as they measure ROI and conduct ROI evaluations: (1) collecting post-program data, (2) isolating the effects of the program, and (3) converting data to monetary values. A book is devoted to each of these critical issues, allowing researchers and consultants to easily find details on each issue.

A fourth audience is those who are curious about the ROI Methodology and its use. The first book in this series focuses specifically on ROI, its use, and how to determine whether it is appropriate for an organization. When interest is piqued, the remaining books provide more detail.

Flow of the Books

The six books are presented in a logical sequence, mirroring the ROI process model. Book one, *ROI Fundamentals: Why and When to Measure ROI,* presents the basic ROI Methodology and makes the business case for measuring ROI as it explores the benefits and barriers to implementation. It also examines the type of organization best suited for the ROI Methodology and the best time to implement it. Planning for an ROI evaluation is also explored in this book.

Book two, *Data Collection: Planning For and Collecting All Types of Data,* details data collection by examining the different techniques, processes, and issues involved in this process, with an emphasis on collecting post-program data. It examines the different data collection methods: questionnaires, interviews, focus groups, observation, action plans, performance contracts, and monitoring records.

Book three, *Isolation of Results: Defining the Impact of the Program,* focuses on the most valuable part of the ROI Methodology and the essential step for ensuring credibility. Recognizing that factors other than the program being measured can influence results, this book shows a variety of ways in which the effects of a program can be isolated from other influences. Techniques include comparison analysis using a control group, trend line analysis and forecasting methods, and expert input from a variety of sources.

Book four, *Data Conversion: Calculating the Monetary Benefits,* covers perhaps the second toughest challenge of ROI evaluation: placing monetary value on program benefits. To calculate the ROI, data must be converted to money, and *Data Conversion* shows how this conversion has been accomplished in a variety of organizations. The good news is that standard values are available for many items. When they are not, the book shows different techniques for converting them, ranging from calculating the value from records to seeking experts and searching databases. When data cannot be

converted to money credibly and with minimum resources, they are considered intangible. This book explores the range of intangible benefits and the necessary techniques for collecting, analyzing, and recording them.

Book five, *Costs and ROI: Evaluating at the Ultimate Level*, focuses on costs and ROI. This book shows that all costs must be captured in order to create a fully loaded cost profile. All the costs must be included in order to be conservative and to give the analysis additional credibility. Next, the actual ROI calculation is presented, showing the various assumptions and issues that must be addressed when calculating the ROI. Three different calculations are presented: the benefit-cost ratio, the ROI percentage, and the payback period. The book concludes with several cautions and concerns about the use of ROI and its meaning.

Book six, *Communication and Implementation: Sustaining the Practice*, explores two important issues. The first issue is reporting the results of an evaluation. This is the final part of the ROI Methodology and is necessary to ensure that audiences have the information they need so that improvement processes can be implemented. A range of techniques is available, including face-to-face meetings, brief reports, one-page summaries, routine communications, mass-audience techniques, and electronic media. All are available for reporting evaluation results. The final part of the book focuses on how to sustain the ROI evaluation process: how to use it, keep it going, and make it work in the long term to add value to the organization and, often, to show the value of all the programs and projects within a function or department.

Terminology: Programs, Projects, Solutions

In this series the terms *program* and *project* are used to describe many processes that can be evaluated using the ROI Methodology. This is an important issue because readers may vary widely in their perspectives. Individuals involved in technology applications may

Table I.1 Terms and Applications

Term	Example
Program	Leadership development skills enhancement for senior executives
Project	A reengineering scheme for a plastics division
System	A fully interconnected network for all branches of a bank
Initiative	A faith-based effort to reduce recidivism
Policy	A new preschool plan for disadvantaged citizens
Procedure	A new scheduling arrangement for truck drivers
Event	A golf outing for customers
Meeting	A U.S. Coast Guard conference on innovations
Process	Quality sampling
People	Staff additions in the customer care center
Tool	A new means of selecting hotel staff

use the terms *system* and *technology* rather than *program* or *project*. In public policy, in contrast, the word *program* is prominent. For a professional meetings and events planner, the word *program* may not be pertinent, but in human resources, *program* is often used. Finding one term for all these situations would be difficult. Consequently, the terms *program* and *project* are used interchangeably. Table I.1 lists these and other terms that may be used in other contexts.

Features

Each book in the series takes a straightforward approach to make it understandable, practical, and useful. Checklists are provided, charts are included, templates are presented, and examples are explored. All are intended to show how the ROI Methodology works. The focus of these books is implementing the process and making it successful within an organization. The methodology is based on the work of hundreds of individuals who have made the ROI Methodology a successful evaluation process within their organizations.

About Pfeiffer

Pfeiffer serves the professional development and hands-on resource needs of training and human resource practitioners and gives them products to do their jobs better. We deliver proven ideas and solutions from experts in HR development and HR management, and we offer effective and customizable tools to improve workplace performance. From novice to seasoned professional, Pfeiffer is the source you can trust to make yourself and your organization more successful.

Essential Knowledge Pfeiffer produces insightful, practical, and comprehensive materials on topics that matter the most to training and HR professionals. Our Essential Knowledge resources translate the expertise of seasoned professionals into practical, how-to guidance on critical workplace issues and problems. These resources are supported by case studies, worksheets, and job aids and are frequently supplemented with CD-ROMs, Web sites, and other means of making the content easier to read, understand, and use.

Essential Tools Pfeiffer's Essential Tools resources save time and expense by offering proven, ready-to-use materials—including exercises, activities, games, instruments, and assessments—for use during a training or team-learning event. These resources are frequently offered in looseleaf or CD-ROM format to facilitate copying and customization of the material.

Pfeiffer also recognizes the remarkable power of new technologies in expanding the reach and effectiveness of training. While e-hype has often created whizbang solutions in search of a problem, we are dedicated to bringing convenience and enhancements to proven training solutions. All our e-tools comply with rigorous functionality standards. The most appropriate technology wrapped around essential content yields the perfect solution for today's on-the-go trainers and human resource professionals.

Pfeiffer *Essential resources for training and HR professionals*
www.pfeiffer.com

Data Collection

Planning For and Collecting All Types of Data

Patricia Pulliam Phillips, Ph.D.
Cathy A. Stawarski, Ph.D.

Pfeiffer
A Wiley Imprint
www.pfeiffer.com

Copyright © 2008 by John Wiley & Sons, Inc. All rights reserved.

Published by Pfeiffer
An Imprint of Wiley
989 Market Street, San Francisco, CA 94103-1741
www.pfeiffer.com

No part of this publication may be reproduced, stored in a retrieval system, or transmitted in any form or by any means, electronic, mechanical, photocopying, recording, scanning, or otherwise, except as permitted under Section 107 or 108 of the 1976 United States Copyright Act, without either the prior written permission of the publisher, or authorization through payment of the appropriate per-copy fee to the Copyright Clearance Center, Inc., 222 Rosewood Drive, Danvers, MA 01923, 978-750-8400, fax 978-646-8600, or on the web at www.copyright.com. Requests to the publisher for permission should be addressed to the Permissions Department, John Wiley & Sons, Inc., 111 River Street, Hoboken, NJ 07030, 201-748-6011, fax 201-748-6008, or online at http://www.wiley.com/go/permissions.

Limit of Liability/Disclaimer of Warranty: While the publisher and author have used their best efforts in preparing this book, they make no representations or warranties with respect to the accuracy or completeness of the contents of this book and specifically disclaim any implied warranties of merchantability or fitness for a particular purpose. No warranty may be created or extended by sales representatives or written sales materials. The advice and strategies contained herein may not be suitable for your situation. You should consult with a professional where appropriate. Neither the publisher nor author shall be liable for any loss of profit or any other commercial damages, including but not limited to special, incidental, consequential, or other damages.

Readers should be aware that Internet Web sites offered as citations and/or sources for further information may have changed or disappeared between the time this book was written and when it is read.

For additional copies/bulk purchases of this book in the U.S. please contact 800-274-4434.

Pfeiffer books and products are available through most bookstores. To contact Pfeiffer directly call our Customer Care Department within the U.S. at 800-274-4434, outside the U.S. at 317-572-3985, fax 317-572-4002, or visit www.pfeiffer.com.

Pfeiffer also publishes its books in a variety of electronic formats. Some content that appears in print may not be available in electronic books.

Library of Congress Cataloging-in-Publication Data

Phillips, Patricia Pulliam.
   Data collection: planning for and collecting all types of data / Patricia Pulliam Phillips, Ph.D., and Cathy A. Stawarski, Ph.D.
     p. cm.—(The measurement and evaluation series)
   Includes bibliographical references and index.
   ISBN: 978-0-7879-8718-3 (pbk.)
   1. Project management—Evaluation. 2. Rate of return. 3. Employees—Rating of.
4. Organizational learning—Evaluation. 5. Social sciences—Research—Methodology.
I. Stawarski, Cathy A. II. Title.
   HD69.P75P496 2008
   001.4'33—dc22

2007035758

Production Editor: Michael Kay   Editorial Assistant: Julie Rodriguez
Editor: Matthew Davis   Manufacturing Supervisor: Becky Morgan
Printed in the United States of America

PB Printing 10 9 8 7 6 5 4 3 2 1

Contents

Acknowledgments from the Editors   xxi

Principles of the ROI Methodology   xxiii

Chapter 1: Using Questionnaires and Surveys   1

Types of Questions   1
Questionnaire Design Steps   2
    Determine the Specific Information Needed   2
    Involve Stakeholders in the Process   3
    Select the Types of Questions   3
    Develop the Questions   3
    Check the Reading Level   3
    Test the Questions   4
    Address the Anonymity Issue   4
    Design for Ease of Tabulation and Analysis   4
    Develop the Completed Questionnaire and Prepare a Data Summary   5
Improving the Response Rate for Questionnaires and Surveys   5
    Provide Advance Communication   5
    Communicate the Purpose   6
    Describe the Data Integration Process   6
    Keep the Questionnaire as Simple as Possible   6

Simplify the Response Process ... 6
Use Local Manager Support ... 7
Let the Participants Know That They Are Part of a Sample ... 7
Consider Incentives ... 7
Have an Executive Sign the Introductory Letter ... 8
Use Follow-Up Reminders ... 8
Provide a Copy of the Results to the Participants ... 8
Review the Questionnaire with Participants ... 9
Consider a Captive Audience ... 9
Communicate the Timing of Data Flow ... 9
Select the Appropriate Medium ... 10
Consider Anonymous or Confidential Input ... 10
Pilot Test the Questionnaire ... 10
Explain How Long Completing the Questionnaire Will Take ... 11
Personalize the Process ... 11
Provide an Update ... 11
Final Thoughts ... 12

Chapter 2: Using Tests ... 13

Types of Tests ... 13
    Norm-Referenced Tests ... 13
    Criterion-Referenced Tests ... 14
    Performance Tests ... 14
Simulations ... 16
    Electromechanical Simulation ... 17
    Task Simulation ... 17
    Business Games ... 17
    In-Basket Simulation ... 17
    Case Study ... 18
    Role-Playing ... 18
Informal Tests ... 19
    Exercises, Problems, or Activities ... 19
    Self-Assessment ... 20
    Facilitator Assessment ... 20
Final Thoughts ... 21

Chapter 3: Using Interviews, Focus Groups, and Observation — 23

- Interviews — 23
  - Types of Interviews — 24
  - Interview Guidelines — 24
    - Develop the Questions to Be Asked — 24
    - Test the Interview — 24
    - Prepare the Interviewers — 25
    - Provide Clear Instructions to the Participants — 25
    - Schedule the Interviews — 25
- Focus Groups — 25
  - Applications of Focus Groups — 26
  - Guidelines — 27
    - Plan Topics, Questions, and Strategy Carefully — 27
    - Keep the Group Size Small — 27
    - Use a Representative Sample — 27
    - Use Experienced Facilitators — 28
- Observations — 28
  - Guidelines for Effective Observation — 28
    - Observations Should Be Systematic — 29
    - Observers Should Be Knowledgeable — 29
    - The Observer's Influence Should Be Minimized — 29
    - Observers Should Be Selected Carefully — 30
    - Observers Must Be Fully Prepared — 30
  - Observation Methods — 30
    - Behavior Checklist — 30
    - Delayed Report — 31
    - Video Recording — 31
    - Audio Monitoring — 32
    - Computer Monitoring — 32
- Final Thoughts — 32

Chapter 4: Using Other Data Collection Methods — 35

- Business Performance Monitoring — 35
  - Using Current Measures — 36

Identify Appropriate Measures	36
Convert Current Measures to Usable Ones	36
Developing New Measures	37
Action Planning	38
Developing an Action Plan	40
Using Action Plans Successfully	42
Communicate the Action Plan Requirement Early	42
Describe the Action Planning Process at the Beginning of the Program	42
Teach the Action Planning Process	42
Allow Time to Develop the Plan	43
Have the Facilitator Approve Action Plans	43
Require Participants to Assign a Monetary Value to Each Improvement	43
Ask Participants to Isolate the Effects of the Program	44
Ask Participants to Provide a Confidence Level for Estimates	44
Require That Action Plans Be Presented to the Group	45
Explain the Follow-Up Process	45
Collect Action Plans at the Stated Follow-Up Time	46
Summarize the Data and Calculate the ROI	46
Applying Action Plans	48
Identifying Advantages and Disadvantages of Action Plans	51
Performance Contracts	51
Final Thoughts	54

Chapter 5: Measuring Reaction and Planned Action   **55**

Why Measure Reaction and Planned Action?	55
Customer Satisfaction	55
Immediate Adjustments	56
Team Evaluation	56
Predictive Capability	56
Importance of Other Levels of Evaluation	58
Areas of Feedback	58
Data Collection Issues	63

Timing	63
Methods	64
Administrative Guidelines	65
Uses of Reaction Data	67
Final Thoughts	69

Chapter 6: Measuring Learning and Confidence — 71

Why Measure Learning and Confidence?	71
The Learning Organization	71
Compliance Issues	72
Development of Competencies	73
Certification	73
Consequences of an Unprepared Workforce	73
The Role of Learning in Programs	74
Measurement Issues	75
Challenges	75
Program Objectives	75
Typical Measures	76
Timing	77
Data Collection Methods	79
Administrative Issues	81
Validity and Reliability	81
Consistency	82
Pilot Testing	83
Scoring and Reporting	83
Confronting Failure	84
Uses of Learning Data	84
Final Thoughts	85

Chapter 7: Measuring Application and Implementation — 87

Why Measure Application and Implementation?	87
Obtain Essential Information	88
Track Program Focus	88

Discover Problems and Opportunities	89
Reward Effectiveness	90
Challenges	**90**
Linking Application with Learning	90
Building Data Collection into the Program	90
Ensuring a Sufficient Amount of Data	91
Addressing Application Needs at the Outset	91
Measurement Issues	**92**
Methods	92
Objectives	92
Areas of Coverage	93
Data Sources	93
Timing	95
Responsibilities	96
Data Collection Methods	**96**
Questionnaires	96
Progress with Objectives	97
Use of Program Materials and Handouts	97
Application of Knowledge and Skills	97
Changes in Work Activities	104
Improvements or Accomplishments	105
Definition of the Measure	105
Amount of Change	105
Unit Value	105
Basis for Value	106
Total Annual Impact	106
Other Factors	106
Improvements Linked with the Program	107
Confidence Level	107
Perception of Investment in the Program	107
Link with Output Measures	107
Other Benefits	108
Barriers	108
Enablers	108
Management Support	108
Other Solutions	109
Target Audience Recommendations	109
Suggestions for Improvement	109

Interviews, Focus Groups, and Observation 110
Action Plans 110
Barriers to Application 111
Uses of Application Data 112
Final Thoughts 112

Chapter 8: Measuring Impact and Consequences — 115

Why Measure Business Impact? 115
  Impact Data Provide Higher-Level Information on Performance 115
  Impact Data Represent the Business Driver of a Program 116
  Impact Data Provide Value for Sponsors 117
  Impact Data Are Easy to Measure 117
Effective Impact Measures 117
  Hard Data Measures 118
  Soft Data Measures 120
  Tangible Versus Intangible Measures 121
  Impact Objectives 122
  Linking Specific Measures to Programs 123
  Sources of Impact Data 126
Data Collection Methods 127
  Monitoring Business Performance Data 127
    Identify Appropriate Measures 128
    Convert Current Measures to Usable Ones 128
    Develop New Measures 129
  Action Plans 129
    Set Goals and Targets 130
    Define the Unit of Measure 130
    Place a Monetary Value on Each Improvement 131
    Implement the Action Plan 131
    Document Specific Improvements 132
    Isolate the Effects of the Program 132
    Provide a Confidence Level for Estimates 133
    Collect Action Plans at Specified Time Intervals 133
    Summarize the Data and Calculate the ROI 133

Performance Contracts	134
Questionnaires	134
Final Thoughts	138

Chapter 9: Selecting the Proper Data Collection Method — 139

Matching Exercise	139
Selecting the Appropriate Method for Each Level	143
Type of Data	143
Investment of Participants' Time	143
Investment of Managers' Time	144
Cost	144
Disruption of Normal Work Activities	144
Accuracy	145
Built-In Design Possibility	145
Utility of an Additional Method	146
Cultural Bias of Data Collection Method	146
Final Thoughts	146
Index	147
About the Authors	153

Acknowledgments from the Editors

From Patti

No project, regardless of its size or scope, is completed without the help and support of others. My sincere thanks go to the staff at Pfeiffer. Their support for this project has been relentless. Matt Davis has been the greatest! It is our pleasure and privilege to work with such a professional and creative group of people.

Thanks also go to my husband, Jack. His unwavering support of my work is always evident. His idea for the series was to provide readers with a practical understanding of the various components of a comprehensive measurement and evaluation process. Thank you, Jack, for another fun opportunity!

From Jack

Many thanks go to the staff who helped make this series a reality. Lori Ditoro did an excellent job of meeting a very tight deadline and delivering a quality manuscript.

Much admiration and thanks go to Patti. She is an astute observer of the ROI Methodology, having observed and learned from hundreds of presentations, consulting assignments, and engagements. In addition, she is an excellent researcher and student of the process, studying how it is developed and how it works. She has become an ROI expert in her own right. Thanks, Patti, for your many contributions. You are a great partner, friend, and spouse.

Principles of the ROI Methodology

The ROI Methodology is a step-by-step tool for evaluating any program, project, or initiative in any organization. Figure P.1 illustrates the ROI process model, which makes a potentially complicated process simple by breaking it into sequential steps. The ROI process model provides a systematic, step-by-step approach to ROI evaluations that helps keep the process manageable, allowing users to address one issue at a time. The model also emphasizes that the ROI Methodology is a logical, systematic process that flows from one step to another and provides a way for evaluators to collect and analyze six types of data.

Applying the model consistently from one program to another is essential for successful evaluation. To aid consistent application of the model, the ROI Methodology is based on twelve Guiding Principles. These principles are necessary for a credible, conservative approach to evaluation through the different levels.

1. When conducting a higher-level evaluation, collect data at lower levels.
2. When planning a higher-level evaluation, the previous level of evaluation is not required to be comprehensive.
3. When collecting and analyzing data, use only the most credible sources.

Figure P.1. The ROI Process Model

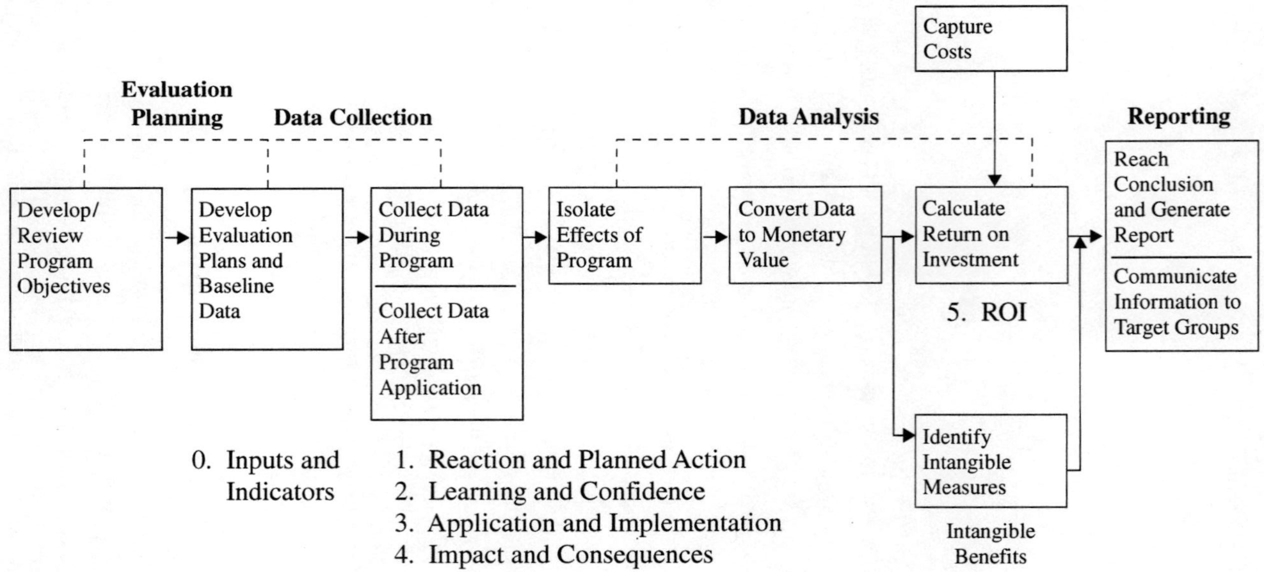

Evaluation Planning | **Data Collection** | **Data Analysis** | **Reporting**

Develop/Review Program Objectives → Develop Evaluation Plans and Baseline Data → Collect Data During Program / Collect Data After Program Application → Isolate Effects of Program → Convert Data to Monetary Value → Calculate Return on Investment ← Capture Costs

Identify Intangible Measures → Intangible Benefits

5. ROI

Reporting: Reach Conclusion and Generate Report / Communicate Information to Target Groups

0. Inputs and Indicators
1. Reaction and Planned Action
2. Learning and Confidence
3. Application and Implementation
4. Impact and Consequences

4. When analyzing data, select the most conservative alternative for calculations.
5. Use at least one method to isolate the effects of a project.
6. If no improvement data are available for a population or from a specific source, assume that little or no improvement has occurred.
7. Adjust estimates of improvement for potential errors of estimation.
8. Avoid use of extreme data items and unsupported claims when calculating ROI.
9. Use only the first year of annual benefits in ROI analysis of short-term solutions.
10. Fully load all costs of a solution, project, or program when analyzing ROI.
11. Intangible measures are defined as measures that are purposely not converted to monetary values.
12. Communicate the results of the ROI Methodology to all key stakeholders.

1

Using Questionnaires and Surveys

Data collection is the first operational part of the ROI process model. Data are collected in different time frames and from different sources. This is the first of four chapters on data collection methods. Collectively, these four chapters will provide a variety of ways to meet any application, budget, or time constraint.

Probably the most common data collection method is the questionnaire (Alreck and Settle, 1995). Ranging from short reaction forms to detailed follow-up tools, questionnaires can be used both to obtain subjective information about participants and to document objective, measurable impact results for an ROI analysis. Because of this versatility, the questionnaire is the preferred method for capturing data at Levels 1, 2, 3, and 4 in some organizations.

A survey is a specific type of questionnaire with several applications in measuring program success. Surveys are used in situations in which only attitudes, beliefs, and opinions are captured; questionnaires are much more flexible, capturing a wide range of data from attitudes to specific improvement statistics. The principles of survey construction and design are similar to those of questionnaire design. This chapter explains how to develop both types of instruments.

Types of Questions

In addition to the types of data sought, the types of questions distinguish surveys from questionnaires. Surveys may elicit yes-or-no responses, if absolute agreement or disagreement is required, or they may solicit a range of responses, often on a five-point scale from "strongly agree" to "strongly disagree."

A questionnaire may contain any or all of these types of questions:

- *Open-ended questions* allow unlimited answers. Questions are followed by ample blank space for the responses.
- *Checklists* provide a list of items, and the participant is asked to check those that apply in the situation.
- *Two-way questions* limit answers to a pair of alternative responses, such as yes and no.
- *Multiple-choice questions* provide several possible answers, and the participant is asked to select the one that is most applicable.
- *Ranking scales* require the participant to rank a list of items.

Questionnaire Design Steps

Nothing is more confusing, frustrating, and potentially embarrassing than a poorly designed or improperly worded questionnaire. Fortunately, with thought and planning, these problems can be easily avoided. Questionnaire design is a logical process that can be divided into simple steps. Use the following steps to help you develop a valid, reliable, and effective instrument (Robson, 2002).

Determine the Specific Information Needed

The first step in questionnaire design is reviewing the objectives, topics, skills, or attitudes presented in the program for potential questionnaire items. Developing this information in outline form is sometimes helpful so that related questions or items can be grouped.

At this time, also explore issues related to the application and impact of the program for inclusion in the questionnaire.

Involve Stakeholders in the Process

To the extent possible, stakeholders—clients, sponsors, supporters, or other interested parties—should be involved in the questionnaire design process. Ask those most familiar with the program to provide information on specific issues and concerns that might affect how the actual questions are framed for the questionnaire. In some cases, stakeholders may want to provide input on specific issues or items. Not only is stakeholder input useful in questionnaire design but it also builds ownership in the measurement and evaluation process and supports content validity.

Select the Types of Questions

From the five types of questions described previously, select the type or types that will result in the specific data needed. The planned data analysis and variety of data needed should be considered when deciding which types of questions to use.

Develop the Questions

The next step is to develop specific questions based on the type of questions selected and the information needed. Questions should be simple and straightforward, to avoid confusing the participants or leading them toward a desired response. Each question should address only one issue. If multiple issues need to be addressed, divide questions into multiple parts or develop separate questions for each issue. Avoid terms or expressions that might be unfamiliar to participants.

Check the Reading Level

To ensure that the questionnaire can be easily understood by the target audience, assess the reading level of the questionnaire. Many word processing programs have a function that can determine the reading difficulty of a text, indicating what grade level of education would be needed to read it. This important check ensures that the reading level of the questionnaire matches that of the target audience.

Test the Questions

Proposed questions should be tested to make sure that they will be correctly understood. Ideally, the questions should be tested on a sample group of participants. If this is not feasible, the sample group of employees should be at approximately the same job level as the participants. Seek feedback, critiques, and suggestions from the sample group so that the questionnaire design can be improved before it is administered to participants. Ensure that questions reflect program objectives and content.

Address the Anonymity Issue

Participants must feel free to respond openly to questions, without fear of reprisal. The confidentiality of their responses is of the utmost importance because there is usually a link between a questionnaire's anonymity and respondents' honesty. Therefore, questionnaires and surveys should be anonymous unless individuals must be identified for specific reasons. In situations in which participants must complete the questionnaire as a captive audience or submit a completed questionnaire directly to an individual, have a neutral third party collect and process the data, to ensure that participants' identities are not revealed. In cases in which individual identities must be known (for example, to compare output data with previous data or to verify the data), make every effort to keep respondents' identities from being revealed to those who might be biased by their responses. Confidentiality goes a long way when collecting data for current or future evaluation projects.

Design for Ease of Tabulation and Analysis

Consider how each potential question will affect data tabulation, data summary, and data analysis. If possible, outline and review the data analysis process at this point. This step will help you avoid problems of inadequate, cumbersome, or lengthy data analysis caused by improper wording or design of questionnaire items.

Develop the Completed Questionnaire and Prepare a Data Summary

Integrate and develop the questions into an attractive questionnaire with instructions that will allow it to be administered effectively. In addition, develop an analysis spreadsheet so that the data can be tabulated quickly for analysis. Developing the questionnaire and planning data analysis in tandem will ensure appropriate and efficient reporting in the end.

Improving the Response Rate for Questionnaires and Surveys

The items on a questionnaire represent a wide range of potential issues to explore. Obviously, asking all of the possible questions could result in a reduced response rate. The challenge, therefore, is to design and administer the questionnaire so as to maximize the response rate while ensuring reliable responses. Asking too many questions can reduce the number of questionnaires returned; asking too few can negatively affect the reliability of the results. Response rate management is a critical issue if the questionnaire is the primary data collection method and most of the evaluation hinges on the response of the participants. Taking the actions discussed in this section can help increase response rates.

Provide Advance Communication

If it is appropriate and feasible, communicate with participants in advance about the requirement of completing the questionnaire. Advance warning reduces some of the resistance to the process, provides an opportunity to explain in more detail the circumstances surrounding the evaluation, and positions the follow-up evaluation as an integral part of the program, not an add-on activity.

Communicate the Purpose

Make sure that participants understand the reason for the questionnaire, including who or what has initiated this specific evaluation and how the data from the questionnaire will be used. Participants should know whether the questionnaire—and the evaluation it is a part of—is the result of an ongoing systematic process or a special request for this program. Let the participants know who will see the data and the results of the questionnaire. If the questionnaire is anonymous, communicate clearly to participants the steps that will be taken to ensure anonymity. If senior executives will see the aggregate results, let participants know.

Describe the Data Integration Process

If other data are being collected for the same evaluation, help participants understand how the questionnaire results will be combined with those other data. The questionnaire may be only one of several data collection methods used. Participants should know how the data will be weighted and integrated into the final report.

Keep the Questionnaire as Simple as Possible

While a simple questionnaire does not always provide the full scope of data necessary for an ROI analysis, a simple approach should be a goal. When questions are developed and the total scope of the questionnaire is finalized, keep it as simple and brief as possible. But, as mentioned earlier, take care to design a questionnaire that provides reliable results as well as one that will ensure high response.

Simplify the Response Process

To the extent possible, responding to the questionnaire should be easy. If appropriate, a pre-addressed, stamped envelope should be included. Perhaps e-mail can be used to respond, if that is easier. In some situations, Web-based questionnaires are better. In still other situations, a response box can be provided near the participants' workstations.

Use Local Manager Support

Management involvement at the departmental or even functional level is critical to response rate success. Ask participants' managers to distribute the questionnaire, refer to the questionnaire in staff meetings, follow up to see whether the questionnaire has been completed, or generally show support for completing the questionnaire. Direct manager support will cause some participants to respond with usable data.

Let the Participants Know That They Are Part of a Sample

If it is appropriate, let participants know that they are part of a carefully selected sample and that their input will be used to make decisions that will affect a much larger target audience. This knowledge often appeals to participants' sense of responsibility, motivating them to provide usable, accurate data on the questionnaire.

Consider Incentives

A variety of incentives can be offered. Usually, incentives fall into three categories. The first type of incentive is provided in exchange for the completed questionnaire. For example, if participants return the questionnaire personally or through the mail, they receive a small gift, such as a mouse pad or coffee mug. If anonymity is an issue, a neutral third party can distribute the gifts.

The second type of incentive is provided to make participants feel guilty about not responding. Examples are a dollar bill (or equivalent international currency) clipped to the questionnaire or a pen enclosed in the envelope. Participants are asked to "take the money, buy a beverage, and fill out the questionnaire" or to "please use this pen to complete the questionnaire."

The third type of incentive is designed to obtain a quick response. This approach is based on the assumption that quick responses will ensure a greater response rate. If an individual puts off completing the questionnaire, the odds of completing it diminish. The initial group of participants who send in the questionnaire may receive a more expensive gift, or members of this group may be entered in a drawing for a gift. For example, in one study involving seventy-five participants, the first twenty-five who returned questionnaires were placed in a drawing for a $500 gift certificate. The next twenty-five were added to the first twenty-five for another drawing. After the first fifty, there was no incentive. The longer a participant waited, the lower his or her odds of winning were.

Have an Executive Sign the Introductory Letter

Participants are always interested in who signed the letter that accompanies a questionnaire. For maximum effectiveness, a senior executive who is responsible for a major area in which the participants work should sign the letter. Employees may be more willing to respond to a senior executive's request than a staff member's.

Use Follow-Up Reminders

Send a follow-up reminder one week after participants receive the questionnaire and another reminder two weeks after the questionnaire is received. In some situations, a third follow-up is recommended. Don Dillman (2006) suggests a tried-and-true approach that includes four follow-ups to an initial invitation to participate in the survey. Sometimes, it is effective to send the follow-ups through different media. For example, a questionnaire might be sent through the regular mail, the first follow-up reminder might be a telephone call, and a second follow-up reminder might be sent through e-mail.

Provide a Copy of the Results to the Participants

Make sure that participants see the results of the study, even if in an abbreviated form. More important, tell participants at the time they are asked to provide the data how and when they will receive a copy of the study. This promise often increases the response rate because some individuals want to see the results for the entire group.

Review the Questionnaire with Participants

The participants must understand the questionnaire. Seeing a copy in advance of the data collection can be helpful to them. Ideally, the questionnaire should be distributed and reviewed at the program launch or during the initial project meeting. Each question should be briefly discussed, and any issues or concerns about the questions should be clarified. This not only helps the response rate but also improves the quality and quantity of data.

Consider a Captive Audience

The best way to obtain a high response rate is to collect data from a captive audience. As part of a program follow-up session, a routine meeting, or a mandatory session designed for data collection, ask participants to provide input, usually during the first few minutes of the meeting. Sometimes, a routine meeting (such as a weekly sales meeting or staff meeting) provides the perfect setting for collecting data. This approach is ideal in a major program with a series of meetings; in that case, each subsequent meeting is an opportunity to collect data about the previous one.

Communicate the Timing of Data Flow

Give participants a specific deadline for completing the questionnaire. In addition, let them know when the results will be available. The best approach is to provide the date when the last questionnaires will be accepted and the date they will receive the results of the evaluation. It may also be prudent to advise participants when the sponsor will receive the results so that they can anticipate potential feedback, changes, or opportunities. Informing participants about specific points on the timetable builds respect for the entire evaluation process. This commitment of a timetable also builds accountability into management of the evaluation project.

Select the Appropriate Medium

It is important that the medium of the questionnaire (for example, paper, Web, or e-mail) match the culture of the participants. The medium should be selected for the convenience of the respondents, not the evaluator. Sometimes, an optional response medium can be offered in order to make responding more convenient for some participants.

Consider Anonymous or Confidential Input

Anonymous data are often more objective and, sometimes, more free-flowing than data not provided anonymously. If participants know that their input is anonymous, they will be more constructive and candid in their feedback, and their response rates will, in most situations, be higher. Sometimes, however, it is important to know who is responding. When this is the case, it is still important to ensure confidentiality. A confidentiality statement indicating that participants' names will not be revealed to anyone other than those collecting and analyzing data can play a positive role in gaining a high response rate. An explanation of how the confidentiality will be managed reinforces the commitment to keeps names separate from data.

Pilot Test the Questionnaire

Consider running a pilot test on a sample of the target audience. Conducting a pilot test is one of the best ways to ensure that a questionnaire is designed properly and that the questions flow adequately. Pilot testing can be accomplished quickly with a very small sample and can reveal problems with a questionnaire before it is administered to the whole audience. This will alleviate potential confusion, which sometimes negatively influences participants' willingness to respond.

Explain How Long Completing the Questionnaire Will Take

Participants need a realistic guideline on how long it will take them to provide the data. Although this issue seems simple, it should not be overlooked. Nothing is more frustrating than grossly underestimating how much time will be needed to complete a questionnaire. If the questionnaire is online, consider placing an indicator in a visible location on the screen in order to give the respondents an idea of how many more questions to expect. The pilot test should provide the information needed to allocate adequate time for participants to respond.

Personalize the Process

Participants usually respond well to personal messages and requests. Personalize the letter accompanying the questionnaire, if possible. In addition, if it is possible, use personal phone calls to deliver follow-up reminders. Calls may be made by the program facilitator, a manager or supervisor, an executive, or even the expert in the field being introduced to participants. A personal touch brings sincerity and a sense of responsibility to the process. It also further encourages participants to respond by explaining to them the importance of their data.

Provide an Update

In some cases, it may be appropriate to provide an update on current response totals and the progress of the evaluation project. If individuals understand how others are doing and how many responses have been returned, they may feel subtle pressure and be reminded to provide data by completing their questionnaire.

Used together, the steps in this section help boost response rates on follow-up questionnaires. Using all of these strategies can result in a 50 to 60 percent response rate, even for lengthy questionnaires that take forty-five minutes to complete.

Final Thoughts

This chapter has briefly described some of the issues involved in using questionnaires and surveys. More detail on questionnaire content will be given in the chapters that discuss the different levels of evaluation and examples of each type of questionnaire.

References

Alreck, P. L., and Settle, R. B. *The Survey Research Handbook: Guidelines and Strategies for Conducting a Survey.* (2nd ed.) New York: McGraw-Hill, 1995.

Dillman, D. A. *Mail and Internet Surveys: The Tailored Design Method.* (2nd ed.) New York: Wiley, 2006.

Robson, C. *Real World Research: A Resource for Social Scientists and Practitioner-Researchers.* (2nd ed.) Malden, Mass.: Blackwell, 2002.

2

Using Tests

Testing is important for measuring learning in program evaluations. Pre- and post-program comparisons using tests are common. An improvement in test scores shows the change in skills, knowledge, or attitude attributed to the program. The principles of test development are similar to those for the design and development of questionnaires and surveys. This chapter presents information on types of formal testing instruments and on informal tools used to assess knowledge acquisition.

Types of Tests

Three types of formal tests are commonly used in program evaluation: norm-referenced tests, criterion-referenced tests, and performance tests. In this section, we will examine each of these types of tests.

Norm-Referenced Tests

Norm-referenced tests compare participants with each other or with other groups rather than against specific instructional objectives. Norm-referenced tests use data to compare the participants with the norm or average. Although in some evaluations, norm-referenced tests can be of only limited use, they may be useful in programs in which large numbers of participants are involved and average scores and relative rankings are important. In some situations, participants who score highest on the exams receive special recognition or awards or are made eligible for other special activities.

Criterion-Referenced Tests

A criterion-referenced test is an objective test in which a predetermined cut-off score indicates acceptable performance. A criterion-referenced test is a measure against carefully written objectives for a specific program. In a criterion-referenced test, the interest lies in whether participants meet the desired minimum standard, not in how participants rank against one another. The primary concern is measuring, reporting, and analyzing participant performance as it relates to the instructional objectives. Table 2.1 shows a printout of the results of a criterion-referenced test.

Criterion-referenced testing is a popular measurement method (Shrock and Coscarelli, 2001). Its use is becoming widespread, with frequent use in e-learning. Criterion-referenced tests have the advantages of being objective, precise, and relatively easy to administer. However, their use requires programs with clearly defined objectives that can be measured by tests.

Performance Tests

Performance testing allows a participant to exhibit a skill or, occasionally, knowledge or attitudes that have been learned in a program. The skill can be manual, verbal, analytical, or a combination of the three. Performance testing is used frequently in job-related training in which the participants need to demonstrate what they have learned. In supervisory and management training, performance testing comes in the form of skill practices or role-playing. Participants are asked to demonstrate the discussion or problem-solving skills that they have acquired.

Table 2.1. Reporting Format for Data from a Criterion-Referenced Test

	Objective 1		Objective 2			Objective 3			Total Objectives Passed	Minimum Program Standard	Overall Program Score
	Pass/Fail	Raw Score	Standard	Pass/Fail	Raw Score	Standard	Pass/Fail				
Participant 1	P	4	10	F	87	90	F		1	2 of 3	Fail
Participant 2	F	12	10	P	110	90	P		2	2 of 3	Pass
Participant 3	P	10	10	P	100	90	P		3	2 of 3	Pass
Participant 4	P	14	10	P	88	90	F		2	2 of 3	Pass
Totals (4)	3 Pass, 1 Fail			3 Pass, 1 Fail			2 Pass, 2 Fail		8 Pass, 4 Fail		3 Pass, 1 Fail

Source: Phillips, 1997, p. 124. Used with permission.

To design and administer an effective performance test, as well as other types of tests, follow these recommendations:

- Make sure that the test accurately represents the content of the program and allows the participants to demonstrate as many of the skills that were taught in the program as possible.

- Thoroughly plan every phase of the test, including collection of necessary materials and tools, preparation of the participants, use of time, and evaluation of results.

- Prepare thorough and consistent instructions. As in other types of tests, the quality of the instructions can affect the outcome of a performance test. All participants should be provided with the same instructions.

- Develop standards for a performance test so that participants know in advance what must be accomplished in order for their performance to be considered satisfactory.

- Include relevant information that will keep participants on track and maintain objectivity in responses.

By following these general guidelines, you can develop performance tests into effective tools for program evaluation. Although they are more costly than written tests, performance tests are essential in situations in which the test conditions must mirror the work environment.

Simulations

Job simulations are another technique for measuring learning. This method involves creating and implementing a procedure or task that simulates or models the activity that the program teaches. The simulation is designed to represent the actual job situation as closely as possible. Simulations may be used as an integral part of the program's instruction as well as for evaluation. When a simulation is used for evaluation, participants have an opportunity to try performing the simulated activity as well as to have their performance evaluated. Simulations may be used during a program, at the end of a program, or as part of follow-up evaluation. A variety of simulation techniques that are used to evaluate program results will be discussed in this section.

Electromechanical Simulation

Electromechanical simulation uses a combination of electronic and mechanical devices to simulate real-life situations; this technique is often used in conjunction with programs to develop operational and diagnostic skills.

Task Simulation

As its name implies, task simulation requires participants, as part of the evaluation process, to perform a simulated task similar to what they would do on the job.

Business Games

Business games have grown in popularity in recent years. Business games simulate part or all of a business enterprise; participants change the variables of the business and observe the effects of those changes. The game not only reflects the real-world situation but also is a synopsis of the program of which it is a part.

In-Basket Simulation

The in-basket simulation is particularly useful for assessing learning in supervisory and management training programs. Portions of a supervisor's job are simulated through a series of items that would normally appear in the participant's in-basket, such as memos, notes, letters, and reports, which simulate real-life conditions that the supervisor will face. The participant's performance in the in-basket simulation represents an evaluation of the program.

Case Study

Another popular technique is the case study. A case study gives a detailed description of a problem and usually includes a list of several questions. The participant is asked to analyze the case and determine the best course of action. Case studies allow participants to analyze a real-life situation. Although case studies are often ideal for assessing some programs (for evaluating a project or the leadership style of a corporate executive, for example), it is difficult to actually place a score on a person's level of knowledge acquisition. However, case studies do require that participants examine various aspects of program content and transfer that information to the case situation.

Role-Playing

In role-playing (sometimes referred to as *skill practice*), participants practice a newly learned skill while they are being observed by other individuals. Participants are given specific instructions about their assigned roles, which may include an ultimate course of action. Participants then practice the skill with the other assigned individuals, trying to accomplish the desired objectives and demonstrate the knowledge that they acquired during the program.

Simulations come in many varieties. They offer opportunities for participants to practice what was taught in a program and to have those performances observed in conditions similar to those they will face on the job. Job simulations can provide extremely accurate evaluations if objective, clearly measurable criteria are set for performance in the simulation.

Informal Tests

In some situations, an informal check of learning is necessary to provide some assurance that participants acquired the desired skills, knowledge, or perhaps changes in attitudes as a result of a program. This approach is appropriate when levels of evaluation other than Level 2, learning, are being pursued. For example, if you are planning a Level 3 evaluation of on-the-job application of skills learned in the program, a comprehensive Level 2 evaluation may not be necessary. An informal assessment of learning may be sufficient. After all, resources are scarce and a comprehensive evaluation at all levels can be expensive. The following are some alternative approaches to in-depth learning measurement that might suffice when inexpensive, low-key, informal assessments are needed.

Exercises, Problems, or Activities

Many programs contain specific activities, exercises, or problems that must be explored, developed, or solved during the program. Some of these are constructed as exercises for group involvement, while others require individual problem-solving skills. When these types of activities are integrated into the program, several specific ways to measure learning are available:

- Submit the results of the exercise for review and evaluation by the facilitator.

- Discuss the results in a group, comparing the different approaches and solutions. Ask the group to assess how much each individual has learned.

- Share the solutions to the problem or exercises, and ask the group or individual participants to provide a self-assessment indicating the degree to which the skills or knowledge have been obtained from the exercise.

- Have the facilitator review the progress or success of individual participants in order to determine their relative success.

Self-Assessment

In many applications, a self-assessment may be appropriate. Participants are provided an opportunity to assess the extent of their skills or knowledge acquisition. Self-assessment is suitable when Level 3, 4, or 5 evaluations are planned and knowing whether learning has improved is important. Use the following techniques to ensure that the self-assessment process is effective.

- Allow participants to perform the self-assessment anonymously so that they feel free to provide a realistic and accurate assessment of what they have learned.
- Explain the purpose of the self-assessment, along with the plans for the data. Specifically, discuss the implications for course design or individual testing.
- Explain what the implications of the results will be and how self-assessment and post-program follow-up evaluation may be compared. This may help in reducing the subjectivity and perceived bias that sometimes results when self-assessment evaluations are conducted.

Facilitator Assessment

A final informal technique is for facilitators to provide an assessment of the learning that has taken place. Although this is a subjective approach, it may be adequate when a Level 3, 4, or 5 evaluation is planned. One effective way to accomplish such an assessment is to provide a checklist of the specific skills that need to be acquired during the course. Facilitators can then check off their assessment of a participant's knowledge of a particular skill or issue. It may be appropriate to provide rating scales to guide facilitators in their assessment; a simple yes-or-no checklist is also sufficient if the knowledge area or skill is one that can easily be observed.

Final Thoughts

This chapter explored a variety of techniques to measure learning. While formal testing provides the greatest opportunity for objective learning assessment, other forms of assessment are also available when tests are inappropriate, unappreciated, or too expensive. Also, it is important to remember that tests provide information on a respondent's success with the test questions. Other forms of assessment used in combination with formal tests will provide a broader and more balanced perspective on success with knowledge and understanding.

References

Phillips, J. J. *Handbook of Training Evaluation and Measurement Methods.* (3rd ed.) Boston: Butterworth-Heinemann, 1997.

Shrock, S. A., and Coscarelli, W. C. *Criterion-Referenced Test Development.* (2nd ed.) San Francisco: Pfeiffer, 2001.

Westgaard, O. *Tests That Work: Designing and Delivering Fair and Practical Measurement Tools in the Workplace.* San Francisco: Pfeiffer, 1999.

3

Using Interviews, Focus Groups, and Observation

Several methods are available for capturing qualitative data. Three of these—interviews, focus groups, and observation—are the focus of this chapter. Each is a rich and powerful method of data collection.

Interviews

Although not used in evaluation as frequently as questionnaires, interviews are a useful data collection method. Program staff, the participant's supervisor, or an outside third party can conduct interviews. Interviews can secure data that are not available in performance records or data that are difficult to obtain through written responses or observations (Kvale, 1996). Also, interviews may uncover success stories that can be used when communicating the evaluation results. Participants may be reluctant to list their results on a questionnaire, but they will volunteer the information to a skillful interviewer who asks the right questions and probes for more information. While the interview process uncovers reaction, learning, and impact data, it is primarily used for collecting application data. Interviews may be time-consuming, and they require interviewer preparation to ensure that the process is consistent—both major disadvantages of the process.

Types of Interviews

Interviews fall into two basic categories: structured and unstructured. A structured interview is much like a questionnaire. Interviewers ask specific questions with little room for deviation from the desired responses. One of the major advantages of structured interviews over questionnaires is that interviews ensure that all the participants respond to all the questions and that the interviewer understands the participant's responses.

An unstructured interview allows the interviewer to probe for additional information. This type of interview uses a few general questions that can lead to more detailed information as important data are uncovered. The interviewer must be skilled in asking follow-up questions and probing for more information when needed.

Interview Guidelines

The design issues and steps for interviews are similar to those for questionnaires. A few key steps can ensure a successful interview process.

Develop the Questions to Be Asked

After determining the type of interview that will be used, develop specific questions. The questions should be brief, precise, and designed for easy response. As with questionnaires, interview questions should reflect the objectives of the program.

Test the Interview

A small number of participants should be interviewed in order to test the interview's design. If possible, these interviews should be conducted as part of the trial run of the program. The responses should be analyzed, and if necessary, the interview should be revised.

Prepare the Interviewers

The interviewer should have the appropriate level of core skills, including active listening, asking probing questions, and collecting and summarizing information. Interviewers should also be familiar enough with program content and the evaluation purpose that they can probe for detail when a response infers there is more to the story.

Provide Clear Instructions to the Participants

Make sure that the participants understand why the interview is being conducted and that they know how the information will be used. The expectations, conditions, and rules of the interview should also be thoroughly discussed. For example, the participants should know whether their statements will be kept confidential and, if not, who will see them.

Schedule the Interviews

Like other evaluation instruments, interviews must be conducted according to a predetermined plan. The timing of the interview, the individual who will conduct it, and its location should all be determined when developing the plan. Commitment from the interviewee should be obtained early. For a program with a large number of participants, interviewing a sample instead of all the participants may be necessary in order to save time and reduce evaluation costs. As with questionnaires, a plan is necessary to ensure that interviewees will follow through on their commitment to participate.

Focus Groups

Focus groups are a specific type of interview. They are particularly helpful when in-depth feedback is needed for a Level 3 evaluation. A focus group is a small-group discussion conducted by an experienced facilitator and designed to solicit qualitative data on a topic or issue. The basic premise of focus groups is that when quality judgments are subjective, several individual judgments are better than one. Each group member is required to provide input, for individual input builds on input from others in the group (Subramony, Lindsay, Middlebrook, and Fosse, 2002). Compared with questionnaires, surveys, tests, and interviews, focus groups have several advantages. The group process, in which participants stimulate ideas in others, is an effective method for generating qualitative data. Conducting a focus group is less expensive than carrying out one-on-one interviews, given the longer time it takes to interview the same number of people individually. Focus groups can usually be scheduled quickly, but an incentive needs to be put forth to ensure that targeted respondents participate. The flexible format of a focus group makes it possible to explore a program's unexpected outcomes or applications. Flexibility, however, does not mean lack of structure. The key to a focus group is to keep it focused on a single issue. Otherwise, the focus group will go down many paths, ultimately leaving you with much data, little of which you sought at the outset.

Applications of Focus Groups

Focus groups are particularly helpful when qualitative information is needed about a program's success. For example, focus groups can be used in the following situations:

- To evaluate reactions to specific exercises, cases, simulations, or other components of a program
- To assess the overall effectiveness of program application
- To assess the impact of a program in a post-program evaluation

Essentially, focus groups are helpful when evaluation information is needed but cannot be collected adequately with questionnaires, interviews, or quantitative methods. Situations in which it is helpful for respondents to build off the thoughts of others are good opportunities for focus groups.

Guidelines

No specific rules have been set on how to use focus groups during an evaluation, though much has been written about various techniques to facilitate and manage focus groups and the resulting data. The guidelines provided in this section can help you plan and conduct a successful focus group.

Plan Topics, Questions, and Strategy Carefully

As in the implementation of any evaluation instrument, when developing focus groups, planning is critical. The topics, specific questions, and issues to be discussed must be carefully planned and sequenced in order to facilitate the comparison of results of different groups and to ensure that the group process is effective and stays on track.

Keep the Group Size Small

While there is no magic group size, eight to twelve is appropriate for most focus groups. A group needs to be large enough to ensure different points of view but small enough to provide a chance for each participant to freely exchange comments.

Use a Representative Sample

If possible, sample groups should be selected to represent the target population. The sample group should match the target population in its mix of job experience, rank, and job level. The best way to select a representative sample is through the random selection process, in which everyone in the population has an equal opportunity to participate; however, this technique is not always feasible.

Use Experienced Facilitators

A focus group's success rests with the facilitator, who must be skilled in conducting focus groups. Facilitators must know how to control aggressive members of the group and how to diffuse the input from those who may want to dominate the group. Also, facilitators must be able to create an environment in which participants feel comfortable enough to freely and openly offer comments. To facilitate a free flow of comments, some organizations use external facilitators.

In summary, a focus group is an inexpensive and quick way to determine the strengths and weaknesses of a program. However, the data represent only the views of those participating in the focus group. This can limit the perspective being given about a program. Used in combination with a questionnaire, however, a focus group can provide additional information on a specific area covered in the questionnaire, thereby broadening the understanding of program impact.

Observations

Another potentially useful data collection method is observing participants and recording any changes in their behavior. The observer may be a member of the staff, the participants' supervisor, a member of a peer group, or an external party. The most common and probably the most practical type of observer is a staff member; however, external, third-party observers often offer a more objective view, although they also increase the cost of data collection.

Guidelines for Effective Observation

Observation is often misused or misapplied to evaluation situations, causing some to lose faith in the process. The effectiveness of observation can be improved by following the guidelines discussed in this section.

Observations Should Be Systematic

The observation process must be planned so that it can be executed effectively and without surprises. The individuals observed should know in advance that they will be observed and why they will be observed, but not necessarily when, unless the observation is used to measure learning or knowledge acquisition. If the observation is used to collect data regarding a participant's routine application of knowledge, the observer should go unnoticed; otherwise, the behavior may be influenced. The timing of observations should be part of the plan as well. There are right times and wrong times to observe a participant. If a participant is observed when times are not normal (such as during a crisis), the data that are collected may be useless.

Observers Should Be Knowledgeable

Observations involve judgment decisions. The observers should know how to interpret and report what they see. They must analyze which behaviors are being displayed and what actions the participants are taking. They should know how to summarize the behaviors and report the results in a way that is meaningful to management and senior executives.

The Observer's Influence Should Be Minimized

Except for mystery observers and electronic observations, completely isolating the effect of an observer is impossible. If participants know that they are being observed, they may display the behavior they think is appropriate and they will usually be at their best. The presence of the observer must be minimized. To the extent possible, the observer should blend into the work environment or extend the observation period to allow participants to become accustomed to his or her presence.

Observers Should Be Selected Carefully

Observers should be independent of the participants—for example, program staff members. An observer from outside the participants' department is often more skilled at recording behavior and making interpretations of behavior than a department person would be and therefore may not need any special preparation. Observers from outside the participating department are usually unbiased in their interpretations. However, an observer from another area of the organization may be perceived as an outsider who is checking up on the work of others. Participants may overreact and possibly resent this kind of observer. Thus, recruiting an observer from outside the organization may sometimes be a better choice. Hiring a consultant has the advantage of avoiding the prejudices that might otherwise affect the observer's decisions; however, as mentioned earlier, this increases the cost of the evaluation. Therefore, when deciding who will observe, a balance must be found between objectivity and cost.

Observers Must Be Fully Prepared

Observers must completely understand the information that is needed and what skills were covered during the program. They must be trained for the assignment and provided with a chance to practice their observation skills.

Observation Methods

Five methods of observation are used; the choice of method depends on the type of information that is needed. Each method is briefly described in this section.

Behavior Checklist

A behavior checklist is useful for recording the presence, absence, frequency, or duration of a participant's behavior as it occurs. A checklist will not usually provide information on the quality or intensity of the observed behavior or on the circumstances surrounding the behavior. Measuring the duration of a behavior is more difficult and requires a stopwatch and a place on the checklist to record the time interval. Duration, however, is usually not as important as whether a particular behavior was observed or how often it was observed. The number of behaviors listed on the checklist should be small, and they should be listed in a logical sequence if they normally occur in a sequence. A variation of this approach involves coding behaviors on a form, entering a predefined code for each specific behavior. Whether using a checklist or a coded form, the behaviors should be described clearly enough that if multiple observers observe the same person at the same time, they will all give the same response. Ensuring the reliability of the observation is an important issue when using observation methods of any type, particularly checklists.

Delayed Report

In the delayed report method, the observer uses no forms or written materials during the observation period. The information is either recorded after the observation is completed or at intervals during the observation. The observer attempts to reconstruct what has been observed during the observation period. The advantage of this approach is that the observer is not as noticeable, and no forms are completed or notes taken during the observation. The observer can blend into the situation and be less distracting. An obvious disadvantage is that information written after the fact may not be as accurate and reliable as information collected at the time that it occurred. A variation of this approach is 360° feedback, a process in which surveys by peers, supervisors, and direct reports are completed based on observations within a specific time frame.

Video Recording

Video recording as an observation method has the obvious advantage: the video camera registers every detail of behavior and provides a permanent record. However, this intrusion may be awkward and cumbersome, and participants may be nervous or self-conscious about being videotaped. If the camera is concealed, participants' privacy may be invaded. For this reason, video recording of on-the-job behavior is not frequently used.

Audio Monitoring

Monitoring the conversations of participants who are using the skills they were taught in a program is an effective observation technique. For example, in a large communications company's telemarketing department, sales representatives are trained to sell equipment by telephone. To determine whether employees are using the skills properly, telephone conversations are monitored on a selective and sometimes random basis. While this approach may cause some controversy, it is an effective way to determine whether skills are being applied consistently and effectively. For audio monitoring to work smoothly, it must be fully explained and the rules must be clearly communicated.

Computer Monitoring

For employees who work regularly with a keyboard, computer monitoring is becoming an effective way to observe how participants perform job tasks. The computer monitors times, sequences of steps, and other activities to determine whether the participant is performing the work according to what was learned in a program. Because technology continues to be a significant part of many jobs, computer monitoring holds promise for effective observation of the actual application of skills on the job—in other words, Level 3 data.

Final Thoughts

This chapter discusses three methods of collecting data: interviews, focus groups, and observation. Interviews are similar to questionnaires, except that the interviewer ensures that all the questions are answered and that the answers are understood. In unstructured interviews, the interviewer can ask further questions if needed. Focus groups are helpful for acquiring input from participants when it is important for them to hear what others have to say. Observation can also be used for data collection, but depending on the observer, quality, objectivity, and costs are considerations.

References

Kvale, S. *InterViews: An Introduction to Qualitative Research Interviewing.* Thousand Oaks, Calif.: Sage, 1996.

Subramony, D. P., Lindsay, N. R., Middlebrook, R. H., and Fosse, C. E. "Using Focus Group Interviews." *Performance Improvement,* 2002, *41*(8), 38–45.

4

Using Other Data Collection Methods

To round out our description of data collection methods, we now discuss three important approaches: monitoring the records of an organization, which is particularly helpful in collecting impact data; using action plans, which fits many different projects or programs; and performance contracting, which can be very powerful when it is appropriate.

Business Performance Monitoring

Data that measure performance are available in every organization. Monitoring performance data enables management to measure performance in terms of output, quality, costs, and time. When you are searching for data to use in an evaluation, the first place to look is existing databases and reports. In most organizations, performance data that can be used to show the improvement resulting from a program are available (Mondschein, 1999). If they are not, additional record-keeping systems will have to be developed for measurement and analysis. At this stage, as with many other stages in the process, the question of economics enters. Is it economical to develop the record-keeping system necessary to evaluate a program? Obviously, if the costs are greater than the expected return for the entire program, then developing a new system is not worth the expense.

Using Current Measures

The recommended approach to collecting performance data is to use existing performance measures, if they are available. Use the guidelines in this section to ensure that analyzing current measures is easy and cost-effective.

Identify Appropriate Measures

Performance measures should be researched in order to identify those that are related to the proposed objectives of the program. Frequently, an organization will have several performance measures related to the same item. For example, the efficiency of a production unit can be measured in a variety of ways:

- Number of units produced per hour
- Number of on-schedule production units
- Percentage of equipment used
- Percentage of equipment downtime
- Labor cost per unit of production
- Overtime required per piece of production
- Total unit cost

Each of these, in its own way, measures the efficiency or effectiveness of the production unit. All related measures should be reviewed in order to identify those most relevant to the program.

Convert Current Measures to Usable Ones

Occasionally, existing performance measures are integrated with other data. Keeping them isolated from unrelated data can be difficult. In this situation, all existing measures should be extracted and recalculated as necessary to render them more appropriate for comparison in an evaluation. At times, conversion factors may be necessary. For example, the average number of new sales orders per month may be presented regularly in the performance measures for the sales department. In addition, the sales costs per sales representative may be presented. However, in the course of evaluating a new program, the average cost per new sale is needed. The two existing performance records can be used to develop the data needed for the comparison.

Developing New Measures

In some cases, data needed to measure the effectiveness of a program are not available. The staff must work with the organization to develop record-keeping systems, if this is economically feasible. In one organization, a new employee orientation system was implemented company-wide. Several measures were planned, including early turnover—represented by the percentage of employees who left the company during the first six months of their employment. An improved employee orientation program that would influence this measure was planned. At the time of the program's inception, this measure was not monitored. When the program was implemented, the organization began collecting early turnover figures for comparison.

Following are some typical questions to consider when creating new measures:

- Which department will develop the measurement system?
- Who will record and monitor the data?
- Where will the measures be recorded?
- Will forms be used?

Answering these questions will usually involve other departments or management decisions beyond the scope of the staff members who are planning the program. An organization's administration division, finance and accounting departments, or information technology function may be instrumental in helping to determine whether new measures are needed and, if so, how they will be collected.

Action Planning

The action plan is a versatile follow-up process. In this approach, participants—the individuals directly involved in the program who must apply the objectives of the program on the job—are required to develop action plans as part of the program. Action plans contain detailed steps for accomplishing specific objectives related to the program. The plan is typically prepared on a printed form such as the one shown in Exhibit 4.1. The action plan shows what is to be done, by whom, and by what date the objectives should be accomplished. The action plan approach is a straightforward, easy-to-use method for determining how participants will change their behavior on the job and achieve success as a result of the program. Action plans produce data that answer such questions as

- What steps or action items have been accomplished, and when?
- What on-the-job improvements or accomplishments have been realized since the program was conducted?
- What is the monetary value of the improvement?
- How much of these improvements is linked to the program versus other factors?
- What may have prevented participants from accomplishing specific action items?

With the information provided in the action plan, professionals can decide whether a program should be modified and in what ways, while managers can assess the findings to determine the value of the program.

Exhibit 4.1. Action Plan

Name: _____ Instructor Signature: _____ Follow-Up Date: _____

Objective: _____ Evaluation Period: _____ to _____

Improvement Measure: _____ Current Performance: _____ Target Performance: _____

Action Steps	Analysis
1. _____	A. What is the unit of measure? _____
_____	B. What is the value (cost) of one unit? $ _____
2. _____	C. How did you arrive at this value? _____
_____	_____
3. _____	_____
_____	_____
4. _____	D. How much did the measure change during the evaluation period? _____ (monthly value)
_____	E. List the other factors that may have caused this change: _____
5. _____	_____
6. _____	F. What percentage of this change was actually caused by this program? _____ %
7. _____	G. What level of confidence do you place on the above information? (100% = certainty; 0% = no confidence) _____ %

Intangible Benefits: _____

Comments (i.e., barriers or enablers affecting completion of action items): _____
_____
_____

Developing an Action Plan

Development of an action plan requires that two tasks be completed during the program: (1) determining the areas for action and (2) writing the action items. The areas or measures for action should stem from the original need for the program and from the content of the program; at the same time, they should be related to on-the-job activities. Participants can independently develop a list of potential areas for action, or a list can be generated during group discussions. The list may include a specific business measure needing improvement, or it may represent an opportunity for increased performance in a certain area. Typical categories are

- Productivity
- Sales, revenue
- Quality or process improvement
- Efficiency
- Time savings
- Cost savings
- Complaints
- Job satisfaction
- Work habits
- Customer satisfaction
- Customer service

The specific action items should support business measures; therefore, writing them is usually more difficult than simply identifying the action areas. The most important characteristic of an action item is that it be written so that everyone involved will understand it and will know when it has been achieved. One way to help attain this goal is to use specific action verbs. Here are some examples of action items:

- *Learn* how to use Microsoft Vista software by [date].
- *Identify* and *secure* five new customer accounts by [date].
- *Handle* every piece of paper only once, to improve my personal time management, by [date].
- *Learn* to talk with my employers directly about problems that arise rather than avoiding a confrontation, by [date].

Some questions that typically are asked when developing action items are

- How much time will this action take?
- Are the skills to accomplish this action item available?
- Who has the authority to implement the action plan?
- Will this action have an effect on other individuals?
- Are there any organizational constraints on accomplishing this action item?

If appropriate, each action item should have a completion date and should indicate any resources or actions by other individuals that are required for completion. Also, planned behavior changes should be observable. Completion of the action item should be obvious to the participant and to others when it occurs. Action plans, as used in this context, do not require prior approval or input from the participant's supervisor, although that may be helpful in gaining the supervisor's support for the process. Ultimately, it is the participant involved in the program or project who is accountable for completion of the action plan, though his or her success is sometimes influenced by others.

Using Action Plans Successfully

The action plan process should be an integral part of a program, not an add-on or optional activity. To obtain maximum effectiveness from action plans and to collect data for ROI calculations, the following steps should be implemented.

Communicate the Action Plan Requirement Early

Participants often react negatively to action plans when they are surprised by them. When program participants are asked to develop a detailed action plan that they were not expecting, there is often immediate, built-in resistance. Communicating the need for an action plan to participants in advance and presenting action plans as an integral part of the program will often minimize resistance. When participants fully realize the benefits of formulating an action plan before they attend the first session, they often take the process more seriously and will usually perform the extra steps to make it a success. In this scenario, the action plan is positioned as an application tool, not an evaluation tool.

Describe the Action Planning Process at the Beginning of the Program

During the first session, discuss action plan requirements, including an explanation of the purpose of the process, why it is necessary, and the basic participant requirements during and after the program. Some facilitators provide a separate notepad so that participants can collect ideas and useful techniques to use in developing their action plans. This productively focuses more attention and effort on the process.

Teach the Action Planning Process

An important prerequisite for successful use of action plans for collecting data is ensuring that the participants understand how an action plan works and how to develop one. A portion of the program's agenda should be allocated to teaching participants how to develop plans. During this session, the requirements are outlined, special forms and procedures are discussed, and a completed example is distributed and reviewed. Sometimes, an entire program module is allocated to the action planning process so that participants will fully understand it and use it. Any available support tools—such as key measures, charts, graphs, suggested topics, or sample calculations—should be used in this session to help facilitate the plan's development.

Allow Time to Develop the Plan

When action plans are used to collect data for an ROI evaluation, participants must be allowed time to develop their plans during the program. Sometimes, it is helpful to have participants work in teams so that they can share ideas as they develop their individual plans. During these sessions, facilitators often monitor the progress of individuals or teams in order to keep the process on track and to answer questions. In some programs, action plans are developed in an evening session as a scheduled part of the program.

Have the Facilitator Approve Action Plans

The action plan must be related to program objectives and, at the same time, represent an important accomplishment for the organization when it is completed. Participants may stray from the intent and purpose of action planning and not give it the attention that it requires. Therefore, it is helpful to have the facilitator or program director sign off on the action plan, ensuring that the plan reflects all the requirements and is appropriate for the program. In some cases, a space on the action plan is provided for the facilitator's signature.

Require Participants to Assign a Monetary Value to Each Improvement

Participants are asked to determine, calculate, or estimate the monetary value of each improvement listed in the plan. When the actual improvement occurs, participants can use these values to capture the annual monetary benefits of the plan. For this step to be effective, it may be helpful to provide examples of typical ways in which values can be assigned to the actual data.

Ask Participants to Isolate the Effects of the Program

Although the action plan was developed because of the program, the actual improvements resulting from participants' completion of the actions may have occurred as a result of other factors. It is, therefore, imperative that participants recognize the other influencing factors and give credit only for the improvement actually due to their completion of the actions on the action plan. For example, a participant may target a reduction in employee turnover as the measure he or she intends to improve. Specific actions are listed on the action plan based on information or knowledge the participant acquired during the program. When follow-up on the action plan occurs, employee turnover may well have been reduced, but this reduction could have been the result of a number of factors as well as the completion of the action. Factors such as leadership changes or bonus-driven pay plans or new hiring practices can all affect employee turnover. Therefore, when completing the action plan during the follow-up evaluation, participants should isolate the impact of their actions from the impacts of those other influences (Phillips and Phillips, 2002). While at least nine ways to isolate the effects of a program are available, participant estimation is usually appropriate when action plans are used. Consequently, participants are asked to estimate the percentage of the improvement that is directly related to the program. This question can be asked on the action plan or on a follow-up questionnaire.

Ask Participants to Provide a Confidence Level for Estimates

Estimates of program impact and monetary values of business impact measures may not be exact. Therefore, participants are asked to indicate their level of confidence in those two values, collectively.

Assigning a value on a scale of 0 to 100 percent (in which 0 percent means no confidence and 100 percent means complete confidence) provides participants with a way to express any uneasiness or lack of confidence in their estimate. This error adjustment results in the most conservative estimate given the range of possibilities based on the participant's input.

Require That Action Plans Be Presented to the Group

There is no better way to secure commitment to and ownership of the action planning process than to have a participant describe his or her action plan to fellow participants. Having participants present their action plans helps ensure that the process is thoroughly developed and that it will be implemented on the job. Sometimes, the process causes competition among the group. If the number of participants is too large for individual presentations, perhaps one participant can be selected from each team (if the plans are developed in teams). Under these circumstances, a team will usually select the best action plan for presentation to the group, raising the bar for others.

Explain the Follow-Up Process

Participants must leave the session with a clear understanding of the timing of action plan implementation and planned follow-up. How the data will be collected, analyzed, and reported should also be openly discussed. Five options are available for following up on the implementation of action plans:

1. The group is reconvened to discuss the progress on the plans.
2. Participants meet with their immediate supervisor to discuss the success of the plan. Copies of the minutes from those meetings are forwarded to the program team.
3. The program evaluator, the participant, and the participant's manager meet to discuss the plan and how it was implemented.

4. Participants send their plan to the evaluator, and they discuss it in a telephone call.
5. Participants send the plan directly to the evaluation team, with no meetings or discussions. This is the most commonly used option.

Other data collection options are available. Select a method that fits the culture, requirements, and constraints of the organization.

Collect Action Plans at the Stated Follow-Up Time

Because having an excellent response rate is critical to the success of data collection through action plans as well as other data collection techniques, it is important to take the necessary steps to ensure that the action plans are completed and the data are returned to the appropriate individual or group for analysis. Once a collection time has been determined, every effort must be made to get the action plans returned to the evaluation team. Some organizations use follow-up reminders by mail or e-mail to encourage participants to complete their action plans. Others periodically call participants to check on their progress. Still others offer assistance in completing the final plan. These steps may require additional resources, however, and these costs must be weighed against the importance of having more data.

When the action plan process is implemented as outlined in this book, response rates will normally be very high: in the 60 to 90 percent range. Usually, participants see the importance of the process, so they develop their plans in detail before leaving the program and complete them at the assigned time.

Summarize the Data and Calculate the ROI

If developed and implemented properly, each action plan will have annualized monetary values associated with improvements in the targeted business measures. Also, each individual will have indicated the percentage of the improvement that is directly related to the program. Finally, each participant will have provided a confidence percentage that reflects any uncertainty about the process and the subjective nature of some of the data provided.

Because this process involves estimates, it may not appear credible. Several adjustments can be made during the analysis to improve the credibility of the process. Make adjustments by following these steps:

1. For participants who do not provide data, assume that they had no improvement to report. This is a conservative assumption. (Guiding Principle 6)
2. Check each value for realism, usability, and feasibility. Discard extreme values, omitting them from the analysis. (Guiding Principle 8)
3. Assume only first-year benefits, even though some programs will add value in the second and third year. (Guiding Principle 9)
4. Adjust the improvement from step 3 according to the confidence level provided by the participant, multiplying it by the confidence percentage. The confidence level represents the error in the estimate as suggested by the participant. For example, a participant indicating 80 percent confidence in the data provided is reflecting a 20 percent possibility of error. In a $10,000 estimate with an 80 percent confidence factor, the participant is suggesting that the value could be in the range of $8,000 to $12,000. To be conservative, the lower number is used. Thus, the amount of improvement is multiplied by the confidence factor. (Guiding Principle 7)
5. Adjust the new values according to the percentage of improvement related directly to the program, using straight multiplication. This calculation isolates the effects of the program from other influences. (Guiding Principle 5)

The monetary values that participants determine by following these five steps are combined to arrive at a total program benefit. Since the values are already annualized (assuming first-year benefits only), the total represents the annual benefit of the program. This value is placed in the numerator of the formula for calculating the ROI.

Applying Action Plans

The impact of the action plan process can be impressive. For example, consider the following case. In a medium-sized manufacturing facility, a program that focused on improving interpersonal skills with employees was developed for first-level supervisors. Several of the areas addressed were productivity improvement, scrap reduction, absenteeism, turnover, grievances, and safety. These areas were discussed, and supervisors learned the skills to make improvements in each area. Supervisors were required to develop action plans for improvement and to report their results in a follow-up six months after the program. In this situation, the improvement measures were predetermined on the basis of the needs assessment. The following results were documented from a pilot group:

- The department unit hour was increased from 65 to 75. The unit hour is a basic measure of productivity; a unit hour of 60 is considered average and acceptable work.

- Scrap was reduced from 11 percent to 7.4 percent.

- Absenteeism was reduced from 7 percent to 3.25 percent.

- The annual turnover rate was drastically reduced from 30 percent to 5 percent.

- Grievances were reduced by 80 percent.

- Lost-time accidents were reduced by 95 percent.

These results were achieved by supervisors' practicing what they had learned and reporting the results of their action plans. Although these results are impressive, three additional steps are needed to develop the ultimate evaluation, the ROI. First, the amount of the improvement that is actually linked to the program must be determined, working with each measure. In this situation, supervisors estimated the percentage of the improvement that could be directly linked to the program. For example, while absenteeism showed an overall decrease of 3.75 percent, the supervisors collectively estimated that only 46 percent of the reduction was actually linked to the program. Therefore, the 3.75 percent reduction in absenteeism was reduced to 1.725 percent. This figure was then further adjusted by factoring in the participants' confidence levels. In this example, supervisors were 84 percent confident about their allocation of the absenteeism improvement. When adjusted for the 84 percent confidence level, 1.725 percent became 1.45 percent. These two adjustments isolated the effects of the program on the output measures; this process is fully described in the next book in this series, *Isolation of Results*.

The second step in developing the ROI measurement is converting the data to monetary values. In our example, a value for a single absence needed to be determined and used to calculate the annual benefit of the improvement in absenteeism. There are at least ten ways to place values on data, and they are fully described in the fourth book in this series, *Data Conversion*. In this case, the supervisors had developed an estimated value of one absence, which had been used in several previous applications that required a value for the cost of absenteeism. Consequently, the total number of absences avoided was calculated and multiplied by the value of one absence to obtain the training program's annual impact through reduction of absenteeism. This process shows the economic value of the program on that specific output measure. The two steps of isolating the effects of the program and converting data to monetary values were performed for each of the six improvement measures;

after the total annual value of each of the six improvements was calculated, the total value of all six represented the annual economic benefit of the program.

The third step necessary to calculate ROI is developing the fully loaded costs of the program. In this step, the costs related to needs assessment and program development are prorated based on the number of people involved or the number of times a program is implemented over the lifetime of the program. In addition, all direct program costs are captured, along with the cost of the participants' salaries and benefits during the time that they are involved. The fully loaded cost for all participants reflects the total investment in the program for this group. The process of arriving at the total cost figure is fully explained in the fifth book in this series, *Costs and ROI*.

After the preceding three additional steps have been completed, ROI can be calculated, using the formulas described in *ROI Fundamentals* (net benefits divided by costs multiplied by 100). In our example, after all six improvement items were converted to monetary units, the annual benefits directly attributed to the program totaled $775,000. The fully loaded costs for the program—which included the costs of needs assessment and program development, delivery, and evaluation—came to $65,000. Thus, the ROI was calculated as follows:

$$\text{ROI} = \frac{\text{Net Program Benefits}}{\text{Program Costs}} \times 100$$

$$\text{ROI} = \frac{\$775{,}000 - \$65{,}000}{\$65{,}000} \times 100 = 1092\%$$

This impressive ROI has credibility because the adjustments made to the data make it a conservative estimate. Without these three steps, the target audience might have wondered what part of the results was actually linked to the program and whether the benefits actually exceeded the costs.

Identifying Advantages and Disadvantages of Action Plans

Although action plans have many advantages, their use raises at least two concerns. First, the process relies on direct input from participants, usually with no assurance of anonymity. Therefore, the information may be biased and unreliable. Also, action plans can be time-consuming for participants; as a result, if a participant's supervisor is not active in the process, the participant may not complete the assignment.

As this section has illustrated, the use of action plans offers many advantages. Action plans are simple and easy to administer, easily understood by participants, appropriate for a wide variety of programs, and appropriate for collecting all types of data. In addition, they can be used to measure reaction, learning, application, and business impact. They can be used with or without other evaluation methods. The two disadvantages can be overcome with careful planning and implementation. Building action plans into the program mitigates the presence of an evaluation. It suggests, instead, that follow-through on actions that drive business performance is an important part of the program itself. It also provides participants the opportunity to track how successful they are with their implementation. When participants are prepared in advance, their apprehension about participating is reduced. Ensuring participants that their results will be used for program or process improvement provides some comfort that their individual job performance is not being examined. Because of their tremendous versatility and the adjustments that can be made during analysis to render more conservative estimates, action plans have become an important data collection tool for ROI evaluations.

Performance Contracts

Performance contracts are a slight variation of action plans, with the added feature of a pre-program commitment. Based on the principle of mutual goal setting, a performance contract is a written agreement between a participant and the participant's manager. The participant agrees to improve performance in an area of mutual concern related to the content of the program. The agreement takes the form of a project to be completed or a goal to be accomplished soon after the program's completion. The agreement spells out what should be accomplished, at what time, and with what results.

Performance contracting is administered in much the same way as the action planning process. Although the steps depend on the specific kind of contract and on the organization, a common sequence of events is as follows:

1. With his or her manager's approval, the participant decides to be involved in a program or project.
2. The participant and his or her manager agree on a topic for improvement and specific measures of that improvement.
3. Specific, measurable goals are set.
4. The participant undergoes the program, during which the contract is discussed and plans are developed to accomplish the determined goals.
5. Following the program, the participant works on the contract, adhering to a specific deadline.
6. The participant reports the results to his or her immediate manager.
7. The manager and participant document the results and forward a copy of the documentation to the evaluation team, along with appropriate comments.

Participants and their managers together select the area or measure to be improved prior to the start of the program. The process of selecting the area for improvement is similar to the process of developing an action plan, described earlier in this chapter. The proposed improvement can cover one or more of the following areas:

- *Routine performance*, which includes specific improvements in routine performance measures such as production targets, efficiency, or error rates
- *Problem solving*, which focuses on specific problems such as an unexpected increase in accidents, a decrease in efficiency, or a loss of morale
- *Innovative or creative applications*, which include initiating changes or improvements in work practices, methods, procedures, techniques, or processes
- *Personal development*, which involves learning new information or acquiring new skills in order to increase individual effectiveness

The proposed improvement should be stated in terms of one or more objectives. The objectives should state what will be accomplished when the contract is complete. These objectives should be

- Written
- Understandable (by all involved)
- Challenging (requiring unusual effort to achieve)
- Achievable (something that can be accomplished)
- Largely under the control of the participant
- Measurable
- Time sensitive

The detailed steps needed to accomplish the contract objectives are developed by following the guidelines for developing action plans items, which were presented earlier in this chapter. The methods for analyzing the data and reporting progress are also essentially the same as those used in the action planning process.

Final Thoughts

This chapter has provided an overview of three data collection approaches that can be used in ROI evaluation. Use of these methods in collecting data for ROI calculations is gaining more acceptance. Performance monitoring, action plans, and performance contracting are often used to collect data for ROI evaluations.

References

Mondschein, M. *Measurit: Achieving Profitable Training*. Leawood, Kans.: Leathers, 1999.

Phillips, J. J., and Phillips, P. P. "Evaluating the Impact of a Graduate Program in a Federal Agency." In P. P. Phillips and J. J. Phillips (eds.), *In Action: Measuring ROI in the Public Sector*. Alexandria, Va.: ASTD, 2002.

5

Measuring Reaction and Planned Action

This chapter focuses on measurement of reaction and planned action (Level 1 in the ROI Methodology), which involves collecting data at the beginning of and during a program. Participant feedback supplies powerful information that can be used to make adjustments and measure success. This chapter outlines the most common approaches to collecting Level 1 data and explores ways to use the information for maximum value.

Why Measure Reaction and Planned Action?

It is difficult to imagine a program being conducted without the collection of feedback from those involved in the program or, at least, from the participants. Collecting reaction data serves several purposes. Participant feedback is critical to understanding how well a program serves the customer and the potential of the program to meet identified business needs.

Customer Satisfaction

Reaction is a measure of customer satisfaction with a program. Without sustained favorable reactions, a program may not succeed. The individuals who have a direct role in planning and implementing a program are immediately affected by reaction data and often have to change processes or procedures or make other adjustments in response. Participant feedback on preferences is critical to making adjustments and changes in a program as it unfolds. Feedback from program supporters is also important because this group is in a position to influence the program's continuation and development. The sponsors—who approve budgets, allocate resources, and ultimately, live with the program's success or failure—must be completely satisfied with the program, and their overall satisfaction must be verified early and often.

Immediate Adjustments

A program can go astray quickly, and sometimes a program ends up being the wrong solution for the specified problem. A program can also be mismatched to the problem from the beginning, so getting feedback early in the process is necessary so that immediate adjustments can be made. This can help prevent misunderstandings, miscommunications, and, more important, misappropriations. Gathering and using reaction data promptly can allow an improperly designed program to be changed before more serious problems arise.

Team Evaluation

In some projects and programs, reaction or feedback data are used to evaluate the effectiveness of the team that has implemented the program. In learning and development, consulting, and change management, facilitator evaluation is critical. These data can reveal how well facilitators have fulfilled their responsibilities. Reaction data may also be used to evaluate other team members, including program coordinators, program planners, or sponsors. Such input also sometimes leads the program team to make quick adjustments in order to ensure that the program progresses properly.

Predictive Capability

A relatively recent use of reaction data is predicting the success of a program through analytical techniques. Participants are asked to predict the effectiveness of the application of learning from the

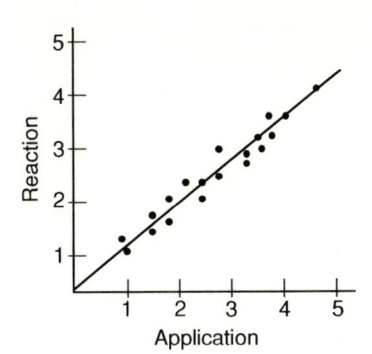

Figure 5.1. Correlations Between Reaction and Application Data

program and, in some cases, the resulting value of that application. The reaction data thus become a forecast. Figure 5.1 shows the correlation between reactive feedback and application data. Studies have been conducted that verify this correlation.

In this type of analysis, the reaction measures are taken as the program is introduced, and the success of the application (or implementation) is later judged using the same scale (a rating from 1 to 5). When significant positive correlations between reaction and application measures are present, reaction measures can have predictive capability. Some reaction measurement items shown to have predictive capability are

- The program is relevant to my job.
- The program is necessary.
- The program is important to my success.
- I intend to implement the program.
- I would recommend that others pursue similar programs.

Measurement items such as these consistently lead to strong positive correlations and consequently represent more powerful feedback than typical measures of satisfaction with a program. Some organizations collect these or similar reaction measures for every project or program initiated.

Importance of Other Levels of Evaluation

Feedback data are critical to a program's success and should be collected for every program. Unfortunately, however, in some organizations, feedback alone has been used to measure program success. In the meetings and events industry, which is a $150 billion industry, it is estimated that 95 percent of meetings and events are evaluated only at the reaction level (Phillips, Myhill, and McDonough, 2007). For example, in a financial services firm in Israel, the traditional method of measuring the effectiveness of an ethics program relied entirely on feedback data from employees, asking them whether the ethics policy was appropriate, fair, and necessary. Positive feedback is obviously critical to the policy's acceptance but is no guarantee that the new policy will be successfully executed. As subsequent policy changes were made, executives became interested in more realistic evaluation, which included the extent to which employees actually understood the policy (learning), the extent to which employees followed the policy in their work (application), and the effectiveness of the policy in reducing ethical violations and infractions (impact). Only when these additional measures were taken could the full scope of success be identified.

Collecting only reaction data for a project or program is risky. Research shows that a positive reaction to a program does not always correlate to positive program results Although reaction data are easy to collect, they are based on many elements and contain potential bias. Data collected later in the evaluation chain are more helpful for evaluating projects or programs.

Areas of Feedback

In capturing reaction and planned action data, it is important to focus on the content of the project, program, or initiative. Too often,

Table 5.1. Noncontent Issues Versus Content Issues for a Marketing Event

Noncontent Issues	Content Issues
Demographics	Service quality
Facilities	Learning environment
Location	Relevance of program to
Transportation	participant's clients
Registration	Importance of program to
Logistics	participant's success
Hotel service	Timing of program
Media	Use of participant's time
Food	Amount of new information
Breaks and refreshments	Quality of presentations
Cocktail reception	Usefulness of materials
Gala party	Perceived value of program
Closing dinner	Value of contacts made
Opening keynote	Planned use of material
Quality of speakers	Forecast of impact on sales
Future needs	Confidence of estimate of impact
Overall satisfaction	Overall satisfaction with program content

feedback data reflect aesthetic issues that are not relevant to the substance of the project. Table 5.1 shows two types of reaction data that could be captured at a marketing event for customer relationship managers by using a reaction questionnaire. The difference is more than subtle. The traditional way to evaluate activities is to focus on noncontent issues or inputs. In Table 5.1, the column on the left represents areas important to the activity surrounding the marketing event but contains nothing indicating results or possible results achieved from the event. The column on the right reflects a focus on content. This is not to suggest that the nature of the service, the atmosphere of the event, and the quality of the logistics are not important; it is assumed that these issues will be taken care of and addressed appropriately. However, a more important set of data, focused on results, incorporates detailed information about the perceived value of the meeting, the importance of the content, and the planned use of material or a forecast of the impact—indicators that successful results were achieved.

Many topics are targets for reaction feedback. Feedback data are needed in connection with almost every major issue, step, or process in order to make sure that things are working properly. The areas of feedback used for reaction data depend, to a large extent, on the organization and the purpose of the evaluation. Some requests for feedback are simple, while others are detailed and require more time for participants to answer and for evaluators to collect. Feedback requests should be designed to supply the information needed to satisfy the purpose of the evaluation. Following is a comprehensive list of over twenty common types of feedback:

- *Progress on objectives.* To what degree were the objectives met?

- *Program content.* Was the content appropriate? Important? Motivational?

- *Program materials.* Were the materials useful? Practical?

- *Pre-work materials.* Were the pre-work, or introductory, materials necessary? Helpful?

- *Assignments.* Were the assignments helpful?

- *Method of delivery.* Was the method of delivery appropriate? Efficient? Timely?

- *Facilitator.* Was the facilitator effective? Knowledgeable? Responsive?

- *New information.* How much new information was included?

- *Motivation to learn.* Were you motivated to learn the content?

- *Relevance.* Was the program relevant to your needs?

- *Importance.* How important was the content to your success?

- *Value of program.* Was this a good investment? A good use of your time?

- *Rewarding.* Was the program rewarding?

- *Challenging.* Was the program difficult?

- *Logistics.* Were the scheduling and coordination efficient?

- *Facilities.* Did the facilities enhance the program? The learning environment?

- *Potential barriers.* What are the potential barriers to application of the program material?

- *Use of material.* How will you apply what you have learned?

- *Planned improvements.* What improvements will you make?

- *Recommendations for target audiences.* What is the appropriate audience for this program? Will you recommend it to others?

- *Overall evaluation.* What is your overall rating of the program?

Objective questions covering each of the areas listed will ensure thorough feedback from participants; although, if the data are not going to be used to improve the program or provide relevant information, then a type may be eliminated. Such feedback can be extremely useful in making adjustments in a program and may assist in predicting performance after the program.

In training, learning, development, consulting, and change management programs, evaluation of the facilitator deserves additional comment. In some organizations, the primary evaluation centers on the facilitator (a separate form may be used for each facilitator, if there are several), covering a variety of areas such as the following:

- Preparation for sessions
- Knowledge of the subject matter, including familiarity with content and depth of understanding
- Presentation skills, including clarity of the presentation, pacing of material, and eye contact
- Communication skills, including use of understandable language and real-life examples, as well as promotion of discussion
- Assessment of learners' understanding, and responses appropriate to learners' needs and questions
- Use of appropriate technology and ability to respond effectively to technical requirements of learners
- Encouragement of application of learning through the use of real-life examples, job-related discussions, and relevant exercises

In organizations in which significant learning activity occurs, reaction data collection is usually automated, employing computerized scanning and reporting. Typical questions can easily be developed for a scan sheet, and reports that will help decision makers understand and use the data can be programmed. Some organizations use direct input into a Web site to develop not only detailed reports but also databases, allowing feedback data to be compared with data from other programs or from the same program with other facilitators.

Data Collection Issues

Several issues can affect the quality and quantity of data collected at Level 1. These issues should be addressed professionally and efficiently in order to ensure that data are sufficient in quality, quantity, and objectivity.

Timing

The timing of data collection centers on particular events connected with the program. For example, reaction data collection for any industry conference may occur at the end of every session as well as at the end of the conference itself. Reaction data may be collected immediately after content or information is presented and then again after participants have had time to put that content into action. As discussed previously, feedback during the early stages of program implementation can be extremely useful. Ideally, early feedback will validate the decision to go forward with the project and confirm that the project aligns with business needs. Noting problems in the initial feedback allows adjustments to be made early in the program's implementation. In practice, however, many organizations omit early feedback and wait until significant parts of the project have been implemented, when feedback may be more meaningful.

Longer projects may require data collection at multiple points, which may require increased coordination and project management than when data are collected only once. However, automation makes data collection at multiple points in time more manageable. Measures can be taken at the beginning of the project and then at routine intervals once the project is under way.

Methods

A variety of methods can be used to collect reaction data. Instruments range from simple surveys to comprehensive interviews. The appropriate method depends on the type of data needed (quantitative or qualitative), the convenience of the method for potential respondents, the culture of the organization, and cost.

Questionnaires or surveys are the most common method of collecting and measuring reaction data. Questionnaires and surveys come in all sizes, ranging from short forms to detailed, multiple-page instruments. They can be used to obtain subjective data about participants' reactions as well as to document responses for use in a projected ROI analysis. Here participants forecast improvement in business measures as well as attempt to identify a monetary contribution from those improvements. Proper design of questionnaires and surveys is presented in Chapter One.

Interviews, though not used as frequently as questionnaires to capture reaction data, may be conducted to secure data that are difficult to obtain through written responses. Interviews may be desirable when a program is new or has a long duration. They can uncover success stories that may help to communicate early achievements of the program. Respondents may be reluctant to describe their experiences using a questionnaire but may volunteer the information to a skillful interviewer using probing techniques. A major disadvantage of interviews is that they are time-consuming, which increases the cost of data collection. They also require interviewer preparation in order to ensure that the process is consistent. Thus, for most reaction data collection, interviews are too expensive.

As previously discussed, focus groups are a useful tool when in-depth feedback is needed. Focus groups can be used in lieu of or in addition to the standard end-of-program questionnaire. In lieu of the questionnaire, the evaluator will gather limited data, and those data will be focused on one or two key issues in the program content and delivery. When using a focus group in addition to a questionnaire, specific follow-up on the initial results can occur. For example, a large-scale performance improvement initiative took place in a federal government agency. The reaction data from the end-of-program questionnaire indicated that even though participants were satisfied overall, they saw neither the relevance nor the value of the program itself. Focus groups allowed participants to express their concerns with the program more adequately than they could through the questionnaire.

Administrative Guidelines

Several administrative guidelines can improve the effectiveness of data collected at Level 1.

Keep responses anonymous. Anonymous feedback is recommended. It allows participants to be open with their comments, resulting in helpful and constructive feedback. Otherwise, the input may be biased or stifled because of concerns about the facilitator's reaction.

Have a neutral person collect the data. In addition to anonymous responses, it is helpful to have a neutral person to collect the feedback data. In some organizations, the program coordinator or sponsor conducts the evaluation at the end of the program, independent of the facilitator. This action increases the objectivity of the input and decreases the likelihood of the facilitator reacting unfavorably to criticism contained in the feedback.

Provide questions in advance. For lengthy evaluations involving programs that span several days, distribute the feedback questions early in the program so that participants can familiarize themselves with the issues. Participants can address specific topics as they are discussed during the program and will have more time to think through particular issues. They should be cautioned, however, not to reach a final conclusion on general issues until the end of the program or project.

Explain the purpose of the feedback and how it will be used. Although this is sometimes understood, repeating where the information goes and how it is used in the organization can be helpful. There may still be some mystery surrounding the use of feedback data. Restating the process in terms of the flow of data and the use of data may clarify this issue.

Consider ongoing evaluation. In lengthy programs, an end-of-program evaluation may suffer because participants are unable to remember their reactions from earlier in the program. An ongoing evaluation can be used to improve this situation. One approach is to distribute evaluation forms at the beginning of the program and then explain when and how to supply the information. After each topic is presented, participants evaluate that topic. That way, the information can be easily recalled by participants, and the feedback is more useful to program evaluators. Another approach is to use a daily or routine feedback form to collect input on program pacing, degree of involvement, unclear items, and so on. Exhibit 5.1 shows a routine feedback form.

Collect information related to improvement. Although it is difficult to secure realistic input related to cost reductions or savings as part of feedback data, it is worth a try. The response may be surprising. At times, a simple question will cause participants to focus on savings or improvements. A statement to elicit this sort of data might look like this:

> Please estimate the savings in monetary values that will be realized (for example, from increased productivity, improved methods, or reduced costs) over a period of one year as a result of this program: $ _____
>
> Please explain the basis of your estimate.
>
> Express as a percentage the confidence you place on your estimate (0% = no confidence, 100% = certainty): _____

Allow ample time for participants to provide data. A time crunch can cause problems. If participants are asked to provide feedback in a hurry, they may provide incomplete information, cutting their feedback short in an effort to finish and leave. One way to avoid

Exhibit 5.1. Routine Feedback Form

1. What issues still remain confusing or unclear?
   _____
   _____
   _____

2. The most useful information was
   _____
   _____
   _____

3. It would help me if you would
   _____
   _____
   _____

4. The pacing of the program was
   ☐ Just right
   ☐ Too slow
   ☐ Too fast

5. Three important items that you should cover soon are
   1) _____
   2) _____
   3) _____

6. Comments
   _____
   _____
   _____

this problem is to allow ample time for evaluation in a scheduled session before the end of the program. The evaluation session could be followed by a wrap-up of the program. A thirty-minute session would provide an opportunity for thorough feedback, enhancing the quality and quantity of information.

Uses of Reaction Data

Sometimes, feedback is solicited, tabulated, summarized, and then disregarded. Too often, program evaluators use the material to feed their egos and then let it quietly disappear in the files, forgetting the original purposes for its collection. Information should be collected and used for one or more of the purposes of evaluation; otherwise, the exercise is a waste of time. Typical purposes of collecting reaction data include these:

Monitoring customer satisfaction. Reaction data indicate participants' and other stakeholders' overall reaction to and satisfaction with the program, allowing program developers and owners some insight into how satisfied the customers are with their product.

Identifying strengths and weaknesses of a program. Feedback helps identify the weaknesses as well as the strengths of a program. Finding weaknesses often leads to adjustments and changes as a result of the feedback. Identifying strengths so that they can be replicated in future designs is an important use of reaction data.

Developing norms and standards. Because reaction data are usually collected for 100 percent of programs and because tabulation of the data can be automated, it is relatively easy to develop norms and standards for reaction data within an organization. Target ratings can be set, and later, the actual ratings can be compared against those norms and standards.

Evaluating facilitators and team members. Perhaps one of the most common uses of reaction data is program team evaluation. If data collection is properly planned and executed, helpful feedback can be provided to facilitators and program leaders, allowing them to make adjustments that increase their program's effectiveness. Some caution needs to be exercised because facilitator and program leader evaluations are sometimes biased due to the presence of a facilitator during the evaluation or to relationships with team leaders and members. When a concern with bias does exist, other evidence may be necessary to provide a complete performance assessment.

Evaluating planned improvements. Feedback data from program participants can provide a profile of their planned improvements. This profile can be compared with the on-the-job actions that were anticipated results of the program when it began. Thus, reaction data can be a rich source of information on what processes, methods, or behaviors participants may be changing or implementing because of what they have learned.

Linking with follow-up data. If a follow-up evaluation is planned, linking reaction data with follow-up data may be helpful in order to see whether planned improvements became reality. In most cases, planned actions are inhibited in some way by on-the-job barriers.

Obtaining material for marketing programs. For some organizations, participant feedback data provides helpful marketing information. Direct participant statements or reactions on particular issues can provide information that may be convincing to potential participants. Program brochures and other marketing pieces often contain quotes from and summaries of feedback data.

Final Thoughts

This chapter discussed data collection at the first level of evaluation, reaction and planned action. Measuring reaction is a component of every study and is a critical factor in a program's success. Data are collected by means of a variety of techniques, although surveys and questionnaires are most often used, due to their cost-effectiveness and convenience. Level 1 data are important because they allow immediate adjustments to be made to a program. While reaction data are important to those who are directly involved in implementing a program, their value to executives is usually low. The value of data to executives increases as the evaluation moves up the chain of impact.

Reference

Phillips, J. J., Myhill, M., and McDonough, J. B. *Proving the Value of Meetings and Events.* Birmingham, Ala.: ROI Institute; Meetings Professional International, 2007.

6

Measuring Learning and Confidence

Measuring learning is an important part of the evaluation process, especially when a program is intended to change on-the-job behaviors or processes. Participants' knowledge of what to do and how to do it is critical to a program's success. This chapter focuses on simple, commonly used techniques for measuring learning and begins with a look at the reasons for measuring learning.

Why Measure Learning and Confidence?

Several key principles illustrate the importance of measuring learning during the course of a program. Each in itself is sufficient to justify measurement of learning; together, they provide an indication of the full range of benefits that result from measuring the changes in skills, knowledge, and other qualities that occur during a program.

The Learning Organization

During the past two decades, organizations have experienced a rapid transformation of competitive global markets as a result of economic changes. Organizations need new ways to serve customers, and they need new technology and innovations to enhance efficiency, to restructure, to reorganize, and to execute their functions globally. In response to this need for strategic change, the concept known as the learning organization evolved. This concept requires organizations to use learning in proactive and integrated ways to support growth for individuals, teams, and entire organizations. Peter Senge popularized the idea of the learning organization, suggesting that organizations capture, share, and use knowledge so that their members can work together to change how the organization responds to challenges (Senge, 1990). Managers must question old social constructs and practice new ways of thinking.

Learning must take place within and must support a framework of teams and larger groups in which individuals can work together to generate new knowledge. The process must be continual, because a learning organization is a never-ending journey (Watkins and Marsick, 1996).

With the new focus on creating learning organizations in which countless activities and processes are in place to promote continual learning, measurement of learning has become an important issue. How can we know whether an organization has become a learning organization? How is learning in such an organization measured? Can learning be measured on a large scale?

Compliance Issues

Organizations face an increasing number of regulations with which they must routinely comply. These regulations involve all aspects of business, and governing bodies consider them essential to protect customers, investors, and the environment. Employees must have some knowledge of the regulations in order to remain in compliance. Therefore, an organization must measure the extent of employee learning and understanding of the regulations to ensure that compliance does not become a problem.

Some programs are compliance-driven. For example, one large banking organization had to implement a major program to ensure that its employees were all familiar with regulations on money laundering. This program was precipitated by the bank's continuing failure to comply with the regulations. The problem appeared to arise from a lack of knowledge of the rules. When programs such as this are initiated, learning must be measured.

Development of Competencies

The use of competencies and competency models has increased dramatically in recent years. In the struggle for competitive advantage, many organizations have focused on people as the key to their success. Competency models are used to ensure that employees do the right things, clarifying and articulating what is required for effective performance. Competency models help organizations align behavior and skills with the strategic direction of the company. A competency model describes a particular combination of knowledge, skills, and characteristics necessary to perform a role in an organization. Competency models are used as tools for recruiting, selecting, training, reviewing performance, and even removing individuals from the organization (Lucia and Lepsinger, 1999). With the increased focus on competencies, measuring learning is a necessity.

Certification

The learning and development field has gone crazy over certification. Employees are becoming certified in many processes, ranging from Microsoft™ products and service to Six Sigma implementation. With this focus on certification comes an increased emphasis on measuring learning. Almost every certification program (if not all of them) requires that individuals demonstrate that they know something or know how to do something. Certification programs place much more emphasis on measurement than typical learning and development programs.

Consequences of an Unprepared Workforce

Perhaps the most important reason to focus on learning measurement is to ensure that the workforce is prepared. Many sad and disappointing stories have detailed how employees are not capable of performing the skills needed to do their jobs and deliver excellent customer service. Hearing about or experiencing such gaps in workers' skills has motivated many management teams to work hard to ensure that their workers are prepared. The only way to make sure that employees have learned the knowledge and skills needed to perform their jobs successfully is to measure learning through some credible, valid, and reliable process.

The Role of Learning in Programs

Although some programs involve new equipment, processes, and technology, the human factor remains critical to the success of most programs. Whether an organization is restructuring or adding new systems, employees must learn how to work in the new environment, a process that requires them to develop new knowledge and skills. Simple tasks and procedures do not necessarily come with new processes. Instead, complex environments, procedures, and tools must be used in an intelligent way to reap the desired benefits for the organization. Employees must learn in different ways—not just in a formal classroom environment but through technology-based learning and on-the-job practice. Team leaders and managers serve as coaches or mentors in some programs. In a few cases, learning coaches or on-the-job trainers are used to ensure that learning is transferred to the job and is implemented as planned.

Participants don't always fully understand what they must do. Although the chain of impact can be broken at any level, a common place for such a break is at Level 2, learning and confidence. Employees simply may not know what to do or how to do it properly. When application and implementation of program skills do not go smoothly, program leaders need to determine whether a learning deficiency is the problem; if it is, they may be able to eliminate it. In other words, measurement of learning is necessary to leaders' understanding of why employees are or are not performing as they should.

Measurement Issues

Several factors affect the nature and scope of measurement at the learning level. These factors include challenges of testing, program objectives, the measures themselves, and timing.

Challenges

The greatest challenge when measuring learning is maintaining objectivity without crossing ethical or legal lines while keeping costs low. A common method of measuring learning is testing (discussed in Chapter Two). This approach generates its own unique challenges.

The first challenge is the fear factor. Few people enjoy being tested. Many are offended by it and feel that their professional expertise is being questioned. Some people are intimidated by tests, which bring back memories of their third-grade math teacher, red pen in hand.

Another challenge raised by tests is the legal and ethical repercussions of basing decisions about employees' job status on test scores. Therefore, organizations often use other techniques to measure learning, such as surveys, questionnaires, role-playing, and simulations. These methods, however, bring their own challenges as well—most notably, the financial burden they impose and the potential for inaccurate measures. Trade-offs often must be made between resources and the accuracy of the learning measurement process.

Program Objectives

The starting point for any level of measurement is development of the program's objectives. Measurement of learning is built on a program's learning objectives. Learning and development professionals are skilled at generating detailed learning objectives by following the process described in book one of this series, *ROI Fundamentals*. However, even for programs in which the focus is not necessarily on a learning activity but on, for example, implementing a new policy, initiating a new procedure, or creating a wellness and fitness center, the first step is ensuring that learning objectives are in place. Following are some examples of learning objectives:

- Identify the six features of the new ethics policy.
- Demonstrate the use of each software routine within the standard time.
- Score 75 or better on the new-product quiz.
- Explain the value of diversity in a work group.
- Successfully complete the leadership simulation.
- Know how to apply for housing assistance.

Typically, the objectives of a program are broad and indicate only major skills or general knowledge areas that should be achieved as the program is implemented. These are sometimes called a program's key learning objectives. Key learning objectives can be broken into specific measures that define the criteria for success or failure. Such detail is necessary when a tremendous number of tasks, procedures, or new skills must be learned in order to make a program successful. For other programs, this level of detail might not be needed; identifying the major objectives and indicating what must be accomplished in order to meet each objective is often sufficient.

Typical Measures

Measurement of learning focuses on knowledge, skills, and attitudes as well as on an individual's confidence in applying or implementing the project or program as desired. Typical measures at this level involve

- Skills
- Knowledge
- Awareness
- Understanding
- Contacts
- Attitudes
- Capacity
- Readiness
- Confidence

Obviously, the more detailed the knowledge area, the greater the number of possible objectives. The concept of knowledge is quite broad and often includes the assimilation of facts, figures, and ideas. Instead of knowledge, terms such as *awareness, understanding,* and *information* may be used to identify specific categories of knowledge. Sometimes, a participant's perceptions or attitudes change based on what he or she has learned. For example, participants' perceptions of a diverse work group are often changed when a major diversity program is implemented. In some cases, the focus of a program is development of a reservoir of knowledge and related skills in order to improve capability, capacity, or readiness. Networking is often part of a program; in that case, developing contacts who may be valuable later is important. Networking may occur within or outside of an organization. For example, within an organization, a program may include people from different functional areas of the organization, and an expected outcome from a learning perspective might be knowing who to contact at particular times in the future. In programs that involve different organizations, such as a marketing event, new contacts that result from the event may be important and may ultimately pay off in terms of efficiency or revenue growth.

Timing

The timing of learning measurement can vary depending on the program content and design as well as the participants involved in the program. In some situations, a preliminary measure needs to be taken, so a pretest is generated to determine the extent to which participants understand the specific objectives or content of the program. A pretest can be important in assessing participants' current skills and knowledge so that the learning of additional skills and knowledge can be planned more efficiently. This step may prevent participants from being taught information they already know. When a pretest has been used, it is common to administer a posttest in order to obtain data to compare with those from the pretest. The posttest can be administered early in the program or as soon as the learning portion is completed. The pretest and posttest should be conducted under the same or similar conditions, using questions or other test items that are identical or very similar. A factor to consider in using pretests and posttests is participants' existing level of knowledge. Participants who have no previous knowledge of the content presented should not be pretested. The baseline for them is zero. When they are pretested, the results may reflect what participants think they know, and the corresponding posttest may result in lower scores, because through the program process participants have realized what they don't know. Participants who are expected to have some level of knowledge are good targets for pretesting as the program is intended to enhance their current level of knowledge.

If no pretest is administered, measurement of learning can occur at various times. If formal learning sessions connected with the program are offered, a measure will be taken at the end of each session to ensure that participants are ready to apply their newly acquired knowledge. If a program has no formal learning sessions, measurement may occur at different intervals. In long-term programs, as skills and knowledge grow, routine assessment may be necessary to measure both the acquisition of additional skills and the retention of previously acquired skills. The timing and frequency of measurement are aligned with the need to know the new information and are always balanced against the cost of obtaining, analyzing, and responding to the data. Ideally, the timing of measurement is considered as part of the development of a data collection plan, as discussed in Chapter Six of *ROI Fundamentals*, the first book in this series.

Data Collection Methods

One of the most important considerations in measuring learning is the specific way in which data are collected. Learning data can be collected using many different methods. The following list of instruments includes just some of the data collection methods that are used:

- Questionnaires
- Performance tests
- Technology simulations and task simulations
- Case studies
- Role-playing or skill practice
- Informal assessments

These methods were discussed in earlier chapters.

Many times, learning will be measured by means of a self-assessment instrument on which participants indicate the extent to which they have learned the material. Self-assessments were discussed briefly in Chapter Two. They are discussed here because of their frequent use in measuring learning. Exhibit 6.1 shows an end-of-the-conference questionnaire for an annual business development conference for insurance agents. The questionnaire includes questions that cover reaction and learning, a typical data collection method that provides an opportunity to raise the percentage of programs that are evaluated at Level 2. In essence, the learning measures are taken at the same time as the reaction measures; in

Exhibit 6.1. End-of-Conference Questionnaire

	Strongly Disagree				Strongly Agree	
	1	2	3	4	5	n/a
Reaction						
1. The meeting was organized and efficient.	○	○	○	○	○	○
2. The speakers were effective.	○	○	○	○	○	○
3. The meeting was valuable for business development.	○	○	○	○	○	○
4. The meeting content was important to my success.	○	○	○	○	○	○
5. The meeting was motivating.	○	○	○	○	○	○
6. The meeting was challenging.	○	○	○	○	○	○
7. The meeting contained new information.	○	○	○	○	○	○
8. The meeting represented an excellent use of my time.	○	○	○	○	○	○
9. I will use the material from this conference.	○	○	○	○	○	○
Learning						
10. I can identify the five steps for a business development strategy.	○	○	○	○	○	○
11. I can develop a business development plan.	○	○	○	○	○	○
12. I can select the best community service group to join for business development.	○	○	○	○	○	○
13. I can explain the changes in products.	○	○	○	○	○	○
14. I can identify the five most effective ways to turn a contact into a sale.	○	○	○	○	○	○
15. I can identify at least five agents to call for suggestions and advice.	○	○	○	○	○	○
Suggestions for Improvement						
16. What suggestions do you have for improving this conference?	○					

this instance, as mentioned, the data are collected at the end of the conference.

Another common method of measuring learning is the true-false test. This basic form of objective learning assessment tests recall of key concepts and information presented during a program. Answers are either right or wrong, unless the answers are intended to generate discussion rather than to actually test knowledge. If this is the case, it may be more appropriate to refer to this type of assessment as a true-false survey, as testing rules have probably not been followed.

Administrative Issues

Several administrative issues must be addressed when learning is measured. Each issue is briefly discussed in this section and should be considered as part of the overall plan for collecting learning data.

Validity and Reliability

Two important issues in test design are validity and reliability. Validity is the extent to which an instrument measures what it is designed to measure. Reliability is the extent to which the results provided by an instrument are stable or consistent over time. Any instrument used to collect data should be both valid (measure what it should measure) and reliable (provide consistent results over time). An instrument is reliable when the same questions, asked at different times, with no intervening processes or variables changing in the respondent's knowledge, yield the same responses. Significant deviations indicate that an instrument is unreliable.

Validity and reliability become particularly important criteria when a human resource action (job status change) is taken as a result of a person's failing a specific test or failing to meet a specific standard when learning is measured. For example, if an individual is promoted, denied promotion, provided an increase in pay, or assigned a job because of his or her performance on a test, the

Figure 6.1. Relationship Between Validity and Reliability

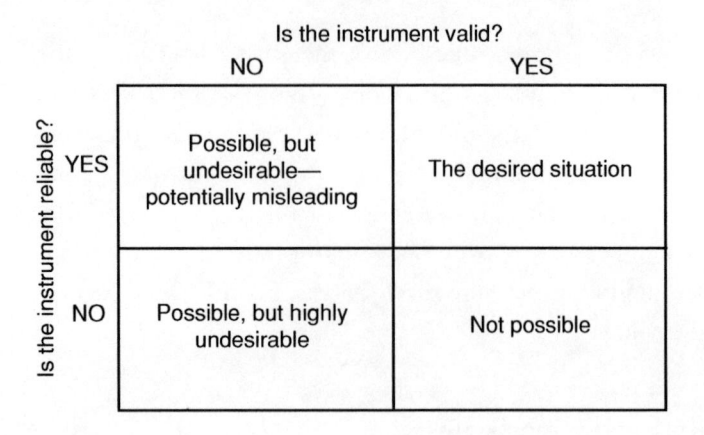

	Is the instrument valid? NO	Is the instrument valid? YES
Is the instrument reliable? YES	Possible, but undesirable—potentially misleading	The desired situation
Is the instrument reliable? NO	Possible, but highly undesirable	Not possible

instrument must be defensible. Of course, in the vast majority of programs, the consequences of not passing a test will not be so severe. The concepts of validity and reliability and how to check for adequate levels of the two are beyond the scope of this book, but other sources provide more detail (for example, see Phillips and Phillips, 2007).

Understanding the relationship between validity and reliability is important (see Figure 6.1). An instrument cannot be valid unless it is also reliable, although, it can be reliable without being valid. Validity should be strived for when developing data collection instruments.

Consistency

Tests, exercises, and assessments for measuring learning must be administered consistently from one group to another in order to effectively measure and compare learning between groups. Consistency refers to the time allotted to respond, the conditions under which participants complete the process, the resources available to them, and the amount of assistance they receive from other members of the group. These concerns can easily be addressed in the instructions.

When formal testing is used, participants should be monitored as they complete the test. Monitoring ensures that individuals work independently and that someone is available to provide assistance or answer questions as needed. These considerations may not apply in all situations, but they should be addressed in the evaluation plan.

Pilot Testing

It is advisable to test an instrument with a small group to ensure that the instrument is both valid and reliable. A pilot test provides an opportunity to resolve anything that is confusing about the instructions, questions, or statements. When a pilot test is administered, it should be timed to see how long individuals take to complete it. Also, the individuals taking the pilot test should provide input on other ways to ask the questions, improve the flow of information, and generally improve the test. At a minimum, a test should be pilot-tested in order to examine its content. All too often, a test or survey is administered that does not cover the content necessary to support implementation of the program.

Scoring and Reporting

Scoring instructions for the measurement process need to be developed in such a way that the person evaluating the responses will be objective and consistent in the scoring. Ideally, the potential for bias from the individual scoring the instrument will be completely eliminated by providing proper scoring instructions and other information necessary to guarantee an objective evaluation.

In some situations—for example, when self-scoring tests or group-based scoring mechanisms are used—participants are given the results immediately. In other situations, the results may not be known until later. In these situations, a method for providing the scores should be built into the evaluation plan unless it has been determined that participants will not know the scores. The worst course of action is to promise that participants will receive their test scores and then deliver them late or not at all.

Confronting Failure

Failure to pass the test may not be an issue, particularly if the data are collected informally through a self-assessment process. However, when more rigorous and formal methods are used and individuals do not demonstrate the required competency to pass the test, the issue of failures must be confronted. An important principle is to ensure that the test and the testing procedures are defensible. As described earlier, a test must be both reliable and valid, and the cut-off score for passing must be defensible. Written material should be developed to address these issues, and participants should be familiar with this material before they take the test. The outcomes and consequences of taking the test should also be discussed with the individuals. Repeating the test may be allowed, if appropriate, as long as all individuals receive the same treatment.

Uses of Learning Data

Data must be used to add value and to improve processes. Several uses of learning data are appropriate; those described in this section are the most common.

Ensuring that learning has been acquired. Sometimes, knowing the extent and scope of learning is essential. Measuring learning, even informally, will provide input on this issue, indicating whether the learning component of the chain of input is successful.

Providing individual feedback in order to build confidence. Learning data, when provided directly to participants, support the learning process by providing reinforcement of correct answers and enhancing confidence.

Improving a program. Perhaps the most important use of learning data is improving a program. Learning data provide designers, developers, facilitators, and team leaders with information and impetus for process improvement. Consistently low responses on certain learning measures may indicate that inadequate facilitation has been provided on that topic. Consistently low scores from all participants may indicate that the objectives and scope of coverage are misdirected or too ambitious.

Evaluating facilitators. In addition to reaction and planned action data, learning measures can be used to evaluate program leaders and facilitators, providing evidence of their success (or lack thereof). A facilitator has the responsibility of ensuring that participants learn the new skills and knowledge needed for program success. Learning measures reflect the degree to which the skills and knowledge have been acquired and internalized for application.

Building a database. In major programs that are repeated, building a database to track competency improvement, skills acquisition, or required knowledge may be helpful. Such data sets may be beneficial in indicating how one program compares with others. Over time, they can also be used to set expectations and judge success.

Final Thoughts

This chapter discusses some of the key issues involved in measuring learning—an important ingredient in program success. Even if it is accomplished informally, learning must be assessed to determine the extent to which the participants in a program have learned new skills, techniques, processes, tools, and procedures. By measuring learning, facilitators and program leaders can ascertain the degree to which participants are capable of successfully implementing the program. Measuring learning provides an opportunity to quickly make adjustments and improvements in order to facilitate program success. While learning measures indicate potential success with implementation, measurement at the next level, application and implementation (Level 3), indicates actual progress.

References

Lucia, A. D., and Lepsinger, R. *The Art and Science of Competency Models: Pinpointing Critical Success Factors in Organizations.* San Francisco: Pfeiffer, 1999.

Phillips, J. J., and Phillips, P. P. *Handbook of Training Evaluation and Measurement Methods.* (4th ed.) Woburn, Mass.: Butterworth-Heinemann, 2007.

Senge, P. *The Fifth Discipline: The Art and Practice of the Learning Organization.* New York: Random House, 1990.

Watkins, K. E., and Marsick, V. J. (eds.). *Creating the Learning Organization.* (J. J. Phillips, series ed.) Alexandria, Va.: ASTD, 1996.

7

Measuring Application and Implementation

Many programs fail because of breakdowns in implementation. Participants just don't do what is expected, at the time expected, and as often as expected. Measuring application and implementation is critical to understanding the success of implementation. Without successful implementation, positive business impact will not occur and no positive return will be achieved.

This chapter explores the most common ways to evaluate the application and implementation of projects, processes, and programs. The possibilities vary from the use of questionnaires to observation to action planning. In addition to describing the techniques used to evaluate implementation, this chapter addresses the challenges and benefits of each technique.

Why Measure Application and Implementation?

Measuring application and implementation is absolutely necessary for some programs. It provides the most critical data set because it helps evaluators understand the degree to which successful program implementation has occurred and the barriers and enablers that influence success.

Obtain Essential Information

As Chapter One of *ROI Fundamentals* briefly discusses, the value of information to senior executives increases as evaluation progresses up the chain of impact from reaction (Level 1) to ROI (Level 5). Therefore, information concerning application and implementation (Level 3) is more valuable to clients than reaction and learning data (Levels 1 and 2). This fact does not discount the importance of evaluation at the first two levels but emphasizes the importance of moving up the chain of impact. Measuring the extent to which a program is implemented provides data about its success and about factors that can contribute to greater success as the program is fully implemented.

Level 1 and Level 2 measures occur during a program's early stages, when more attention is focused on participants' direct involvement in the program. Application and implementation measurement occurs after the program has been implemented. The data captured at this level reflect the program's success as participants apply the knowledge learned in the program to their job tasks. Essentially, this measure shows how well the system in which the participant works supports the transfer of knowledge to the job. Initial implementation of a program is the first step of a transition to a new state, behavior, or process. Understanding how successfully participants make the transition from applying skills in the program to applying them on the job requires measuring application and implementation.

Track Program Focus

Because many projects and programs focus directly on implementation and application of new behaviors and processes, a program sponsor often speaks in these terms and has concerns about measures of implementation success. The sponsor of a major program designed to transform an organization will be concerned with implementation and application and thus will want to know the extent to which key stakeholders adjust to and implement the desired new behaviors, processes, and procedures.

Discover Problems and Opportunities

If the chain of impact breaks at this level (application and implementation), little or no corresponding impact data will be available. Without impact, there is no return on the sponsor's investment. This breakdown most often occurs because participants in the program encounter barriers, inhibitors, or obstacles that deter implementation. A dilemma arises when reactions to the program are favorable and participants learn what is intended. Positive results at the reaction and learning levels set an expectation that knowledge transfer to the job will occur. Unfortunately, participants fail to overcome the barriers presented in the organization and don't accomplish what is necessary for success.

When a program goes astray, the first question usually asked is "What happened?" More important, when a program appears to add no value, the first question should be "What can we do to change its direction?" In responding to either question, it is important to identify the barriers to success, the problems with implementation, and the obstacles to application. At Level 3, implementation and application, these problems are addressed, identified, and examined. In many cases, the stakeholders directly involved in the process can provide important recommendations on making changes or using a different approach in the future.

When a program is successful, the obvious question is "How can we repeat this or improve it in the future?" The answer to this question is also found at Level 3. Identifying the factors that contribute directly to the success of a program is critical. Often, those same elements can be used to replicate the process and, possibly, to produce better results in the future. When key stakeholders identify critical elements and issues, they make the program successful and provide an important case history on what is necessary for success.

Reward Effectiveness

Measuring application and implementation allows the sponsor and the program team to reward those who do the best job of applying the processes and implementing the program. Measures taken at this level provide clear evidence of success and achievement and also provide a basis for performance reviews. Rewards often have a reinforcing value, helping to keep employees on track and communicating strong encouragement for future improvement.

Challenges

Collecting application and implementation data involves key challenges that must be addressed in order to attain a successful evaluation at this level.

Linking Application with Learning

Application data should be linked closely with the learning data discussed in the preceding chapter. Program leaders need to know what has been accomplished, what has been done differently, and what activities have been implemented, all in comparison with what the participants learned to do in the program. This level of evaluation measures the extent to which participants accurately took what they learned and applied it to their jobs.

Building Data Collection into the Program

Application data are collected after the program's implementation. Because of the time lag between program implementation and data collection, it is difficult to secure high-quality data and a large quantity of data. One of the most effective ways to ensure that the appropriate quality and quantity of data are collected is to build data collection into the program from the beginning. Data collection tools positioned as application tools must be built in as part of the implementation. By analogy, consider that many software applications contain overlay software that shows a user performance profile. Essentially, the software invisibly tracks the user, capturing the steps, pace, and difficulties encountered while using the software. When the process is complete, a credible data set has been captured, simply because program leaders built it into the process at the beginning.

Ensuring a Sufficient Amount of Data

Regardless of whether data were collected through questionnaires, action plans, interviews, or focus groups, poor response rates are a problem in most organizations. Motivating individuals to participate in the data collection process is a challenge. Ensuring that adequate amounts of high-quality data are available requires a serious effort to achieve adequate response rates.

When the program is intended to improve business impact and ultimately show a positive ROI, there is less emphasis on application and implementation measures; in many cases, they are omitted or slighted during the analysis. This is unfortunate as attention must be given to changing processes, procedures, and tasks, as well as to removing barriers in order to achieve the business goal. Doing things differently can result in substantial benefits, but knowing the degree to which things are done differently and the supporting or deterring influences is essential to guaranteeing those benefits in the future.

Addressing Application Needs at the Outset

During needs assessment, one question that is asked is "What is being done (or not being done) on the job that's inhibiting [business measure]?" When this question is answered adequately, a connection is made between the solution and the business measure. When this issue is addressed, the activities or behaviors that need to change are identified, serving as the basis of the data collection. The bottom line is that too many evaluations focus either on impact measures, which define the business measure intended to be improved, or on learning measures, which uncover what people do not know. More focus is needed at Level 3, which involves the tasks, processes, procedures, and behaviors that need to be in place for success on the job.

Measurement Issues

In measuring program application and implementation, the key issues are largely similar to those encountered in measuring reaction and learning. There are slight differences due to the later time frame in which these data are collected.

Methods

Methods for collecting data at Level 3 include traditional surveys and questionnaires, observation, interviews, and focus groups. Other powerful methods include action planning and follow-up sessions.

Objectives

As at the other levels of evaluation, the starting point for Level 3 data collection is the objectives set for program application and implementation. Without clear objectives, collecting data would be difficult. Objectives define what activity is expected. They provide specific milestones that indicate when one part or all of the process has been implemented. Typical application objectives are as follows:

- At least 99.1 percent of software users will be following the correct sequences after three weeks of use.

- Within one year of program implementation, 10 percent of employees will submit documented suggestions for cutting costs.

- Ninety-five percent of high-potential employees will complete individual development plans within two years of program implementation.

- Forty percent of the city's homeless population will apply for special housing within one year of program launch.

- Eighty percent of employees will use one or more of the three cost containment features of the health care plan in the next round of annual enrollment.

- Fifty percent of conference attendees will follow up with at least one contact from the conference within six months.

Areas of Coverage

To a certain extent, the areas of coverage for application and implementation measurement in a given program will parallel the areas that were identified for learning measurement. The later time frame for implementation data collection changes the measurement from a predictive measure to a post-program measure. The key point is that this level focuses on action, not on the ability to act (Level 2) and not on the consequences of acting (Level 4).

The sheer number of activities to measure can be mind-boggling. Action areas for application will vary from program to program, depending on the need for the program and the objectives and measures that represent program success. Table 7.1 shows some typical areas.

Data Sources

The many sources of evaluation data were identified in Chapter Six of *ROI Fundamentals*. Essentially, all key stakeholders are potential data sources. Perhaps the most important sources of data are the users of the solutions—that is, those directly involved in the application and implementation of the project or program. Members of the program team or team leaders charged with the implementation may also be good sources of implementation data. In some cases,

Table 7.1. Examples of Action Areas for Application of Program Learning

Action	Explanation	Example
Increase	Increasing an activity or action	Use negotiation skills with a certain level of frequency.
Decrease	Decreasing an activity or action	Decrease the number of times water temperature is checked during manufacturing.
Eliminate	Stopping a task or activity	Eliminate the formal follow-up meeting and replace it with a virtual meeting.
Maintain	Keeping the same level of activity for a particular process	Continue to monitor the manufacturing process on the same schedule previously used.
Create	Designing or implementing a new procedure, process, or activity	Create a procedure for resolving the differences between two divisions.
Use	Using a process, procedure, skill, or activity	Use communication skills in difficult customer service situations.
Perform	Performing a task, process, or procedure	Conduct a post-audit review at the end of each marketing cycle.
Participate	Becoming involved in an activity or program	Submit a suggestion for reducing R&D costs.

Table 7.1. Examples of Action Areas for Application of Program Learning (*Continued*)

Action	Explanation	Example
Enroll	Signing up for a process, program, or project	Enroll in a career advancement program.
Respond	Reacting to groups, individuals, or systems	Respond to customer inquiries within fifteen minutes.
Network	Facilitating relationships with others who are involved in or have been affected by a program	Continue networking with contacts on at least a quarterly basis.

the best source of application data may be organizational records such as audit reports, time sheets, and databases.

Timing

The timing of application data collection varies. Because application data collection is a follow-up activity after the program launch, the key issue is determining the best time for a post-implementation evaluation. The challenge is to analyze the nature and scope of the application and implementation in order to determine the earliest point by which a trend or pattern may evolve. At this point, the application of skills has become routine and the implementation is making progress. Determining this point is a judgment call. Collecting data as early as possible is important so that adjustments to the implementation, if necessary, can still be made. At the same time, evaluators must wait long enough so that behavior changes have a chance to occur and implementation makes enough progress to be observed and measured. In programs spanning a considerable length of time, measures may be taken at three- to six-month intervals. Using effective measures at well-timed intervals will provide successive input on the progress of implementation and clearly show the extent of improvement.

Convenience and project constraints also influence the timing of data collection. If the participants are meeting to observe a milestone or a special event, the meeting provides an excellent opportunity to collect data. Sometimes, constraints are placed on data collection. Consider, for example, the time constraint that sponsors may impose. If they are anxious to have the data in order to make program decisions, they may request that data collection be moved to an earlier time than is ideal.

Responsibilities

Measuring application and implementation usually requires many people to share the responsibility and the work. In Level 3 data collection, an important issue is determining who is responsible for following up on the progress of implementation. Application data collection may fall to personnel ranging from program staff and sponsors to external consultants. This matter should be addressed during the planning stages so that no misunderstanding arises about the distribution of responsibilities. More important, those who are responsible should fully understand the nature and scope of their role and what will be needed to collect the data.

Data Collection Methods

Some techniques for collecting application and implementation data are easy to administer and provide quality data. Other techniques provide greater detail about program success but raise more challenges in administration.

Questionnaires

Questionnaires have become a mainstream tool for collecting application and implementation data because of their flexibility, low cost, and ease of administration. The discussion of questionnaire design in Chapter One can be applied to the development of questionnaires that measure application and implementation. One of the most difficult tasks is determining the issues to include in a follow-up questionnaire. Exhibit 7.1 presents an example of a questionnaire used to capture application, implementation, and impact data (Level 3 and Level 4 data).

A questionnaire like this might serve as the primary method of data collection for follow-up data. This example will be used to illustrate many of the issues involved in designing questionnaire items, especially items for collecting application (Level 3) and impact (Level 4) data.

Progress with Objectives

Sometimes, using a program's objectives to assess progress in the follow-up evaluation is helpful, as illustrated in question 1 in Exhibit 7.1. While program objectives are usually assessed during the program (when Level 1 data are collected), it can be beneficial to revisit the objectives after the participants have had an opportunity to apply what has been learned.

Use of Program Materials and Handouts

If participants have been provided with materials to use on the job, determining the extent to which these materials are used is important. This is particularly helpful when operating manuals, reference books, and job aids have been distributed and explained during the program and are expected to be used on the job. Question 2 in Exhibit 7.1 focuses on this issue.

Application of Knowledge and Skills

Knowing the level of improvement in the skills directly linked to the program is important (see question 3). A more detailed variation of this question lists each skill and asks participants to indicate their frequency of use and effectiveness of use for each. For many skills, frequent use soon after acquisition is critical so that the skills

Exhibit 7.1. Sample Questionnaire

Pharma Company

Note: This example is used only to illustrate a sampling of questions that may be asked on a follow-up questionnaire. It is not intended to represent a document that is ready for implementation.

Instructions

Please complete this questionnaire as promptly as possible and return it to the address shown on the last page. To provide responses, you will need to reflect on the leadership development program and think about specific ways in which you have applied what you learned from each session. It may be helpful to review the materials from each session.

Please take your time as you provide responses. Accurate and complete responses are very important. You should be able to provide thorough responses in about 25 minutes.

Please be objective in providing responses. In no way will your name be linked to your input. Your questionnaire and action plan will be viewed only by a representative from an external firm, the ROI Institute. Specific responses or comments related to any individual will not be communicated to your employer.

Your responses will help determine the impact of this program and provide data for making adjustments. In exchange for your participation in this evaluation, a summary of the success of the entire class will be sent to you within two weeks. Three weeks later, you will receive a summary of the changes made to the program based on your input. Please make sure that your input is included along with that of your classmates.

Should you need clarification or more information, please contact your instructor, your representative, or a representative from the ROI Institute.

For each person returning the questionnaire, we are pleased to provide a copy of Marshall Goldsmith's book *What Got You Here Won't Get You There.* When you have returned the questionnaire, please let Crystal know, and she will be happy to send you a copy of the book. Thanks for your cooperation on this very important issue.

Jim Rogers
Chief Executive Officer

Exhibit 7.1. Sample Questionnaire (*Continued*)

Leadership Development Program Impact Questionnaire

Are you currently in a supervisory or management role or capacity? Yes ❑ No ❑

1. Listed below are the objectives of the leadership program. After reflecting on the program, please indicate your degree of success in achieving these objectives. *Please check the appropriate response beside each item.*

	No Success	Very Little Success	Limited Success	Generally Successful	Completely Successful
A. Apply the 11-step goal-setting process	❑	❑	❑	❑	❑
B. Apply the 12-step leadership planning process	❑	❑	❑	❑	❑
C. Identify the 12 core competencies of outstanding leaders	❑	❑	❑	❑	❑
D. Identify 10 ways to create higher levels of employee loyalty and satisfaction	❑	❑	❑	❑	❑
E. Apply the concept of deferred judgment in 5 scenarios	❑	❑	❑	❑	❑
F. Apply the creative problem-solving process to an identified problem	❑	❑	❑	❑	❑
G. Identify the 7 best ways to build positive relationships	❑	❑	❑	❑	❑
H. Given a work situation, apply the 4-step approach to deal with errors	❑	❑	❑	❑	❑
I. Practice 6 ways to improve communication effectiveness	❑	❑	❑	❑	❑

2. Have you used the written materials since you participated in the program?
   Yes ❑   No ❑
   Please explain: _____

3. In the following result areas, please indicate the level of improvement during the last few months as influenced by your participation in the leadership program. *Check the appropriate response beside each item.*

Exhibit 7.1. Sample Questionnaire (*Continued*)

Result Area	No Opportunity to Apply	No Change	Some Change	Moderate Change	Significant Change	Very Significant Change
A. ORGANIZING						
1) Prioritizing daily activities	❏	❏	❏	❏	❏	❏
2) Applying creative techniques	❏	❏	❏	❏	❏	❏
3) Organizing daily activities	❏	❏	❏	❏	❏	❏
4) Raising level of performance standards in area of responsibility	❏	❏	❏	❏	❏	❏
B. WORK CLIMATE						
1) Applying coaching	❏	❏	❏	❏	❏	❏
2) Applying techniques or initiatives that influence motivational climate	❏	❏	❏	❏	❏	❏
3) Implementing actions that influenced retaining people	❏	❏	❏	❏	❏	❏
4) Implementing job enrichment opportunities for valued associates	❏	❏	❏	❏	❏	❏
5) Implementing better control and monitoring systems	❏	❏	❏	❏	❏	❏
6) Applying techniques that influenced better teamwork	❏	❏	❏	❏	❏	❏
C. PERSONAL OUTCOMES						
1) Realizing improved written communications	❏	❏	❏	❏	❏	❏
2) Realizing improved oral communications	❏	❏	❏	❏	❏	❏
3) Realizing greater self-confidence	❏	❏	❏	❏	❏	❏
4) Working personal leadership plan	❏	❏	❏	❏	❏	❏

Exhibit 7.1. Sample Questionnaire (*Continued*)

4. List the three behaviors or skills from the above list that you have used most frequently as a result of the program.
   A) _____
   B) _____
   C) _____

5. What has changed about you or your work as a result of your participation in this program? (Specific behavior change such as increased delegation to employees, improved communication with employees, employee participation in decision making, improved problem solving, and so forth.)
   _____
   _____
   _____
   _____

6. How has Pharma Company benefited from your participation in the program? Please identify specific business accomplishments or improvements that you believe are linked to participation in this program. (Think about how the improvements actually resulted in influencing business measures, such as increased revenue, increased overall shipments, improved customer satisfaction, improved employee satisfaction, decreased costs, saved time, and so forth.)
   _____
   _____
   _____

7. Please define the measure(s) listed for Question 6. Be specific.
   _____
   _____

8. Indicate the amount of change in this measure since your participation in the program.
   _____

   Indicate the frequency of the measure.
   ❑ Daily   ❑ Weekly   ❑ Monthly   ❑ Quarterly   ❑ Annually

9. Think of specific ways to convert your accomplishments into a monetary value.
   Estimated unit monetary amount: $ _____

10. What is the basis for the value listed in Question 9? _____
    ❑ Standard value
    ❑ Expert input (indicate who the expert is) _____
    ❑ Estimate (Indicate how you arrived at the value) _____

11. Calculate the total annual value of this measure, considering the change that has occurred following the program. Annualize that value, based on the frequency of the measure. Multiply the unit value by the amount of change times the needed adjustment for a whole year of change. _____

Exhibit 7.1. Sample Questionnaire (*Continued*)

12. List factors other than the program that could have contributed to the improvement you listed in Question 7.
    _____
    _____

13. What percentage of the improvement above was actually influenced by the application of knowledge and skills from the leadership program? _____ %

14. What level of confidence do you place on the above estimations?
    _____ % Confidence (0% = no confidence; 100% = certainty)

15. Do you think this leadership program represented a good investment for Pharma Company?
    Yes ❑   No ❑
    Please explain: _____

16. Indicate the extent to which you think your application of the knowledge, skills, and behavior learned from the leadership program had a positive influence on the following business measures in your own work or your work unit. *Please check the appropriate response beside each measure.*

Business Measure	Not Applicable	Applies But No Influence	Some Influence	Moderate Influence	Significant Influence	Very Significant Influence
A. Work output	❑	❑	❑	❑	❑	❑
B. Quality	❑	❑	❑	❑	❑	❑
C. Cost control	❑	❑	❑	❑	❑	❑
D. Efficiency	❑	❑	❑	❑	❑	❑
E. Response time to customers	❑	❑	❑	❑	❑	❑
F. Cycle time of products	❑	❑	❑	❑	❑	❑
G. Sales	❑	❑	❑	❑	❑	❑
H. Employee turnover	❑	❑	❑	❑	❑	❑
I. Employee absenteeism	❑	❑	❑	❑	❑	❑
J. Employee satisfaction	❑	❑	❑	❑	❑	❑
K. Employee complaints	❑	❑	❑	❑	❑	❑
L. Customer satisfaction	❑	❑	❑	❑	❑	❑
M. Customer complaints	❑	❑	❑	❑	❑	❑
N. Other (please specify)	❑	❑	❑	❑	❑	❑

Exhibit 7.1. Sample Questionnaire (*Continued*)

17. Please cite specific examples or provide more details: _____

18. What additional benefits have been derived from this program? _____

19. What barriers, if any, have you encountered that have prevented you from using skills or behaviors gained in the leadership program? *Check all that apply.*
    - ❏ I have had no opportunity to use the skills.
    - ❏ I have not had enough time to apply the skills.
    - ❏ My work environment does not support the use of these skills or behaviors.
    - ❏ My supervisor does not support this type of program.
    - ❏ This material does not apply to my job situation.
    - ❏ Other (please specify): _____

    If any of the above is checked, please explain, if possible. _____

20. What enablers, if any, are present to help you use the skills or knowledge gained from this program? Please explain.

21. What additional support could be provided by management that would influence your ability to apply the skills and knowledge learned from the program?

22. What additional solutions do you recommend that would help to achieve the same business results that the leadership program has influenced?

Exhibit 7.1. Sample Questionnaire (*Continued*)

23. Would you recommend the leadership program to others?
    Yes ❏   No ❏
    Please explain. If no, why not? If yes, what groups or jobs, and why?
    _____
    _____
    _____
    _____

24. What specific suggestions do you have for improving this program?
    _____
    _____
    _____
    _____

25. Other comments:
    _____
    _____
    _____
    _____
    _____
    _____
    _____
    _____

become internalized. In our example, question 4 addresses the skill frequency issue in a more concise format.

Changes in Work Activities

Sometimes it is helpful to determine what specific work activities or processes have changed as a result of employees' participation in the program. Question 5 asks participants to explore how the application of skills learned in the program (listed earlier) has changed their work habits or processes.

Improvements or Accomplishments

Question 6 in Exhibit 7.1 begins a series of questions about business impact that are appropriate for most follow-up questionnaires. This question seeks specific accomplishments or improvements that are directly linked to the program, focusing on specific measurable successes that can be easily identified by the participants. Since this question is open-ended, providing examples that indicate the nature and range of responses requested may be helpful. However, when writing questions, consider that examples may also be constraining and may limit responses.

Definition of the Measure

Defining business measures precisely is important. Using general terms. such as quality or productivity or even sales. does not define a specific measure. A precise definition is necessary in order to provide an accurate accounting of improvement. Question 7 in Exhibit 7.1 allows participants to supply their definition of the business measure or measures they listed.

Amount of Change

In question 8, it is important for the participant to indicate how much the business measure listed earlier has changed. For example, if customer complaints are the measure, then the actual change in the number of complaints from before the program to after the program would be listed. In addition, the frequency of the measure is included. This information is important so that results can be annualized.

Unit Value

In order for a particular business measure to be used in ROI analysis, it must be assigned a unit monetary value. Many methods are available for assigning monetary value to data. Capturing this value directly from participants is important (see question 9).

Participants have three feasible sources for an estimate of unit value. First, a standard value for the measure may already be used within the organization. Fortunately, most measures that matter to an organization already have a unit value assigned to them. Second, an expert may be able to estimate a unit value. Finally, if the other two options are not available, the participant can estimate the unit value.

Basis for Value

To support the credibility of the estimated unit value, it is important to understand where it came from. Question 10 asks participants to indicate whether the unit value they are using is a standard value in the organization, whether it is based on expert input, or whether it is their own estimate. If the value comes from an expert, they are asked to indicate who the expert is. If it is an estimate, they are asked to show how the value was developed.

Total Annual Impact

Question 11 asks participants to show the total monetary value of the change that has occurred as a result of their participation in the program. The question asks participants to calculate the value of change for only one year. Participants can calculate this value by using the unit value, the amount of change, and the frequency of the data. For example, if the number of customer complaints has been reduced from 250 to 200 per month, and the unit value is $900 per complaint, then the total annual value is $50 \times \$900 \times 12$, which is $540,000.

Other Factors

When isolating the effects of a program on a business measure, it is important to think about other factors that might have caused the change. In question 12, participants are asked to list what other factors are in play that could have influenced the measure they listed.

Improvements Linked with the Program

The next question in the impact series (question 13) isolates the effects of the program. Participants estimate the percentage of the improvement that is directly related to the program. As an alternative, participants may be provided with various factors that may have influenced their results and asked to allocate percentages to each factor.

Confidence Level

To adjust for the uncertainty of the data provided in question 13, question 14 asks participants to offer a level of confidence for the estimate, expressed as a percentage from 0 to 100. This question allows participants to reflect their level of uncertainty about the estimating process.

Perception of Investment in the Program

Participants' views on the value of a program can be useful information. Question 15 of Exhibit 7.1 asks participants whether they perceive the program as an appropriate investment. Another option for a question on this topic is to present the actual cost of the program so that participants can respond from more accurate knowledge of the actual investment amount. It may be useful to express the cost as a per-participant cost. Also, the question can be divided into two parts—one reflecting on the investment of funds by the company and the other on the investment of the participant's time.

Link with Output Measures

Sometimes, it is helpful to determine the degree to which a program has influenced specific output measures, as shown in question 16. In some situations, a detailed analysis of the responses to such a question may reveal specifically which measures the program has influenced. However, when a program's effects are uncertain, it may be helpful to list the business performance measures that may have been influenced by the program and seek input from the participants. The question should be worded so that the frame of reference is the time period after the program was conducted.

Other Benefits

In most programs, additional benefits—in particular, intangible benefits—will begin to emerge as the program is implemented. Participants should be asked to detail any benefits not represented elsewhere in the survey. In our example, question 18 is an open-ended query about additional benefits.

Barriers

A variety of barriers may detract from the successful application of the skills and knowledge learned in a program. Question 19 asks participants to identify such barriers. Some perceived barriers are listed, and the participants are asked to check all that apply. One alternative to the question in the exhibit is an open-ended question on this topic. Still another variation is listing the barriers with a range of responses that indicate the extent to which each barrier inhibited results.

Enablers

Just as important as barriers are enablers—issues, events, or situations that enable a process to be applied successfully on the job. Question 20 provides an open-ended question about enablers. The same options apply for this question as for question 19, only in reverse.

Management Support

For most programs, management support is critical to the successful application of newly acquired skills. At least one question on management support, such as question 21 in Exhibit 7.1, should be included in the data collection instrument. Sometimes, this question is structured so that various descriptions of management support are detailed and participants are asked to check the one that applies to their situation. The information collected from questions about management support is very beneficial in helping to remove or minimize barriers.

Other Solutions

A program is only one of many potential solutions to a performance problem. If the needs assessment is faulty or if there are alternative approaches to developing the desired skills or knowledge, other potential solutions could be more effective in achieving the same success. In question 22, the participant is asked to identify other solutions that might be effective in obtaining the same or similar results.

Target Audience Recommendations

Sometimes, soliciting input about the most appropriate target audience for a program is useful. In question 23, participants are asked to indicate which groups of employees would most benefit from attending the program.

Suggestions for Improvement

For a wrap-up, participants are asked to provide suggestions for improving any part of the program. Illustrated in question 24, the open-ended structure is intended to solicit qualitative responses that can be used to make improvements.

The questionnaire in Exhibit 7.1 is quite comprehensive, soliciting a tremendous amount of data. All the data are needed to calculate the actual ROI and develop the full profile of data sets required for complete analysis. Obviously, many variations on these questions could work well, and other questions could explore many other issues pertaining to program application and implementation.

Interviews, Focus Groups, and Observation

Interviews and focus groups can be used during implementation or on a follow-up basis to collect data on implementation and application. Guidelines for designing and administering these instruments were covered in Chapter Three and will not be repeated here. Other resources also cover this area well (for example, Phillips and Phillips, 2007).

Observing participants on the job and recording changes in behavior and specific actions taken is another method of collecting Level 3 data. While observation is also used to collect learning data, a fundamental difference is that participants do not necessarily know they are being observed when observation is used to collect application data. Observation of participants is often used in sales and sales support programs. The observer may be a member of the program staff, the participant's manager, a peer, or an external resource such as a mystery shopper. Observation is most commonly (and, often, most practically) performed by a member of the program staff. Technology also provides tools to assist with observations. Audio recorders, video cameras, and computers play an important role in capturing application data.

Action Plans

Action plans are a common follow-up approach. Participants are required to develop action plans as part of a program. The action plans contain the detailed steps necessary to accomplish specific objectives related to the program. The action planning process is one of the most effective ways to build participant support and the sense of ownership needed for successful program application and implementation. Level 3 data are collected during the follow-up phase, when participants report on implementation of the action plans. Details of the design of action plans were discussed in Chapter Four, with an example provided in Exhibit 4.1.

Barriers to Application

One of the important reasons for collecting application and implementation data is to uncover barriers and enablers. Although both groups are important, barriers can kill a program. Barriers must be identified, and actions must be taken to minimize, remove, or go around them.

Barriers are a serious problem in every program implementation. When they can be removed or minimized, the program can be implemented. When barriers are identified, they become important reference points for change and improvement. Typical barriers that can stifle the success of programs include the following:

- My immediate manager does not support the program.
- The culture in our work group does not support the program.
- We have no opportunity to use the program skills, knowledge, or information.
- We have no time to implement the program.
- Technology was not available for the program.
- Resources are not available to implement the program.
- We didn't see a need to implement the program.
- Another program got in the way.
- The program is not appropriate for our work unit.
- My job changed, and this no longer applies.

The important point is to identify all barriers and to use the data in meaningful ways to make them less of a problem.

Uses of Application Data

Data become meaningless if they are not used properly. As evaluation moves up the chain of impact, the data become more valuable in the minds of sponsors, key executives, and others who have a strong interest in a program. Although data can be used in dozens of ways, the principal uses for Level 3 data after they are collected are as follows:

- To report results and review them with various stakeholders
- To adjust program design and implementation
- To identify and remove barriers
- To identify and enhance enablers
- To recognize individuals who have contributed to program success
- To reinforce in current and future program participants the value of desired actions
- To improve management support for programs
- To market future programs

Final Thoughts

Measuring application and implementation is critical in determining whether a program has been successful. This essential type of measurement not only determines the success achieved but also identifies areas in which improvement is needed and in which success can be replicated in the future. Understanding success in application is important in providing evidence that business needs have been met, but it is only through measurement at Level 4, impact and consequences, that a direct link between a program and business impact can be made.

Reference

Phillips, J. J., and Phillips, P. P. *Handbook of Training Evaluation and Measurement Methods.* (4th ed.) Woburn, Mass.: Butterworth-Heinemann, 2007.

8

Measuring Impact and Consequences

Most clients regard business impact data as the most important data type because of its connection to business success. In many programs, inadequate performance in one or more business measures (the business need) is what led executives to initiate the program. Business impact evaluation data close the loop by showing a program's success in meeting business needs. This chapter examines a variety of business impact measures and the specific processes needed to collect the measurement data within a program. First, however, this chapter addresses the reasons that impact data are measured.

Why Measure Business Impact?

Several rationales support the collection of business impact data related to a program.

Impact Data Provide Higher-Level Information on Performance

If we go with the assumption that higher-level data create more value for key stakeholders, business impact measures offer a more valuable data set than measures at Level 1, 2, or 3. Why are Level 4 data more valuable? Impact data are the consequence of application and implementation of a program. They represent the bottom-line measures that are positively influenced when a program is successful.

The chain of impact can be broken at Level 4, and unfortunately, in many programs, it is. If the program does not drive business impact data, results at lower levels may be less than satisfactory. However, in some cases, the program is successful at the lower levels but fails at Level 4. Participants may react positively to the program, may learn successfully to implement the program, and may follow the correct implementation steps or use the skills needed to implement the program. However, if the business impact measure that was thought to be influenced by the program does not change, the program does not add value. What could cause this? There are two possibilities. First, the program may not have been properly aligned with the business, which would mean that the program is not the right solution. Although the program may have been well implemented, it has driven activity and not results. The second possibility is that factors other than those addressed by the program are driving the business measure. Although the program may be connected to the business measure, other influences may be negatively affecting the same measure. Thus, at first glance, it may appear that the program has no value, but in reality it may have. This brings into focus the importance of isolating the effects of a program. The business data may be disappointing, but it is possible that they would be even more disappointing without the program. The important process of isolating the effects of a program is presented in book three of this series, *Isolation of Results*.

Impact Data Represent the Business Driver of a Program

For most programs, business impact data represent the initial drivers of the program. The problem of deteriorating or poorer-than-expected performance or the opportunity for improvement of performance on a business measure usually leads to initiation of a program. If the business needs defined by a business measure are driving a program, then the key measure for evaluating the program is that business measure. The extent to which that measure changes is the principal determinant of success.

Impact Data Provide Value for Sponsors

From the perspective of a sponsor, business impact data represent key measures of a program's payoff. These key measures are the ones often desired by the sponsor and the ones that the sponsor wants to see changed or improved. They often represent hard, indisputable facts about business performance, which is critical at the business unit or operating unit level of the organization. Business impact leads to "the money"—the actual return on investment in the program. Without credible business impact data linked directly to the program, it would be difficult, if not impossible, to establish a credible monetary value for the program. These business realities make this level of data collection one of the most critical.

Impact Data Are Easy to Measure

One unique feature of business impact data is that they are often easy to measure. Hard and soft data measures at this level often correspond to key measures that are plentiful throughout an organization. It is not unusual for an organization to have hundreds or even thousands of measures reflecting specific business impact items. The challenge is to connect the objectives of the program with the appropriate business measures. This linkage begins during the needs assessment process, continues as program objectives are developed, and is made clear during the evaluation process with the step to isolate the program's impact on Level 4 measures.

Effective Impact Measures

Any process, item, or perception can be measured, and such measurement is critical to Level 4 analysis. If the program focuses on solving a problem, preventing a problem, or seizing an opportunity, the measures are usually identifiable. The important point is that the measures are present in the system, ready to be captured for this level of analysis. The challenge is to define the measures and to find them economically and swiftly.

Hard Data Measures

In choosing desired measures, a distinction between hard data and soft data is often used to categorize the various types of business measures. Hard data are measures of improvement presented in the form of quantitative, undisputed facts that are usually gathered within functional areas throughout an organization. These are the most desirable type of data because they are easy to quantify and are easily converted to monetary values. The fundamental criteria for gauging the effectiveness of an organization are hard data items such as revenue, productivity, and profitability, as well as measures of quality, costs, and time.

Hard data are objective and credible measures of an organization's performance. Hard data are usually grouped in four categories, as shown in Table 8.1. These categories—output, quality, costs, and time—are typical performance measures in any organization.

Hard data from a particular program often involve improvements in the output of a work unit, section, department, division, or entire organization. Every organization, regardless of type, must have basic measures of output, such as number of patients treated, students graduated, tons produced, or packages shipped. Since these values are monitored, changes can easily be measured by comparing outputs before and after a program.

Quality is a very important category of hard data. If quality is a major priority for an organization, processes are likely in place to measure and monitor quality. The rising prominence of quality improvement processes (such as total quality management, continuous quality improvement, and Six Sigma) has contributed to tremendous recent successes in pinpointing an organization's proper quality measures, as well as assigning monetary values to them.

Table 8.1. Examples of Hard Data

Output	Quality	Costs	Time
Units produced	Failure rates	Shelter costs	Cycle time
Tons manufactured	Dropout rates	Treatment costs	Equipment downtime
Items assembled	Scrap	Budget variances	Overtime
Money collected	Waste	Unit costs	On-time shipments
Items sold	Rejects	Cost by account	Time to program completion
New accounts generated	Error rates	Variable costs	Processing time
Forms processed	Rework	Fixed costs	Supervisory time
Loans approved	Shortages	Overhead costs	Time to proficiency
Inventory turnover	Product defects	Operating costs	Learning time
Patients visited	Deviation from standard	Program cost savings	Adherence to schedules
Applications processed	Product failures	Accident costs	Repair time
Students graduated	Inventory adjustments	Program costs	Efficiency
Tasks completed	Time card corrections	Sales expense	Work stoppages
Output per hour	Incidents		Order response time
Productivity	Compliance discrepancies		Late reporting
Work backlog	Agency fines		Lost-time days
Incentive bonus			
Shipments			
Completion rate			

Cost is another important category of hard data. Many projects and programs are designed to lower, control, or eliminate the cost of a specific process or activity. Achieving cost targets has an immediate effect on the bottom line. Some organizations focus narrowly on cost reduction. For example, consider Wal-Mart, whose tagline is "Always low prices. Always." All levels of the organization are dedicated to lowering costs on processes and products and passing the savings along to customers.

Time is a critical measure in any organization. Some organizations gauge their performance almost exclusively in relation to time. When asked what business FedEx is in, company executives say, "We engineer time."

Soft Data Measures

Soft data are probably the most familiar measures of an organization's effectiveness, yet collecting them can present a challenge. Values representing attitude, motivation, and satisfaction are examples of soft data. Soft data are more difficult to gather and analyze than hard data; therefore, they are used when hard data are not available or to supplement hard data. Soft data are also more difficult to convert to monetary values, a process that requires subjective methods. Performance measurements using soft data are less objective than those using hard data and are usually behavior-related, yet organizations place great emphasis on them.

Improvements in soft data measures represent important business needs, but many organizations omit them from the ROI equation due to the challenges in converting them to money. However, soft data measures can contribute to economic value to the same extent as hard data measures. Table 8.2 shows common examples of soft data by category. The key is not to focus too much on the hard versus soft data distinction. A better approach is to consider data as tangible or intangible.

Table 8.2. Examples of Soft Data

Work Habits
   Excessive breaks
   Tardiness
   Visits to the dispensary
   Violations of safety rules
   Communication breakdowns

Work Climate and Job Satisfaction
   Grievances
   Discrimination charges
   Employee complaints
   Job satisfaction
   Organization commitment
   Employee engagement
   Employee loyalty
   Intent to leave the organization
   Stress

Initiative and Innovation
   Creativity
   Innovation
   New ideas
   Suggestions
   New products and services
   Trademarks
   Copyrights and patents
   Process improvements
   Partnerships and alliances

Customer Service
   Customer complaints
   Customer satisfaction
   Customer dissatisfaction
   Customer impressions
   Customer loyalty
   Customer retention
   Lost customers

Employee Development and Advancement
   Promotions
   Capability
   Intellectual capital
   Requests for transfer
   Performance appraisal ratings
   Readiness
   Networking

Image
   Brand awareness
   Reputation
   Leadership
   Social responsibility
   Environmental friendliness
   Social consciousness
   Diversity
   External awards

Tangible Versus Intangible Measures

The fundamental difference between hard and soft data involves the objectivity in their measurement. The key is to remember that, ultimately, all roads lead to hard data. Although creativity may be categorized as a form of soft data, a creative workplace can develop new products or new patents, which leads to greater revenue—which clearly is a hard data measure. Although it is possible to convert soft data to monetary value, it is often more realistic and practical to leave them in nonmonetary form. This decision is based on considerations of credibility and the cost of the conversion.

According to the Guiding Principles of the ROI Methodology, an intangible measure is defined as a measure that is intentionally not converted to a monetary value. If a soft data measure can be credibly converted to a monetary amount, using minimal resources, it is considered tangible, reported as a monetary value, and incorporated in the ROI calculation. If a data item cannot be credibly converted to money, using minimal resources, it is listed as an intangible measure. Therefore, the key difference between measures in terms of ROI calculation is not whether they represent hard or soft data but whether they are tangible or intangible. In either case, they are important contributions toward measurement of the desired payoff and of important business impact data.

Impact Objectives

Impact objectives indicate key business measures that should improve as the application and implementation objectives are achieved. Following are some typical impact objectives:

- Grievances should be reduced from three per month to no more than two per month at the Golden Eagle tire plant within one year of program launch.

- Tardiness at the Newbury foundry should decrease by 20 percent within the next calendar year.

- The average number of product defects should decrease from 214 to 153 per month at all Amalgamated Rubber extruding plants in the Midwest region by the end of the current fiscal year.

- The company-wide job satisfaction index should rise by 2 percent during the next calendar year.

- There should be a 10 percent increase in Pharmaceuticals Inc. brand awareness among physicians during the next two years.

- The dropout rate for high school students in the Barett County system should decrease by 5 percent within three years.

Impact objectives are critical to measuring business performance because they define the ultimate expected outcome of the project. They describe the business unit performance that should result from the project. Above all, impact objectives emphasize achievement of the bottom-line results that key client groups expect and demand.

Linking Specific Measures to Programs

An important issue that often surfaces when considering ROI applications is how to understand which specific measures are driven by specific programs. Although no standard answers are available, Table 8.3 summarizes some typical payoff measures for specific types of programs. The measures are quite broad for some programs. For example, a reward systems program can pay off in a variety of measures, such as improved productivity, enhanced sales and revenues, improved quality, cycle-time reduction, and even direct cost savings. Essentially, the reward systems program should drive the measure that the rewards are designed to influence. In other programs, the influenced measures are quite narrow. For example, in labor-management cooperation programs, the payoffs are typically in reduced grievances, fewer work stoppages, lower absenteeism, and improved employee satisfaction. Orientation programs

Table 8.3. Typical Impact Measures in ROI Applications

Program	Key Impact Measurements
Absenteeism control or reduction	Absenteeism, customer satisfaction, job satisfaction, stress
Business coaching	Productivity, output, quality, time savings, efficiency, costs, employee satisfaction, customer satisfaction
Career development and career management	Turnover, promotions, recruiting expenses, job satisfaction
Communications	Errors, stress, conflicts, productivity, job satisfaction
Compensation plans	Costs, productivity, quality, job satisfaction
Compliance	Penalties and fines, charges, settlements, losses
Diversity	Turnover, absenteeism, complaints, allegations, legal settlements, losses
E-Learning	Cost savings, productivity improvement, quality improvement, cycle times, error reductions, job satisfaction
Employee benefits plans	Costs, time savings, job satisfaction
Employee relations	Turnover, absenteeism, job satisfaction, engagement
Gainsharing plans	Production costs, productivity, turnover
Labor-management cooperation	Work stoppages, employee grievances, absenteeism, job satisfaction
Leadership development	Productivity, output, quality, efficiency, cost savings, time savings, employee satisfaction, engagement
Marketing and advertising	Sales, market share, customer loyalty, cost of sales, wallet share, customer satisfaction, brand recognition
Meeting planning	Sales, productivity, output, quality, time savings, job satisfaction, customer satisfaction
Orientation and on-boarding	New hire turnover, training time, productivity

Table 8.3. Typical Impact Measures in ROI Applications (*Continued*)

Program	Key Impact Measurements
Personal productivity and time management	Time savings, productivity, stress reduction, job satisfaction
Procurement	Costs, time savings, quality, stability, schedule
Project management	Time savings, quality improvement, budgets
Public policy	Time savings, cost savings, quality, stakeholder satisfaction, image
Public relations	Image, branding, customer satisfaction, investor satisfaction
Recruiting sources	Costs, yield, early turnover
Retention management	Turnover, engagement, job satisfaction
Safety incentive plan	Accident frequency, accident severity, first aid treatments
Selection process	New hire turnover, training time, productivity
Self-directed teams	Productivity, output, quality, customer satisfaction, turnover, absenteeism, job satisfaction
Sexual harassment prevention	Complaints, turnover, absenteeism, employee satisfaction
Six Sigma	Defects, rework, response times, cycle times, costs
Skill-based pay	Labor costs, turnover, absenteeism
Strategy and policy	Productivity, output, sales, market share, customer service, quality or service levels, cycle times, cost savings, job satisfaction
Stress management	Medical costs, turnover, absenteeism, job satisfaction
Technical training (job-related)	Productivity, sales, quality, time, costs, customer service, turnover, absenteeism, job satisfaction
Technology implementation	Cycle times, error rates, productivity, efficiency, customer satisfaction, job satisfaction
Wellness and fitness	Turnover, medical costs, accidents, absenteeism

typically pay off in measures of early turnover (turnover in the first ninety days of employment), initial job performance, and productivity. The measures that are influenced depend on the objectives and the design of the program.

Table 8.3 also illustrates the immense number of applications of the ROI Methodology and the even larger set of measures that can be driven or influenced. In most of these situations, assigning monetary values to the impact measures (so that the benefits of a given program can be compared with the costs) and developing the ROI become reasonable tasks.

A word of caution: Presenting specific measures linked to a typical program may give the impression that these are the only measures influenced. In practice, a given program can have many outcomes, and this can make calculation of the ROI a difficult process. The good news is that most programs are driving business measures. The monetary values are based on what is being changed in various business units, divisions, regions, and individual workplaces. These are the measures that matter to senior executives. The difficulty often comes in establishing that a connection to the program exists. This connection is deduced through a variety of techniques that isolate the effects of the program on particular business measures, as will be discussed in *Isolation of Results*, the third book in this series.

Sources of Impact Data

The potential sources of impact data are diverse. Many data items come from routine reporting systems in the organization. In many situations, poor performance in regard to these items has led to the perceived need for the program. A vast array of documents, systems, databases, and reports can be consulted in selecting the specific measure or measures to be monitored throughout a program. Impact data sources include quality reports, service records, suggestion systems, and employee engagement data.

Some evaluators assume that corporate data sources are scarce because the data are not readily available to them. However, data can usually be located by investing a small amount of time. Rarely do new data collection systems or processes need to be developed in order to gather data that represent the business needs of an organization.

In searching for the proper measures to connect to the program and to identify business needs, it is helpful to consider all possible measures that could be influenced. Sometimes, collateral measures move in harmony with the program. For example, efforts to improve safety may also improve productivity and increase job satisfaction. Weighing adverse impacts on certain measures may also help. For example, when cycle times are reduced, quality may suffer; or when sales increase, customer satisfaction may deteriorate. Finally, evaluators must anticipate unintended consequences and capture them as other data items that might be connected to or influenced by the program.

Data Collection Methods

As with the previous levels of measurement, there are a variety of ways by which we can collect Level 4 business impact data. Many of these techniques are also used to collect data for lower levels of evaluation and are described in detail in Chapter Four. This section serves as a review of those techniques and describes how they are used with Level 4 measurement.

Monitoring Business Performance Data

Data are available in every organization to measure business performance. Monitoring performance data enables management to measure performance in terms of output, quality, costs, time, job satisfaction, customer satisfaction, and other measures. In selecting sources of data for evaluation, the first consideration should be existing databases, reports, and scorecards. In most organizations, performance data will be available that are suitable for measuring improvement resulting from a program. If such data are not available, additional record-keeping systems may have to be developed for measurement and analysis. At this point, the question of economics surfaces. Is it economical to develop the record-keeping systems necessary to evaluate a program or project? If the costs will be greater than the expected benefits, developing those systems is pointless.

Identify Appropriate Measures

Existing performance measures should be thoroughly researched to identify those most closely related to the proposed objectives of the program. Often, several performance measures are related to the same item. For example, the efficiency of a production unit can be measured in several ways:

- Number of units produced per hour
- Number of units produced on schedule
- Percentage of equipment used
- Percentage of equipment downtime
- Labor cost per unit of production
- Overtime required per unit of production
- Total unit cost

Each of these measures the effectiveness or efficiency of the production unit in its own way. All related measures should be reviewed to determine those most relevant to the program.

Convert Current Measures to Usable Ones

As discussed in Chapter Four, it is sometimes necessary to convert existing measures to usable measures. To do this, performance measures are integrated with other data. An example of this process is described in Chapter Four.

Develop New Measures

In some cases, data needed to measure the effectiveness of a program are not available, and new data are needed. This need can be met by working with the client or others in the organization to develop record-keeping systems. The first step is to identify the department that will develop the measurement system. This department is typically the department that "owns" the measure. For example, if absenteeism is a problem, which job category represents the position for which absenteeism is the problem? Determining the job category will often assist in isolating the department or function that should track the measure. If the problem is cross-organizational (meaning that absent employees are an issue across multiple job categories) and it is determined that the measure should be monitored from a corporate perspective, then it may be prudent to house the measurement system in the human resources or accounting and finance department.

Next, the person(s) who will actually monitor the measure should be identified. Third, it must be decided where the measures will be recorded—a database, a paper-based system, or some other system. Will there be a journal or a record book, or will automation be used to track the measure? Finally, what forms will be used to support various departments in tracking absenteeism in their function?

Action Plans

In Chapter Seven, action plans were presented as a tool to capture application and implementation data. Action plans are also a useful tool for capturing business impact data. The business impact data gathered through use of an action plan are more focused and credible than those gathered through a questionnaire. The basic design principles and issues involved in developing and administering action plans to gather business impact data are the same as those discussed in Chapter Four. However, a few issues unique to collecting business impact and ROI data are presented here. The following steps are recommended when an action plan is developed and implemented to capture business impact data and to convert the data to monetary values.

Set Goals and Targets

An action plan can be developed to focus directly on business impact data. Participants develop an overall objective for the plan, which is usually the primary objective of the program. In some cases, a program may have more than one objective, which requires additional action plans—one for each objective. In addition to the objective, the improvement measure and current levels of performance are identified. Providing this information on objectives requires the participant to anticipate the application and implementation of the program and to set goals for specific performances that can be realized.

The action plan is completed during program implementation, often with the input, assistance, and facilitation of the program team. The evaluator or program leader approves the plan, indicating that it meets the requirements of being specific, motivational, achievable, realistic, and time-based (SMART). The plan can be developed in one to two hours and often begins with action steps related to implementation of the program. These action steps are Level 3 activities that detail the application and implementation of learning from the program. All these steps build support for and are linked to business impact measures.

Define the Unit of Measure

The next important issue is defining the unit of measure for the desired change in performance. In some cases, more than one measure may be used, resulting in additional action plans—again, one for each measure. The unit of measure is necessary in order to break the process into simple steps so that its ultimate value can be determined. The unit may be a unit of output data—such as one unit manufactured or one package delivered—or it may be a unit of sales and marketing data—such as $1 of sales revenue or a 1 percent increase in market share. If quality is being measured, the unit may be one reject, one error, or one defect. Time-based units are usually measured in minutes, hours, days, or weeks. Other units are specific to their particular type of data, such as one grievance, one complaint, one absence, or one person receiving welfare payments. The important point is to break impact data into the simplest terms possible.

Place a Monetary Value on Each Improvement

During program implementation, participants are asked to locate, calculate, or estimate the monetary value of each improvement outlined in their plan. The unit monetary value is determined through a variety of methods, including standard values, expert input, external databases, and estimates. The process to be used in arriving at the unit monetary value is described in the instructions of the action plan. When the actual improvement occurs, participants use the unit monetary values to calculate the annual monetary benefits of the plan. To be effective in this step of assigning monetary values to improvements, it is helpful to understand the ways in which values can be assigned to the data, which are discussed in *Data Conversion*, the fourth book of this series.

In the worst-case scenario, participants are asked to estimate unit monetary values themselves, although use of standard values and consultation with an expert are better courses of action. When it is necessary for participants themselves to make the calculations, they must explain the assumptions they made in their calculations.

Implement the Action Plan

Participants implement their action plan during program implementation, which often lasts for weeks or months following the launch of a program. Participants complete the activities described in the action plan, and business impact results are achieved.

Document Specific Improvements

At the end of the specified follow-up period—usually three months, six months, nine months, or one year—participants indicate the specific improvements that have been achieved, usually expressed as a daily, weekly, or monthly amount that represents the actual amount of change observed, measured, or recorded. Participants must understand the need for accuracy as data are recorded. In most cases, only the changes are recorded because these are the amounts needed to calculate the monetary value of the program. In other cases, data from before and after program implementation may be recorded, allowing the evaluator to calculate the difference.

Isolate the Effects of the Program

As discussed in Chapter Four, while the action plan may have been initiated because of the program, the improvements reported on the action plan may have been caused or influenced by factors other than those put in play by the program. Consequently, the program should not be given full credit for the improvement. For example, an action plan to implement a new computer system in a division may be given only partial credit for a business improvement because other variables may have affected the impact measures. Although there are several ways to isolate the effects of a program, participant estimation is usually most appropriate in the action planning process, because participants will typically be focusing on measures specific to their work rather than targeting improvement in one specific, universal measure. Consequently, participants are asked to estimate the percentage of the improvement that is related to a particular program. This information can be requested on the action plan form or in a follow-up questionnaire. Sometimes it is beneficial to precede the request for an estimate with a request that the participant identify the entire range of factors that could have influenced the results. This encourages participants to think through the relationships among all the factors before allocating a portion of the results to the program under evaluation.

Provide a Confidence Level for Estimates

The process of isolating the amount of improvement related to the program is not always precise. Participants are asked to indicate their level of confidence in their estimate. By using a scale of 0 to 100 percent in which 0 indicates that the values are completely false and 100 percent indicates that the values are absolutely certain, participants can express their uncertainty about their estimate.

Collect Action Plans at Specified Time Intervals

Because a high response rate is essential to a credible evaluation process, several steps may be necessary to ensure that action plans are completed and returned. Participants usually see the importance of the process and develop their plans in detail at the beginning of the program. Some organizations send follow-up reminders by mail or e-mail; others phone participants to check on their progress. Still others offer assistance in developing the final plan. These steps may require expending additional resources, the value of which must be weighed against the importance of having more data. Specific ways to improve response rates for questionnaires were discussed in Chapter One, but many of the techniques apply to action plans, too.

Summarize the Data and Calculate the ROI

If developed properly, each action plan will include annualized monetary values associated with improvements. Also, each individual should have indicated the percentage of the improvement that is directly related to the program. Finally, each participant should have provided a confidence percentage to reflect his or her uncertainty about the process and the subjective nature of some of the data provided.

Because this process involves estimates, it may appear to be inaccurate, although adjustments during analysis can make the process more credible and more accurate. These adjustments reflect the Guiding Principles that form the basis of the ROI Methodology. Exhibit 8.1 shows an example of a completed action plan with the impact data reported.

Performance Contracts

Another technique for collecting business impact data is the performance contract. This technique is described in Chapter Four. As described, a performance contract is a slight variation on the action plan. Based on the principle of mutual goal setting, a performance contract is a written agreement between a participant and the participant's manager. The participant agrees to improve performance in an area of mutual concern related to the program. The agreement establishes a goal for the employee to accomplish during the program or after the program's completion. It will sometimes include the manager's commitment to the employee to ensure success. The agreement details what is to be accomplished, at what time, and with what results. Exhibit 8.2 presents a simple performance contract.

Questionnaires

As described in previous chapters, the questionnaire is one of the most versatile data collection tools and can be used to collect Level 1, 2, 3, and 4 data. Essentially, the design principles and content issues are the same as at other levels, except that questionnaires developed for a business impact evaluation will include additional questions to capture data specific to business impact. A detailed example of such a questionnaire was included in the preceding chapter.

The use of questionnaires for impact data collection brings both good news and bad news. The good news is that questionnaires are easy to implement and low in cost. Data analysis is efficient, and the time required for participants to provide the data is often minimal, making questionnaires among the least disruptive of data collection methods. The bad news is that the data can be distorted

Exhibit 8.1. Example of an Action Plan

Action Plan

Name: _John Mathews_   Instructor's Signature: _____   Follow-Up Date: _1 September_

Objective: _Reduce team's weekly rate of absenteeism_   Evaluation Period: _March to September_

Improvement Measure: _Rate of absenteeism_   Current Performance: _8%_   Target Performance: _5%_

Action Steps

1. _Meet with team to discuss reasons for absenteeism, using problem-solving skills._ — 10 March
2. _Review absenteeism records for each employee; look for trends and patterns._ — 20 March
3. _Counsel problem employees to help them correct habits and explore opportunities for improvement._
4. _Conduct a brief performance discussion with an employee returning to work after an unplanned absence._
5. _Provide recognition to employees who have perfect attendance._ — 31 March
6. _Follow up on each discussion: discuss improvement or lack of improvement, and plan other action._
7. _Monitor improvement and provide recognition when appropriate._

Analysis

A. What is the unit of measure? _One absence_
B. What is the value (cost) of one unit? _$41.00_
C. How did you arrive at this value? _Standard value_
D. How much did the measure change during the evaluation period? (monthly value) _2.5%_
E. List the other factors that could have caused this. _Job market and new discipline policy._
F. What percentage of this change was actually caused by this program? _65%_
G. What level of confidence do you place on the above information? (100% = certainty; 0% = no confidence) _80%_

Intangible Benefits: _Less stress, greater job satisfaction_

Comments: _Great program—it kept me on track with this problem._

Exhibit 8.2. Example of Simple Performance Contract

ROI RESOURCE CENTER™
Performance Contract

To: Carrie Luke

From: Patti Phillips

Date: April 5

We are happy to have your talents added to the staff. Your expertise will undoubtedly promote the program's overall success that is important to ROI Resource Center. To ensure that we are all in agreement about deliverables and timelines, this document summarizes the expected performance from the upcoming program.

The program we plan to implement was designed specifically to help us develop innovative products that support clients' evaluation practices.

Desired performance: 10 new products by year end

Current performance: 5 new products annually

The program will be considered successful to the extent we see improvement in the performance from the current to desired level.

In order to complete your part of the project, you will receive the following from us by the dates indicated:

Items (that your organization will provide)	Date
A copy of the entire performance improvement action plan.	April 15
Draft product criteria	April 30
Focus group participant list	May 15
Final product selection matrix	May 30
Product selection	June 15
Focus group logistics	June 30

We expect that you will deliver the following items on the date(s) indicated:

Deliverables (items that your organization will need)	Date
Comments on product criteria	May 10
Suggestions and quotes for new products	June 15
Sample products to demo in focus group	July 10
Conduct focus group	July 15
Focus group results	July 20

We agree to provide the deliverables specified above on the dates noted.

Signature _____ Director_____

Date _____ Date_____

and inaccurate, and data are sometimes missing. Poor design, lack of understanding of program objectives, and misalignment between questions and measures can undermine attempts to gather good data. The challenge is to take all the steps necessary to ensure that questionnaires are complete, accurate, and clear, and that they are returned with all the necessary data.

Unfortunately, questionnaires are the weakest method of data collection due to the subjectivity inherent in the use of this instrument. Paradoxically, they are the most commonly used because of their advantages. Of the first one hundred case studies published on the ROI Methodology, roughly half used questionnaires as a method of data collection. Questionnaires are popular, convenient, and low in cost, and they have become a way of life. The challenge is to improve them. The philosophy of the ROI Methodology is to take processes that represent the weakest method and make them as credible as possible. Here the challenge is to make questionnaires credible and useful by ensuring that they request all the data needed, that participants provide accurate and complete data, and that return rates are in at least the 70 to 80 percent range.

The reason that return rates must be high is explained in Guiding Principle 6 of the ROI Methodology: no data, no improvement. If an individual provides no improvement data, it is assumed that the person had no improvement to report. This is a very conservative principle, but it is necessary to bring credibility to the evaluation process. Consequently, using questionnaires will require effort, discipline, and personal attention in order to ensure proper response rates. Chapter One presented many ways to ensure high response rates for Level 1 data collection. The same techniques should be considered for Level 4 data collection. It is helpful to remember that questionnaires are the least preferred method for collecting Level 4 data and should be used only when other methods do not work (that is, when business performance data cannot be easily monitored, when action plans are not feasible, or when performance contracting is not suitable).

Final Thoughts

This chapter has explored the issues of collecting impact data, illustrating the common ways in which this important data set is captured. The good news is that these data are very common and readily available in virtually every organization. They can usually be collected by simply monitoring the organization's record-keeping systems. If not, action plans, performance contracts, and questionnaires can be used to capture this data set.

9

Selecting the Proper Data Collection Method

Confused? Maybe so. There are many ways to collect data, leaving some people in a state of confusion as to which data collection method is most appropriate for their situation. This brief chapter will provide some practice in the use of the data collection tools described in this book. It also provides guidelines to consider when selecting the best technique(s) for collecting data when evaluating your programs.

Matching Exercise

Perhaps an exercise will illustrate some of the key differences among the data collection methods. While this book focused on many approaches, seven are routinely used in data collection: surveys, tests, questionnaires, interviews, focus groups, observations, and performance records. The exercise that follows explores the use of each of these data collection methods.

Instructions

For each of the following situations, please indicate the most appropriate type of instrument to use in collecting the data needed to evaluate a program. Select from these types:

A. Survey
B. Test
C. Questionnaire
D. Interview
E. Focus group
F. Observation
G. Performance records

Write the letter of the most appropriate instrument in the box to the right of each question. Also indicate the level of evaluation to be pursued (1, 2, 3, or 4).

Situation	Instrument
1. Customer service representatives have learned to resolve customer complaints in the most effective manner. An integral part of the program required customer service representatives to follow a series of planned steps to resolve complaints, using empathy and listening skills. As part of the evaluation, the human resources staff must determine the extent to which participants are actually using the newly acquired skills.	☐ ☐
2. Intact team members are involved in a conflict resolution program in which they acquired skills to resolve conflicts and disputes among themselves. Team members in this work group have a high degree of interaction and some of their responsibilities include checking the work of others. There had been an unusually high level of friction, with displays of open conflict in the group. In the program, participants learned how to deal with these issues and work together as a smooth operating team. The human resources staff needs to collect information about the group's progress, ideally in an environment in which there is an opportunity for	☐ ☐

group members to listen to comments from others.

3. Technicians participate in an e-learning program on basic mathematics and are required to achieve a predetermined level of competence in mathematics after completing the program. Human resources staff members measure the participants' level of mathematical ability before and after the program. ☐ ☐

4. The front desk staff at a major hotel have participated in a program to teach them how to use a new reservation system that is being installed. As part of the evaluation, it is important to obtain participants' reactions to the program and capture their planned actions. ☐ ☐

5. A company has implemented a new compensation plan in which the employees share in the overall profits of the company. Employees have attended a roll-out meeting in which they had the opportunity to learn how the program works and what is required of them to make it successful. As part of the evaluation, management is interested in finding out what the employees think about the new plan after attending the briefing. ☐ ☐

6. Sales representatives have a new commission program designed to improve sales. One objective of the program is to improve sales volume, and the human resources staff must determine exactly how much of an increase has been achieved by each individual since the program was conducted. ☐ ☐

7. Supervisors attended a problem-solving program in which they learned a logical ☐ ☐

approach to solving significant problems facing their work units. As a part of the program's evaluation, the human resources staff needs feedback from participants concerning their use of the acquired skills. The staff thinks there is a possibility that there is a success story here and will need to probe for details.

Responses

1. *Data collection method F, Level 3.* The key issue is the last sentence of the description. Observation is the only way to understand how someone is actually using these skills on the job. For the observation to work effectively, it must be invisible or unnoticeable. It would be Level 3 evaluation because data need to be collected about post-program skill usage.
2. *Data collection method E, Level 3.* The key to this issue is also in the last sentence. A focus group is the only method in which an opportunity to listen to the comments of others is available. This is important for capturing qualitative data. Data will be collected at Level 3 because the situation involves the use of skills.
3. *Data collection method B, Level 2.* This is a classic example of measuring learning, and a test is one of the most common ways of doing this. Testing for competencies is Level 2 data collection.
4. *Data collection method C, Level 1.* The desired instrument is considered a questionnaire because planned actions are to be captured. There is a clear distinction between surveys and questionnaires. A survey captures only attitudes, beliefs, and opinions, and responses are often solicited in an agree-or-disagree format or by means of a Likert scale representing the extent of agreement. A questionnaire may have survey data plus all other types of questions, including multiple-choice, yes-or-no, and fill-in-the-blank questions. This example captures Level 1 (reaction) data.

5. *Data collection method A, Level 1.* A survey can collect opinions about the participants' reactions to the plan. Gathering reactions is Level 1 evaluation.
6. *Data collection method G, Level 4.* This example requires data collection from record-keeping systems, which will provide credible hard data. Impact data (Level 4) are being collected in this example.
7. *Data collection method D, Level 3.* The interview is the only method that allows probing for more information in order to understand the responses or to explore an issue in more detail. In this case, Level 3 (application) data are collected.

Selecting the Appropriate Method for Each Level

The data collection methods presented in this and earlier chapters offer a wide range of opportunities to collect data in a variety of situations. Nine issues should be considered when you are deciding on the most appropriate method of collecting data.

Type of Data

One of the most important issues to consider when selecting a data collection method is the type of data to be collected. Some methods are more appropriate for collecting business impact data. Follow-up questionnaires, observations, interviews, focus groups, action planning, and performance contracting are best suited for application data; in fact, some of these methods are suited only for application data. Performance monitoring, action planning, and questionnaires can easily capture business impact data.

Investment of Participants' Time

Another important factor in selecting a data collection method is the amount of time participants must spend with data collection and evaluation systems. Time requirements should always be minimized, and the method should be positioned so that it is a value-added activity. Participants must understand that data collection is a valuable undertaking, not an activity to be resisted. Sampling can be helpful in keeping total time spent by participants to a minimum. Methods like performance monitoring require no participant time, whereas others, such as interviews and focus groups, require a significant investment of participants' time.

Investment of Managers' Time

The time that a participant's manager must allocate to data collection is another issue in method selection. Time requirements for managers should always be minimized. Methods like performance contracting require significant involvement from the manager before and after program implementation, whereas other methods, such as participants' completion of a questionnaire, require no manager time.

Cost

Cost is always a consideration in selecting the data collection method. Some data collection methods are more expensive than others. For example, interviews and observations are expensive, whereas surveys, questionnaires, and performance monitoring are usually inexpensive.

Disruption of Normal Work Activities

Perhaps the issue that generates the greatest concern among managers is the degree of work disruption that data collection will create. Routine work processes should be disrupted as little as possible. Data collection techniques like performance monitoring require very little employee time and cause little distraction from normal activities. Questionnaires generally do not disrupt the work environment and can often be completed in just a few minutes, sometimes even after normal work hours. At the other extreme, techniques such as focus groups and interviews may disrupt the work unit.

Accuracy

The accuracy of the technique is another factor to consider in selecting a data collection method. Some data collection methods are more accurate than others. For example, performance monitoring is usually very accurate, whereas questionnaires are subject to distortion and may be unreliable, whether due to poor design or the mere subjectivity residing in individuals' responses. If on-the-job behavior must be captured, observation is clearly one of the most accurate methods. However, there is often a trade-off between the accuracy and the cost of a method.

Built-In Design Possibility

Because building data collection into many evaluation plans is important, how easily the method can be built into a program is another consideration; it must become an integral part of the program. Some methods, such as action plans, can be easily built into the design of a program. Other methods, such as observation, are more difficult to integrate into a program.

In some situations, a program is redesigned to provide a follow-up session in which evaluation is addressed and additional training is offered. For example, an interactive selling skills program (a consecutive three-day program) was redesigned as a two-day workshop to build skills, followed by a one-day session three weeks later. The follow-up session provided an opportunity for additional training and evaluation. During the first part of the last day, Level 3 evaluation data were collected through a focus group. In addition, specific barriers and problems encountered when applying the skills were discussed. The second half of the day was devoted to additional skill building and refinement, along with techniques to overcome barriers to using the skills. The redesigned program provided a method for follow-up in both evaluation and training.

Utility of an Additional Method

Because there are so many methods of collecting data, using too many methods is tempting. Multiple data collection methods add time and cost to an evaluation and may result in very little added value. Utility refers to the value added by each additional data collection method. When more than one method is used, this question should always be addressed: Does the value obtained from the additional data warrant the extra time and money that would need to spent on the method? If the answer is no, the additional method should not be implemented. The same issue must be addressed when considering multiple data sources and multiple time frames.

Cultural Bias of Data Collection Method

The culture or philosophy of the organization may dictate which data collection methods would be best to use. For example, if an organization or audience is accustomed to using questionnaires, they will work well within the culture of that organization. If, however, an organization tends to overuse questionnaires, this may not be the best choice for collecting program data. Some organizations routinely use third-party observation. However, others view the technique as invasive—an attitude that is a clear deterrent to using observation to evaluate a program at that organization.

Final Thoughts

This brief chapter has explored the issue of selecting an appropriate data collection method. In choosing a method, some straightforward criteria are useful. Most of the criteria detailed in this chapter will fit well in any organizational setting.

Index

A

Action plans
　advantages and disadvantages of, 51
　for application/implementation data, 110–111
　applications of, 48–50
　calculating ROI, 49–50, 133
　description and example of, 38–39
　developing an, 40–42
　for impact data collection, 129–133, 135
　successful implementation of, 42–48
Activities, 19–20
Alreck, P. L., 1
Anonymity issue, 4, 10, 65
Application and Implementation (Level 3)
　action areas for, 93, 94–95
　barriers to application, 111–112
　data collection methods for, 96–111
　measurement issues for, 92–96
　reasons for measuring, 87–92
　uses of application data, 112
Attitude, knowledge, skills, 76–77, 97, 104
Audio monitoring observation, 32

B

Behavior checklist, 30–31
Business games, 17
Business performance monitoring, 35–38

C

Captive audience, 9
Case study, 18
Certification, 73
Checklists
　behavior, 30–31
　questionnaire use of, 2
Competency development, 73
Compliance issues, 72–73
Computer monitoring observation, 32
Confidentiality issue, 4, 10
Consistency, 82–83
Coscarelli, W. C., 14
Cost issues, 144
Criterion-referenced tests, 14, 15
Cultural bias issue, 146
Customer satisfaction, 55–56, 68

D

Data
　measures of, 118–120
　measures of soft, 120–121
　tangible versus intangible measures of, 121–122

147

Index

Data collection
  action plans for, 38–51, 110–111, 129–133, 135
  for application data, 96–111
  built into the program, 90–91
  business performance monitoring for, 35–38
  focus groups for, 25–28, 64–65, 110
  interviews for, 23–25, 64, 110
  of learning measurements, 79–81
  observations for, 28–32, 110
  performance contracts for, 51–54, 134, 136
  questionnaires and surveys for, 1–12, 64, 96–110, 134, 137
  reaction feedback, 55–67
  tests used for, 13–21
Data collection selection
  matching exercise for, 139–143
  selecting method appropriate for each level, 143–146
Data sources
  for application data, 93, 95
  for impact data, 126–127
Database building, 85
Delayed report method, 31

E
Electromechanical simulation, 17
Employees
  certification of, 73
  consequences of unprepared, 73–74
  developing competencies, 73
  rewarding effective, 90
  See also Participants; Work activities
End-of-conference questionnaire, 80
Evaluation
  considering end-of-the program, 66
  increasing value of, 88
  Reaction and Planned Action (Level 1), 55–69
Exercises, 19–20

F
Facilitators
  action plan approval by, 43
  assessment of, 20–21
  collecting feedback on, 60
  evaluating, 68, 85
  focus group interviews by, 28
Failure (test), 84
Focus groups
  for application/implementation data, 110
  data collection using, 25–28
  for gathering reaction feedback, 64–65
Follow-up
  action plan, 45–46
  reminders for, 8
Fosse, C. E., 26

I
Impact and Consequences (Level 4)
  data collection methods for, 127–137
  effective impact measures used for, 117–127
  reasons for measuring, 115–117
In-basket simulation, 17–18
Incentive methods, 7–8
Informal tests, 19–21
Intangible measures, 121–122
Interviews
  for application/implementation data, 100
  focus group, 25–28, 64–65, 110
  for gathering reaction feedback, 64
  types and guidelines for, 23–25
Introductory letters, 8
Isolating program effects
  action plan and, 132
  ROI calculations adjusted for, 49

K
Knowledge, skills, attitudes, 76–77, 97, 104
Kvale, S., 23

L

Learning
  knowledge, skills, attitudes measurements of, 76–77
  linking application to, 90
  measuring levels of, 71–85
  objectives for, 75–76
  programs and role of, 74–75
Learning and Confidence (Level 2)
  administrative issues for, 81–84
  measurement issues for, 75–81
  reasons for measuring, 71–75
  timing of measuring, 77–79
  uses of learning data, 84–85
Learning organizations, 71–72
Lindsay, N. R., 26

M

Managers
  data collection method and investment of, 144
  questionnaire support by, 7
Marketing programs, 69
Marsick, V. J., 72
McDonough, J. B., 58
Middlebrook, R. H., 26
Mondschein, M., 35
Monetary value units
  assigning data, 105–106
  basis for assigned, 106
  impact data providing, 117
  of program improvements, 131
Multiple-choice questions, 2
Myhill, M., 58

N

Needs assessment, 91–92
Norm-referenced tests, 13–14

O

Objectives
  impact, 122–123
  performance, 53
  program, 75–76
  program application and implementation, 92–93
  reaction feedback on, 60

Observations
  for application/implementation data, 100
  described, 28
  guidelines for effective, 28–32
Open-ended questions, 2
Organizations
  compliance issues for, 72–73
  learning, 71–72

P

Participants
  action plan measurements by, 43–45
  allowing ample response time for, 66–67
  anonymity of, 4, 10, 65
  improving questionnaire response rates by, 5–12
  interviewing, 23–25
  providing incentives for, 7–8
  See also Employees; Work activities
Performance contracts, 51–54, 134, 136
Performance data, 115–116, 127–129
Performance tests, 14, 16
Pharma Company Questionnaire, 98–104
Phillips, J. J., 15, 44, 58, 82, 110
Phillips, P. P., 44, 82, 110
Pilot testing
  of learning measurements, 83
  questionnaire for, 10
  See also Tests
Problems
  identifying program, 89
  testing by using, 19–20
Programs
  building data collection into, 90–91
  evaluating planned improvements of, 68–69
  identifying business driver of, 116–117
  identifying problems of, 89

Programs (*Continued*)
   identifying strengths and weaknesses of, 68
   measuring reaction and planned action for, 55–69
   objectives of, 75–76
   obtaining data for marketing, 69
   role of learning in, 74–75
   tracking focus of, 88–89

Q
Questionnaires
   for application/implementation data, 96–110
   design steps for, 2–5
   end-of-conference, 80
   example of Pharma Company, 98–104
   for gathering reaction feedback, 64
   for impact data collection, 134, 137
   improving response rate for, 5–12
   ROI Methodology use of, 137
   types of questions used for, 1–2

R
Reaction and Planned Action (Level 1)
   areas of feedback on, 58–63
   data collection issues for, 55–67
   reaction and application data correlations, 57
   reasons for measuring, 55–58
   routine feedback form for, 67
   timing of data collection for, 63
   uses of data on, 67–69
Reliability, 81–82
Reporting learning measures, 83–84
Robson, C., 2
ROI Methodology
   Application and Implementation (Level 3) of, 87–112
   on data and improvement, 137
   Impact and Consequences (Level 4) of, 115–137
   Learning and Confidence (Level 2) of, 71–85
   questionnaires as used in the, 137
   Reaction and Planned Action (Level 1), 55-69
   selecting data collection method for each level of, 143–146
ROI (return on investment)
   calculating action plan, 49–50, 133
   impact measures in applications of, 123–126
   isolating program effects adjustments for, 49
   measuring action plan, 46–47
Role-playing (or skill practice), 18

S
Scoring learning measures, 83–84
Self-assessment, 20
Senge, P., 72
Settle, R. B., 1
Shrock, S. A., 14
Simulations, 16–18
Skill practice (or role-playing), 18
Skills, knowledge, attitudes, 76–77, 97, 104
SMART plan, 130
Structured interview, 24
Subramony, D. P., 26
Surveys. *See* Questionnaires

T
Tangible measures, 121–122
Task simulation, 17
Tests
   failure to pass, 84
   informal, 19–21
   simulations used as, 16–18
   true-false, 81
   types of, 13–16
   See also Pilot testing

360° feedback, 31
Time issues
  allowing participants response
    time, 66–67
  timing of application/
    implementation data collection,
    95–96
  timing of impact action plans, 133
  timing of learning measurement,
    77–79
  timing of reaction feedback
    collection, 63
True-false test, 81
Two-way questions, 2

U
Unstructured interview, 24

V
Validity, 81–82
video recording observation, 31–32

W
Watkins, K. E., 72
Work activities
  data collection disruption of,
    144–145
  measuring changes in, 104
  See also Employees; Participants

About the Authors

Patricia Pulliam Phillips, Ph.D., is president of the ROI Institute, Inc., the leading source of ROI competency building, implementation support, networking, and research. She supports organizations in their efforts to build accountability into their training, human resources, and performance improvement programs with a primary focus on building accountability in public sector organizations. She helps organizations implement the ROI Methodology in countries around the world, including South Africa, Singapore, Japan, New Zealand, Australia, Italy, Turkey, France, Germany, Canada, and the United States.

In 1997, after a thirteen-year career in the electrical utility industry, she embraced the ROI Methodology by committing herself to ongoing research and practice. To this end, Phillips has implemented the ROI Methodology in private sector and public sector organizations. She has conducted ROI impact studies of programs in leadership development, sales, new-hire orientation, human performance improvement, K–12 educator development, National Board Certification mentoring for educators, and faculty fellowship. Phillips is currently expanding her interest in public sector accountability by applying the ROI Methodology in community- and faith-based initiatives.

Phillips teaches others to implement the ROI Methodology through the ROI certification process, as a facilitator for ASTD's

ROI and Measuring and Evaluating Learning workshops, and as an adjunct professor for graduate-level evaluation courses. She speaks on the topic of ROI at conferences such as ASTD's International Conference and Exposition and the International Society for Performance Improvement's International Conference.

Phillips's academic accomplishments include a master's degree in public and private management and a Ph.D. degree in international development. She is certified in ROI evaluation and has earned the designation of certified performance technologist (CPT) and certified professional in learning and performance (CPLP). She has authored a number of publications on the subject of accountability and ROI, including *Show Me the Money: How to Determine ROI in People, Projects, and Programs* (Berrett-Koehler, 2007); *The Value of Learning* (Pfeiffer, 2007); *Return on Investment (ROI) Basics* (ASTD, 2005); *Proving the Value of HR: How and Why to Measure ROI* (Society for Human Resource Management, 2005); *Make Training Evaluation Work* (ASTD, 2004); *The Bottomline on ROI* (Center for Effective Performance, 2002), which won the 2003 ISPI Award of Excellence; *ROI at Work* (ASTD, 2005); the ASTD In Action casebooks *Measuring Return on Investment*, Volume 3 (2001), *Measuring ROI in the Public Sector* (2002), and *Retaining Your Best Employees* (2002); the ASTD Infoline series, including *Planning and Using Evaluation Data* (2003), *Mastering ROI* (1998), and *Managing Evaluation Shortcuts* (2001); and *The Human Resources Scorecard: Measuring Return on Investment* (Butterworth-Heinemann, 2001). Phillips's work has been published in a variety of journals. She can be reached at patti@roiinstitute.net.

Cathy A. Stawarski, Ph.D., is program manager of the Strategic Performance Improvement and Evaluation program at the Human Resources Research Organization (HumRRO) in Alexandria, Virginia. She has more than twenty-five years experience in research, training and development, and program evaluation. Throughout her nearly twenty years at HumRRO, she has worked primarily with clients in the federal sector. Her work includes leading and conducting the evaluation of leadership and human capital initiatives as well as assisting organizations in developing comprehensive evaluation strategies. Stawarski is a certified practitioner in the ROI Methodology and a member of the American Society for Training and Development and the International Society for Performance Improvement. She has authored nearly one hundred technical reports and training manuals during her career at HumRRO and has spoken at a variety of conferences on the topic of evaluation and ROI, including the Training Officers Conference, which supports the development of leaders in the federal government. She can be reached at cstawarski@humrro.org.

Pfeiffer Publications Guide

This guide is designed to familiarize you with the various types of Pfeiffer publications. The formats section describes the various types of products that we publish; the methodologies section describes the many different ways that content might be provided within a product. We also provide a list of the topic areas in which we publish.

FORMATS

In addition to its extensive book-publishing program, Pfeiffer offers content in an array of formats, from fieldbooks for the practitioner to complete, ready-to-use training packages that support group learning.

FIELDBOOK Designed to provide information and guidance to practitioners in the midst of action. Most fieldbooks are companions to another, sometimes earlier, work, from which its ideas are derived; the fieldbook makes practical what was theoretical in the original text. Fieldbooks can certainly be read from cover to cover. More likely, though, you'll find yourself bouncing around following a particular theme, or dipping in as the mood, and the situation, dictate.

HANDBOOK A contributed volume of work on a single topic, comprising an eclectic mix of ideas, case studies, and best practices sourced by practitioners and experts in the field.

An editor or team of editors usually is appointed to seek out contributors and to evaluate content for relevance to the topic. Think of a handbook not as a ready-to-eat meal, but as a cookbook of ingredients that enables you to create the most fitting experience for the occasion.

RESOURCE Materials designed to support group learning. They come in many forms: a complete, ready-to-use exercise (such as a game); a comprehensive resource on one topic (such as conflict management) containing a variety of methods and approaches; or a collection of like-minded activities (such as icebreakers) on multiple subjects and situations.

TRAINING PACKAGE An entire, ready-to-use learning program that focuses on a particular topic or skill. All packages comprise a guide for the facilitator/trainer and a workbook for the participants. Some packages are supported with additional media—such as video—or learning aids, instruments, or other devices to help participants understand concepts or practice and develop skills.

- *Facilitator/trainer's guide* Contains an introduction to the program, advice on how to organize and facilitate the learning event, and step-by-step instructor notes. The guide also contains copies of presentation materials—handouts, presentations, and overhead designs, for example—used in the program.

- *Participant's workbook* Contains exercises and reading materials that support the learning goal and serves as a valuable reference and support guide for participants in the weeks and months that follow the learning event. Typically, each participant will require his or her own workbook.

ELECTRONIC CD-ROMs and web-based products transform static Pfeiffer content into dynamic, interactive experiences. Designed to take advantage of the searchability, automation, and ease-of-use that technology provides, our e-products bring convenience and immediate accessibility to your workspace.

METHODOLOGIES

CASE STUDY A presentation, in narrative form, of an actual event that has occurred inside an organization. Case studies are not prescriptive, nor are they used to prove a point; they are designed to develop critical analysis and decision-making skills. A case study has a specific time frame, specifies a sequence of events, is narrative in structure, and contains a plot structure—an issue (what should be/have been done?). Use case studies when the goal is to enable participants to apply previously learned theories to the circumstances in the case, decide what is pertinent, identify the real issues, decide what should have been done, and develop a plan of action.

ENERGIZER A short activity that develops readiness for the next session or learning event. Energizers are most commonly used after a break or lunch to

stimulate or refocus the group. Many involve some form of physical activity, so they are a useful way to counter post-lunch lethargy. Other uses include transitioning from one topic to another, where "mental" distancing is important.

EXPERIENTIAL LEARNING ACTIVITY (ELA) A facilitator-led intervention that moves participants through the learning cycle from experience to application (also known as a Structured Experience). ELAs are carefully thought-out designs in which there is a definite learning purpose and intended outcome. Each step—everything that participants do during the activity—facilitates the accomplishment of the stated goal. Each ELA includes complete instructions for facilitating the intervention and a clear statement of goals, suggested group size and timing, materials required, an explanation of the process, and, where appropriate, possible variations to the activity. (For more detail on Experiential Learning Activities, see the Introduction to the *Reference Guide to Handbooks and Annuals*, 1999 edition, Pfeiffer, San Francisco.)

GAME A group activity that has the purpose of fostering team spirit and togetherness in addition to the achievement of a pre-stated goal. Usually contrived—undertaking a desert expedition, for example—this type of learning method offers an engaging means for participants to demonstrate and practice business and interpersonal skills. Games are effective for team building and personal development mainly because the goal is subordinate to the process—the means through which participants reach decisions, collaborate, communicate, and generate trust and understanding. Games often engage teams in "friendly" competition.

ICEBREAKER A (usually) short activity designed to help participants overcome initial anxiety in a training session and/or to acquaint the participants with one another. An icebreaker can be a fun activity or can be tied to specific topics or training goals. While a useful tool in itself, the icebreaker comes into its own in situations where tension or resistance exists within a group.

INSTRUMENT A device used to assess, appraise, evaluate, describe, classify, and summarize various aspects of human behavior. The term used to describe an instrument depends primarily on its format and purpose. These terms include survey, questionnaire, inventory, diagnostic, survey, and poll. Some uses of instruments include providing instrumental feedback to group

members, studying here-and-now processes or functioning within a group, manipulating group composition, and evaluating outcomes of training and other interventions.

Instruments are popular in the training and HR field because, in general, more growth can occur if an individual is provided with a method for focusing specifically on his or her own behavior. Instruments also are used to obtain information that will serve as a basis for change and to assist in workforce planning efforts.

Paper-and-pencil tests still dominate the instrument landscape with a typical package comprising a facilitator's guide, which offers advice on administering the instrument and interpreting the collected data, and an initial set of instruments. Additional instruments are available separately. Pfeiffer, though, is investing heavily in e-instruments. Electronic instrumentation provides effortless distribution and, for larger groups particularly, offers advantages over paper-and-pencil tests in the time it takes to analyze data and provide feedback.

LECTURETTE A short talk that provides an explanation of a principle, model, or process that is pertinent to the participants' current learning needs. A lecturette is intended to establish a common language bond between the trainer and the participants by providing a mutual frame of reference. Use a lecturette as an introduction to a group activity or event, as an interjection during an event, or as a handout.

MODEL A graphic depiction of a system or process and the relationship among its elements. Models provide a frame of reference and something more tangible, and more easily remembered, than a verbal explanation. They also give participants something to "go on," enabling them to track their own progress as they experience the dynamics, processes, and relationships being depicted in the model.

ROLE PLAY A technique in which people assume a role in a situation/scenario: a customer service rep in an angry-customer exchange, for example. The way in which the role is approached is then discussed and feedback is offered. The role play is often repeated using a different approach and/or incorporating changes made based on feedback received. In other words, role playing is a spontaneous interaction involving realistic behavior under artificial (and safe) conditions.

SIMULATION A methodology for understanding the interrelationships among components of a system or process. Simulations differ from games in that they test or use a model that depicts or mirrors some aspect of reality in form, if not necessarily in content. Learning occurs by studying the effects of change on one or more factors of the model. Simulations are commonly used to test hypotheses about what happens in a system—often referred to as "what if?" analysis—or to examine best-case/worst-case scenarios.

THEORY A presentation of an idea from a conjectural perspective. Theories are useful because they encourage us to examine behavior and phenomena through a different lens.

TOPICS

The twin goals of providing effective and practical solutions for workforce training and organization development and meeting the educational needs of training and human resource professionals shape Pfeiffer's publishing program. Core topics include the following:

    Leadership & Management

    Communication & Presentation

    Coaching & Mentoring

    Training & Development

    E-Learning

    Teams & Collaboration

    OD & Strategic Planning

    Human Resources

    Consulting

What will you find on pfeiffer.com?

- The best in workplace performance solutions for training and HR professionals
- Downloadable training tools, exercises, and content
- Web-exclusive offers
- Training tips, articles, and news
- Seamless on-line ordering
- Author guidelines, information on becoming a Pfeiffer Affiliate, and much more

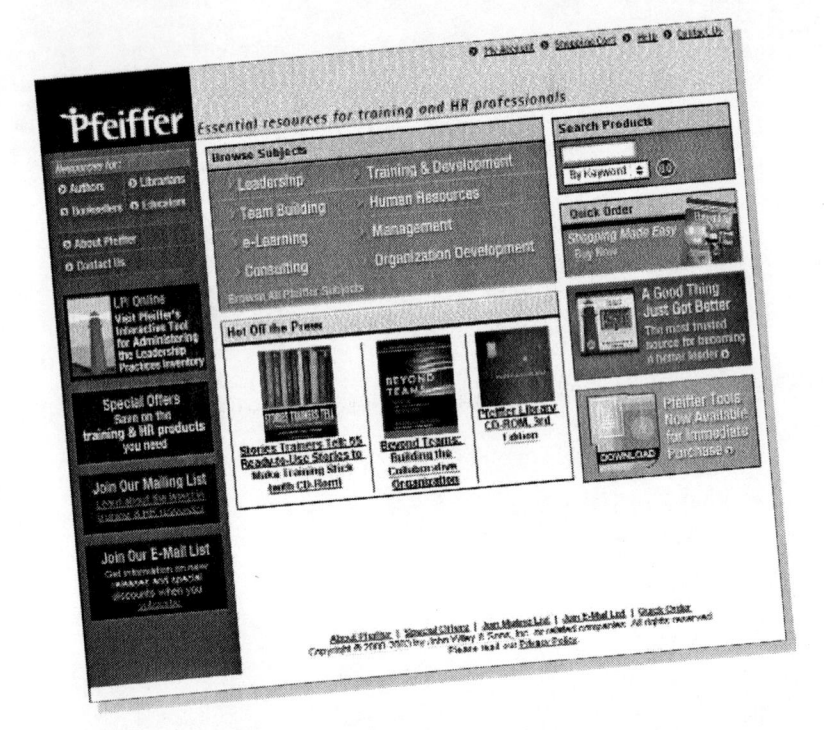

Discover more at www.pfeiffer.com

Measurement and Evaluation Series

Series Editors
Patricia Pulliam Phillips, Ph.D., and Jack J. Phillips, Ph.D.

A six-book set that provides a step-by-step system for planning, measuring, calculating, and communicating evaluation and Return-on-Investment for training and development, featuring:

- Detailed templates
- Complete plans
- Ready-to-use tools
- Real-world case examples

The M&E Series features:

1. *ROI Fundamentals: Why and When to Measure ROI* (978-0-7879-8716-9)
2. *Data Collection: Planning For and Collecting All Types of Data* (978-0-7879-8718-3)
3. *Isolation of Results: Defining the Impact of the Program* (978-0-7879-8719-0)
4. *Data Conversion: Calculating the Monetary Benefits* (978-0-7879-8720-6)
5. *Costs and ROI: Evaluating at the Ultimate Level* (978-0-7879-8721-3)
6. *Communication and Implementation: Sustaining the Practice* (978-0-7879-8722-0)

Plus, the *ROI in Action Casebook* (978-0-7879-8717-6) covers all the major workplace learning and performance applications, including Leadership Development, Sales Training, Performance Improvement, Technical Skills Training, Information Technology Training, Orientation and OJT, and Supervisor Training.

The **ROI Methodology** is a comprehensive measurement and evaluation process that collects six types of measures: Reaction, Satisfaction, and Planned Action; Learning; Application and Implementation; Business Impact; Return on Investment; and Intangible Measures. The process provides a step-by-step system for evaluation and planning, data collection, data analysis, and reporting. It is appropriate for the measurement and evaluation of *all* kinds of performance improvement programs and activities, including training and development, learning, human resources, coaching, meetings and events, consulting, and project management.

Special Offer from the ROI Institute

Send for your own ROI Process Model, an indispensable tool for implementing and presenting ROI in your organization. The ROI Institute is offering an exclusive gift to readers of The Measurement and Evaluation Series. This 11" × 25" multicolor foldout shows the ROI Methodology flow model and the key issues surrounding the implementation of the ROI Methodology. This easy-to-understand overview of the ROI Methodology has proven invaluable to countless professionals when implementing the ROI Methodology. Please return this page or e-mail your information to the address below to receive your free foldout (a $6.00 value). Please check your area(s) of interest in ROI.

Please send me the ROI Process Model described in the book. I am interested in learning more about the following ROI materials and services:

- ☐ Workshops and briefing on ROI
- ☐ Books and support materials on ROI
- ☐ Certification in the ROI Methodology
- ☐ ROI software
- ☐ ROI consulting services
- ☐ ROI Network information
- ☐ ROI benchmarking
- ☐ ROI research

Name _____

Title _____

Organization _____

Address _____

Phone _____

E-mail Address _____

Functional area of interest:

- ☐ Learning and Development/Performance Improvement
- ☐ Human Resources/Human Capital
- ☐ Public Relations/Community Affairs/Government Relations
- ☐ Consulting
- ☐ Sales/Marketing
- ☐ Technology/IT Systems
- ☐ Project Management Solutions
- ☐ Quality/Six Sigma
- ☐ Operations/Methods/Engineering
- ☐ Research and Development/Innovations
- ☐ Finance/Compliance
- ☐ Logistics/Distribution/Supply Chain
- ☐ Public Policy Initiatives
- ☐ Social Programs
- ☐ Other (Please Specify) _____

Organizational Level

- ☐ executive ☐ management ☐ consultant ☐ specialist
- ☐ student ☐ evaluator ☐ researcher

Return this form or contact The ROI Institute
P.O. Box 380637
Birmingham, AL 35238-0637

Or e-mail information to info@roiinstitute.net
Please allow four to six weeks for delivery.

About This Book

Why This Book Is Important

This third book in the M&E Series explores the techniques that can be used to isolate the effects of programs on business measures from the effects of other factors. Many factors can affect business performance; some are direct effects of the program, and others are not. Top organizations use the techniques in this book to isolate the program effects of a variety of programs, an important step in measuring return on investment.

A direct cause-and-effect relationship between a program and business performance can be difficult to prove, but it can be accomplished. This book shows how up-front planning can ensure that this important step in program evaluation is accomplished successfully. It also discusses why isolation of program effects is important.

What This Book Achieves

This book shows how to isolate the effects of a program from other influences, using the following techniques:

- Control groups
- Trend lines and forecasts
- Expert estimates

In addition, this volume explains how to select the appropriate technique for any situation and any level of evaluation.

How This Book Is Organized

This book begins with a brief introduction to the ROI process model and the Twelve Guiding Principles. Chapter One discusses why isolating program effects is so important.

The book then introduces and describes the techniques that can be used to isolate the effects of a program. Chapter Two examines the use of control groups, which is the most credible way to isolate the effects of a program. This chapter also describes many of the issues surrounding this technique and includes several examples of how organizations have used control groups.

Chapter Three discusses another method of isolating the effects of a program: trend line analysis and forecasting. Several case examples are provided to illustrate the use of these methods. Chapter Four examines the least credible way to isolate the effects of a program: estimates. The chapter discusses possible sources of expert input, including program participants, participants' immediate managers, senior management, customers, and experts. Several case examples show how estimates can be used to isolate the effects of the program.

In Chapter Five, a matching exercise illustrates situations that are appropriate for each method. The importance of isolating program effects is discussed once again, along with several myths surrounding this issue. How to build credibility into the process of isolating program effects is also examined.

The Measurement and Evaluation Series

Editors

Patricia Pulliam Phillips, Ph.D.

Jack J. Phillips, Ph.D.

Introduction to the Measurement and Evaluation Series

The ROI Six Pack provides detailed information on developing ROI evaluations, implementing the ROI Methodology, and showing the value of a variety of functions and processes. With detailed examples, tools, templates, shortcuts, and checklists, this series will be a valuable reference for individuals interested in using the ROI Methodology to show the impact of their projects, programs, and processes.

The Need

Although financial ROI has been measured for over one hundred years to quantify the value of plants, equipment, and companies, the concept has only recently been applied to evaluate the impact of learning and development, human resources, technology, quality, marketing, and other support functions. In the learning and development field alone, the use of ROI has become routine in many organizations. In the past decade, hundreds of organizations have embraced the ROI process to show the impact of many different projects and programs.

Along the way, professionals and practitioners need help. They need tools, templates, and tips, along with explanations, examples, and details, to make this process work. Without this help, using the ROI Methodology to show the value of projects and

programs is difficult. In short, practitioners need shortcuts and proven techniques to minimize the resources required to use this process. Practitioners' needs have created the need for this series. This series will provide the detail necessary to make the ROI Methodology successful within an organization. For easy reference and use, the books are logically arranged to align with the steps of the ROI Methodology.

Audience

The principal audience for these books is individuals who plan to use the ROI Methodology to show the value of their projects and programs. Such individuals are specialists or managers charged with proving the value of their particular project or program. They need detailed information, know-how, and confidence.

A second audience is those who have used the ROI Methodology for some time but want a quick reference with tips and techniques to make ROI implementation more successful within their organization. This series, which explains the evaluation process in detail, will be a valuable reference set for these individuals, regardless of other ROI publications owned.

A third audience is consultants and researchers who want to know how to address specific evaluation issues. Three important challenges face individuals as they measure ROI and conduct ROI evaluations: (1) collecting post-program data, (2) isolating the effects of the program, and (3) converting data to monetary values. A book is devoted to each of these critical issues, allowing researchers and consultants to easily find details on each issue.

A fourth audience is those who are curious about the ROI Methodology and its use. The first book in this series focuses specifically on ROI, its use, and how to determine whether it is appropriate for an organization. When interest is piqued, the remaining books provide more detail.

Flow of the Books

The six books are presented in a logical sequence, mirroring the ROI process model. Book one, *ROI Fundamentals: Why and When to Measure ROI*, presents the basic ROI Methodology and makes the business case for measuring ROI as it explores the benefits and barriers to implementation. It also examines the type of organization best suited for the ROI Methodology and the best time to implement it. Planning for an ROI evaluation is also explored in this book.

Book two, *Data Collection: Planning For and Collecting All Types of Data*, details data collection by examining the different techniques, methods, and issues involved in this process, with an emphasis on collecting post-program data. It examines the different data collection methods: questionnaires, interviews, focus groups, observation, action plans, performance contracts, and monitoring records.

Book three, *Isolation of Results: Defining the Impact of the Program*, focuses on the most valuable part of the ROI Methodology and the essential step for ensuring credibility. Recognizing that factors other than the program being measured can influence results, this book shows a variety of ways in which the effects of a program can be isolated from other influences. Techniques include comparison analysis using a control group, trend line analysis and forecasting methods, and expert input from a variety of sources.

Book four, *Data Conversion: Calculating the Monetary Benefits*, covers perhaps the second toughest challenge of ROI evaluation: placing monetary value on program benefits. To calculate the ROI, data must be converted to money, and *Data Conversion* shows how this conversion has been accomplished in a variety of organizations. The good news is that standard values are available for many items. When they are not, the book shows different techniques for converting them, ranging from calculating the value from records to seeking experts and searching databases. When data cannot be

converted to money credibly and with minimum resources, they are considered intangible. This book explores the range of intangible benefits and the necessary techniques for collecting, analyzing, and recording them.

Book five, *Costs and ROI: Evaluating at the Ultimate Level*, focuses on costs and ROI. This book shows that all costs must be captured in order to create a fully loaded cost profile. All the costs must be included in order to be conservative and to give the analysis additional credibility. Next, the actual ROI calculation is presented, showing the various assumptions and issues that must be addressed when calculating the ROI. Three different calculations are presented: the benefit-cost ratio, the ROI percentage, and the payback period. The book concludes with several cautions and concerns about the use of ROI and its meaning.

Book six, *Communication and Implementation: Sustaining the Practice*, explores two important issues. The first issue is reporting the results of an evaluation. This is the final part of the ROI Methodology and is necessary to ensure that audiences have the information they need so that improvement processes can be implemented. A range of techniques is available, including face-to-face meetings, brief reports, one-page summaries, routine communications, mass-audience techniques, and electronic media. All are available for reporting evaluation results. The final part of the book focuses on how to sustain the ROI evaluation process: how to use it, keep it going, and make it work in the long term to add value to the organization and, often, to show the value of all the programs and projects within a function or department.

Terminology: Programs, Projects, Solutions

In this series the terms *program* and *project* are used to describe many processes that can be evaluated using the ROI Methodology. This is an important issue because readers may vary widely in their perspectives. Individuals involved in technology applications may

Table I.1. Terms and Applications

Term	Example
Program	Leadership development skills enhancement for senior executives
Project	A reengineering scheme for a plastics division
System	A fully interconnected network for all branches of a bank
Initiative	A faith-based effort to reduce recidivism
Policy	A new preschool plan for disadvantaged citizens
Procedure	A new scheduling arrangement for truck drivers
Event	A golf outing for customers
Meeting	A U.S. Coast Guard conference on innovations
Process	Quality sampling
People	Staff additions in the customer care center
Tool	A new means of selecting hotel staff

use the terms *system* and *technology* rather than *program* or *project*. In public policy, in contrast, the word *program* is prominent. For a professional meetings and events planner, the word *program* may not be pertinent, but in human resources, *program* is often used. Finding one term for all these situations would be difficult. Consequently, the terms *program* and *project* are used interchangeably. Table I.1 lists these and other terms that may be used in other contexts.

Features

Each book in the series takes a straightforward approach to make it understandable, practical, and useful. Checklists are provided, charts are included, templates are presented, and examples are explored. All are intended to show how the ROI Methodology works. The focus of these books is implementing the process and making it successful within an organization. The methodology is based on the work of hundreds of individuals who have made the ROI Methodology a successful evaluation process within their organizations.

About Pfeiffer

Pfeiffer serves the professional development and hands-on resource needs of training and human resource practitioners and gives them products to do their jobs better. We deliver proven ideas and solutions from experts in HR development and HR management, and we offer effective and customizable tools to improve workplace performance. From novice to seasoned professional, Pfeiffer is the source you can trust to make yourself and your organization more successful.

Essential Knowledge Pfeiffer produces insightful, practical, and comprehensive materials on topics that matter the most to training and HR professionals. Our Essential Knowledge resources translate the expertise of seasoned professionals into practical, how-to guidance on critical workplace issues and problems. These resources are supported by case studies, worksheets, and job aids and are frequently supplemented with CD-ROMs, Web sites, and other means of making the content easier to read, understand, and use.

Essential Tools Pfeiffer's Essential Tools resources save time and expense by offering proven, ready-to-use materials—including exercises, activities, games, instruments, and assessments—for use during a training or team-learning event. These resources are frequently offered in looseleaf or CD-ROM format to facilitate copying and customization of the material.

Pfeiffer also recognizes the remarkable power of new technologies in expanding the reach and effectiveness of training. While e-hype has often created whizbang solutions in search of a problem, we are dedicated to bringing convenience and enhancements to proven training solutions. All our e-tools comply with rigorous functionality standards. The most appropriate technology wrapped around essential content yields the perfect solution for today's on-the-go trainers and human resource professionals.

Pfeiffer
www.pfeiffer.com   *Essential resources for training and HR professionals*

Isolation of Results

Defining the Impact of the Program

Jack J. Phillips, Ph.D.
Bruce C. Aaron, Ph.D.

Pfeiffer
A Wiley Imprint
www.pfeiffer.com

Copyright © 2008 by John Wiley & Sons, Inc. All rights reserved.

Published by Pfeiffer
An Imprint of Wiley
989 Market Street, San Francisco, CA 94103-1741
www.pfeiffer.com

No part of this publication may be reproduced, stored in a retrieval system, or transmitted in any form or by any means, electronic, mechanical, photocopying, recording, scanning, or otherwise, except as permitted under Section 107 or 108 of the 1976 United States Copyright Act, without either the prior written permission of the publisher, or authorization through payment of the appropriate per-copy fee to the Copyright Clearance Center, Inc., 222 Rosewood Drive, Danvers, MA 01923, 978-750-8400, fax 978-646-8600, or on the web at www.copyright.com. Requests to the publisher for permission should be addressed to the Permissions Department, John Wiley & Sons, Inc., 111 River Street, Hoboken, NJ 07030, 201-748-6011, fax 201-748-6008, or online at http://www.wiley.com/go/permissions.

Limit of Liability/Disclaimer of Warranty: While the publisher and author have used their best efforts in preparing this book, they make no representations or warranties with respect to the accuracy or completeness of the contents of this book and specifically disclaim any implied warranties of merchantability or fitness for a particular purpose. No warranty may be created or extended by sales representatives or written sales materials. The advice and strategies contained herein may not be suitable for your situation. You should consult with a professional where appropriate. Neither the publisher nor author shall be liable for any loss of profit or any other commercial damages, including but not limited to special, incidental, consequential, or other damages.

Readers should be aware that Internet Web sites offered as citations and/or sources for further information may have changed or disappeared between the time this book was written and when it is read.

For additional copies/bulk purchases of this book in the U.S. please contact 800-274-4434.

Pfeiffer books and products are available through most bookstores. To contact Pfeiffer directly call our Customer Care Department within the U.S. at 800-274-4434, outside the U.S. at 317-572-3985, fax 317-572-4002, or visit www.pfeiffer.com.

Pfeiffer also publishes its books in a variety of electronic formats. Some content that appears in print may not be available in electronic books.

Library of Congress Cataloging-in-Publication Data

Phillips, Jack J., date.
  Isolation of results: defining the impact of the program/Jack J. Phillips and Bruce C. Aaron.
    p. cm.
  Includes bibliographical references and index.
  ISBN 978-0-7879-8719-0 (pbk.)
  1. Project management.   2. Project management—Evaluation.   3. Rate of return.
I. Aaron, Bruce C.   II. Title.
  HD69.P75P488   2008
  658.4'04—dc22
                                                                                2007035497

Production Editor: Michael Kay   Editorial Assistant: Julie Rodriguez
Editor: Matthew Davis   Manufacturing Supervisor: Becky Morgan
Printed in the United States of America

PB Printing 10 9 8 7 6 5 4 3 2 1

Contents

Acknowledgments from the Editors — xix

Principles of the ROI Methodology — xxi

Chapter 1: The Importance of Isolating the Effects of Programs — 1

Challenges in Understanding a Program's Impact — 2
Case Study: What Caused the Improvement? — 2
Preliminary Issues in Isolating Program Effects — 5
    The Need to Isolate Program Effects — 6
    Chain of Impact: Initial Evidence of Program Effects — 8
    Identification of Factors Other Than the Program:
        A First Step — 10
Final Thoughts — 12

Chapter 2: Use of Control Groups — 15

Control Group Design — 15
    Threats to Validity — 15
    Basic Control Group Design — 17
    Ideal Experimental Design — 18
    Posttest-Only Control Group Design — 20
    Which Design to Choose — 21
Issues When Considering Control Groups — 22
    Viability — 22
    Practicality — 22

Ethical Considerations	23
Potential Problems with Control Groups: A Case Example	24
Feasibility	29

Control Group Example 1: Retail Merchandise Company — 31

Setting	31
Audience	32
Solution	32
Measures That Matter	32
Selection Criteria	33
Size of Groups	33
Duration of Experiment	33

Control Group Example 2: Federal Information Agency — 34

Setting	34
Audience	34
Solution	35
Measures That Matter	35
Selection Criteria	35
Size of Groups	36
Duration of Experiment	36

Control Group Example 3: Midwest Electric, Inc. — 36

Setting	36
Needs Assessment	37
Audience	38
Solution	39
Measures That Matter	39
Selection Criteria	39
Size of Groups	40
Duration of Experiment	40

Control Group Example 4: International Software Company — 41

Setting	41
Audience	41
Solution	41
Measures That Matter	41
Selection Criteria	42

Size of Groups	42
Duration of Experiment	42
Final Thoughts	43

Chapter 3: Use of Trend Lines and Forecasts — 45

Trend Lines	46
Forecasts	50
Trend Line Analysis Example 1: Micro Electronics	53
Setting	53
Audience	53
Solution	53
Measures That Matter	54
Conditions Test	54
Trend Line Analysis Example 2: Healthcare, Inc.	54
Setting	54
Audience	55
Solution	55
Measures That Matter	56
Conditions Test	56
Trend Line Analysis Example 3: National Book Company	57
Setting	57
Audience	57
Solution	57
Measures That Matter	58
Conditions Test	58
Final Thoughts	59

Chapter 4: Use of Expert Estimates — 61

Participants' Estimates of Program Impact	62
Using Focus Groups to Obtain Participant Estimates	63
Using Questionnaires to Obtain Participant Estimates	68
Using Interviews to Obtain Participant Estimates	74
Advantages and Disadvantages of Participant Estimates	75

Case Study	76
Setting	76
Audience	76
Solution	77
Measures	78
Estimates Provided	78
Credibility Check	78
Methodology	79
Immediate Managers' Estimates of Program Impact	80
Senior Management's Estimates of Program Impact	82
Customers' Estimates of Program Impact	83
Experts' Estimates of Program Impact	84
Determining the Impact of Other Factors	84
Estimate Example 1: Global Financial Services	85
Setting	85
Audience and Solution	86
Measures	86
Estimates Provided	87
Estimate Example 2: Cracker Box	87
Setting	87
Audience and Solution	88
Measures	88
Estimates Provided	89
Estimate Example 3: Public Bank of Malaysia	89
Setting	89
Audience and Solution	89
Measure	89
Estimates Provided	90
Estimate Example 4: Multi-National, Inc.	90
Setting	90
Audience, Solution, and Measures	91
Estimates Provided	91
The Power of Estimates	92
Research	92
A Demonstration	92
Participant Reaction	93
Management Reaction	94
The Wisdom of Crowds	94

Key Issues in Using Estimates	95
Final Thoughts	96

Chapter 5: Use of Isolation Techniques — 99

Matching Exercise: Isolating the Effects of a Program	99
Case Study: National Computer Company	102
Why Isolation Is a Key Issue	105
Other Factors Are Always There	105
Without It, There Is No Business Link: Evidence Versus Proof	105
Other Factors and Influences Have Protective Owners	106
To Do It Right Is Not Easy	106
Without It, the Study Is Not Valid	106
Isolation Myths	107
Build Credibility with the Isolation Process	109
Selecting the Technique	109
Using Multiple Methods	110
Building Credibility	111
Final Thoughts	112
Index	113
About the Authors	119

Acknowledgments from the Editors

From Patti

No project, regardless of its size or scope, is completed without the help and support of others. My sincere thanks go to the staff at Pfeiffer. Their support for this project has been relentless. Matt Davis has been the greatest! It is our pleasure and privilege to work with such a professional and creative group of people.

Thanks also go to my husband, Jack. His unwavering support of my work is always evident. His idea for the series was to provide readers with a practical understanding of the various components of a comprehensive measurement and evaluation process. Thank you, Jack, for another fun opportunity!

From Jack

Many thanks go to the staff who helped make this series a reality. Lori Ditoro did an excellent job of meeting a very tight deadline and delivering a quality manuscript.

Much admiration and thanks go to Patti. She is an astute observer of the ROI Methodology, having observed and learned from hundreds of presentations, consulting assignments, and engagements. In addition, she is an excellent researcher and student of the process, studying how it is developed and how it works. She has become an ROI expert in her own right. Thanks, Patti, for your many contributions. You are a great partner, friend, and spouse.

Principles of the ROI Methodology

The ROI Methodology is a step-by-step tool for evaluating any program, project, or initiative in any organization. Figure P.1 illustrates the ROI process model, which makes a potentially complicated process simple by breaking it into sequential steps. The ROI process model provides a systematic, step-by-step approach to ROI evaluations that helps keep the process manageable, allowing users to address one issue at a time. The model also emphasizes that the ROI Methodology is a logical, systematic process that flows from one step to another and provides a way for evaluators to collect and analyze six types of data.

Applying the model consistently from one program to another is essential for successful evaluation. To aid consistent application of the model, the ROI Methodology is based on twelve Guiding Principles. These principles are necessary for a credible, conservative approach to evaluation through the different levels.

1. When conducting a higher-level evaluation, collect data at lower levels.
2. When planning a higher-level evaluation, the previous level of evaluation is not required to be comprehensive.
3. When collecting and analyzing data, use only the most credible sources.

Figure P.1. The ROI Process Model

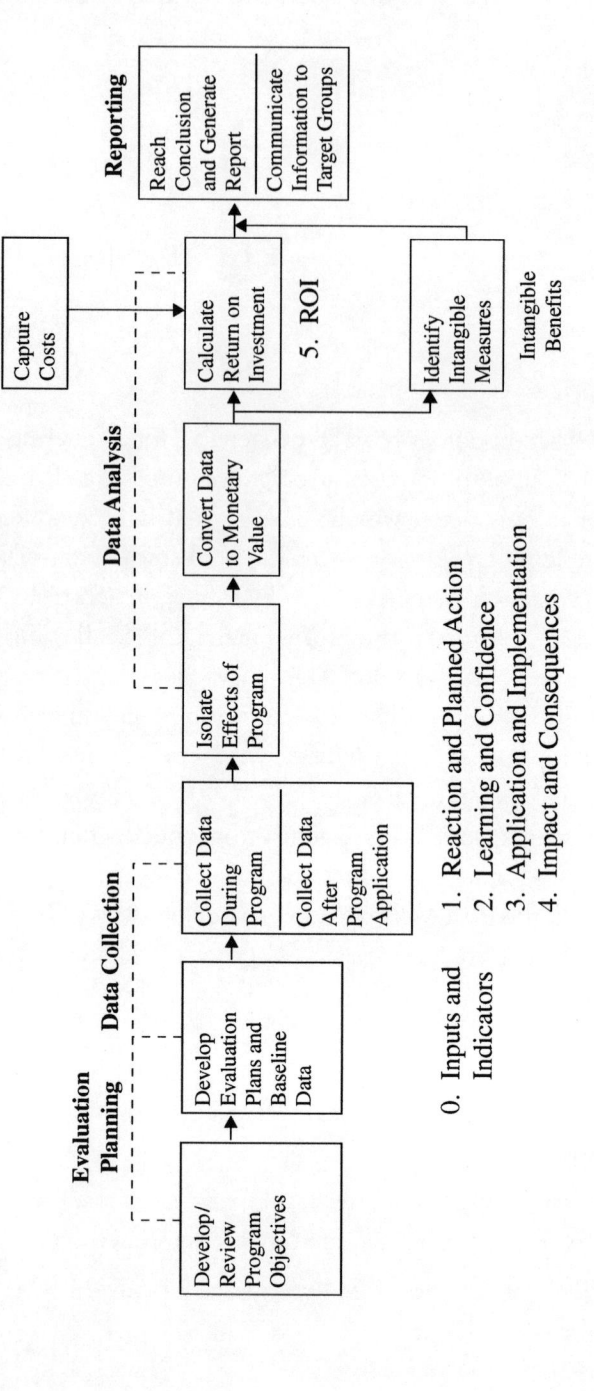

Evaluation Planning

- Develop/Review Program Objectives
- Develop Evaluation Plans and Baseline Data

Data Collection

- Collect Data During Program
- Collect Data After Program Application

- Isolate Effects of Program

Data Analysis

- Convert Data to Monetary Value
- Capture Costs
- Calculate Return on Investment — 5. ROI
- Identify Intangible Measures — Intangible Benefits

Reporting

- Reach Conclusion and Generate Report
- Communicate Information to Target Groups

0. Inputs and Indicators
1. Reaction and Planned Action
2. Learning and Confidence
3. Application and Implementation
4. Impact and Consequences

4. When analyzing data, select the most conservative alternative for calculations.
5. Use at least one method to isolate the effects of a project.
6. If no improvement data are available for a population or from a specific source, assume that little or no improvement has occurred.
7. Adjust estimates of improvement for potential errors of estimation.
8. Avoid use of extreme data items and unsupported claims when calculating ROI.
9. Use only the first year of annual benefits in ROI analysis of short-term solutions.
10. Fully load all costs of a solution, project, or program when analyzing ROI.
11. Intangible measures are defined as measures that are purposely not converted to monetary values.
12. Communicate the results of the ROI Methodology to all key stakeholders.

1

The Importance of Isolating the Effects of Programs

The following situation is repeated often. A significant increase in performance is noted after a major program has been conducted, and the improvement appears to be linked to the program. A key manager asks, "How much of this improvement was caused by the program?" When this potentially embarrassing question is asked, it is rarely answered with any degree of accuracy or credibility. While the change in performance may be linked to the program, other factors have usually contributed to the improvement as well.

This book explores the techniques for isolating the effects of programs from other factors. These techniques are used in top organizations as they measure the return on investment of a variety of programs. This first chapter focuses on the importance of isolating the effects of a program and the challenges faced in doing so.

A cause-and-effect relationship between a program and business performance can be difficult to prove, but such a relationship can be established with an acceptable degree of accuracy. The challenge is to decide upon one or more specific techniques to isolate the effects of the program or project early in the process, usually as part of an evaluation plan. Up-front planning is the best way to ensure that appropriate techniques with minimum costs and time commitments are used.

Challenges in Understanding a Program's Impact

In organizations, initiatives unfold in complex systems of people, processes, and events. The only way to learn about the connection between a program or a project and business performance is to isolate the effects of the program on specific business measures. This step ensures that the data analysis allocates to the program only that part of the performance improvement that is actually connected with the program. If this important step is omitted, the study may be invalid because factors other than the program may have affected the outcome of the program. Factors that can affect business performance include job redesign, incentives, rewards, compensation, technology, operational systems, and other internal processes. Factors external to the targeted department, functional area, or even the organization can also influence performance. Taking full credit for performance results without accounting for other factors is unacceptable. Only the results influenced by the program should be reported to stakeholders.

Case Study: What Caused the Improvement?

The following example illustrates why isolating the effects of a program is a critical step in the evaluation process.

First Bank, a large commercial bank, had experienced a significant increase in consumer loan volume for the quarter. In an executive meeting, the chief executive officer asked the executive group why the volume had increased. The responses were interesting.

- The executive responsible for consumer lending began the discussion by pointing out that his loan officers had become more aggressive: "They have adopted an improved sales approach. They all have sales development plans in place. We are being more aggressive."

- The marketing executive added that she thought the increase was related to a new promotional program and an increase in advertising during the period. "We've had some very effective ads," she remarked.

- The chief financial officer thought the increase in loan volume was the result of falling interest rates. He pointed out that interest rates had fallen by an average of 1 percent for the last six months and added, "Each time interest rates fall, consumers borrow more money."

- The executive responsible for mergers and acquisitions felt that the change was the result of a reduction in competition: "Several competitors closed bank branches during this quarter, which had an impact on our market areas. This has driven those customers to our branches." She added, "When you have more customers, you will have more loan volume."

- The human resources vice president spoke up and said that the incentive plan for consumer loan referrals had been slightly altered, with an increase in the referral bonus for all employees who referred legitimate customers for consumer loans. This new bonus plan, in her opinion, had caused the increase in consumer loans. She concluded, "When you reward employees for bringing in customers, they will bring them in . . . in greater numbers."

- The vice president for human resources development said that a seminar on consumer lending delivered to loan officers had caused the improvement. He indicated that the seminar had been revised in order to present appropriate strategies for increasing customer prospects and was now extremely effective. He concluded, "When you have effective training and build skills in sales, you will increase loan volume."

These responses left the CEO wondering just what had caused the improvement. Was it one or all of the factors? If so, how much of the improvement was influenced by each?

Consider for just a moment: Is this situation unusual? Probably not. As is the case in many settings, the process owners all claim credit for the improvement; yet realistically, each can rightfully claim only a share, if any, of the actual improvement. The challenge is to determine which isolation method would be most appropriate. Unfortunately, because the situation has already occurred, some of the methods for addressing this issue are not feasible. It might be helpful to review some of the data to see whether a time series analysis could determine the various influences and their corresponding impact. It is too late for a control group arrangement because all parts of the bank were subject to the various influences. It is also important to note that the people who understand this issue best—the loan officers who are familiar with the influences—have been omitted from the meeting. Of the many available techniques, asking the participants (the actual performers—that is, the loan officers) to isolate the effects of a particular program or influence may be the most credible and perhaps only way that isolation of program effects can be accomplished in this situation. Unfortunately, in this setting, this option was ignored.

The CEO concluded the meeting with a request for additional details from each of the participants. Unfortunately, only one person, the chief financial officer, provided data. In his response, he said that data from the American Bankers Association indicated that when consumer loan interest rates fall, the volume of consumer loans goes up. He applied this information to the bank's situation to account for a large portion of the increase in loan volume. The other owners of the processes did not respond.

We can draw some important conclusions from this case:

- Isolation of program effects must be addressed in order for any of the functions or processes designed to improve consumer loan volume to gain credibility as a source of performance improvement.

- Sometimes, the most important people in the analysis of program effects are the performers who are actually involved in the process being measured. In this case, the loan officers were most directly involved in the process of increasing loan volume and thus were in the best position to analyze which factors were influencing business performance.

- Failure to address isolation of program effects leaves a concern or even a cloud over the contribution of a particular program; doing nothing is not an option.

- The issue of isolating program effects must be addressed early in the evaluation process so that many options can be considered.

A variety of techniques are available to isolate the effects of a program. Exhibit 1.1 lists the techniques explored in this book.

The techniques can be categorized into three basic approaches: control groups, trends and forecasts, and expert estimates. These approaches can be explained in greater technical detail. A chapter is devoted to each technique, describing the approach and providing examples of its application. The methods for isolation and guidance described here are sufficiently comprehensive and accurate for practical application. They have been proven over many years, clients, and contexts.

Preliminary Issues in Isolating Program Effects

A few preliminary issues should be considered before presenting specific techniques for isolating the effects of programs. These issues

Exhibit 1.1. Techniques for Isolating the Effects of Programs and Projects

- Control group arrangement
- Trend line analysis of performance data
- Forecasting performance data
- Participant's estimate of impact
- Supervisor's estimate of impact
- Management's estimate of impact
- Estimates based on expert opinion or previous studies
- Calculation or estimation of the impact of factors other than the program
- Customer estimate of impact

---

further underscore the need to isolate program effects and to address the reasons for some objections to the process. This section also explores some initial steps that must be taken to make isolation of program effects an easy-to-accomplish piece of the evaluation process.

The Need to Isolate Program Effects

To many practitioners, isolating the effects of programs and projects seems logical, practical, and necessary; among others, however, it is still much debated. Some professionals argue that isolating the effects of a process (for example, training) goes against everything taught in systems thinking and team performance improvement (Brinkerhoff and Dressler, 2002). Others argue that the only way to link a program to actual business results is to isolate its effect on those business measures (Russ-Eft and Preskill, 2001).

Much of the debate centers on misunderstandings about the isolation of program effects and on the challenge of the isolation process. The first point of debate is the issue of complementary processes. It is true that many changes in processes are implemented as part of a total performance improvement initiative; as a result,

Figure 1.1. Finding a Program's Contribution

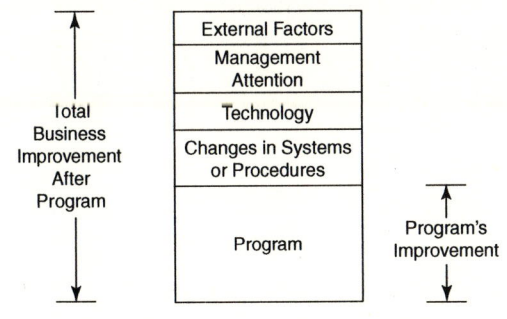

Several factors contribute to an improvement after a program is conducted

Total Business Improvement After Program	External Factors	
	Management Attention	
	Technology	
	Changes in Systems or Procedures	
	Program	Program's Improvement

many influences work in harmony to improve business results. Often, the issue is not whether a particular process is part of the mix but how much it is needed, what specific content is appropriate, and what is the most effective method of implementation to drive its share of improvement.

The principle of isolating the effects of a program is not meant to suggest that any program should stand alone as the single variable influencing or driving significant business performance. The isolation issue comes into play, however, when different processes are influencing business results, as shown in Figure 1.1, and the different owners of the processes need information about their relative contributions. In many situations, they need to address the question "How much of the improvement was caused by the process that I am responsible for?" If they do not have a specific method for answering this question, they lose tremendous credibility, especially with the senior management team.

The second point of debate is the difficulty of isolating program effects. The classic approach—and the most credible one—is to use control group arrangements, in which one group participates in the program and another does not. However, in the majority of studies, control groups are not feasible or appropriate, so other methods must be used. Researchers sometimes use time series analysis, or forecasting. Beyond that, many researchers either give up, suggesting that isolation of program effects cannot be addressed credibly, or choose to ignore the issue, hoping that it will not be noticed by the sponsor. Neither of these responses is acceptable to a senior management team that needs to understand the link between a specific program and business success. The important point is that this issue should *always* be addressed, even if an expert estimation with an adjustment for error must be used. In this way, isolating the effects of a program becomes an essential, required step in the analysis. This requirement is the basis of Guiding Principle 5 of the ROI Methodology: Use at least one method to isolate the effects of a project.

Chain of Impact: Initial Evidence of Program Effects

Before presenting the techniques for isolating program effects, it is helpful to examine the chain of impact implied in the different levels of evaluation. As illustrated in Figure 1.2, the chain of impact must be unbroken for the program to drive business results.

Figure 1.2. The Chain of Impact

Level 1   Participants React to the Program

↓

Level 2   Participants Obtain Skills and Knowledge

↓

Level 3   Participants Apply Skills and Knowledge

↓

Level 4   Business Measures Change   [Isolate the effects of the program]

↓

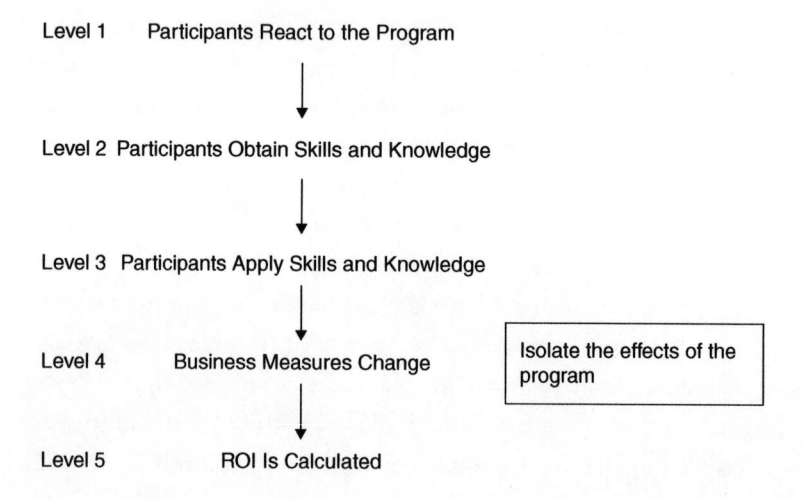

Level 5   ROI Is Calculated

Measurable business impact achieved from a program should be derived from on-the-job application of skills and knowledge over a specified period of time after program completion. On-the-job application occurs at Level 3 of program evaluation (see Figure P.1 in "Principles of the ROI Methodology" in the front of this book; in addition, *ROI Fundamentals*, book one of this series, provides more detail on evaluation levels). Continuing with this logic, successful application of program material on the job should stem from participants learning new skills or acquiring new knowledge through the program, which is measured at Level 2. Therefore, for business results to improve (Level 4), the chain of impact implies that measurable on-the-job applications must be realized (Level 3) after new knowledge and skills are learned (Level 2). Without preliminary evidence based on the chain of impact, it would be difficult to isolate the effects of a program. If there is no learning or on-the-job application of the program material, it would be virtually impossible to conclude that the program caused any performance improvements.

This requirement for different levels of evaluation based on the chain of impact is supported in the literature (Alliger and Janak, 1989). From a practical standpoint, it means that data collection at four levels is required for an ROI evaluation. If data are collected on business results, data should also be collected at the other levels of evaluation to ensure that the program helped to produce the business results. This issue is so critical that it became the first Guiding Principle for the ROI Methodology: When a higher-level evaluation is conducted, collect data at lower levels.

This is consistent with the practices of leading organizations participating in benchmarking projects. Organizations that collect Level 4 data on business results usually report that they also collect data at the lower three levels. It is important to note, however, that the chain of impact does not prove a direct connection between a program and business results; the chain of impact is necessary but not sufficient. Taking the step to isolating the program's effects is necessary to make this connection and to pinpoint the amount of improvement caused by the program.

If the chain of impact is strong, we expect data between evaluation levels to be correlated. Several research efforts have investigated correlations between the different levels (Bledsoe, 1999; Aaron, 2005). If a significant correlation does not exist, then barriers have caused the process to break down—a logical conclusion in light of the chain of impact. However, most research in this area adds very little to the understanding of evaluation.

In different studies, correlations between two levels show varying levels of connection (or disconnection) between the two. The variation in levels of correlation doesn't mean that the concept of the levels of evaluation is flawed. Instead, as we just stated, it implies that in some cases, one or more barriers prevented a process or program from adding value. For example, most of the breakdowns occur between Level 2 and Level 3. Research has shown that as much as 90 percent of what is learned in a program is not applied and implemented (Kaufman, 2002). Even so, it is important to collect data at both levels to understand how the process of learning is working and how the system in which performers work supports the transfer of learning. A correlation analysis between levels of evaluation adds very little understanding to what must occur in practice for programs to add business value. And correlation analysis does not show a cause-and-effect relationship. Even if there is a strong correlation, the critical step of isolating the effects of a program must still be undertaken to establish a causal relationship between the program and the business improvement.

Identification of Factors Other Than the Program: A First Step

As a first step in isolating a program's impact on performance, all the key factors that may have contributed to the performance improvement should be identified. This step reveals factors other than the program that may have influenced the results, underscoring that the program is not the sole source of improvement. As a result, credit for improvement is shared among several possible variables and factors, an approach that is likely to gain the respect of management.

Several sources can potentially be used to identify major influencing variables. Sponsors, if they requested the program, may be able to identify factors that should influence the output measure. Sponsors will usually be aware of other initiatives or programs that may affect the output. Even if the program focuses on operational processes, the program sponsor or client may have insight into the other influences that may have driven performance improvement.

Direct clients as well as sponsors may also be able to provide input. The direct clients of a program are the persons who funded the initiative or provided key support for the program. These individuals are keenly interested in the issue that gave rise to the program and may be able to provide insight into other factors that may be influencing the relevant business measures. They are concerned about those measures and often understand their dynamics.

Program participants are often aware of other influences that may have caused performance improvement. After all, it is the impact of their collective efforts that is being monitored and measured. In many situations, they have witnessed previous movements in the performance measures and can pinpoint the reasons for changes. They are normally the experts on this issue.

Analysts and program developers are another potential source of information about variables that might have had an impact on results. Their needs analysis for the program would routinely have uncovered these influencing variables. In addition, program designers typically analyze such variables in addressing the issue of transfer of the skills and knowledge learned during the program.

In some situations, the participants' immediate manager may be able to identify variables that have influenced performance improvement. This is particularly useful when program participants are entry-level or low-skill employees who may not be fully aware of the variables that can influence performance.

Subject matter experts who represent different functions and processes are available. These experts have often provided input and advice needed for the program or project through all the stages of the process. They understand the dynamics of the workplace and the setting in which the program is implemented. They may be able to identify factors that are influencing the business results.

Finally, members of middle and top management may be able to identify factors other than a program that may be influencing performance, based on their experience and knowledge of the situation. Perhaps they have monitored, examined, and analyzed the other influences. Their authority within the organization often increases the credibility and acceptance of the data they provide.

Taking time to focus attention on all the variables that may have influenced performance brings additional accuracy and credibility to the program evaluation process. This step moves the process beyond the scenario in which results are presented with no mention of other influences, an omission that often destroys the credibility of an impact report. This initial step also provides a foundation for some of the techniques described in this book by identifying the variables that must be isolated in order to show the effects of a particular program.

A word of caution is appropriate here. Halting the process at this step would leave many unknowns about the actual impact of a program and might leave the client or senior management with a negative impression of the program because the analysis might have identified variables that management did not previously consider. Therefore, it is recommended that program staff members go beyond this initial step and use one or more of the techniques for isolating the impact of a program that are the focus of this book.

Final Thoughts

This brief introductory chapter has outlined the reasons why it is necessary to tackle this critical issue, isolating the effects of programs. Without it, credibility is lost, and with it, credibility is gained. That is the key issue. The next chapter focuses on the most credible method for isolating the effects of programs: using control groups.

References

Aaron, B. C. "Use the Chain of Impact to Leverage Data and Demonstrate ROI." Paper presented at the International Conference and Exposition of ASTD, Orlando, Fla., May 2005.

Alliger, G. M., and Janak, E. A. "Kirkpatrick's Levels of Training Criteria: Thirty Years Later." *Personnel Psychology*, 1989, *42*, 331–342.

Bledsoe, M. "Correlations in Kirkpatrick's Evaluation Model." Dissertation. Ann Arbor, Mich.: UMI Microform, 1999.

Brinkerhoff, R. O., and Dressler, D. "Using Evaluation to Build Organizational Performance and Learning Capability: A Strategy and a Method." *Performance Improvement*, July 2002, *41*(6), 14–21.

Kaufman, R. "Resolving the (Often-Deserved) Attacks on Training." *Performance Improvement*, July 2002, *41*(6), pp. 5–6.

Russ-Eft, D., and Preskill, H. *Evaluation in Organizations: A Systematic Approach to Enhancing Learning, Performance, and Change.* Cambridge, Mass.: Perseus, 2001.

2

Use of Control Groups

The most accurate approach to isolating the impact of a program is the use of control groups in an experimental design process (Wang, Dou, and Lee, 2002). This approach involves the use of an experimental group that participates in a specific program and a control group that does not. The composition of both groups should be as similar as possible; therefore, the selection of participants for each group should be random, if that is feasible. When random selection is used and both groups are subjected to the same environmental influences, the difference in performance of the two groups can be attributed to the program.

Control Group Design

A few variations of the control group design are briefly presented in the following sections. However, using a control group is the most credible process only if it is used appropriately. Before looking at the experimental designs, it is appropriate to discuss what factors might threaten the credibility of a control group arrangement.

Threats to Validity

When discussing the merits of various control group arrangements, it is important to address the issue of validity, which is discussed in *Data Collection*, book two of this series. Validity is the extent to which an instrument or experiment measures what it is designed to measure. Several problems may alter the measured results of a program and thus reduce the validity of an evaluation design.

The first threat involves time. Time has a way of changing things. With the passage of time, performance can improve and attitudes can change—even without the implementation of a program or project. When observing output measures of a program, always ask, "Would the same results have occurred without the program?" The control group design addresses threats to validity from events outside of a program that develop over time.

The second threat has to do with the effects of testing (also referred to as test sensitization). The experience of a test or other measurement technique might have an effect on performance or attitudes, even if no program is undertaken. Participants reflect on the pretest or other measurement, and they alter their behavior or actions toward the issue, thereby influencing the results. Studies show that simply administering pretests has substantial positive effect on performance (Wilson and Putnam, 1982).

A third threat to validity is faulty selection of the groups. A biased group might have an effect on the outcome. Naturally, some individuals will perform better than others. If a large number of overachievers or underachievers are selected for one group, the results will be distorted and atypical. This problem can be addressed by using random selection whenever feasible.

Finally, a fourth threat is mortality. Participants may drop out of the program for various reasons. If pretests and posttests are used and the number of participants in the group changes from one measurement to the other, the change makes it difficult to compare the results of the two. This difficulty is compounded by the fact that low-level performers are usually the ones who drop out of a program. The evaluation is compromised when a significant number of participants are not in the same job when the follow-up is conducted.

These challenges are the most common threats to validity, and it is essential that they be addressed when selecting the control group.

Basic Control Group Design

A basic control group design consists of an experimental group and a control group (see Figure 2.1). The experimental group participates in the program, while the control group does not. Data are gathered on both groups before and after the program. The results of the experimental group, when compared with those of the control group, reveal the impact of the program.

This design is acceptable only when the two groups are similar with respect to relevant selection criteria. The participants in each group should have approximately the same experience, ability, and working conditions, and they should be at approximately the same job level and possibly even the same location. For example, it is improper to compare frontline supervisors with middle-level managers when determining the effects of a program on results. Such a difference between groups would make it almost impossible to perform a credible analysis of post-program performance.

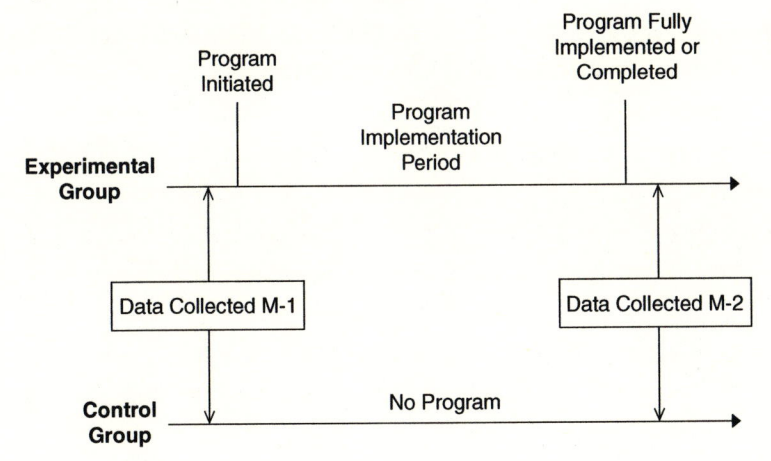

Figure 2.1. Control Group Design

The ideal way to select control and experimental groups is on a random basis. If the participants for the two groups come from the same population and can be randomly assigned, then the evaluation design is a true control group arrangement. Random selection not only tends to equalize the groups prior to the program but also promotes a generalization of the evaluation results to other similar groups and situations. However, from a practical standpoint, selecting participants on a random basis may be difficult: for example, when time is of the essence or when an executive targets a specific group for involvement in a program. If shortcomings of the design are evident, they need to be recognized when the results are reported.

The true experimental design is one of the most powerful evaluation designs available because it combines random selection and the use of a control group. The threats to validity are controlled as tightly as possible with this design. The fact that both groups are subjected to a pretest may have an undetermined effect on performance, however. The design discussed in the next section eliminates the most common threats to validity including the influence of the pretest.

Ideal Experimental Design

Figure 2.2 shows an evaluation design that is more ideal than the classic control group design. This comprehensive design involves the use of three groups, random selection of participants, and pretesting and posttesting of two groups and posttesting only of one group. As Figure 2.2 illustrates, Group A takes a pretest, participates in the program, and takes a posttest. Group B takes a pretest and does not participate in the program but does take a posttest. Group C has no pretest, participates in the program, and does take a posttest.

The control group, Group B, isolates the time and mortality threats to validity. If measurement 1 (M-1) and measurement 2 (M-2) are equal for Group B, then it follows that neither of these

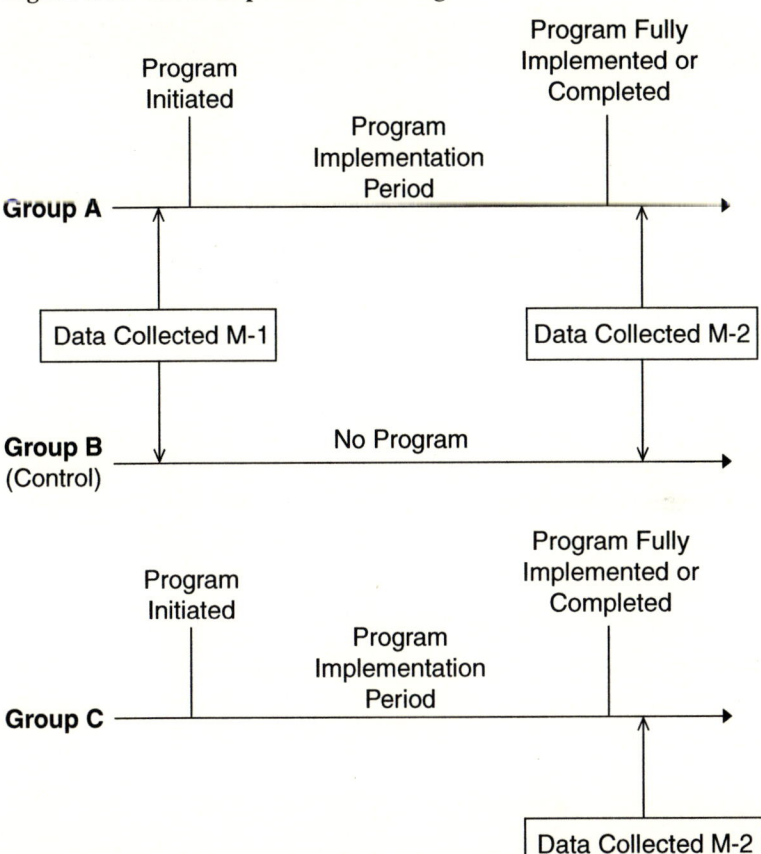

Figure 2.2. Ideal Experimental Design

```
                    Program                    Program Fully
                    Initiated                  Implemented or
                    |                          Completed
                    |        Program           |
                    |        Implementation    |
                    |        Period            |
Group A  ───────────┼──────────────────────────┼──────────▶
                    ↑                          ↑
              ┌─────────────────┐        ┌─────────────────┐
              │ Data Collected M-1 │     │ Data Collected M-2 │
              └─────────────────┘        └─────────────────┘
                    ↓         No Program       ↓
Group B  ───────────┼──────────────────────────┼──────────▶
(Control)

                    Program                    Program Fully
                    Initiated                  Implemented or
                    |                          Completed
                    |        Program           |
                    |        Implementation    |
                    |        Period            |
Group C  ───────────┼──────────────────────────┼──────────▶
                                               ↑
                                        ┌─────────────────┐
                                        │ Data Collected M-2 │
                                        └─────────────────┘
```

factors influenced the result. Randomization isolates the selection threat to validity. If the results for Group B are unequal, with M-2 showing a higher level of performance, then the influence of the pretest comes into play; hence the need for Group C.

Group C is used to rule out the interaction of the pretest with the effects of the program, a weakness in the classic control group design presented previously. If the posttest measurements (M-2) for Group A and Group C do not differ significantly, then the pretest had no effect on performance.

This design approaches the ultimate in experimental design. However, from a practical standpoint, obtaining three randomly selected groups may be difficult. The time, expense, inconvenience, and administrative procedures required for this arrangement may prohibit its use. Alternate designs such as the one presented in the next section can yield similar reliable results.

Posttest-Only Control Group Design

Figure 2.3 shows a more practical and less expensive alternative to the ideal experimental design: the posttest-only control group design. In this design, the randomly selected experimental and control groups are given only a posttest; neither group takes a pretest. This eliminates the effects of a pretest on the participants. Elimination of the pretest reduces the time requirement and expense of the evaluation design. In addition, this design isolates other threats to validity (Aiken, 1991).

Because of the practical nature of the posttest-only control group design, it is recommended for most studies involving measuring ROI. It is often impractical to have the three different groups that

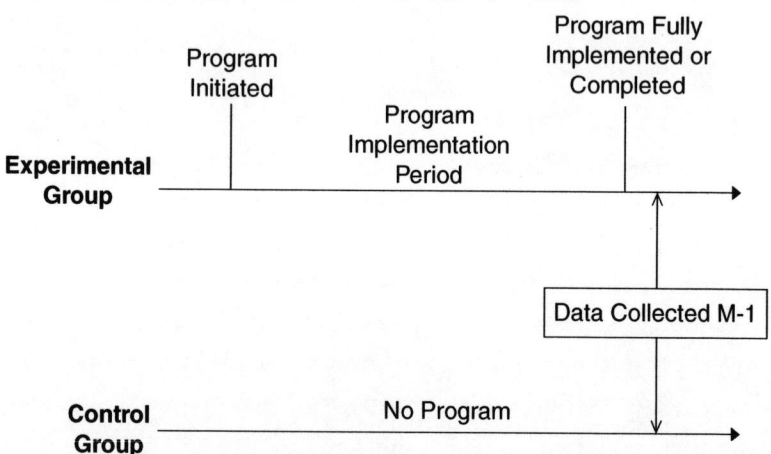

Figure 2.3. Posttest-Only Control Group Design

are required for the ideal experimental design. The posttest-only design is much easier to implement.

Which Design to Choose

Deciding which design you will use seems daunting at first, but answering two basic questions can help you make the decision:

1. Are you evaluating to understand whether there is a change in performance or to understand whether there is a difference in performance between groups?
2. Are data coming from people or systems?

Answering the first question tells you whether or not you need a pretest. If your program or project is intended to change a performance measure for which you have (or can get) baseline data, then understanding the difference between pre-program and post-program performance is necessary. In this case, the classic control group design is what you need. Alternatively, you may be interested only in understanding the difference in performance between two groups when one group participates in a program and another group does not. Here, pretesting is unnecessary, since the comparison is between the groups, and not within each group and then again between groups. If this is the case, then the post-program-only design can be used.

Answering the second question tells you whether there is a possibility that the pretest will influence results. If you intend to gather (with a pretest) pre-program data from people, then there is a possibility that the pretest will influence results. If you are concerned about this influence, then the ideal experimental design, using Groups A, B, and C as described earlier, should be considered. However, if you are gathering pre-program data from a system, the classic design is the approach to take, as a system is not influenced by pretests.

Issues When Considering Control Groups

Several important issues must be considered when control groups are used: viability, practicality, ethical implications, potential problems, and feasibility.

Viability

It is important for evaluators to give fair consideration to the idea of using control groups. Many take the easy way of simply not considering a control group. Thus, in a variety of settings, opportunities to benefit from the use of this isolation technique are ignored or missed because the control group arrangement was not considered. Control groups are a viable option in many organizations; however, the perception of engaging in a scientific approach makes many feel the process is impractical for them.

Practicality

Control group arrangements are used in many settings in both the private and public sectors. For example, in an impact study to measure the return on investment for a program to improve customer service, Verizon Communications used an experimental group and a control group (Keuler, 2001). The program was designed to improve feedback from Verizon's telephone customers and was expected to reduce the overall number of calls that escalated to the supervisory level. The difference between the two groups revealed the extent to which the skills were transferred to the job (Level 3) and the impact the skills were having in the workplace (Level 4). This case shows the practicality of using control groups for both Level 3 and Level 4 evaluation.

In another example, a turnover reduction program for communication specialists in a government agency used a control group and an experimental group (Phillips and Phillips, 2002). The experimental group consisted of individuals in a special program—aimed at employee retention—that allowed participants to achieve a master's degree in information science on agency time and at agency expense. The control group was carefully selected to match the experimental group in terms of job title, tenure with the agency, and college degree obtained. The differences in results between the control group and the experimental group were dramatic, showing the impact of the retention program.

Ethical Considerations

The use of control groups may convey an image that the evaluator is creating a laboratory setting, which appears to some administrators and executives to put the organization in an ethical dilemma. Concerns about purposefully withholding an opportunity from a group send up a red flag in some organizations. However, this concern can be addressed when a program is being piloted. In other words, when a decision to roll out a program to a larger group has not been made, a pilot is often offered. This offers an opportunity to select a control group from those not participating in the pilot. An example will illustrate this approach.

An international specialty manufacturing company in Malaysia developed a program for its customer service representatives, who sell directly to the public. The program was designed to improve selling skills and produce higher levels of sales. Previously, acquisition of sales skills was informal, on the job, through trial and error. The learning and development manager was convinced that formal training would significantly increase sales. Management was skeptical and wanted proof—a familiar scenario.

The program was pilot-tested by teaching sales skills to sixteen customer service representatives randomly selected from the thirty-two most recently hired. The remaining sixteen served as a control group and did not receive training. Prior to training, performance was measured, using average daily sales (sales divided by the number of days) for thirty days (or length of service, if shorter than thirty days for a specific individual), for each of the two groups. After training, the average daily sales were recorded for another thirty days. A significant difference in the sales of the two groups occurred, and because the groups were almost identical and had been subjected to the same environmental influences, it was concluded that the sales difference was a result of the training program and not other factors. In this setting, the pilot group was the experimental group. The comparison group (control group) was easily selected. The technique was used without the publicity and potential criticism that can occur when using the control group arrangement.

Potential Problems with Control Groups: A Case Example

The control group process has some inherent problems that may make it difficult to apply in practice. The problems that can occur when using control groups are illustrated in the following example.

Financial Services, Inc. (FSI), is a growing financial services company with 5,000 employees at eight hundred branch locations. Branch offices are grouped into twelve geographic regions, each headed by a regional manager who supervises eight district sales managers. FSI had experienced annual turnover rates of 48 to 63 percent in the position of branch manager trainee. Although these rates were typical of the industry, they were far too high for management, which took steps to reduce them. A needs assessment revealed that improper selection was a key cause of the turnover. As a result, a comprehensive selection system for branch manager trainees was developed, including recruiting strategies, interviewing guidelines, evaluation guidelines, and individual feedback. After the elements were developed, district sales managers implemented the selection system procedures and were taught how to train their branch managers in the program's concepts.

To measure the impact of the program, a control group arrangement was used. The program was implemented on an experimental basis in one-third of the company's branches. The other two-thirds of the branches served as a control group. During the six months after the program was implemented, significant differences were reported between the program group and the control group. After the six months, when the measurement was to take place, elements of the system had begun to be used in parts of the control group, diluting the purity of the control group for comparison purposes. The program had been so successful in the program group that managers in the rest of the company asked for it to be implemented in their regions and districts.

This scenario reveals several problems that can quickly be identified:

- The selection criteria for the groups are not clear. Having one-third of the branches in the experimental group and two-thirds in the control group suggests that the selection process was far from random and criteria were ill-defined. Specific selection criteria should result in groups that are as similar as possible.

- The groups were much too large, losing their experimental characteristics. Usually, experimental groups involve a small number of people because the project is an experiment. Also, if possible, each group should be of equal size, to facilitate comparison between the two groups.

- The program was much too long. The duration of a program must strike a delicate balance; the program should be long enough for a trend or pattern to emerge in the two groups, yet not so long that contamination occurs.

- Contamination is perhaps the most serious problem. The success identified in the experimental group quickly influenced the control group. This contamination was practically encouraged by the experimental design. District sales managers were prepared for the process but were asked to implement it in only a few locations, withholding the solution from the branches that were part of the control group. This arrangement invited contamination; the managers in the control group quickly began to use the new process when they realized it was working.

- Perhaps a control group was the wrong isolation technique for this situation. If this was indeed the solution that was needed for an expensive problem, was it prudent to wait almost a year to implement it in two-thirds of the organization? The answer is probably no.

Let's look more closely at some of the problems that can occur when using control groups.

The first major problem is that the control group process is inappropriate for many situations. For some types of programs, it is not a good idea to withhold the program from one group while providing it to another. This is particularly important in programs involving critical skills, processes, or technologies that are needed immediately on the job. For example, in entry-level training, employees need basic skills to perform their jobs. It would be inappropriate to withhold training from a group of new employees so that this group can be compared with a group that receives the training. Although this would reveal the impact of initial training, it would be devastating to the individuals who are struggling to learn necessary skills and trying to cope with a new job situation. In the previous example of the Malaysian company, a control group was feasible because the program was not essential to the job and the organization was not completely convinced that it would add value in terms of increasing sales.

This barrier keeps many control groups from being implemented. Often, management is not willing to withhold a process from one area to see how it works in another. However, in practice, a control group arrangement often develops naturally when a program is implemented throughout an organization. If it will take several months for everyone in the organization to participate in a program, there may be enough time for a comparison between the initial group involved and the last group involved. In these cases, it is critical to ensure that the groups are matched as closely as possible so that the first two groups are very similar to the last two groups. The challenge is to address this issue early enough to influence the implementation schedule so that similar groups can be used in the comparison.

The second problem that occurs in control group arrangements involves selection of the groups. From a practical perspective, having identical control and experimental groups is virtually impossible. Dozens of factors can affect employee performance; some of them are individually matched, and others are contextual. When the output can be influenced by as many as forty or fifty factors, considering all the factors is almost impossible, especially if a large number of groups is involved. Using the Pareto principle (20 percent of the variables will influence 80 percent of the outcome) makes the challenge of selecting groups manageable. Take a realistic approach, and address a reasonable number of factors. In practical terms, it is best to select group members on the basis of the three to five variables that would most influence their performance (like number of years on the job, job classification, and score on a written pretest). Ideally, the values of the chosen variables should be exactly the same in each group. Practically, the values of the chosen variables should be as similar as possible within each group. In summary, practical use of control groups must take into consideration the constraints of a work setting and focus on the most critical influences on the output measure (besides the program).

A third potential problem with control group arrangements is contamination, which occurs when participants in the program influence individuals in the control group. Sometimes, members of the control group will observe changes in the behavior of those in the experimental group and model those behaviors, with no consideration of why the behavior has changed. At other times, participants in the control group come to the realization that a program is being implemented to which they have not been invited, thus influencing their behavior. In either case, the experiment becomes contaminated because the influence of the program filters to the control group. Contamination can be minimized by ensuring that control groups and experimental groups are at different locations, have different shifts, or are on different floors in the same building. When this is not possible, it is sometimes helpful to explain to both groups that one group will participate in the program now and another will participate at a later date. Also, it may be helpful to appeal to the sense of responsibility of those involved in the program and ask them not to share the information with others.

Closely related to the problem of contamination is the issue of duration of the control group arrangement. The longer a control group and experimental group comparison operates, the greater the likelihood that influences other than the program will affect the results. More factors will enter into the situation, contaminating the results. Nevertheless, enough time must pass to allow a clear pattern of the relationship between the two groups to emerge. As mentioned earlier, the timing of control group comparisons must strike a delicate balance, waiting long enough for their performance differences to show but not so long that the results become seriously contaminated.

A fifth problem occurs when the different groups function under different environmental influences. If the groups are in different locations, their environmental influences may be different. Sometimes, the way in which the groups are selected can help prevent this problem. Another tactic is to use more groups than necessary and then discard the results from those that turn out to have some environmental discrepancies.

A sixth problem with using control groups is that it may appear too research oriented for many business organizations. For example, management may not want to take the time to experiment before proceeding with a program or may not want to withhold an experimental program from a group just to measure program impact. Because of this concern, some evaluators do not entertain the idea of using control groups. When the process is used, however, some organizations conduct it with pilot participants as the experimental group and nonparticipants as the control group. Under this arrangement, members of the control group are not informed of their control group status.

Because the use of a control group arrangement is an effective technique for isolating the impact of programs, it should be considered as a strategy when a major ROI evaluation is planned. In such situations, it is important for the program impact to be isolated with a high level of accuracy; the primary advantage of the control group process is accuracy. About one-third of the more than two hundred published studies on the ROI Methodology use the control group process.

Feasibility

Several issues must be thought through before use of a control group can be considered feasible. Every attempt should be made to use this technique because it is the most credible process. Here are a few questions to help determine whether a control group arrangement is a feasible isolation technique for a program:

- Is the population large enough to divide into groups?
- Is the population homogeneous—that is, does it represent similar jobs and similar environments?
- What is the particular measure that matters to the organization?
- What variables may be affecting the measure? These variables would be used to select the comparison groups for the control group arrangement.

- Which of the variables most strongly influences the output measure (or measures)?

- Can the program be withheld from a particular group? Sometimes, this situation occurs naturally because it takes a long time to roll out a program. Employees who participate in the program last may be three to six months behind those who participate in the program first, creating an opportunity to compare the last group with the first group.

- Is a pilot offering planned, and could the pilot group be selected to facilitate comparison with other nonparticipating groups?

When the control group arrangement is selected as a viable and feasible process, several rules are helpful.

- Keep the groups separated in different locations, different buildings, different shifts, or different floors.

- Minimize communication between the groups.

- Do not let members of the control group or the experimental group know that they are part of an experiment and are being compared with others.

- Monitor data on a short-term basis, to check for improvements in both groups.

- Try to prevent the Hawthorne effect (improvement that results from the fact of being observed) in the experimental group. Other than that required by the program design, the amount of attention paid to the group should be normal.

- Minimize the effect of the self-fulfilling prophecy by not creating expectations beyond the norm that may influence the results. For example, do not tell people that they are part of a special group and that top performance is expected.

The control group arrangement is a powerful method and can be made practical. The next few sections consist of case studies that detail how control groups have been decided on and structured in real situations.

Control Group Example 1: Retail Merchandise Company

Setting

Retail Merchandise Company (RMC) is a national chain of 420 stores, located in most major U.S. markets. RMC sells small household items, gifts of all types, electronics, jewelry, and personal accessories. It does not sell clothes or major appliances. RMC executives had been concerned about slow sales growth and were experimenting with several programs designed to boost sales. One concern focused on interaction with customers. Sales associates were not actively involved in the sales process; they usually waited for a customer to make a purchasing decision and then processed the sale. Several store managers had analyzed the situation to determine whether more communication with customers would boost sales. The analysis revealed that the use of very simple techniques to probe for a customer's needs and then guide the customer to a purchase should boost sales in each store.

The senior executives asked the learning and development staff to experiment with a simple program to teach customer interaction skills to a small group of sales associates. A program produced by an external supplier was chosen in order to avoid the cost of development, in case the program proved ineffective. The specific charge from the management team was to implement the program in three stores, monitor the results, and make recommendations.

If the program increased sales and provided a significant payoff for RMC, it would be implemented in other stores.

Audience

The participants (sales associates) were typical of retail store employees. Few (if any) were college graduates, and most had only a few months of retail store experience. They were not considered professional employees but rather were seen as clerical and administrative workers. Historically, they had not been involved in discussing sales with customers except in the course of processing transactions. This program was designed to shift that paradigm so that sales associates would be more actively involved in the sales experience.

Solution

The needs analysis determined that the sales staff did not have the skills necessary to be engaged with customers. Therefore, the learning and development staff decided to implement a program called Interactive Selling Skills, which used frequent skill practice to help participants learn the required knowledge and skills and then reinforce the knowledge gained during the program. The program consisted of two days of training, during which participants had an opportunity for skill practice with a fellow classmate. The training was followed by three weeks of on-the-job application. The third and final day of the program included a discussion of problems, issues, barriers, and concerns in regard to the use of the new skills. Additional practice and fine tuning of the skills were also part of this final session. The program, an existing product from an external supplier, was applied in the electronics area of three stores. The program was taught by members of the supplier's staff for a predetermined facilitation fee.

Measures That Matter

The specific measure undergoing analysis was the average weekly sales per associate. These data, by store and by individual, were readily available from each store's sales receipts records. A history of sales data was also available.

Selection Criteria

Although many different factors could influence sales, after discussion with several store executives, four criteria were selected. Stores were selected based on similarities in

- *Previous store performance.* Weekly sales per associate for a six-month period.
- *Sales volume.* Annual sales volume for the store.
- *Traffic flow.* For security purposes, customers were routinely monitored as they came in and out of the store. This monitoring recorded the traffic flow.
- *Market.* The average household disposable income in each area was available in the company's marketing database and was one of the key measures that influenced the selection of each store.

These four factors were used to select two matching groups. (Three stores received the training; three stores did not.) These factors were selected because they influenced sales more than any other factors.

Size of Groups

There were sixteen associates in each of the six stores, providing two equal-sized groups: forty-eight in the experimental group and forty-eight in the control group. This would be enough participants to see whether differences between the groups occurred, yet would not be too expensive.

Duration of Experiment

The experiment ran for three months. The evaluation team thought that would be long enough to allow the team to see the impact of such simple skills on sales. During the three months, participants would have ample opportunity to use the new skills in a variety of situations and with a significant number of customers.

For the rest of the story of RMC, see *Proving the Value of HR: ROI Case Studies*, by Patricia Pulliam Phillips and Jack J. Phillips, published by the ROI Institute.

Control Group Example 2: Federal Information Agency

Setting

The Federal Information Agency (FIA) collects and distributes many types of important and sensitive information to a variety of stakeholders. FIA was experiencing an unacceptable rate of employee turnover among a group of communication specialists—averaging 38 percent in the preceding year alone. The high turnover was placing a strain on the agency's ability to recruit trained replacements. An analysis of exit interviews revealed that employees were leaving for jobs with higher salaries. Because FIA was somewhat limited in its ability to provide competitive salaries, it was having difficulty competing with the private sector. Although salary increases and adjustments in pay would be necessary to avoid turnover, FIA was also exploring other options. The annual employee survey indicated that employees were very interested in attending an on-site master's degree program on agency time.

Audience

The individuals targeted were 1,500 communications specialists who had degrees in various fields: communications, computer science, and electrical engineering. Only a few had master's degrees in their specialty. Among these 1,500, roughly a third were considered high-potential employees who were destined for leadership assignments in the organization. The others were needed for continuing work in their assigned positions.

Solution

The solution was an in-house master's degree program offered by a regional state university. The program would be presented at no cost to the participating employees and conducted during normal work hours. Both morning and afternoon classes were available, each representing three hours of class time per week. Participants were allowed to take one or two courses per semester (and one course during the summer session) but were discouraged from taking more than two courses per term. On this schedule, the program could be completed in three years.

Measures That Matter

The measure that was monitored was the voluntary employee turnover rate, measured monthly. Of particular interest were employees in the first four years of employment. The records showed that once individuals had been employed for four years, they would usually continue for a longer period of time, and the turnover rate went down considerably.

Selection Criteria

The experimental group consisted of participants in the program, and a matching control group was selected, using three criteria, although many factors could affect an employee's decision to leave. The criteria deemed most important and used to match control group participants to participants in the graduate program were

- Possession of an undergraduate (B.S.) degree
- Job status (for example, job title and pay grade)
- Tenure with the agency

Size of Groups

One hundred individuals were selected for the program, and one hundred matching control group members were selected. The individuals not in the program were selected to match those in the program group in regard to the three criteria identified earlier.

Duration of Experiment

The experiment ran for four years—three years to take the first group through the program and one year post-program to continue to measure turnover.

For more details on the FIA case, see *Proving the Value of HR* (Phillips and Phillips, 2007).

Control Group Example 3: Midwest Electric, Inc.

Setting

Midwest Electric, Inc. (MEI) is a growing electric utility that serves several midwestern states. Since deregulation of the industry, MEI has been on a course of diversification and growth. Through a series of acquisitions, MEI has moved outside its traditional operating areas into several related businesses. MEI experienced significant workplace changes as it transformed from a bureaucratic, sluggish organization into a lean, competitive force in the marketplace. These changes placed tremendous pressure on employees to develop multiple skills and perform additional work. Employees, working in teams, had to constantly strive to reduce costs, maintain excellent quality, boost productivity, and generate new and efficient ways to supply customers and improve service.

Like many companies in industries in a deregulated environment, MEI has detected symptoms of employee stress. The company's safety and health department suggested that employee stress could be lowering productivity and reducing employee effectiveness. Stress was also considered a significant risk to employee health. Research has shown that high levels of stress are commonplace in many work groups and that organizations are taking steps to help employees and work groups reduce stress in a variety of ways. The vice president of human resources asked the training and education department, with the help of the safety and health department, to develop a program for work groups to help them alleviate stressful situations and deal more productively and effectively with job-induced stress.

Needs Assessment

Because it was a large organization with sophisticated human resources systems, MEI had an extensive database on employee-related measures. MEI took pride in being one of the leaders in human resources practices in its industry. Needs assessments were routinely conducted, and the human resources vice president was willing to allow sufficient time for an adequate needs assessment before proceeding with the program.

The overall purpose of the needs assessment was to identify the causes of a perceived problem. The needs assessment would

- Confirm that a problem with stress existed and assess the actual impact of this problem

- Uncover potential causes of the problem within work units, the company, and the work environment, and provide insight into potential remedies

Sources of data for the needs assessment included company records, external research, team members, team leaders, and managers. The assessment began with a review of external research that identified the factors usually related to high stress and the consequences of high stress in work groups. The consequences led to identification of relevant business measures that could be monitored at MEI.

The external research then led to a review of several key data items in company records, including attitude surveys, medical claims, Employee Assistance Plan records, safety and health records, and exit interview transcripts. Attitude survey results from the previous year were reviewed for low scores on the specific questions that could yield stress-related symptoms. Medical claims were analyzed by codes to identify the extent of those related to stress-induced illnesses. Employee Assistance Plan data were reviewed to determine the extent to which employees were using the provisions and services of the plan that were perceived to be stress-related. Safety records were reviewed to determine whether specific accidents were stress-related or whether causes of accidents could be traced to high levels of stress. In each of the preceding areas, current data were compared with data from the previous year to determine whether stress-related measures had changed. In addition, data were compared against expected norms found through the external research, where available. Finally, exit interviews from the previous six months were analyzed to determine the extent to which stress-related situations were factors in employees' decisions to voluntarily leave MEI.

A small sample of employees (ten team members) was interviewed in order to discuss their work-life situation and uncover symptoms of stress at work. A small group of managers (five) was interviewed with the same purpose. To provide more detail, a 10 percent sample of employees received a questionnaire that explored the same issues. MEI has 22,550 employees, including 18,220 nonsupervisory team members.

Audience

The audience for this program was members of intact work teams who voluntarily enrolled in the program to reduce stress. These teams had to be experiencing high levels of stress and be willing to participate in a program of planned stress reduction.

Solution

The program, Stress Management for Intact Work Teams, involved several activities occurring in ten sessions. Initially, the entire group completed the comprehensive self-assessment tool called StressMap® so that group members could see where they stood on a scale of twenty-one stress factors. Then a three- to four-hour StressMap debriefing session helped individuals interpret their scores. This was followed by a four-hour module suited to the needs of the group. All this was done in one day. Approximately three to four hours of telephone follow-up was included in the process.

Measures That Matter

This program focused on multiple measures:

- Unplanned and unexpected absenteeism
- Voluntary turnover
- Reported monthly health care costs for employees
- Reported monthly safety costs for employees

Selection Criteria

Six pairs of intact teams were selected. Each pair consisted of a program group and a matching control group. Several criteria were used in selecting the control group:

- The control group and its corresponding program group had to have the same types of performance measures in their operating group. At least 75 percent of the measures had to be common between the two groups.

This action provided an opportunity to compare the performance of the groups in the six months preceding the program.

- Each control group and corresponding experimental group had to have the same function code. (At MEI, all work groups were assigned a function code that indicated the type of work they performed, such as finance and accounting, engineering, or plant operations.)

- Group size was also a factor. The number of employees in the control group and the number in the corresponding program group had to be within 20 percent of each other.

- Average tenure was also used as a selection criterion. The average tenures of employees in the two groups in a pair had to be within two years of each other. At MEI, as at many other utilities, average tenure was high.

Size of Groups

The six pairs of groups represented a total of 138 team members in the experimental groups and 132 team members and six managers in the control groups.

Duration of Experiment

Data on all four measures were reviewed after six months; the results were then extrapolated for a complete year to determine an annual impact.

More details on the MEI case can be found in *Proving the Value of HR* (Phillips and Phillips, 2007).

Control Group Example 4: International Software Company

Setting

International Software Company (ISC) produces payroll software for companies with a small number of employees. Several enhancements can be purchased to perform other routines involving employee statistics and data. In some cases, the data are relevant to staffing and manpower-planning issues. The company has a customer database of over 1,500 users. For the most part, the customers use only the payroll functions of the software.

Each year, ISC hosts a conference during which users discuss issues they have encountered during implementation; new uses of the software; and how the software could be adjusted, modified, or enhanced to add value to their organizations. The conference is also an opportunity for ISC to get referrals and sell enhanced versions of its software.

Audience

The audience for this project was the individuals who attended the users' conference. To attend the conference, they must have purchased the software and used it primarily for the payroll option.

Solution

The solution was a two-day conference designed to improve customer satisfaction with the software, upgrade software users to other options, and obtain referrals to potential clients. There was no charge for attendance; however, the participants had to pay for their own travel arrangements and hotel accommodations.

Measures That Matter

Several measures were monitored in the control group arrangement to ensure the success of this program:

- Sales of upgrades to current customers (sales to existing clients)
- Referrals to new clients
- Increase in customer satisfaction as measured on the annual satisfaction survey

Selection Criteria

Four criteria were used to select individuals for the comparison groups. The conference attendees became the experimental group, and a comparison group of users that did not attend the conference became the control group. The two groups were matched using the following criteria:

- *Type of organization*. Type of business, according to standard industrial classification
- *Extent of use*. The extent to which a customer used the upgraded software options beyond the basic payroll processing
- *Sales*. Sales volume to date, which reflected the number of employees in the client business
- *Longevity*. Longevity of the customer, measured in years of using the current software

Size of Groups

There were 124 users at the conference, and a matching control group of 121 was selected, using the criteria just outlined.

Duration of Experiment

The experiment lasted for one year and tracked the three selected measures, sales, referrals, and customer satisfaction, in order to compare the data from conference participants in the year after the program with the data from users who did not attend the conference. For example, the average number of referrals that came through the conference was compared with the number of referrals from other channels. In addition, the number of upgrades made by users who attended the conference was compared with the number of upgrades made by those who did not attend. Finally, the customer satisfaction data were compared for the two groups.

Final Thoughts

This chapter has explored the most powerful technique for isolating the effects of a program: the classic comparison of performance in an experimental group and a control group. Three designs were introduced in this chapter: the classic design, the ideal design, and the post-program-only design. Each design is useful depending on the needs of the evaluation. Although there are issues concerning the use of control and experimental comparisons, including viability, feasibility, and ethical implications, as shown in the case studies, these comparisons can be made when the conditions warrant.

Due to practical considerations, however, the use of control and experimental groups is at times not feasible in organizational settings, and thus other approaches have to be explored in order to address the issue of isolating the effects of a program on performance. The trade-off often pits research principles against feasibility. In reality, most of the decisions made by management are not based on valid and reliable data. Instead, they are often made on management's intuitive assessment of the data presented to it. In recent years, progress has been made in developing innovative approaches to isolate the effects of a program on output performance, using data appropriate to management needs. The next chapter focuses on such an approach: trends and forecasts.

References

Aiken, L. *Psychological Testing and Assessment.* (7th ed.) Boston: Allyn & Bacon, 1991.

Keuler, D. "Measuring ROI for Telephonic Customer Service Skills." In P. P. Phillips (ed.), *In Action: Measuring Return on Investment*, Vol. 3. Alexandria, Va.: ASTD, 2001.

Phillips, P. P., and Phillips, J. J. "Evaluating the Impact of a Graduate Program in a Federal Agency." In P. P. Phillips (ed.), *In Action: Measuring ROI in the Public Sector.* Alexandria, Va.: ASTD, 2002.

Phillips, P. P., and Phillips, J. J. *Proving the Value of HR: ROI Case Studies.* Birmingham, Ala.: ROI Institute, 2007.

Wang, G., Dou, Z., and Lee, N. "A Systems Approach to Measuring Return on Investment (ROI) for HRD Interventions." *Human Resource Development Quarterly*, 2002, *13*(2), 203–224.

Wilson, V. L., and Putnam, R. R. "A Metanalysis of Pretest Sensitization Effects in Experimental Design." *American Education Research Journal*, 1982, *19*, 249–258.

3

Use of Trend Lines and Forecasts

When a control group analysis is not feasible for isolating the impact of a program, the next logical choice is some type of time series analysis. This chapter describes two closely related techniques. Trend line analysis is a simple process of using pre-program data to forecast the value of a measure at some future point. The actual value of the performance measure after program implementation is compared with the projected trend value, and the difference in performance is attributed to the program. Trend line analysis can be used only when no influences other than the program have affected the measure.

The forecast method is a more general technique that is used when influences outside of a program have entered the process. A mathematical relationship is developed to take the outside influences into account so that the value of a measure can be forecast rather than just projected on a trend line. The forecast measure is compared with the actual measure after program implementation in order to show the program's contribution. The analytical tools involved in these forecasting techniques are fairly simple; nonetheless, forecasting can sometimes become complicated, as will be discussed later in this chapter.

This chapter has good news and bad news. The good news is that the techniques of trend line analysis and forecasting are credible processes that can accurately isolate the effects of programs.

The bad news is that they work less than 25 percent of the time because workplaces are so dynamic and because the mathematical relationships between the variables are often not present in the real world. However, because these methods are relatively easy to use, it is worthwhile for evaluators to pursue them in order to isolate the effects of programs.

Trend Lines

Trend line analysis is a useful technique for approximating the impact of a program. A trend line is drawn, using previous performance as a base and extending the trend into the future. After the program is conducted, actual performance is compared with the projected value, the trend line. Any improvement in performance over what the trend line predicted can then be reasonably attributed to the program, if two conditions are met:

1. The trend prior to the program would have been expected to continue if the program had not been implemented to alter it. Ask this question: "If the program had not been implemented, would this trend have continued on the path that was established before the program was initiated?" The process owner (or owners) should be able to provide input to help answer this question. If the answer is no, trend line analysis will not be used. If the answer is yes, the second condition must still be met.

2. No other new variables or influences entered the process after the program was conducted. The key word is *new*; the trend was established as a result of the influences already in place. Ask this question: "Have influences other than the program entered the process?" If the answer is yes, another method must be used. If the answer is no, the trend line analysis will result in a reasonable and credible estimate of the impact of the program.

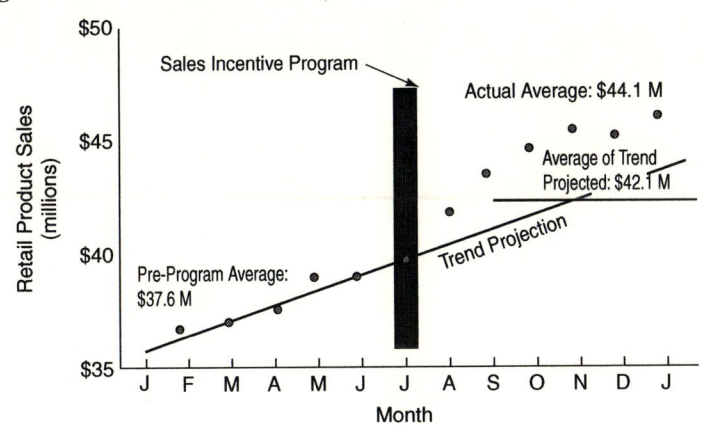

Figure 3.1. Trend Line Analysis of Sales

Figure 3.1 shows the trend line analysis of sales revenue in a retail store chain. The figure presents data from before and after a sales incentive program was introduced in July. The data showed an upward trend prior to implementation of the incentive program. Although the program had a dramatic effect on sales, the trend line shows that some improvement would have occurred anyway, according to the previously established trend. It is tempting to measure the improvement by comparing the average of the six months of sales prior to the program ($37.6 million) with the average of the six months of sales after the program ($44.1 million), yielding a $6.5 million difference. However, it would be more accurate to estimate the program's impact by comparing the six-month average after the program with the trend line average that was projected for the same period ($42.1 million), a difference of $2 million. Using this more conservative estimate increases the accuracy and credibility of the isolation process. In this case, the two conditions outlined earlier were met (the answer was yes on the first question and no on the second question). As a result, the $2 million improvement in sales can reasonably be attributed to the program.

Pre-program data must be available in order for trend line analysis to be used, and the data should have a reasonable degree of stability. If the variance of the data is high, the stability of the trend line becomes an issue. If this is an extremely critical issue and the stability cannot be assessed from a direct plot of the data, more detailed statistical analyses can be used to determine whether the data are stable enough to make the projection (Salkind, 2000).

A trend line projected directly from the historical data by means of graphics software may be acceptable. If additional accuracy is needed, the trend line can be projected by using a simple analytical routine available in many calculators and software packages—for example, Microsoft Excel.

The use of trend line analysis becomes more dramatic and convincing when a measure that was moving in an undesirable direction is completely turned around as a result of a program. For example, Figure 3.2 shows a trend line analysis of voluntary employee turnover in a large hotel chain. As the figure shows, turnover was increasing, moving in an undesirable direction. The retention program turned the situation around so that the actual results were in the other direction: turnover data showed a decreasing trend. The trend line process highlights dramatic improvement. In Figure 3.2, the trend line's projected value for turnover is significantly higher than the actual results.

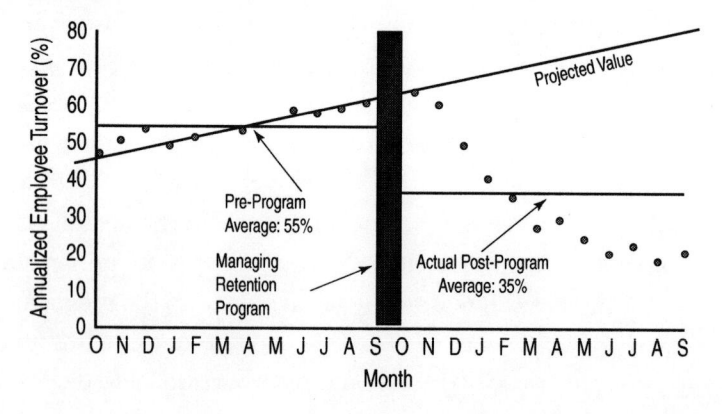

Figure 3.2. Trend Line Analysis of Voluntary Turnover of Hotel Staff

A primary disadvantage of the trend line approach is that it is not always accurate. Use of this approach assumes that the factors that influenced the performance measure prior to the program are still in place after the program, except for the implementation of the program (in other words, that the trends established prior to the program continue in the same direction). Also, trend line analysis assumes that no new influences affected the situation when the program was conducted or subsequently. This is not always the case.

The primary advantage of trend line analysis is that it is simple and inexpensive. If historical data are available, a trend line can quickly be drawn and differences estimated. While trend line analysis is not exact, it does provide a very quick assessment of a program's impact. About 15 percent of the more than two hundred published studies on the ROI Methodology use trend line analysis. However, when variables other than the program being analyzed enter the situation, additional analysis is needed.

Trend line analysis is often easy to perform, and it can yield a credible estimate of a program's impact. To use trend lines effectively, you must be able to answer yes to each of these four questions:

1. Are historical data available for the measure at hand?
2. Are at least six data points available?
3. Do the historical data appear to be stable when they are plotted over time?
4. Do you anticipate that no other new influences, factors, or processes will come into play or be implemented at the same time as the program?

In conclusion, here are some general guidelines for working with trend line analysis:

1. Use pre-program data to draw the trend line for your chosen measure.

2. Trend lines are easily developed in Microsoft Excel. Input the data in columns, then use the chart wizard to create the graph.
3. In addition to drawing the trend line, check with the process owners about whether a trend had begun before the onset of the program. Ask whether the trend probably would have continued during the post-analysis period if the program had not been implemented. If the answer to this question is no, trend line analysis cannot be used for the measure under consideration.
4. After the program has been implemented, ask whether any additional factors entered the process during the evaluation time period. If other factors likely influenced the measure being tracked, trend line analysis cannot be used for the measure under consideration.
5. If the question in item 3 is answered yes and the question in item 4 is answered no, trend line analysis is a credible way of isolating the effects of your program.

Forecasts

A more analytical approach to trend line analysis is the use of forecasting methods that can predict changes in performance measures based on variables other than the program under analysis. This approach represents a mathematical interpretation of the trend line analysis discussed earlier when additional new variables have entered the situation at the time of program implementation. The basic premise is that the actual performance of a measure (which is related to the program) will be compared with the forecast value of that measure (which is based on the other influences). A linear model, in the form $y = ax + b$, is appropriate when only one other variable influences the output performance and that relationship is characterized by a straight line. Instead of drawing the straight line, a linear equation is developed, which calculates a value for the anticipated performance improvement.

An example will help to explain the application of this process. A large retail store chain with a strong sales culture implemented a sales training program for sales associates. The three-day program was designed to enhance sales skills and prospecting techniques. It was assumed that application of the skills taught in the program would increase the sales volume for each associate. An important measure of the program's success was the sales per employee six months after the program compared with the same measure prior to the program. Prior to the program, the average daily sales per employee, using a one-month average, were $1,100 (rounded to the nearest $100). Six months after the program, the average daily sales per employee were $1,500 (average for the sixth month). Both of these sales numbers are average values for a specific group of participants. Two related questions must be answered: (1) Is the difference in the two values attributable to the training program? (2) Did other factors influence the post-program sales level?

A review of potential influencing factors with several store executives found that only one factor, the level of advertising, appeared to have changed significantly during the period under consideration. A review of previous data on sales per employee and levels of advertising revealed a direct relationship between the two. As expected, when advertising expenditures were increased, sales per employee increased proportionately.

The advertising staff had developed a mathematical relationship between advertising and sales. Using the historical values, a simple linear model yielded the following relationship: $y = 140 + 40x$, where y is the daily sales per employee and x is the level of advertising expenditures per week divided by 1,000. This equation was developed by the marketing department, using the method of least squares to derive a mathematical relationship between two columns of data (advertising and sales). The least squares function is a routine option on some calculators and is included in many software packages. Figure 3.3 shows the linear relationship between

Figure 3.3. Relationship Between Advertising and Daily Sales

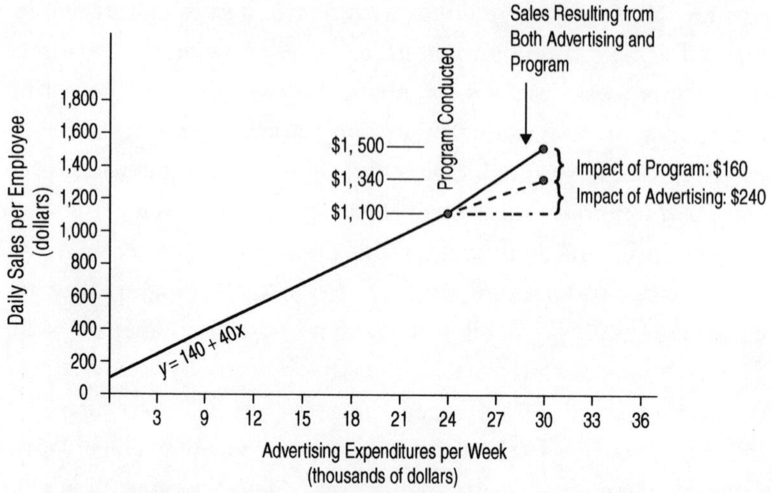

A graph showing Daily Sales per Employee (dollars) on the y-axis (0 to 1,800) versus Advertising Expenditures per Week (thousands of dollars) on the x-axis (3 to 36). The line equation is $y = 140 + 40x$. Key points marked: $1,100, $1,340, and $1,500. Labels: "Program Conducted", "Sales Resulting from Both Advertising and Program", "Impact of Program: $160", "Impact of Advertising: $240".

advertising and sales. It is important to remember that this relationship had already been developed by the advertising department.

The level of weekly advertising expenditures in the month preceding the program was $24,000, and the level of expenditures in the sixth month after the program was $30,000. Assuming that the other factors influencing sales were insignificant, store executives determined the impact of the advertising by plugging in the new advertising expenditure amount (30) for x and calculating the daily sales, which yielded $1,340. Therefore, the new sales level caused by the increase in advertising was $1,340, as shown in Figure 3.3. Because the actual sales value was $1,500, $160 ($1,500 − $1,340) must be attributed to the program. The effects of both the program and advertising are shown in Figure 3.3.

A major disadvantage of this forecasting approach occurs when several variables enter the process. The complexity multiplies, and use of sophisticated statistical packages for multiple variable analyses becomes necessary. Even then, a good fit of the data to the model may not be possible. Unfortunately, some organizations have not developed mathematical relationships for output variables as a function of one or more inputs. Without them, the forecasting method is difficult to use.

The primary advantage of this forecasting process is that it can accurately predict business performance measures without the program, if appropriate data and models are available. The use of more complex models is an option for practitioners familiar with the assumptions and requirements of general linear model techniques. The presentation of more complex methods is beyond the scope of this book and is contained in other publications (see, for example, Armstrong, 2001).

Approximately 5 percent of the published studies on the ROI Methodology use this forecasting technique.

Trend Line Analysis Example 1: Micro Electronics

Setting

A series of programs was conducted as part of an improvement effort for Micro Electronics, a manufacturer of electronics components. One measure of quality was the reject rate—the percentage of items returned for rework. Because of an overall emphasis on quality in the preceding year, there had been a downward trend in the reject rate. However, the movement had been gradual, and there was still room for improvement.

Audience

In one work unit, a continuous process improvement program was implemented in order to improve the reject rate. All twenty-six employees in the process unit were involved in the program.

Solution

The solution was a continuous process improvement program, conducted two hours per day over a one-week period. During this program, employees examined each of the process variables in the work unit and discussed and brainstormed ways to make improvements. The result was improvement in several of the processes, which addressed the measure in question—the reject rate.

Figure 3.4. Reject Rate

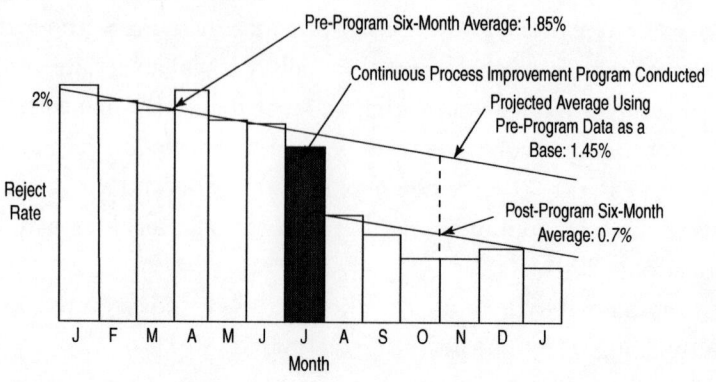

```
                    Pre-Program Six-Month Average: 1.85%
                    Continuous Process Improvement Program Conducted
  2%                Projected Average Using
                    Pre-Program Data as a
                    Base: 1.45%
 Reject
  Rate              Post-Program Six-Month
                    Average: 0.7%

        J  F  M  A  M  J  J  A  S  O  N  D  J
                        Month
```

Measures That Matter

The measure of interest was the reject rate in the work unit, which had been as high as 2 percent at times. The goal was to get the reject rate as close to zero as possible. Figure 3.4 shows a plot of the data.

Conditions Test

The employees, the quality control staff, and the team leader knew of no influences other than those from the program that entered into the process during the evaluation period. They also concluded that the downward trend would most likely have continued—at least for the six months during the evaluation period. With these two conditions met, it is possible to attribute the difference between 1.45 percent and 0.7 percent—a 0.75 percent decrease in the reject rate—to the process improvement program.

Trend Line Analysis Example 2: Healthcare, Inc.

Setting

Healthcare, Inc. (HI), provides a variety of health care services through a chain of hospitals, health maintenance organizations, and clinics. HI, a regional provider, has grown steadily in the last few years and has earned a reputation as a progressive and financially sound company. HI is publicly owned, and its aggressive management team is poised for additional growth.

Sexual harassment is a significant employee relations issue in the United States. Sexual harassment claims in the health care industry and throughout the nation continue to increase, sparked in part by increased public awareness of the issue and victims' increased willingness to report harassment. HI had experienced an increasing number of sexual harassment complaints, and a significant number of them resulted in legal charges and lawsuits. Executives found the complaint record excessive and a persistent and irritating problem. In addition, HI was experiencing an unusually high level of turnover, part of which might have been linked to sexual harassment.

Audience

The audience was all HI employees. There were 6,844 nonsupervisory employees. First- and second-level managers numbered 655, and the senior management team numbered 41.

Solution

A detailed analysis indicated that the major causes of the problem of sexual harassment were a lack of understanding of the company's sexual harassment policy and a lack of understanding about what constitutes inappropriate and illegal behavior. As a result, a one-day workshop was designed to educate all first- and second-level managers about sexual harassment. After the managers attended the program, they were required to conduct a meeting with employees to disseminate information about the company's policy and to discuss what constitutes inappropriate behavior. In essence, the program reached every employee using this process. Seventeen one-day workshops were conducted over a forty-five-day period, and a total of 655 managers participated.

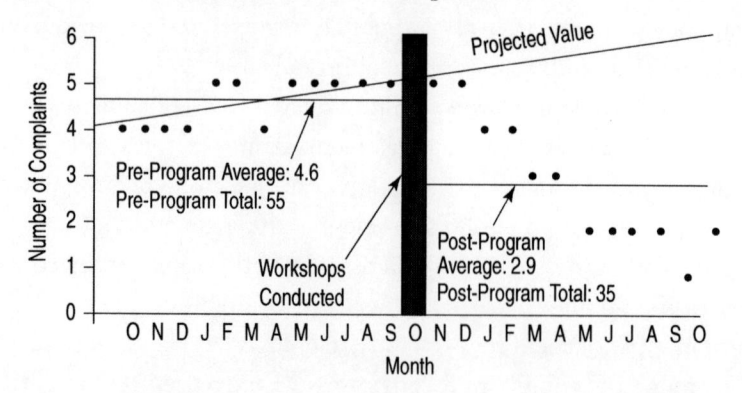

Figure 3.5. Sexual Harassment Complaints

```
6 ┤                            Projected Value
5 ┤    • •   • • •
4 ┤ • • • •      •              • •
3 ┤ Pre-Program Average: 4.6
2 ┤ Pre-Program Total: 55                      • • • •
1 ┤         Workshops    Post-Program                •
0 ┤         Conducted    Average: 2.9
    O N D J F M A M J J A S O N D J F M A M J J A S O
                              Month
```
Number of Complaints

Post-Program Total: 35

Measures That Matter

Two measures are critical in this analysis. The first measure is the number of internal sexual harassment complaints filed with the human resources manager. These formal written complaints had to be investigated, and some resolution had to be reached, whether sexual harassment was confirmed or not. The second measure is avoidable employee turnover, which represents employees who leave voluntarily and thus is turnover that could have been prevented in some way. Figure 3.5 plots the sexual harassment complaints.

Conditions Test

The human resources staff, including the human resources manager, reviewed HI's climate during the one-year period following the program implementation. The group concluded the following:

- The upward trend of sexual harassment complaints probably would have continued if the company had not implemented the program.

- They could not identify any new influences other than the program that could have prevented the sexual harassment complaints. Therefore, the difference between the projected value based on the trend and the actual end-of-program measurement was the decrease in the number of complaints that could be attributed to the sexual harassment prevention program.

For more details of the HI case study, see *Proving the Value of HR: ROI Case Studies* (Phillips and Phillips, 2007).

Trend Line Analysis Example 3: National Book Company

Setting

National Book Company, a publisher of specialty books, was experiencing productivity problems in its shipping department. On any given day, many of the scheduled shipments were not sent out, which meant that promised shipments to some customers were delayed. The company's organization development staff explored the issue, analyzed the problem, and addressed the issue in a team program.

Audience

The audience was all the employees in the shipping department, including the three supervisors.

Solution

The solution was an off-the-job meeting with an organization development consultant during which the employees of the shipping department explored the problem, its causes, suggestions for improvement, and commitments to make changes. Individual and collective follow-up sessions spanned a two-week period.

Figure 3.6. Shipment Productivity

A line chart showing Percentage of Schedule Shipped (y-axis, 85 to 100) versus Month (x-axis, J F M A M J J A S O N D J). Pre-Program Average: 87.3% M. O.D. Program marked around June/July. Post-Program Average: 94.4%. Trend Projection line leading to Projected Average: 92.3%.

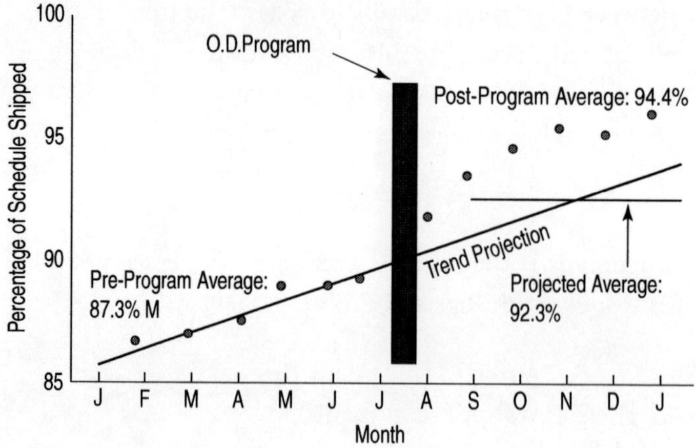

Measures That Matter

The critical measure is shipment productivity—the percentage of scheduled shipments that shipped each day. The results were reported back to the shipping department staff on a routine basis. Figure 3.6 shows the shipment productivity before and after the meeting with the organization development consultant.

Conditions Test

The team members concluded the following:

- The upward trend in shipment productivity prior to the program would probably have continued because of ongoing concern about productivity and discussions of productivity in staff meetings.

- No other new influences on shipment productivity had occurred during the evaluation period, so the total improvement could be attributed to the team-building program. Thus, the difference between the actual average of 94.4 percent and the projected average of

92.3 percent (2.1 percent) represents the improvement directly connected with the program.

Final Thoughts

This chapter shows how simple trend line analysis can be used to isolate the effects of a program. This technique is useful when no new influences other than the program have entered the process during program implementation or subsequently. Trend line analysis is a useful tool, but unfortunately, other processes often do enter the picture; therefore, another isolation technique must used.

Forecasting is a little more complicated than trend line analysis. Its use will be rare because it requires that mathematical relationships between key variables be known or worked out; however, when forecasting can be used, it is a credible method of isolating program effects. If neither trend line analysis nor forecasting can be used, the next step is to consider the use of estimates, which is covered in the next chapter.

References

Armstrong, J. (ed.) *Principles of Forecasting: A Handbook for Researchers and Practitioners.* Boston: Kluwer, 2001.

Phillips, P. P., and Phillips, J. J. *Proving the Value of HR: ROI Case Studies.* Birmingham, Ala.: ROI Institute, 2007.

Salkind, N. *Statistics for People Who (Think They) Hate Statistics.* Thousand Oaks, Calif.: Sage, 2000.

4

Use of Expert Estimates

This chapter moves to a more controversial, yet important set of tools for isolating the effects of programs. Essentially, this approach uses estimates from a variety of experts, among whom the program participants are perhaps the most credible source. The use of estimates has been shunned by some researchers, who contend that if control groups or time series analysis (trend lines or forecasts) cannot be used, no other technique should be attempted. Unfortunately, the need to isolate the effects of a program does not go away just because the preferred tools do not apply. Failure to isolate the effects of a program leaves the owners of that program somewhat vulnerable or at least unable to connect the program to its business impact. Other techniques must be explored in order to at least attempt to get a credible assessment of a program's true impact. In businesses and other organizations with dynamic environments and time constraints, decisions will be made with the best available data. Ultimately, these decisions will be more subjective, not less, to the extent that all reasonable and credible data are not brought to bear.

The good news is that estimates can be phenomenally powerful. A tremendous amount of research shows the effectiveness of expert estimates. When specific guidelines are followed and the estimates are adjusted for error, they become credible and, unfortunately, easy to use. Ease of use is unfortunate when estimates become the method of choice rather than a method of last resort. The methods described in the previous chapters of this book should be considered first, before resorting to estimates. Estimates are not preferred, but evaluators must be prepared to use and defend them when other methods are not available. This chapter explores how estimates can be a powerful and credible way to isolate the effects of a program.

Participants' Estimates of Program Impact

An easily implemented method for isolating the impact of a program is obtaining information directly from the participants. The effectiveness of this approach rests on the assumption that participants are capable of determining or estimating how much of a performance improvement is related to the program. Because their actions have produced the improvement, participants may have accurate input on the issue. They should know how much of the change was caused by applying what they learned in the program. Although it is an estimate, this value will typically have credibility with management because participants are at the center of the change or improvement.

When this technique is used, several assumptions are made:

- The variety of activities, tasks, and learning opportunities that were implemented as a result of the program, project, or initiative were all focused on improving performance.

- One or more business measures were identified prior to program implementation and monitored both before and after the program. Data monitoring has revealed an improvement in the business measure.

- The program needs to be linked to a specific amount of performance improvement, and the monetary impact of the improvement needs to be calculated. This information forms the basis for calculating the ROI.

Given these assumptions, the participants can identify the results that are actually linked to the program and provide the data necessary to develop the ROI. This information can be gathered through a focus group, an interview, or a questionnaire.

Using Focus Groups to Obtain Participant Estimates

Focus groups work extremely well for isolating the effects of a program if the groups can be kept relatively small—eight to twelve participants. If they become much larger, the groups should be divided into smaller groups. Focus groups provide an opportunity for members to share information equally, avoiding domination by any one individual. The process taps the input, creativity, and reactions of all the group members.

The participants in a focus group should be the most credible source of data, according to Guiding Principle 3 of the ROI Methodology. Although some may question the ability of participants to provide these data, if the situation is examined realistically, one can see that it is their performance that is being scrutinized. They often know which influences have caused their performance to improve and, to a certain degree, the relationship between those influences and the outcomes. Even if they are not the ideal source of data, they are often the most credible in comparison with other sources. This is particularly true when the participants are professional, technical, clerical, or managerial employees.

The meeting should take about one hour (slightly more if multiple factors affected the results or if multiple business measures are being evaluated). The facilitator should be neutral during the process. (For example, an individual with an ownership role in the program should not conduct the focus group.) Focus group facilitation and input should be as objective as possible.

The task is to link the business results with the program. The group is presented with the improvement (a fact) and asked to provide input in order to determine the impact of the program on the given improvement.

To arrive at the most credible value for the program's impact, follow these steps:

1. *Explain the purpose of the focus group meeting.* Participants should understand that their team has achieved a specific improvement in performance. While many factors could have contributed to the performance, the task of the focus group is to determine how much of the improvement is related to the program.
2. *Discuss the rules.* Each participant should be encouraged to provide input, limiting his or her comments to two minutes (or less) for each specific factor. Comments are confidential and will not be linked to an individual.
3. *Explain the importance of the process.* The participants' role in the process is critical. Because it is their performance that has improved, participants are in the best position to indicate what caused the improvement; they are the experts in this determination. Without quality input, the contribution of the program (or other processes) may never be known.
4. *Identify the measure, and show the improvement.* Using actual data, present the level of performance before and after the program, showing the change in business results.
5. *Identify the different factors that may have contributed to the performance improvement.* Using input from experts—others who are knowledgeable about the setting and improvements—list any factors that may have influenced the improvement (for example, a change in the volume of work, a new work system or procedure, or enhanced technology).
6. *Ask the group to identify other factors that may have contributed to the performance improvement.* In some situations, only the

participants know of other influencing factors, and those factors should surface at this time. If any other factors are identified, they should be added to the list. At this point, all the factors should have been identified.

7. *Discuss the links.* Taking one factor at a time, have participants individually describe the link between that factor and the business results. For example, for the training influence, participants would describe how the training program has driven improvement by providing examples, anecdotes, and other supporting evidence. All participants should be allowed the same amount of time. Participants may require some prompting to provide comments. If they cannot provide dialogue regarding an issue, there is a good chance that the factor had little or no influence.

8. *Repeat step 7 for each factor.* Explore each factor until all the participants have discussed the linkage between all the factors and the business performance improvement. After the linkages have been discussed, the participants should have a clear understanding of the cause-and-effect relationships between the various factors and the business impact.

9. *Ask participants to allocate a percentage of the improvement to each of the factors discussed.* Provide participants with a pie chart that represents the total amount of improvement for the measure in question, then ask them to carve up the pie, allocating a percentage to each improvement, making sure that the percentages total 100 percent. Some participants may feel uncertain about this process, but they should be encouraged to complete it, using their best estimates. Let them know that their uncertainty will be addressed in the next step.

10. *Ask for confidence estimates.* Ask participants to review their allocations and, for each one, to estimate their level of confidence in each allocation estimate. Using a scale of 0 to 100 percent, in which 0 percent represents no confidence and 100 percent is certainty, have participants express their level

of confidence for each of their estimates in step 9. A participant may be more comfortable with some factors than others, so the confidence estimates may vary. Results will be adjusted according to these confidence estimates.

11. *Ask participants to multiply the two percentages.* For example, if an individual has allocated 30 percent of the improvement to a specific program and is 80 percent confident, she would multiply 30 percent by 80 percent, which results in 24 percent. In essence, the participant is suggesting that at least 24 percent of the team's business improvement is linked to the program. The confidence estimate provides a conservative discount factor, allowing evaluators to adjust for error in the estimate. The pie charts, with the calculations, are collected without names to identify the participants, and the calculations are verified. Another option is to collect the pie charts and make the calculations for the participants.

12. *Report the results.* The average of the adjusted values for the group should be developed and communicated to the group, if possible. Also, a summary of all the information should be communicated to the participants as soon as possible.

Participants who do not provide information should be excluded from the analysis. Table 4.1 illustrates the approach discussed here with an example of one participant's estimates.

The participant allocated 50 percent of the improvement to the training program. The confidence percentage represents the participant's perception of how much error there could be in the estimate. A 70 percent confidence level equates to a potential error range of $\pm$ 30 percent (100% − 70% = 30%). The amount of improvement caused by the training program could be 30 percent more (50% + 15% = 65%), 30 percent less (50% − 15% = 35%), or somewhere in between. Therefore, the participant's allocation is in the range of 35 percent to 65 percent. In essence, the confidence

Table 4.1. One Participant's Estimates

Factor That Influenced Improvement	Percentage of Improvement Caused by Factor	Level of Confidence, Expressed as a Percentage
Training program	50%	70%
Adjustment in procedures	10%	80%
Change in technology	10%	50%
Revision of incentive plan	20%	90%
Increased management attention	10%	50%
Other _____	___%	___%
Total	100%	

estimate frames an error range. To be conservative, the low value of the range (35 percent) is used, following Guiding Principle 7: Adjust estimates of improvement for potential errors of estimation.

The approach described in the preceding paragraph is equivalent to multiplying the isolation estimate by the confidence percentage to develop a usable program factor value of 35 percent (50% × 70%). This adjusted percentage is then multiplied by the actual amount of improvement (post-program value minus pre-program value) to isolate the portion attributed to the program. The adjusted value of improvement attributed to the program is now ready for conversion to monetary values and, ultimately, for use in calculating the return on investment.

The approach detailed in this section provides a credible way to isolate the effects of a program when other methods will not work. It is often regarded as a low-cost solution to the problem of isolation because it takes only a few focus groups and a small amount of time to arrive at a conclusion. In most settings, the conversion to monetary values is not performed by the group but developed in another way. For most data, the company may already have developed a standard conversion rate. The issues involved in converting data to monetary values are detailed in *Data Conversion*, the next book in this series. However, if necessary, participants can provide input on the monetary value of the improvement during the same focus group meeting in which they provide their factor allocations. The steps for estimating monetary values are similar to the steps for estimating program effects.

Using Questionnaires to Obtain Participant Estimates

Sometimes, focus groups are not an available option or are considered unacceptable for collecting data. The participants may not be available for a group meeting, or focus groups may be too expensive. In these situations, a follow-up questionnaire may be administered to collect similar information. By answering a series of questions about the program's impact, participants address the same issues that they would deal with in a focus group.

The questionnaire may focus solely on the issue of isolating the effects of the program, or it may focus on the monetary value derived from the program, so that the information pertaining to the isolation issue is only a part of the data collected. The latter is a more versatile way to use questionnaires when it is not certain exactly how participants will provide business impact data. In some programs, the precise measures that will be influenced by the program may not be known. This is sometimes the case in programs involving leadership, process improvement teams, communications, negotiation, problem solving, innovation, or performance improvement initiatives. In these situations, it is helpful to obtain information from participants through a series of questions about how they have used what they have learned and the subsequent impact on their work or team. It is important for participants to know about these questions before they receive the questionnaire; the surprise element can be disastrous in data collection. Allowing participants to preview the questions early in the program will help them provide better data later on. A recommended series of questions is shown in Exhibit 4.1.

Exhibit 4.1. Questions for Participants Who Are Estimating Program Impact

1. How have you and your job changed as a result of your participation in this program (skills and knowledge application)?
2. What impact do these changes bring to your work or work unit?
3. How is this impact measured (specific measure)?
4. How much did the value of this measure change after you participated in the program (monthly, weekly, or daily amount)?
5. What is the unit value of the measure?
6. What is the basis for this unit value? Please indicate the assumptions made and the specific calculations you performed to arrive at the value.
7. What is the annual value of this change or improvement in your work unit (for the first year)?
8. Recognizing that many factors besides this program may have influenced the output results, please identify other factors that could have contributed to this performance improvement.
9. What percentage of this improvement can be attributed directly to the application of skills and knowledge gained during the program? (0–100%)
10. What confidence do you have in the estimate and data provided for Question 9, expressed as a percentage? (0% = no confidence; 100% = certainty)
11. What other individuals or groups could estimate this percentage or determine the amount?

Perhaps an illustration of the process of using a questionnaire to gather participant estimates of business impact will reveal its effectiveness and acceptability. In a global auto rental company, the impact of a leadership program for new managers was being assessed. Because the decision to calculate the impact of the program was made after it had begun, the control group arrangement was not a feasible method for isolating the effects of the program. A specific business impact measure that was directly linked to the program had not been identified, so participants could select two measures to improve. As a result, using trend line analysis was not appropriate because there were too many measures. Participants' estimates proved to be the most useful way to assess the impact of the program on business performance.

In a detailed follow-up questionnaire, participants were asked a variety of questions about the application and impact of what was learned in the program. The series of questions listed in Exhibit 4.1 provided an assessment of the impact.

Although this series of questions is challenging, when set up properly and presented to participants in an appropriate way, such questions can be very effective for collecting impact data. Table 4.2 shows a sample of the calculations based on these questions for this particular program. In this example, twenty-nine participants were asked to identify two measures for improvement. The table shows the input from fifteen of the twenty-nine. The first column represents the participant who responded (the list is in random order). The second column represents data for Question 7 in Exhibit 4.1; the next five columns represent input for Questions 3, 6, 9, 8, and 10. The last column provides the adjusted monetary value for each measure identified by each participant. These first fifteen measures are added to get the total monetary benefit for these measures. The total contribution of the remaining fourteen of the participants' first measures and the total for the second measure are also shown. Each measure is converted to money, linked to the program through estimation with an adjustment made for error,

Table 4.2. Sample of Input from Participants in a Leadership Program for New Managers

Participant Number	Q7 Annual Improvement	Q3 Measure	Q6 Method for Converting Data to Monetary Value	Q9 Contribution from Program	Q8 Number of Other Factors	Q10 Confidence Estimate	Q7×Q9×Q10 Total Monetary Benefit (Adjusted Value)
1	$13,100	Sales	Standard	60%	3	80%	$6,288
3	41,200	Productivity	Expert	75%	1	95%	29,355
4	5,300	Sales	Standard	80%	1	90%	3,816
6	7,210	Cost	N/A	70%	2	70%	3,533
9	4,215	Efficiency	Standard	40%	3	75%	1,265
10	17,500	Quality	Expert	35%	4	60%	3,675
12	11,500	Time	Standard	60%	2	80%	5,520
14	3,948	Time	Standard	70%	1	80%	2,211
15	14,725	Sales	Standard	40%	3	70%	4,123
17	6,673	Efficiency	Estimate	50%	3	60%	2,002
18	12,140	Cost	N/A	100%	0	100%	12,140
19	17,850	Sales	Standard	60%	2	70%	7,497
21	13,920	Sales	Standard	50%	3	80%	5,568
22	15,362	Cost	N/A	40%	4	90%	5,530
23	18,923	Sales	Standard	60%	1	75%	8,515
						Total for the items above	$101,038
						Total for the next 14 items	$84,398
						Total for 2nd measure	$143,764
						Total benefits	$329,200

and adjusted appropriately, then the amounts are added together to provide the total contribution to the organization. The total value for the program represents the total of the input from all who provided data, following Guiding Principle 6: If no improvement data are available for a population or from a specific source, assume that little or no improvement has occurred. That is, only the data provided were used.

Although these input data are estimates, the approach has an acceptable level of accuracy and credibility. Remember, this technique is a worst-case scenario. Four adjustments have been used to constitute a conservative and thus more credible approach.

1. The individuals who do not respond to the questionnaire or do not provide usable data on the questionnaire are assumed to have no improvements to report. This is probably an overstatement because some individuals will experience improvements but not report them on the questionnaire or not respond to the questionnaire. This adjustment follows Guiding Principle 6, which is discussed in *ROI Fundamentals,* the first book in this series.

2. Extreme data and incomplete or unsupported claims are omitted from the analysis, although they may be included in an "other benefits" category. (Guiding Principle 8)

3. Because only annualized values are used, it is assumed that no benefits from the program occur after the first year of implementation. In reality, leadership development would be expected to add value for several years after the program has been conducted. (Guiding Principle 9)

4. The confidence estimates, expressed as percentages, are multiplied by the improvement values to reduce the amount of the improvement according to the potential error in the estimates. (Guiding Principle 7)

When presented to senior management, the results of this impact study were perceived to be an understatement of the program's success; the data and the process were considered credible.

Collecting an adequate amount of quality data from the series of impact questions is the critical challenge in using questionnaires to collect participant estimates of program impact. Participants must be primed to provide usable data. *Data Collection*, the second book in this series, provides a detailed list of techniques for obtaining a high response rate. Seven techniques are powerful in securing a large return rate (60 to 90 percent).

1. Participants should know in advance that they are expected to provide detailed data and should be given an explanation of why the data are needed and how they will be used.

2. Participants should see a copy of the questionnaire and discuss it while they are involved in the program. If possible, a verbal commitment to provide the data should be obtained at that time.

3. Participants should be reminded of the requirement to provide data prior to the data collection period. The reminder should come from others involved in the process—for example, from the participants' immediate manager.

4. Participants can be provided with examples of how the questionnaire can be completed, using most-likely scenarios and typical data.

5. One or more incentives can be used to stimulate a return.

6. The participants' immediate manager should support, encourage, or be involved in data collection.

7. Participants should be provided with a summary of the data once it is compiled.

Use of these techniques keeps the data collection process, with its chain of impact questions, from being a surprise and accomplishes three critical tasks:

1. *Increases the response rate.* Because participants have committed to providing data during the session, a greater percentage will respond.
2. *Increases the quantity of data.* Because participants will understand the chain of impact and how the data will be used, they will complete more questions.
3. *Improves the quality of the data.* Because expectations are clarified up front, participants have a greater understanding of the type of data needed and improved confidence in the data they provide. Perhaps subconsciously, participants begin to think through the consequences of the program on specific impact measures. The result: improved quality of input.

Using Interviews to Obtain Participant Estimates

In lieu of a questionnaire, an interview can be useful for isolating the effects of a program. An interview may represent a compromise between using a focus group and using a questionnaire. A focus group may not be feasible; perhaps it is not feasible for a significant number of participants to reconvene. Using a questionnaire is easier than using a focus group; participant data for the purpose of isolating program effects can be gathered simply by adding three questions. However, an interview may be far more revealing and useful than a questionnaire and can be conducted by telephone, which is easier than convening a focus group. Of course, a face-to-face interview is more powerful, but it may be too expensive. Essentially, the line of questioning in an interview is similar to that on a questionnaire. To isolate the effects of a program, the same three questions as would be added to a questionnaire can be added to an interview.

Advantages and Disadvantages of Participant Estimates

Participant estimation is an important technique for isolating the effect of a program. However, the process has some disadvantages. It is an estimate and, consequently, does not have the accuracy desired by some professionals. Also, the input data may be unreliable because some participants are incapable of providing these types of estimates. They might not be aware of exactly which factors contributed to the results, or they may be reluctant to provide data. If the questions come as a surprise, the data will be scarce.

Several advantages make participant estimation attractive. It is a simple process, easily understood by most participants and by those who review evaluation data. It is inexpensive and takes very little time and analysis, making the results an efficient addition to the evaluation process. Participant estimates originate from a credible source—the individuals who actually produced the improvement.

The advantages usually offset the disadvantages. Isolating the effects of a program will never be a precise process, and participant estimates are accurate enough for clients and management groups. Participant estimates are appropriate when the participants are managers, supervisors, team leaders, sales associates, engineers, or other professional and technical employees.

Participant estimates are the default isolation method for many types of programs. If nothing else will work, this method is used. A fallback approach is needed if the effect of the program must always be isolated, which is recommended. The reluctance to use this process often rests with the evaluator and his or her immediate manager or with staff and support team members, who typically avoid estimates because they are reluctant to use a technique that is not airtight. However, the key audience for the data—sponsors, clients, or senior executives—will readily accept this approach. Living in an ambiguous world, they understand that estimates have to be made and may be the only way to approach the issue of isolation. They understand the challenge and appreciate the conservative approach, often commenting that the actual value of a program is probably greater than the value presented. Because of the factors outlined here, approximately 50 percent of the published studies on the ROI Methodology use participant estimates to isolate the effects of programs.

Case Study

To show how the estimation process works within an organization, it is best to examine an actual case. This case study shows the power of developing estimates from a group of participants involved in different processes, all with different process owners.

Setting

National Bank had established a carefully planned growth pattern through acquisitions of smaller banks. One recent acquisition was quite large, representing almost $1 billion in total assets. After the acquisition, record-keeping systems and performance-monitoring processes were implemented at all locations. Each branch in the network had a scorecard on which performance was tracked, using several measures such as new accounts, total deposits, and sales growth of specific products. National Bank had an excellent reputation as an organization with a strong sales culture. Through a sales training program, all branch personnel were taught how to aggressively pursue new customers and cross-sell to existing customers in a variety of product lines. The bank used sales training coupled with incentives and management reinforcement to ensure that ambitious sales goals were met. A variety of marketing initiatives also supported the sales process. Six months after the systems were in place in the new acquisition, management was ready to implement the sales culture among all branch personnel.

Audience

The audience was the employees in all thirty new branches. At each branch, the branch manager and the teller supervisors were included in the program, bringing the total to over six hundred participants.

Solution

Recognizing that several factors had influenced the scorecard results, management decided to let the program participants estimate the impact of the program in a focus group facilitated by the branch managers. Branch management initially identified that sales output had been significantly influenced by the following factors: (1) the sales training program, (2) incentive systems, (3) management emphasis on sales and management reinforcement of sales activities, and (4) marketing. After the program was implemented, management tracked performance improvements on the scorecard by product category.

The sales training program covered both product knowledge (products had been adjusted slightly from product offerings prior to the acquisition) and sales techniques (explaining the features and benefits of the products, overcoming resistance to the sale, and pointing out advantages over competitors' products). The program was delivered in half-day increments for a total of one and a half days.

The incentive system for the branch staff who sold credit cards changed slightly under the new ownership. The incentive process was owned by the compensation department. The bonus for selling a credit card was not large, but for some, it was a motivator to sell more. For others, it may not have made much difference.

The goal-setting and reinforcement process was owned by the organization development department. Previously, the employees had had goals, but the goals had not been as detailed as those required after the acquisition. Under the new ownership, goals (which were posted in each branch's break room) were specified by individual and by product line for each day. Each morning, the branch manager had a brief meeting with the staff to discuss the goals that must be achieved that day. At the end of each day, there was a brief review of progress made and a discussion of what could be done to make up for any deficiencies.

The fourth influence on sales output was marketing. Post-acquisition marketing had been low-key. Signs had been changed, and customers had been welcomed to the new company. There had been no specific promotions or advertising beyond those elements. Still, the marketing had had an effect; it had brought existing customers into the branch. Perhaps the newly posted signs had even attracted some new customers. These marketing elements were owned by the marketing department, of course.

Measures

Each branch monitored all major measures, including the number of new credit cards, the number of new checking accounts, increases in deposits, and increases in consumer loans. Although other measures were related to the products, these were the measures that the staff could most directly influence.

Estimates Provided

All participants provided estimates (by branch) in focus groups. Each branch manager was trained in the focus group process and conducted the meeting for his or her branch. The data from each of the thirty branches were captured in this way. Branch managers were considered independent of the change processes, a requirement for being the focus group facilitator. Each manager collected input from his or her entire group, using a summary of estimates for each measure.

Credibility Check

To ensure that the most credible individuals provided estimates, the evaluation team decided that branch staff members should provide the data. It was their performance that was being evaluated, and they should know more than anyone else what had caused their performance to improve.

Methodology

The branch managers in the target metro area conducted focus groups with the team to estimate the percentage of improvement that could be attributed to each of the four influences listed earlier. All branch employees provided input during a meeting facilitated by their branch manager. In each carefully organized meeting, the branch manager

- Described the task.

- Explained why the information was needed and how it would be used.

- Had employees discuss the link between each factor and the specific output measure.

- Provided employees with any additional information needed to estimate the contribution of each factor.

- Asked employees to identify any other influences that may have contributed to the increase.

- Obtained from each employee an estimate of the contribution of each factor. The total had to be 100 percent. Several consensus-reaching tools were offered.

- Obtained the confidence level of each employee for his or her estimate on each factor (100 percent = certainty; 0 percent = no confidence). The values of the estimates and confidence levels were averaged for each factor.

For example, Table 4.3 shows the information collected from one branch for one business measure, the increase in credit-card accounts.

The amount of improvement attributed to the first factor, the sales training program, was determined by multiplying the total amount of improvement (175) by the average percentage of

Table 4.3. One Branch's Allocation of Factors Affecting Number of Credit Accounts, and Corresponding Confidence Levels

Contributing Factor	Average Impact on Results	Average Confidence Level
Sales training program	32%	83%
Incentive systems	41%	87%
Goal setting, management emphasis on sales	14%	62%
Marketing	11%	75%
Other	2%	91%
	100%	

Note: Monthly increase in credit card accounts: 175.

performance attributed to the sales training program (32%). This calculation shows the impact of the program on the credit-card product line. The number was then adjusted by the confidence percentage (83%). Thus, the number of new credit cards attributed to the sales training program was $175 \times 32\% \times 83\% = 46$ (at least). If the same calculation is made for every factor, the total is less than the original 175. In essence, "the error" is removed from the analysis.

Immediate Managers' Estimates of Program Impact

In lieu of (or in addition to) participant estimates, the participants' immediate managers may be asked to assess the extent of a program's role in producing a performance improvement. In some settings, participants' managers may be more familiar with the other factors influencing performance and thus may be better equipped to provide estimates of impact.

After describing the improvement made by a program's participants, ask their supervisors these questions:

1. In addition to this program, what factors could have contributed to this success?

2. What percentage of the performance improvement was a result of the program? (0% to 100%)
3. What is the basis for this estimate?
4. What is your confidence in this estimate, expressed as a percentage? (0 percent = no confidence; 100 percent = complete confidence)
5. What other individuals or groups would know about this improvement and could estimate the percentage of improvement that resulted from the program?

These questions are similar to those asked of participants. Immediate managers' estimates should be analyzed in the same way as participant estimates. To provide a more conservative evaluation, estimates should be adjusted by the confidence percentage. If feasible, it is recommended that input be obtained from both participants and supervisors. If both participants' and supervisors' estimates have been collected, evaluators must decide which estimates to use. If one type of estimate is more credible than another, the more credible one should be used. The most conservative approach is to use the estimate that yields the lowest value and include an appropriate explanation (Guiding Principle 4). Another option is to recognize that each source has its own unique perspective and that an average of the two is appropriate, placing equal weight on each input.

Supervisor estimates have the same disadvantages as participant estimates. They are subjective and therefore may be viewed with skepticism by some. Supervisors may be reluctant to participate or may be incapable of providing accurate impact estimates. They may not know about factors other than the program that may have contributed to the improvement, unless they work closely with the participants they manage.

The advantages of supervisor estimates are similar to the advantages of participant estimation. They are simple and inexpensive and have an acceptable degree of credibility because they come from the managers of those who participated in the program and made the improvements. When supervisor estimates are combined with participant estimates, their credibility may be enhanced. Also, when levels of confidence are used to adjust the results, the credibility of supervisor estimates further increases.

Senior Management's Estimates of Program Impact

In some cases, upper management may estimate the percentage of improvement that should be attributed to the program. For example, in one organization, the senior management team adjusted the results from a program to create self-directed teams. After considering factors external to the program that could have contributed to performance improvement, such as technology, procedures, and process change, management applied a subjective factor of 60 percent to represent the portion of the results that should be attributed to the program. The factor of 60 percent was developed in a meeting with top managers and thus had the benefit of group ownership. Although estimates by top management can be highly subjective, often they represent input from the individuals who approve or provide the funding for a program. Sometimes, their level of comfort with the process is the most important consideration.

Because of their highly subjective nature, senior management estimates of program contributions are not usually recommended. Senior managers may not understand all the factors that could have affected the business measure driven by a program or may have no indication of the relative impact of the factors. Therefore, top management estimates should be avoided or used only when necessary to secure buy-in from the senior management team.

In some situations, a large program impact results in a very high ROI. Top managers may feel more comfortable with the evaluation if they are allowed to adjust the results, even if actual data rather than estimates were used as the basis for the ROI evaluation. Their basis for the adjustment is their perception that the numbers are unrealistic. In essence, they are applying a discount to adjust for an unknown factor, even though attempts have been made to identify each factor. While there is no scientific basis for this technique, discounting the data sometimes helps secure management buy-in.

Customers' Estimates of Program Impact

One helpful approach in some highly specific situations is soliciting input on a program's impact directly from customers. Customers can be asked why they chose a particular product or service or to explain how individuals applying skills and abilities have influenced their reaction to a product or service. This technique focuses directly on what the program is designed to improve. For example, after a teller training program was conducted consequent to a bank merger, market survey data showed that the percentage of customers who were dissatisfied with teller knowledge was reduced by 5 percent compared with market survey data before the training program. Since only the training program had increased teller knowledge, the 5 percent reduction in dissatisfied customers was directly attributable to the program.

In another example, a large real estate company provided a comprehensive training program for agents, focusing on presentation skills. As customers listed their homes with an agent, they received a survey that explored their reasons for deciding to list their home with the company. Among the reasons listed were the presentation skills of the agent. Responses to this question and related questions provided evidence of new listings that could be attributed to the training program.

Of course, customer estimates can be used only in situations in which customer input can be obtained. Even then, customers may not be able to provide accurate data. They must be able to see the influencing factors in order to isolate them. However, because customer input is usually credible, the approach is effective when the situation allows it to be used.

Experts' Estimates of Program Impact

External or internal experts can sometimes estimate the portion of results that can be attributed to a program. When this strategy is used, experts must be selected on the basis of their knowledge of the process, program, and situation. For example, an expert might be able to provide estimates of how much change in a quality measure can be attributed to a specific program such as Six Sigma or continuous quality improvement.

Expert estimates would most likely be used to evaluate the success of a program implemented by an external supplier. In previous evaluations, a certain portion of the results would have been attributed to the program. This percentage, provided by the supplier, is extrapolated to the current situation. This approach should be pursued cautiously because the current situation may be very different from those in the supplier's past implementations. However, if the previous program applications have many similarities to the current situation, the supplier's value may be used as a rough estimate. Because of the concerns listed here, this approach should be used with explanations. In addition, it is important to check the supplier's studies, to ensure that credible, objective processes were used for data collection and analysis.

The use of expert estimates has one advantage: its credibility often reflects the reputation of the expert or independent consultant. It can provide quick input from a reputable source. Sometimes, top management will place more confidence in external experts than in their own internal staff.

Determining the Impact of Other Factors

In some situations, it may be feasible to calculate the impact of factors other than the program in question and then credit the implemented program with the remaining portion. In this approach, the program takes credit for improvement that cannot be attributed to other factors.

An example will help explain the approach. In a large bank, a significant increase in consumer loan volume was generated after a training program was conducted for consumer loan officers. Part of the increase was attributed to the program, and the remainder was attributed to the influence of other factors operating during the same time period. Two other factors were identified by the evaluator: a loan officer's production improves with time, and falling interest rates stimulated an increase in consumer loans.

The first factor considers the fact that the confidence of loan officers improves as they make loans. They use consumer lending policy manuals and gain knowledge and expertise through trial and error. The contribution of this factor to performance improvement was estimated by using input from several internal experts in the marketing department.

For the second factor, industry sources were used to show the relationship between increased consumer loan volume and falling interest rates.

The estimates based on the first and second factors accounted for a certain percentage of increased consumer loan volume. The remaining improvement was attributed to the training program.

The method of isolation by elimination is appropriate when the factors external to the program are easily identified and appropriate mechanisms are available to calculate their impact on the improvement. In some cases, estimating the impact of other factors is just as difficult as estimating the impact of the program in question, leaving this approach less advantageous. This process can be credible if the method used to isolate the impact of the other factors is credible.

Estimate Example 1: Global Financial Services

Setting

Global Financial Services, Inc. (GFS) is a large international firm that offers a variety of financial services to clients. Analyzing its current sales practices and results, the firm identified a need to manage sales relationships more effectively. A task force comprising representatives from field sales, marketing, financial consulting, information technology, and education and training examined several solutions for improving relationships, including customer contact software packages. The firm chose to implement a software package called ACT!™. This software, developed by Symantec and designed to turn contacts into relationships and relationships into increased sales, features a flexible customer database, easy contact entry, a calendar, and a to-do list. ACT! enabled quick and effective customer communication and was designed for use with customized reports. It also had built-in contact and calendar sharing and was Internet-ready.

Audience and Solution

The audience consisted of 4,000 relationship managers. These managers were sales representatives who had direct contact with customers. GFS evaluated the success of the software on a pilot basis, using three groups, each composed of thirty relationship managers. A one-day workshop was designed to teach the relationship managers how to use the software. The ACT! software was distributed and used at the workshop. If the trial program proved successful, yielding an appropriate return on investment, GFS planned to implement ACT! for all its relationship managers.

Measures

Measures were tracked in four categories:

1. Increase in sales to existing customers
2. Reduction of customer complaints about missed deadlines, late responses, and failure to complete transactions
3. Increase in customer satisfaction on the customer survey
4. Reduction in response time on customer inquiries and requests

Estimates Provided

The relationship managers provided estimates of program impact in a focus group meeting. Five groups of twelve—a total of sixty managers—participated. It was decided that the relationship managers were the most credible source of data for this estimate. Their performance was being judged; therefore, they should know the program's impact better than anyone. The method for the estimate was the focus group approach outlined earlier in this chapter.

Estimate Example 2: Cracker Box

Setting

Cracker Box, Inc., was a large, fast-growing restaurant chain located along interstate highways and major thoroughfares. In the past ten years, Cracker Box had grown steadily; it had over four hundred stores and plans for continued growth. Each store had a restaurant and a gift shop. A store manager was responsible for both profit units. Store manager turnover was approximately 25 percent—lower than the industry average of 35 percent but still excessive. Because of the chain's growth and the rate of manager turnover, almost two hundred new store managers had to be developed each year.

Store managers operated autonomously and were held accountable for store performance. Using their store team, managers controlled expenses, monitored operating results, and took action as needed to improve store performance. Each store tracked dozens of performance measures in a monthly operating report. Some measures were reported weekly.

Store managers were recruited both internally and externally and had to have restaurant experience. Many had college degrees. The program for new managers usually lasted nine months. When selected, the store manager trainee reported directly to a store manager who served as a mentor to the trainee. Trainees were usually assigned to a specific store location for the duration of manager training. During the training period, the entire store team reported to the manager trainee as the store manager coached the trainee. As part of the formal training and development, each manager trainee was required to attend at least three one-week programs offered by the company's corporate university. One such program was the Performance Management Program.

Audience and Solution

The audience consisted of new store managers (store manager trainees) who were attending the Performance Management Program as part of the nine-month training program.

The Performance Management Program taught new store managers how to improve store performance. Participants learned how to establish measurable goals for employees, provide performance feedback, measure progress toward goals, and take action to ensure that goals were met. The program focused on using the store team to solve problems and improve performance. Problem analysis and counseling skills were also covered. The one-week program was residential, and evening assignments were often part of the process. Skill practice sessions were integrated with the other sessions during the week. The program was taught by both the corporate university staff and operation managers. Program sessions took place at the corporate university near the company's headquarters.

Measures

The measures in this example varied, depending on where the manager was located and what operational issues were a concern to both the manager and his or her direct supervisor. Measures could include sales and customer service, store operations, efficiency, safety and health, absenteeism and turnover, or any others that were appropriate.

Estimates Provided

The manager trainees provided the estimates. Essentially, it was each store team's performance that was being measured, and the teams reported directly to the manager trainees. The evaluation team concluded that the manager trainees were the most credible source of information about the factors that could have contributed to their store's improvement. The data were obtained on an action planning document, on which each manager trainee was asked to indicate the percentage of improvement directly related to the program. Confidence levels were also provided and were used to adjust the amount of improvement reported.

For more details on this case, see *Proving the Value of HR: ROI Case Studies* (Phillips and Phillips, 2007).

Estimate Example 3: Public Bank of Malaysia

Setting

The Public Bank of Malaysia began offering a new deposit savings product and was interested in measuring the impact of the new product on business performance.

Audience and Solution

A training program on the new product targeted customer service representatives. The training focused on ways to sell the new deposit savings product by convincing customers to buy it.

Measure

The only measure was sales of the deposit savings product.

Estimates Provided

When customers decided to put their money into the new savings product, they were asked to complete a card and leave it in a box as they exited the branch. The card listed reasons why a customer might have selected the product at that time. The customer could check any or all of these factors. One of the factors was the sales approach of the customer service representative, which might have convinced a customer to buy the product. The responses on this factor would be directly related to the training program, assuming that no other factors had influenced the customer service representatives' sales skills. The use of customer estimates often carries a great deal of credibility. However, customers may not be as objective or as accurate as employees in understanding customer choices. The impact of estimates and how they can add credibility has been underscored in other sections of this chapter.

Estimate Example 4: Multi-National, Inc.

Setting

Multi-National, Inc. (MNI) is a large global firm with manufacturing and support facilities in more than twenty-five countries. MNI had experienced tremendous growth and was poised for additional growth in the future. MNI's comprehensive executive development process included a series of programs for the executives. One executive education program, Leadership and Shareholder Value, focused on using leadership and management principles to add shareholder value to the company.

As the program was developed, the company's chief financial officer (CFO) was asked to sponsor it. Because he found the program intriguing, the CFO accepted the challenge and became involved in some of the design issues and the implementation of the program. He made personal visits to as many programs as he could fit into his schedule. His work with the program turned into enthusiasm as he saw an opportunity for an education program to have a measurable business impact, something that he had not seen previously.

Audience, Solution, and Measures

Executives from various functions were the targeted group. Built into the three-day program was a detailed action plan that participants had to develop and implement. The action plan focused on a project to be completed that would add shareholder value to the company. The specific measures influenced included output, quality, cycle time, and customer service.

Because of his enthusiasm about the program and his sincere belief that it was adding significant value to the company, the CFO asked the program designers to follow up on the action plans and determine the success of the program in monetary terms. Two groups were targeted and contacted in order to obtain information on their accomplishments related to the action planning process. Much to the CFO's pleasure, significant improvements were identified as important projects were implemented as a result of the program. Input from the participants was reviewed, and the project items were tallied. To be consistent, only annual values converted to margin were used in the analysis. It was assumed that all the improvements reported were linked directly to the program. The total came to a surprising $3 million for the two groups.

The CFO was unsure of the actual cost of the program but was quite convinced that its benefits exceeded the costs. Eager to show the success of the program, he sent a brief report to senior executives, highlighting the success of the program. Because the executive group had never seen monetary values attached to this type of program, their response was extremely favorable.

Estimates Provided

The CFO was uncomfortable with claiming all the results. He consulted with the leadership development team to explore ways to make the results more credible. The team decided to make two adjustments to the data. In a follow-up e-mail, the participating executives were asked to indicate the percentage of the results that were attributable to the program and their confidence in that allocation, using a scale of 0 to 100 percent. The value of each participant's improvement was adjusted by the percentage attributable to the program and by the confidence percentage. After these adjustments, the total value of the improvements reported by the participants was $950,000. The team assembled the total, fully loaded costs of the program to compare against the benefits and then calculated the ROI, which turned out to be an impressive 87 percent. The CFO felt much better about the results and sent a revised summary to the executive group.

The Power of Estimates

The use of estimates can be a powerful process when the estimates are collected properly, analyzed conservatively, and reported cautiously.

Research

A tremendous amount of research has been compiled on the power of estimates through our work at the ROI Institute and through direct involvement in hundreds of studies. The research suggests that estimates are used in addition to more credible techniques such as control groups and trend line analysis. In the vast majority of cases, using estimates is a conservative and credible approach to isolating the effects of a program. Whenever a control group or trend line analysis is used, estimates should also be used. This provides an opportunity to compare the effectiveness of the estimates with that of more credible methods.

A Demonstration

The power of estimates can be validated in many ways; one of the most effective is to have participants take part in an exercise, especially if a group of individuals has questioned the validity of estimates. The exercise should be discussed for a few minutes and then administered. It takes about ten minutes.

First, pick a measurable fact with a value that the participants will not know precisely but will be able to make a reasonable guess at. A typical example is the distance from the meeting room to the nearest airport, assuming that each individual has been to the airport and thus is capable of providing an estimate. The specific route to the airport should be discussed, examining multiple alternatives, so that all the individuals attempt to estimate the mileage for the same route. Have each participant estimate the mileage and then provide a confidence estimate. Collect all the estimates. Using an Excel spreadsheet, calculate the average of the mileage. Now adjust the estimates based on the confidence levels (multiply the estimated mileage by the confidence percentage), and calculate the adjusted average.

Next, use a mapping service (such as Google Maps or MapQuest) to calculate the precise distance from the meeting room to the airport. Then report the results to the participants. In over two hundred iterations of this exercise, the results have been the same. The estimates before adjustments are made overstate the actual mileage, and the estimates after adjustments are made understate the mileage. This exercise demonstrates what must be done with real estimates; confidence levels must be used to adjust the estimate and provide a conservative result. This quick exercise has even been used during presentations of evaluation results to management groups to show them how powerful and credible estimates can be.

Participant Reaction

Based on the use of estimates in thousands of situations, some interesting conclusions have been drawn about the reaction of participants. Some professionals fear that participants may be unwilling or unable to provide the estimates and may become frustrated or irritated or just not participate. That has not been the case. Participants appreciate being recognized as the authority, the most credible source. They will usually participate, often eagerly, and anxiously await the results of the evaluation. This finding dispels concerns about reluctance on the part of participants.

Management Reaction

One of the fears about using estimates is that management may reject the process and, therefore, the results. This, too, has not been the case. Senior managers understand the difficulty of isolating the effects of a program, especially when many factors are involved. They also realize that the other, more credible techniques may not be appropriate in all cases. They appreciate the way in which the data have been collected and the adjustment for error. To some, a presentation that understates the results is a breath of fresh air. Management reaction is often positive, so much so that it can become a detriment. When management reacts favorably to estimates, there may be a tendency not to use the more credible processes. Avoiding the use of more credible methods can be a mistake.

The Wisdom of Crowds

One of the most significant publications focusing on the power of collective input from average people is *The Wisdom of Crowds: Why the Many Are Smarter Than the Few and How Collective Wisdom Shapes Business, Economies, Societies, and Nations* (Surowiecki, 2004). The book begins with a story about British scientist Francis Galton, who, in 1906, left his home in the town of Plymouth and headed for a country fair. He was eighty-five years old. The story explains that Galton had devoted much of his career to measuring characteristics in breeding. His belief was that breeding mattered—that only a few people had the breeding necessary to keep the society healthy. As the story unfolds, Galton finds himself attending a weight-judging competition at which the audience would guess the weight of a fat ox after it had been slaughtered and dressed. Galton's theory of breeding told him that only the experts could make an accurate guess; however, there he stood, observing 800 ordinary people, mostly commoners, purchasing tickets on which they would place their guesses. Each person completed a ticket with his or her name, occupation, address, and estimate.

Galton wanted to prove that the average voter was capable of very little, so he turned his observation into an experiment. When the contest was over and the prizes had been awarded, Galton borrowed the tickets from the organizers and ran a series of statistical tests on them. Galton arranged the guesses (totaling 787—thirteen were discarded because they were illegible) in order from highest to lowest and graphed them to see if they would form a bell curve. Expecting the crowd members to be way off the mark, he added all their estimates, and calculated the mean. In so doing, he proved himself wrong. The crowd had guessed that the slaughtered and dressed ox would weigh 1,197 pounds. In actuality, it weighed 1,198 pounds. "In other words, the crowd's judgment was essentially perfect. The 'experts' were not close."

This simple story presents an example of the power of groups of people—and their estimates. As Surowiecki (2004) explains, what Francis Galton stumbled on that day in Plymouth was this simple but powerful truth: under the right circumstances, groups are remarkably intelligent and are often smarter than the smartest people in them. Groups do not need to be dominated by exceptionally intelligent people to be smart. Even if most of the people within a group are not especially well informed or rational, they can still reach a collectively wise decision.

Key Issues in Using Estimates

In summary, here are a few guidelines for effective use of estimates:

1. Estimates should be used as the technique of last resort for isolating program effects. When more credible methods are not appropriate for the situation, be prepared to use estimates and defend them.

2. Always use the most credible source of data; in many situations, that source is the participants. Be careful about obtaining data from the immediate managers of the participants; they may not be able to isolate the effects of different factors on performance.
3. Collect data in an unbiased way, ensuring that participants feel free to express their true feelings about how the effects of the program and other factors should be reported.
4. Collect data in the most effective way. The focus group process usually works best. When a focus group is not feasible or appropriate, interviews may be a workable option. As a last resort, collect the data by using questionnaires, adding key questions to capture the isolation data.
5. Adjust for error by collecting a confidence estimate (expressed as a percentage) from each participant and multiplying it by the allocation percentage. The confidence level serves as an error discount factor, allowing you to remove the error inherent in the estimation process.
6. Report the data carefully, explaining to management why estimation is being used and that it may not be completely accurate but that the value of the measured improvement has been adjusted in two ways: (1) only a portion of it has been attributed to the program, and (2) it has been adjusted to remove the error introduced through the estimation process.

Final Thoughts

This chapter discusses the use of estimates, perhaps the most unsettling and controversial yet nonetheless powerful technique for isolating the effects of a program. When more credible methods cannot be used, the fallback method is the use of estimates. While they represent the weakest method, estimates can still be accurate and credible if they are collected appropriately and adjusted for error. When estimation becomes commonplace or readily accepted, there is a danger that it will be preferred over more credible techniques, which is not recommended.

References

Phillips, P. P., and Phillips, J. J. *Proving the Value of HR: ROI Case Studies.* Birmingham, Ala.: ROI Institute, 2007.

Surowiecki, J. *The Wisdom of Crowds: Why the Many Are Smarter Than the Few and How Collective Wisdom Shapes Business, Economies, Societies, and Nations.* New York: Doubleday, 2004.

5

Use of Isolation Techniques

This chapter provides summary information and advice about using the different techniques for isolating the effects of programs. The chapter also includes exercises to ensure understanding of the use of the different methods.

Matching Exercise: Isolating the Effects of a Program

Perhaps it would be helpful to review some of the techniques by participating in an exercise.

Instructions

For each of the following situations, please indicate the best method for isolating the effects of the program. Select from these methods:

A. Control group
B. Trend line analysis
C. Forecasting
D. Participant's estimate
E. Use of customer input
F. Expert's estimate

In each box, write the letter that corresponds to the method used.

Situation	Method

1. A manufacturing company has recently implemented a new incentive plan to boost sales for client partners. Just as the plan was implemented, the company increased its promotional budget for each product line. Both the sales incentive plan and the sales promotion have driven an increase in sales. It appears that no other factors have contributed to this increase. Historical data show a mathematical relationship between the promotional budget and sales. This equation has been used to predict the sales increase, based on the increase in the promotional budget. This forecast is compared with actual figures to isolate the impact of the sales incentive program.

2. Absenteeism of bus drivers in a large metropolitan area had been a deteriorating situation for some time. A human resources program that included a no-fault absence policy and a change in the selection process was implemented. After the program was conducted, the rate of absenteeism decreased. No other influences appear to have contributed to the decrease. The pre-program data on absenteeism are very stable, and a trend was projected for the post-program period to compare with the actual figures. The difference between the projection and the actual figure represents the contribution of the project.

3. An agent training program in a real estate firm was designed to increase listings by teaching agents how to improve their presentation skills. Customers are asked to provide their rationale for deciding to list a home with a particular agent. Three months after the training program was completed, listings increased.

Situation	Method

Many factors caused the increase; however, according to customer feedback, one factor was the quality of the presentation made by the agent, which was the basis of the program. This information was used to understand the impact of the agent training program on the actual number of houses listed.

4. One year after an energy company opened a new wellness and fitness center for employees, the company's health care expenditures decreased. Given the amount of the decrease, the staff assembled several experts who could understand why health care costs have changed. These individuals have been asked to explain all the contributing factors and isolate the effects of the wellness and fitness center on that measure. ☐

5. A large automobile company implemented a sales consulting process on a pilot basis. Twelve dealerships were used in the initial pilot program. A comparison group of twelve other dealerships was selected against which to judge performance on several measures: sales volume, economy in the market, the sales versus service mix, incentives provided to sales staff, and the quality rating of the dealership. The difference between the two groups shows the impact of the sales consulting. ☐

6. In a leadership development program for a biotech company, the participating managers were asked to provide details on the impact of their use of leadership skills, using actual data from their work unit. As part of the exercise, the participants estimated the percentage of improvement that was directly related to the leadership development program. ☐

Responses

1. C. The mathematical relationship between sales, the program measure, and another factor, the promotional budget, makes forecasting possible.
2. B. The trend line of the rate of absenteeism can be projected on the basis of the pre-program data.
3. E. Customers can recognize a presentation's effectiveness, which stems directly from the training program.
4. F. Experts may be able to figure out what factors they think contributed to the improvement, although it would be a rare feat for outsiders to accomplish this.
5. A. This is a classic control group arrangement, the most effective method of isolating program effects.
6. D. Participants estimate the improvement generated by the program. Participant estimation will be the dominant method in many evaluations.

Case Study: National Computer Company

This case study shows how different methods for isolating program effects evolve as more credible methods are pursued or considered.

National Computer Company (NCC) sells computers to businesses and consumers. To ensure that customer service and support were sufficient, NCC established customer care centers in six geographic regions. All of the care centers were similar in size and employee characteristics. In recent years, NCC care centers had experienced a high employee turnover rate. To reduce turnover, a new program was developed to help managers improve employee engagement, appreciate employee concerns and differences, and communicate with employees effectively. NCC decided to implement this new program in one customer care center and compare the results with others.

Figure 5.1. Turnover Trend at the National Computer Company

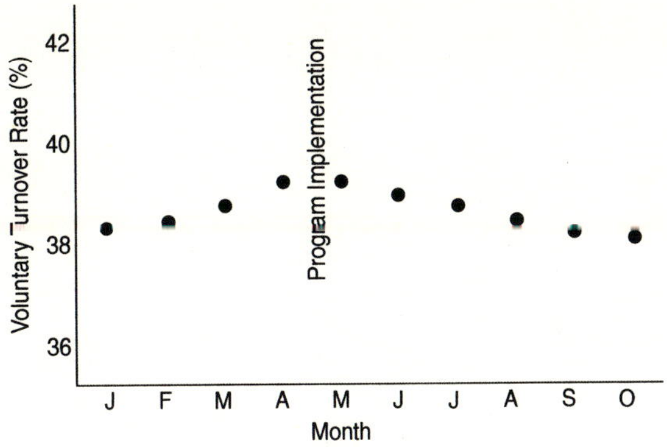

[Scatter plot showing Voluntary Turnover Rate (%) on the y-axis (ranging from 36 to 42) versus Month (J, F, M, A, M, J, J, A, S, O) on the x-axis. A vertical label between April and May indicates "Program Implementation". Data points hover around 38–39%.]

The NCC program staff decided that, for a variety of reasons, the customer care centers did not match appropriately. As a result, the control group arrangement for isolating program effects would not work. Therefore, projecting a data trend was considered. Figure 5.1 shows the trend of the annual turnover rate (reported monthly) during the four months before the program and the six months after the program.

In considering the impact of the new program on employee turnover, the staff identified an additional factor that was driving improvement. This factor was the change in the unemployment rate. In the area of the customer care center where the program was implemented, the unemployment rate increased from 5 percent to 6 percent. Figure 5.2 shows the relationship between the unemployment rate and the voluntary turnover rate. The mathematical relationship is $y = 50 - 3x$, where x is the unemployment rate and y is the voluntary turnover rate. As the unemployment rate increased from 5 percent to 6 percent, the turnover rate went down. The mathematical relationship between the unemployment rate and the turnover rate can be used to estimate how much of the reduced turnover was caused by the increased unemployment rate, not the program. When no other factors are involved other

Figure 5.2. Relationship Between Unemployment and Voluntary Turnover

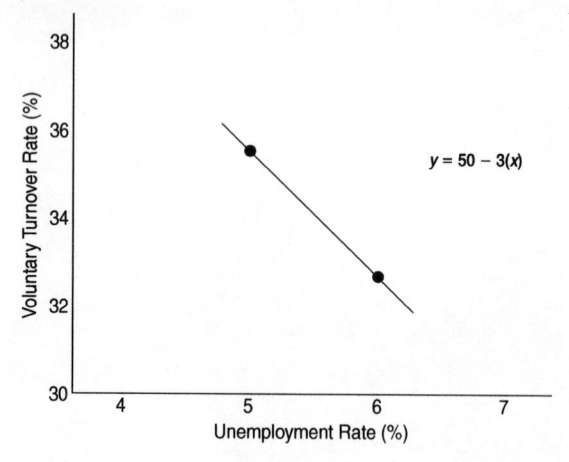

```
Voluntary Turnover Rate (%)
38
36                    •
                              y = 50 – 3(x)
34
                          •
32
30
   4       5       6       7
      Unemployment Rate (%)
```

than the program, the improvement in turnover rate not allocated to increased unemployment is attributed to the program

However, after further examination, it was determined that not only was the unemployment rate increasing, resulting in lower turnover, but that other key factors were contributing to the turnover. First, the customer care management team placed emphasis on this issue, working diligently with employees and team leaders to make the organization a more attractive place to work, to understand the problems that might lead to an employee's departure, and to avoid turnover, if possible. This emphasis on reducing turnover had had an impact on the turnover rate. In addition, one of NCC's competitors in the local market that had often recruited employees from NCC customer care was experiencing a downturn and laying off employees. This development had minimized opportunities at the competitor company, stopped the recruiting, and contributed to the reduction in turnover. In essence, turnover was reduced by three factors in addition to the program designed to improve the skills and capabilities of the management team. As a result, a decision was made to use estimates from team leaders as a

Table 5.1. One Team Leader's View of Factors Contributing to Turnover

Contributing Factors	Impact on Results	Confidence Level
Program	30%	80%
Unemployment rate	50%	100%
Management emphasis	5%	70%
Competition	15%	90%

technique for isolating the effects of the program. Table 5.1 shows an example of one team leader's evaluation of the four factors that affected turnover at NCC.

Why Isolation Is a Key Issue

Isolating the effects of a program on business impact data is one of the most challenging steps in the ROI Methodology, yet it is essential. When addressed credibly, this step links learning directly to business impact.

Other Factors Are Always There

In almost every situation, multiple factors create business results. The world does not just stand still while programs are implemented. Many functions in an organization may be attempting to improve the same metrics. A situation in which no other factors enter into the process is almost impossible.

Without It, There Is No Business Link: Evidence Versus Proof

Without taking steps to show the contribution, there is no business linkage—only evidence that the program could have made a difference. Results have improved; however, other factors may have influenced the data. The proof that the program has made a difference on the business measure comes from this step in the process—isolating the effects of the program.

Other Factors and Influences Have Protective Owners

The owners of the other processes that influence results are convinced that their processes made the difference. For example, employees in marketing, technology, and quality functions are convinced that improvements are entirely due to their efforts. They present a compelling case to management, stressing their achievements. In real situations, other processes, such as performance improvement, reward systems, and job redesign, also have protective owners, and they often are convinced and are prepared to convince others that they made the difference.

To Do It Right Is Not Easy

The challenge of isolating the effects of a program on impact data is critical and can be achieved, but it is not an easy process for complex programs, especially when strong-willed owners of other processes are involved. Determination is needed to address this situation every time an ROI evaluation is conducted. Fortunately, a variety of approaches are available, as has been shown in this book.

Without It, the Study Is Not Valid

A study is not valid unless it addresses the issue of isolation of program effects, because other factors are almost always in the mix, so a direct connection to the program is not apparent. In any study, three things should never be done by an evaluator:

1. Taking all the credit for the improvement without addressing the issue of isolating the program's effects

2. Doing nothing, attempting to ignore the critical issue of isolation
3. Admitting that he or she does not have the knowledge to address the issue of how to isolate the program's effects

Doing any of these things will lower the credibility of the case for the program's connection to business improvement.

Isolation Myths

Several myths about isolating the effects of a program often create concerns, confusion, and frustration with the process. Some researchers, professionals, and consultants inflame the situation by suggesting that isolating program effects is not necessary. Here are the most common myths:

1. *Most programs are complementary with other processes; therefore, an attempt to isolate the effects of a program should not be made.* New initiatives complement other factors, all of which drive results. However, if the sponsor of a program needs to understand the relative contribution of that program, this issue must be tackled. If accomplished properly, it will show how all the complementary factors work together to drive the improvements.
2. *Other functions in the organization do not isolate the effects of their programs, so we don't need to either.* While managers in some functions avoid this issue and try to make a convincing case that all improvement is related to their own processes, others are effectively addressing the issue of demonstrating that their programs produce tangible results. Using a credible approach to address this issue is necessary if the linkage to results is to be perceived as likely. Many organizations ask customers to complete

a customer survey after they make a purchase or open a new account. These organizations usually ask customers why they made their purchases. The organizations are trying to isolate the effects of multiple variables that influence why customers make purchases.

3. *If a control group analysis cannot be used, then no attempt to isolate the effects of the program should be made.* Although a control group analysis is the most credible approach, it will not be feasible in the majority of situations. As a result, other methods must be used to isolate program effects. The problem does not go away just because a desired or favorite technique cannot be used. The challenge is to find other processes that are effective and that will work anytime, even if they are not as credible as the control group method.

4. *The stakeholders will understand the link; therefore, an attempt to isolate the effects of a program on impact measures is not necessary.* Unfortunately, stakeholders see and understand what is presented to them. Absence of information makes understanding the link difficult for them, especially when others are claiming full credit for the improvement.

5. *Estimates of improvement provide no value.* Although the use of estimates is a choice of last resort for isolating program effects, it can provide value and be a credible process, particularly when the estimates are adjusted for error. Using estimates from the individuals who best understand the process is certainly better than not isolating program effects at all. Estimates are used routinely to isolate the effects of programs in many organizations.

6. *If we ignore the issue of isolating program effects, maybe management won't think about it.* Unfortunately, audiences are becoming more sophisticated on this issue, and they are aware of multiple influences. If no attempt is made to isolate the effects of a program, the audience will assume that the other factors have

had a tremendous effect—perhaps, all the effect. As a result, the credibility of the program will deteriorate.

These myths underscore the importance of tackling the issue of isolating program effects. All of this is not to suggest that a specific program is not implemented in harmony with other processes. All groups should work as a team to produce the desired results. However, when funding is provided to different functions in the organization—with different process owners—there is always a struggle to show and, sometimes even to understand, the connection between the programs of each function and the results. If the issue is not addressed by the program team, others will address it, leaving the program owners with less-than-desired budgets, resources, and respect.

Build Credibility with the Isolation Process

Several items must be addressed in regard to credibility. This step—isolation of program effects—is the most significant credibility issue in the ROI Methodology.

Selecting the Technique

Table 5.2 shows the frequency with which isolation techniques are used by over two hundred organizations that have been applying the ROI Methodology for five years or more. The table shows a high percentage for control group analysis; the use of this method in all impact studies would be lower. After all, the organizations represented in Table 5.2 are the best-practice organizations, and they have worked diligently to use the most credible analyses. "Other" encompasses a variety of techniques that are less likely to be used.

Table 5.2. Use of Techniques for Isolating Program Effects in Best-Practice Organizations

Technique[1]	Frequency of Use[2]
Control group analysis	35%
Trend line analysis or forecasting	20%
Expert estimation	50%
Other	20%

[1]Techniques are listed in order of credibility.
[2]Percentages exceed 100% because some organizations use more than one technique.

With several techniques available to isolate the impact of a program, selecting the most appropriate method (or methods) for a specific program can be difficult. Estimates are simple and inexpensive, while other techniques are more time-consuming and costly. When selecting an isolation technique, consider these factors:

- Feasibility of the technique
- Accuracy provided by the technique, compared to the accuracy needed
- Credibility of the technique with the target audience
- Cost of implementing the technique
- Amount of disruption of normal work activities that will result from implementation of the technique
- Participant, staff, and management time needed to implement the technique

Using Multiple Methods

Multiple isolation techniques or sources of data input should be considered, because two sources are usually better than one. When multiple sources are used, it is recommended that a conservative method be used to combine the inputs—for example, using the results that are least favorable to the program. A conservative approach builds acceptance and credibility. The target audience should always be provided with explanations of the process and the various subjective factors involved. Multiple sources allow an organization to experiment with different methods and build confidence with a particular technique. For example, if management is concerned about the accuracy of the participants' estimates, a combination of a control group arrangement and participants' estimates could be used to check the accuracy of the estimation process.

Building Credibility

It is not unusual for the ROI for a program to be extremely large. Even when a portion of the improvement is allocated to other factors, in many situations the numbers are still impressive. The audience should understand that although every effort was made to isolate the program's impact, it is still a figure that may not be precise and may contain error. It represents the best estimate of the program's impact, given the constraints, conditions, and resources available.

One way to strengthen the credibility of the ROI is to consider the different factors that influence the credibility of data. Exhibit 5.1 lists factors that typically influence the credibility of data

---

Exhibit 5.1. Issues That Affect the Credibility of Data

- Reputation of the source of the data
- Motives of the researchers
- Personal bias of audience
- Methodology of the study
- Assumptions made in the analysis
- Realism of the outcome data
- Type of data
- Scope of analysis

---

presented to a particular group. The issue of isolating the effects of a program is influenced by several of these credibility factors. First, the reputation of the source of the data is critical. The most knowledgeable expert must provide input and be involved in the analysis. The motives of the researchers can also be a critical issue. For example, to increase credibility, a third party should facilitate any focus group that is completed and the data must be collected in an objective way. The personal biases of the audience members can make a difference, and steps should be taken to alleviate concerns that might arise from known biases in the audience. Also, the assumptions made in the analysis and in the methodology of the study should be clearly defined so that the audience will understand the steps that were taken to increase credibility. The type of data may affect how credible it is perceived to be. Managers prefer to deal with hard data that can be linked to the direct output of a program. Finally, by isolating the effects of only one program, the scope of analysis is kept narrow, enhancing credibility.

Final Thoughts

This chapter reviews the variety of methods that can be used to isolate the effects of programs. These techniques represent the most effective ways to address this issue and are used by some of the most progressive organizations. Too often, results are reported and linked to a program without any attempt to isolate the portion of the results that can be attributed to the program. This chapter also discusses issues pertaining to the necessity of performing this step and how to maximize the credibility of the analysis.

Index

A
Advertising–daily sale relationship forecast, 51–53
Alliger, G. M., 9
Armstrong, J., 53

B
Basic control group design, 17–18
Brinkerhoff, R. O., 6

C
Case studies
  Crack Box, Inc., 87–89
  Federal Information Agency (FIA), 34–36
  First Bank, 2–5
  Global Financial Services, Inc. (GFS), 85–87
  Healthcare, Inc. (HI), 54–57
  International Software Company, 41–43
  Micro Electronics, 53–54
  Midwest Electric, Inc., 36–40
  Multi-National, Inc., 90–92
  National Bank, 76–80
  National Book Company, 57–59
  National Computer Company (NCC), 102–105
  Public Bank of Malaysia, 89–90
  Retail Merchandise Company (RMC), 31–34

Chain of impact, 7, 8–10
Contaminated control groups, 25–26
Control group design
  basic, 17–18
  deciding which design to select, 21
  ideal experimental, 18–20
  posttest-only, 20–21
  threats to validity of, 15–17
Control group issues
  ethical considerations, 23–24
  feasibility as, 29–31
  FSI case example of potential problems, 24–29
  practicality as, 22–23
  viability as, 22
Control groups
  designing, 15–21
  Federal Information Agency (FIA) example of, 34–36
  frequency of use for isolating effects, 109–110
  International Software Company (ISC) example of, 41–43
  as isolating program effects technique, 6, 7–8
  isolation myth regarding use of, 108
  issues when considering, 22–31
  Midwest Electric, Inc. example of, 36–40

113

Control groups (*Continued*)
　National Computer Company
　　(NCC) example of, 102–103
　Retail Merchandise Company
　　(RMC) example of, 31–34
　See also Participants
Crack Box, Inc. case study, 87–89
Customer expert estimates, 6, 83,
　94–95

D
Data
　building credibility regarding,
　　111–114
　control groups, 6, 7–8, 15–44
　expert estimates, 6, 61–97
　forecast method for, 6, 50–53
　issues that affect credibility of, 114
　trend line analysis, 6, 45, 46–50,
　　53–59
Dou, Z., 15
Dressler, D., 6

E
Ethical control group issue, 23–24
Expert estimates
　Crack Box, Inc. example of, 87–89
　of customers, 6, 83
　demonstrating power of, 92–93
　of focus groups, 63–66, 94–95
　frequency of use for isolating
　　effects, 110
　Global Financial Services, Inc.
　　(GFS) example of, 85–87
　of immediate managers, 80–82, 94
　isolating program effects using, 6,
　　61–62, 84
　key issues in using, 95–96
　Multi-National, Inc. example of,
　　90–92
　National Computer Company
　　(NCC) example of, 104–105
　of participants, 62–80, 93–94
　Public Bank of Malaysia example
　　of, 89–90

　research on power of, 92
　of senior management, 82–83, 94

F
Feasibility control group issue,
　29–31
Federal Information Agency (FIA)
　case study, 34–36
Financial Services, Inc. (FSI),
　24–26
First Bank case study, 2–5
Focus groups
　participant estimates from, 63–64
　steps for most credible estimates
　　from, 64–66
　validity of estimates by, 94–95
　See also Participants
Forecast method
　advertising–daily sales
　　relationship example of, 51–52
　described, 45–46
　disadvantages of, 52–53
　frequency of use for isolating
　　effects, 110
　isolating program effects using, 6
　linear model of, 50
　National Computer Company
　　(NCC) example of, 102–105

G
Glaton, F., 94–95
Global Financial Services, Inc.
　(GFS) case study, 85–87

H
Healthcare, Inc. (HI) case study,
　54–57
Hotel staff turnover trend line
　analysis, 48–49

I
Ideal experimental control group
　design, 18–20
Immediate manager estimates,
　80–82, 94

Impact of other factors, 10–12, 84–85
Improvement
 First Bank case study identifying reasons for, 2–5
 identifying other factors contributing to, 10–12
 isolating program effects to identify reasons for, 1–12
 isolation myth regarding, 108
International Software Company (ISC) case study, 41–43
Interviews, 74
Isolating program effects
 building credibility regarding, 109–112
 First Bank case study showing importance of, 2–5
 matching exercise for, 99–102
 myths related to, 107–109
 preliminary issues in, 5–12
 recognizing importance of, 1, 105–107
 required to understand program's impact, 2
 See also Programs
Isolating program effects issues
 identifying chain of impact, 8–10
 identifying factors other than program, 10–12, 84–85
 need to isolate program effects, 6–8
Isolating program effects techniques
 control groups, 6, 7–8, 15–44, 102–103, 108, 110
 expert estimates, 6, 61–97, 104–105, 108
 forecast method, 6, 50–53, 110
 frequency of use of specific, 110
 listed, 6
 National Computer Company (NCC) case study on different, 102–105
 using multiple, 110–111
 selecting the right, 109–110
 trend line analysis, 6, 45, 46–50, 53–59, 103, 112

J
Janak, E. A., 9

K
Kaufman, R., 10
Keuler, D., 22

L
Lee, N., 15

M
Management
 expert estimates from immediate, 80–82, 94
 expert estimates from senior, 82–83, 94
 isolation myth regarding, 108–109
Matching exercise, 99–102
Micro Electronics case study, 53–54
Midwest Electric, Inc., case study, 36–40
Mortality of participants, 16
Multi-National, Inc., case study, 90–92

N
National Bank case study, 76–80
National Book Company case study, 57–59
National Computer Company (NCC) case study
 using control group, 103
 using expert estimates, 104–105
 using mathematical forecasting, 103–104
 using trend line analysis, 103

O
Other factors impact, 10–12, 84–85

P

Participants
  advantages/disadvantages of estimates from, 75–76
  expert estimates from, 62–80, 93–94
  interviews to obtain estimates from, 74
  mortality of, 16
  National Bank case study on estimates from, 76–80
  questionnaires to obtain estimates from, 68–74
  testing effects on, 16
  See also Control groups; Focus groups
Phillips, J. J., 22, 34, 36, 40, 57, 89
Phillips, P. P., 22, 34, 36, 40, 57, 89
Posttest-only control group design, 20–21
Practicality issue, 22–23
Preskill, H., 6
Programs
  identifying chain of impact, 7, 8–10
  identifying contribution of, 7
  impact of factors other than, 10–12, 84–85
  isolating program effects for understanding impact of, 2
  See also Isolating program effects
Proving the Value of HR: ROI Case Studies (Phillips and Phillips), 34, 36, 40, 57, 89
Public Bank of Malaysia case study, 89–90

Q

Questionnaires
  examples of questions used in, 69–70
  Guiding Principles used to create, 72–73
  participant estimates using, 68–74
  sample of input from, 71

R

Retail Merchandise Company (RMC) case study, 31–34
ROI Guiding Principles
  for immediate managers' estimates, 81
  for participant estimate questionnaire, 72–73
ROI Methodology
  Guiding Principles of, 72–73, 81
  isolation as credibility issue in, 109–112
  isolation as key issue for, 105–107
Russ-Eft, D., 6

S

Sale revenue trend line analysis, 47–48
Salkind, N., 48
Senior management estimates, 82–83, 94
Sexual harassment trend line analysis, 54–57
Shipment productivity trend line analysis, 57–59
Stakeholder isolation myth, 108
Surowiecki, J., 94, 95

T

Testing effects, 16
Time issue, 16
Trend line analysis
  conditions required for, 46, 49
  described, 45–46
  frequency of use for isolating effects, 110
  guidelines for working with, 49–50
  Healthcare, Inc. (HI) example of, 54–57

hotel staff turnover example of, 48–49
isolating program effects using, 6
Micro Electronics example of, 53–54
National Book Company example of, 57–59
National Computer Company (NCC) example of, 103–104
sale revenue example of, 47–48
True experimental control group design, 18

V
Validity
isolating program effects for study, 109
threats to control group, 15–17
Verizon Communications, 22
Viability issue, 22

W
Wang, G., 15
The Wisdom of Crowds: (Surowiecki), 94

About the Authors

Jack J. Phillips, Ph.D., a world-renowned expert on accountability, measurement, and evaluation, provides consulting services for Fortune 500 companies and major global organizations. The author or editor of more than fifty books, Phillips conducts workshops and makes conference presentations throughout the world.

His expertise in measurement and evaluation is based on more than twenty-seven years of corporate experience in the aerospace, textile, metals, construction materials, and banking industries. Phillips has served as training and development manager at two Fortune 500 firms, as senior human resources officer at two firms, as president of a regional bank, and as management professor at a major state university. This background led Phillips to develop the ROI Methodology, a revolutionary process that provides bottom-line figures and accountability for all types of learning, performance improvement, human resources, technology, and public policy programs.

Phillips regularly consults with clients in manufacturing, service, and government organizations in forty-four countries in North and South America, Europe, Africa, Australia, and Asia.

Books most recently authored by Phillips include *Show Me the Money: How to Determine ROI in People, Projects, and Programs* (Berrett-Koehler, 2007); *The Value of Learning* (Pfeiffer,

2007); *How to Build a Successful Consulting Practice* (McGraw-Hill, 2006); *Investing in Your Company's Human Capital: Strategies to Avoid Spending Too Much or Too Little* (Amacom, 2005); *Proving the Value of HR: How and Why to Measure ROI* (Society for Human Resource Management, 2005); *The Leadership Scorecard* (Butterworth-Heinemann, 2004); *Managing Employee Retention* (Butterworth-Heinemann, 2003); *Return on Investment in Training and Performance Improvement Programs*, 2nd edition (Butterworth-Heinemann, 2003); *The Project Management Scorecard* (Butterworth-Heinemann, 2002); *How to Measure Training Results* (McGraw-Hill, 2002); *The Human Resources Scorecard: Measuring the Return on Investment* (Butterworth-Heinemann, 2001); *The Consultant's Scorecard* (McGraw-Hill, 2000); and *Performance Analysis and Consulting* (ASTD, 2000). Phillips served as series editor for the In Action casebook series of the American Society for Training and Development (ASTD), an ambitious publishing project featuring thirty titles. He currently serves as series editor for Butterworth-Heinemann's Improving Human Performance series and for Pfeiffer's new Measurement and Evaluation series.

Phillips has received several awards for his books and his work. The Society for Human Resource Management presented him with an award for one of his books and honored a Phillips ROI study with its highest award for creativity. ASTD gave him its highest award, Distinguished Contribution to Workplace Learning and Development. *Meeting News* named Phillips one of the twenty-five most influential people in the meetings and events industry, based on his work on ROI within the industry.

Phillips holds undergraduate degrees in electrical engineering, physics, and mathematics; a master's degree in decision sciences from Georgia State University; and a Ph.D. degree in human resources management from the University of Alabama.

Jack Phillips has served on the boards of several private businesses—including two NASDAQ companies—and several associations, including ASTD, and nonprofit organizations. He is

chairman of the ROI Institute, Inc., and can be reached at (205) 678-8101, or by e-mail at jack@roiinstitute.net.

Bruce C. Aaron, Ph.D., is responsible for research and evaluation of learning and knowledge management initiatives within Accenture, a global management consulting, technology services, and outsourcing company. During his tenure, Accenture Education has received several awards from professional associations for excellence in measurement and evaluation, including the 2004 ASTD ROI Impact Study of the Year award.

Bruce joined Accenture in 1998 after several years as a public sector evaluation consultant for district and state educational agencies in Florida. He has presented to a wide range of professional audiences for organizations such as the International Society for Performance Improvement (ISPI), ASTD, SALT, American Educational Research Association (AERA), and the Psychometric Society on topics in statistics, measurement, evaluation, instructional technology, and group decision-making systems.

Bruce has authored and coauthored dozens of papers, presentations, articles, and books. He has recently coauthored *Return on Learning, Part 4: Maximizing the Business Impact of Enterprise Learning* (Accenture, 2007), *Handbook of Research on Electronic Surveys and Measurements* (IGI Publishing, 2007), and a chapter in *Instructional Design in the Real World: A View from the Trenches* (Information Science Publishing, 2004).

Bruce has served on the advisory committee for the ASTD ROI Network, and is a certified professional in learning and performance (CPLP). He received his M.A. degree in school psychology and his Ph.D. degree in educational measurement and evaluation from the University of South Florida.

Pfeiffer Publications Guide

This guide is designed to familiarize you with the various types of Pfeiffer publications. The formats section describes the various types of products that we publish; the methodologies section describes the many different ways that content might be provided within a product. We also provide a list of the topic areas in which we publish.

FORMATS

In addition to its extensive book-publishing program, Pfeiffer offers content in an array of formats, from fieldbooks for the practitioner to complete, ready-to-use training packages that support group learning.

FIELDBOOK Designed to provide information and guidance to practitioners in the midst of action. Most fieldbooks are companions to another, sometimes earlier, work, from which its ideas are derived; the fieldbook makes practical what was theoretical in the original text. Fieldbooks can certainly be read from cover to cover. More likely, though, you'll find yourself bouncing around following a particular theme, or dipping in as the mood, and the situation, dictate.

HANDBOOK A contributed volume of work on a single topic, comprising an eclectic mix of ideas, case studies, and best practices sourced by practitioners and experts in the field.

An editor or team of editors usually is appointed to seek out contributors and to evaluate content for relevance to the topic. Think of a handbook not as a ready-to-eat meal, but as a cookbook of ingredients that enables you to create the most fitting experience for the occasion.

RESOURCE Materials designed to support group learning. They come in many forms: a complete, ready-to-use exercise (such as a game); a comprehensive resource on one topic (such as conflict management) containing a variety of methods and approaches; or a collection of like-minded activities (such as icebreakers) on multiple subjects and situations.

TRAINING PACKAGE An entire, ready-to-use learning program that focuses on a particular topic or skill. All packages comprise a guide for the facilitator/trainer and a workbook for the participants. Some packages are supported with additional media—such as video—or learning aids, instruments, or other devices to help participants understand concepts or practice and develop skills.

- *Facilitator/trainer's guide* Contains an introduction to the program, advice on how to organize and facilitate the learning event, and step-by-step instructor notes. The guide also contains copies of presentation materials—handouts, presentations, and overhead designs, for example—used in the program.

- *Participant's workbook* Contains exercises and reading materials that support the learning goal and serves as a valuable reference and support guide for participants in the weeks and months that follow the learning event. Typically, each participant will require his or her own workbook.

ELECTRONIC CD-ROMs and web-based products transform static Pfeiffer content into dynamic, interactive experiences. Designed to take advantage of the searchability, automation, and ease-of-use that technology provides, our e-products bring convenience and immediate accessibility to your workspace.

METHODOLOGIES

CASE STUDY A presentation, in narrative form, of an actual event that has occurred inside an organization. Case studies are not prescriptive, nor are they used to prove a point; they are designed to develop critical analysis and decision-making skills. A case study has a specific time frame, specifies a sequence of events, is narrative in structure, and contains a plot structure—an issue (what should be/have been done?). Use case studies when the goal is to enable participants to apply previously learned theories to the circumstances in the case, decide what is pertinent, identify the real issues, decide what should have been done, and develop a plan of action.

ENERGIZER A short activity that develops readiness for the next session or learning event. Energizers are most commonly used after a break or lunch to

stimulate or refocus the group. Many involve some form of physical activity, so they are a useful way to counter post-lunch lethargy. Other uses include transitioning from one topic to another, where "mental" distancing is important.

EXPERIENTIAL LEARNING ACTIVITY (ELA) A facilitator-led intervention that moves participants through the learning cycle from experience to application (also known as a Structured Experience). ELAs are carefully thought-out designs in which there is a definite learning purpose and intended outcome. Each step—everything that participants do during the activity—facilitates the accomplishment of the stated goal. Each ELA includes complete instructions for facilitating the intervention and a clear statement of goals, suggested group size and timing, materials required, an explanation of the process, and, where appropriate, possible variations to the activity. (For more detail on Experiential Learning Activities, see the Introduction to the *Reference Guide to Handbooks and Annuals*, 1999 edition, Pfeiffer, San Francisco.)

GAME A group activity that has the purpose of fostering team spirit and togetherness in addition to the achievement of a pre-stated goal. Usually contrived—undertaking a desert expedition, for example—this type of learning method offers an engaging means for participants to demonstrate and practice business and interpersonal skills. Games are effective for team building and personal development mainly because the goal is subordinate to the process—the means through which participants reach decisions, collaborate, communicate, and generate trust and understanding. Games often engage teams in "friendly" competition.

ICEBREAKER A (usually) short activity designed to help participants overcome initial anxiety in a training session and/or to acquaint the participants with one another. An icebreaker can be a fun activity or can be tied to specific topics or training goals. While a useful tool in itself, the icebreaker comes into its own in situations where tension or resistance exists within a group.

INSTRUMENT A device used to assess, appraise, evaluate, describe, classify, and summarize various aspects of human behavior. The term used to describe an instrument depends primarily on its format and purpose. These terms include survey, questionnaire, inventory, diagnostic, survey, and poll. Some uses of instruments include providing instrumental feedback to group

members, studying here-and-now processes or functioning within a group, manipulating group composition, and evaluating outcomes of training and other interventions.

Instruments are popular in the training and HR field because, in general, more growth can occur if an individual is provided with a method for focusing specifically on his or her own behavior. Instruments also are used to obtain information that will serve as a basis for change and to assist in workforce planning efforts.

Paper-and-pencil tests still dominate the instrument landscape with a typical package comprising a facilitator's guide, which offers advice on administering the instrument and interpreting the collected data, and an initial set of instruments. Additional instruments are available separately. Pfeiffer, though, is investing heavily in e-instruments. Electronic instrumentation provides effortless distribution and, for larger groups particularly, offers advantages over paper-and-pencil tests in the time it takes to analyze data and provide feedback.

LECTURETTE A short talk that provides an explanation of a principle, model, or process that is pertinent to the participants' current learning needs. A lecturette is intended to establish a common language bond between the trainer and the participants by providing a mutual frame of reference. Use a lecturette as an introduction to a group activity or event, as an interjection during an event, or as a handout.

MODEL A graphic depiction of a system or process and the relationship among its elements. Models provide a frame of reference and something more tangible, and more easily remembered, than a verbal explanation. They also give participants something to "go on," enabling them to track their own progress as they experience the dynamics, processes, and relationships being depicted in the model.

ROLE PLAY A technique in which people assume a role in a situation/scenario: a customer service rep in an angry-customer exchange, for example. The way in which the role is approached is then discussed and feedback is offered. The role play is often repeated using a different approach and/or incorporating changes made based on feedback received. In other words, role playing is a spontaneous interaction involving realistic behavior under artificial (and safe) conditions.

SIMULATION A methodology for understanding the interrelationships among components of a system or process. Simulations differ from games in that they test or use a model that depicts or mirrors some aspect of reality in form, if not necessarily in content. Learning occurs by studying the effects of change on one or more factors of the model. Simulations are commonly used to test hypotheses about what happens in a system—often referred to as "what if?" analysis—or to examine best-case/worst-case scenarios.

THEORY A presentation of an idea from a conjectural perspective. Theories are useful because they encourage us to examine behavior and phenomena through a different lens.

TOPICS

The twin goals of providing effective and practical solutions for workforce training and organization development and meeting the educational needs of training and human resource professionals shape Pfeiffer's publishing program. Core topics include the following:

Leadership & Management

Communication & Presentation

Coaching & Mentoring

Training & Development

E-Learning

Teams & Collaboration

OD & Strategic Planning

Human Resources

Consulting

What will you find on pfeiffer.com?

- The best in workplace performance solutions for training and HR professionals
- Downloadable training tools, exercises, and content
- Web-exclusive offers
- Training tips, articles, and news
- Seamless on-line ordering
- Author guidelines, information on becoming a Pfeiffer Affiliate, and much more

Discover more at www.pfeiffer.com

Measurement and Evaluation Series

Series Editors
Patricia Pulliam Phillips, Ph.D., and Jack J. Phillips, Ph.D.

A six-book set that provides a step-by-step system for planning, measuring, calculating, and communicating evaluation and Return-on-Investment for training and development, featuring:

- Detailed templates
- Complete plans
- Ready-to-use tools
- Real-world case examples

The M&E Series features:

1. *ROI Fundamentals: Why and When to Measure ROI*
   (978-0-7879-8716-9)
2. *Data Collection: Planning For and Collecting All Types of Data*
   (978-0-7879-8718-3)
3. *Isolation of Results: Defining the Impact of the Program*
   (978-0-7879-8719-0)
4. *Data Conversion: Calculating the Monetary Benefits*
   (978-0-7879-8720-6)
5. *Costs and ROI: Evaluating at the Ultimate Level*
   (978-0-7879-8721-3)
6. *Communication and Implementation: Sustaining the Practice*
   (978-0-7879-8722-0)

Plus, the *ROI in Action Casebook* (978-0-7879-8717-6) covers all the major workplace learning and performance applications, including Leadership Development, Sales Training, Performance Improvement, Technical Skills Training, Information Technology Training, Orientation and OJT, and Supervisor Training.

The **ROI Methodology** is a comprehensive measurement and evaluation process that collects six types of measures: Reaction, Satisfaction, and Planned Action; Learning; Application and Implementation; Business Impact; Return on Investment; and Intangible Measures. The process provides a step-by-step system for evaluation and planning, data collection, data analysis, and reporting. It is appropriate for the measurement and evaluation of *all* kinds of performance improvement programs and activities, including training and development, learning, human resources, coaching, meetings and events, consulting, and project management.

Special Offer from the ROI Institute

Send for your own ROI Process Model, an indispensable tool for implementing and presenting ROI in your organization. The ROI Institute is offering an exclusive gift to readers of The Measurement and Evaluation Series. This 11"×25" multicolor foldout shows the ROI Methodology flow model and the key issues surrounding the implementation of the ROI Methodology. This easy-to-understand overview of the ROI Methodology has proven invaluable to countless professionals when implementing the ROI Methodology. Please return this page or e-mail your information to the address below to receive your free foldout (a $6.00 value). Please check your area(s) of interest in ROI.

Please send me the ROI Process Model described in the book. I am interested in learning more about the following ROI materials and services:

- ☐ Workshops and briefing on ROI
- ☐ Books and support materials on ROI
- ☐ Certification in the ROI Methodology
- ☐ ROI software
- ☐ ROI consulting services
- ☐ ROI Network information
- ☐ ROI benchmarking
- ☐ ROI research

Name _____
Title _____
Organization _____
Address _____
Phone _____
E-mail Address _____

Functional area of interest:

- ☐ Learning and Development/Performance Improvement
- ☐ Human Resources/Human Capital
- ☐ Public Relations/Community Affairs/Government Relations
- ☐ Consulting
- ☐ Sales/Marketing
- ☐ Technology/IT Systems
- ☐ Project Management Solutions
- ☐ Quality/Six Sigma
- ☐ Operations/Methods/Engineering
- ☐ Research and Development/Innovations
- ☐ Finance/Compliance
- ☐ Logistics/Distribution/Supply Chain
- ☐ Public Policy Initiatives
- ☐ Social Programs
- ☐ Other (Please Specify) _____

Organizational Level

- ☐ executive   ☐ management   ☐ consultant   ☐ specialist
- ☐ student   ☐ evaluator   ☐ researcher

Return this form or contact   The ROI Institute
P.O. Box 380637
Birmingham, AL 35238-0637

Or e-mail information to info@roiinstitute.net
Please allow four to six weeks for delivery.

About This Book

Why This Book Is Important

This fourth book in the M&E Series explains a critical step of the ROI Methodology: converting impact data to monetary values. After isolating the effects of a program, the only way to understand the true impact of a program is to determine the monetary value of the business impact. This book examines the different techniques for translating data into monetary terms.

Although executives want to see the monetary value of programs, other benefits occur that we often choose not to convert to monetary values; these are intangible benefits. This book explains intangible measures and why they are important. These intangible benefits are often as important to some organizations as monetary benefits.

What This Book Achieves

This book shows how to convert impact data to monetary values by means of the following techniques:

- Using standard values
- Calculating the value
- Consulting sources in order to find the value
- Estimating the value

The book also explains how to select the appropriate technique for any situation and any level of evaluation.

How This Book Is Organized

This book introduces and describes the techniques that can be used to convert data to monetary values and ends by discussing the methods that are best for each situation. It begins with a brief introduction to the ROI process model and the Twelve Guiding Principles of the ROI Methodology. Chapter One discusses why data conversion is important. Converting data to monetary values helps executives see the value of programs and projects in terms that they understand. The first chapter also examines the different kinds of data and the steps that must be taken to convert each type to a monetary value.

The remainder of the book explains the techniques that can be used to convert data to monetary values. Chapter Two details the use of standard values that have been developed by others who measured the same items. This is the most credible technique for data conversion. This chapter explains why standard values have been developed and provides some examples of standard values. Chapter Three discusses the many ways in which monetary values can be calculated—for example, by using historical costs or by linking the data with other measures.

Chapter Four describes how to locate sources of monetary values, such as internal and external experts and external databases. Chapter Five illustrates how estimates can be used to convert impact data to monetary values. Estimates, the least credible technique, can be obtained from program participants, participants' supervisors and managers, or program staff.

Chapter Six explains how to select the appropriate technique, ensure accuracy and credibility, and make adjustments in order to improve credibility. At the end of the chapter, a matching exercise tests the reader on how to select the correct technique for a given situation. Finally, Chapter Seven discusses why intangible measures are important. It also examines how to decide whether to convert intangible measures to money.

The Measurement and Evaluation Series

Editors

Patricia Pulliam Phillips, Ph.D.

Jack J. Phillips, Ph.D.

Introduction to the Measurement and Evaluation Series

The ROI Six Pack provides detailed information on developing ROI evaluations, implementing the ROI Methodology, and showing the value of a variety of functions and processes. With detailed examples, tools, templates, shortcuts, and checklists, this series will be a valuable reference for individuals interested in using the ROI Methodology to show the impact of their projects, programs, and processes.

The Need

Although financial ROI has been measured for over one hundred years to quantify the value of plants, equipment, and companies, the concept has only recently been applied to evaluate the impact of learning and development, human resources, technology, quality, marketing, and other support functions. In the learning and development field alone, the use of ROI has become routine in many organizations. In the past decade, hundreds of organizations have embraced the ROI process to show the impact of many different projects and programs.

Along the way, professionals and practitioners need help. They need tools, templates, and tips, along with explanations, examples, and details, to make this process work. Without this help, using the ROI Methodology to show the value of projects and

programs is difficult. In short, practitioners need shortcuts and proven techniques to minimize the resources required to use this process. Practitioners' needs have created the need for this series. This series will provide the detail necessary to make the ROI Methodology successful within an organization. For easy reference and use, the books are logically arranged to align with the steps of the ROI Methodology.

Audience

The principal audience for these books is individuals who plan to use the ROI Methodology to show the value of their projects and programs. Such individuals are specialists or managers charged with proving the value of their particular project or program. They need detailed information, know-how, and confidence.

A second audience is those who have used the ROI Methodology for some time but want a quick reference with tips and techniques to make ROI implementation more successful within their organization. This series, which explains the evaluation process in detail, will be a valuable reference set for these individuals, regardless of other ROI publications owned.

A third audience is consultants and researchers who want to know how to address specific evaluation issues. Three important challenges face individuals as they measure ROI and conduct ROI evaluations: (1) collecting post-program data, (2) isolating the effects of the program, and (3) converting data to monetary values. A book is devoted to each of these critical issues, allowing researchers and consultants to easily find details on each issue.

A fourth audience is those who are curious about the ROI Methodology and its use. The first book in this series focuses specifically on ROI, its use, and how to determine whether it is appropriate for an organization. When interest is piqued, the remaining books provide more detail.

Flow of the Books

The six books are presented in a logical sequence, mirroring the ROI process model. Book one, *ROI Fundamentals: Why and When to Measure ROI*, presents the basic ROI Methodology and makes the business case for measuring ROI as it explores the benefits and barriers to implementation. It also examines the type of organization best suited for the ROI Methodology and the best time to implement it. Planning for an ROI evaluation is also explored in this book.

Book two, *Data Collection: Planning For and Collecting All Types of Data*, details data collection by examining the different techniques, methods, and issues involved in this process, with an emphasis on collecting post-program data. It examines the different data collection methods: questionnaires, interviews, focus groups, observation, action plans, performance contracts, and monitoring records.

Book three, *Isolation of Results: Defining the Impact of the Program*, focuses on the most valuable part of the ROI Methodology and the essential step for ensuring credibility. Recognizing that factors other than the program being measured can influence results, this book shows a variety of ways in which the effects of a program can be isolated from other influences. Techniques include comparison analysis using a control group, trend line analysis and forecasting methods, and expert input from a variety of sources.

Book four, *Data Conversion: Calculating the Monetary Benefits*, covers perhaps the second toughest challenge of ROI evaluation: placing monetary value on program benefits. To calculate the ROI, data must be converted to money, and *Data Conversion* shows how this conversion has been accomplished in a variety of organizations. The good news is that standard values are available for many items. When they are not, the book shows different techniques for converting them, ranging from calculating the value from records to seeking experts and searching databases. When data cannot be

converted to money credibly and with minimum resources, they are considered intangible. This book explores the range of intangible benefits and the necessary techniques for collecting, analyzing, and recording them.

Book five, *Costs and ROI: Evaluating at the Ultimate Level*, focuses on costs and ROI. This book shows that all costs must be captured in order to create a fully loaded cost profile. All the costs must be included in order to be conservative and to give the analysis additional credibility. Next, the actual ROI calculation is presented, showing the various assumptions and issues that must be addressed when calculating the ROI. Three different calculations are presented: the benefit-cost ratio, the ROI percentage, and the payback period. The book concludes with several cautions and concerns about the use of ROI and its meaning.

Book six, *Communication and Implementation: Sustaining the Practice*, explores two important issues. The first issue is reporting the results of an evaluation. This is the final part of the ROI Methodology and is necessary to ensure that audiences have the information they need so that improvement processes can be implemented. A range of techniques is available, including face-to-face meetings, brief reports, one-page summaries, routine communications, mass-audience techniques, and electronic media. All are available for reporting evaluation results. The final part of the book focuses on how to sustain the ROI evaluation process: how to use it, keep it going, and make it work in the long term to add value to the organization and, often, to show the value of all the programs and projects within a function or department.

Terminology: Programs, Projects, Solutions

In this series the terms *program* and *project* are used to describe many processes that can be evaluated using the ROI Methodology. This is an important issue because readers may vary widely in their perspectives. Individuals involved in technology applications may

Table I.1. Terms and Applications

Term	Example
Program	Leadership development skills enhancement for senior executives
Project	A reengineering scheme for a plastics division
System	A fully interconnected network for all branches of a bank
Initiative	A faith-based effort to reduce recidivism
Policy	A new preschool plan for disadvantaged citizens
Procedure	A new scheduling arrangement for truck drivers
Event	A golf outing for customers
Meeting	A U.S. Coast Guard conference on innovations
Process	Quality sampling
People	Staff additions in the customer care center
Tool	A new means of selecting hotel staff

use the terms *system* and *technology* rather than *program* or *project*. In public policy, in contrast, the word *program* is prominent. For a professional meetings and events planner, the word *program* may not be pertinent, but in human resources, *program* is often used. Finding one term for all these situations would be difficult. Consequently, the terms *program* and *project* are used interchangeably. Table I.1 lists these and other terms that may be used in other contexts.

Features

Each book in the series takes a straightforward approach to make it understandable, practical, and useful. Checklists are provided, charts are included, templates are presented, and examples are explored. All are intended to show how the ROI Methodology works. The focus of these books is implementing the process and making it successful within an organization. The methodology is based on the work of hundreds of individuals who have made the ROI Methodology a successful evaluation process within their organizations.

About Pfeiffer

Pfeiffer serves the professional development and hands-on resource needs of training and human resource practitioners and gives them products to do their jobs better. We deliver proven ideas and solutions from experts in HR development and HR management, and we offer effective and customizable tools to improve workplace performance. From novice to seasoned professional, Pfeiffer is the source you can trust to make yourself and your organization more successful.

Essential Knowledge Pfeiffer produces insightful, practical, and comprehensive materials on topics that matter the most to training and HR professionals. Our Essential Knowledge resources translate the expertise of seasoned professionals into practical, how-to guidance on critical workplace issues and problems. These resources are supported by case studies, worksheets, and job aids and are frequently supplemented with CD-ROMs, Web sites, and other means of making the content easier to read, understand, and use.

Essential Tools Pfeiffer's Essential Tools resources save time and expense by offering proven, ready-to-use materials—including exercises, activities, games, instruments, and assessments—for use during a training or team-learning event. These resources are frequently offered in looseleaf or CD-ROM format to facilitate copying and customization of the material.

Pfeiffer also recognizes the remarkable power of new technologies in expanding the reach and effectiveness of training. While e-hype has often created whizbang solutions in search of a problem, we are dedicated to bringing convenience and enhancements to proven training solutions. All our e-tools comply with rigorous functionality standards. The most appropriate technology wrapped around essential content yields the perfect solution for today's on-the-go trainers and human resource professionals.

Pfeiffer *Essential resources for training and HR professionals*
www.pfeiffer.com

Data Conversion

Calculating the Monetary Benefits

Patricia Pulliam Phillips, Ph.D.
Holly Burkett, M.A.

Pfeiffer
A Wiley Imprint
www.pfeiffer.com

Copyright © 2008 by John Wiley & Sons, Inc. All rights reserved.

Published by Pfeiffer
An Imprint of Wiley
989 Market Street, San Francisco, CA 94103-1741
www.pfeiffer.com

No part of this publication may be reproduced, stored in a retrieval system, or transmitted in any form or by any means, electronic, mechanical, photocopying, recording, scanning, or otherwise, except as permitted under Section 107 or 108 of the 1976 United States Copyright Act, without either the prior written permission of the publisher, or authorization through payment of the appropriate per-copy fee to the Copyright Clearance Center, Inc., 222 Rosewood Drive, Danvers, MA 01923, 978-750-8400, fax 978-646-8600, or on the web at www.copyright.com. Requests to the publisher for permission should be addressed to the Permissions Department, John Wiley & Sons, Inc., 111 River Street, Hoboken, NJ 07030, 201-748-6011, fax 201-748-6008, or online at http://www.wiley.com/go/permissions.

Limit of Liability/Disclaimer of Warranty: While the publisher and author have used their best efforts in preparing this book, they make no representations or warranties with respect to the accuracy or completeness of the contents of this book and specifically disclaim any implied warranties of merchantability or fitness for a particular purpose. No warranty may be created or extended by sales representatives or written sales materials. The advice and strategies contained herein may not be suitable for your situation. You should consult with a professional where appropriate. Neither the publisher nor author shall be liable for any loss of profit or any other commercial damages, including but not limited to special, incidental, consequential, or other damages.

Readers should be aware that Internet Web sites offered as citations and/or sources for further information may have changed or disappeared between the time this book was written and when it is read.

For additional copies/bulk purchases of this book in the U.S. please contact 800-274-4434.

Pfeiffer books and products are available through most bookstores. To contact Pfeiffer directly call our Customer Care Department within the U.S. at 800-274-4434, outside the U.S. at 317-572-3985, fax 317-572-4002, or visit www.pfeiffer.com.

Pfeiffer also publishes its books in a variety of electronic formats. Some content that appears in print may not be available in electronic books.

Library of Congress Cataloging-in-Publication Data

Phillips, Patricia Pulliam.
   Data conversion: calculating the monetary benefits / Patricia Pulliam Phillips, Holly Burkett.
      p. cm.
   Includes bibliographical references and index.
   ISBN 978-0-7879-8720-6 (pbk.)
    1. Project management—Cost effectiveness. 2. Rate of return. 3. Activity-based costing. 4. Project management—Evaluation. I. Burkett, Holly. II. Title.
   HD69.P75.P4962 2008
   658.15'54—dc22

                                                                               2007045002

Production Editor: Michael Kay   Editorial Assistant: Julie Rodriguez
Editor: Matthew Davis   Manufacturing Supervisor: Becky Morgan
Printed in the United States of America

PB Printing 10 9 8 7 6 5 4 3 2 1

Contents

Acknowledgments from the Editors — xvii

Principles of the ROI Methodology — xix

Chapter 1: The Importance of Converting Data to Monetary Values — 1

Why Convert Data to Monetary Values? — 2
    Value Equals Money — 2
    Impact Is More Understandable — 2
    Programs Start Because of Money — 3
    Converting Data to Money Is Similar to Budgeting — 4
    Monetary Value Is Vital to Organizational Operations — 4
    Monetary Values Are Necessary to Understand Problems — 5

Hard and Soft Data — 5

Converting Data to Monetary Values — 7
    1. Focus on a Unit of Measure — 7
    2. Determine the Value of Each Unit — 9
    3. Calculate the Change in Performance — 10
    4. Determine the Annual Amount of Change — 10
    5. Calculate the Total Value of the Improvement — 10
    Case Example of Converting Data to Monetary Values — 11

Final Thoughts — 11

Chapter 2: Use Standard Values 13

Converting Output Data to Monetary Values 13
   Case Example: A Commercial Bank 14
   Case Example: Snapper Lawn Mowers 15
   More Examples of Standard Values for Output Measures 16
Converting Quality to Monetary Value 17
   Quality Cost Categories 19
   Examples of Measures Converted to Quality Cost 21
Converting Employee Time to Monetary Value 22
   Case Example: A Technology Company 23
   A Word of Caution 24
Why Standard Values Are Developed 25
Standard Values Are Everywhere 26
Final Thoughts 27

Chapter 3: Calculate the Value 31

Using Historical Costs 31
   Key Issues in Using Records and Reports 32
   Case Study: A Metropolitan Transit Authority 33
Linking with Other Measures 35
   Classic Relationships 36
   Case Example: A European Postal Service 37
   Case Example: Sears, Roebuck and Company 38
   Concerns When Using Relationships Between Measures
      to Assign Monetary Values 40
Final Thoughts 41

Chapter 4: Find the Value 43

Using Internal and External Experts 43
   Working with Internal Experts 44
   Working with External Experts 45
   Case Example: A Manufacturing Plant 45
   Case Example: A Health Care Firm 46
Using External Databases 47
   Internet Searches 48
   Case Example: A Regional Bank 50

Case Example: A Federal Agency	53
Other Sources of Databases	56
Final Thoughts	56

Chapter 5: Estimate the Value — 59

Using Estimates from Participants	59
Case Example: A Manufacturing Plant	59
Key Issues in Using Participant Estimates	60
Using Estimates from Supervisors and Managers	61
Using Estimates from Senior Management	62
Using Staff Estimates	63
Final Thoughts	64

Chapter 6: Use of Data Conversion Techniques — 65

Selecting the Appropriate Technique	65
Ensuring the Accuracy and Credibility of Data	67
Credibility: The Key Issue	67
How the Credibility of Data Is Influenced	69
Rules for Determining Credibility	72
Reputation of the Source of the Data	73
Reputation of the Source of the Study	73
Motives of the Evaluators	73
Audience Bias	73
Methodology of the Study	74
Assumptions Made During the Analysis	74
Realism of the Outcome Data	74
Type of Data	74
Scope of Analysis	75
How to Address the Issue of Credibility	75
Use the Most Credible and Reliable Sources for Estimates	75
Remain Unbiased and Objective	75
Prepare for Potential Audience Bias	77
Fully Explain Your Methodology at Each Step in the Process	77
Define Assumptions Made During the Analysis	77
Prepare for an Unrealistic Value	77

Use Hard Data Whenever Possible	78
Keep the Scope of Analysis Narrow	79
Making Adjustments	79
Consider the Possibility of Management Adjustment	79
Consider the Issue of Short-Term Versus Long-Term Programs	80
Consider an Adjustment for the Time Value of Money	81
Converting Data to Money: Matching Exercise	81
Final Thoughts	86

Chapter 7: Intangible Measures — 87

Why Intangibles Are Important	88
Intangibles Are the Invisible Advantage	89
We Are Entering the Intangible Economy	89
Intangibles Are Being Converted to Tangibles	90
Intangibles Drive Programs	90
Measuring Intangibles	90
Converting Intangibles to Monetary Values	93
Identifying and Collecting Intangibles	96
Analyzing Intangibles	97
Confronting Intangibles	98
Example 1: Customer Service	98
Example 2: Innovation and Creativity	102
Innovation	102
Creativity	105
Example 3: Employee Attitudes	107
Employee Satisfaction	107
Organizational Commitment	108
Employee Engagement	108
Example 4: Leadership	109
360° Feedback	110
Leadership Inventories	110
Leadership Perception	111
Business Impact	111
Final Thoughts	112
Index	115
About the Authors	121

Acknowledgments from the Editors

From Patti

No project, regardless of its size or scope, is completed without the help and support of others. My sincere thanks go to the staff at Pfeiffer. Their support for this project has been relentless. Matt Davis has been the greatest! It is our pleasure and privilege to work with such a professional and creative group of people.

Thanks also go to my husband, Jack. His unwavering support of my work is always evident. His idea for the series was to provide readers with a practical understanding of the various components of a comprehensive measurement and evaluation process. Thank you, Jack, for another fun opportunity!

From Jack

Many thanks go to the staff who helped make this series a reality. Lori Ditoro did an excellent job of meeting a very tight deadline and delivering a quality manuscript.

Much admiration and thanks go to Patti. She is an astute observer of the ROI Methodology, having observed and learned from hundreds of presentations, consulting assignments, and engagements. In addition, she is an excellent researcher and student of the process, studying how it is developed and how it works. She has become an ROI expert in her own right. Thanks, Patti, for your many contributions. You are a great partner, friend, and spouse.

Principles of the ROI Methodology

The ROI Methodology is a step-by-step tool for evaluating any program, project, or initiative in any organization. Figure P.1 illustrates the ROI process model, which makes a potentially complicated process simple by breaking it into sequential steps. The ROI process model provides a systematic, step-by-step approach to ROI evaluations that helps keep the process manageable, allowing users to address one issue at a time. The model also emphasizes that the ROI Methodology is a logical, systematic process that flows from one step to another and provides a way for evaluators to collect and analyze six types of data.

Applying the model consistently from one program to another is essential for successful evaluation. To aid consistent application of the model, the ROI Methodology is based on twelve Guiding Principles. These principles are necessary for a credible, conservative approach to evaluation through the different levels.

1. When conducting a higher-level evaluation, collect data at lower levels.
2. When planning a higher-level evaluation, the previous level of evaluation is not required to be comprehensive.
3. When collecting and analyzing data, use only the most credible sources.

Figure P.1. The ROI Process Model

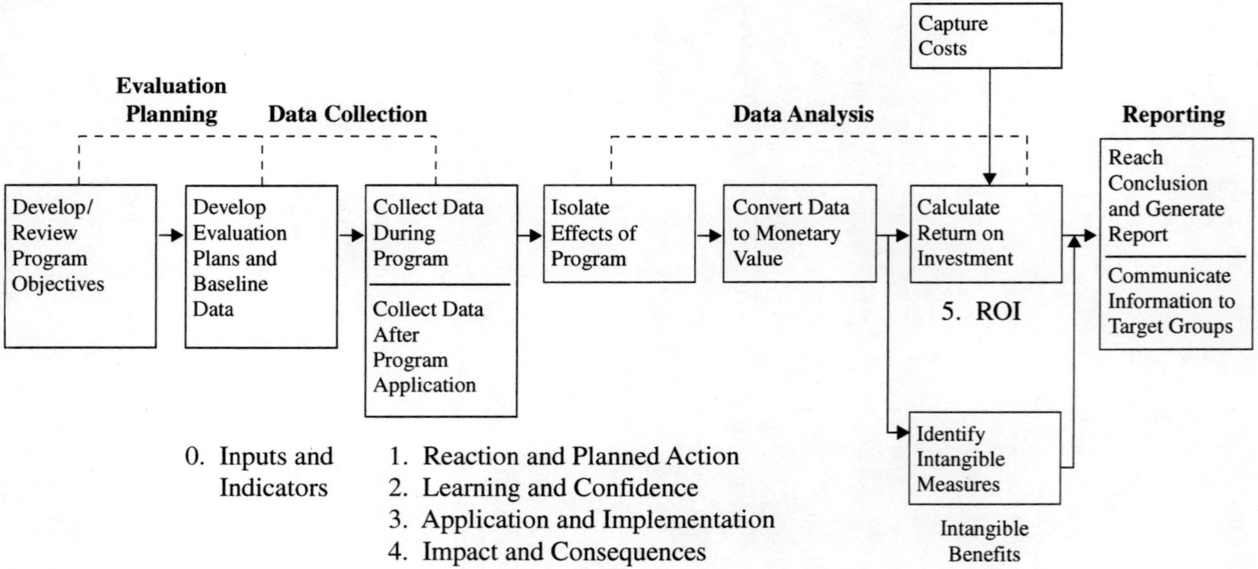

Evaluation Planning

- Develop/Review Program Objectives
- Develop Evaluation Plans and Baseline Data

Data Collection

- Collect Data During Program
- Collect Data After Program Application

Data Analysis

- Isolate Effects of Program
- Convert Data to Monetary Value
- Capture Costs
- Calculate Return on Investment → **5. ROI**
- Identify Intangible Measures → Intangible Benefits

Reporting

- Reach Conclusion and Generate Report
- Communicate Information to Target Groups

0. Inputs and Indicators
1. Reaction and Planned Action
2. Learning and Confidence
3. Application and Implementation
4. Impact and Consequences

4. When analyzing data, select the most conservative alternative for calculations.
5. Use at least one method to isolate the effects of a project.
6. If no improvement data are available for a population or from a specific source, assume that little or no improvement has occurred.
7. Adjust estimates of improvement for potential errors of estimation.
8. Avoid use of extreme data items and unsupported claims when calculating ROI.
9. Use only the first year of annual benefits in ROI analysis of short-term solutions.
10. Fully load all costs of a solution, project, or program when analyzing ROI.
11. Intangible measures are defined as measures that are purposely not converted to monetary values.
12. Communicate the results of the ROI Methodology to all key stakeholders.

1

The Importance of Converting Data to Monetary Values

Traditionally, most impact evaluation studies stop with a tabulation of business results. In these situations, the program is considered successful if it produced improvements such as productivity increases, quality enhancements, absenteeism reductions, or customer satisfaction improvements. While these results are important, converting the data to monetary values and showing the total monetary impact of the improvement provides more concrete data for determining and validating program success. This calculation responds to the request "Show me the money." Also, the monetary value of program benefits is needed for comparison with the cost of the program in developing the return on investment (ROI). This evaluation is the ultimate level of the evaluation framework on which the ROI Methodology is based.

This book shows how leading organizations are moving beyond simply tabulating business results and are adding the step of converting data to monetary values.

This initial chapter focuses on the importance of taking this extra step. It also explores some of the preliminary issues that must be considered before addressing the specific techniques available for converting data to money.

Why Convert Data to Monetary Values?

The need to convert data to monetary amounts is not always clearly understood. A program or project can be shown to be a success just by providing business impact data showing the amount of change directly attributable to the program. For example, a change in quality, cycle time, market share, or customer satisfaction could represent a significant improvement linked directly to a new program. For some programs, this may be sufficient. However, many sponsors require the actual monetary value, and increasingly, evaluators are taking the extra step of converting data to monetary values.

Value Equals Money

For some stakeholders, the most important value is money. Although there are many different types of value, monetary value is one of the primary criteria of success. Executives, sponsors, clients, administrators, and other leaders are concerned with the allocation of funds and want to see evidence of the contribution of a program in terms of monetary value. Often, for these key stakeholders, outcomes stated in any other terms are unsatisfactory.

Impact Is More Understandable

For some programs, the impact is more understandable when it is stated in terms of monetary value. Consider, for example, the impact of a major program to improve the creativity of an organization's employees and thereby enhance the innovation of the organization. Suppose this program involved all employees and had an impact on all parts of the organization. Across all departments, functions, units, and divisions, employees were being more creative, suggesting new ideas, taking on new challenges, driving new products—in short, helping the organization in a wide variety of ways. The easiest way to understand the value of such a program is to convert the individual efforts and their consequences to monetary values. Totaling the monetary values of all the innovations can provide a sense of the value of the program.

Consider the impact of a leadership development program directed at all of the middle managers in an organization. As part of the program, the managers were asked to select at least two measures of importance to them and to indicate what would need to change or improve for them to meet their specific goals. The measures numbered in the dozens. When the program's impact was studied, a large number of improvements were identified but were hard to quantify. Converting them to monetary values allowed these improvements to be expressed in the same terms, enabling the outcomes to be more clearly reported.

As described in earlier books in this series, the monetary value of program benefits is needed to compare against costs in order to develop the benefit-cost ratio, the ROI (as a percentage), and the payback period. Calculating ROI is impossible without converting data to monetary amounts.

Programs Start Because of Money

Sometimes, the monetary value of a particular issue provides the impetus for a program. For example, a company might be experiencing huge fines due to compliance violations, and these fines result in a program to prevent further violations. In another example, excessive accidents, when converted to monetary values, might illustrate the magnitude of a problem, which leads directly to new programs to lower the number of accidents. Essentially, the best way to get the attention of a potential sponsor for a program is to place the problem or opportunity in the context of money. This almost guarantees that the program will be implemented, if the data are credible and the resources are available.

Converting Data to Money Is Similar to Budgeting

Professionals and administrators work with budgets and are expected to develop budgets for programs with an acceptable degree of accuracy; thus they are comfortable with tabulating costs. When it comes to benefits, however, many are not comfortable, even though some of the same techniques used to develop budgets are used to determine benefits. Defining the benefits of a program in terms of cost savings or cost reductions may make identification of the costs or value of the program easier for some managers. The monetary benefit resulting from a program becomes a natural extension of the budget.

Monetary Value Is Vital to Organizational Operations

With global competitiveness and the drive to improve the efficiency of operations, awareness of the costs related to particular processes and activities is essential. In the 1990s, this emphasis gave rise to activity-based costing (ABC) and activity-based management. ABC is not a replacement for traditional general ledger accounting. Rather, it is a translator or medium between cost accumulations—that is, the specific expenditure account balances in the general ledger—and the end users who must apply cost data in decision making. In typical cost statements, the actual cost of a process or problem is not readily discernible. ABC converts inert cost data to relevant, actionable information. ABC has become increasingly useful for identifying improvement opportunities and measuring the benefits realized from performance initiatives (Cokins, 1996). Over 80 percent of the ROI impact studies that have been conducted show that a program has benefited an organization through cost savings (cost reduction or cost avoidance). Understanding the cost of a problem and the payoff of the corresponding solution is essential to proper management of a business.

Monetary Values Are Necessary to Understand Problems

In any business, costs are essential to understanding the magnitude of a problem. Consider, for example, the cost of employee turnover. Traditional records and even those available through activity-based costing will not indicate the full cost of the problem. A variety of estimates and expert inputs may be necessary to supplement cost statements in order to arrive at a specific value. The good news is that organizations have developed a number of standard procedures for identifying undesirable costs. For example, Wal-Mart has calculated the cost of one truck sitting idle at a store for one minute, waiting to be unloaded. When this cost is multiplied by hundreds of deliveries per store and then multiplied by five thousand stores, the cost becomes enormous. Understanding the enormity of the cost gives the retailer an undisputable reason why strides must be taken to ensure the trucks are unloaded as quickly as possible.

Hard and Soft Data

When collecting business impact data, some managers find it helpful to divide the data into two categories: hard data and soft data. Hard data are obtained through the traditional measures of organizational performance. Hard data are objective, easy to measure, and easy to convert to monetary values. Because hard data are often obtained through common performance measures, they enjoy high credibility with management and are available in almost every organization. They are destined to be converted to monetary values and included in the ROI calculation.

Hard data represent the output, quality, cost, and time of work-related processes. Table 1.1 shows examples of data in these four categories. Almost every department or function will have performance measures that yield hard data. For example, a government

Table 1.1. Examples of Hard Data

Output	Quality	Cost	Time
Units produced	Failure rates	Shelter costs	Cycle time
Tons manufactured	Dropout rates	Treatment costs	Equipment downtime
Items assembled	Scrap	Budget variances	Overtime
Money collected	Waste	Unit costs	On-time shipments
Items sold	Rejects	Cost by account	Time to project completion
New accounts generated	Error rates	Variable costs	Processing time
Forms processed	Rework	Fixed costs	Supervisory time
Loans approved	Shortages	Overhead cost	Time to proficiency
Inventory turnover	Product defects	Operating costs	Learning time
Patients visited	Deviation from standard	Program cost savings	Adherence to schedules
Applications processed	Product failures	Accident costs	Repair time
Students graduated	Inventory adjustments	Program costs	Efficiency
Tasks completed	Time card corrections	Sales expense	Work stoppages
Output per hour	Incidents		Order response time
Productivity	Compliance discrepancies		Late reporting
Work backlog	Agency fines		Lost-time days
Incentive bonus			
Shipments			
Completion rate			

office that approves applications for work visas might track the following four performance measures: number of applications processed (output), number of errors made in processing applications (quality), cost per application processed (cost), and average time taken to process and approve an application (time). Most projects or programs in this unit should be linked to one or more hard data measures.

Because many programs are designed to develop soft skills, soft data must also be collected during evaluation. Soft data are usually subjective, are sometimes difficult to measure, are almost always difficult to convert to monetary values, and are behavior-oriented. Compared with hard data, soft data are usually perceived as less credible although we use them frequently when managing organization processes. Soft data measures may or may not be converted to monetary values.

Soft data items can be grouped into several categories; Table 1.2 shows one such grouping. Measures such as employee complaints and grievances are listed as soft data items not because they are difficult to measure but because they are difficult to convert accurately to monetary values.

Converting Data to Monetary Values

Before describing the techniques to convert either hard or soft data to monetary values, we will briefly summarize the steps used to convert data in each category. These steps should be followed each time a measure is converted to monetary value.

1. Focus on a Unit of Measure

First, identify a unit of measure targeted for improvement. For output data, the unit of measure might be an item produced, a service provided, or a sale completed. Time measures are varied and include items such as the time to complete a program, cycle time, or customer response time. Units of time measures are usually

Table 1.2. Examples of Soft Data

Work Habits	Customer Service
Excessive breaks	Customer complaints
Tardiness	Customer satisfaction
Visits to the dispensary	Customer dissatisfaction
Violations of safety rules	Customer impressions
Communication breakdowns	Customer loyalty
	Customer retention
	Lost customers
Work Climate and Job Satisfaction	**Employee Development and Advancement**
Grievances	Promotions
Discrimination charges	Capability
Employee complaints	Intellectual capital
Job satisfaction	Requests for transfer
Employee organizational commitment	Performance appraisal ratings
Employee engagement	Readiness
Employee loyalty	Networking
Intent to leave the organization	
Stress	
Initiative and Innovation	**Image**
Creativity	Brand awareness
Innovation	Reputation
New ideas	Leadership
Suggestions	Social responsibility
New products and services	Environmental friendliness
Trademarks	Social consciousness
Copyrights and patents	Diversity
Process improvements	External awards
Partnerships and alliances	

expressed in minutes, hours, or days. For quality the unit might be one error, reject, defect, or rework item. Soft data measures are varied; a unit of improvement might be one sale or a change of one point in the employee engagement score. Here are some specific examples of units of improvement:

- One student enrolled
- One patient served
- One loan approved
- One full-time employee hired
- One reworked item
- One grievance
- One voluntary turnover
- One hour of downtime
- One hour of cycle time
- One hour of employee time
- One customer complaint
- One person removed from welfare
- One less day of incarceration (prison)
- One point increase in customer satisfaction

2. Determine the Value of Each Unit

Now, the challenge: place a value (V) on the unit of measure identified in the first step. This step is the focus of this book. For measures of production, quality, cost, and time, this process is relatively easy. Most organizations have records or reports that state the value of items such as one unit of production or the cost of a defect. Soft data are more difficult to convert to a value; the cost of one absence, one grievance, or a change of one point in the employee attitude survey is often difficult to pinpoint. The techniques in this book provide an array of possibilities for making this conversion. When more than one value is available, either the most credible or the lowest value is used.

3. Calculate the Change in Performance

The change in output data is calculated after the effects of the program have been isolated from other influences. The change (Δ) is the performance improvement, expressed in hard or soft data, which is directly attributable to the program. The value may represent the performance improvement for an individual, a team, a group, or several groups of participants.

4. Determine the Annual Amount of Change

Annualize the value by calculating the total change in the performance data that would occur in one year if improvement were to continue at the same rate that was recorded during the program (ΔP). In many organizations, calculating the benefits for one year has become a standard approach to defining the total benefits of a program. Although the benefits may not be realized at the same level for an entire year, some programs will continue to produce benefits beyond one year. In some cases, the stream of benefits may continue for several years. Using one year of benefits is considered a conservative approach, leading to Guiding Principle 9: Use only the first year of annual benefits in ROI analysis of short-term solutions.

5. Calculate the Total Value of the Improvement

Compute the total value of improvement that can be attributed to the program by multiplying the unit value (V) by the annual performance change (ΔP). For example, if a group of fifteen supervisors attended a program designed to reduce the number of complaints filed by a specific employee group, the annual change in performance would be the total number by which grievances were reduced for the entire year, not just up to the point in time at which the data were collected. This annual improvement is then multiplied by the value of one unit to calculate the total monetary benefits to the organization.

Another example of this calculation is annualizing the measure representative of a large population. If a group of twenty managers attended a program designed to reduce absenteeism, the annualized performance change would reflect the reduction in absenteeism for the entire target population (say two hundred employees working in operations) over the course of one year. This value is then multiplied by the unit value of one absence to calculate the annual monetary benefits of the program. This value for the total annual program benefits is then compared with the cost of the program, usually by using the return on investment formula presented in *ROI Fundamentals*, the first book of this series.

Case Example of Converting Data to Monetary Values

An example taken from a team-building program at a manufacturing plant illustrates the five-step process of converting data to monetary values. This program was developed and implemented after a needs assessment revealed that lack of teamwork was causing an excessive number of grievances. The number of grievances resolved at step 2 in the four-step grievance process was selected as an impact measure. Exhibit 1.1 shows the steps taken to assign monetary values to the reduction in grievances.

Final Thoughts

This brief chapter sets the stage for addressing one of the critical issues in an ROI evaluation: converting data to monetary values. This chapter shows the rationale for this step and some of the key issues that must be addressed when beginning the process.

As this book will illustrate, many techniques can be used to convert data to monetary values; the good news is that often much of the conversion work has already been done. Several techniques are available for converting data to monetary values. Some methods are appropriate only for a specific type of data, while others can be used with virtually any type of data. The challenge is to select the

Exhibit 1.1. Converting Data to Monetary Values: Evaluation of a Team-Building Program in a Manufacturing Plant

Step 1:	**Define the unit of measure.**
	Unit of measure = one less grievance reaching step 2 in the four-step grievance resolution process.
Step 2:	**Determine the value of each unit.**
	Using internal experts on the labor relations staff, the cost of an average grievance was estimated to be $6,500, considering time and direct costs. ($V = \$6,500$)
Step 3:	**Calculate the change in performance.**
	Six months after the program was completed, total grievances per month reaching step 2 had declined by ten. Supervisors isolated the effects of the program, determining that seven of the ten grievance reductions were related to the program. ($\Delta = 7$)
Step 4:	**Determine an annual amount of change.**
	Using the adjusted Δ value of seven per month yields an annual improvement of eighty-four (7 fewer grievances × 12 months) for the first year. ($\Delta P = 84$)
Step 5:	**Calculate the total value of the improvement.**
	Annual value = $\Delta P \times V$
	= 84 × $6,500
	= $546,000

technique that best matches the type of data and situation. Each method is presented in the next four chapters, beginning with the most credible approach. The next chapter focuses on the easiest method for getting to the monetary value: finding standard values that have already been converted.

Reference

Cokins, G. *Activity-Based Cost Management: Making It Work—A Manager's Guide to Implementing and Sustaining an Effective ABC System.* New York: McGraw-Hill, 1996.

2

Use Standard Values

Perhaps the best news about converting data to monetary values is that it has already been done for most of the measures that matter in an organization. It is estimated that 80 percent of the measures that are important to an organization have been converted to monetary values. That is, if it is important enough to drive a program or project, then someone has been concerned enough about it to convert it to a monetary value.

This chapter highlights the progress that has been made in developing standard values. A standard value is defined as a value that is accepted by an organization as the monetary cost or value of a particular unit of measure. This chapter divides the standard values into output, quality, and time—three of the four major categories of hard data that are described in Chapter One.

Converting Output Data to Monetary Values

When a program has produced a change in output, the value of the increased output can be determined from the organization's accounting or operating records. Output measures include revenue and productivity measures. For organizations operating on a profit basis, this value is usually the marginal profit contribution of an additional unit of production or unit of service provided. For example, if a production team in a major appliance manufacturer is able to boost production of small refrigerators with a series of comprehensive programs, the unit of improvement is the profit margin on the sale of one refrigerator. In organizations that are performance-driven rather than profit-driven, the value of increased output is reflected in the savings accumulated when additional output is realized without increasing input requirements. For example, in a university, if an additional student application is processed at no additional cost, the increase in output translates into a cost savings equal to the original unit cost of processing an application.

The formulas and calculations used to measure the value of the increased output depend on the organization and its records. Most organizations have this type of data readily available for use in performance monitoring and goal setting. Managers often use marginal cost statements and sensitivity analyses to pinpoint the value associated with changes in output. If a value for the desired output measure is not available, staff members must initiate or coordinate the development of an appropriate value.

Case Example: A Commercial Bank

In one case involving a commercial bank, a sales seminar for consumer loan officers was conducted, resulting in increased consumer loan volume (output). To measure the return on investment in the program, it was necessary to calculate the value (profit contribution) of one additional consumer loan, which could be calculated rather easily by using data from the bank's records. Table 2.1 shows

Table 2.1. Loan Profitability Analysis

Profit Component	Unit Value
Average loan size	$15,500
Average loan yield	9.75%
Average cost of funds (including branch costs)	5.50%
Direct costs for consumer lending	0.82%
Corporate overhead	1.61%
Net profit per loan	1.82%

the components that went into the calculation of the net profit per loan.

The first step was to determine the yield from the loans, which was available from bank records. Next, the average difference between the cost of funds and the yield received on the loans was calculated. For example, the bank could obtain funds from depositors at 5.5 percent on average, including the cost of operating the branches. Next, the direct costs of making the loan, such as salaries of employees directly involved in consumer lending and advertising costs for consumer loans, had to be subtracted. Historically, such direct costs had amounted to 0.82 percent of the loan value. To cover overhead costs for other corporate functions, an additional 1.61 percent was subtracted. The remaining 1.82 percent of the average loan value represented the bank's profit margin on a loan. For example, if a loan is made in the amount of $1.5 million, the profit (value) of the loan to the bank would be $27,300 ($1.5 million × 1.82% profit margin = $27,300).

The advantage of this technique for calculating the value of increased output is that standard values are often available for many measures. The challenge is to quickly find appropriate and credible values for the desired measures. In the preceding bank example, the desired values had already been developed for other purposes and thus were available for use in the evaluation of the sales seminar program.

Case Example: Snapper Lawn Mowers

One of the more important measures of output is productivity, particularly for organizations in a highly competitive environment. Today, most organizations competing in the global economy do an excellent job of monitoring productivity and placing a value on it. Consider, for example, the Snapper lawn mower factory in McDonough, Georgia. Ten years ago, it produced 40 models of outdoor equipment items; now it makes 145. Ten years ago, all the manufacturing processes were performed by humans. Today robots do the welding, lasers cut parts, and computers control the steel-stamping process. Productivity at the factory is three times what it was ten years ago, and the workforce has been cut by half (Fishman, 2006). The value of this increased productivity can be calculated by the value of one new mower produced with the same resources. The value would be the portion of the revenue generated from the sale of the mower that is gross operating profit. At Snapper, each factory worker's output is measured every hour, every day, every month, and every year. And each person's performance is posted publicly every day for all to see. Production at the Snapper plant is rescheduled every week according to the pace of store sales across the nation. A computer juggles work assignments and balances the various parts of the assembly process. At Snapper, productivity is important; therefore, it is measured and valued. Snapper knows the value of improving productivity by an infinitesimal amount; the president knows that the factory must be aggressively efficient to compete in a global market with low-cost products. This requires that the performance of every factory worker be measured every hour of every day.

More Examples of Standard Values for Output Measures

In the Snapper case, monetary values for output have been developed. Snapper calculates the value of one unit of productivity; other organizations calculate the value of one item sold or some other output measure. For example, in a large retail store chain, a program was developed to increase sales at the store level. To determine the payoff, the evaluation team used the store-level profit margin of 2 percent, a measure that had been previously developed and that was listed in the company's annual report. When converting a sale to profit, this 2 percent margin was the multiplier that resulted in the monetary contribution to the store.

Using a profit margin instead of actual sales in an ROI calculation is an important issue. If this is done the true picture of the value added to the organization is not presented. A product sold or a service provided always incurs a cost, and the profit margin is a measure that subtracts out that cost. So the profit margin alone does not show the impact of the program; it needs to be applied to the actual sales data. Therefore, the true value added by a program, which must go into an ROI calculation, is the sales data multiplied by the profit margin.

In another example, the value of a new policyholder for an insurance company was calculated based on how long a customer could be expected to be with the insurance company and the money that would be made from a typical policy. Obviously, this value would vary with the product line—for example, automobile insurance versus homeowner's insurance versus life insurance. The insurance company has historical data on the length of time that policies have been held and the profit that has been made from the policies. This information is used to calculate the value of a new client (that is, the amount of money the company can expect to make, on average, when a new policy is written).

Table 2.2 provides additional detail on common measures of output data. As the table shows, standard values for output data are almost always available within an organization. However, if no value has been developed for a measure, one of the techniques discussed in this book can be used to develop the value.

Converting Quality to Monetary Value

Because quality is a critical issue, its cost is an important measure in most manufacturing and service firms. And because many programs are designed to improve quality, the program staff must place a value on improvement in relevant quality measures. For some quality measures, the task of assigning a monetary value is easy. For example, if quality is measured by means of a defect rate, the value of improvement is the cost of repairing or replacing a defective product. The most obvious cost of poor quality is the scrap or waste generated by mistakes. Defective products, spoiled raw materials, and discarded paperwork are all the results of poor quality.

Table 2.2. Common Output Measures and the Methods for Converting Output Data to a Monetary Value

Output Measure	Example	Method for Conversion to a Monetary Value	Comments
Unit of production	One unit assembled	Standard value	Value is available in almost every manufacturing unit.
Unit of service provided	One package delivered on time	Standard value	Value is developed in most service companies.
Sales	Monetary increase in revenue	Standard value (profit margin)	The profit from one additional dollar of sales is usually a standard value.
Market share	10 percent increase in market share in one year	Standard value	Margin on increased sales is usually a standard value.
Productivity	10 percent change in productivity index. For example an improvement in percentage of shipments per month.	Standard value	Such measures are specific to the type of production or productivity measured. Such measures may represent productivity per unit of time.

This scrap and waste translates directly to a monetary value. For example, in a production environment, the cost of a defective product is the total cost incurred to the point the mistake is identified minus the salvage value. In a service environment, the cost of a defective service is the cost incurred up to the point at which the deficiency is identified plus the cost to correct the problem, plus the cost to make the customer happy, plus the cost of the loss of customer loyalty.

Employee errors can cause expensive rework. The most costly rework occurs when a defective product is delivered to a customer and must be returned for correction. The cost of rework includes both labor and direct costs. In some organizations, the cost of rework can be as much as 35 percent of operating costs (Campanella, 1999).

Quality Cost Categories

Quality costs can be grouped into six major categories (Rust, Zahorik, and Keiningham, 1994):

1. *Internal failure* represents costs associated with problems detected prior to product shipment or service delivery. Typically, such costs are for rework and retesting.
2. *Penalty costs* are fines or penalties incurred as a result of unacceptable quality.
3. *External failure* refers to problems detected after product shipment or service delivery. Typical items in this category include technical support, complaint investigation, remedial upgrades, and fixes.
4. *Appraisal costs* are the expenses involved in determining the condition of a particular product or service. Typical appraisal costs involve testing and related activities, such as product quality audits.

5. *Prevention costs* involve efforts undertaken to avoid unacceptable products or service quality. These efforts include service quality management, inspections, process studies, and improvements.

6. *Customer dissatisfaction* is perhaps the costliest element of inadequate quality. In some cases, serious mistakes result in lost business. Customer dissatisfaction is difficult to quantify, and arriving at a monetary value through direct methods may be impossible. The judgment and expertise of sales, marketing, or quality managers are usually the best resources to draw on in measuring the impact of dissatisfaction. Increasingly, quality experts are measuring customer and client dissatisfaction through market surveys.

A tremendous number of quality measures have been converted to standard values. These measures include, but are not limited to, the following:

- Defects
- Rework
- Processing errors
- Accidents
- Grievances
- Equipment downtime
- System downtime
- Delay
- Fines
- Number of days sales uncollected
- Queues

Examples of Measures Converted to Quality Cost

In one example, a program focused on customer service provided by dispatchers in an oil company. The dispatchers processed orders and scheduled deliveries of fuel to service stations. A level of quality that was considered unsatisfactory was the number of pullouts experienced. A pullout occurs when a delivery truck cannot fill an order for fuel at a service station and the truck must return to the terminal for an adjustment to the order. In essence, this is a rework item. The average cost of a pullout was developed by tabulating the cost from a sampling of actual pullouts. The elements of the tabulation included driver time, the cost of the truck while adjusting the load, the cost of terminal use, and extra administrative expenses. The value that was developed became the accepted standard in the company. Organizations like this one have made great progress in developing standard values for the cost of quality.

In another example, a program was implemented for new couriers with DHL Worldwide Express in Spain. Several measures were used to evaluate the payoff of the program. One was a quality measure known as repackaging error. A repacking error occurs when a parcel is damaged due to mishandling and has to be repackaged before it can be delivered to the customer. The time and repackaging costs are small; nevertheless, when the repackaging errors across the country are tabulated, the value can be significant. It turned out that the quality office in Brussels had already developed a cost for this error, so that standard value was used in the ROI evaluation of the courier program.

This next example involves the cost of customer complaints. A large international firm, Global Financial Services, which offers a variety of financial services to its clients, embarked on a technological solution to improve management of customer contact. The software, called ACT!™, was designed to turn contacts into relationships and relationships into increased sales. The software was rolled out in a one-day workshop that taught participants how to use the software. The workshop consisted of three groups of thirty relationship managers, for a total of ninety. Among the impact measures driven by the program were customer complaints. The program was designed to reduce the number of customer complaints caused by excessive delays in responding or by miscommunications in those responses. Because this was a critical measure, the company had taken some steps to develop the value for a complaint. Also, because costs often increase over time, the value of a complaint needs to be adjusted each year, using the producer price index. At the time of this study, $4,610 was used as the cost of a complaint. In other words, if a complaint could be avoided, it would save the organization $4,610. This value included the time involved in resolving the complaint, the value of services and adjustments provided to the complaining party, and the potential loss of business as a result of the situation.

In many organizations, a great deal of effort has been put into developing and improving values for quality measures, due, in part, to total quality management, continuous process improvement, and Six Sigma. All these processes have focused on individual quality measures and the cost of quality. As a result, specific standard values have been developed.

Converting Employee Time to Monetary Value

A reduction in the use of employee time is a typical objective for an organizational program. In a team environment, a program might enable teams to perform tasks in a shorter time frame or with fewer people. On an individual basis, time management workshops are designed to help professional, sales, supervisory, and managerial employees save time in performing daily tasks. The value of time saved is often an important measure of a program's success; fortunately, converting data on time saved to a monetary value is a relatively easy process.

The most obvious value involved in employee time savings is reduction of the labor costs of performing the work. The monetary savings are found by multiplying the hours saved by the labor cost per hour. For example, after attending a time management program, participants estimated that they saved an average of seventy-four minutes per day, worth $31.25 per day or $7,500 per year. These values for the time savings were based on the participants' average salary plus benefits.

Using the average wage with a percentage added for employee benefits is appropriate for most calculations. However, employee time may be worth more. For example, additional costs in maintaining an employee (office space, furniture, telephone, utilities, computers, secretarial support, and other overhead expenses) could be included in the average labor cost. Therefore, the average wage rate could quickly escalate to a larger number. However, the conservative approach is to use the salary plus employee benefits.

In addition to reduced labor cost per hour, other benefits can result from a time savings. Such benefits include improved service, avoidance of penalties for late projects, and creation of additional opportunities for profit.

Case Example: A Technology Company

A case example will illustrate the conversion of time savings to a monetary value. A firm that produced telecommunication equipment was concerned about the excessive amount of time that engineers were spending in meetings. The initial assessment indicated that meetings might be longer than necessary, that some of the meetings could be avoided, and that too many individuals participated in meetings. Project-related meetings occupied a significant amount of time in the organization. A meeting management program was implemented to address all three concerns uncovered through the initial assessment: number of meetings, meeting duration, and number of meeting participants. The result was significant reductions in those three measures, which translated into time savings. The value used for the time savings was the average salary of the participants, estimated from human resources records by using the midpoint value of the job classifications of the meeting participants. The average salary was adjusted by the standard benefits factor to arrive at a cost of $31 per hour. To add credibility to the calculation, the evaluators took two additional steps. First, participants were asked what percentage of their time saved was actually spent on other productive work. Next, participants were asked to provide examples of other productive work. Addressing these two issues helped make the value more credible.

A Word of Caution

A word of caution is in order when a value for time savings is being developed. Benefits from time savings are realized only when the amount of time saved translates into an additional contribution. If a program results in a time savings for a specific manager, a monetary benefit will be realized only if the manager uses the additional time productively. If a team-based program generates a new process that eliminates several hours of work each day, actual savings will be realized only if costs decrease because of a reduction in employees, a reduction in overtime pay, or increased productivity. Therefore, an important preliminary step in developing a value for time savings is to determine whether a *true* savings will be realized.

True time savings can be arrived at in a variety of ways:

- A reduction of people employed, if the time savings involves a large number of individuals

- A reduction in hours worked, especially if the individuals involved are contract employees or are working overtime

- Finding out how much of the time savings is related directly to the program (isolating the effects of the program)

- Determining what percentage of the time savings has been used for other productive work

- Providing examples of the productive work facilitated by the time savings (such examples may also provide insight into how the time savings have been generated)

Such adjustments are critical in order to ensure that reporting of time savings is credible. Otherwise, key audience members may view the time savings as "funny money"; some chief financial officers indicate that if a benefit does not show up in the cost statements, then they will not count it. This is a hard-nosed approach that increases the importance of taking steps to ensure that time savings data are credible.

Why Standard Values Are Developed

Perhaps a recap of why standard values have been developed, particularly in recent years, will be helpful. Measures that matter are labeled as such because they are important to an organization, and therefore executives need to know their contribution or their value. Naturally, the impact of problems that lead to the implementation of programs is often defined in terms of these measures that matter and also needs to be converted to a monetary value. Most organizations have experienced a variety of process improvement programs—for example, transformation, reengineering, and reinvention. These programs provide structure and a process for driving improvements. Often, an important part of process improvement programs is not only fine tuning, revising, or amplifying the measurement process but also converting the measures to monetary values so that the magnitude of the process improvements can be shown.

Finally, activity-based costing has become important as the accounting field has placed more emphasis on calculating the monetary value of activities and processes. Often, a new measure, such as the cost of providing a service, is based on a series of activities that have already been valued in monetary terms. Thus research on these activities and their applications has resulted in more standard values for a variety of output items.

Standard Values Are Everywhere

As this chapter has illustrated, standard values have been developed for and are located in various parts of every organization. Exhibit 2.1 lists some of the many functions that have developed standard values. As we mentioned at the beginning of this chapter, in the ROI Methodology, a standard value is defined as an accepted monetary value placed on a unit of measure. The output measures so valued represent cost savings or profits. Output in the form of sales, new customers, market share, or customer loyalty adds value through additional profits obtained from additional sales. Output that is not connected to profits, such as the output of an individual work group, can be converted to cost savings. For example, if the output of a work group can be increased as a result of a program, with no additional resources required to drive the output, then the

Exhibit 2.1. Functions That Generate Standard Values

- Finance, accounting
- Production, manufacturing
- Operations, methods
- Engineering, technical support
- Information technology
- Marketing, customer service
- Procurement, logistics, supply chain
- Research and development
- Human resources

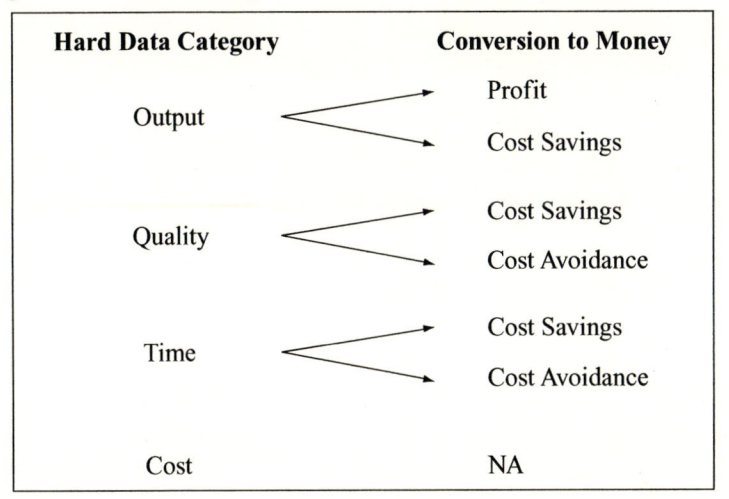

Figure 2.1. Converting Hard Data to Monetary Values

Hard Data Category	Conversion to Money
Output	Profit
	Cost Savings
Quality	Cost Savings
	Cost Avoidance
Time	Cost Savings
	Cost Avoidance
Cost	NA

corresponding value of the program is a cost savings (that is, additional output achieved for the same cost or decreased cost per unit of output). In the end, when converting data to money, the conversion is based on making money (profit), saving money, or avoiding costs. Figure 2.1 summarizes this process.

Perhaps no field has better developed standard values than sales and marketing. Table 2.3 shows examples of standard values from sales and marketing. As this table demonstrates, a tremendous number of standard values have been developed in sales and marketing, illustrating the strides in collecting standard values for output made in that field.

Final Thoughts

Standard values are everywhere. This chapter reinforces this statement by discussing several sources of standard values. The chapter also shows how standard values can be used as part of an ROI evaluation. They should come from credible sources, and when more than one standard value is located, the most credible—or if

Table 2.3. Examples of Standard Values from Sales and Marketing

Metric	Definition	Notes on Conversion to Monetary Value
Sales	Sale of the product or service, recorded in a variety of ways—for example, by product, by time period, by customer	The data must be converted to a monetary value by applying the profit margin for a particular sales category.
Profit margin (percentage)	$\frac{\text{Price} - \text{Cost}}{\text{Cost}}$ for the product, customer, or time period	Factor for converting sales to monetary value added to the organization.
Unit margin	Unit price less unit cost	This measure shows the value of incremental sales.
Channel margin	Channel profits as a percentage of the product's selling price in that channel	This measure shows the value of sales through a particular marketing channel.
Retention rate	Ratio of customers retained to the number of customers at risk of leaving	The value of this measure is the money saved by not having to acquire a replacement customer.
Churn rate	Ratio of customers who leave to the number who are at risk of leaving	The value of this measure is the money saved by not having to acquire a replacement customer.
Customer profit	Difference between the revenues earned from and the cost associated with a customer relationship during the specified period	The monetary value added is the profit obtained from customers. It all goes toward the bottom line.
Customer value, lifetime	Present value of the future cash flows attributed to a customer relationship	This is a bottom-line measure; as customer value increases, it adds directly to profits. Also, when a customer is added, the incremental value is the customer lifetime value average.

Cannibalization rate	Percentage of new product sales taken from existing product lines	This measure should be minimized because it represents an adverse effect on existing products; the value added is the loss of profits due to the loss of sales in the existing product lines.
Workload	Hours required to service clients and prospects	The cost of this measure includes the salaries, commissions, and benefits paid for workload hours.
Inventories	Total amount of product or brand available for sale in a particular channel	Because inventories are valued at the cost of carrying the inventory, costs involve space, handling, and the time value of money. Insufficient inventory results in the cost of expediting the new inventory or the loss of sales because of the inventory outage.
Market share	Sales revenue as a percentage of total market sales	Actual sales are converted to monetary values through the profit margins. This is a measure of competitiveness.
Loyalty	The length of time the customer stays with the organization, the willingness to pay a premium, and the willingness to search for a brand or product	The value of this measure is calculated as the profit from the sale or the additional profit on the premium.

Source: Adapted from Farris, Bendle, Pfeifer, and Ribstein, 2006, pp. 46–47.

all are credible, the lowest—should be used. When standard values are not available, other methods must be used to find the monetary value of the measures that matter. The next chapter discusses one such method: calculating the value.

References

Campanella, J. (ed.). *Principles of Quality Costs*. (3rd ed.) Milwaukee, Wis.: American Society for Quality, 1999.

Farris, P. W., Bendle, N. T., Pfeifer, P. E., and Ribstein, D. J. *Marketing Metrics: 50+ Metrics Every Executive Should Master*. Upper Saddle River, N.J.: Wharton School Publishing, 2006.

Fishman, C. *The Wal-Mart Effect: How the World's Most Powerful Company Really Works—and How It's Transforming the American Economy*. New York: Penguin Books, 2006.

Rust, R., Zahorik, A., and Keiningham, R. *Return on Quality: Measuring the Financial Impact of Your Company's Quest for Quality*. Chicago: Probus, 1994.

3

Calculate the Value

If a standard value is not available for a desired measure, one logical approach is to calculate its monetary value. This chapter discusses two basic approaches. One is to use cost statements, reports, or records to develop the value. This approach can be time-consuming and is not always recommended because of the excessive resources that may be required. The second approach is to try to develop links between the measure in question, one that is difficult to convert to a monetary value, and some other measure that can be converted more easily. The upside is that much progress has been made in showing links between hard-to-measure data and other, easy-to-measure data. The downside is that finding these connections is difficult. We suggest that evaluators should not try to calculate a relationship but should try to find one that has already been developed.

Using Historical Costs

Sometimes, historical records contain the value of a measure or reveal the cost (or value) of a unit of improvement. This technique involves identifying the appropriate records and tabulating the cost components of the measure in question. For example, a large construction firm implemented a program to improve safety performance. The program improved several safety-related performance measures, ranging from OSHA fines to total workers' compensation costs. Using one year of data from the company's records, the staff calculated the average value of improvements in each safety measure.

Key Issues in Using Records and Reports

The technique of developing monetary values from historical records, while credible, can be difficult to use for several reasons. The first and perhaps the most important issue is the amount of time required to calculate the values. This technique often involves securing a variety of records and calculating an average. For example, a financial services firm in Tel Aviv was interested in demonstrating the value of an ethics program. One of the payoff measures was a reduction in expense account violations, whether intentional or unintentional. Calculating the cost of an expense account violation required that an evaluator add up the last fifty violations. It took a lot of effort to pore over the records, determine the money lost due to each violation, add the numbers, and determine the average value. Again, using historical records is a credible method, but it often requires too much time.

Another issue is availability of data. Sometimes, all the data are not available and exhaustive searching may be necessary to find exactly what is needed. Still another issue is access to the data. In some situations, the individual conducting the evaluation may not have access to the data. Some of the data may be considered off-limits or proprietary and thus may not be available for use in the evaluation. Accuracy of the data is yet another consideration. Records, although they appear precise, may not be accurate.

Inaccuracy leads to a final concern: estimation. While records may clearly indicate direct expenses, this information often represents only part of the cost. Other costs may have to be estimated. For example, the cost of employee turnover may include costs that are not indicated in the records. While the direct costs of replacing an individual—for instance, the costs of recruiting, selection, orientation, and initial training—are easily available from the records, other costs—such as those associated with disruption, bottlenecks, lost productivity, or lost knowledge—are not readily available from the records, if at all. Therefore, even though historical records are being used to develop a monetary value, estimates would have to be used in the calculation.

For all of these reasons, historical records are usually used to convert data to a monetary value only when the sponsor, the key client, wants to know the cost of the item because it has not been previously developed.

A word of caution is in order. If the historical records approach is used to convert data to monetary value, this part of the evaluation may require more time, effort, or money than has been budgeted for the entire ROI evaluation. The client should be made aware of this possibility, and it might be desirable to assign responsibility for developing the value of the data to other, more suitable parties.

All of the issues in this section need to be addressed during the evaluation planning stage discussed in *ROI Fundamentals*, the first book in this series.

Case Study: A Metropolitan Transit Authority

Here is a detailed example of the historical records approach.

A large city had implemented an absenteeism reduction program for its bus drivers. The vice president of human resources was interested in presenting the return on investment for the program. To show the impact of the program, a value for the cost of one absence was needed. As part of the study, an external consulting firm developed a detailed cost of one absence, including the full costs of a driver pool that included 231 substitute drivers, in order to cover unexpected absences.

While several approaches could have been taken in order to determine the cost of absenteeism, the analysis at Metro Transit Authority was based on the cost of replacement driver staffing. Substitute drivers, as well as the regular drivers, were expected to work an average of 240 days per year, leaving 20 days for vacation, holidays, and sick days. The average wage for a substitute driver was $33,500 per year, and the employee benefits factor was 38 percent of payroll. When a regular driver was unexpectedly absent, he or she could charge the absence to either sick leave or vacation, substituting a planned paid day (vacation) for the unexpected absence. This was almost always what occurred. Because of this system, the cost of absenteeism was minimized. When there was a perfect match between the number of absences and the number of substitute drivers, the cost of the driver pool was for vacation coverage.

However, substitute driver staffing was not always at the exact level needed for a specific day's unscheduled absences. The planned number of substitute drivers was a function of expected absenteeism. Because of the service problems that could develop as a result of understaffing, for most days overstaffing of substitute drivers was planned. To minimize potential delays, all substitute drivers were required to report to work each day. Substitute drivers not used in driver seats essentially performed no productive work that could be counted as added value. During the previous year, overstaffing had occurred on about 75 percent of the weekdays and nonholidays. This overstaffing represented 4,230 days of wasted time. On weekends and holidays, overstaffing had occurred almost half the time, representing a total of 570 wasted days.

On some days, a shortage of substitute drivers occurred, which caused the buses to run late; in those cases, overtime was used to make the adjustment. During the last year, there had been sixty-five instances in which a driver was not available, and it was estimated that in forty-five of those situations, a regular driver was paid double time to fill in the schedule.

A final and significant cost of absenteeism, beyond the salaries and benefits of the substitute drivers, was the cost of recruiting, training, maintaining, and supervising the substitute driver pool. This item included recruiting and employment, training and preparation, office space, administration and coordination, and

Exhibit 3.1. The Cost of Absenteeism at Metro Transit Authority

Average daily cost of wages and benefits for a substitute driver:

$$\$33,500 \times 1.38 \div 240 = \$192.63$$

Cost of overstaffing, weekdays:

$$\$192.63 \times 4,230 = \$814,800$$

Cost of overstaffing, weekends and holidays:

$$\$192.63 \times 570 = \$109,800$$

Cost of understaffing, overtime:

$$\$192.63 \times 45 = \$8,670$$

Cost of recruiting, training, maintaining, and supervising the driver pool:

$$\$33,500 \times 231 \times 0.25 = \$1,934,600$$

Total cost of absenteeism = $2,867,070

---

supervision. This item was estimated to be equal to 25 percent of the substitute drivers' annual pay. Exhibit 3.1 illustrates how the total direct cost of absenteeism was developed from the preceding information.

As this impact study revealed, developing historical costs can sometimes be expensive and time-consuming, leading evaluators to look for an easier way. Using historical cost data may not be the technique of choice because of the time, effort, and costs involved. In those situations, one or more of the other techniques discussed in this book should be used.

Linking with Other Measures

When standard values and historical records are unavailable or inappropriate, a feasible approach might be to find a relationship between the measure in question and some other measure that can

Exhibit 3.2. Classic Relationships

Job satisfaction	connected to	Turnover
Job satisfaction	connected to	Absenteeism
Job satisfaction	connected to	Customer satisfaction
Organizational commitment	connected to	Productivity
Engagement	connected to	Productivity
Customer satisfaction	connected to	Revenue
Conflicts	connected to	Productivity

be easily converted to a monetary value. This approach involves identifying relationships in which there is a strong correlation between one measure and another with a standard value.

Classic Relationships

Fortunately, in the last two decades, many relationships between measures within organizations have been found. Exhibit 3.2 lists some of these classic relationships. Success in using the linking technique comes from finding these relationships that have already been worked out. These relationships have been figured out because the organization has an interest in understanding the connections between the measures.

For example, consider the classic relationship shown in Figure 3.1: the relationship between customer satisfaction and revenue from those customers. This is perhaps the relationship that is most commonly examined because it seems logical to conclude that customer satisfaction and revenue are related. Customers are more satisfied, so they purchase more products or they continue to be a customer. In most organizations, this relationship exists, and today a majority of larger organizations have examined this connection.

Figure 3.1. A Classic Relationship Between Customer Satisfaction and Revenue

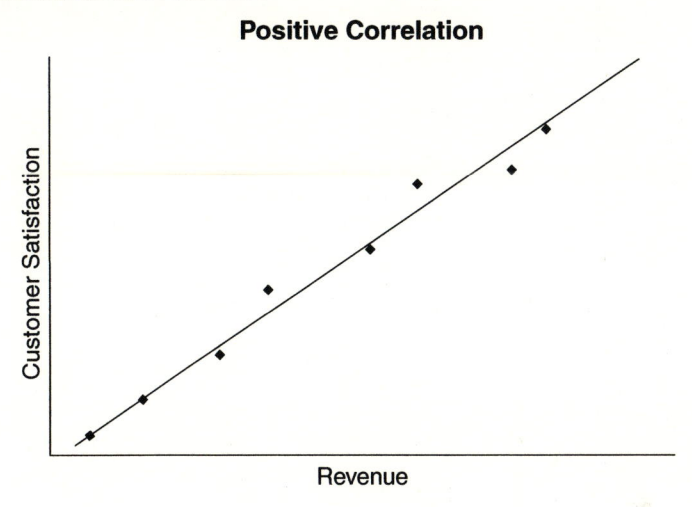

Positive Correlation

[Scatter plot with Customer Satisfaction on y-axis and Revenue on x-axis showing positive linear correlation]

The important point is that when a program results in increased customer satisfaction, then revenue increases, giving the organization a direct payoff. Both customer satisfaction and revenue may be program objectives, and both may be payoff measures that are driven by the program. In that situation, customer satisfaction would be listed as an intangible measure, because the method of converting customer satisfaction to a monetary value (making it tangible) uses the connection of customer satisfaction to revenue, which is already included in the evaluation as a payoff measure. It is important not to count this value twice. However, if revenue is not used as a measure in the evaluation but is used only to show the monetary value of the improved customer satisfaction, the established relationship between the two measures provides an opportunity to show that payoff.

Case Example: A European Postal Service

The relationship illustrated in Figure 3.2 represents a correlation between job satisfaction and employee turnover. In a postal

Figure 3.2. The Relationship Between Job Satisfaction and Turnover

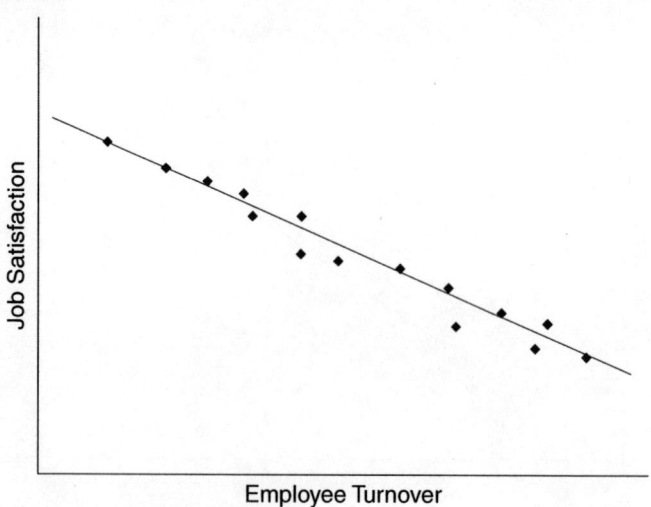

[Figure: scatter plot with downward-sloping trend line; y-axis labeled "Job Satisfaction", x-axis labeled "Employee Turnover"]

service program designed to improve job satisfaction, a monetary value needed to be assigned to changes in the job satisfaction index. A predetermined relationship showing a correlation between improvements in job satisfaction and reductions in turnover for specific groups linked the changes in job satisfaction directly to turnover. These data sets were taken from the human capital system. Through the use of a standard value, the cost of turnover can easily be calculated. As a result, a change in job satisfaction is converted to an approximate monetary value. Such a valuation is not always exact because of error and other factors, but this type of estimate may be sufficient for converting job satisfaction to a monetary value.

Case Example: Sears, Roebuck and Company

In some situations, a chain of relationships may be established to show the connection between two or more variables. In this approach, a measure that may be difficult to convert to a monetary

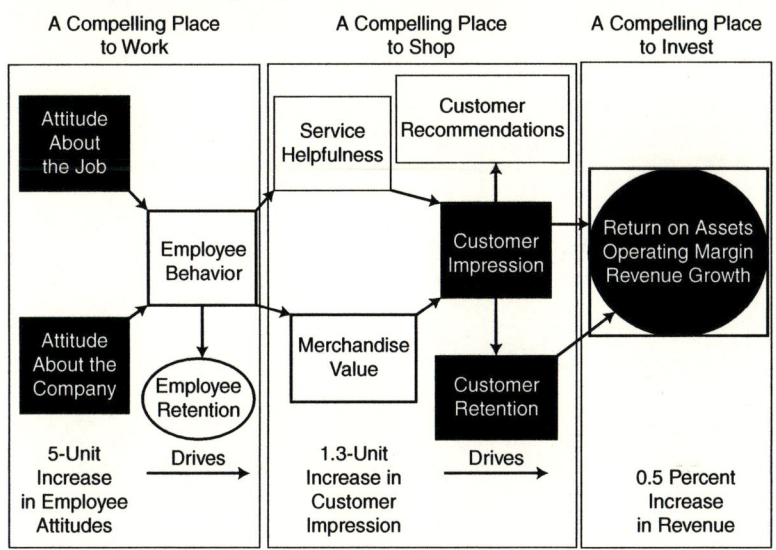

Figure 3.3. Link Between Job Satisfaction and Revenue at Sears, Roebuck and Company

A Compelling Place to Work	A Compelling Place to Shop	A Compelling Place to Invest
Attitude About the Job → Employee Behavior ← Attitude About the Company; Employee Retention	Service Helpfulness, Customer Recommendations, Customer Impression, Merchandise Value, Customer Retention	Return on Assets, Operating Margin, Revenue Growth
5-Unit Increase in Employee Attitudes — Drives →	1.3-Unit Increase in Customer Impression — Drives →	0.5 Percent Increase in Revenue

Source: Rucci, Kirn, and Quinn, 1998, p. 83. Used with permission. Copyright 1998 by the President and Fellows of Harvard College.

value is linked to other measures that, in turn, are linked to measures on which a value can be placed. Ultimately, the measures are linked to a monetary value that is often based on profits. Figure 3.3 shows the model used by Sears, one of the world's largest retail chains (Rucci, Kirn, and Quinn, 1998). The model connects job attitudes (collected directly from the employees) with customer service, which is directly related to revenue growth. The shaded measures are collected and distributed in the form of Sears total performance indicators. The rectangles in the chart represent survey information, while the ovals represent hard data.

As the model shows, a 5-point improvement in employee attitudes will drive a 1.3-point improvement in customer satisfaction. This, in turn, drives a 0.5 percent increase in revenue growth.

Therefore, if employee attitudes at a local store improved by 5 points and previous revenue growth was 5 percent, the new revenue growth would be 5.5 percent.

Links between measures such as those just described, often called the *service-profit chain*, create a promising way to place monetary values on measures that are difficult to quantify.

Concerns When Using Relationships Between Measures to Assign Monetary Values

This section presents some pros and cons about the use of relationships between measures to assign monetary values. One advantage is that many of these relationships have been figured out, though not necessarily as part of an ROI study. However, if a relevant relationship has not been worked out, attempting to figure out one of these relationships simply to convert one data item to a monetary value would likely allocate too much time and too many resources to that one issue. One must keep the issue in perspective, remembering that the item is only one measure in one part of the ROI evaluation. To exhaust days or weeks of time and resources in an attempt to convert one data item to a monetary value would be unadvisable. For this reason, the recommended approach is to find a relationship between measures that has already been established.

However, if no relevant relationship has been worked out, that fact may bring up an important issue. When attempting to convert soft data—a typical category of hard-to-value data—to a monetary value, it may be helpful to raise the issue that there has been no work within the organization to convert it to money; that is, classical relationships have not been developed. Calling attention to this need may lead to another project, but that project will be beyond the scope of the team conducting the ROI evaluation. As discussed earlier, the cost in time and money of such a study would likely exceed the value of the evaluation itself.

Final Thoughts

This chapter has presented two credible approaches for converting data to monetary values. The first, calculating the cost of a data item by using records, cost statements, and reports, often involves adding up the costs of repeated incidents and averaging them to get the cost of one unit. The second technique involves finding a link between the hard-to-value measure and an easy-to-value measure. While both of these are credible methods, they may require too much time and effort if the data are not readily available or the relevant relationships have not already been determined. These techniques are useful, but they must be used with caution. When the techniques described in this chapter are not feasible, then the next source of data is research—conducted either by speaking with experts or by perusing the databases. These techniques are described in the next chapter.

Reference

Rucci, A., Kirn, S., and Quinn, R. "The Employee-Customer-Profit Chain at Sears." *Harvard Business Review*, Jan./Feb. 1998, 76(1), 82–98.

4

Find the Value

This chapter presents two easy and credible techniques for converting data to monetary values. The first is to have experts from within or outside an organization place a monetary value on a unit of measure, using their knowledge and experience. The second technique is to search databases in order to find a value for the unit of measure in question. Many databases are accessible on the Internet, making this an easy-to-use method that generates abundant information.

Using Internal and External Experts

When faced with converting soft data items to monetary values when historical records or standard values are often not available, obtaining input from experts may be an appropriate solution. In this approach, experts provide the value of one unit of measure. Individuals who have knowledge of the situation under evaluation as well as the respect of the management group are often the best choices to provide expert input. These experts must understand the processes and must be willing to provide values as well as the assumptions used in arriving at the values. When requesting input from experts, it is best to explain the full scope of what is needed, providing as many specifics as possible. Most experts will have their own method of determining a value.

Working with Internal Experts

Internal experts are relatively easy to find. Many times, the expert is located in the obvious department or has an obvious job title. For example, in a BlueCross BlueShield affiliate, a program was being implemented to lower the number of customer appeals. An appeal occurs when a customer requests that an insurance company reconsider its decision in regard to the payment or coverage of an item. To calculate the ROI, the cost of one appeal was needed. A standard value had not been developed for this measure, so a logical choice was to go to the customer appeals department (the obvious department), which had several customer appeals coordinators (the obvious job title). These individuals were knowledgeable about the issues involved when an insurance claim was appealed and dealt with these issues daily. They were credible and were in the best position to offer a credible value for the measure.

Another way to find an expert is to trace the origin of a report. Many data items come from a report generated by a department or a function. The individual who sends the report may know the value of the measure or may know the person who would be in the best position to provide relevant data. If the identity of the individual who generated the report is unknown or unclear, the organization directory might indicate who within the organization could address the issue. If all else fails, ask someone. Asking others can narrow the search to the individual or individuals who know the information best.

Several issues must be addressed when asking an internal expert to provide a monetary value. First is the expert's experience. The most experienced individuals should provide the value. Another issue is conflicts of interest. Do the experts have a reason for wanting the value of the measure to be large or small? Sometimes, a bias is present. For example, in the BlueCross BlueShield case, if the customer appeals coordinators providing the information had felt that their workload was too heavy and that they did not have time to handle the appeals, they might have placed a higher value on the number of appeals processed in order to bring the matter to the attention of the management team. It is important that the experts who provide the monetary value be neutral.

Working with External Experts

When internal experts are not available, external experts are often sought. Like internal experts, external experts must be selected on the basis of their experience with the unit of measure. Fortunately, many experts are available who work directly with important measures such as creativity, innovation, employee attitudes, customer satisfaction, employee turnover, absenteeism, and grievances. They are often willing to provide values for these items. Consider the credibility and reputation of the expert carefully; these factors are critical, because the credibility of the value will be directly related to the expert's reputation.

The credibility of external experts is often determined by their credentials. Sometimes, the expert's credentials involve certifications, degrees, or experience in a relevant area. Credibility could also be based on an individual's publications; writing articles, studies, or books about the subject in question can add to an expert's credibility. Consulting experience can also qualify an individual as an expert. Finally, a track record in offering a value for a measurement and having that value verified through other analysis is another positive credential. Above all, the individual must be neutral in regard to the value, with no bias toward assigning either a high or a low value.

Case Example: A Manufacturing Plant

An example will help clarify the process of consulting an internal expert. In one manufacturing plant, a team-building program was designed to reduce the number of grievances that proceeded to step 2 in the plant's four-step grievance resolution process. Step 2 was when the grievance was recorded in writing and became a measurable data item. Except for the costs of settlements and direct external costs, the company had no records on the total costs of grievances. (For example, there were no data on the time required to resolve a grievance.) Therefore, a value from an expert was needed. The manager of labor relations, who had credibility with senior management and thorough knowledge of the grievance process, provided an estimate of the cost. He based his estimate on the average settlement when a grievance was lost; direct costs related to grievances (arbitration, legal fees, printing, research); the estimated amount of supervisory, staff, and employee time associated with grievances; and a factor for reduced morale and other "soft" consequences. This internally generated, estimated value, while not a precise figure, was appropriate for this analysis and had adequate credibility with management.

Case Example: A Health Care Firm

Sometimes, two or more methods may be used in combination to develop monetary values. In a study involving a health care firm, the cost of a formal complaint filed with the vice president of human resources was evaluated. In this analysis, it was assumed that if no complaints were filed, there would be no costs of communication, investigation, or defense associated with sexual harassment. Two approaches were used to arrive at the cost of a complaint. First, the direct cost of all activities and processes connected with sexual harassment for an entire year was captured. This figure was taken directly from cost statements. Second, the other costs (for example, staff and management time spent on these activities) were estimated, using input from internal experts—the EEOC and affirmative action staff. Figure 4.1 shows how these two values were combined to arrive at a total value of $852,000 for

Figure 4.1. Converting Data to Monetary Values by Combining Historical Costs and Expert Input

```
The Cost of a Sexual Harassment Complaint
```

                  Actual Costs   Legal Fees,
                  from Records   Settlements, Losses,
                                        Material,
                                        Direct Expenses
    35 $852,000
    Complaints   Annually

                  Estimated   EEO/AA Staff
                  Additional Costs   Time, Management
                  from Staff   Time

$$\text{Cost Per Complaint: } \frac{\$852,000}{35} = \$24,343$$

thirty-five complaints, or an approximate value of $24,000 for one complaint.

Using External Databases

For some soft data items, it may be appropriate to assign monetary values that are taken from the research of others. This strategy taps external databases containing studies and research projects that focus on the cost of data items. Fortunately, many databases contain cost studies on a variety of data items related to programs. Information is available on the cost of turnover, absenteeism, grievances, accidents, and even customer satisfaction. The difficulty lies in finding a database with studies or research on a situation similar to the program that is being evaluated. Ideally, the information would come from a similar setting in the same industry, but that is not always possible. Sometimes, information that relates to all industries or organizations can be sufficient, perhaps with an adjustment to fit the industry under consideration.

Internet Searches

For some, the Web holds the most promise for finding monetary values that are not readily available from standard values, historical records, or experts. Progress continues to be made in the use of Web searches to develop monetary values. A few guidelines for using the Web are presented later in this section.

General Web directories and portals may be very helpful. Although they have a bit in common with Web search engines, general Web directories such as Yahoo, Open Directory, and Look Smart also differ greatly. Although their databases may include less than 1 percent of what search engines cover, general Web directories can still help an evaluator locate needed information and in many cases may be the best starting point (Hock, 2004).

A specialized directory is more appropriate than the general Web directories for accessing Web resources on a specific topic. Such sites bring together well-organized collections of Internet resources on specific topics and provide an important starting point for research on monetary values of measures.

Search engines provide more possibilities for searches because of their vast coverage. General Web search engines such as AltaVista, AllTheWeb, and Google stand in contrast to a Web directory in three primary ways:

1. They are much larger, containing over a billion instead of a few million records.
2. Virtually no human selectivity is involved in determining which Web pages are included in the search engine's database.
3. They are designed for searching (responding to a user's specific query) rather than browsing and, therefore, provide much more substantial searching capabilities than directories.

Groups, mailing lists, and other interactive forums form a class of Internet resources that too few researchers take advantage of. They can be useful for a broad range of applications, including finding the monetary value of data. Because they can tap knowledge held only in people's minds, these tools can be gold mines of information not found elsewhere.

A range of news resources are also available online, including news services, newswires, newspapers, news consolidation services, and more. Because some studies centering on particular values are newsworthy, online news items can be excellent sources for those who are seeking to capture the value of specific types of data.

In general, Web searches are an important tool for the evaluator when it comes to collecting information on monetary values.

A typical concern about Web searches is the quality of the content. Some think that the Internet has low-quality content, although in reality, it is no different from other sources; for example, right alongside the high-quality publications available on newsstands are those with low-quality content. Nonetheless, here are a few guidelines to help evaluators obtain high-quality information from Web searches:

- *Consider the source*. From what organization does the content originate? Check to see that the organization is identified both on the Web page and in the URL. The URL will identify the owner, and the owner may be revealing in regard to the quality. Is the content identified as coming from known sources, such as a news organization, the government, an academic journal, a professional association, or a major investment firm?

- *Consider the motivation*. What is the purpose of this site—dissemination of academic research, consumer protection, sales, entertainment, or political dialogue? Considering the motivation behind a posting can be helpful in assessing the degree of objectivity.

- *Look at the quality of the writing*. If the content contains spelling and grammatical errors, the data may have quality problems as well.

- *Look at the quality of the source documentation.* First, remember that the number of footnotes is not necessarily an accurate measure of the quality of a work. On the other hand, if facts are cited, does the page identify the origin of the facts? Check out some of the cited sources to see whether the facts actually appear there.
- *Check whether the site and its content are as current as they should be.* If the site is reporting on current events, the need for currency and the answer to the question of currency will be apparent.
- *Use multiple sources to verify the facts used in the data conversion, or choose the most authoritative source.* Unfortunately, many facts given on Web pages are simply wrong, due to carelessness, exaggeration, guessing, or other factors. Often, they are wrong because the person creating the page content did not check the facts.

The preceding list provides some helpful ways to focus on the quality of information, which is crucial in a search for a credible monetary value for a particular measure.

Critical thinking should be applied to the information found and the claims that are made. Exhibit 4.1 provides some critical thinking questions to help the serious searcher find the right information (Berkman, 2004).

Case Example: A Regional Bank

An example will illustrate the use of databases to find a monetary value for a measure. A new program was designed to reduce turnover of branch employees in a regional banking group. To complete the evaluation and calculate the ROI, the cost of turnover was needed. To develop the turnover value internally, several costs would have to be identified, including the costs of recruiting, employment processing, orientation, training new employees, lost productivity while a new employee was being trained, quality problems, scheduling difficulties, and customer satisfaction problems. Additional costs included regional manager time spent on turnover issues and, in some cases, exit costs of litigation, severance, and unemployment. Obviously, these costs were significant. However, most

Exhibit 4.1. Ask the Right Questions When Searching the Web

Before going to the Web for business research, ask yourself:

- Why am I choosing the Web to perform this research?

  If it's because the Web is fast, why is that good?

  If it's because it's free, why is free information best? How much would I pay for good information?

- Is a search engine the best tool to find what I'm looking for on the Web?

- Where else might I find the same type of information?

- Would a library or a fee-based database contain the information I'm looking for?

When you find a source of interest on the Web, ask yourself:

- Who put this information on the Web? Why?
- If it's free, why did the creator make it that way?
- Who gains from having this information on the Web?

When evaluating the authority of the publisher or creator of the information, ask yourself:

- What are the qualifications of this person or organization?
- Why should I trust this person or organization?
- Why are these opinions being offered here?

If a search engine doesn't return the information you're looking for, ask yourself:

- Did I use all the appropriate keywords and phrases?
- Did I follow the search engine's instructions?

Exhibit 4.1. Ask the Right Questions When Searching the Web (*Continued*)

- Could the search engine have failed to index the site that includes the information?

- Could the information be online, but as part of the "invisible Web" that's inaccessible to search engines?

- Could it mean that the information isn't on the Web? If so, might it be available from other sources (for example, the library, a journal database, a book or directory, an association, an expert)?

- Could it be that what I'm looking for isn't the kind of information that's easily found on the Web? If so, am I better off trying a different type of resource altogether?

- Could it mean that the information simply doesn't exist?

When you find statistical data, ask yourself:

- What (or who or where) is the original source or creator of the data?

- Is this the most recent version or series of the data?

- Do I know the larger context from which these data were derived?

- Where can I find the methodologies and assumptions used to create these statistics?

On an online news site, ask yourself:

- What makes this a legitimate news-gathering and reporting site?

- What is a legitimate news-gathering and reporting site?

- Can I distinguish editorial content from advertising on this site?

Source: Adapted from Berkman, 2004.

program managers do not have the time to calculate the cost of turnover, particularly when it is needed only for a one-time event such as evaluating a program. In this case, turnover cost studies in the same industry placed the value at about 1.1 to 1.25 times the average annual salary of the employees. Most turnover cost studies report the cost of turnover as a multiple of annual base salaries. In this case, management decided to be conservative and adjusted the value down to 0.9 times the average annual base salary of the employees.

Case Example: A Federal Agency

In another example, a federal government agency wanted to reduce turnover among its communication specialists. The agency was experiencing turnover in the range of 35–40 percent in these highly specialized jobs. Over 1,500 individuals were in the job group, so the results of this turnover were disastrous. Unable to increase pay, the agency decided on a unique approach to the turnover problem, offering a master's degree program for communication specialists, to be attended on agency time. This program took three years to complete and was offered to specialists who had at least one year of service. The individuals involved in the program had to agree to two years of service after they received their master's degree. (For more details on this case study, see Phillips and Phillips, 2007.)

Although the monetary value of the program derived primarily from turnover reduction, value was also received from the graduate projects that were required for the specialists' degrees. To calculate the cost of turnover, an Internet search was conducted through ERIC. The search, available through EBSCO*host*, yielded a variety of studies that, when arranged by job group, yielded the information found in Table 4.1. The target group closely fit the specialist category, a fact that suggested that the cost of turnover was two to four times the annual salary. This number was higher than the human resources staff anticipated. As a compromise, a value of 1.75 times the annual salary was used. While this value was probably lower than the actual fully loaded cost of turnover, it was conservative to assign this value. It is much better to use a conservative value than to calculate the fully loaded costs, which would involve all the categories shown in note 2 of Table 4.1.

Table 4.1. Summary of Turnover Costs from an External Database

Job Type or Category	Turnover Costs as a Percentage of Annual Wages or Salary
Entry-level workers—hourly, nonskilled (for example, fast-food worker)	30–50%
Service and production workers—hourly (for example, courier)	40–70%
Skilled workers—hourly (for example, machinist)	75–100%
Clerical and administrative (for example, scheduler)	50–80%
Professional (for example, sales representative, nurse, accountant)	75–125%
Technical (for example, computer technician)	100–150%
Engineers (for example, chemical engineer)	200–300%
Specialists (for example, computer software designer)	200–400%
Supervisors and team leaders (for example, section supervisor)	100–150%
Middle managers (for example, department manager)	125–200%

General notes:

1. Percentages are rounded, to reflect the general range of costs from the studies.

Table 4.1. Summary of Turnover Costs from an External Database (*Continued*)

2. Costs are fully loaded to include all the costs of replacing an employee and bringing him or her to the level of productivity and efficiency of the former employee. The turnover included in the studies is usually unexpected and unwanted. The following cost categories are usually included:

   - Exit cost of previous employee
   - Recruiting cost
   - Employee cost
   - Orientation cost
   - Training cost
   - Wages and salaries while training
   - Lost productivity
   - Quality problems
   - Customer dissatisfaction
   - Loss of expertise and knowledge
   - Supervisor's time on turnover issues
   - Temporary replacement costs

3. Turnover costs are usually calculated when excessive turnover is an issue and turnover costs are high. The actual cost of turnover for a specific job in an organization may vary considerably. The ranges listed in this table are intended to reflect what has been generally reported in the literature when turnover costs are analyzed.

4. The sources of the data in this table fall into three general categories:

   (a) Industry and trade magazines that have reported the cost of turnover for a specific job within an industry.

   (b) Publications in general management (for both academics and practitioners), human resources management, human resources development, training, and performance improvement that publish ROI cost studies because of the importance of turnover to senior managers and human resources managers.

   (c) Independent studies that have been conducted by organizations and not reported in the literature. Some of these studies have been provided privately to the ROI Institute. In addition, the ROI Institute has conducted several turnover cost studies; these results are included in the table.

This brief example shows the potential value of using the Internet. Table 4.1 could serve as a useful guide to monetary values for other turnover studies. Other information similar to that in Table 4.1 can be easily obtained online.

Exhibit 4.2. Finding Data: A Variety of Databases

- Search engines
- Research databases
- Academic databases
- Industry and trade databases
- Government databases
- Commercial databases
- Association databases
- Professional databases

Other Sources of Databases

A variety of databases are available, and they are not found only on the Internet. Exhibit 4.2 lists some types of databases that are available. Industries, trade associations, government organizations, commercial organizations, and professional associations all represent excellent potential sources of databases. Often, these databases can be downloaded from the organization. Sometimes, they are only available on hard copy and obtaining them may involve a charge. Regardless of the source, the key is to find the most credible data available for the measures in question.

Final Thoughts

This chapter presents two techniques that hold promise for capturing the monetary value of a measure. Input from internal or external experts is usually easy to obtain and is often credible. Obtaining a value from an expert may take no more time than an e-mail or a phone call. The challenge in using this method is to ensure that the expert is the most credible source of information (Guiding Principle 3). Sometimes, external databases of data from previously developed studies are available. Using the Internet is an excellent way to find and use these databases. If the needed data are not found in Internet databases, other databases may provide the information needed to convert a measure to a monetary value. Using experts and drawing on information from external databases are credible techniques for finding the monetary value of a measure and are feasible for most programs. When experts and databases are unavailable, the next technique to consider is estimations. Their use in converting data to money is described next.

References

Berkman, R. *The Skeptical Business Searcher: The Information Advisor's Guide to Evaluating Web Data, Sites, and Sources.* Medford, N.J.: Information Today, 2004.

Hock, R. *The Extreme Searcher's Internet Handbook.* Medford, N.J.: CyberAge Books, 2004.

Phillips, P. P., and Phillips, J. J. *Proving the Value of HR: ROI Case Studies.* Birmingham, Ala.: ROI Institute, 2007.

5

Estimate the Value

This final chapter on the techniques for converting data to monetary values shows how to use estimates from a variety of sources. Using estimates is the technique of last resort for converting data to monetary values because of the perceived inaccuracy of estimates. The challenge when using estimates is to ensure that the data are taken from the most credible source, that they are adjusted for the error of the estimate, and that they are reported cautiously.

Using Estimates from Participants

In some situations, program participants are in the best position to estimate the value of improvement in soft data. This method is appropriate when participants are capable of providing estimates of the value of the unit of measure that was improved by implementation of the program. Participants should be provided with clear instructions, along with examples of the type of information needed. The advantage of this method is that the individuals closest to the improvement are often able to provide the most reliable estimates of its value.

Case Example: A Manufacturing Plant

An example will illustrate the process of having participants estimate the monetary value of a measure. A group of supervisors in a manufacturing plant attended an interpersonal skills program,

"Improving Work Habits," which was designed to lower the rate of absenteeism of employees in their work units. It was hoped that successful application of the program would result in a reduction in absenteeism. To calculate the ROI for the program, it was necessary to determine the average cost of one absence. As in most organizations, historical records on the cost of absenteeism were not available. Experts were not available, and external databases for that particular industry were sparse. As a result, supervisors (the program participants) were asked to estimate the cost of an absence.

In a group interview, each participant was asked to recall the last time an employee in his or her work group was unexpectedly absent and to describe what had to be done to compensate for the absence. Because the impact of an absence varies considerably from one employee to another even within the same work unit, the group listened to all explanations. After reflecting on what had to be done when an employee was absent, each supervisor was asked to provide an estimate of the average cost of an absence within the company. As is sometimes the case, some of the supervisors were reluctant to provide estimates, but with prodding and encouragement, they provided a value. They were also asked to state how confident they were in their estimates.

Each value given was adjusted by the confidence percentage of the person who provided the estimate. The adjusted values for the group were averaged, and the result was the estimated cost of an absence for use in the program evaluation. Although it was an estimate, this value was probably more accurate than data from external databases, calculations using internal records, or estimates from experts would have been. Because it came from supervisors who dealt with the issue daily, it was likely to have credibility with senior management.

Key Issues in Using Participant Estimates

One of the fundamental issues in using participants to estimate the monetary value of a measure is the credibility of those providing the estimate. In some cases, participants are in a position to provide the data, as the preceding example illustrates. However, in many cases, they are not. They may not know the full scope of the measure. This issue is different from the issue that occurs when participants isolate the effects of a program, which is discussed in *Isolation of Results*, book three in this series. In that situation, participants are often the most credible source because their performance has caused the change, and they can isolate the effects of the program based on their own changes in performance. However, when the task is placing a monetary value on a data item, the individual driving the performance may not appreciate all the consequences or all the impacts of the measure, all of which affect the monetary value.

Another issue is adjusting for the error of the estimate, as explained in the previous example. Asking the question "What is your confidence in the value that you have provided, on a scale of 0 percent (no confidence) to 100 percent (complete confidence)?" provides an adjustment factor that can be multiplied by the estimated value. Essentially, the confidence percentage is an error discount factor.

Using Estimates from Supervisors and Managers

In some situations, participants may be incapable of placing an accurate value on the improvement resulting from a program. Their work may be so far removed from the output of the process that they cannot reliably provide estimates. In these cases, their team leader, supervisor, or manager may be capable of providing estimates and may therefore be asked to provide a monetary value for a unit of improvement linked to the program. For example, a program for customer service representatives was designed to reduce customer complaints. Applying the skills and knowledge learned from the program resulted in a reduction in complaints, and the value of a single customer complaint was needed to determine the value of the improvement. Although customer service representatives had knowledge of some issues involved in customer complaints, they were not well versed in the full impact, so their supervisors were asked to provide a value.

In other situations, supervisors are asked to review and approve participants' estimates. After program completion, participants estimate the value of the improvements that are directly related to their own participation in the program. Their immediate managers are then asked to review the estimates and the process used by participants to arrive at the final estimates. Supervisors may confirm, adjust, or discard the values provided by the participants.

A key concern in the use of estimates is ensuring that the person providing the estimate has a clear picture of the full impact of the measure. In some cases, the participants' immediate supervisor has a better picture of the impact. For example, evaluation of a program in a call center required a value for the cost of one call escalation. The participants in the program to reduce call escalations were also the individuals who escalated calls to a higher level. While participants were the ones who made the decision to escalate a call, they sometimes were unaware of the consequences of the escalation for those at the next level. However, their immediate supervisor was in an excellent position to determine the value of eliminating an escalated call. The value was likely to include the cost of the supervisor's time and the cost of having a more disgruntled customer. At any rate, the supervisor would be a more credible source than the participants for the value in question.

Using Estimates from Senior Management

In rare cases, senior management provides estimates of a measure's value. In this approach, senior managers interested in the process or program are asked to place a value on the improvement based on their perception of its worth. This approach is used in situations in which calculating the value is difficult or in which other sources of estimation are unavailable or unreliable.

Here is an example of the use of supervisor estimates to assign a monetary value to a measure. A hospital chain was attempting to improve customer satisfaction through a program for all employees. The program was designed to improve customer service and, therefore, to improve the external customer satisfaction index. To determine the value of the program, a value for the unit of improvement (one point on the index) was needed. Because senior managers were interested in improving the index, they were asked to provide input on the value of a one-point increase. In a regular executive staff meeting, each senior manager and hospital administrator was asked to describe what it means for a hospital when the index increases.

After some discussion, each individual was asked to provide an estimate of the monetary value gained when the index moved one point. Although the senior managers were initially reluctant to provide the information, after some encouragement, monetary values were provided, adjusted for error, totaled, and averaged. The result was an estimate of the worth of one unit of improvement, which was used as a basis for calculating the benefits of the program. Although this process was subjective, it had the advantage of being owned by the senior executives—the same executives who approved the program budget.

Using Staff Estimates

The final method for converting data to monetary values is the use of staff estimates. Using all the available information as well as their experience, the staff members most familiar with the program provide estimates of the value of improvement. For example, an international oil company created a dispatcher training program in order to reduce dispatcher absenteeism and other performance problems. The staff estimated the cost of an absence to be $200. This value was then used to calculate the savings represented by the reduction in absenteeism that followed the training of the dispatchers. Although the staff may be capable of providing accurate estimates, this approach may be perceived as biased. In this case, for example, the staff might want the value of each absence to be large so that the savings generated by the program they created will be impressive. Therefore, staff should be used to estimate the monetary value of a measure only when other approaches are not possible.

Final Thoughts

This brief chapter discusses the method of last resort for converting data to monetary values: using estimates from the most knowledgeable and credible sources. The likely choices to provide estimates are the participants in the program, the immediate manager of the participants, and managers at other levels. In addition, the staff members involved in developing the program may provide estimates.

Credibility is the key issue in obtaining estimates of monetary values. If credibility becomes a problem in evaluating measures of improvement, there is an alternative. If data cannot be converted to monetary values credibly and with minimum resources, then they are left as intangible measures. Intangible measures are covered in Chapter Seven. Now that we have presented techniques to convert measures to monetary value, it is important to review some issues involved with the use of these techniques. This discussion is presented in Chapter Six.

6

Use of Data Conversion Techniques

This book has presented a variety of ways to convert data to monetary values. Sometimes, choosing the best method can be confusing. This chapter focuses on the use of the techniques, exploring some of the issues that must be addressed for successful and consistent practice within the ROI Methodology.

Selecting the Appropriate Technique

When so many techniques for data conversion are available, it can be challenging to select one or more techniques appropriate to the situation. The guidelines in this section can help you determine the proper method.

Use the technique that is appropriate for the type of data. Some techniques are designed specifically for hard data, while others are more appropriate for soft data. Therefore, the type of data will often dictate the technique. Hard data, while always preferred, are not always available. Soft data are often required and must be addressed through techniques that are appropriate for soft data. For example, hard data such as quality measures often have standard values. Soft data measures such as employee satisfaction can be converted to money by linking them with customer satisfaction.

Move from the most accurate technique to the least accurate. The techniques in this book are presented in order of accuracy and credibility, beginning with the most credible. Using standard, accepted values is the most credible method; staff estimates are the least credible. Work down the list, considering the feasibility of each technique, given the situation. Use of the technique with the most accuracy and credibility is recommended.

Consider availability and convenience. Sometimes, the availability of a particular method will drive the selection. In other situations, the convenience of a technique may be an important factor in making a selection.

For estimates, use the source with the broadest perspective—the person who knows the measure and its value best. To improve the accuracy of an estimate, the broadest possible perspective on the issue is needed. The individual providing an estimate must be knowledgeable on all the processes and issues involved in the value of the data item.

Use multiple techniques when feasible. Sometimes, using more than one technique to obtain a value is helpful. When multiple sources are readily available, more than one source should be used, for comparison or to provide another perspective. When multiple sources are used, the data must be integrated by applying a rule, such as using the lowest value, which is a preferred approach because it is the conservative choice. (This approach follows Guiding Principle 4: When analyzing data, select the most conservative alternative for calculations.)

The most conservative approach yields the lowest ROI. Therefore, if benefits are under consideration, remember that benefits are in the numerator of the ROI equation, so selecting the lowest value will yield the lowest ROI.

Minimize the amount of time. As in other processes, keeping the time invested as low as possible is important, so that the total time and effort for the evaluation does not become excessive. Some techniques can be implemented in less time than others. This step in the ROI Methodology can quickly absorb more time than all the other steps combined. Too much time spent on this step may dampen enthusiasm for the process and increase total program costs.

Ensuring the Accuracy and Credibility of Data

Credibility: The Key Issue

The techniques presented in this book assume that each data item collected and linked with a program can be converted to a monetary value. Although estimates can be developed using one or more of these techniques, the process of converting data to monetary values may lose credibility with the target audience, who may doubt its use in the analysis. Very subjective data, such as a change in employee morale or a reduction in the number of employee conflicts, are difficult to convert to monetary values. The key question in this determination is "Could these results be presented to senior management with confidence?" If the process does not meet this credibility test, the data should not be converted to monetary values and instead should be listed as an intangible benefit. Other data, especially hard data items, can be used in the ROI calculation, leaving the very subjective data as intangibles.

When it is unclear whether a data item should be converted, use the four-part test shown in Figure 6.1. Note the importance of the final question: "Can we convince our executive in two minutes that the value is credible?" This is the ultimate reality test, for time is limited when results are communicated to management. If buy-in is not achieved quickly, then the credibility of the entire process may be questioned.

When converting data to a monetary value, it is important to be consistent and methodical in your approach. Specific rules for making conversions will ensure this consistency and, ultimately, enhance the reliability of the study. Using the Guiding Principles will help with this issue.

Figure 6.1. Four-Part Test for Data Conversion

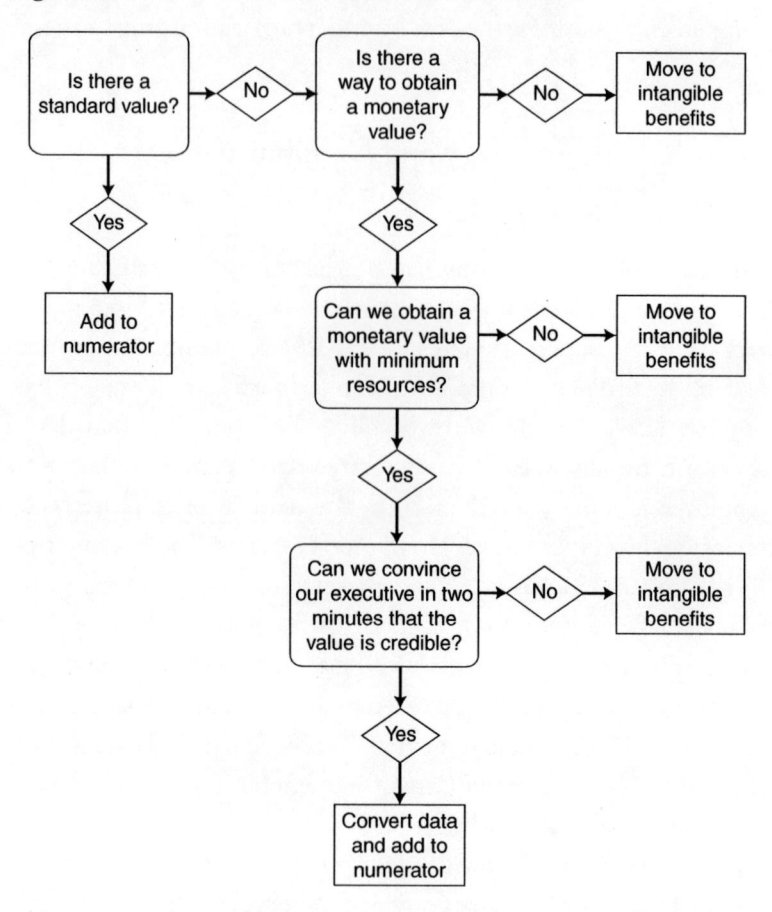

```
                          Is there a
  Is there a    No    →   way to obtain    No   →   Move to
  standard value?          a monetary                intangible
       │                    value?                   benefits
       │                       │
      Yes                     Yes
       ↓                       ↓
   Add to                Can we obtain a
   numerator             monetary value     No   →   Move to
                         with minimum                intangible
                         resources?                  benefits
                              │
                             Yes
                              ↓
                         Can we convince
                         our executive in two   No  →  Move to
                         minutes that the              intangible
                         value is credible?            benefits
                              │
                             Yes
                              ↓
                         Convert data
                         and add to
                         numerator
```

The accuracy of data and the credibility of the data conversion process are important concerns, causing some professionals to avoid converting data to monetary values. They are more comfortable reporting, for example, that a program reduced absenteeism from 6 percent to 4 percent, without attempting to place a value on the improvement. They assume that each person receiving the information will place a value on the reduction in absenteeism. Unfortunately, the target audience may know little about the cost of absenteeism and may underestimate the actual value of the improvement. Because stakeholders may undervalue the benefits of a program, some attempt should be made to include data conversion in the ROI analysis.

How the Credibility of Data Is Influenced

When ROI data are presented to selected target audiences, its credibility will be an issue. The degree to which the target audience believes the data are credible will be influenced by many factors. Credibility issues surface during the isolation step, during which estimates are sometimes used to isolate the effects of the program, and during data conversion, when estimates are used as well.

Completing an exercise on the credibility of data may be helpful. Exhibit 6.1 presents seven data items. Each item is presented as fact, and individuals are asked to believe each one. They represent annual values and the source of the item is included. Take a few minutes to indicate which of these items are the most credible by ranking them from 1 to 7, with 1 being the most credible and 7 being the least credible.

Next, for each item, list the factors that make it credible and the factors that make it not so credible. Essentially, the purpose of this exercise is to understand what makes people believe data. This is sometimes an eye-opening exercise, because it shows that many factors can affect credibility.

Exhibit 6.1. How Credible Are These Data Items?

	Rank
1. The cumulative expenditure on child sex abuse claims in the United States for the Roman Catholic Church is $1.5 billion. *Source:* U.S. Conference of Catholic Bishops.	☐
2. Vulcan Materials Company produced 275 million tons of crushed stone during the year. *Source:* Vulcan Materials Company Annual Report, audited by Deloitte & Touche.	☐

Exhibit 6.1. How Credible Are These Data Items? (*Continued*)

	Rank
3. A pharmaceutical firm in Ireland received a –42% ROI (negative) in a management training program. *Source:* Jack J. Phillips and Patti P. Phillips (eds.), *ROI at Work*, Alexandria, Va.: American Society for Training and Development.	☐
4. Wachovia Bank received a 932% ROI in a training program for relationship managers. *Source:* Patti P. Phillips (ed.), *In Action: Measuring Return on Investment,* Vol. 3. Alexandria, Va.: American Society for Training and Development.	☐
5. The annual cost of absenteeism and diminished productivity resulting from employee depression is $23.8 billion. *Source:* Massachusetts Institute of Technology study, reported in *Nation's Business.*	☐
6. The annual value of the market for wildlife trafficking—the second largest illegal trade in the world after drugs—is $10 billion. *Source:* U.S. Department of State.	☐
7. Presenteeism (working while sick) is costing employers $15 billion each year.	☐

Source: The Today Show, NBC.

Here are a few comments about these data items.

1. This item about the Roman Catholic Church is suspect because the church has not been forthcoming in addressing the issue of sex abuse. Some may not believe the value, suggesting that it could be understated.
2. This example from Vulcan Materials seems to be specific and is often rated as the most credible item. However, note that the data item presented here is not shipments to customers but

production. The company measures its shipments to customers but does not measure the crushed rock produced. Instead, an estimation process based on the concept of inventory adjustment is used. If the inventory at the end of the year is the same from one year to the next, then the customer shipments equaled the production. However, if the inventory goes up when compared to the customer shipments, which are known, the production equals the customer shipments plus the adjustment. To measure the inventory, an airplane flies over the quarry, allowing an individual in the plane to estimate the circumference of the rock piles, from which the volume of the piles and then the weight of the stone in inventory can be estimated. This appears to be an accurate number, yet it includes error. It is an estimate. Operating managers are also allowed to make minor adjustments in the inventory values based on the idea that they may know more about the amount of stone in inventory than the estimation reveals. In summary, the figure that is reported in the financial documents is at best a rough estimate of the amount of production. It suffices for the company, but it seems more credible than it actually is.

3. This item usually receives high credibility marks. Respondents reason that if a firm is willing to present a negative ROI, then the ROI must not be biased and might be accurate.

4. This often gets low marks because the ROI seems unrealistic or unbelievable. Also, the method used to arrive at the number is questionable. If the method described in the cited book was used, then it may be credible. If not, perhaps it is not so credible.

5. Several issues are raised in this item. First, the method for connecting absenteeism and productivity due to depression is a major issue. Obviously, it would be impossible to go to employers and find this information, because the specific reason for an absence is not usually recorded. If the data are clinical—that is, if employees have been diagnosed as clinically depressed—limited information may be obtained from the employees about the

number of absences caused by depression and the approximate productivity lost for this reason. However, the number may still be hard to believe.

Another issue, which is not apparent in the statement, is that this study was funded by a pharmaceutical firm that manufactures a drug to treat depression. Also this study was reported in a business publication and not in a medical journal.

6. This data item brings up issues about its source and how the number was determined.
7. This item also raises issues about its source and the method used to determine the number.

What does all this mean? The second part of the exercise begins to identify some issues that can affect the credibility of data or an individual's perception of the credibility.

Rules for Determining Credibility

The previous exercise can be summarized by the issues shown in Exhibit 6.2, which are the major influences on credibility. The

Exhibit 6.2. The Major Influences on Credibility

- Reputation of the data source
- Reputation of the study source
- Motives of the evaluators
- Personal biases of the audience
- Methodology of the study
- Assumptions made during the analysis
- Realism of the outcome data
- Type of data
- Scope of the analysis

concerns about the data set presented in the exercise can usually be categorized as one of these influences.

Reputation of the Source of the Data

The source of the data represents the first credibility issue. How credible are the individuals or the groups providing the data? Do they understand the issues? Are they knowledgeable about all the processes? Are they biased? The target audience will often give more credibility to data obtained from those who are closest to the source of the improvement or change.

Reputation of the Source of the Study

The target audience scrutinizes the reputation of the individuals, groups, or organizations that present the data. Do they have a history of providing accurate reports? Are they unbiased in their analyses? Are they fair in their presentation? Answers to these and other questions will help the audience form an impression about the source's reputation.

Motives of the Evaluators

The audience will look for motives of the person or persons conducting the study. Do the individuals presenting the data have a motive for exaggerating the results? Do they have a personal interest in creating a favorable or unfavorable result? Do they claim "ownership" of the program or part of it? Are the stakes high if the study is unfavorable? The audience will examine these and other issues in order to determine motives.

Audience Bias

The audience may have a bias—positive or negative—toward a particular study or toward the data presented from the study. Some executives may have a positive feeling about a program and will need fewer data to convince them of its value. Other executives may have a negative attitude toward the program and will need more data in order to be convinced of the data's accuracy. The potential bias of the audience should be understood early so that the presentation can be designed to counter any biases.

Methodology of the Study

The audience will want to know specifically how the research was conducted. How were the calculations made? What steps were followed? What processes were used? A lack of information about the methodology will cause the audience to become wary and suspicious of the results. Audience members will substitute their own perceptions and conclusions about the methodology if information is not provided.

Assumptions Made During the Analysis

The audience will try to understand the basis for the analysis. What definitions are used? What are the assumptions in the evaluation? Are they standard? How do they compare with assumptions in other studies? When assumptions are omitted, the audience members will substitute their own, often-unfavorable assumptions. In studies using the ROI Methodology, the conservative Twelve Guiding Principles are used in performing calculations and arriving at conclusions, in order to maximize credibility.

Realism of the Outcome Data

When outcomes appear to be unrealistic, the target audience may have difficulty believing them. Huge claims often fall on deaf ears, causing reports to be thrown away before they are reviewed. Impressive ROI values could cause problems.

Type of Data

Members of the target audience will usually have a preference for hard data. They are seeking business performance data tied to output, quality, costs, and time. These measures are easily understood and closely related to organizational performance. Conversely, soft data are sometimes viewed suspiciously from the outset; many senior executives will be concerned about their soft nature and the limitations of analysis of soft data.

Scope of Analysis

Do the data represent one organization or many? The smaller the scope, the more credible the data. Is the scope of the analysis narrow? Does it involve just one group or all the employees in the organization? Limiting the study to a small group or a small series of groups makes the process more accurate and believable.

How to Address the Issue of Credibility

The factors listed in the preceding section will influence the credibility of an ROI impact study and provide a framework from which to develop the ROI report. Therefore, in addition to considering each of the factors, consider the following key points when you are developing an ROI impact study for presentation to senior management.

Use the Most Credible and Reliable Sources for Estimates

This fundamental principle (Guiding Principle 3) must be addressed throughout an ROI evaluation, and therefore, it has been consistently discussed throughout these books. In some cases, the program participants are the most credible source, particularly when the evaluator is attempting to isolate the effects of the program. However, when the evaluator is converting data to monetary values, a higher-level manager may be more credible because he or she may have a broader view of the issues.

Remain Unbiased and Objective

This is a difficult issue, but it must be addressed. In an ideal setting, the person conducting the evaluation does not own the program. The ideal situation does occur in some organizations—evaluators are independent of the program's design, development, and delivery and of any other forms of ownership. When this ideal cannot be achieved, other methods are often available to help with credibility.

During data collection, the credibility issue may surface. If the person collecting the data wanted to influence the results of the evaluation, the data could be adjusted in a variety of ways. Negative data could be eliminated, neutral data could be made positive, and positive data could be enhanced. While this scenario may seem improbable, it does happen. Therefore, the data collection needs to be as independent as possible.

A variety of options can help build the credibility of the data:

1. A person or group within the organization (for example, a colleague, the finance and accounting department, or the organizational effectiveness unit) may agree to collect the data. The data are then included in the report in a summarized form. The audience should be informed that the data collection was independent.

2. Sometimes when data are collected by electronic means, the independence is built into the process. The data go to a server, and the server sends a data summary. The raw data are never visible to the evaluator.

3. In other situations, a person or small firm specializing in evaluation will agree to collect data, summarize it, and return it at a low cost.

4. External consultants are readily available to collect the data, analyze it, and report it.

5. If none of the preceding options is available, then the issue should be addressed early in the communication. The audience should understand at the beginning that the person conducting the study also owns the program, and it should be stated that the data were not changed or altered in any way and that a summary of the data is contained in an appendix of the report.

Prepare for Potential Audience Bias

Preparation involves understanding the audience who will receive the report or be present during the meeting in which the study is presented. Audiences sometimes have biases. When the biases are understood, preparation to address those biases becomes important. Ideally, addressing the issues that might feed audience biases would be an effective strategy. Ensuring that efforts are made to moderate negative and positive bias is important.

Fully Explain Your Methodology at Each Step in the Process

An explanation of methodology is important because understanding the method used to capture and analyze the data leads to an understanding of the data's credibility. In this context, the audience must understand that a systematic, accepted method has been used, with logical steps and sequences, and that there were options along the way. This is sometimes helpful when executives and audience members want to know whether a proven method was used to convert the data to monetary values.

Define Assumptions Made During the Analysis

Assumptions are critical. They need to be logical and, most of all, conservative. In the ROI Methodology, the assumptions are the Guiding Principles, which are listed in the section titled "Principles of the ROI Methodology" at the beginning of this book. They become an evaluator's best friend when the evaluator is dealing with credibility issues. Conservative assumptions help increase the credibility of the process.

Prepare for an Unrealistic Value

In a sense, this is a good problem to have. If the ROI number is high, which for some people would be good news, the challenge is to make the audience believe the number. Executives, managers, and chief financial officers are used to ROI values in the range of

15 to 20 percent. If ten or twenty times this amount is reported, it may be difficult for them to believe the figure.

Two issues must be underscored. First, if the conservative Twelve Guiding Principles of the ROI Methodology are used, the value that is being presented is an understatement of the results, so the ROI is even greater than the value reported. Second, it is possible and sometimes routine for successful programs to drive high ROIs. This phenomenon is explored in more detail in the next book in the series, *Costs and ROI*. Essentially, this is the leverage effect. That is, spending money on one group of individuals can have an effect on a larger group. This is particularly true in a program such as executive development in which a change in an executive's behavior can affect the entire department, division, region, or company under that executive's influence. As a result, investing in one person can have a multiplicative effect.

Finally, performing sensitivity analysis may be helpful. That is, the audience needs to know that if some assumptions were changed and made even more conservative, the value would be different. The audience needs to understand that while the figure is high, it is probably less than what has actually been achieved. Depending on the assumptions made, the figure could be higher or lower; however, the figure reported is based on conservative assumptions.

Use Hard Data Whenever Possible

If an evaluation includes an ROI calculation, then the data are converted to monetary values and those are the hard data—and are tangible. If soft data are involved, an attempt should be made to convert these data to monetary values. If they are converted, then they have become tangible. However, some data will not be converted, and they will remain intangible. Every effort should be made to convert the data to monetary values.

Executives prefer the data to be hard data. When soft data are converted, credibility will be an issue. Are they credible data? See if they meet the credibility test shown in Figure 6.1. An important point, however, is that intangible benefits are still important, as the next chapter explains.

Keep the Scope of Analysis Narrow

The narrower the scope, the more credible the evaluation. This means that an ROI evaluation is more credible when it is conducted on one program than it is when it is conducted on multiple programs and more credible when it involves one group of employees rather than all the employees in the company. It is not as credible when an entire function is subjected to the evaluation—for example, when the effort is to calculate the payoff of the entire learning and development function or the whole technology budget.

In conclusion, these guidelines provide rules for presenting data credibly. Credibility is king when ROI studies are communicated. Credibility issues must be acknowledged and addressed at each step in order to maintain high credibility with the target audience and to collect believable data.

Making Adjustments

Consider the Possibility of Management Adjustment

In organizations in which soft data are common and values are derived through imprecise methods, senior managers and administrators are sometimes offered the opportunity to review and approve the data. Because of the subjective nature of this process, management may wish to factor out parts of the data in order to make the final results more credible.

This approach is not recommended, because there is no valid reason to do this on a routine basis. However, if the management team members who support and sponsor programs need to make an adjustment in order to accept the data, evaluators should allow them to do it formally. If evaluators don't allow it, the management team may do it anyway.

Consider the Issue of Short-Term Versus Long-Term Programs

When data are converted to monetary values, usually one year of data is included in the analysis. This practice follows Guiding Principle 9, which states that for short-term solutions, only the first-year benefits are used in the ROI analysis. However, some programs are long-term rather than short-term programs. Whether a program is short-term or long-term is defined by how long it takes to complete or implement the program. If one individual participating in the program and working through the process takes months to complete it, then it probably is not a short-term program. Some programs take years to implement with one particular group. A good rule of thumb is to consider a program short-term when an individual takes a month or less to learn what needs to be done to make the program successful.

When a program is long-term, the time period during which benefits will be assumed to accrue should be set before program evaluation. Input should be secured from all stakeholders, including the sponsor, champion, implementer, designer, and evaluator. After some discussion, the final estimate of the time period for program effects should be conservative and perhaps should be reviewed by finance and accounting. When a long-term solution is under consideration, forecasting will need to be used to estimate multiple years of value; no sponsor will wait several years to see how a program turns out. Some assumptions will need to be made so that the forecast can be completed.

Consider an Adjustment for the Time Value of Money

Since a program investment is made in one time period and the return is realized at a later time, some organizations adjust program benefits to reflect the time value of money by using discounted cash-flow techniques. The monetary benefits of the program are discounted on the basis of the time period between outlay and return. The amount of adjustment, however, is usually small compared with the typical benefits of programs.

Although the time value of money may not be an issue for every program, it should be considered, and some type of standard discount rate should be used. Consider an example of how this is calculated. A program cost of $100,000 and a two-year period will be used before the full value of the investment will be covered. (This is a long-term solution spanning two years.) Using a discount rate of 6 percent, the adjusted cost for the program for the first year would be $100,000 × 106% = $106,000. For the second year it would be $106,000 × 106% = $112,360. Therefore, the program cost has been adjusted for a two-year value with a 6 percent discount rate. This calculation assumes that the program sponsor could have invested the money in some other program and obtained at least a 6 percent return on that investment; hence another cost has been added to the program cost.

Converting Data to Money: Matching Exercise

As a review of the techniques for converting data to monetary values, we have provided a matching exercise. This exercise will serve as a reminder of the methods described in this book.

This exercise shows the versatility of the methods for converting data to monetary values. The good news is that many credible methods are available. Some are easy to use, and most of the values have already been developed. Even better news is that if the data

Instructions

For each of the following situations, please indicate the method used to convert data to monetary values. Select from these methods:

A. Profit or savings from output (standard value)
B. Cost of quality (standard value)
C. Employee time as compensation (standard value)
D. Historical costs or savings from records
E. Expert input
F. External database
G. Linking with other measures
H. Participant estimation
I. Management estimation
J. Staff estimation

In each box, write the letter that corresponds to the method used.

Situation	Conversion Technique
1. The Veteran's Administration was experiencing a high turnover rate among its nurses. A new human resources program was designed to reduce turnover. To obtain the value of one voluntary turnover, the Internet was used to find a health care study that showed the average cost (fully loaded) of replacing a nurse. This number, expressed as a percentage of salary, was used in the calculation.	☐
2. A new program for couriers at DHL was designed to reduce the number of repackaging errors. A repackaging error occurs when a package is damaged by the couriers and has to be repackaged before delivery. The quality office in Brussels had previously determined the standard cost for a repackaging error. This amount was used to develop the total monetary value for the reduction in errors.	☐

Use of Data Conversion Techniques 83

Situation	Conversion Technique
3. Middle-level managers at an electric utility were involved in a time management program. Each manager estimated the number of hours saved each week that were directly attributable to this program. The value calculated for each hour saved was based on the average annual salary of the managers, adjusted for employee benefits and divided by the number of hours worked in one year to reach an hourly cost.	☐
4. An Australian government agency was implementing a new human resources program to reduce the number of stress claims filed by employees. The employees, who worked with angry and upset people, were suffering from extreme stress on the job, resulting in many claims. To obtain the monetary value of a stress claim, medical and health staff provided an average value for one claim based on their expertise in managing stress claims for several years.	☐
5. A new customer call center program at a home appliance company was designed to reduce the number of calls that were escalated to the next level of management. The individuals involved in the program were the immediate supervisors of the employees taking the calls. To determine the cost of a call escalation, the participants (supervisors) estimated the cost attached to one escalated call.	☐
6. A pharmaceutical company was implementing a new ethics program for all employees. While several outcomes were expected from this program, one performance measure was expense account violations. To obtain the average cost of an expense account violation, the cost of all of the	☐

Situation	Conversion Technique
violations for a two-month period was taken directly from the records and divided by the total violations.	
7. Employee engagement data were collected for a global computer company. After the data were analyzed, a new human resources program was designed in order to improve engagement scores. To place a value on a change in engagement score, the staff examined the correlation between engagement scores and employee turnover in different job groups. This correlation analysis was easily performed as part of the company's human capital management system. As engagement scores improved, voluntary turnover decreased. The cost savings from the corresponding turnover reduction was used as the value for each change in the engagement score.	☐
8. A small equipment manufacturing company was interested in reducing absenteeism. A program was implemented, and the cost of one absence was needed in order to calculate the monetary impact. The human resources staff member who conducted the study estimated the cost of one absence to be $300 per day.	☐
9. A major retail store chain was anxious to reduce the number of customer complaints that it received. A new program was implemented for that purpose; naturally, the cost of a complaint was needed in order to evaluate the program. To obtain the cost of one complaint, the management of the customer service area and the vice president of customer care estimated the average cost of one complaint.	☐

Situation	Conversion Technique
10. Wachovia Bank implemented an advanced negotiation program in which commercial bankers learned how to increase revenue from new and existing clients. The outcome of the program was increased revenue in specific product lines. To calculate the monetary value of a sale, the revenue amount was multiplied by the profit margin for the product line, which was considered a standard value in the organization.	☐

Responses

1. **F**. In this example, the evaluator used the Internet to find a value for turnover in a particular setting, health care, and a particular job group, nursing. This should be a credible value.
2. **B**. This is a standard value located in the quality department. It is an accepted value that has already been calculated and used for this measure. This conversion is credible.
3. **C**. This example uses a standard value for time. The cost per hour of manager time is not an estimate of the value. In the example, the time is an estimate, but the value is a standard value that reflects fully loaded compensation—salary plus benefits.
4. **E**. The medical staff are experts who can provide a credible value for the measure in question.
5. **H**. In this example, the value for one escalated call is obtained directly from the program participants. The credibility of this value will rest on the participants' understanding of the full scope of this measure—that is, how well they know and understand the issue.
6. **D**. While this method is credible, it is very time-consuming. Adding all the expense account violations and dividing by the number of violations takes a large amount of resources and time.

7. **G.** This method can be credible if the correlation analysis is credible. The important issue is that the data were developed with the input of someone outside the owners of the program. A calculation was not performed by the staff for this program. If the staff had had to develop the value, it would have taken too much time.
8. **J.** This is perhaps the least credible data conversion because the human resources staff has a stake in the value of one absence being large because it affects the ROI. This method of estimating the value of a measure is not recommended, except as a last resort, and even then, it may not meet the credibility test when the program evaluation is presented to management. The measure may have to be left as intangible.
9. **I.** The credibility of the value rests on the credibility of the managers who provided it. They may well be in a good position to place a monetary value on this item.
10. **A.** This method is very credible. The example uses a standard value profit margin for the product.

---

cannot be converted to a monetary value, the measure can be left as an intangible. The next chapter discusses intangible measures in detail.

Final Thoughts

This chapter provides a quick review of the data conversion methods in this book and discusses several issues involved in their use. When conversion is attempted, the most critical issue is credibility, and the second most important issue is the required resources. These two issues must be considered in tandem; the conversion may take too much time and effort, and it could lose credibility. The final chapter in this book covers intangible measures, the measures that cannot be or are not converted to monetary values.

7

Intangible Measures

Program results usually include both tangible and intangible measures. Intangible measures represent the benefits or detriments directly linked to a program that cannot or should not be converted to monetary values. By definition, according to Guiding Principle 11 of the ROI Methodology, an intangible measure is one that is purposely not converted to a monetary value. (If a conversion cannot be accomplished with minimum resources and with credibility, the measure is considered an intangible.) Intangible measures are often monitored after the program has been implemented. Although they are not converted to monetary values, intangible measures are nonetheless an important part of the evaluation process. This chapter explores the role of intangibles, how to measure them, when to measure them, and how to report them.

The range of intangible measures is almost limitless. Exhibit 7.1 highlights over two dozen examples of these measures. Some measures make the list because of the difficulty in measuring them; others because of the difficulty in converting them to money. Others are on the list for both reasons. Being labeled as intangible does not mean that these items can never be measured or converted to monetary values. In one study or another, each of these items has been monitored and quantified in financial terms. However, in typical programs, these measures are considered intangible benefits

Exhibit 7.1. Common Intangibles

• Accountability	• Innovation and creativity
• Alliances	• Job satisfaction
• Attention	• Leadership
• Awards	• Loyalty
• Branding	• Networking
• Capability	• Organizational commitment
• Capacity	• Partnering
• Clarity	• Reputation
• Communication	• Stress
• Corporate social responsibility	• Sustainability
• Customer service (customer satisfaction)	• Team effectiveness
• Employee attitudes	• Timeliness
• Engagement	• Work/life balance
• Image	

because of the difficulty in measuring them or the difficulty in converting them to monetary values.

Why Intangibles Are Important

Although intangible measures are not new, they are becoming increasingly important. Intangibles secure funding and drive the economy, and organizations are built on them. Everywhere we look, intangibles are becoming not only increasingly important but also critical to organizations. Here's a recap of why they have become so important.

Intangibles Are the Invisible Advantage

When the elements behind the success of many well-known organizations are examined, intangibles are often found. A highly innovative company continues to develop new and improved products; a government agency reinvents itself; a company with highly involved and engaged employees attracts and keeps talent. A large consulting firm shares knowledge with employees, providing a competitive advantage. Still another organization is successful because of its strategic partners and alliances. These intangibles do not often appear in cost statements or other records, but they are there, and they make a huge difference.

Trying to identify, measure, and react to intangibles may be difficult, but it is possible to do so. Intangibles transform the way organizations work, the way employees are managed, the way products are designed, the way services are sold, and the way customers are treated. The implications are profound, and an organization's strategy must address them. Although they are invisible, the presence of intangibles is felt and the results of their presence are concrete.

We Are Entering the Intangible Economy

Our economy has been constantly changing since before the Iron Age. One of the biggest changes was the transition to the agricultural age. In the late nineteenth century and early twentieth century, the world took another leap forward, moving into the industrial age. From the 1950s on, the world has moved into the technology and knowledge age; this evolution translates into an emphasis on intangibles.

During all of these changes, a natural evolution of technology has occurred. During the industrial age, companies and individuals invested in tangible assets, like manufacturing plants and equipment. In the technology and knowledge age, companies invest in intangible assets, like brands or systems. The future will hold more of the same, as intangibles continue to evolve as an important part of the overall economic system (Boulton, Libert, and Samek, 2000).

Intangibles Are Being Converted to Tangibles

Data once regarded as intangible are now being converted into monetary values. As a result of this trend, once-classic intangibles are now accepted as tangible measures because their value is more easily understood. Consider, for example, customer satisfaction. Just a decade ago, few organizations had a clue about the monetary value of customer satisfaction. Now, more firms have taken the step of linking customer satisfaction directly to revenues and profits. Companies are seeing the tremendous value that can be derived from intangibles. As this chapter illustrates, more information is being accumulated in order to show monetary values for intangible data, moving some intangible measures into the tangible category.

Intangibles Drive Programs

Some programs are implemented because of intangibles. For example, the need to have greater collaboration, partnering, communication, teamwork, or better customer service drives new programs. In the public sector, the need to reduce poverty, employ disadvantaged citizens, and save lives often drives programs. From the outset, the intangibles are the important drivers and become the most important measures. Consequently, an increasing number of executives include a string of intangibles on their scorecards, reports on key performance indicators, dashboards, and other routine reporting systems. In some cases, the intangibles represent nearly half of all measures that are monitored.

Measuring Intangibles

In some programs, intangibles are more important than monetary measures and therefore should be monitored and reported as part of the evaluation. In practice, almost every program, regardless of its nature, scope, or content, produces intangible measures. The challenge is to identify them effectively and report them appropriately.

From time to time, it is necessary to explore the issue of measuring the difficult to measure. Responses to this exploration usually occur in the form of comments instead of questions. "You can't measure it" is a typical response. This is not true, because anything can be measured. What the frustrated observer suggests by that comment is that the intangible is not something you can count, examine, or see in quantities, like items produced on an assembly line. In reality, a quantitative value can be assigned to or developed for any intangible. If it exists, it can be measured. Consider human intelligence, for example. Although human intelligence is vastly complex and abstract, with myriad facets and qualities, IQ scores are assigned to many people, and most people seem to accept them. The software engineering institute at Carnegie-Mellon University assigns software organizations a score of 1 to 5 to represent their maturity in software engineering. This score has enormous implications for the organizations' business development capabilities, yet the measure goes practically unchallenged (Alden, 2006).

Several approaches to measuring intangibles are available. Intangibles that can be counted include customer complaints, employee complaints, and conflicts. These can be recorded easily and constitute one of the most acceptable types of measures for intangibles. Unfortunately, many intangibles are based on attitudes and perceptions that must be measured in order to provide a value. The key is in the development of the measurement instrument. Instruments are usually developed with scales of 3, 5, or even 10 points to represent levels of perception. The methods for measuring intangibles represent three basic varieties.

The first method is use of a survey instrument. One type of instrument lists the intangible items and asks respondents to agree or disagree on a 5-point scale (on which the midpoint represents a neutral opinion). Other instruments define various qualities of the intangible, such as its reputation. A 5-point scale can easily

Figure 7.1. The Link Between Hard-to-Measure and Easy-to-Measure Items

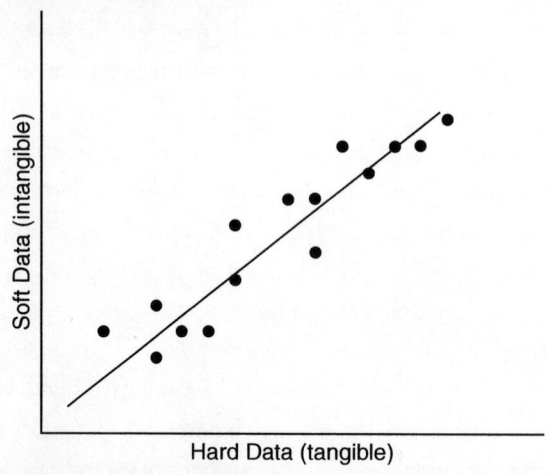

[Scatter plot with "Soft Data (intangible)" on the y-axis and "Hard Data (tangible)" on the x-axis, showing data points clustered along an upward-sloping trend line.]

be developed to describe degrees of reputation, ranging from the worst rating (a horrible reputation) to the best rating (an excellent reputation). Still other instruments solicit ratings of agreement or disagreement on a scale of 1 to 10 after respondents review a description of the intangible.

A second way to measure an intangible connects it to a measure that is easier to measure or easier to value. As shown in Figure 7.1, a hard-to-measure item is linked to an easy-to-measure item. In the classic situation, a soft measure (typically the intangible) is connected to a hard measure (typically the tangible). Although this link can be developed through logical deductions and conclusions, gathering some empirical evidence through a correlation analysis (as shown in the figure) that demonstrates a significant correlation between the items is the best approach. However, a detailed analysis would have to be conducted to ensure the existence of a causal relationship between the items. In other words, just because a correlation is apparent, it does not mean that one caused the other. Consequently, additional analysis, other empirical evidence, and supporting data would be needed to provide evidence of a causal effect.

A final method of measuring an intangible is development of an index. An index is a single score representing some complex factor; it is constructed by aggregating the values of several different measures. These may be a combination of both hard and soft data items. Measures making up the index are sometimes weighted according to their importance as elements of the abstract factor being measured. Some index measures are based strictly on hard data items. For example, the U.S. poverty level is a family income equal to three times the cost of feeding a family of four as determined by the U.S. Department of Agriculture, adjusted for inflation using the consumer price index. Sometimes an index is completely intangible—for example, the customer satisfaction index developed by the University of Michigan.

Intangibles are often combined with a variety of tangibles to reflect the performance of a business unit or program. Intangibles are often associated with nonprofit, nongovernment, and public sector organizations. Table 7.1 shows the performance measures that reflect greatness at the Cleveland Orchestra. For the Cleveland Orchestra, intangibles include such items as comments from cab drivers; tangibles include ticket sales. Collectively and regardless of how difficult they are to obtain, these data sets reflect the overall performance of the orchestra.

Converting Intangibles to Monetary Values

Converting hard-to-measure data items to monetary values is challenging, to say the least. When working with intangibles, interest in the monetary contribution expands considerably compared to, for example, measures of productivity, where the monetary value can be more clearly interpreted. Three major groups have an interest in the monetary value of intangibles.

1. The sponsors who fund a particular program almost always seek monetary values among the measures.

Table 7.1. Measuring Greatness at the Cleveland Orchestra

Superior Performance	Distinctive Impact	Lasting Endurance
• Emotional response of audience; increase in number of standing ovations • Wide technical range; can play any piece with excellence, no matter how difficult—from soothing and familiar classical pieces to difficult and unfamiliar modern pieces • Increased demand for tickets; demand for more complex, imaginative programs in Cleveland, New York, and Europe • Invited to Salzburg Festival (first time in twenty-five years), signifying elite status among top European orchestras	• Cleveland's style of programming increasingly copied; becoming more influential • A key point of civic pride; cab drivers say, "We're really proud of our orchestra" • Orchestra leaders increasingly sought for leadership roles and perspectives in elite industry groups and gatherings	• Excellence sustained across generations of conductors—from George Szell through Pierre Boulez, Christoph von Dohnányi, and Franz Welser-Möst • Supporters donate time and money, invest in long-term success of orchestra; endowment tripled

Source: Adapted from Collins, 2005.

Intangible Measures 95

2. The public is involved in some way with many intangibles. Even private sector organizations are trying to improve their image, their reputation, and confidence in their organizations in the mind of the public.
3. The individuals who are actively involved with the program and who support it often need and sometimes demand that a monetary value be developed.

The path most commonly used to capture monetary values for intangibles is shown in Figure 7.2. The first challenge is to locate an existing value or to compute or measure the value in some way, making sure that the information is accurate and reliable. If it is not possible to locate an existing value, an expert may be able to assign a credible monetary value to the measure, based on his or her experience, knowledge, credentials, and track record. If an expert opinion is not available, stakeholders may provide their input, estimating the monetary value of the measure, although their estimates should be adjusted for bias. Some stakeholders are biased in one way or another; they may want the value to be smaller or larger, depending on their particular motives. Their estimates

Figure 7.2. Converting an Intangible Measure: Valuing the Hard-to-Value

Approach	Challenge
Existing data	Finding the right database
⇩	
Expert input	Locating a credible expert
⇩	
Stakeholder input	Making the data credible
⇩	
Analysis of data	Resources

may have to be adjusted or thrown out altogether. Finally, the data are converted, using conservative processes and adjusting for error as necessary. Unfortunately, no specific rule exists for converting each intangible measure to a monetary value. By definition, an intangible is a measure that is not converted to money. If the conversion cannot be accomplished with minimum resources and with credibility, it is left as an intangible.

Identifying and Collecting Intangibles

Intangible measures can be taken from different sources and at different times during the program life cycle, as depicted in Figure 7.3. They can be uncovered early in the process, during the needs assessment, and their collection can be planned as part of the overall data collection strategy. For example, one program might have several hard data measures linked to it. Job stress, an intangible measure, is also identified and monitored, with no plans to convert it to a monetary value. From the beginning, this measure is destined to be a nonmonetary, intangible benefit that is reported along with the ROI results.

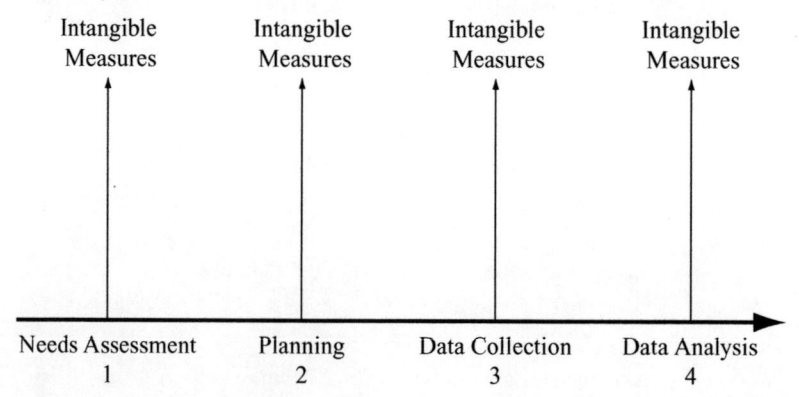

Figure 7.3. Identifying Intangible Measures During the Program Life Cycle

Intangible Measures	Intangible Measures	Intangible Measures	Intangible Measures
↑	↑	↑	↑
Needs Assessment 1	Planning 2	Data Collection 3	Data Analysis 4

A second opportunity to identify intangible benefits is during the planning process, when clients or sponsors of the program agree on an evaluation plan. Key stakeholders can usually identify the intangible measures they expect to be influenced by the program. For example, a change management program in a large multinational company was conducted, and an ROI analysis was planned. Program leaders, participants, participants' managers, and experts identified potential intangible measures that were perceived to be influenced by the program, including collaboration, communication, and teamwork.

A third opportunity to collect intangible measures presents itself during data collection. Although the measure may not be anticipated in the initial design, it may surface on a questionnaire, in an interview, or during a focus group. Questions are often asked about other improvements linked to a program, and participants usually provide several intangible measures for which no plans are available for assigning a value. For example, in the evaluation of one program, participants were asked what specifically had improved about their work area and their relationships with customers as a result of the program. Participants provided more than a dozen intangible benefits that managers attributed to the program.

The fourth opportunity to identify intangible measures is during data analysis, while attempting to convert data to monetary values. If the conversion loses credibility, the measure should be reported as an intangible benefit. For example, in one sales improvement program, customer satisfaction was identified early in the process as a measure of program success. Conversion to a monetary value was attempted, but it lacked accuracy and credibility. Consequently, customer satisfaction was reported as an intangible benefit.

Analyzing Intangibles

For each intangible measure identified, some evidence of its connection to the program must be shown. However, in many cases, no specific analysis is planned beyond tabulation of responses. Early attempts to quantify intangible data sometimes resulted in aborting the entire process, with no further data analysis being conducted. In some cases, isolating the effects of the program may be undertaken, using one or more of the methods outlined in *Isolation of Results*, book three of this series. This step is necessary when an evaluator needs to know the specific amount of change in the intangible measure that is linked to the program. Intangible data often reflect improvement. However, neither the precise amount of improvement nor the amount of improvement directly related to a program is always identified. Because the value of these data is not included in the ROI calculation, intangible measures are not normally used to justify another program or to justify continuing an existing program. A detailed analysis is not necessary. Intangible benefits are often viewed as additional evidence of the program's success and are presented as supportive qualitative data.

Confronting Intangibles

There are so many intangibles that addressing them appropriately can be difficult. Many advances have been made in measuring intangibles effectively and in converting them to monetary values. Of course, when they are converted to monetary values, they are no longer intangible; they are tangible. This issue is not easy, but progress is being made and will continue to be made. The next section covers four examples in which organizations focus on measuring intangibles in the public sector and the private sector. These measures include only a few of the examples listed in Exhibit 7.1.

Example 1: Customer Service

Because of the importance of building and improving customer service, related measures are typically monitored to track payoff. Several types of customer service programs have a direct influence on these measures. This metric makes our list because it is perceived as difficult to measure and to convert to monetary value. However,

Figure 7.4. Customer Service Linkage: Awareness, Attitudes, and Usage

Type	Measures	Typical Questions
Awareness ⇩	Awareness and knowledge	Have you heard of Brand X? What brand comes to mind when you think "luxury car"?
Attitudes ⇩	Beliefs and intentions	Is Brand X for me? On a scale of 1 to 5, is Brand X for young people?
Usage ⇩	Purchasing habits and loyalty	Did you use Brand X this week? What brand did you last buy?

Source: Adapted from Farris, Bendle, Pfeifer, and Ribstein, 2006.

in the last two decades, much progress has been made, and some of these measures are routinely considered tangible because they are converted to monetary values by using the methods described in this chapter. The technique of linking to other measures that is used in our example is the most common way in which intangible measures of customer service are converted to monetary values. This technique follows the sequence shown in Figure 7.4. The first step is to create awareness of a particular product, service, or brand. The next step is to develop attitudes that define the beliefs, opinions, and intentions in regard to the product, service, or brand, and lead to usage, the final step that confirms the purchasing habits and loyalty of the customer.

The important links between awareness, attitudes, and usage are ingrained in most marketing and promotion programs and processes and have led to a variety of measures that are becoming standard in the field. Table 7.2 shows intangibles associated with

Table 7.2. Customer Service Intangibles

Metric	Definition	Issues	Purpose
Awareness	Percentage of total population who are aware of a brand.	Is awareness prompted or unprompted?	Consideration of who has heard of the brand.
Top of mind	First brand to be considered.	May be subject to most recent advertising or experience.	Saliency of brand.
Knowledge	Percentage of population who know product, have recollection of its advertising.	Not a formal metric. Is knowledge prompted or unprompted?	Extent of familiarity with product beyond name recognition.
Beliefs	Customers' or consumers' view of product, generally captured via survey (responses, often through ratings on a scale).	Customers or consumers may hold beliefs with varying degrees of conviction.	Perception of brand by attribute.
Purchasing intentions	Probability of intention to purchase.	To estimate probability of purchase, aggregate and analyze ratings of stated intentions.	Measures pre-shopping disposition to purchase.
Willingness to recommend	Intention to recommend to potential new customer (generally measured by ratings on scale of 1 to 5).	Nonlinear in impact.	Shows strength of loyalty, potential impact on others.

Customer satisfaction	Customers' satisfaction with brand in general or with specific attributes (generally measured on scale of 1 to 5).	Subject to response bias; captures views of current customers, not lost customers; satisfaction is a function of expectations.	Indicates likelihood of repurchase; reports of dissatisfaction show aspects requiring improvement to enhance loyalty.
Willingness to search	Percentage of customers willing to delay purchases, change stores, or reduce quantities to avoid switching brands.	Hard to capture.	Indicates importance of distribution coverage.
Loyalty	Customers' willingness to pay premium, to search, to stay.	"Loyalty" itself is not a formal metric, but specific metrics do measure aspects of this dynamic. New product entries may alter loyalty levels.	Indicates base future revenue stream.

Source: Adapted from Farris, Bendle, Pfeifer, and Ribstein, 2006, p. 16.

customer service and underscores the array of possibilities, all aimed at developing awareness, attitudes, and usage. The most common intangible is customer satisfaction, which is generally measured on scales of 1 to 5, 1 to 7, or 1 to 10 (although other scales are used, too). A tremendous amount of research has been accumulated about the value of satisfied customers and the loss connected with dissatisfied customers. Using elaborate processes of decision tree analysis, probability theories, expected value, and correlations, organizations have developed detailed relationships between customer service intangibles and monetary values, showing that movement in sales and profits is connected to a variety of measures. The most important measure is customer satisfaction. Within an organization, a variety of specific measures can be developed, including customer response time, sensitivity to costs and pricing issues, and creativity with customer responses. Of particular importance is the matter of response time. Providing prompt customer service is critical for most organizations. Therefore, organizations monitor the time required to respond to specific customer service requests or problems. Although reducing response times is a common objective, this measure is not usually converted to a monetary value. Therefore, customer response time is usually reported as an important intangible measure.

Example 2: Innovation and Creativity

Innovation and creativity are related. Creative employees create innovative products, services, and solutions. In our knowledge- and technology-based economy, innovation and creativity are becoming important factors in organizations' success.

Innovation

Innovation is critical to most organizations. Just how important is innovation? Let's put it in perspective. If it were not for the intellectual curiosity of employees—thinking things through, trying out new ideas, and taking wild guesses in R&D labs across the country—the United States would have half the economy it has today. In a recent report on research and development, the American Association for the Advancement for Science estimated that as much as 50 percent of U.S. economic growth in the half century since the Fortune 500 came into existence is the result of advances in technology (Brown, 2004).

After a few years' retrenchment and cost cutting, senior executives from a variety of industries now share the conviction that innovation—the ability to define and create new products and services and quickly bring them to market—is an increasingly important source of competitive advantage. Executives are setting aggressive performance goals for their innovation and product development organizations, targeting 20 to 30 percent improvements in such areas as time to market, development cost, product cost, and customer value (Kandybihn and Kihn, 2004).

There is a vast disconnect between hope and reality, however. A recent survey of fifty companies conducted by Booz Allen Hamilton shows that companies are only marginally satisfied that their innovation organizations are delivering their maximum potential. Worse, executives say that only half the improvement efforts they launch end up meeting expectations. Several waves of improvement in innovation and product development have already substantially enhanced companies' ability to deliver differentiated, high-quality products to markets quickly and efficiently. However, the degree of success achieved has varied greatly among companies and among units within companies. The differences in success stem from the difficulty in managing change in the complex processes and organizations associated with innovation and product development.

Some companies have managed to assemble an integrated "innovation chain" that is truly global and that allows them to outflank competitors that innovate using knowledge in a single cluster. They have been able to implement a process for innovating that transcends local clusters and national boundaries, becoming metanational innovators. This strategy of using localized pockets of technology, market intelligence, and human capabilities has provided a powerful new source of competitive advantage: more high-value innovation at lower cost (Santos, Doz, and Williamson, 2004).

Innovation is both easy and difficult to measure. Measuring outcomes in areas such as new products and processes, improved products and processes, copyrights, patents, inventions, and employee suggestions is easy. Many companies track these items. They can be documented in order to reflect the innovative profile of an organization. Unfortunately, comparing these data with previous data or benchmarking with other organizations is sometimes meaningless because these measures are typically unique to each organization and may not provide an accurate point of reference by which to gauge success.

Perhaps the most obvious way to measure innovation is by tracking patents—both those used internally and those licensed for others' use through a patent and license exchange. For example, IBM has been granted more patents than any other company in the world—more than 25,000 U.S. patents. IBM's licensing of patents and technology generates several billion dollars in profits each year. IBM and Microsoft are at the top of the list, but most organizations in the new economy monitor trademarks, patents, and copyrights as important measures of the innovative talent of their employees.

It is helpful to remember that the registration of patents stems from employees' inventive spirit. This means that employees do not have to be highly degreed scientists or engineers to be inventive. Although invention is often thought of in the context of technology, computing, materials, or energy, in fact it spans all disciplines and can therefore be extracted from any technological realm for application to problems in any area (Schwartz, 2004).

Through the years, inventors have been viewed as nerds, with much of their inventiveness explained by the quirky makeup of their personality. This image is popular because history is laced with well-known inventors endowed with an eccentric personality. In fact, however, inventors are usually ordinary people who possess extraordinary imagination. Many modern organizations of wide-ranging focus are devoting resources to the encouragement of employee creativity, from which they hope to gain advantages over their competition. Organizations intent on sparking ingenuity will consider innovation, monitor it, and take action to enhance it.

BusinessWeek uses a widely recognized evaluation process to develop its annual list of the world's most innovative companies (McGregor, 2006). This list of companies that have produced the top twenty-five innovations of the year is both comprehensive and respected. In partnership with Boston Consulting Group, the evaluation begins with a survey of innovation distributed electronically to executives worldwide early in the year, targeting 1,500 global corporations (determined by market capitalization). The executives are instructed to distribute the survey to their top ten executives. The survey is also accessible on several Web sites. The survey consists of nineteen general questions on innovation, as well as questions that focus on innovation metrics. In 2006, Apple, Google, 3M, Toyota, and Microsoft constituted the list's top five. Although the survey is comprehensive, it is deficient in measuring the actual monetary value attributable to innovation. Figure 7.5 shows how survey respondents measured the success of innovation. It is disappointing that only 30 percent indicated that they measure the actual ROI on innovation.

Creativity

Creativity, often considered the precursor to innovation, encompasses the creative experience, actions, and input of organizations. Measuring the creative spirit of employees may prove more difficult than measuring innovation. The employee suggestion system, a longtime measure of the creative processes of an organization, flourishes today in many organizations. Employees are rewarded for their suggestions if they are approved and implemented. Tracking the suggestion rates and benchmarking them against those of other

Figure 7.5. Measuring the Success of Innovation

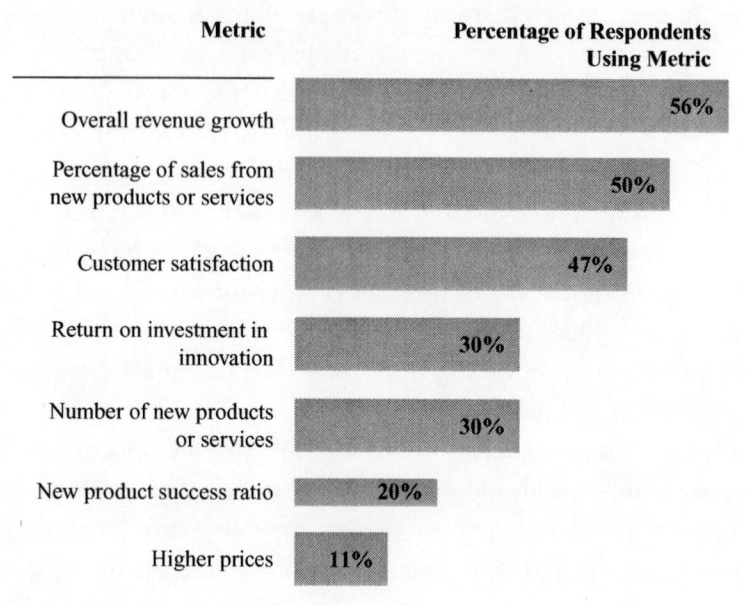

Metric	Percentage of Respondents Using Metric
Overall revenue growth	56%
Percentage of sales from new products or services	50%
Customer satisfaction	47%
Return on investment in innovation	30%
Number of new products or services	30%
New product success ratio	20%
Higher prices	11%

Source: Adapted from McGregor, 2006, p. 63.

organizations is an important way to measure creative capability. Another measure that can be monitored is the number of new ideas. Formal feedback systems often generate creative suggestions that can lead to improved processes.

Some organizations measure the creative capabilities of employees by distributing inventories or instruments at meetings or training sessions. In other organizations, a range of statements about employee creativity is included in the annual employee feedback survey. Using a rating scale, employees agree or disagree with the statements. Comparing the ratings of groups of employees over time reflects the degree to which employees perceive improvement in creativity in the workplace. Having consistent and comparable measures is still a challenge. Other organizations may monitor the number, duration, and participation rate of creativity training programs. These methods illustrate the proliferation of creativity tools, programs, and activity in the last decade.

Example 3: Employee Attitudes

Employee Satisfaction

An important item monitored by most organizations is employee job satisfaction. Using feedback surveys, executives can monitor the degree to which employees are satisfied with their employer's policies, work environment, and supervision and leadership; with the work itself; and with other factors. A composite rating may be developed in order to provide an overall satisfaction value or an index for an organization, division, department, or region.

Although job satisfaction has always been an important factor in employee relations, in recent years it has taken on a new dimension because of the link between job satisfaction and other measures. The relationship between job satisfaction and the attraction and retention of employees is classic: firms with excellent ratings in job satisfaction have better success in attracting the most desirable employees. Organizations with job satisfaction ratings high enough that they are listed among the employers of choice or best places to work have gained a powerful recruiting tool. Recent heightened emphasis on the relationship between job satisfaction and employee retention has resulted from the reality that turnover and retention are now such critical issues. These relationships can now be easily worked out by using human capital management software featuring modules that calculate the correlation between turnover rates and job satisfaction scores for various job groups, divisions, and departments.

Job satisfaction has taken on new dimensions in connection with customer service. Dozens of applied research projects are beginning to show a high correlation between job satisfaction scores and customer satisfaction scores. Intuitively, one understands that a more satisfied employee is likely to provide more productive, friendly, and appropriate customer service. Likewise, a disgruntled employee will provide poor service. Research has established that job attitudes (job satisfaction) relate to customer impression (customer satisfaction), which relates to revenue growth (profits). Therefore, it follows that if employee attitudes improve, revenues will increase. These links, often referred to as a *service profit chain*, create a promising way to identify important relationships between attitudes within an organization and the profits that the organization earns.

Organizational Commitment

In recent years, organizational commitment (OC) measures have complemented or replaced job satisfaction measures. OC measures go beyond employee satisfaction to include the extent to which employees identify with an organization's goals, mission, philosophy, values, policies, and practices. The concept of involvement and commitment to the organization is key. OC often closely correlates with productivity and other performance improvement measures, whereas job satisfaction usually does not. OC is often measured in the same way as job satisfaction, using an attitude survey with a 5- or 7-point scale that is administered directly to employees. As organizational commitment scores (usually measured by a standard index) improve, a corresponding improvement in productivity should be seen.

Employee Engagement

A different twist on the OC measure is one that reflects employee engagement. Measures are taken that indicate the extent to which employees are actively engaged in the organization. Consider the case of the Royal Bank of Scotland Group (RBS). With more than 115,000 employees, RBS considered it a strategic imperative to measure the effectiveness of its investment in people and the impact of this investment on business performance. As a result, RBS built, validated, and introduced a human capital model that demonstrably links "people strategies" to performance (Bates, 2003).

RBS moved beyond monitoring employee satisfaction and commitment to measuring whether employees actively improved business results. The bank accomplished this by using an employee engagement model that assesses employees' likelihood of contributing to business profits. The model links separate elements of human resources (HR) information in a consistent way, then links them to key business indicators. The outputs enabled RBS to understand how to influence the bank's results through its workforce.

To test and validate its model, RBS's HR research and measurement team reviewed the array of survey instruments used in HR activities. The HR team decided to put the employee engagement model into practice in the processing and customer contact centers, where productivity measures related to customer service are very important. Using the amount of work processed as a throughput measure, the team found that productivity increased in tandem with engagement levels. They were also able to establish a correlation between increasing engagement and decreasing staff turnover.

Hundreds of organizations now use engagement data to understand the extent to which employees are engaged and how their engagement relates to productivity and turnover.

Example 4: Leadership

Leadership is perhaps the most difficult measure to address. On the surface, it would seem easy to measure the outcome, because effective leadership leads to an effective organization. However, putting a monetary value on the consequences of new leadership behavior is not as easy as it appears.

Leadership can (and usually does) determine the success or failure of an organization. Without appropriate leadership behaviors throughout an organization, resources can be misapplied or wasted, and opportunities can be missed. The news and literature are laced with examples of failed leadership at the top, as well as accounts of mismanagement of employees, shareholders, investors, and the public. Some of these high-profile failed leadership stories have been painful. At the same time, there are positive examples of leaders—for example, former General Electric CEO Jack Welch—who have earned extraordinary success at many levels of their organization over a sustained period. These leaders are often documented in books, articles, and lists of admiration. They clearly make a difference in their organization.

How can that difference be measured? Obviously, the ultimate measure of leadership is the overall success of an organization. Whenever overall measures of success have been achieved or surpassed, they are always attributed to great leadership, perhaps rightly. However, attempting to use overall success as the only measure of leadership is a cop-out in terms of accountability. Other measures must be in place to provide systemwide monitoring of leaders and leadership in an organization.

360° Feedback

Leadership can be measured in many different ways, the most common of which is known as 360° feedback. Here, a prescribed set of leadership behaviors desired in the organization is assessed by different sources to provide a composite of overall leadership capability and behavior. The sources often consist of the immediate manager of the leader being assessed, a colleague in the same area, the employees directly supervised by the leader, internal or external customers, and the leader's self-assessment. Combined, these assessments form a circle of influence (360°). The measure is basically an observation of behavior captured in a survey, often reported electronically. The practice of 360° feedback has been growing rapidly in the United States, Europe, and Asia as an important way to capture overall leadership behavior change. Because the consequences of behavior change are usually measured as business impact, leadership improvement should be linked to business performance in some way.

Leadership Inventories

Another way to measure leadership is to require the management team to participate in a variety of leadership inventories in which they assess themselves by responding to a series of leadership competency statements. The inventories reflect the extent to which a particular leadership style, a particular approach, or even success is in place. These inventories, though they were popular in the 1970s and 1980s, are now being replaced by the 360° feedback process in many organizations.

Leadership Perception

It is also useful to capture the quality of leadership from the perspective of employees. In some organizations, employees regularly rate the quality of their leadership. Top executives and middle managers are typically the subjects of this form of evaluation. The measure is usually taken in conjunction with the annual feedback survey, in the form of direct statements about the executive or immediate manager, with which respondents agree or disagree, using a 5-point scale. This type of survey attempts to measure how the followers in a particular situation perceive the quality, success, and appropriateness of the leadership exercised by their managers.

Business Impact

The outcomes of leadership development are clearly documented in many case studies involving ROI analysis. Of the thousands of studies conducted annually, leadership development ROI studies are at the top of the list of applications, not because conducting them is easier but because of the uncertainty and the unknown aspects of investing in leadership development.

Most leadership development will have an impact in a particular leader's area. Leadership development creates new skills that are applied on the job and produce improvements in the leader's work unit. These improvements can vary significantly from leader to leader and from unit to unit. The best way to evaluate a general leadership development program involving executives and leaders from a variety of areas is to calculate its monetary impact. When particular improvements are made, examining those improvements individually makes little sense. Examining the monetary value of each measure as a whole is more worthwhile. The measures are converted to monetary values using one of the methods discussed earlier in this book. The monetary values of the improvements for the first year are combined into a total value, which ultimately feeds into an ROI calculation. Leadership development programs aimed at improving leadership behavior and driving business improvement often yield a high payoff, with ROI values that range from 500 percent to 1,000 percent (Phillips and Schmidt, 2004). This high yield is primarily due to the multiplicative effect as leaders are developed and changes of behavior influence important measures within the leaders' teams.

Final Thoughts

It should be clear by now that intangible measures are crucial to gauging the success of a program. Although they may not carry the weight of measures expressed in monetary terms, they are nevertheless an important part of the overall evaluation. Intangible measures should be identified, explored, examined, and monitored for changes linked to programs. Collectively, they add a unique dimension to the program report because most if not all programs involve intangible variables. We have explored five common intangible measures in some detail in this chapter, but the fact is that the range of intangible measures is practically limitless.

References

Alden, J. "Measuring the 'Unmeasurable.'" *Performance Improvement*, May/June 2006, 45(5), 7.

Bates, S. *Linking People Measures to Strategy*. Research report R-1342-03-RR. New York: Conference Board, 2003.

Boulton, R., Libert, B., and Samek, S. *Cracking the Value Code*. New York: HarperBusiness, 2000.

Brown, S. "Scientific Americans." *Fortune*, Sept. 20, 2004, p. 175.

Collins, J. *Good to Great and the Social Sector*. New York: HarperCollins, 2005.

Farris, P. W., Bendle, N. T., Pfeifer, P. E., and Ribstein, D. J. *Marketing Metrics: 50+ Metrics Every Executive Should Master*. Upper Saddle River, N.J.: Wharton School Publishing, 2006.

Kandybihn, A., and Kihn, M. "Raising Your Return on Innovation Investment." *Strategy + Business: Resilience Report*, May 11, 2004, no. 35, 1–12.

McGregor, J. "The World's Most Innovative Companies." *BusinessWeek*, Apr. 24, 2006, p. 63.

Phillips, J., and Schmidt, L. *The Leadership Scorecard*. Woburn, Mass.: Butterworth-Heinemann, 2004.

Santos, J., Doz, Y., and Williamson, P. "Is Your Innovation Process Global?" *MIT Sloan Management Review*, Summer 2004, 45(4), 31–37.

Schwartz, E. *Juice: The Creative Fuel That Drives World-Class Inventors*. Boston: Harvard Business School Press, 2004.

Index

A
ABC (activity-based costing), 4
ACT! (software), 21–22
Adjusting monetary values
  by management, 79–80
  for short-term vs. long-term
    programs, 80
  for time value of money, 81
Alden, J., 91
AllTheWeb, 48
AltaVista, 48
American Association for the
  Advancement of Science,
  103
Appraisal costs, 19

B
Bates, S., 108
Bendle, N. T., 99
Berkman, R., 50, 52
BlueCross BlueShield, 44
Brown, S., 103
BusinessWeek innovation list, 105

C
Campanella, J., 19
Case studies
  commercial bank, 14–15
  European postal service, 38
  federal agency employee turnover,
    53–55

manufacturing plant and
  estimating value, 59–60
manufacturing plant and using
  expert help, 45–46
measuring customer service
  intangibles, 98–102
measuring employee attitudes,
  107–109
measuring employee
  innovation/creativity, 102–106
measuring leadership, 109–111
Metropolitan Transit Authority,
  33–35
regional bank, 50, 53
Sears, Roebuck and Company,
  38–40
sexual harassment complaint,
  46–47
snapper lawn mowers, 15–16
team-building program, 11, 12
time savings to technology
  company, 23–24
Classic relationships, 36–40
Cleveland Orchestra measures, 93,
  94
Cokins, G., 4
Commercial bank case study, 14–15
Costs
  ABC (activity-based costing), 4
  appraisal, 19
  categories for quality, 19–20

Costs (*Continued*)
  examples of quality evaluations of, 21–22
  historical, 31–35
  penalty, 19
  prevention, 20
  ROI and importance of saving, 4
Creativity, 105–106
Credibility issue
  four-part test for data conversion, 67–68
  how credibility is influenced, 69–72
  how to address the, 75–79
  as key to data conversion, 67–69
  rules for determining credibility, 72–75
Customer dissatisfaction, 20
Customer satisfaction
  case study on measuring intangibles of, 98–102
  relationship between revenue and, 36–37
  University of Michigan index for, 93
Customer service case study, 98–102

D

Data
  credibility of, 67–79
  hard, 5–7, 92
  historical cost, 31–35
  See also Soft data
Data conversion
  case example of, 1, 11
  using experts for soft data, 43–57
  four-part test of, 67–68
  steps for, 7, 9–11
  why to figure monetary values from, 2–5
Data conversion of output
  commercial bank case of, 14–15
  described, 13–14
  methods for, 18
  more examples of standard values for, 16–17
  snapper lawn mowers case study on, 15–16
Data conversion steps
  1: focus on unit of improvement, 7, 9
  2: determine value of each unit, 9
  3: calculate change in performance, 10
  4: determine annual amount of change, 10
  5: calculate the total value of improvement, 10–11
Data conversion techniques
  ensuring accuracy/credibility of data, 67–79
  for making adjustments, 79–81
  matching exercise for, 81–86
  selecting the appropriate, 65–67
Databases
  using external, 47–53
  sources of external, 48–50, 51–52, 56
DHL Worldwide Express (Spain), 21
Doz, Y., 104

E

EBSCO*host*, 53
Employees
  case study on customer service provided by, 98–102
  case study on innovation and creativity of, 102–107
  case study on measuring attitudes of, 107–109
  case study on turnover of, 53–55
  converting their time to monetary value, 22–25
  job satisfaction of, 36–40, 107–108
ERIC, 53
Estimating value
  from participant estimates, 59–61
  from senior management estimates, 62–63
  from staff estimates, 63–64
  from supervisor/manager estimates, 61–63

European postal service case study, 38
Experts
  combining historical costs and, 47
  using internal and external, 43–47
External databases
  benefits of using, 47–48
  case studies on using, 50, 53
  Internet searches for, 48–50, 51–52, 56
  sources of, 56
External experts
  case study on using, 46–47
  used to convert soft data, 45
External failure, 19

F
Farris, P. W., 99
Federal agency employee turnover case study, 53–55

G
Global Financial Services, 21–22
Google, 48

H
Hard data
  converting to monetary values, 27
  described, 5, 7
  examples of, 6
  as tangible measure, 92
Historical costs
  combining expert input and, 47
  types and sources of, 31–35
Hock, R., 48

I
Innovation, 102–105, 106
Intangible measures
  converting to monetary values, 93, 95–98
  customer service, 98–102
  of employee attitudes, 107–109
  of employee innovation and creativity, 102–106
  importance of, 88–90

  of leadership, 109–111
  process of measuring the, 90–93
  during program life cycle, 96
  range and types of common, 87–88
  See also Soft data
Internal experts
  case study on using, 45–46
  used to convert soft data, 44–45
Internal failure, 19
Internet searches
  asking right questions during, 51–52
  database sources found during, 56
  overview of, 48–50

J
Job satisfaction
  relationship between revenue and, 38–40
  relationship between turnover and, 37–38

K
Kandybihn, A., 103
Keiningham, R., 19
Kihn, M., 103
Kim, S., 39

L
Leadership measures case study, 109–111
Loan profitability analysis, 14

M
Management
  using estimates provided by, 61–63
  monetary value adjustments by, 79–80
Manufacturing plant case studies
  on estimating value, 59–60
  on using external experts, 45–46
Marketing standard values, 28–29
McGregor, J., 105, 106
Measure relationships
  classic, 36–40
  concerns regarding, 40
  identifying, 35–36

Index

Measures
  Cleveland Orchestra, 93, 94
  intangible, 87–112
  link between hard-to-measure/easy-to-measure items, 92
  relationships between, 35–40
Metropolitan Transit Authority case study, 33–35
Monetary values
  concerns when using relationships to assign, 40
  conversion of time savings to, 23–24
  converting employee time to, 22–25
  converting hard data to, 27
  converting intangibles to, 93, 95–98
  converting output data to, 13–17, 18
  converting quality to, 17, 19–22
  estimating the value, 59–64
  making adjustments to, 79–81
  reasons for converting data to, 2–5
  ROI calculation and role of, 1
  of time, 81
  See also Standard values

O

Organizations
  monetary values role in operations of, 4
  OC (organizational commitment) to, 108

P

Participant estimates, 59–61
Penalty costs, 19
Performance
  calculating change in, 10
  calculating total value of improved, 10–11
  unit of improvement in, 7, 9
Pfeifer, P. E., 99
Phillips, J. J., 53, 112
Phillips, P. P., 53
Prevention costs, 20
Programs
  adjusting for short-term vs. long-term, 80
  case study on team-building, 11, 12
  identifying intangible measures during life cycle of, 96
  intangibles as driving, 90
  role of monetary values in, 3
  time value of money factor of, 81

Q

Quality
  benefits of monetary value conversion of, 17, 19
  cost categories for, 19–20
  examples of cost evaluations of, 21–22
  measures of, 20
Quinn, R., 39

R

Regional bank case study, 50, 53
Revenue
  relationship between customer satisfaction and, 36–37
  relationship between job satisfaction and, 38–40
Ribstein, D. J., 99
ROI (return on investment)
  cost saving importance to, 4
  using profit margin instead of actual sales in, 16–17
  role of monetary values in calculating, 1
Royal Bank of Scotland Group (RBS), 108–109
Rucci, A., 39
Rust, R., 19

S

Sales standard values, 28–29
Santos, J., 104
Schmidt, L., 112

Schwartz, E., 104
Sears, Roebuck and Company case study, 38–40
Senior management
  using estimates provided by, 62–63
  monetary value adjustments by, 79–80
Service-profit chain, 40
Sexual harassment complaint case study, 46–47
Snapper lawn mowers case study, 15–16
Soft data
  described, 5
  examples of, 8
  using experts to convert, 43–57
  link between measuring hard and, 92
  See also Data; Intangible measures
Staff estimates, 63–64
Standard values
  calculating, 31–41
  for converting output data, 16–17
  definition of, 13, 26
  development of, 25–26
  examples from sales and marketing, 28–29
  functions that generate, 26–27
  See also Monetary values

Standard values calculation
  concerns when using relationships in, 40
  using historical costs, 31–35
  linking with other measures, 35–40
Supervisor estimates, 61–62

T
Team-building program case study, 11, 12
360° feedback, 110, 111
Time savings
  caution regarding converting, 24–25
  monetary value conversion of, 23–24
Time value, 81

U
University of Michigan, 93

W
Web search engines, 48–52, 56
Williamson, P., 104

Z
Zahorik, A., 19

About the Authors

Patricia Pulliam Phillips, Ph.D., is president of the ROI Institute, Inc., the leading source of ROI competency building, implementation support, networking, and research. She supports organizations in their efforts to build accountability into their training, human resources, and performance improvement programs with a primary focus on building accountability in public sector organizations. She helps organizations implement the ROI Methodology in countries around the world, including South Africa, Singapore, Japan, New Zealand, Australia, Italy, Turkey, France, Germany, Canada, and the United States.

In 1997, after a thirteen-year career in the electrical utility industry, she embraced the ROI Methodology by committing herself to ongoing research and practice. To this end, Phillips has implemented the ROI Methodology in private sector and public sector organizations. She has conducted ROI impact studies of programs in leadership development, sales, new-hire orientation, human performance improvement, K–12 educator development, National Board Certification mentoring for educators, and faculty fellowship. Phillips is currently expanding her interest in public sector accountability by applying the ROI Methodology in community- and faith-based initiatives.

Phillips teaches others to implement the ROI Methodology through the ROI certification process, as a facilitator for ASTD's

ROI and Measuring and Evaluating Learning workshops, and as an adjunct professor for graduate-level evaluation courses. She speaks on the topic of ROI at conferences such as ASTD's International Conference and Exposition and the International Society for Performance Improvement's International Conference.

Phillips's academic accomplishments include a master's degree in public and private management and a Ph.D. degree in international development. She is certified in ROI evaluation and has earned the designation of certified performance technologist (CPT) and certified professional in learning and performance (CPLP). She has authored a number of publications on the subject of accountability and ROI, including *Show Me the Money: How to Determine ROI in People, Projects, and Programs* (Berrett-Koehler, 2007); *The Value of Learning* (Pfeiffer, 2007); *Return on Investment (ROI) Basics* (ASTD, 2005); *Proving the Value of HR: How and Why to Measure ROI* (Society for Human Resource Management, 2005); *Make Training Evaluation Work* (ASTD, 2004); *The Bottomline on ROI* (Center for Effective Performance, 2002), which won the 2003 ISPI Award of Excellence; *ROI at Work* (ASTD, 2005); the ASTD In Action casebooks *Measuring Return on Investment*, Volume 3 (2001), *Measuring ROI in the Public Sector* (2002), and *Retaining Your Best Employees* (2002); the ASTD Infoline series, including *Planning and Using Evaluation Data* (2003), *Mastering ROI* (1998), and *Managing Evaluation Shortcuts* (2001); and *The Human Resources Scorecard: Measuring Return on Investment* (Butterworth-Heinemann, 2001). Phillips's work has been published in a variety of journals. She can be reached at patti@roiinstitute.net.

Holly Burkett, M.A., SPHR, CPT, is principal of Evaluation Works and has been a certified ROI professional (CRP) since 1997. As an internal and external consultant, she has more than eighteen years of experience assisting diverse public and private sector organizations to design and measure a wide range of evaluation processes, programs, and systems. Formerly with Apple Computer, she led the operation's first HRD impact studies. Editor-in-chief of ISPI's *Performance Improvement Journal* and a certified performance technologist (CPT), she is a frequent conference presenter, workshop leader, and author on performance measurement topics. Most recently, she coauthored *The ROI Fieldbook* (with Jack Phillips, Patricia Phillips, and Ron Stone, 2006). She earned her M.A. degree in human resources and organization development from the University of San Francisco and is currently pursuing doctoral studies in human capital development. She can be reached at burketth@earthlink.net.

Pfeiffer Publications Guide

This guide is designed to familiarize you with the various types of Pfeiffer publications. The formats section describes the various types of products that we publish; the methodologies section describes the many different ways that content might be provided within a product. We also provide a list of the topic areas in which we publish.

FORMATS

In addition to its extensive book-publishing program, Pfeiffer offers content in an array of formats, from fieldbooks for the practitioner to complete, ready-to-use training packages that support group learning.

FIELDBOOK Designed to provide information and guidance to practitioners in the midst of action. Most fieldbooks are companions to another, sometimes earlier, work, from which its ideas are derived; the fieldbook makes practical what was theoretical in the original text. Fieldbooks can certainly be read from cover to cover. More likely, though, you'll find yourself bouncing around following a particular theme, or dipping in as the mood, and the situation, dictate.

HANDBOOK A contributed volume of work on a single topic, comprising an eclectic mix of ideas, case studies, and best practices sourced by practitioners and experts in the field.

An editor or team of editors usually is appointed to seek out contributors and to evaluate content for relevance to the topic. Think of a handbook not as a ready-to-eat meal, but as a cookbook of ingredients that enables you to create the most fitting experience for the occasion.

RESOURCE Materials designed to support group learning. They come in many forms: a complete, ready-to-use exercise (such as a game); a comprehensive resource on one topic (such as conflict management) containing a variety of methods and approaches; or a collection of like-minded activities (such as icebreakers) on multiple subjects and situations.

TRAINING PACKAGE An entire, ready-to-use learning program that focuses on a particular topic or skill. All packages comprise a guide for the facilitator/trainer and a workbook for the participants. Some packages are supported with additional media—such as video—or learning aids, instruments, or other devices to help participants understand concepts or practice and develop skills.

- *Facilitator/trainer's guide* Contains an introduction to the program, advice on how to organize and facilitate the learning event, and step-by-step instructor notes. The guide also contains copies of presentation materials—handouts, presentations, and overhead designs, for example—used in the program.

- *Participant's workbook* Contains exercises and reading materials that support the learning goal and serves as a valuable reference and support guide for participants in the weeks and months that follow the learning event. Typically, each participant will require his or her own workbook.

ELECTRONIC CD-ROMs and web-based products transform static Pfeiffer content into dynamic, interactive experiences. Designed to take advantage of the searchability, automation, and ease-of-use that technology provides, our e-products bring convenience and immediate accessibility to your workspace.

METHODOLOGIES

CASE STUDY A presentation, in narrative form, of an actual event that has occurred inside an organization. Case studies are not prescriptive, nor are they used to prove a point; they are designed to develop critical analysis and decision-making skills. A case study has a specific time frame, specifies a sequence of events, is narrative in structure, and contains a plot structure—an issue (what should be/have been done?). Use case studies when the goal is to enable participants to apply previously learned theories to the circumstances in the case, decide what is pertinent, identify the real issues, decide what should have been done, and develop a plan of action.

ENERGIZER A short activity that develops readiness for the next session or learning event. Energizers are most commonly used after a break or lunch to

stimulate or refocus the group. Many involve some form of physical activity, so they are a useful way to counter post-lunch lethargy. Other uses include transitioning from one topic to another, where "mental" distancing is important.

EXPERIENTIAL LEARNING ACTIVITY (ELA) A facilitator-led intervention that moves participants through the learning cycle from experience to application (also known as a Structured Experience). ELAs are carefully thought-out designs in which there is a definite learning purpose and intended outcome. Each step—everything that participants do during the activity—facilitates the accomplishment of the stated goal. Each ELA includes complete instructions for facilitating the intervention and a clear statement of goals, suggested group size and timing, materials required, an explanation of the process, and, where appropriate, possible variations to the activity. (For more detail on Experiential Learning Activities, see the Introduction to the *Reference Guide to Handbooks and Annuals*, 1999 edition, Pfeiffer, San Francisco.)

GAME A group activity that has the purpose of fostering team spirit and togetherness in addition to the achievement of a pre-stated goal. Usually contrived—undertaking a desert expedition, for example—this type of learning method offers an engaging means for participants to demonstrate and practice business and interpersonal skills. Games are effective for team building and personal development mainly because the goal is subordinate to the process—the means through which participants reach decisions, collaborate, communicate, and generate trust and understanding. Games often engage teams in "friendly" competition.

ICEBREAKER A (usually) short activity designed to help participants overcome initial anxiety in a training session and/or to acquaint the participants with one another. An icebreaker can be a fun activity or can be tied to specific topics or training goals. While a useful tool in itself, the icebreaker comes into its own in situations where tension or resistance exists within a group.

INSTRUMENT A device used to assess, appraise, evaluate, describe, classify, and summarize various aspects of human behavior. The term used to describe an instrument depends primarily on its format and purpose. These terms include survey, questionnaire, inventory, diagnostic, survey, and poll. Some uses of instruments include providing instrumental feedback to group

members, studying here-and-now processes or functioning within a group, manipulating group composition, and evaluating outcomes of training and other interventions.

Instruments are popular in the training and HR field because, in general, more growth can occur if an individual is provided with a method for focusing specifically on his or her own behavior. Instruments also are used to obtain information that will serve as a basis for change and to assist in workforce planning efforts.

Paper-and-pencil tests still dominate the instrument landscape with a typical package comprising a facilitator's guide, which offers advice on administering the instrument and interpreting the collected data, and an initial set of instruments. Additional instruments are available separately. Pfeiffer, though, is investing heavily in e-instruments. Electronic instrumentation provides effortless distribution and, for larger groups particularly, offers advantages over paper-and-pencil tests in the time it takes to analyze data and provide feedback.

LECTURETTE A short talk that provides an explanation of a principle, model, or process that is pertinent to the participants' current learning needs. A lecturette is intended to establish a common language bond between the trainer and the participants by providing a mutual frame of reference. Use a lecturette as an introduction to a group activity or event, as an interjection during an event, or as a handout.

MODEL A graphic depiction of a system or process and the relationship among its elements. Models provide a frame of reference and something more tangible, and more easily remembered, than a verbal explanation. They also give participants something to "go on," enabling them to track their own progress as they experience the dynamics, processes, and relationships being depicted in the model.

ROLE PLAY A technique in which people assume a role in a situation/scenario: a customer service rep in an angry-customer exchange, for example. The way in which the role is approached is then discussed and feedback is offered. The role play is often repeated using a different approach and/or incorporating changes made based on feedback received. In other words, role playing is a spontaneous interaction involving realistic behavior under artificial (and safe) conditions.

SIMULATION A methodology for understanding the interrelationships among components of a system or process. Simulations differ from games in that they test or use a model that depicts or mirrors some aspect of reality in form, if not necessarily in content. Learning occurs by studying the effects of change on one or more factors of the model. Simulations are commonly used to test hypotheses about what happens in a system—often referred to as "what if?" analysis—or to examine best-case/worst-case scenarios.

THEORY A presentation of an idea from a conjectural perspective. Theories are useful because they encourage us to examine behavior and phenomena through a different lens.

TOPICS

The twin goals of providing effective and practical solutions for workforce training and organization development and meeting the educational needs of training and human resource professionals shape Pfeiffer's publishing program. Core topics include the following:

Leadership & Management

Communication & Presentation

Coaching & Mentoring

Training & Development

E-Learning

Teams & Collaboration

OD & Strategic Planning

Human Resources

Consulting

What will you find on pfeiffer.com?

- The best in workplace performance solutions for training and HR professionals
- Downloadable training tools, exercises, and content
- Web-exclusive offers
- Training tips, articles, and news
- Seamless on-line ordering
- Author guidelines, information on becoming a Pfeiffer Affiliate, and much more

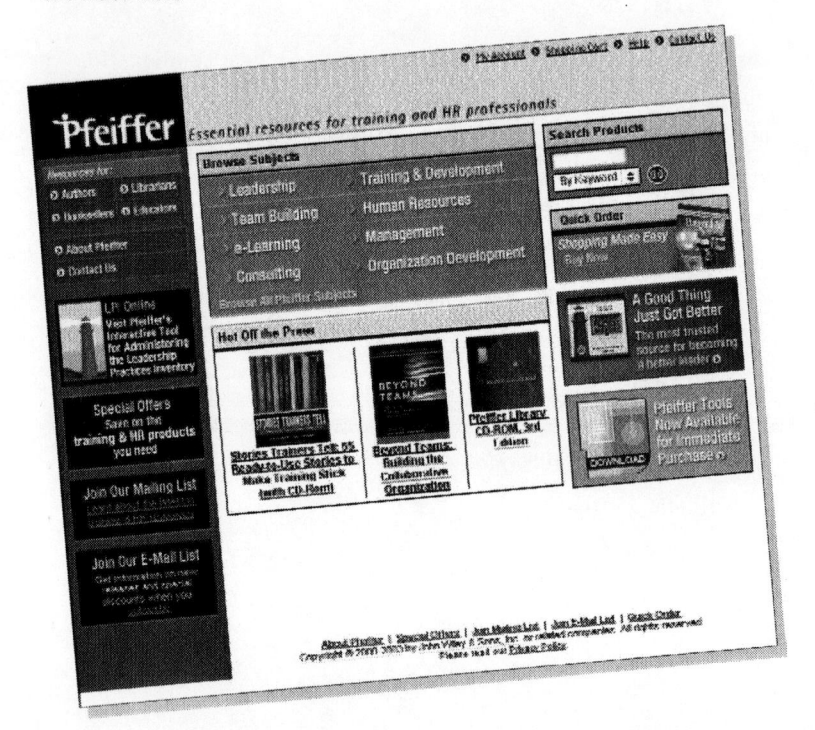

Discover more at www.pfeiffer.com

Measurement and Evaluation Series

Series Editors
Patricia Pulliam Phillips, Ph.D., and Jack J. Phillips, Ph.D.

A six-book set that provides a step-by-step system for planning, measuring, calculating, and communicating evaluation and Return-on-Investment for training and development, featuring:

- Detailed templates
- Ready-to-use tools
- Complete plans
- Real-world case examples

The M&E Series features:

1. *ROI Fundamentals: Why and When to Measure ROI*
   (978-0-7879-8716-9)
2. *Data Collection: Planning For and Collecting All Types of Data*
   (978-0-7879-8718-3)
3. *Isolation of Results: Defining the Impact of the Program*
   (978-0-7879-8719-0)
4. *Data Conversion: Calculating the Monetary Benefits*
   (978-0-7879-8720-6)
5. *Costs and ROI: Evaluating at the Ultimate Level*
   (978-0-7879-8721-3)
6. *Communication and Implementation: Sustaining the Practice*
   (978-0-7879-8722-0)

Plus, the *ROI in Action Casebook* (978-0-7879-8717-6) covers all the major workplace learning and performance applications, including Leadership Development, Sales Training, Performance Improvement, Technical Skills Training, Information Technology Training, Orientation and OJT, and Supervisor Training.

The **ROI Methodology** is a comprehensive measurement and evaluation process that collects six types of measures: Reaction, Satisfaction, and Planned Action; Learning; Application and Implementation; Business Impact; Return on Investment; and Intangible Measures. The process provides a step-by-step system for evaluation and planning, data collection, data analysis, and reporting. It is appropriate for the measurement and evaluation of *all* kinds of performance improvement programs and activities, including training and development, learning, human resources, coaching, meetings and events, consulting, and project management.

Special Offer from the ROI Institute

Send for your own ROI Process Model, an indispensable tool for implementing and presenting ROI in your organization. The ROI Institute is offering an exclusive gift to readers of The Measurement and Evaluation Series. This 11"×25" multicolor foldout shows the ROI Methodology flow model and the key issues surrounding the implementation of the ROI Methodology. This easy-to-understand overview of the ROI Methodology has proven invaluable to countless professionals when implementing the ROI Methodology. Please return this page or e-mail your information to the address below to receive your free foldout (a $6.00 value). Please check your area(s) of interest in ROI.

Please send me the ROI Process Model described in the book. I am interested in learning more about the following ROI materials and services:

- ☐ Workshops and briefing on ROI
- ☐ Books and support materials on ROI
- ☐ Certification in the ROI Methodology
- ☐ ROI software
- ☐ ROI consulting services
- ☐ ROI Network information
- ☐ ROI benchmarking
- ☐ ROI research

Name _____
Title _____
Organization _____
Address _____
Phone _____
E-mail Address _____

Functional area of interest:

- ☐ Learning and Development/Performance Improvement
- ☐ Human Resources/Human Capital
- ☐ Public Relations/Community Affairs/Government Relations
- ☐ Consulting
- ☐ Sales/Marketing
- ☐ Technology/IT Systems
- ☐ Project Management Solutions
- ☐ Quality/Six Sigma
- ☐ Operations/Methods/Engineering
- ☐ Research and Development/Innovations
- ☐ Finance/Compliance
- ☐ Logistics/Distribution/Supply Chain
- ☐ Public Policy Initiatives
- ☐ Social Programs
- ☐ Other (Please Specify) _____

Organizational Level

☐ executive ☐ management ☐ consultant ☐ specialist
☐ student   ☐ evaluator   ☐ researcher

Return this form or contact The ROI Institute
P.O. Box 380637
Birmingham, AL 35238-0637

Or e-mail information to info@roiinstitute.net
Please allow four to six weeks for delivery.

About This Book

Why This Book Is Important

Costs and ROI: Evaluating at the Ultimate Level, the fifth book in the M&E series, discusses the ultimate level of evaluation: calculating ROI. Executives want to know whether specific programs and projects add value to their organization; calculating the ROI gives them the accountability they seek.

Part of calculating ROI is tabulating the fully loaded program costs. Fully loaded costs include all direct and indirect costs. Using fully loaded costs is critical in order to maintain a conservative approach.

What This Book Achieves

This book shows how to tabulate the fully loaded costs of a program and explains what costs should be included in this total. It also presents the different formulas that can be used to calculate ROI. Finally, measures other than ROI that can show the value of programs and projects are defined and explained.

How This Book Is Organized

This book begins with a brief introduction to the ROI process model and the Twelve Guiding Principles. Chapter One discusses why tabulating costs and calculating the ROI are important. It also examines why the ROI should be forecast. Chapter Two discusses how to efficiently track costs and explores the issues involved in cost tracking and cost categories. Cost reporting, cost accumulation, and cost estimation are also discussed.

Chapter Three details the calculation of ROI. The chapter includes examples as well as different ways to calculate the return and other measures. Chapter Four reviews the many concerns, issues, and myths surrounding the ROI Methodology.

In Chapter Five, the many benefits of developing an ROI forecast are discussed. Forecasts can be developed prior to a program's implementation by using a pilot program, reaction data, learning data, or skills and competencies. Finally, the guidelines for forecasting are examined.

The Measurement and Evaluation Series

Editors
Patricia Pulliam Phillips, Ph.D.
Jack J. Phillips, Ph.D.

Introduction to the Measurement and Evaluation Series

The ROI Six Pack provides detailed information on developing ROI evaluations, implementing the ROI Methodology, and showing the value of a variety of functions and processes. With detailed examples, tools, templates, shortcuts, and checklists, this series will be a valuable reference for individuals interested in using the ROI Methodology to show the impact of their projects, programs, and processes.

The Need

Although financial ROI has been measured for over one hundred years to quantify the value of plants, equipment, and companies, the concept has only recently been applied to evaluate the impact of learning and development, human resources, technology, quality, marketing, and other support functions. In the learning and development field alone, the use of ROI has become routine in many organizations. In the past decade, hundreds of organizations have embraced the ROI process to show the impact of many different projects and programs.

Along the way, professionals and practitioners need help. They need tools, templates, and tips, along with explanations, examples, and details, to make this process work. Without this help, using the ROI Methodology to show the value of projects and

programs is difficult. In short, practitioners need shortcuts and proven techniques to minimize the resources required to use this process. Practitioners' needs have created the need for this series. This series will provide the detail necessary to make the ROI Methodology successful within an organization. For easy reference and use, the books are logically arranged to align with the steps of the ROI Methodology.

Audience

The principal audience for these books is individuals who plan to use the ROI Methodology to show the value of their projects and programs. Such individuals are specialists or managers charged with proving the value of their particular project or program. They need detailed information, know-how, and confidence.

A second audience is those who have used the ROI Methodology for some time but want a quick reference with tips and techniques to make ROI implementation more successful within their organization. This series, which explains the evaluation process in detail, will be a valuable reference set for these individuals, regardless of other ROI publications owned.

A third audience is consultants and researchers who want to know how to address specific evaluation issues. Three important challenges face individuals as they measure ROI and conduct ROI evaluations: (1) collecting post-program data, (2) isolating the effects of the program, and (3) converting data to monetary values. A book is devoted to each of these critical issues, allowing researchers and consultants to easily find details on each issue.

A fourth audience is those who are curious about the ROI Methodology and its use. The first book in this series focuses specifically on ROI, its use, and how to determine whether it is appropriate for an organization. When interest is piqued, the remaining books provide more detail.

Flow of the Books

The six books are presented in a logical sequence, mirroring the ROI process model. Book one, *ROI Fundamentals: Why and When to Measure ROI,* presents the basic ROI Methodology and makes the business case for measuring ROI as it explores the benefits and barriers to implementation. It also examines the type of organization best suited for the ROI Methodology and the best time to implement it. Planning for an ROI evaluation is also explored in this book.

Book two, *Data Collection: Planning For and Collecting All Types of Data,* details data collection by examining the different techniques, methods, and issues involved in this process, with an emphasis on collecting post-program data. It examines the different data collection methods: questionnaires, interviews, focus groups, observation, action plans, performance contracts, and monitoring records.

Book three, *Isolation of Results: Defining the Impact of the Program,* focuses on the most valuable part of the ROI Methodology and the essential step for ensuring credibility. Recognizing that factors other than the program being measured can influence results, this book shows a variety of ways in which the effects of a program can be isolated from other influences. Techniques include comparison analysis using a control group, trend line analysis and forecasting methods, and expert input from a variety of sources.

Book four, *Data Conversion: Calculating the Monetary Benefits,* covers perhaps the second toughest challenge of ROI evaluation: placing monetary value on program benefits. To calculate the ROI, data must be converted to money, and *Data Conversion* shows how this conversion has been accomplished in a variety of organizations. The good news is that standard values are available for many items. When they are not, the book shows different techniques for converting them, ranging from calculating the value from records to seeking experts and searching databases. When data cannot be

converted to money credibly and with minimum resources, they are considered intangible. This book explores the range of intangible benefits and the necessary techniques for collecting, analyzing, and recording them.

Book five, *Costs and ROI: Evaluating at the Ultimate Level*, focuses on costs and ROI. This book shows that all costs must be captured in order to create a fully loaded cost profile. All the costs must be included in order to be conservative and to give the analysis additional credibility. Next, the actual ROI calculation is presented, showing the various assumptions and issues that must be addressed when calculating the ROI. Three different calculations are presented: the benefit-cost ratio, the ROI percentage, and the payback period. The book concludes with several cautions and concerns about the use of ROI and its meaning.

Book six, *Communication and Implementation: Sustaining the Practice*, explores two important issues. The first issue is reporting the results of an evaluation. This is the final part of the ROI Methodology and is necessary to ensure that audiences have the information they need so that improvement processes can be implemented. A range of techniques is available, including face-to-face meetings, brief reports, one-page summaries, routine communications, mass-audience techniques, and electronic media. All are available for reporting evaluation results. The final part of the book focuses on how to sustain the ROI evaluation process: how to use it, keep it going, and make it work in the long term to add value to the organization and, often, to show the value of all the programs and projects within a function or department.

Terminology: Programs, Projects, Solutions

In this series the terms *program* and *project* are used to describe many processes that can be evaluated using the ROI Methodology. This is an important issue because readers may vary widely in their perspectives. Individuals involved in technology applications may

Table I.1. Terms and Applications

Term	Example
Program	Leadership development skills enhancement for senior executives
Project	A reengineering scheme for a plastics division
System	A fully interconnected network for all branches of a bank
Initiative	A faith-based effort to reduce recidivism
Policy	A new preschool plan for disadvantaged citizens
Procedure	A new scheduling arrangement for truck drivers
Event	A golf outing for customers
Meeting	A U.S. Coast Guard conference on innovations
Process	Quality sampling
People	Staff additions in the customer care center
Tool	A new means of selecting hotel staff

use the terms *system* and *technology* rather than *program* or *project*. In public policy, in contrast, the word *program* is prominent. For a professional meetings and events planner, the word *program* may not be pertinent, but in human resources, *program* is often used. Finding one term for all these situations would be difficult. Consequently, the terms *program* and *project* are used interchangeably. Table I.1 lists these and other terms that may be used in other contexts.

Features

Each book in the series takes a straightforward approach to make it understandable, practical, and useful. Checklists are provided, charts are included, templates are presented, and examples are explored. All are intended to show how the ROI Methodology works. The focus of these books is implementing the process and making it successful within an organization. The methodology is based on the work of hundreds of individuals who have made the ROI Methodology a successful evaluation process within their organizations.

About Pfeiffer

Pfeiffer serves the professional development and hands-on resource needs of training and human resource practitioners and gives them products to do their jobs better. We deliver proven ideas and solutions from experts in HR development and HR management, and we offer effective and customizable tools to improve workplace performance. From novice to seasoned professional, Pfeiffer is the source you can trust to make yourself and your organization more successful.

Essential Knowledge Pfeiffer produces insightful, practical, and comprehensive materials on topics that matter the most to training and HR professionals. Our Essential Knowledge resources translate the expertise of seasoned professionals into practical, how-to guidance on critical workplace issues and problems. These resources are supported by case studies, worksheets, and job aids and are frequently supplemented with CD-ROMs, websites, and other means of making the content easier to read, understand, and use.

Essential Tools Pfeiffer's Essential Tools resources save time and expense by offering proven, ready-to-use materials—including exercises, activities, games, instruments, and assessments—for use during a training or team-learning event. These resources are frequently offered in looseleaf or CD-ROM format to facilitate copying and customization of the material.

Pfeiffer also recognizes the remarkable power of new technologies in expanding the reach and effectiveness of training. While e-hype has often created whizbang solutions in search of a problem, we are dedicated to bringing convenience and enhancements to proven training solutions. All our e-tools comply with rigorous functionality standards. The most appropriate technology wrapped around essential content yields the perfect solution for today's on-the-go trainers and human resource professionals.

Pfeiffer
www.pfeiffer.com   *Essential resources for training and HR professionals*

Costs and ROI

Evaluating at the Ultimate Level

Jack J. Phillips, Ph.D.
Lizette Zúñiga, M.A.

Pfeiffer
A Wiley Imprint
www.pfeiffer.com

Copyright © 2008 by John Wiley & Sons, Inc. All rights reserved.

Published by Pfeiffer
An Imprint of Wiley
989 Market Street, San Francisco, CA 94103-1741
www.pfeiffer.com

Wiley Bicentennial logo: Richard J. Pacifico

No part of this publication may be reproduced, stored in a retrieval system, or transmitted in any form or by any means, electronic, mechanical, photocopying, recording, scanning, or otherwise, except as permitted under Section 107 or 108 of the 1976 United States Copyright Act, without either the prior written permission of the Publisher, or authorization through payment of the appropriate per-copy fee to the Copyright Clearance Center, Inc., 222 Rosewood Drive, Danvers, MA 01923, 978-750-8400, fax 978-646-8600, or on the web at www.copyright.com. Requests to the Publisher for permission should be addressed to the Permissions Department, John Wiley & Sons, Inc., 111 River Street, Hoboken, NJ 07030, 201-748-6011, fax 201-748-6008, or online at http://www.wiley.com/go/permissions.

Limit of Liability/Disclaimer of Warranty: While the publisher and author have used their best efforts in preparing this book, they make no representations or warranties with respect to the accuracy or completeness of the contents of this book and specifically disclaim any implied warranties of merchantability or fitness for a particular purpose. No warranty may be created or extended by sales representatives or written sales materials. The advice and strategies contained herein may not be suitable for your situation. You should consult with a professional where appropriate. Neither the publisher nor author shall be liable for any loss of profit or any other commercial damages, including but not limited to special, incidental, consequential, or other damages.

Readers should be aware that Internet websites offered as citations and/or sources for further information may have changed or disappeared between the time this book was written and when it is read.

For additional copies/bulk purchases of this book in the U.S. please contact 800-274-4434.

Pfeiffer books and products are available through most bookstores. To contact Pfeiffer directly call our Customer Care Department within the U.S. at 800-274-4434, outside the U.S. at 317-572-3985, fax 317-572-4002, or visit www.pfeiffer.com.

Pfeiffer also publishes its books in a variety of electronic formats. Some content that appears in print may not be available in electronic books.

Library of Congress Cataloging-in-Publication Data

Phillips, Jack J., date.
  Costs and ROI: evaluating at the ultimate level/Jack J. Phillips, Lizette Zúñiga.
    p. cm.
  Includes bibliographical references and index.
  ISBN: 978-0-7879-8721-3 (pbk.)
  1. Employees—Training of—Cost effectiveness. 2. Employees—Training of—Evaluation. 3. Personnel management—Evaluation. 4. Rate of return—Evaluation. I. Zúñiga, Lizette. II. Title.
  HF5549.5.T7P427 2008
  658.3'124—dc22

2007045001

Production Editor: Michael Kay	Editorial Assistant: Julie Rodriguez
Editor: Matthew Davis	Manufacturing Supervisor: Becky Morgan

Printed in the United States of America

PB Printing 10 9 8 7 6 5 4 3 2 1

Contents

Acknowledgments from the Editors   xix

Principles of the ROI Methodology   xxi

Chapter 1: The Importance of Costs and ROI   1

  Why Be Concerned About Costs?   2
    Benchmarking   2
    Evaluation   5
    Cost Forecasting   6
    Efficiency   6
    Other Reasons for Monitoring Costs   6
  The Importance of ROI   7
    The Ultimate Level of Evaluation   8
    Types of Values   9
    ROI Is King   10
    The "Show Me" Generation   10
    The New Definition of Value   11
  Why ROI Now?   12
    Program Failures   12
    Increased Total Program Costs   13
    Trend Toward Greater Accountability   13
    Staff Support Managers' New Business Focus   14
    Evidence-Based or Fact-Based Management   14
    Limitations of Benchmarking   15
    Executive Appetite for Evaluation of ROI   16

Why Forecast ROI?	16
Expensive Programs and Projects	16
High Risks and Uncertainty	17
Post-Program Comparison	17
Compliance	18
Final Thoughts	18

Chapter 2: Cost Tracking and Classification 21

Cost Issues	21
Pressure to Disclose All Costs	21
Fully Loaded Costs as a Conservative Approach	23
The Danger of Accumulating Costs Without Tracking Benefits	26
Policies and Guidelines	26
Cost Tracking Issues	27
Sources of Program Costs	27
Process Steps and Costs	28
Prorated Versus Direct Costs	29
Employee Benefits Factor	30
Major Cost Categories	30
Needs Assessment and Analysis	30
Design and Development	31
Acquisition	33
Technological Support	33
Delivery and Implementation	33
Facilitators' and Coordinators' Salaries and Benefits	34
Participants' Salaries and Benefits	34
Travel, Lodging, and Meals	34
Facilities	34
Program Materials and Fees	35
Evaluation	36
Overhead	36
Cost Reporting	38
Cost Accumulation and Estimation	40
Cost Classification Matrix	40
Cost Accumulation	42
Cost Estimation	43

Case Study: Federal Information Agency	46
Overview	46
Problem and Solution	47
Program Description	48
Selection Criteria	49
Program Administration	50
Drivers of Evaluation	51
Program Costs	52
Final Thoughts	53

Chapter 3: The ROI Calculation   57

Basic Issues in Calculating ROI	57
Definitions Are Critical	57
Annualized Values	58
Benefit-Cost Ratio	59
ROI Formula	60
ROI Examples	62
Example 1: Retail Merchandise Company	62
Example 2: Global Financial Services	66
Example 3: Healthcare, Inc.	67
Example 4: Metro Transit Authority	68
Example 5: Midwest Electric	69
Positioning ROI Evaluation	71
Choosing the Right Formula	71
Developing ROI Objectives	73
Determining ROI Targets	75
Other ROI Measures	75
Payback Period	76
Discounted Cash Flow	76
Internal Rate of Return	78
Utility Analysis	78
ROI, the Profit Center, and EVA	80
Final Thoughts	83

Chapter 4: ROI Issues   85

ROI Can Be Very Large	85
What Happens When the ROI Is Negative?	87

ROI Is Not for Every Program 89
Concerns About ROI 91
   Cautions 91
      Take a Conservative Approach When Developing
         Benefits and Costs 92
      Make Sure That ROI of Programs Is Not Confused with
         Other Financial Measures of Return 92
      Involve Management in Calculating ROI 92
      Fully Disclose Assumptions and Methodology 92
      Approach Sensitive and Controversial Issues with Caution 93
      Teach Others the Methods for Calculating ROI 93
      Recognize That Not Everyone Will Buy into ROI 93
      Do Not Boast About a High Return 93
      Choose the Place for Debates 94
      Use ROI to Evaluate Selected Programs 94
   ROI Myths 94
      ROI Is Too Complex for Most Users 95
      ROI Is Expensive, Consuming Too Many Critical
         Resources 95
      If Senior Management Does Not Require ROI, There Is
         No Need to Pursue It 96
      ROI Is a Passing Fad 96
      ROI Is Only One Type of Data 97
      ROI Is Not Future-Oriented; It Reflects Only Past
         Performance 97
      ROI Is Rarely Used by Organizations 97
      The ROI Methodology Cannot Be Easily Replicated 97
      The ROI Methodology Is Not a Credible Process; It Is
         Too Subjective 98
      ROI Cannot Be Evaluated for Soft-Skill Programs; It Is
         Only for Production and Sales 98
      ROI Is Only for Manufacturing and Service Organizations 99
      It Is Not Always Possible to Isolate the Effects of a Program 99
      Measurement of On-the-Job Activities Is Impossible
         Because Post-Program Control of Participants
         Is Impossible 100
      ROI Is Appropriate Only for Large Organizations 100
      The ROI Methodology Has No Standards 101
Final Thoughts 101

Chapter 5: ROI Forecasting — 103

- The Trade-Offs of Forecasting — 103
- Pre-Program ROI Forecasting — 106
  - Basic Model — 106
  - Steps for Forecasting ROI — 108
  - Sources of Expert Input — 113
  - Securing Input — 114
  - Conversion to Money — 115
  - Estimating Program Costs — 115
  - Case Study: Retail Merchandise Company—Part A: Pre-Program ROI Forecasting — 116
    - Situation — 116
    - Proposed Solution — 117
- ROI Forecast with a Pilot Program — 119
- ROI Forecast with Reaction Data — 119
  - Case Study: Retail Merchandise Company—Part B: Level 1 ROI Forecasting — 123
- ROI Forecast with Learning Data — 125
  - Case Study: Retail Merchandise Company—Part C: Level 2 ROI Forecasting — 126
  - Cautions — 128
  - Advantages — 128
- ROI Forecast with Application Data — 129
  - Case Study: Retail Merchandise Company—Part D: Level 3 ROI Forecasting — 130
  - Advantages — 131
- Guidelines for Forecasting — 132
  - If You Must Forecast, Forecast Frequently — 132
  - Consider Forecasting an Essential Evaluation Tool — 132
  - Forecast Different Types of Data — 133
  - Secure Input from Those Who Know the Process Best — 133
  - Understand That Long-Term Forecasts Will Usually Be Inaccurate — 134
  - Expect Forecasts to Be Biased — 134
  - Commit to the Hard Work of Serious Forecasting — 134
  - Routinely Review the Success of Forecasting — 134
  - Be Aware That Assumptions Are the Most Serious Errors in Forecasting — 135

  Keep in Mind That Decision Making Is the Purpose of
    Forecasting 135
  Final Thoughts 135

Index 137

About the Authors 141

Acknowledgments from the Editors

From Patti

No project, regardless of its size or scope, is completed without the help and support of others. My sincere thanks go to the staff at Pfeiffer. Their support for this project has been relentless. Matt Davis has been the greatest! It is our pleasure and privilege to work with such a professional and creative group of people.

Thanks also go to my husband, Jack. His unwavering support of my work is always evident. His idea for the series was to provide readers with a practical understanding of the various components of a comprehensive measurement and evaluation process. Thank you, Jack, for another fun opportunity!

From Jack

Many thanks go to the staff who helped make this series a reality. Lori Ditoro did an excellent job of meeting a very tight deadline and delivering a quality manuscript.

Much admiration and thanks go to Patti. She is an astute observer of the ROI Methodology, having observed and learned from hundreds of presentations, consulting assignments, and engagements. In addition, she is an excellent researcher and student of the process, studying how it is developed and how it works. She has become an ROI expert in her own right. Thanks, Patti, for your many contributions. You are a great partner, friend, and spouse.

Principles of the ROI Methodology

The ROI Methodology is a step-by-step tool for evaluating any program, project, or initiative in any organization. Figure P.1 illustrates the ROI process model, which makes a potentially complicated process simple by breaking it into sequential steps. The ROI process model provides a systematic, step-by-step approach to ROI evaluations that helps keep the process manageable, allowing users to address one issue at a time. The model also emphasizes that the ROI Methodology is a logical, systematic process that flows from one step to another and provides a way for evaluators to collect and analyze six types of data.

Applying the model consistently from one program to another is essential for successful evaluation. To aid consistent application of the model, the ROI Methodology is based on twelve Guiding Principles. These principles are necessary for a credible, conservative approach to evaluation through the different levels.

1. When conducting a higher-level evaluation, collect data at lower levels.
2. When planning a higher-level evaluation, the previous level of evaluation is not required to be comprehensive.
3. When collecting and analyzing data, use only the most credible sources.

Figure P.1. The ROI Process Model

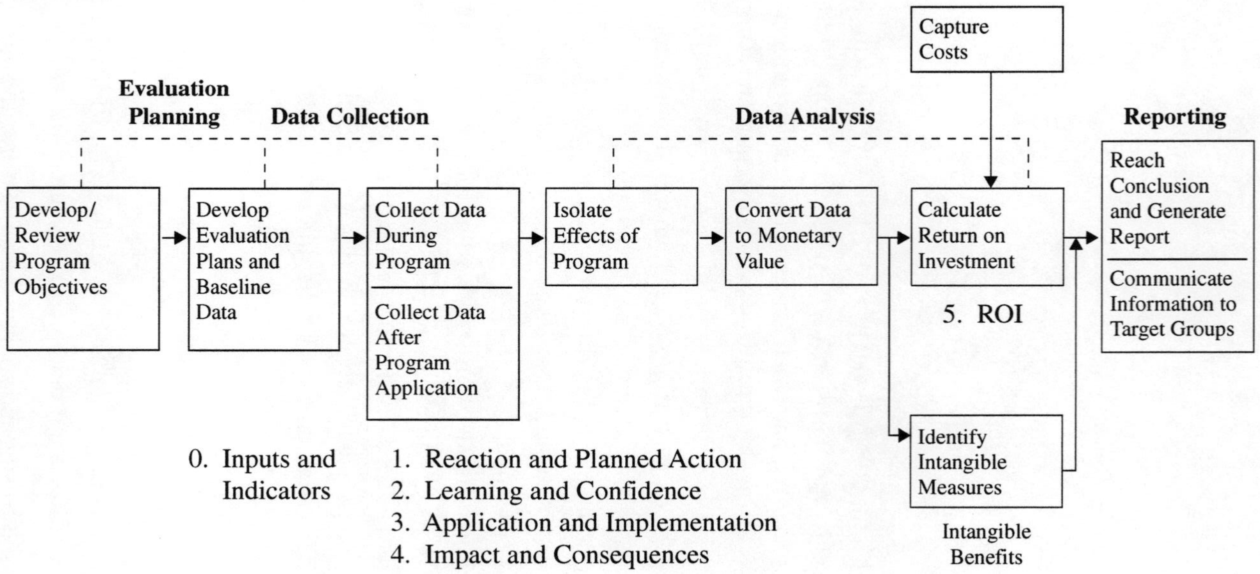

Evaluation Planning | **Data Collection** | **Data Analysis** | **Reporting**

- Develop/Review Program Objectives
- Develop Evaluation Plans and Baseline Data
- Collect Data During Program
- Collect Data After Program Application
- Isolate Effects of Program
- Convert Data to Monetary Value
- Capture Costs
- Calculate Return on Investment
- Identify Intangible Measures
- Intangible Benefits
- Reach Conclusion and Generate Report
- Communicate Information to Target Groups

5. ROI

0. Inputs and Indicators
1. Reaction and Planned Action
2. Learning and Confidence
3. Application and Implementation
4. Impact and Consequences

4. When analyzing data, select the most conservative alternative for calculations.
5. Use at least one method to isolate the effects of a project.
6. If no improvement data are available for a population or from a specific source, assume that little or no improvement has occurred.
7. Adjust estimates of improvement for potential errors of estimation.
8. Avoid use of extreme data items and unsupported claims when calculating ROI.
9. Use only the first year of annual benefits in ROI analysis of short-term solutions.
10. Fully load all costs of a solution, project, or program when analyzing ROI.
11. Intangible measures are defined as measures that are purposely not converted to monetary values.
12. Communicate the results of the ROI Methodology to all key stakeholders.

1

The Importance of Costs and ROI

The costs of programs and projects are increasing, creating more pressure on managers to know how and why money is spent. Sometimes, the total cost of a program is required, which means that the cost profile must go beyond the direct costs to include all indirect costs as well. Cost information is used to manage resources, develop standards, measure efficiencies, and examine alternative delivery processes.

Tabulating program costs is an essential step in calculating ROI; program costs are the denominator in the ROI formula. Thus, it is just as important to focus on costs as it is to focus on benefits. In practice, costs are often more easily captured than benefits. This chapter explores the costs accumulation and tabulation steps, outlines the specific costs that should be captured, and presents economical ways to develop costs.

When ROI calculations are developed, understanding the alternatives to the ROI calculation and their relationship to each other is important. In addition, it is necessary to know what ROI means and how it should be used in an organization. This book shows how costs and ROI calculations are developed and how the ROI Methodology can be used as a forecasting tool. This opening chapter outlines the importance of tracking and monitoring costs, developing the ROI, and forecasting.

Why Be Concerned About Costs?

Apart from the fact that cost figures are required for the ROI calculation, costs should be tracked and monitored for many reasons. Today's organizations focus on understanding and controlling costs; having an appropriate framework for keeping track of costs and using them in different ways allows a department or organization to be more efficient—an important advantage in a globally competitive market.

Benchmarking

Many factors have contributed to the increased attention now given to monitoring costs accurately and thoroughly. Every organization must know how much money it spends on programs and projects and functions. Many organizations calculate these expenditures and compare the amounts with those of other organizations, although comparisons are difficult to make because organizations often have different bases for cost calculations. For example, some organizations calculate learning and development costs as a percentage of payroll costs and set targets for increased investment. In the United States, the average is about 2 percent, whereas in Europe it is 3 percent, and in Asia and Latin America it is 3.8 percent. The benchmarks are often the basis for developing financial allocation.

An effective system of cost monitoring enables an organization to calculate the magnitude of total expenditures. Collecting this information also helps management answer two important questions:

- How much do we spend on our function compared with other functions?
- How much should we be spending?

Exhibit 1.1 presents an exercise that may be helpful in addressing these two questions. The table focuses on setting a spending

Exhibit 1.1. Setting Spending Amounts: How Much Should You Spend on Human Resources?

Overall Expenditures	Your Estimate	Actual	Target
Total expenditures for human resources[1]	_____	_____	_____
Total expenditures for human capital[2]	_____	_____	_____
Spending on human resources as a percentage of payroll	_____	_____	_____
Spending on human resources as a percentage of revenues	_____	_____	_____
Spending on human resources as a percentage of operating costs	_____	_____	_____
Spending on human resources per employee	_____	_____	_____

Functional Area	Your Estimate (percentage)	Actual (percentage)	Target (percentage)
Needs assessment	_____	_____	_____
Development	_____	_____	_____
Delivery and implementation	_____	_____	_____
Operations, maintenance	_____	_____	_____
Evaluation	_____	_____	_____
Total	**100%**	**100%**	**100%**

(*Continued*)

Exhibit 1.1. Setting Spending Amounts: How Much Should You Spend on Human Resources? (*Continued*)

Questions for Discussion

1. Is there a significant difference between estimated and actual costs?
   ☐ Yes   ☐ No

   Explain: _____

   _____

   _____

2. How did you determine what your targets would be?

   _____

   _____

3. What should you spend?

   _____

   _____

[1]Total expenditures for human resources = all costs associated with human resources (for example, recruitment, selection, development, compensation).
[2]Total expenditures for human capital = total expenditures for human resources plus the total salaries and benefits of all employees.

amount for the human resources function. The human resources manager could compare actual expenditures with those of organizations considered best practice.

Although this exercise focuses on setting the value for human resources spending, it can be adapted for any function—for example, learning and development, meetings and events, technology, or quality. In the first part of the exercise, estimate the expenditures in each of the areas. Make rough estimates, without making any calculations or searching for the data. Then fill in the actual expenditure in each area if it can easily be found or developed. If estimates must be developed, use a more reliable value than the initial estimate, including input from other individuals. Next, set a target for the expenditure, based on a desire to follow best practices, to overcome gaps in current spending levels, or to pursue other specific goals. Overall expenditures represent expenditures as they relate to organizational funding. Functional area expenditures are those for specific programming functions. The remainder of the exercise consists of questions that reflect on the issues in the exercise.

This exercise focuses on the process of setting spending levels, which are not clearly defined and are not given enough attention in many organizations. Although total spending levels are set by budgets, the process of arriving at those values is sometimes less comprehensive and less thought out than is desirable.

Evaluation

The staff of any functional area should know the relative cost-effectiveness of their programs and the components of those programs. Monitoring costs by program allows the staff to evaluate the relative contribution of a program and determine how those costs are changing. If a program's cost rises, it might be appropriate to reevaluate the program's impact and overall success. Comparing specific cost components with those of other programs or organizations may be useful. For example, the cost per participant for one program could be compared with the cost per participant for a similar program. A huge difference may indicate a problem. Also, costs associated with design, development, or delivery of a program could be compared with those costs for other programs within the organization and used to develop cost standards.

When a return on investment or cost benefit analysis is needed for a specific program, costs must be developed. One of the most significant reasons for collecting costs is to obtain data for use in a benefit-cost comparison. In this comparison, cost data are as important as the program's economic benefits.

Cost Forecasting

Accurate costs are necessary in order to predict future costs. Historical costs for a program provide the basis for predicting future costs of a similar program or budgeting for a program. When an ROI forecast is needed, predicted costs must be developed. Sophisticated cost models make it possible to estimate or predict costs with reasonable accuracy.

Efficiency

Controlling costs is necessary in order to improve the efficiency of a functional area. Competitive pressures place increased attention on the need for efficiencies. Most departments have monthly budgets with cost projections listed by various accounts and, in some cases, by program. Cost monitoring is an excellent tool for identifying problem areas and taking corrective action. From a mere management standpoint, accumulation of cost data is a necessity.

Other Reasons for Monitoring Costs

Exhibit 1.2 summarizes why costs should be developed. As this list illustrates, there are many reasons why capturing costs is necessary, beyond calculating ROI.

Exhibit 1.2. Why Develop Costs?

- To determine overall expenditures
- To determine the relative cost of individual programs
- To predict future program costs
- To calculate benefits versus costs for a specific program
- To improve the efficiency of a department
- To evaluate alternatives to a proposed program
- To plan and budget for next year's operation
- To develop a marginal cost pricing system
- To integrate data into other systems

The Importance of ROI

"Show me the money." There's nothing new about this statement, especially in business. Organizations of all types want to see the money – specifically they want to see a return on their investments. What's new is the method that organizations can use to get there. While "showing the money" is the ultimate report of value, organization leaders recognize that value lies in the eye of the beholder; therefore, the method used to show the money must also show the value as it is perceived by all stakeholders. Just as important, organizations need a methodology that provides data to help improve investment decisions. This book presents an approach that does both: it assesses the value that organizations receive for investing in programs and projects, and it develops data to improve those programs by providing all stakeholders with the information they need to make decisions. These decisions will drive change, improvement, and ultimately value for the organization.

The Ultimate Level of Evaluation

ROI represents the newest way to state value. In the past, the success of a program, project, or process was measured by activity: number of people involved, money spent, days to complete. For example, Motorola measured success by ensuring that every employee must complete forty hours of learning annually. Other companies also used forty hours of learning as a benchmark of success. While utilization metrics describe the level of activity and consumption, these measures do not define value. Little consideration is given to the benefits derived from the activity. Value is defined by results, not activity. More frequently than ever before, value is defined as monetary benefits compared with costs: ROI. ROI is the ultimate level of evaluation. The following examples illustrate this point.

- The U.S. Air Force developed the ROI for an information assurance program to prevent intrusion into its computer databases.
- Apple calculated the ROI for its process improvement teams.
- Sprint/NEXTEL computed the ROI on its diversity program.
- The Australian Capital Territory Community Care agency forecast the ROI for the implementation of a client relationship management system.
- Accenture calculated the ROI on a new sales platform for its consultants.
- Wachovia developed an ROI forecast and then measured the actual ROI for its negotiations program.
- A major hotel chain calculated the financial value and ROI of its coaching program.

- The cities of New York, San Francisco, and Phoenix showed the monetary value of investing in programs to reduce the number of homeless citizens on the streets.
- Cisco Systems is measuring the ROI for its key meetings and events.
- A major U.S. Defense Department agency calculated the ROI for a master's degree program offered by a major university.

Although the ROI Methodology had its beginnings in the 1970s, it has expanded in recent years to become the most comprehensive and far-reaching approach to demonstrating the value of program investment.

Types of Values

Value is determined by stakeholders' perspectives, which may include organizational, spiritual, personal, and social values. Value is defined by consumers, taxpayers, and shareholders in many different ways. Capitalism defines value as the economic contribution to shareholders. The global reporting initiative, established in 1997, defines value from three perspectives: environmental, economic, and societal.

Even as projects, processes, and programs are implemented to improve the social, environmental, and economic climates, their monetary value is often sought in order to ensure that resources are allocated appropriately and that investments reap a return. No longer is it enough to report the number of programs offered, the number of participants or volunteers trained, or the dollars generated through a fundraising effort. Stakeholders at all levels—including executives, shareholders, managers and supervisors, taxpayers, project designers, and participants—are looking for outcomes—improvement in output, quality, costs, and time—and in many cases they want a specific outcome: the ROI.

ROI Is King

Some people are concerned that too much focus is placed on economic value, but it is economics, or money, that allows organizations and individuals to contribute to the greater good. Monetary resources are limited; they can be put to best use, or they can be underused or overused. In the French language, *roi* is the word for king, and ROI is indeed king, for determining ROI is the best way for organizations to show that their programs deliver monetary value to the organization. Organizations and individuals have choices about where they invest their resources. To ensure that monetary resources are put to best use, they must be allocated to the programs, processes, and projects that yield the greatest return.

For example, if a process improvement initiative is designed to improve efficiencies and it subsequently does improve efficiencies, one might assume that the initiative was successful. But if the initiative cost more than the efficiency gains are worth, has value been added to the organization? Could a less expensive process have yielded similar or even better results, possibly reaping a positive ROI? Questions like these should be asked on a routine basis. No longer will activity suffice as a measure of program results. A new generation of decision makers is defining value in a new way, by measuring programs' impact on business performance.

The "Show Me" Generation

Figure 1.1 illustrates the requirements of the new "show me" generation. "Show me" implies that stakeholders want to see actual data (that is, numbers and measures). This impulse accounted for the initial attempt to see value in programs. This evolved into "show me the money," a direct call for financial results. But financial results alone do not provide the evidence needed to ensure that programs add value. Often, a connection between programs and value is assumed, but that assumption soon must give way to the need to show an actual connection by isolating the effects of the program from other influences. Hence, "show me the real money" was an

Figure 1.1. The Evolution of "Show Me"

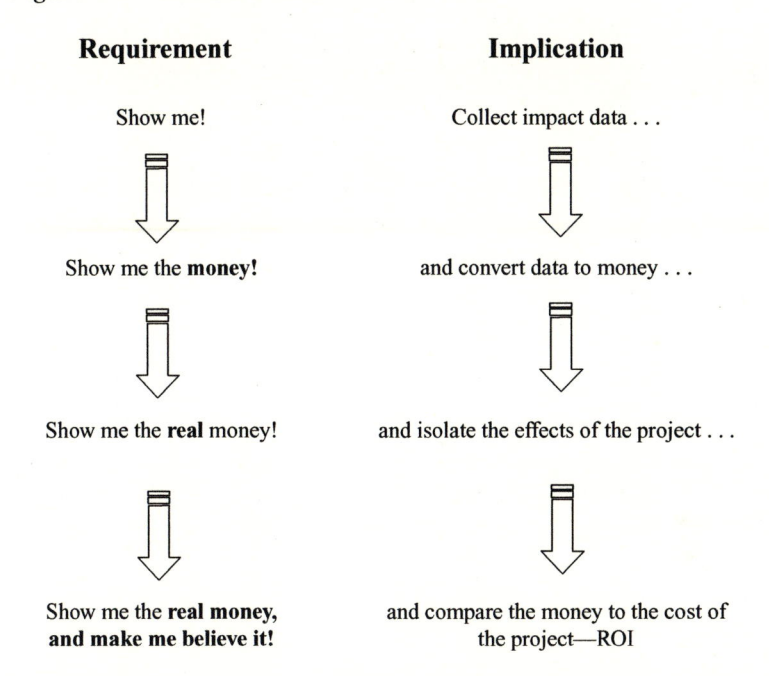

Requirement	Implication
Show me!	Collect impact data . . .
⬇	⬇
Show me the **money**!	and convert data to money . . .
⬇	⬇
Show me the **real** money!	and isolate the effects of the project . . .
⬇	⬇
Show me the **real money, and make me believe it!**	and compare the money to the cost of the project—ROI

attempt at establishing credibility. This phase, though critical, still left stakeholders with an unanswered question: "Do the monetary benefits linked to the program outweigh the costs?" This question is the mantra for the new "show me" generation: "Show me the real money, and make me believe it." This demand is answered by measuring ROI. But this new generation of program sponsors also recognizes that value is more than just a single number: value is what motivates the entire organization. Hence, the need to report value based on the definitions of various people throughout the organization has arisen.

The New Definition of Value

The changing perspectives on value and the shifts that are occurring in organizations have all led to a new definition of value. Value is not defined as a single number. Rather, value is defined by a variety of data points. Value must be balanced with quantitative and qualitative data, as well as financial and nonfinancial data. The data sometimes reflect tactical issues, such as activity, as well as strategic issues, such as ROI. Value must be derived from different time frames and not necessarily represent a single point in time. It must reflect the value systems that are important to stakeholders. The data that are used to assess value must be collected from credible sources, using cost-effective methods; and value must be action-oriented, compelling individuals to make adjustments and changes.

The processes used to calculate ROI must be consistent from one program to another. Standards must be in place so that results can be compared. These standards must support conservative outcomes, leaving broader assumptions to decision makers. The ROI Methodology presented in this book meets all the preceding criteria for assessing value. The ROI Methodology generates six types of data that address the issues raised by the new definition of value: reaction and perceived value, learning and confidence, application and implementation, impact and consequences, return on investment, and intangible benefits.

Why ROI Now?

In recent years, a variety of forces have driven additional focus on measuring the impact of programs, including the financial contribution and ROI. These forces have challenged old ways of defining program success.

Program Failures

Almost every organization has undertaken unsuccessful programs—programs that go astray, costing far too much and failing to deliver on promises. Program disasters occur in business organizations and in government and nonprofit organizations. Some program disasters are legendary. Some are swept into closets or covered up, but they are there, and their numbers are far too large to tolerate (Nickson and Siddons, 2005). The large number of failures has generated increased concerns about measuring project and program success before, during, and after implementation. Many critics suggest that program failure might be avoided more often if (1) programs are based on a legitimate need; (2) adequate planning is in place at the outset; (3) data are collected throughout the program to confirm that the implementation is on track; (4) an impact study is conducted to detail the program's contribution; and (5) the program's monetary benefits are compared to the program's costs (in other words, ROI is calculated). Unfortunately, sometimes these steps are unintentionally omitted, are not fully understood, or are purposely ignored; to counteract these tendencies, greater emphasis is being placed on processes of accountability. This book shows how these five elements can come together to create value-adding projects and programs.

Increased Total Program Costs

As the costs of programs and projects continue to rise, their budgets become targets for others who would like to have that money for their own programs. What was once considered a mere cost of doing business is now considered an investment that must be wisely allocated. For example, consider the field of learning and development in the United States. Of course, learning and development programs are necessary in order to introduce new skills and technology to employees, but twenty years ago they were regarded by some company executives as a frivolous expense. These days, the annual direct cost of organizational learning and development is estimated to be over $100 billion in the United States. A few large organizations spend as much as $1 billion every year on corporate learning and development. With numbers like these, learning and development is no longer considered a frivolous expense; rather, it is regarded as an investment, and many executives expect a return on that investment.

Trend Toward Greater Accountability

A consistent and persistent trend in accountability is evident in organizations across the globe: almost every function, process, program, or initiative is judged against higher standards than in the past. Various functions in organizations are attempting to show their worth by capturing and demonstrating the value they add to the organization. They compete for funds; therefore, they have to show value, including ROI. For example, in many organizations, the research and development function must show its value in monetary terms in order to compete with mainstream processes such as sales and production, which have been showing their value in direct monetary terms for more than a century.

Staff Support Managers' New Business Focus

In the past, managers of many support functions in government, nonprofit, and private-sector organizations had no business experience. Today, things have changed; many managers of support functions have a business background, a formal business education, or a business focus. These managers are more aware of bottom-line issues in their organization and are more knowledgeable about operational and financial concerns. They often take a business approach to their processes, and evaluating ROI is a part of that strategy. Because of their background, they are familiar with the concept of ROI. They have used ROI calculations in their academic studies to evaluate decisions to purchase equipment, build new facilities, or buy a company. As a result, they understand and appreciate the applications of ROI and are eager to apply it in their own operations.

Support functions are often regarded as overhead, a burden on the organization, and an unnecessary expense. These days, the approach of many managers is to outsource, automate, or eliminate overhead operations. Great strides have been made in all three approaches. Consequently, staff support departments must prove their value in order to be accepted as viable support functions or administrative processes, and this proof often includes ROI calculations on major programs.

Evidence-Based or Fact-Based Management

In recent years, there has been an important trend toward fact-based or evidence-based management. Traditionally, many key decisions were based on instinct and gut feelings; now, more managers are using sophisticated, detailed processes to show the value of their projects and programs. Quality decisions must be based on more than gut feelings experienced in the blink of an eye. With a comprehensive set of measures, including financial ROI, better organizational decisions about people, products, programs, and processes are possible.

When taken seriously, evidence-based management can change how a manager thinks and acts. It is a way of seeing the world and thinking about the craft of management. Evidence-based management proceeds from the premise that using better, deeper logic and facts to the extent possible helps leaders do their jobs better. It is based on the belief that facing the hard facts about what works and what doesn't work and understanding and rejecting the total nonsense that often passes for sound advice will help organizations perform better (Pfeffer and Sutton, 2006). Moving to fact-based management makes it easier to expand performance measurement to include ROI calculations.

Limitations of Benchmarking

Many managers have been obsessed with benchmarking, using it to compare every type of process, function, and activity. Unfortunately, benchmarking has its limitations. First, best practices are sometimes elusive. Not all participants in a benchmarking program or report necessarily employ the best practices. In fact, just the opposite may be true: many benchmarking studies are developed by organizations that are willing to pay to participate. Second, what is needed by one organization is not always needed by another. A specific benchmarked measure or process may be of limited use in actual practice. Finally, benchmarking data are often devoid of financial information, reflecting few measures of actual financial contributions. Therefore, many managers are now asking for more specific internal processes that can evaluate those important financial measures.

Executive Appetite for Evaluation of ROI

Evaluation of monetary contribution and ROI is receiving increased interest in the executive suite. Top managers who have watched budgets continue to grow without the implementation of appropriate accountability measures are frustrated, and they are responding to the situation by turning to ROI assessment. Top executives now demand ROI calculations and proof of monetary contributions from departments and functions that previously were not required to provide them. For years, function managers and department heads convinced executives that their processes could not be measured and that the value of their activities should be taken at face value. Executives no longer buy that argument; they demand the same accountability from these functions as they do from the sales and production units of the organization. Such demands for accountability require organizations to shift their measurement processes to include the evaluation of financial impact and ROI.

Why Forecast ROI?

Although ROI calculations based on post-program data are the most accurate, sometimes it is important to forecast ROI before a program is initiated or before final results are tabulated. Several critical issues drive the need for a forecast before a program is completed or perhaps even before a program is pursued.

Expensive Programs and Projects

Because forecasting reduces uncertainty, it may be especially appropriate for costly programs. In these cases, implementation is not practical until the program has been analyzed to determine the potential ROI. For example, if a program involves a significant amount of effort in design, development, and implementation, a client may not even want to expend the resources for a pilot test unless some assurance of a positive ROI can be given. In another example, an expensive equipment purchase may be needed in order to launch a program. It may be necessary to forecast ROI prior to making the purchase, to ensure that the monetary value of the process outcomes outweighs the costs of equipment and implementation.

While there may be trade-offs in deploying a lower-profile, lower-cost pilot, the pre-program ROI is still important, prompting some clients to stand firm until an ROI forecast is produced.

High Risks and Uncertainty

Sponsors want to remove as much uncertainty as possible from the program and act on the best data available. This concern sometimes pushes the program team to forecast ROI before any resources are expended to design and implement the program. Some programs are high-risk opportunities or solutions. In addition to being expensive, they may represent critical initiatives that can make or break an organization. Or the situation may be one in which failure would be disastrous and there is only one chance to get it right. In these cases, the decision maker must have the best possible data, and the best possible data often include an ROI forecast.

For example, one large restaurant chain developed an unfortunate reputation for racial insensitivity and discrimination. The fallout brought many lawsuits and caused a public relations nightmare. The company undertook a major program to transform the organization, changing its image, attitudes, and actions. Because of the program's high stakes and critical nature, company executives requested a forecast before pursuing the program. They needed to know not only whether this major program would be worthwhile financially but also what specifically would change and how specifically the program would unfold. This analysis required a comprehensive forecast involving various levels of data, including the ROI.

Post-Program Comparison

An important reason for forecasting ROI is to see how well the forecast holds up under the scrutiny of post-program analysis. Whenever a plan is in place to collect data on a program's success, comparing actual results with pre-program expectations is helpful. In an ideal world, a forecast ROI would have a defined relationship with the actual ROI, or, at least, one would lead to the other, after adjustments. The forecast is often an inexpensive process because it involves estimates and assumptions. If the forecast becomes a reliable predictor of the post-program analysis, then the forecast ROI might substitute for the actual ROI. This could save money on post-program analysis.

Compliance

More than ever, organizations are requiring a forecast ROI before they undertake major programs. For example, one organization requires any program with a budget exceeding $500,000 to have a forecast ROI before it can receive program approval. Some units of government have enacted legislation that requires program forecasts. With increasing frequency, formal policy and legal structures are reasons for developing ROI forecasts. All of these reasons are leading more organizations to develop ROI forecasts so that their sponsors will have an estimate of programs' expected payoff.

Final Thoughts

This brief introductory chapter describes the rationale for tackling the key issues in this book. It shows why costs must be developed and reported on a routine basis for reasons other than the ROI calculation. This chapter also discusses the importance of measuring ROI and why ROI is evolving into a principal measurement requirement. In addition, this chapter explains when it is important to look into the future and forecast the ROI of a program before it is initiated. The next chapters will amplify these areas in much more detail.

References

Nickson, D., and Siddons, S. *Project Disasters and How to Survive Them*. London: Kogan Page, 2005.

Pfeffer, J., and Sutton, R. *Hard Facts, Dangerous Half-Truths and Total Nonsense: Profiting from Evidence-Based Management*. Boston: Harvard Business School Press, 2006.

2

Cost Tracking and Classification

Capturing costs is challenging because the figures must be accurate, reliable, and realistic. Although most organizations can calculate costs much more easily than they can calculate the economic value of benefits, the true cost of a program is often an elusive figure, even in some of the best organizations. While the total direct budget of a program can usually be easily obtained, determining all of the costs of a program, including the indirect costs related to it, is more difficult. In order for evaluators to calculate a realistic ROI, costs must be accurate and credible; otherwise, painstaking attention to evaluating the benefits will be wasted.

Cost Issues

Before we describe the ways to monitor and classify costs, it will be helpful to discuss a few important cost issues that affect the ways in which costs are tracked and classified.

Pressure to Disclose All Costs

The pressure to report all the costs of a program (the fully loaded costs) has increased. This takes the cost profile beyond the direct cost of the program to include the cost of the time that participants are involved in the program, including the benefits they earn during that time, as well as other overhead costs. For years, senior managers have realized that programs involve many indirect costs. Now, they are asking for an accounting for these costs.

The impact of indirect costs is illustrated by a situation in which management's control of a large state agency was being audited. A portion of the audit focused on training costs. The following comments are based on the auditor's report (ROI Institute, 2005, p. 37). Costs tracked at the program level focused on direct costs ("hard" costs) and ignored the cost of time that employees spent on preparing for, participating in, or supporting the training. For one program, including these costs raised the total training cost dramatically. The agency stated that the total two-year cost for the program was about $600,000. This figure included only direct costs and therefore was substantially low because it did not include the cost of the time spent by staff in preparing for and attending the program. The figure for time spent in preparatory work and attendance came to $1.39 million. When the statewide average of 45.5 percent for benefits was considered, the total indirect cost of staff time spent to prepare for and attend the program was more than $2 million. Finally, when the agency's direct costs of $600,000 were added to the more than $2 million indirect cost just noted, the total was more than $2.6 million. Among other factors that would drive actual costs higher still were the following:

- Cost of travel, meals, and lodging for participants in the training

- Allocated salaries and benefits of staff members who provided administrative and logistic support to the program

- Opportunity costs of productivity lost by staff in doing preparatory work and attending training

Failure to consider all indirect costs ("soft" costs) could have caused the agency to be out of compliance with the Fair Labor

Standards Act (FLSA), particularly as training filtered down to rank-and-file staff. Because FLSA requires that such staff be directly compensated for overtime, it would not be appropriate for the agency to ask such employees to complete preparatory work for the training sessions on their own time. Continuing to handle such overtime work in this way might also encourage false overtime reporting and skew overtime data through incorrect reporting, as well as increase the amount of uncompensated overtime.

Numerous barriers hampered agency efforts to determine "how much training costs."

- Cost systems tended to hide administrative, support, internal, and other indirect or soft costs.

- Costs generally were monitored at the division level rather than at the level of individual programs or activities.

- Cost information required by activity-based cost systems was not being generated.

As this case vividly demonstrates, the cost of training is much more than direct expenditures, and it is important that learning and development departments be expected to report fully loaded costs in their reports.

Fully Loaded Costs as a Conservative Approach

The conservative approach to calculating ROI encourages a specific approach to cost accumulation. Guiding Principle 10 states, "Fully load all costs of a solution, project, or program when analyzing ROI."

In this approach, all costs that can be identified and linked to a particular program are included. The rule is simple: in the denominator of the ROI formula, when in doubt, put it in. (That is, if it is questionable whether a cost should be included, it is recommended that it be included, even if the cost guidelines for an organization do not require it.). This parallels a rule for the numerator of the ROI formula, which states, "When in doubt, leave it out." (That is, if it is questionable whether a benefit should be included, it should be omitted from the ROI analysis.) When an ROI is calculated and reported to target audiences, the accuracy and credibility of the process should be capable of withstanding even the closest scrutiny. The only way to meet this test is to ensure that all costs are included. Of course, from a realistic viewpoint, if the controller or chief financial officer insists on not using certain costs, then it is best to leave them out.

Many professionals ask, "Why include items such as salaries of participants and in-house training and meeting facilities when reporting costs?" They rationalize that salaries are paid and in-house facility costs would be incurred even if the program were not implemented. Also, some would argue that the initial costs of analysis, design, and development should not be included because they represent "sunk" costs. Perhaps the most compelling reason to account for salaries, facilities, and other indirect cost items is that if they are not included, then the ROI will likely be overstated. An example of contrasting approaches is presented in Table 2.1. This table shows the data for a two-day program on negotiation skills, a one-time offering that included all thirty-six professional employees reporting to a manager (the client). The program was delivered by a supplier, using the supplier's materials and process. The annualized monetary benefit of the thirty-six participants' use of their improved skills was $240,000. Table 2.1 shows two approaches to calculating the costs of the program, one used by the program manager (Approach A) and one used by the client (Approach B).

The ROI calculations using both cost scenarios are shown here. ROI using Approach A cost tabulation:

$$\text{ROI (\%)} = \frac{\$240{,}000 - \$111{,}109}{\$111{,}109} \times 100 = 116\%$$

Table 2.1. Comparison of Cost Scenarios for a Negotiation Skills Program

Cost Item	Approach A: Tabulation of Fully Loaded Costs	Approach B: Tabulation of Direct Costs
Needs assessment (one-time cost)	$12,000	_____
Design and development (minimal redesign required to revise role-playing scenarios)	$2,000	_____
Delivery		
• Facilitator and coaching fees	$38,000	$38,000
• Travel expenses, facilitator	$2,900	$2,900
• Materials	$5,000	$5,000
• Refreshments	$900	$900
• Salaries and benefits, coordinator	$317	$317
• Travel expenses, coordinator	$700	$700
• Salaries and benefits, participants	$33,413	_____
• Travel expenses, participants	$3,600	$3,600
• In-house training facility and audiovisual equipment costs	$1,100	_____
Evaluation (one-time cost)	$9,000	$9,000
Overhead (2% of total program cost)	$2,179	$1,208
Total	$111,109	$61,625

Note: Annualized value of benefits from participation of thirty-six employees, after isolation of program effects, is $240,000.

ROI using Approach B cost tabulation:

$$\text{ROI}(\%) = \frac{\$240{,}000 - \$61{,}625}{\$61{,}625} \times 100 = 289\%$$

Approach B, which did not include participant salaries, the cost of in-house facilities, or the cost of the initial analysis and design, yielded an ROI that was more than twice that yielded by Approach A, which was fully loaded. The ROI was significantly overstated in Approach B.

Executives frequently review salaries and benefits in connection with other organizational costs. For example, when a request is made to hire additional staff, the central issue is how to justify spending the additional resources (that is, how will incurring this new cost benefit the organization?). The prospective expenditure for staff is analyzed in terms of "loaded cost," or the cost of one FTE (full-time equivalent). Even the expenses that will likely be incurred by the new employee are detailed as a separate item, increasing the benefit required to justify the hire. Executives are accustomed to using "all costs," direct and indirect. Anything short of this would be viewed as inadequate accounting.

The Danger of Accumulating Costs Without Tracking Benefits

Communicating the costs of a program without presenting benefits can be dangerous. Unfortunately, many organizations have fallen into this trap for years. Costs are presented to management in all types of ingenious ways, such as the cost of the program or the cost per employee. While these costs may be helpful for efficiency comparisons, presenting them without also presenting the benefits of a program may not be a good idea. When most executives review costs, they logically ask, "What benefit was received from this program?" This is a typical management reaction, particularly when costs seem too high. In deference to this logic, some organizations have adopted a policy of not communicating cost data for a program unless the benefits can be captured and presented along with the costs. Even if the benefit data are subjective and intangible, they are included with the cost data. This practice helps maintain a balanced perspective that examines both costs and benefits.

Policies and Guidelines

An organization's philosophy and policy on costs should be detailed in guidelines for staff members and others who monitor and report costs. Cost guidelines specify which costs should be included and how cost data should be captured, analyzed, and reported.

Cost guidelines can range from a one-page document to a fifty-page manual. The simpler approach is better. When fully developed, cost guidelines should be reviewed by the organization's finance and accounting staff. The final document serves as the guiding force for collecting, monitoring, and reporting costs. When ROI is calculated and reported, the costs are included in a summary and the cost guidelines are referenced in a footnote or attached as an appendix.

Cost Tracking Issues

We will now discuss how costs are collected and classified within organizations.

Sources of Program Costs

The three major sources of program costs are illustrated in Table 2.2. Staff expenses usually represent the greatest portion of costs and are sometimes transferred directly to the client or program sponsor. The second major cost category consists of participant expenses, both direct and indirect. These costs are not identified in

Table 2.2. Sources of Program Costs

Source of Costs	Cost Reporting Issues
Staff expenses	• Costs are usually accurate. • Variable expenses may be underestimated.
Participant expenses (direct and indirect)	• Direct expenses are usually not fully loaded. • Indirect expenses are rarely included in program costs.
External expenses (equipment and services)	• External expenses are sometimes understated. • It may be difficult to hold external vendors accountable for their expenditures.

many programs; nevertheless, they represent a significant amount. The third source of program costs is payments made to external resources, including payments to hotels and conference centers, equipment suppliers, and providers of services prescribed in the program. As Table 2.2 shows, many of the costs in these categories are often understated. Financial and accounting systems should be able to track and report the costs from these sources. The process presented in this book is capable of tracking these costs, too.

Process Steps and Costs

Another important way to consider costs is in the context of how a program unfolds. Figure 2.1 shows the typical program cycle,

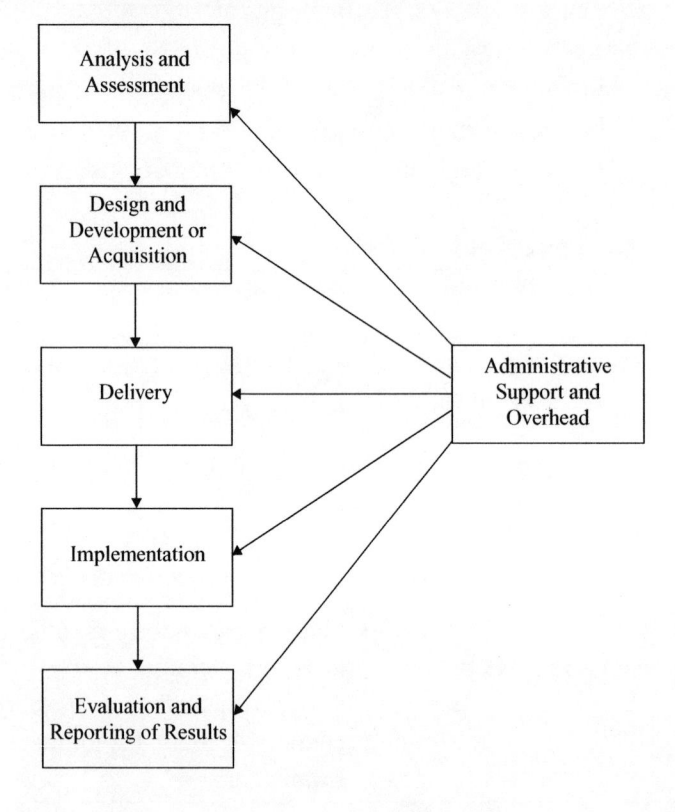

Figure 2.1. Program Cycle

```
┌───────────────┐
│ Analysis and  │
│  Assessment   │
└───────┬───────┘
        │
        ▼
┌───────────────┐
│   Design and  │
│ Development or│◄──┐
│  Acquisition  │   │
└───────┬───────┘   │
        │           │
        ▼           │       ┌───────────────┐
┌───────────────┐   │       │Administrative │
│   Delivery    │◄──┼───────│  Support and  │
└───────┬───────┘   │       │   Overhead    │
        │           │       └───────────────┘
        ▼           │
┌───────────────┐   │
│Implementation │◄──┤
└───────┬───────┘   │
        │           │
        ▼           │
┌───────────────┐   │
│ Evaluation and│◄──┘
│Reporting of Results│
└───────────────┘
```

beginning with initial analysis and assessment and progressing to evaluation and reporting the results. These functional process steps represent the typical flow of work. After a performance problem is identified, a solution is developed or acquired and implemented within the organization. Implementation is often grouped with delivery. The entire process is routinely reported to the client or sponsor, and evaluation is undertaken to assess the program's success. There are also costs involved in supporting the entire process—administrative support and overhead costs. To fully understand the costs, the program should be analyzed according to these process categories, as described later in this chapter.

Prorated Versus Direct Costs

Usually, all costs related to a program are captured and expensed to that program. However, three categories are often prorated over several sessions of the same program. Needs assessment, design and development, and acquisition are all significant costs that should be prorated over the shelf life of a program. If the evaluators are using a conservative approach, the shelf life should be very short. Some organizations will prorate program costs over one year of operation; others may prorate costs over two or three years. If a dispute about the time period arises, the shorter period should be used. If possible, the finance and accounting staff should be consulted.

A brief example will illustrate how development costs are prorated. In a large pharmaceutical company, a program was developed at a cost of $150,000. It was anticipated that the program would have a three-year life before it would need to be updated. About nine hundred participants would be involved in the program over the three-year period, and an ROI calculation for fifty participants was planned. To be conservative, the total cost should be written off at the end of three years. Therefore, the $150,000 development cost would be spread over the nine hundred participants as a prorated development cost of $167 per participant. Thus, the ROI calculation for fifty participants would include a development cost of $8,350.

Employee Benefits Factor

When the cost of participant and staff time associated with programs is presented, the cost of employee benefits should be included along with the salary costs. Most organizations use a "benefits factor" to calculate the cost of benefits. The benefits factor is the cost of all employee benefits expressed as a percentage of total base salaries. This number is usually well known within an organization and typically has been generated by the human resources or finance and accounting staff for use in other costing applications. In some organizations, the benefits factor is as high as 50 percent or 60 percent. In others, it may be as low as 25 percent or 30 percent. The average in the United States is approximately 44 percent (U.S. Chamber of Commerce, 2006).

Major Cost Categories

The most important task in a tabulation of program costs is to define which costs should be included. These decisions will be made by the staff and usually approved by management. The finance and accounting staff may also need to approve the list. Table 2.3 shows the recommended cost categories for a fully loaded, conservative approach to estimating costs. Each category is described in this section.

Needs Assessment and Analysis

One cost category that is often overlooked is costs associated with conducting a needs assessment. In some programs, this cost is zero because the program is conducted without a needs assessment. However, as more organizations focus increased attention on needs assessments, this item will become a more significant cost. All costs associated with the needs assessment should be captured or estimated. These costs include the time of staff members who conduct the assessment, direct fees and expenses of external consultants who conduct the assessment, and internal services and supplies

Table 2.3. Recommended Cost Categories for Tabulation of Fully Loaded Program Costs

Cost Item	Prorated	Expensed
Needs assessment and analysis	✓	
Design and development	✓	
Acquisition	✓	
Technological support	✓	
Delivery and implementation		
Salaries and benefits, facilitators		✓
Salaries and benefits, coordinators		✓
Salaries and benefits, participants		✓
Travel, lodging, meals		✓
Facilities		✓
Program materials and fees		✓
Evaluation		✓
Overhead	✓	

used in the analysis. The total cost of the needs assessment is usually prorated over the life of the program. The estimated shelf life of the program should be kept reasonable—usually one to two years, depending on the nature of the program. The exception would be expensive programs and projects that are not expected to change significantly for several years.

Design and Development

One of the most significant cost categories is the costs associated with designing and developing a program. These costs include internal staff time for both design and development, as well as the cost of supplies, videos, software, and other material directly related to the program. These costs might also include consultant fees. Like needs assessment costs, design and development costs are usually prorated, perhaps using the same time frame. One to two years is recommended as the estimated shelf life of a program, unless the program is not expected to change for many years and the costs are significant.

When pilot programs are implemented, a prorating dilemma may surface. For expensive pilots, the complete design and development costs may be very significant. In this situation, prorating may not be an issue because the program is completely at risk. If all the costs are included in the ROI analysis, it may be difficult or impossible for a program to produce a positive ROI. The following rules can help evaluators work through this dilemma.

1. If the program is completely at risk, all the costs should be placed in the ROI evaluation decision. (That is, if the pilot does not have a positive ROI with all the costs included, the program will not be implemented.) This is rarely the case. However, if it is, the design and development costs should be kept to a minimum. Perhaps the program can be implemented without all the "bells and whistles." Development of videos, software, and other expensive tools can be delayed until the usefulness of the skills and content taught in the program is proven. Often, however, this approach is not feasible. Sometimes a program is developed in its entirety, but launched to an initial group in order to make adjustments before it is offered to the larger group. Rather than a true pilot, this is referred to as a "soft" launch, meaning that the program is not at risk.

2. If program implementation is not at risk, the cost of the development should be prorated over the anticipated life cycle of the program. This is the approach taken in most situations. Executives often find it reasonable to make a significant investment in the design and development of a pilot, with the understanding that if the program does not add value, it can be adjusted, changed, or modified so that it does add value. In these cases, a prorated development cost would be appropriate.

Regardless of the approach taken, it should be discussed during the planning stages, before the ROI evaluation begins. A dispute over prorating should not occur when the results are being tabulated. This discussion should also involve the sponsor of the program and a representative from finance and accounting.

Acquisition

In lieu of incurring development costs, some project leaders purchase programs to use directly or in a modified format. The acquisition costs for such programs include the purchase price for facilitator materials, train-the-trainer sessions, licensing agreements, and other costs associated with the right to deliver the program. These acquisition costs should be prorated using the same rationale that was detailed in earlier sections; an estimated shelf life of one to two years should be sufficient for acquired programs. If a program needs to be modified or some additional development is required, the associated costs should be categorized as development costs. In practice, many programs have both acquisition costs and development costs.

Technological Support

Some programs require technological support. For example, computers may be used to deliver the content of a program. The finance and accounting department can provide information on how to spread the costs of technology over the life of a program based on how the equipment is depreciated. Some programs are associated with new work processes or implementation of technology that require the use of a help desk for a period of time following the program. When it is appropriate to capture these costs, they may also be prorated over the life of the program.

Delivery and Implementation

Usually the largest segment of program costs are those associated with delivery or implementation. Five major subcategories are discussed in this section.

Facilitators' and Coordinators' Salaries and Benefits

The salaries of facilitators or program coordinators should be included in the program's cost. Salaries should be proportionally allocated according to how much time was spent on a program. If a coordinator is involved in more than one program, that person's time should be proportionally allocated to the specific program under review. If external facilitators are used, all charges for the session should be included. The important issue is to capture all the direct time of internal employees or external consultants who work directly with the program. Each time direct labor costs are involved, the benefits factor should be used to figure the cost of employee benefits so that it can be included. As we discussed earlier in this chapter, the benefits factor is usually in the range of 30 to 50 percent in the United States.

Participants' Salaries and Benefits

The salaries and benefits of participants are an expense that should be included in the program cost. Again, they should be allocated according to how much time was spent participating in the program. For situations in which the program has already been conducted, these costs can be estimated by using average or midpoint values for the salaries in typical job classifications. When a program is targeted for an ROI calculation, participants can provide their salaries directly and confidentially.

Travel, Lodging, and Meals

Direct travel costs for participants, facilitators, and coordinators should be included in the program cost. Lodging and meals for participants, facilitators, and coordinators during travel, as well as meals during their stay for the program, should also be included. Refreshments should be included in the program cost as well.

Facilities

The cost of the facilities should be included in the program cost. For meetings or sessions held at external facilities, this cost is the direct charge from the conference center or hotel. If the program is conducted in-house, the use of the conference room represents a cost for the organization, and that cost should be estimated and included even if it is not the practice within the organization to include in-house facilities' costs in other reports. The cost of internal facilities can easily be estimated by obtaining the rental rate of a room of the same size at a local hotel. Sometimes, a cost figure, calculated on a square footage basis, is available from the finance and accounting staff or the facilities management team (that is, the cost of organizational facilities per square foot per day). In other situations, the cost of commercial real estate on a square footage basis can be determined from commercial real estate agents or the local newspaper. The important point is to come quickly to a credible estimate for the cost of the room.

The cost of facilities is an important issue that is often overlooked. With encouragement from the finance and accounting staff, some staff members do not show an amount for the use of internal facilities, arguing that the overhead cost of the room would be regardless. However, the complete cost of a program should include this item, because the room would probably be used for other purposes if programs were not conducted. In the total cost picture, this is a very minor charge. The fact of its being included might be of more value from a credibility standpoint than from the standpoint of its influence on the ROI calculation.

Program Materials and Fees

Specific program materials such as notebooks, textbooks, how-to manuals, instruction guides, software, case studies, exercises, and participant workbooks should be included in the delivery costs of a program, along with license fees, user fees, and royalty payments. Pens, paper, certificates, calculators, and personal copies of software are also included in this category.

For major programs, implementation may be a separate cost category. If the program involves meetings, follow-ups, manager reinforcement, or other activities beyond the program, an additional category for implementation may be appropriate. In some cases, on-site coordinators are available to provide assistance and support for employees as the program is implemented throughout the region, branch, or division. The total cost of these coordinators is an implementation expense that should be included in the program cost.

The specific cost categories for implementation often mirror the categories for delivery. However, in most situations, the implementation is considered part of the delivery and is placed in that category. The remainder of this book presents delivery and implementation as a combined category.

Evaluation

Usually, the total evaluation cost is included in the program cost so that the figure is fully loaded. Evaluation costs include the cost of developing the evaluation strategy, designing instruments, collecting data, data analysis, and report preparation and distribution. Cost categories include time, materials, hardware or software used to collect or analyze data, and purchased instruments or surveys. A case can be made for prorating evaluation costs over several programs instead of charging the total amount as an expense to one program. For example, twenty-five sessions of a program are conducted in a three-year period, and one group is selected for an ROI calculation. The costs of the ROI evaluation could logically be prorated over the twenty-five sessions because the results of the ROI analysis should reflect the success of the other programs and will perhaps result in changes that will affect the other programs as well.

Overhead

A final charge is the cost of overhead, the additional costs within the functional unit that are not directly related to a particular program. The overhead category represents any department costs not considered in the preceding categories. Typical overhead items include the cost of clerical support, departmental office expenses, salaries of managers, and other fixed costs. Some organizations obtain an estimate for overhead allocation by dividing the total overhead by an appropriate number in order to prorate the costs. The number may be the total participants or programs during the year. The result becomes a standard value to use in calculations.

An example will illustrate the simplicity of prorating overhead costs. An organization with fifty training and development programs tabulated all the expenditures in the budget not allocated directly to a particular program ($548,061). This part of the budget represented total overhead. Next, this number was divided by the total number of participant days or hours (for example, if a five-day program is offered ten times a year, 50 days would be put in the total days category, or 400 hours in the total hours category, based on an eight-hour workday). Using participant hours may be helpful if there is a significant amount of e-learning and participants are involved in programs an hour at a time. In other situations, allocation of participant days may be appropriate. In this example, participant days for the year totaled approximately 7,400. The total unallocated overhead of $548,061 was divided by 7,400 days to arrive at $74. Therefore, $74 is charged for overhead for each day of training. A three-day leadership program would be charged $222 for overhead. The overhead amount is usually small and will have very little impact on the ROI calculation. However, including overhead cost as part of a fully loaded cost profile builds credibility with sponsors and senior executives.

Another example illustrates a slightly different approach. In this case, the overhead for a human resources unit is needed in order to place a value on an individual's participation in a human resources (HR) program. Exhibit 2.1 summarizes the relevant information. For simplicity, a $1 million HR budget is assumed and it is estimated that $200,000 of that budget is not allocated to specific programs. The total number of participants in all HR programs (with some duplication) is 8,000. Therefore, the allocation per participant is $25. Thus, if a program is destined for an ROI calculation and 500

Exhibit 2.1. Example of Overhead Allocation

Total HR budget:	$1,000,000
Portion of budget not allocated to specific HR programs:	$200,000
Total number of participants in HR programs:	8,000
Allocation per participant:	$25

people participate, then the amount of overhead allocated to the program would be 500 × $25, or $12,500.

The key to allocating overhead is to use a simple approach that logically and systematically allocates the costs in the department that are not allocated to specific programs. Also, it is important not to spend too much time on this issue. Estimates are appropriate in most situations. Some organizations estimate an amount of overhead for a program, using some logical rationale, spending no more than ten or fifteen minutes on the issue. The overhead will not be a deal breaker in the ROI calculation for most programs.

Cost Reporting

An example from an actual case shows how total program costs are presented. Table 2.4 shows the cost of a major executive leadership program. The extensive program involved four one-week, off-site training sessions in which personal coaches and learning coaches were assigned to the participants. Working in teams, participants tackled a project that was important to top executives. Each team reported their results to management. The project teams could hire consultants as well. These costs are listed as program costs. The costs for the first group of twenty-two participants are detailed in the table.

The issue of prorating costs was an important consideration. In this case, it was reasonably certain that a second group would participate in the program; therefore, the analysis, design, and development expenses of $580,657 could be prorated over two sessions. As

Table 2.4. Reporting of Fully Loaded Costs for an Executive Leadership Development Program

Analysis, Design, and Development	
External consultants	$ 525,330
Training department salaries and benefits	
(for direct work on the program)	28,785
Management committee salaries and benefits	
(for direct work on the program)	26,542
Delivery	
Conference facilities (hotel)	142,554
External consultants	812,110
Training department salaries and benefits	
(for direct work on the program)	15,283
Training department travel expenses	37,500
Management committee	
(for direct work on the program)	75,470
Program costs ($25,000 × 4 weeks)	100,000
Participant salaries and benefits (class sessions)	
(average daily salary × benefits factor × number	
of program days)	84,564
Participant salaries and benefits (program work)	117,353
Travel and lodging for participants	100,938
Cost of materials (handouts, purchased materials)	6,872
Research and Evaluation	
Research	110,750
Evaluation	125,875
Total costs	**$2,309,926**

a result, in the actual ROI calculation, half of the total cost figure ($290,328) was used as the cost for analysis, design, and development. This left a total program cost of $2,019,598 ($2,309,926 − $290,328) to include in the analysis. This total represented $91,800 per participant, or $22,950 per participant for each week of formal sessions. Although this program was very expensive, it was close to a rough benchmark for weekly costs of other senior executive leadership programs.

Cost Accumulation and Estimation

There are two basic ways to accumulate costs. One is to categorize them according to the nature of the expenditure—for example, labor, materials, supplies, travel, and so on. These are expense account classifications. The other is to categorize costs according to the process or function that they apply to—for example, program development, delivery, or evaluation. An effective system monitors costs in expense account categories but also includes a method for accumulating costs in process or functional categories. However, in practice, many systems stop short of this second step. While the first grouping is sufficient to provide a total program cost, it does not allow useful comparison with other programs in order to identify areas in which costs might be excessive.

Cost Classification Matrix

Costs are accumulated in both expense account and functional classifications. The two are obviously related, and the relationship depends on the organization. For instance, the specific costs involved in analysis of a program may vary substantially from organization to organization.

An important part of the classification process is to define the kinds of costs in the account classification system that normally fall in each of the process or functional categories. Table 2.5 is a matrix that shows the categories for accumulating all program-related costs within a particular organization. The costs that normally fall in each process or functional category are checked in the matrix.

Each member of a program team should know how to charge expenses properly. For example, if equipment is rented to use in the development and delivery of a program, should all or part of the cost be charged to development? Or should it be charged to

Table 2.5. Cost Classification Matrix for Program-Related Costs

	Expense Account Classification	Analysis	Development	Delivery	Operations and Maintenance	Evaluation
00	Salaries and benefits—department staff	X	X	X	X	X
01	Salaries and benefits—other staff		X	X		
02	Salaries and benefits—participants			X	X	X
03	Meals, travel, and incidental expenses—department staff	X	X	X	X	X
04	Meals, travel, and accommodations—participants			X		
05	Office supplies and expenses	X	X		X	X
06	Program materials and supplies		X	X		
07	Printing and reproduction	X	X	X		
08	Outside services	X	X	X	X	X
09	Equipment expenses	X	X	X	X	X
10	Equipment—rental		X	X	X	
11	Equipment—maintenance			X	X	
12	Registration fees	X				
13	Facilities expense allocation			X	X	
14	Facilities rental			X		
15	General overhead allowance	X	X	X	X	X
16	Other miscellaneous expenses	X	X	X	X	X

Process or Functional Categories

delivery? More than likely, the cost will be allocated in proportion to the extent to which the item was used for each function.

Cost Accumulation

With expense account classifications clearly defined and the process or functional categories determined, tracking the costs of individual programs is easy. This feat is accomplished by using account numbers and program numbers. The following example illustrates the use of these numbers.

A program number is a three-digit number representing a specific program. Here are some examples:

New professional on-boarding	112
New team leader training	215
Statistical quality control	418
Valuing diversity	791

Numbers are assigned to the process or functional categories. Using the example presented earlier, the following numbers are assigned.

Analysis	1
Development	2
Delivery	3
Operations and maintenance	4
Evaluation	5

The two-digit numbers assigned to account classifications in the left-hand column in Table 2.5 complete the accounting system. For example, if workbooks are reproduced for a statistical quality control workshop, the appropriate charge number for that reproduction is 07-3-418. The first two digits denote the account classification (printing and reproduction); the next digit indicates the process or functional category (delivery); and the last three digits are the program number (statistical quality control). This system enables rapid accumulation and monitoring of program costs. Total costs can then be presented by

- Program (for example, statistical quality control)
- Process or functional category (for example, delivery)
- Expense account classification (for example, printing and reproduction)

Cost Estimation

The preceding sections cover procedures for classifying and monitoring costs related to programs. Monitoring and comparing ongoing costs with the budget or with projected costs is important. However, a significant reason for tracking costs is to predict the cost of future programs. Usually, this goal is accomplished through a formal cost estimation method that is unique to an organization.

Some organizations use cost estimating worksheets to arrive at the total cost for a proposed program. Exhibit 2.2 shows a cost estimating worksheet that summarizes analysis, development, delivery, operations and maintenance, and evaluation costs. The worksheet contains a few formulas that make it easier to estimate the costs. In addition to cost estimating worksheets, organizations often provide the current rates for services, supplies, and salaries. These data become outdated quickly and are usually updated periodically.

The most appropriate way to predict costs is by tracking the actual costs incurred in all phases—from analysis to evaluation—of all programs. This way, it is possible to see how much is spent on programs and how much is being spent in the different categories. Until adequate cost data are available, however, detailed analysis on the worksheets for cost estimation will be necessary.

Exhibit 2.2. Cost Estimating Worksheet

Cost Items	Total
Analysis Costs	
Salaries and employee benefits—department staff (number of people × average hourly salary × employee benefits factor × number of hours on project)	____
Meals, travel, and incidental expenses	____
Office supplies and expenses	____
Printing and reproduction	____
Outside services	____
Equipment expenses	____
Registration fees	____
Other miscellaneous expenses	____
Total Analysis Cost	____
Development Costs	
Salaries and employee benefits—department staff (number of people × average hourly salary × employee benefits factor × number of hours on project)	____
Salaries and employee benefits—other staff	____
Meals, travel, and incidental expenses	____
Office supplies and expenses	____
Program materials and supplies	____
Printing and reproduction	____
Outside services	____
Equipment expenses	____
Other miscellaneous expenses	____
Total Development Cost	____
Delivery Costs	
Salaries and employee benefits—participants (number of participants × average hourly or daily salary × employee benefits factor × hours or days on project)	____
Meals, travel, and accommodations—participants (number of participants × average daily expenses × number of days on project)	____

Exhibit 2.2. Cost Estimating Worksheet (*Continued*)

Cost Items	Total
Program materials and supplies	____
Printing and reproduction	____
Participant replacement costs (if applicable)	____
Lost production (explain basis)	____
Facilitator costs	
Salaries and benefits	____
Meals, travel, and incidental expenses	____
Outside services	____
Facility costs	
Facilities rental	____
Facilities expense allocation	____
Equipment expenses	____
Other miscellaneous expenses	____
Total Delivery Cost	____

Operations and Maintenance

Salaries and employee benefits—department staff
    (number of people × average hourly or daily salary ×
    employee benefits factor × number of hours on project)   ____

Meals, travel, and incidental expenses   ____

Salaries and employee benefits—participants
    (number of participants × average hourly or daily
    salary × employee benefits factor × hours or days
    spent on project)   ____

Office supplies and expenses   ____
Outside services   ____
Equipment expenses   ____
Other miscellaneous expenses   ____
Total Operations and Maintenance Cost   ____

Evaluation Costs

Salaries and employee benefits—department staff
    (number of people × average hourly or daily salary ×
    employee benefits factor × number of hours on project)   ____

Meals, travel, and incidental expenses   ____

(*Continued*)

Exhibit 2.2. Cost Estimating Worksheet (*Continued*)

Cost Items	Total
Salaries and employee benefits—participants (number of participants × average hourly or daily salary × employee benefits factor × hours or days on project)	____
Office supplies and expenses	____
Printing and reproduction	____
Outside services	____
Equipment expenses	____
Other miscellaneous expenses	____
Total Evaluation Cost	____
General Overhead Allocation	____
Total Program Cost	____

Case Study: Federal Information Agency

To illustrate the importance of tracking costs and detailing them, the following case study is presented in its entirety. The introductory and explanatory material is presented so that the complete costs can be better appreciated. As a practice exercise, the costs, representing three years of data, should be entered on the cost worksheet shown in Exhibit 2.3. The completed cost worksheet is shown at the end of the case study.

Overview

The Federal Information Agency (FIA) provides information to other government agencies and businesses as well as state and local organizations, agencies, and interested groups. Several hundred communication specialists with backgrounds in information systems, computer science, electrical engineering, and information science operate across the United States in order to perform their work. Almost all the specialists have bachelor's degrees in one of

Exhibit 2.3. Cost Worksheet

	Year 1	Year 2	Year 3	Total
Initial analysis (prorated)	___	___	___	___
Development (prorated)	___	___	___	___
Tuition—regular	___	___	___	___
Tuition—premium	___	___	___	___
Salaries and benefits—participants	___	___	___	___
Salaries and benefits—program administrator	___	___	___	___
Program coordination	___	___	___	___
Facilities	___	___	___	___
Salaries and benefits—managers	___	___	___	___
Evaluation	___	___	___	___
Total	___	___	___	___

these fields. The headquarters and operation center where 1,500 of the specialists are employed is in the Washington, D.C., area.

Problem and Solution

FIA was experiencing two problems that had senior agency officials concerned. The first problem was an unacceptable rate of employee turnover among the communication specialists—the rate averaged 38 percent in the year before the program was implemented. The need to recruit and train replacements due to the high rate of turnover was placing a strain on the agency. An analysis of exit interviews indicated that employees left primarily for higher salaries. Because FIA was somewhat constrained in its ability to increase salaries, competing with the salaries and benefits offered in the private sector had become difficult. Although salary increases and adjustments in pay levels would be necessary in order to lower turnover, FIA was also exploring other options.

The second problem concerned the need to continually update the technical skills of the staff. While the vast majority of the 1,500 specialists had a bachelor's degree, only a few had a master's degree in their specialty. In this work environment, formal education was quickly outdated. The annual feedback survey of employees indicated a strong interest in an in-house master's degree program in information science. Therefore, FIA explored the possibility of offering such a program. The program would be conducted by the School of Engineering and Science at Regional State University (RSU), and it would be implemented at no cost to the participating employees and conducted on the agency's time during regular work hours. Designed to address both employee turnover and skill updates, the program would normally take three years for participants to complete.

Program Description

RSU was selected to offer the master's program because of its reputation and because its curriculum matched FIA's needs. The program allowed participants to take one or two courses per semester. Taking two courses per semester schedule would enable participants to complete the program in three years. Both morning and afternoon classes were available, each representing three hours per week of class time. Participants were discouraged from taking more than two courses per term. Although a thesis option was normally available at RSU, FIA requested that a graduate project for six hours of credit be required instead of a thesis. The project would begin in Year 2 of the program. A professor would supervise the project. Designed to add value, the project would be applied within the agency.

Classes were usually taught live by professors at the agency's center. Participants were asked to prepare for classroom activities on their own time but were allowed to attend classes on the agency's time. A typical three-year schedule for the program is shown in Table 2.6.

Senior management approved the master's degree curriculum, which represented a mix of courses normally offered in the program

Table 2.6. Typical Three-Year Schedule for Master's Program in Information Science at the Federal Information Agency

	Year 1	Year 2	Year 3
Fall	2 courses (6 hours)	2 courses (6 hours)	2 courses (6 hours)
Spring	2 courses (6 hours)	2 courses (6 hours)	2 courses (6 hours)
Summer	1 course (3 hours)	1 course (3 hours)	Graduate project (3 hours)
		Graduate project (3 hours)	

Total semester hours: 48

and others specially selected for FIA staff. Two new courses were designed by university faculty for the curriculum. These two represented a slight modification of existing courses and were tailored to the communication requirements of the agency. Elective courses were not allowed, for two reasons. First, it would complicate the offerings, requiring additional courses, facilities, and professors—and adding costs to the program. Second, FIA wanted a prescribed, customized curriculum that would add value to the agency while meeting the requirements of the university.

Selection Criteria

An important issue involved the selection of employees to participate in the program. Most employees who voluntarily left the agency resigned within the first four years and were often considered to have high potential for advancement within the agency. Taking these considerations into account, the program designers established the following criteria in order to identify and select employees for the program.

1. A candidate must have at least one year of service prior to beginning classes.
2. A candidate must meet the normal requirements for acceptance into the graduate school at the university.

3. A candidate must be willing to sign a commitment to stay with the agency for two years beyond program completion.
4. A candidate's immediate manager must nominate the employee for consideration.
5. A candidate must be rated "high potential" by the immediate manager.

The management team was provided initial information on the program, kept informed of its development and progress prior to its launch, and briefed as selection criteria were finalized. It was emphasized that selection of participants should be based on objective criteria, following the guidelines offered. At the same time, managers were asked to provide feedback on the level of interest and specific issues about the nomination of candidates.

One hundred participants per year were allowed to enter the program. This limit was based on two key issues:

1. The ability of the university to staff the program had limits; RSU could not effectively teach more than one hundred participants each semester.
2. The program was an experiment that could be modified or enhanced in the future if it was successful.

Program Administration

Because of the magnitude of the anticipated enrollment, FIA appointed a full-time program administrator who was responsible for organizing and coordinating the program. The administrator's duties included registration of the participants, all correspondence and communication with the university and participants, facilities and logistics (including materials and books), and resolving problems as they occurred. FIA absorbed the total cost of the coordinator. The university assigned an individual to serve as a liaison with the agency. This individual was not an additional hire, and the university absorbed the cost of the liaison's time as part of the cost of doing business, covered by tuition.

Drivers of Evaluation

The in-house master's program was selected for comprehensive evaluation. The program's impact on the agency would be assessed, using a four-year time frame. Several influences had brought about the mandate for such detailed accountability.

1. Senior administrators had requested detailed evaluations for certain programs that were considered strategic and that were highly visible and designed to add a great deal of value to the agency.
2. This program was perceived to be very expensive; thus, senior management demanded a higher level of accountability, including return on investment.
3. Because retention was a critical issue for the agency, it was important to determine whether this solution was the appropriate one. A detailed measurement and evaluation would assess the success of the program.
4. The passage of federal legislation and other initiatives aimed at providing more accountability for the use of taxpayers' funds had resulted in a shift toward more public sector accountability in the United States.

As a result, the implementation team planned a detailed evaluation of the master's program that went beyond traditional program evaluation processes. In addition to tracking costs, the team would determine the monetary payoff, including the ROI. Because the master's program was a very complex and comprehensive solution, other important measures would be tracked in order to provide a balanced approach to the measurement.

Recognizing the shift toward public sector accountability, the human resources staff had developed the necessary skills to implement the ROI Methodology; a small group of HR staff members had been certified to implement the ROI Methodology within the agency.

Program Costs

The costs of the program were tabulated and monitored. The evaluation used a fully loaded cost profile, which included all direct and indirect costs. One of the major costs was the tuition for the participants. The university charged the customary tuition, which included the cost of books and materials plus $100 per semester course per participant to offset the additional travel expenses and the faculty expenses of conducting and coordinating the program. The tuition per semester hour was $200 (that is, $600 per three-hour course).

The full-time program administrator was an FIA employee, receiving a base salary of $37,000 per year, with a 45 percent employee benefits factor. The administrator had expenses of approximately $15,000 per year.

Salaries for the participants represented another significant cost category. The average salary for the job categories of the employees involved in the program was $47,800, with a 45 percent employee benefits factor. Salaries usually increased approximately 4 percent per year. Participants attended class a total of 18 hours for each semester hour of credit. Therefore, a three-hour course represented 54 hours of off-the-job time in the classroom. The total hours of off-the-job class time needed for one participant to complete the program was 756 hours (14 courses × 54 hours).

Classroom facilities were another significant cost category. For the one hundred participants, four different courses were offered each semester, and each course was repeated at a different time.

With a class size of twenty-five, eight separate semester courses were presented. Although the classrooms used for this program were normally used for other training and education programs offered at the agency, the cost of providing the facilities was included. (Because of the unusual demand, an additional conference room was built in order to provide ample meeting space.) The estimate for the average cost of all meeting rooms was $40 per hour of use.

The cost of the initial assessment that led to the program, including the turnover analysis, was included in the cost profile. This charge, estimated to be $5,000, was prorated for the first three years. FIA's development costs for the program were estimated to be $10,000 and were also prorated for three years. Management time spent on the program was minimal but was estimated to cost $9,000 over the three-year period. Management time was primarily spent on attending meetings and writing memos about the program. Finally, the evaluation costs, representing the cost of tracking the success of the program and reporting the results to management, were estimated to be $10,000 (see Exhibit 2.4).

Final Thoughts

Costs are important in a variety of applications. Tracking costs helps program staff manage resources carefully, consistently, and efficiently. Tracking costs also allows comparisons between cost items and cost categories over time or across projects. There are several systems of cost categorization; the most common ones are presented in this chapter.

Costs should be fully loaded for an ROI calculation. From a practical standpoint, including certain cost items may be optional because of an organization's cost guidelines or cost philosophy. However, because ROI calculations are often closely scrutinized,

Exhibit 2.4. Completed Cost Worksheet for FIA's In-House Master's Program

	Year 1	Year 2	Year 3	Total
Initial analysis (prorated)	$1,667	$1,667	$1,666	$5,000
Development (prorated)	3,333	3,333	3,334	10,000
Tuition—regular	300,000	342,000	273,000	915,000
Tuition—premium	50,000	57,000	45,500	152,500
Salaries and benefits—participants	899,697	888,900	708,426	2,497,023
Salaries and benefits—program administrator	53,650	55,796	58,028	167,474
Program coordination	15,000	15,000	15,000	45,000
Facilities	43,200	43,200	34,560	120,960
Salaries and benefits—managers	3,000	3,000	3,000	9,000
Evaluation	3,333	3,333	3,334	10,000
Total	$1,372,880	$1,413,229	$1,145,848	$3,931,957

all costs should be included, even if their inclusion goes beyond the requirements of an organization's policy.

References

ROI Institute. *ROI Certification Handbook*. Birmingham, Ala.: ROI Institute, 2005.
U.S. Chamber of Commerce. *Annual Employee Benefits Study*. Washington, D.C.: U.S. Chamber of Commerce, 2006.

3

The ROI Calculation

The monetary values for the program benefits (described in *Data Conversion*, book four of this series) are combined with program cost data (described in Chapter Two of this book) to calculate return on investment (ROI). This chapter explores several approaches to calculating ROI, describing the techniques, processes, and issues involved. Before presenting the formulas for calculating ROI and benefit-cost ratio (BCR), this chapter discusses a few basic issues. An adequate understanding of these issues is necessary to complete an ROI calculation, one of the major steps in the ROI Methodology. The uses and abuses of ROI are also fully explored in this chapter.

Basic Issues in Calculating ROI

Before presenting the methods for calculating ROI, we will review a few issues that are key to understanding the calculation process and the ROI values.

Definitions Are Critical

The term *return on investment* is often misused, sometimes intentionally. In some situations, ROI is defined broadly to mean any benefit from a program. In these situations, ROI is a vague concept in which even the most elusive data associated with a program are included in the concept of return on investment. In this book, *return on investment* is a precise term, signifying an actual value that is calculated by comparing a program's costs with its benefits. The two most common measures of return on investment are the benefit-cost ratio and the ROI formula. Both are presented in this chapter.

For many years, practitioners and researchers have sought to calculate the actual return on investment for all types of programs and projects. For example, if formal employee learning and development is considered an investment, not an expense, then learning and development investments should be subject to the same funding mechanism as other investments, such as the investments in equipment and facilities. Although investments in learning are quite different from these other investments, management often views them in the same way. Therefore, developing specific measures that reflect the return on the investment in learning and development programs is critical to the success of the field of learning and development.

Annualized Values

All the formulas presented in this chapter use annualized values, which means that the impact of the program investment in the first year is measured. Using annual values is becoming a generally accepted practice in evaluating ROI in many organizations. This practice is a conservative approach to measuring ROI, because many short-term programs continue to add value in the second or third year after they are implemented. For long-term programs, annualized values are inappropriate and longer time frames need to be used. For example, in an ROI analysis of a program to send employees to the United States to obtain MBA degrees, a Singapore-based company used a seven-year time frame. The program itself required two years, after which post-program impact data were collected over five years and eventually used to calculate the ROI for the program. However, for most programs lasting one day to one month, basing values on the program's impact in the first year is appropriate.

When selecting the approach to measuring ROI, it is important to communicate to the target audience the formula used and the assumptions made in deciding to use it. This action can avoid misunderstandings and confusion about how the ROI value was developed. Although several approaches are described in this chapter, two stand out as preferred methods: the benefit-cost ratio and the basic ROI formula. These two approaches are described next, along with the interpretation of ROI and brief coverage of other approaches.

Benefit-Cost Ratio

One of the earliest methods for evaluating investments is the benefit-cost ratio. This method compares the benefits of a program to its costs. The ratio is expressed in this formula:

$$BCR = \frac{\text{Program Benefits}}{\text{Program Costs}}$$

In simple terms, the BCR compares the annual economic benefits of a program to the costs of the program. A BCR of 1, written 1:1, means that the benefits equal the costs. A BCR of 2, written 2:1, indicates that for each dollar spent on the program, two dollars in benefits were returned.

The following example illustrates the use of the benefit-cost ratio. A large metropolitan bus system introduced a new program to reduce unscheduled absences. An increase in absences had left the system facing many delays; to prevent the delays, a large pool of drivers had been created to fill in for the absent drivers. The pool had become substantial, representing a significant expenditure. The program involved a change in policy and a change in the selection process for regular drivers, coupled with meetings and communication. Significant improvements were generated. The benefits of the program were captured in a one-year follow-up and compared with the total cost of the program. The benefits from the first year of the program were valued at $662,000. The fully loaded implementation costs totaled $67,400. Thus, the benefit-cost ratio is as follows:

$$BCR = \frac{\$662,000}{\$67,400} = 9.82$$

For every dollar invested in this program, almost ten dollars in benefits were returned. Later in this chapter, the ROI for this program will be calculated.

The BCR is not a traditional financial measure, so no confusion arises when comparing program investments with investments in plants, equipment, or subsidiaries, which use other indicators in the cost-benefit comparison. Some managers prefer not to use the same method to evaluate the return on their program investments that is used to evaluate the return on other investments.

There are no standards for what constitutes an acceptable benefit-cost ratio. A standard should be established within an organization; however, in some organizations, the standard may vary depending on the type of program. Nonetheless, a 1:1 benefit-cost ratio, reflecting break-even return, is unacceptable for most programs, and in some organizations, a 1.25:1 benefit-cost ratio is required, signifying that 1.25 times the cost of the program is the required benefit.

ROI Formula

Another common formula for evaluating program investments is net program benefits divided by costs. The ratio is expressed as a percentage, so the value yielded by the basic formula is multiplied by 100. The formula for ROI is as follows:

$$ROI(\%) = \frac{\text{Net Program Benefits}}{\text{Program Costs}} \times 100$$

Net benefits are the program benefits minus program costs. The ROI value can be obtained from the BCR by subtracting one. For example, a BCR of 2.45 is the same as an ROI value of 1.45, or 145 percent.

This ROI formula is essentially the same as the ROI formula for other types of investments. For example, when a firm builds a new plant, the ROI is calculated by dividing annual earnings by the investment. The annual earnings (annual revenue minus expenses) are comparable to net benefits (annual benefits minus costs). The investment is comparable to program costs, which are the investment in the program.

An ROI of 50 percent for a program means that the costs have been recovered and an additional amount equal to 50 percent of the costs has been gained as "earnings." So, if one dollar is invested, the dollar would be recovered plus an additional fifty cents. An ROI of 150 percent indicates that the costs have been recovered and additional "earnings" equal to 1.5 times the costs have been received. In other words, for every dollar invested, the dollar investment is recovered plus a gain of an additional one dollar and fifty cents.

The following example illustrates the ROI calculation. Hewlett-Packard took a unique approach to increasing telephone-based sales (Seagraves, 2001). An innovative, multistep sales skills intervention drove tremendous improvement in sales skills. The sales improvement, when translated into increased profit, yielded impressive results. The monetary benefits were $3,296,977, and the total, fully loaded costs were $1,116,291. Thus, the net benefits were $2,180,686 ($3,296,977 − $1,116,291). The ROI calculation looks like this:

$$\text{ROI}(\%) = \frac{\$2,180,686}{\$1,116,291} \times 100 = 195\%$$

After the costs of the program had been recovered, Hewlett-Packard received almost two dollars for each dollar invested.

Using the ROI formula places program investments on a level playing field with other investments by using the same formula and similar concepts. The ROI calculation is easily understood by key management and financial executives, who regularly use the ROI formula to evaluate other investments.

ROI Examples

To illustrate how the ROI and BCR calculations are developed, five brief examples are presented in this section. Some of these cases are briefly discussed in some of the other books in this series. Here, the ROI calculations from the cases are presented, showing the monetary results of each program. Working through these examples to become familiar with what goes into the analysis and the actual calculations may be helpful.

Example 1: Retail Merchandise Company

Retail Merchandise Company (RMC), a large national store chain located in most major markets in the United States, piloted a program to boost sales by teaching interactive selling skills to sales associates. The program, developed and delivered by an outside vendor, was a response to a clearly identified need to increase interaction between sales associates and customers. The program consisted of two days of skills training, followed by three weeks of on-the-job skill application. The third day of the program was used for follow-up and additional training. Three groups representing the electronics departments of three stores were initially trained in a pilot implementation. A total of forty-eight employees participated.

Post-program data collection was accomplished through three methods. First, the average weekly sales of each associate were monitored (business performance monitoring of output data). Second, a follow-up questionnaire was distributed three months after the program was completed in order to assess Level 3 success (actual application of skills on the job). Third, Level 3 data were solicited in a follow-up session, which was conducted on the third day of the program. In this session, participants disclosed their success (or lack of success) in applying the new skills. They also discussed the techniques they used to overcome the barriers to program implementation.

The method used to isolate the effects of the program was a control group arrangement. Three store locations (control group) were identified and compared with the three groups that participated in the pilot program (experimental group). The variables of previous store performance, annual sales volume, average household disposable income in the area, and customer traffic levels were used to match the two groups so that they could be as similar as possible. The method of converting data to monetary values was extrapolation of direct profit contribution, based on the value of increased output. The amount of profit that resulted from one additional dollar of sales (profit margin) was a readily available figure that was used in the calculation.

Although the program was evaluated at all five levels outlined in the ROI Methodology, the emphasis of this study was on Levels 4 and 5. The data at Levels 1, 2, and 3 met or exceeded expectations. Table 3.1 shows the Level 4 data—the average weekly sales of both groups after the program. For convenience and at the request of management, a three-month follow-up period was used. Management wanted to implement the program at other locations if it appeared to be successful in the first three months of operation. Evaluation after three months may be premature in terms of determining the total impact of the program, but in practice, evaluation after three months is common because it is convenient. Data from the first three weeks after the program are shown in Table 3.1, along with data from the last three weeks of the evaluation period (weeks 13, 14, and 15). The data show what appears to be a significant difference in the two values.

Two steps were required to move from the Level 4 impact data to Level 5, ROI evaluation. First, the Level 4 data had to be converted to monetary values. Second, the costs of the program had to be tabulated.

First, we will discuss the conversion of the data to monetary values. Exhibit 3.1 shows the annualized program benefits. Only forty-six participants were still in their job after three months; to be

Table 3.1. Level 4 Data: Average Weekly Sales per Associate

Weeks After Program	Post-Program Data for Experimental Groups	Post-Program Data for Control Groups
1	$9,723	$9,698
2	9,978	9,720
3	10,424	9,812
13	13,690	11,572
14	11,491	9,683
15	11,044	10,092
Average for weeks 13, 14, 15	$12,075	$10,449

conservative, the other two participants' potential improvements were excluded from the benefits. The profit contribution at the store level, obtained from the accounting department, was 2 percent of sales. Out of every dollar of additional sales attributed to the program, only two cents would be considered added value.

First-year values were used to reflect the total impact of the program. The annual benefits were calculated using forty-eight weeks rather than fifty-two weeks to account for holidays and vacation. Ideally, if new skills had been acquired, as the Level 3 evaluation

Exhibit 3.1. Annualized Program Benefits

Number of participants who were still in their job after three months: 46

Average weekly sales per associate—program groups	$12,075
Average weekly sales per associate—control groups	10,449
Increase in weekly sales per associate	1,626
Profit contribution from sales increase (2% of sales)	32.50
Total weekly improvement in profit ($32.50 × 46 associates)	1,495
Total annual benefits ($1495 × 48 weeks)	$71,760

Table 3.2. Cost Summary

Item	Cost
Facilitation fees (3 courses @ $3,750)	$11,250
Program materials (48 sets @ $35)	1,680
Meals and refreshments (3 days @ $28/participant)	4,032
Facilities (9 days @ $120)	1,080
Participants' salaries plus benefits (35% of salaries)	12,442
Coordination and evaluation	2,500
Total costs	$32,984

Note: There were forty-eight participants in three courses.

indicated, some value from the use of those skills would occur in the second year or perhaps even in the third year after program implementation. However, for short-term programs, only first-year values are used, requiring the investment to have an acceptable return in a one-year time period. Thus, Guiding Principle 9 states, "Use only the first year of annual benefits in ROI analysis of short-term solutions." The total benefits were $71,760.

Second, we address the tabulation of costs. Table 3.2 shows the cost summary for this program. Costs were fully loaded, including data for all forty-eight participants. The need for the program was identified by senior managers, so a formal needs assessment was not conducted. Since an external supplier conducted the program, there were no direct development costs. The facilitation fee covered the prorated development costs as well as the delivery costs.

The participants' salaries plus a 35 percent factor for employee benefits were included in the costs. Facilities costs were included, although the company did not normally capture the costs when internal facilities were used, as they were for this program. The estimated cost for coordination and evaluation of the program was also included. The total cost of the program was $32,984. Thus, the benefit-cost ratio was as follows:

$$\text{BCR} = \frac{\$71,760}{\$32,984} = 2.18{:}1$$

And the ROI was as follows:

$$\text{ROI}(\%) = \frac{\$71{,}760 - \$32{,}984}{\$32{,}984} \times 100 = 118\%$$

The acceptable ROI, defined by the client, was 25 percent. Therefore, the pilot program had an excellent ROI after three months of on-the-job skill applications. As a result, the decision to implement the program throughout the other store locations became much easier. Six types of data had been collected to show the full range of success, including the actual ROI.

This example, in which the payoff on a pilot program was developed, represents an excellent use of the ROI Methodology. Historically, the decision to go from pilot to full implementation is often based on reaction (Level 1) data alone. Sometimes, learning (Level 2) data and, in limited cases, application (Level 3) data are used. In this case, those types of data were collected, but more important, business impact, ROI, and intangibles added to the rich database that influenced this critical decision. It is much less risky when a full implementation is recommended from a pilot program based on a full range of data.

Example 2: Global Financial Services

Global Financial Services conducted a program for relationship managers to teach them how to use software that would help them manage customer contacts. The program consisted of a one-day workshop, and 120 managers were trained on a pilot basis. Only sixty of the managers participating in the pilot were part of the evaluation project.

Payoff Measures

- Increased sales from existing customers
- Reduction in customer complaints

Key Intangibles

- Taking less time to respond to customers
- Customer satisfaction

Business Impact Measures

Value of increased sales to existing customers	$539,280
Value of reduced customer complaints	575,660
Total	$1,114,940

Program Costs

Development costs	$10,500
Materials and software	18,850
Equipment	6,000
Instructor (including expenses)	7,200
Facilities, food, and refreshments (60 @ $58)	3,480
Participants' time (salaries and benefits)	22,330
Coordination and evaluation	15,600
Total	$83,960

ROI Calculation

$$\text{ROI}(\%) = \frac{\$1{,}114{,}940 - \$83{,}960}{\$83{,}960} \times 100 = 1{,}228\%$$

Example 3: Healthcare, Inc.

Healthcare, Inc., conducted a one-day sexual harassment prevention workshop designed for all first- and second-level supervisors and managers. Seventeen sessions, involving 655 managers, took place over a period of forty-five days.

Payoff Measures

- Reduction in sexual harassment complaints
- Reduced turnover

Key Intangibles

- Job satisfaction
- Absenteeism
- Stress reduction
- Image of Healthcare, Inc.
- Recruiting

Business Impact Measures

Internal complaints	$360,276
Turnover reduction	2,840,632
Total	$3,200,908

Program Costs

Needs assessment (estimated cost of time)	$9,000
Program development and acquisition	15,000
Program coordination and facilitation time	9,600
Travel and lodging for facilitators and coordinators	1,520
Program materials (655 @ $12)	7,860
Food and refreshments (655 @ $30)	19,650
Facilities (17 @ $150)	2,550
Participant salaries and benefits ($130,797 × 1.39)	181,807
Evaluation	31,000
Total	$277,987

ROI Calculation

$$\text{ROI}(\%) = \frac{\$3{,}200{,}908 - \$277{,}987}{\$277{,}987} \times 100 = 1{,}052\%$$

Example 4: Metro Transit Authority

Metro Transit Authority conducted a program that initiated two processes: a no-fault disciplinary system was implemented, and the selection process for new drivers was modified. This program was implemented throughout the company, which employed 2,900 drivers.

Payoff Measure

- Reduced driver absenteeism

Key Intangible

- Improve customer service and satisfaction by reducing schedule delays caused by absenteeism

Business Impact Measures

Contribution of the no-fault policy	$518,000
Contribution of the new screening process	144,000
Total	$662,000

Program Costs

Cost of no-fault policy	
Development cost	$11,000
Materials	3,800
Meeting time	16,500
Total	$31,300
Cost of screening process	
Development cost	$20,000
Interviewer preparation	5,000
Administrative time (1,200 interviews × $7.25)	8,700
Materials (1,200 interviews × $2.00)	2,400
Total	$36,100

ROI Calculation

$$\text{ROI}(\%) = \frac{\$662,000 - \$67,400}{\$67,400} \times 100 = 882\%$$

Example 5: Midwest Electric

In a stress management program conducted by Midwest Electric, managers and representative employees participated in focus groups to identify work satisfiers and de-stressors and then collaborated on alleviating systemic sources of stress.

Payoff Measures

- Reduced medical care costs
- Reduced absenteeism
- Reduced turnover

Key Intangibles

- Improved communication
- Time savings
- Fewer conflicts
- Teamwork
- Improvement in problem solving

Business Impact Measures

Reduced medical costs	$198,720
Reduced absenteeism	67,684
Reduced turnover	157,553
Total	$423,957

Project Costs

Needs assessment	$16,500
Program development	4,800
Program materials (144 @ $95)	13,680
Participant salaries and benefits (based on 1 day)	24,108
Travel and lodging (144 @ $38)	5,472
Facilitation, coordination (including travel and overhead)	10,800
Meeting room, food, and refreshments (144 @ $22)	3,168
Evaluation costs	22,320
Total	$100,848

ROI Calculation

$$\text{ROI}(\%) = \frac{\$423{,}957 - \$100{,}848}{\$100{,}848} \times 100 = 320\%$$

Positioning ROI Evaluation

When ROI evaluation is undertaken, some important issues must be considered. This section presents information on how to position ROI measurement to harness the power of the ROI Methodology and the organizational resources that will support the process.

Choosing the Right Formula

What quantitative measure best represents top management goals? Many managers are preoccupied with the measures of sales, profits (net income), and profit percentages (the ratio of profits to dollar sales). However, the ultimate test of profitability is not the absolute amount of profit or the relationship of profit to sales. The critical test is the relationship of profit to invested capital. The most popular expression of this relationship is return on investment (Anthony and Reece, 1983).

Profits can be generated through increased sales or through cost savings. In practice, more opportunities are available for cost savings than for increased sales. Cost savings can be generated when productivity, quality, efficiency, cycle time, or actual cost reduction is improved. Among almost five hundred ROI studies that we have been involved in, the vast majority of the programs were based on cost savings. Approximately 85 percent of the studies had a payoff based on improvement of output, quality, or efficiency or on reduction of cost or time spent. The other studies had a payoff based on sales increases, in which benefits were derived from the profit margin. It is important for nonprofits and public sector organizations to take note of this situation. Because most performance improvement initiatives are aimed at cost savings, ROI evaluations can still be developed in those settings, even though the opportunity for profit is often unavailable.

In the finance and accounting literature, return on investment is defined as net income (earnings) divided by investment. In the context of performance improvement, net income is equivalent to net monetary benefits (program benefits minus program costs). Investment is equivalent to program costs. The term *investment* is used in three different senses in financial analysis, resulting in three different ROI ratios: return on assets (ROA), return on owners' equity (ROE), and return on capital employed (ROCE).

Financial executives have used ROI for centuries. Still, ROI did not become widespread in industry as a performance measure until the early 1960s. Conceptually, ROI has innate appeal because it blends all the major ingredients of profitability in one number; the ROI statistic by itself can be used to compare opportunities internally or externally. Practically, however, ROI should be used in conjunction with other performance measurements (Horngren, 1982).

The formula presented in this chapter should be the same formula that is used in the entire organization. Deviations from or misuse of the formula may create confusion among users or among the finance and accounting staff. Your chief financial officer (CFO) and your finance and accounting staff should be your partners in implementing the ROI Methodology. Without their support, involvement, and commitment, using the ROI Methodology on a wide-scale basis will be difficult. In recognition of this important relationship, the same financial terms used and expected by the CFO should be used when conducting and reporting the results of an evaluation.

Table 3.3 shows some common misuses of financial terms that appear in the literature. Terms such as *return on intelligence* (or *return on information*) abbreviated as ROI do nothing but confuse a CFO, who thinks that ROI is *return on investment*, as was described earlier. Sometimes, *return on expectations* (ROE), *return on*

The ROI Calculation 73

Table 3.3. Misuse of Financial Terms

Term	Misuse	CFO Definition
ROI	Return on information Return on intelligence	Return on investment
ROE	Return on expectation	Return on equity
ROA	Return on anticipation	Return on assets
ROCE	Return on client expectations	Return on capital employed
ROP	Return on people	??
ROR	Return on resources	??
ROT	Return on training	??
ROW	Return on Web	??

anticipation (ROA), or *return on client expectations* (ROCE) is used, also confusing the CFO, who thinks that those abbreviations stand for *return on equity, return on assets,* and *return on capital employed,* respectively. Use of misleading terms or abbreviations in calculating the payback of a program will confuse the finance and accounting staff and may cause them to withdraw their support from the evaluation project. Other terms such as *return on people, return on resources, return on training,* and *return on Web* are often used, with almost no consistent financial calculations. The bottom line: don't confuse the CFO. This individual (or her representative) should be considered an ally, and the same terminology, processes, and concepts used by her and her department should be used when describing the financial returns of programs.

Developing ROI Objectives

When reviewing the ROI calculation, it is helpful to position the ROI calculation in the context of all the data. The ROI calculation is only one measure generated with the ROI Methodology. Six types of data are developed and categorized along the five-level evaluation framework. The data collected at each level of evaluation are driven by a specific objective, as was described earlier

Figure 3.1. The Chain of Impact Drives ROI

Level	Objective	Results
1 Reaction and Planned Action	• Obtain a positive reaction to the program • At least 75% of participants provide a list of action items	• Average overall rating of 4.11 out of a possible 5 • 93% provided list of action items
2 Learning	• Knowledge of policy on sexual harassment; knowledge of inappropriate and illegal behavior • Skills to investigate and discuss sexual harassment	• Posttest scores averaged 84; pretest scores averaged 51—improvement of 65% ([84–51]/51=65) • Participants demonstrated that they could use the skills successfully
3 Application and Implementation	• Conduct meeting with employees • Administer policy to ensure that workplace is free from sexual harassment • Complete action items	• 100% of participants conducted meetings with employees two weeks after the program • When confronted with a violation of policy, managers took appropriate action • 80% of participants completed 3 out of 3 action items.
4 Business Impact	• Reduce the number of formal internal sexual harassment complaints • Reduce turnover related to sexual harassment • Reduce absenteeism related to sexual harassment	• Complaints reduced from 55 to 35 • Turnover reduced from 24.2% to 19.9% • Increased job satisfaction • Increased teamwork • Reduced stress
5 ROI	• Obtain at least a 25% ROI	• ROI = 1052%

in this series. Specific objectives are often set for ROI, creating expectations about an acceptable ROI value.

Figure 3.1 shows the payoff of a program to prevent sexual harassment. The results at the different levels are clearly linked to the specific objectives of the program. As objectives are established, data are collected to indicate the extent to which the objectives were met. This framework clearly shows the powerful connection between objectives, measurement, and evaluation data. The table also shows the chain of impact: reaction leads to learning, which leads to application, which leads to business impact and to ROI. The intangible benefits shown in the business impact category are items that were purposely not converted to monetary values. Some of those outcomes could have been anticipated before the program was implemented. Others may not have been anticipated but were described as a benefit by those involved in the program. In this example, an ROI of 25 percent was expected. This organization uses 25 percent as a standard for all programs slated for an ROI evaluation. The result of 1,052 percent clearly exceeded that objective by a huge amount.

Determining ROI Targets

Specific expectations for ROI should be developed before an evaluation study is undertaken. While there are no generally accepted standards, *ROI Fundamentals*, the first book of this series, discusses four strategies for setting ROI targets:

- Setting the goal at the same level as other capital investments
- Setting the target at a higher level than other investments
- Aiming for a 0% ROI—that is, breaking even
- Letting the client set the ROI target

This issue should always be addressed before a program begins.

Other ROI Measures

In addition to the traditional ROI and BCR formulas described earlier in this chapter, several other measures are occasionally used to evaluate return on investment in a broad sense. These measures are designed primarily to evaluate other types of financial investments but sometimes work their way into program evaluations.

Payback Period

The payback period is a common method of evaluating capital expenditures. In this approach, the original cash outlay is divided by the annual cash proceeds (savings) produced by that investment to arrive at some multiple of cash proceeds that is equal to the original investment. Measurement is usually in terms of years and months. For example, if the cost savings generated by a program are constant each year, the payback period is determined by dividing the total original cash investment (development costs, outside program purchases, and so on) by the amount of the expected or actual annual savings.

To practice this calculation, assume that a program's cost is $100,000 and that the program has a three-year useful life. The annual net savings from the program are expected to be $40,000. The payback period is as follows:

$$\text{Payback period} = \frac{\text{Total Investment}}{\text{Annual Savings}} = \frac{\$100{,}000}{\$40{,}000} = 2.5 \text{ years}$$

The program will "pay back" the original investment in 2.5 years.

Payback period is a simple concept to use, but it has the limitation of ignoring the time value of money. It has not enjoyed widespread use in evaluating program investments.

Exhibit 3.2 compares BCR, ROI, and payback period for the same program. These calculations are obviously related, and sometimes, all three are reported because of the different perspectives they provide. The payback period figure answers the question "How long will it take to get the investment back (or break even, or achieve a 0% ROI)?" Sometimes, this is referred to as a *break-even analysis*.

Discounted Cash Flow

Discounted cash flow is a method of evaluating investment opportunities in which values assigned are based on the timing of the

Exhibit 3.2. Comparison of ROI, BCR, and Payback Period

Defining Benefit-Cost Ratio

$$BCR = \frac{\text{Program Benefits}}{\text{Program Costs}}$$

Example
Program Benefits = $71,760
Program Costs = $32,984

$$BCR = \frac{\$71,760}{\$32,984} = 2.18$$

Defining Return on Investment

$$ROI(\%) = \frac{\text{Net Program Benefits}}{\text{Program Costs}} \times 100$$

Example
Net Program Benefits = $38,776
Program Costs = $32,984

$$ROI(\%) = \frac{\$38,776}{\$32,984} \times 100 = 118\%$$

Defining Payback Period

$$\text{Payback Period} = \frac{\text{Total Investment}}{\text{Annual Savings}} \times 12$$

Example
Total Investment = $32,984
Annual Savings = $71,760

$$\text{Payback Period} = \frac{\$32,984}{\$71,760} = .46 \times 12 = 5.52 \text{ months}$$

---

proceeds from the investment. The assumption, based on interest rates, is that money earned today is more valuable than money earned a year from now. Discounted cash flow is used when it is important to understand the value of future returns.

There are several ways of using the concept of discounted cash flow to evaluate capital expenditures. The most popular is probably the net present value of an investment. This approach compares the savings, year by year, with the outflow of cash required by the investment. The expected savings for each year is discounted by a selected interest rate. The outflow of cash is also discounted by the same interest rate. If the present value of all the savings is expected to exceed the present value of all the outlays after discounting at a common interest rate, the investment is usually acceptable in the eyes of management. The discounted cash flow method has the advantage of allowing managers to rank investments, but it can be difficult to calculate.

Internal Rate of Return

The internal rate of return (IRR) method determines the interest rate required to make the present value of the cash flow equal to zero. It represents the maximum rate of interest that could be paid if all program funds were borrowed and the organization had to break even on the programs. The IRR considers the time value of money and is unaffected by the scale of the program. It can be used to rank alternatives and to make accept-or-reject decisions when a minimum rate of return is specified. A major weakness of the IRR method is that it assumes that all returns are reinvested at the same internal rate of return. This can make an investment alternative with a high rate of return look even better than it really is, and a program with a low rate of return may look even worse. In practice, the IRR is rarely used to evaluate program investments.

Utility Analysis

An interesting approach to calculating the payoff of a program is utility analysis. Utility analysis measures the economic contribution of a program according to how effective the program was in identifying and modifying behavior and, hence, the future service contribution of employees. Utility is a function of the duration of a program's effect on employees' performance, the number of employees involved, the validity of the program, the value of the job for which the program was provided, and the total program cost (Schmidt, Hunter, and Pearlman, 1982). The following formula is offered for assessing the dollar value of a program:

$$\Delta U = T \times N \times dt \times SDy - N \times C$$

where

ΔU = Monetary value of the program
T = Duration of a program's effect on performance, in years
N = Number of employees involved
dt = True difference in average job performance between employees in the program and those not in the program, in units of standard deviation
SDy = Standard deviation of job performance of those not involved in the program, in dollars
C = Cost of the program per employee

Of all the factors in this formula, the true difference in job performance (dt) and the value of the target job (SDy) are the most difficult to place a value on. The validity of the program (dt) is determined by noting the performance differences between employees participating in the program and those not participating. The simplest way to obtain this information is to have supervisors rate the performance of each group. Supervisors and experts can estimate the value of the target job (SDy).

Utility analysis has advantages and disadvantages. It has two primary flaws. First, it is basically a Level 3 ROI analysis. Essentially, the process converts behavior change (Level 3) into monetary value, ignoring the consequences of that behavior change, which is the business impact (Level 4). As a result, it stops short of following the chain of impact all the way to the new behavior's consequences within the organization. Simply having new behavior in place does not mean that it is being used productively or adding value to the organization.

The second disadvantage is that utility analysis is based on estimates. Because of the subjective nature of estimates and many managers' reluctance to use them, the process has not achieved widespread acceptance among professionals as a practical tool for evaluating return on investment. A recent survey of two hundred published case studies on ROI found that less than 5 percent use utility analysis.

One possible advantage is that researchers have developed an abundance of models. One of the principal proponents of the process identifies six models that use the concept of utility analysis (Cascio, 2000).

Also, the notion of putting a value on behavior change is a novel idea for many practitioners. Given the increased interest in leadership behaviors and job competencies, the prospect of placing a value on those behaviors in the workplace has some appeal and explains the application of utility analysis in some situations. For example, the Eastman Chemical Company used this process to evaluate an empowerment program for employees (Bernthal and Byham, 1997).

Utility analysis should be one of the tools in a manager's ROI arsenal. In the framework presented in this series of books, utility analysis is a Level 3 ROI analysis, which, in essence, forecasts the value or impact of a program based on behavior change.

ROI, the Profit Center, and EVA

Given increased interest in converting various organizational functions to profit centers, distinguishing between the ROI Methodology and the profit center strategy is important. The ROI Methodology described in this series of books shows the payoff of a program (or a group of programs) with highly integrated objectives. It is a microlevel process showing the economic value derived from these programs. The profit center concept usually applies to an entire function, which operates like a privately owned business, with profit as the true measure of its economic success. Its customers, usually the key managers in the organization, have complete discretion on whether to use the internal services of the function or to purchase those services externally. When the services are purchased internally, competitive prices are usually charged and transferred from the operating department, providing revenue to the function. The function's expenses include salaries, office space, materials, fees, and services. Thus, the function operates as a wholly owned subsidiary of the organization, receiving revenues for all services provided and paying out expenses for its staff and operations. The function realizes a profit if the revenue received from the transfer of funds exceeds the costs. This approach holds much interest, particularly for senior executives who want to bring complete accountability to their organization's functions. Also, the profit center approach provides a true test of the perceived value of an organizational function when managers have complete autonomy in their decisions to use each function's services or not.

The profit center concept can be seen as a higher level of evaluation, as depicted in Figure 3.2, which shows the progression of

Figure 3.2. Relationship of the Profit Center to the Evaluation Levels of the ROI Methodology

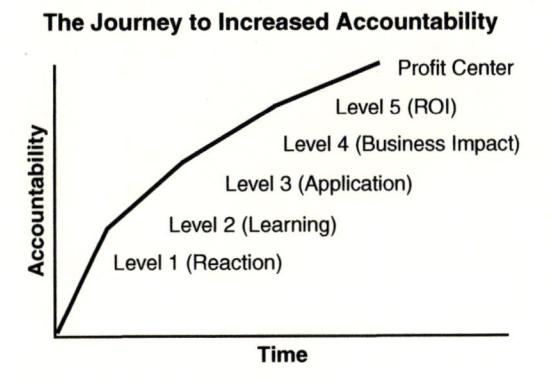

The Journey to Increased Accountability

Accountability vs. Time:
- Profit Center
- Level 5 (ROI)
- Level 4 (Business Impact)
- Level 3 (Application)
- Level 2 (Learning)
- Level 1 (Reaction)

evaluation levels, including the profit center. Level 1 has been used for many years and represents the most common and accepted evaluation data. Level 2 followed, as did Levels 3, 4, and 5. The profit center concept is a higher level of accountability, if it can be achieved. In essence, this level of measurement places a value on the entire function and can show its economic value added (EVA) to the organization. This concept is particularly important because of recent emphasis on economic value added (Young and O'Byrne, 2001). This concept can be applied to functions that generate revenue to offset expenses.

Figure 3.2 also underscores the fact that the previous levels of evaluation must be in place in order for the next level to work. If Level 4 and 5 evaluations have not become a routine part of the measurement scheme, running an effective profit center will be difficult. Some organizations that have failed in the move to the profit center arrangement relied on their success with Level 1 and 2 evaluations, skipping Levels 3, 4, and 5. Because participants reacted positively or developed skills, the program staff perceived that the programs were adding value. Operating managers, on the other hand, were unable to recognize this value, and were reluctant to purchase the programs, when given an option. They were not convinced of the added value because they had not seen any previous data that showed the impact of the programs in their operating departments.

The profit center and EVA are excellent concepts for evaluating the impact of an entire organizational function. Using these concepts is a goal of many executives and managers. In reality, there are many barriers to making the process operational. Not every program should be optional; some programs are necessary. In addition, some programs and initiatives need to be consistent, so their quality needs to be controlled in some way. Allowing managers to opt out of programs and purchase their own may cause them to develop a wide variety of programs that do not necessarily add value. Still, many managers have made the establishment of profit centers one of their goals.

Final Thoughts

This chapter has shown the different ways in which ROI can be calculated, as well as some of the basic interpretations of those calculations. It has also shown the relationships between the different methods of calculation. The ROI formula and the benefit-cost ratio are emphasized because these are the two principal ways in which Level 5 ROI is expressed. The next chapter covers some basic issues involved in ROI calculation.

References

Anthony, R., and Reece, J. *Accounting: Text and Cases.* (7th ed.) Homewood, Ill.: Irwin, 1983.

Bernthal, P., and Byham, B. "Evaluation of Techniques for an Empowered Workforce." In J. J. Phillips (ed.), *In Action: Measuring Return on Investment*, Vol. 2. Alexandria, Va.: American Society for Training and Development, 1997.

Cascio, W. *Costing Human Resources: The Financial Impact of Behavior in Organizations.* London: South-Western College Pub and Thomson Learning, 2000.

Horngren, C. *Cost Accounting.* (5th ed.) Englewood Cliffs, N.J.: Prentice-Hall, 1982.

Schmidt, F., Hunter, J., and Pearlman, K. "Assessing the Economic Impact of Personnel Programs on Workforce Productivity." *Personnel Psychology*, 1982, 35, 333–347.

Seagraves, T. "Mission Possible: Selling Complex Services over the Phone." In J. J. Phillips (ed.), *In Action: Measuring Return on Investment*, Vol. 3. Alexandria, Va.: American Society for Training and Development, 2001.

Young, S., and O'Byrne, S. *EVA® and Value-Based Management: A Practical Guide to Implementation.* New York: McGraw-Hill, 2001.

4

ROI Issues

This chapter describes some of the basic issues involved in the use of the ROI Methodology. Some of these issues have been covered in other books, but they are summarized and integrated here in a thorough discussion of the use of ROI, emphasizing its advantages and disadvantages and some of the concerns that arise at this level of accountability.

ROI Can Be Very Large

As the examples in this book have demonstrated, the actual ROI value can be quite large, far exceeding what might be expected from other types of investments in plants, equipment, and companies. Programs for leadership, team building, management development, supervisor training, and sales training can generate ROIs in the 100 percent to 700 percent range. This does not mean that all ROI studies result in a positive ROI; many ROIs are negative. However, the impact of programs can be quite impressive. It is helpful to remember what constitutes the ROI value. For example, the investment in a one-week program for a team leader could generate an impressive ROI. If the leader's behavior changes as he works directly with his team, a chain of impact might produce a measurable change in performance from the team. That behavior change, translated into a measurement improvement for the entire

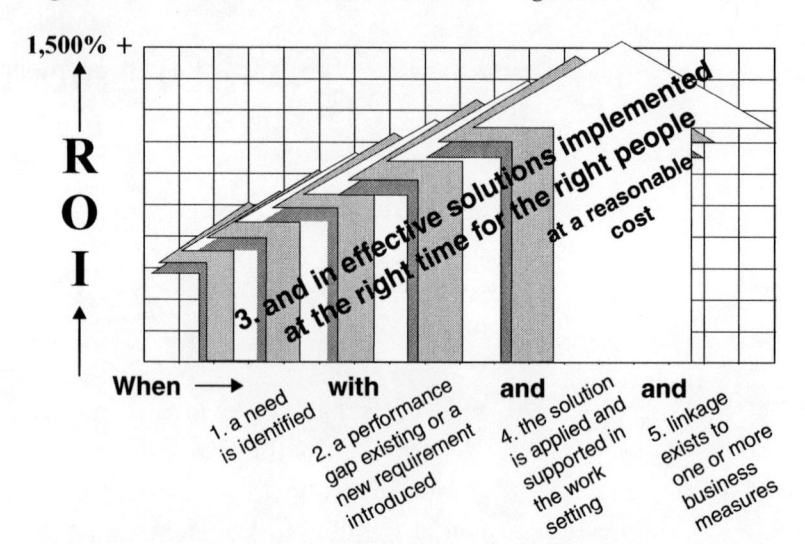

Figure 4.1. Factors That Contribute to High ROI Values

ROI (1,500% +)

When → 1. a need is identified — with 2. a performance gap existing or a new requirement introduced — 3. and in effective solutions implemented at the right time for the right people at a reasonable cost — and 4. the solution is applied and supported in the work setting — and 5. linkage exists to one or more business measures

year, might be quite significant. When the monetary value of the team's improvement is considered for an entire year and compared with the relatively small amount of investment in one team leader, it is easy to see why this number can be quite large.

More specifically, as Figure 4.1 shows, some important factors contribute to high ROI values. The impact can be large when a specific need has been identified and a performance gap exists; a new requirement is introduced and the solution is implemented at the right time for the right people at a reasonable cost; the solution is applied and supported in the work setting; and the solution is linked to one or more business measures. When these conditions are met, high ROI values can be achieved.

It is important to understand that a very high ROI can occur and not necessarily relate directly to the health of the rest of the organization. For example, a high-impact ROI can be generated in an organization that is losing money (or in bankruptcy) because the impact is restricted to the individuals involved in the program and the monetary value of their improvement is connected to that program. At the same time, a disastrous program can generate a very negative ROI in a company that is profitable. ROI evaluations are microlevel activities that evaluate the success of one program within a particular time frame.

What Happens When the ROI Is Negative?

Perhaps one of the greatest fears in using ROI is the possibility of having a negative ROI. This fear concerns not only the program sponsor or owner but also those who are involved in the design, development, and delivery of the program. Few individuals want to be involved in a process that exposes a failure. Those who are involved will naturally be concerned that failure may reflect unfavorably on them.

On the positive side, a negative ROI provides the best opportunity for learning (process improvement). The ROI Methodology reveals problems and barriers. As data are collected throughout the chain of impact, the reasons for failure become clear. Data on barriers and enablers to the transfer of skills captured at Level 3 (Application) usually reveal why the program did not work.

While a negative result from an ROI evaluation is the ultimate learning situation, no one wants to invite that opportunity to his or her door. The preference is to learn from others! Sometimes the damage created by a negative ROI is the sense of expectations that were not managed properly up front and fear of the consequences of the negative ROI. The following steps can help minimize or avoid this dilemma.

1. Raise questions about the feasibility of an impact study: Is it appropriate to use the ROI Methodology for this particular program? Sometimes, a program by its very nature may appear to be a failure, at least in terms of ROI.

2. Make sure that all interested parties have a clear understanding of the consequences of a negative ROI. This issue should be addressed early and often. The ROI Methodology is a process improvement tool, not a performance evaluation tool. No one

wants to be involved in a process that may reflect unfavorably on his or her performance. The individuals involved should not necessarily be penalized or have their performance evaluated unfavorably because of a negative ROI.

3. Look for warning signs early in the process; they are usually everywhere. Level 1 data often send strong signals that an evaluation may result in a negative ROI. Some signals of a potential negative ROI may be that the participants react negatively, do not see the relevance of the program to their jobs, perceive the content to be inappropriate, consider the information outdated, offer no intent to use the material, or refuse to recommend the program to anyone else.

4. Manage expectations. Lower expectations about the ROI are better. Anticipating a high ROI and communicating that prospect to the client or other stakeholders may create an expectation that might not materialize. Keep expectations low and the delivery performance high.

5. Use negative data to reposition the story. Rather than communicating that great results have been achieved with a very effective program, the story becomes, "We have some great information that tells us how to change the program to obtain better results." This story line is more than a nice turn of phrase; it underscores the importance of learning what went wrong and what can be done in the future to positively affect the ROI.

6. Use the information to drive change. Sometimes, the negative ROI can be transformed into a positive ROI with some minor alterations of the program. Implementation issues—for example, providing more support for the use of knowledge and skills in the workplace—may need to be addressed. In other situations, a complete redesign of the program may be necessary. In a few isolated cases, discontinuing the program may be the only option. Whatever the option, use the data to drive action so that the overall value of conducting the study has been realized.

These strategies can help minimize the unfavorable and sometimes disastrous perceptions that can result from a negative ROI.

ROI Is Not for Every Program

The ROI Methodology should not be applied to every program. It takes time and resources to create a valid and credible ROI study. Although this issue is addressed in other books in this series, underscoring the types of programs for which this technique is best suited is appropriate at this stage. ROI is appropriate for programs that

- Have a long life cycle; at some point in the life of the program, this level of accountability should be applied to the program.

- Are important to the organization in meeting its operational goals; these programs are designed to add value, and ROI may be helpful in showing that value.

- Are closely linked to the organization's strategic initiatives; anything this important needs a high level of accountability.

- Are expensive to implement; an expensive program that deploys large amounts of resources should be subjected to this level of accountability.

- Are highly visible and sometimes controversial; these programs often require this level of accountability in order to satisfy the critics.

- Have a large target audience; if a program is designed for all employees, it may be a candidate for ROI.

- Command the interest of the top executive group; if top executives are interested in knowing the impact, the ROI Methodology should be applied.

These are only guidelines and should be considered in the context of the organization in which they are being applied. Other criteria may also be appropriate. Criteria can be prioritized in a scheme to identify the programs most appropriate for this level of accountability.

It is also helpful to consider the type of programs for which the ROI Methodology is not appropriate. ROI is seldom appropriate for programs that

- Are very short in duration, such as two-hour briefings; changing behavior in such a short time frame is difficult.

- Are legislated or required by regulation; changing anything as a result of an evaluation might be difficult if the program is obligatory, legally mandated, or regulated.

- Are required by senior management; it may be that these programs will continue regardless of the findings.

- Serve as operator training and technical skills development; it may be more appropriate to measure at Levels 1, 2, and 3 to ensure that participants know how to do the job and are doing it properly.

These guidelines do not imply that the ROI Methodology cannot be implemented for these types of programs. However, careful use of limited resources and time for measurement and evaluation will result in evaluating more strategic programs. It is also helpful to think about what kind of programs are appropriate for an organization's first one or two ROI studies. Initially, the use of this process will be met with some anxiety and tentativeness. The programs initially evaluated should not only meet the requirements listed earlier but should also meet other requirements. These programs should

- Be as simple as possible; reserve the complex programs for later.
- Be a known commodity, with the perception of positive results; this will help to ensure that the first study does not have a negative result.
- Be free of hidden agendas and political sensitivity; the first study should not be caught up in the organization's politics.

Deciding the level at which to allocate resources to the process of ROI evaluation, which programs to evaluate for ROI, and the number of programs to pursue in any given time frame are important issues.

Concerns About ROI

Following are some cautions to observe when you are evaluating ROI, as well as a discussion of myths that practitioners may struggle with as they begin to assess ROI in their programs.

Cautions

Caution is needed when developing, calculating, and communicating ROI. The implementation of the ROI Methodology is a very important issue and a goal of many managers and professionals. In addition to the guiding principles, a few issues should be addressed to keep the process from going astray. The following cautions are offered to aid you in evaluating ROI.

Take a Conservative Approach When Developing Benefits and Costs

Conservatism in an ROI evaluation builds accuracy and credibility. What matters most is how the target audience perceives the value of the data. A conservative approach is always recommended for both the numerator of the ROI formula (benefits) and the denominator (program costs). A conservative approach is the basis for the Guiding Principles that are described throughout this series.

Make Sure That ROI of Programs Is Not Confused with Other Financial Measures of Return

The return on funds invested or assets employed can be calculated in many ways. ROI is just one of them. Although the calculation for the ROI of programs and projects uses the same basic formula as the formula used for the ROI for capital investment evaluations, it may not be fully understood by the target audience. Its calculation method and its meaning should be clearly communicated. More important, it should be accepted by management as an appropriate measure for program evaluation.

Involve Management in Calculating ROI

Management ultimately decides whether an ROI value is acceptable. To the extent possible, management should be involved in setting the parameters for calculations and establishing the targets for determining whether programs are acceptable within the organization.

Fully Disclose Assumptions and Methodology

When you are discussing the ROI Methodology and communicating data, fully disclosing the process, steps, and assumptions used in the process is very important. Strengths should be clearly communicated as well as weaknesses and shortcomings.

Approach Sensitive and Controversial Issues with Caution

Occasionally, sensitive and controversial issues will be raised during a discussion of an ROI value. It is best to avoid debates over what is measurable and what is not measurable unless clear evidence on the issue in question is available. Also, some programs are so fundamental to the survival of an organization that measuring them is unnecessary. For example, a program designed to improve customer service in a customer-focused company may escape the scrutiny of an ROI evaluation based on the assumption that if the program is well designed, it will improve customer service.

Teach Others the Methods for Calculating ROI

Each time an ROI is calculated, there is an opportunity to educate other managers and colleagues within the organization. Even if they are not responsible for the program, these individuals will be able to see the value of this approach to program evaluation. Also, when possible, each project should serve as a case study in order to educate the staff on specific techniques and methods.

Recognize That Not Everyone Will Buy into ROI

Not every audience member will understand, appreciate, or accept the ROI calculation. For a variety of reasons, one or more individuals may not agree with the values. These individuals may be highly emotional about the concept of showing accountability for specific types of programs. Attempts to persuade them may be beyond the scope of the task at hand. This may be a long-term program, and you may need to use some of the techniques presented in *Communication and Implementation*, book six of this series, to persuade these members of your audience.

Do Not Boast About a High Return

It is not unusual for a high-impact program to generate a high ROI. Several examples in this book have illustrated such possibilities.

An evaluator who boasts about a high rate of return will be open to criticism from others unless the calculation is based on indisputable facts.

Choose the Place for Debates

The time to debate the ROI Methodology is not during a presentation (unless it can't be avoided). Choose appropriate situations in which to constructively debate the ROI Methodology: in a special forum, among staff, in an educational session, in professional literature, on panel discussions, or even during the development of an ROI impact study. The time and place for debate should be carefully selected so as not to detract from the quality and quantity of information presented.

Use ROI to Evaluate Selected Programs

As we discussed earlier, some programs are difficult to quantify and for those, an ROI calculation may not be feasible. Other methods of presenting the benefits may be more appropriate. Targets should be set for the percentage of programs in which ROI will be assessed. Also, specific criteria should be established in order to select programs for ROI analysis.

ROI Myths

Although most practitioners recognize the ROI Methodology as an important addition to measurement and evaluation, they often struggle with how to address the issue. Many professionals see the ROI Methodology as a ticket to increased funding and prosperity for programs. They believe that without it, they may be lost in the shuffle, and with it, they may gain the respect they need to continue moving their department or function forward. Regardless of their motivation for pursuing ROI evaluation, the key questions are "Is it a feasible process that can be implemented with reasonable resources?" and "Will it provide the benefits necessary to make it a useful, sustainable tool?" The answer to these questions may lead to debate and even controversy.

The controversy surrounding the ROI Methodology stems from misunderstandings about what it can and cannot do and how it can or should be implemented within an organization. To conclude this chapter, these misunderstandings are summarized as myths about the ROI Methodology. The myths are based on years of experience with ROI evaluation and the perceptions observed during hundreds of studies and workshops conducted by the ROI Institute. Along with each myth, we present an appropriate explanation.

ROI Is Too Complex for Most Users

This myth is a problem because of a few highly complex ROI models that have been publicly presented. Unfortunately, these models have done little to help users and have caused confusion about ROI. The ROI Methodology is a basic financial formula for accountability that is simple and understandable: earnings are divided by investment; earnings are the net benefits from a program, and the investment equals the total cost of the program. Straying from this basic formula can add confusion and create tremendous misunderstanding. The ROI model provides a step-by-step, systematic process. Each step is taken separately, and issues are addressed for that particular step; the decisions are made incrementally throughout the process. This method helps reduce a complex process to simple, manageable efforts.

ROI Is Expensive, Consuming Too Many Critical Resources

The ROI Methodology can become expensive if it is not carefully organized, controlled, and implemented. While the cost of an external ROI evaluation can be significant, many actions can be taken to keep costs down. Ways to save costs when evaluating ROI are presented in *Communication and Implementation*, book six of this series.

If Senior Management Does Not Require ROI, There Is No Need to Pursue It

This myth affects the most innocent bystanders. It is easy to be lulled into providing measurement and evaluation that simply preserves the status quo, believing that no pressure or request for ROI means no requirement. The truth is that if senior executives have seen only Level 1 reaction data, they may not be asking for higher-level data because they think that those types of data are not available. In some cases, leaders have convinced top management that their programs cannot be evaluated at the ROI level or that the specific impact of some types of programs cannot be determined. Given these conditions, it comes as no surprise that some top managers are not asking for ROI data.

There is another problem with the laid-back approach. Paradigms are shifting. Senior managers are beginning to request this level of data more and more often. Changes in corporate leadership sometimes initiate important paradigm shifts. New leaders often require higher levels of accountability for current and future programs. The process of integrating the ROI Methodology into an organization takes time—about twelve to eighteen months in many organizations; it is not a quick fix. However, when senior executives suddenly ask for ROI measurement, they may expect results to be produced quickly. Because this type of sudden request could occur at any time, proactive leaders will initiate implementation of the ROI Methodology and begin to develop ROI evaluations long before senior management asks for ROI data.

ROI Is a Passing Fad

Unfortunately, many of the processes being introduced in organizations today are indeed fads. However, the need to account for expenditures will always be present, and the ROI Methodology provides the ultimate level of accountability. ROI has been used for years to measure the investment of equipment and new manufacturing plants. Now, it is being used in many other areas, for all types of programs and projects. Drawing on its rich history, evaluators will continue to use ROI as an important tool in measurement and evaluation, extending it into other applications.

ROI Is Only One Type of Data

This is a common misunderstanding. The ROI calculation represents one type of data that shows the benefits versus the costs of a program. However, when the complete five-level evaluation framework is used, six types of data are generated, representing both qualitative and quantitative data and, often, data from different sources, making the ROI Methodology a rich source for a variety of data.

ROI Is Not Future-Oriented; It Reflects Only Past Performance

Unfortunately, many evaluation processes are past-oriented and reflect only what has already happened in a program; this is the only way to accurately assess impact. However, the ROI Methodology can easily be adapted to forecast ROI, as the next chapter describes.

ROI Is Rarely Used by Organizations

This myth is easily dispelled when the evidence is fully examined. More than 3,000 organizations use the ROI Methodology, and more than two hundred case studies on the ROI Methodology have been published. Leading organizations throughout the world, including businesses of all sizes and sectors, use the ROI Methodology to increase accountability and improve programs. This process is also being used in the nonprofit, educational, and government sectors. There is no doubt that it is a widely used process that is growing in use.

The ROI Methodology Cannot Be Easily Replicated

This is an understandable concern. In theory, any process worthy of implementation is one that can be replicated from one study to another. For example, if two different people conducted an ROI evaluation on the same program, would they obtain the same results? Fortunately, the ROI Methodology is a systematic process with standards and guiding principles; the likelihood of two evaluators obtaining the same results is high. And because it is a process that involves step-by-step procedures, the ROI Methodology can also be replicated from one program to another.

The ROI Methodology Is Not a Credible Process; It Is Too Subjective

This myth has evolved because some ROI studies involving estimates have been promoted in the literature and at conferences. Many ROI studies have been conducted without the use of estimates. Estimates are often used when evaluators are attempting to isolate the effects of a program. Using estimates from the participants is only one of several techniques that can be used to isolate the effects of a program. Other techniques involve analytical approaches such as the use of control groups and trend line analysis. Sometimes, estimating is used in other steps of the ROI process, such as converting data to monetary values or estimating output in the data collection phase. In each of these situations, other options are often available, but for reasons of convenience or economics, estimation is often used. While the use of estimates often represents the least ideal scenario in the ROI Methodology, estimates can be extremely reliable when they are obtained carefully, adjusted for error, and reported appropriately. Practitioners in the fields of accounting, engineering, and technology routinely use estimates, often without question or concern.

ROI Cannot Be Evaluated for Soft-Skill Programs; It Is Only for Production and Sales

ROI measurement is often most effective in soft-skill programs, such as those in leadership development, culture, customer satisfaction, and employee engagement. Programs in soft skills such as learning often drive hard data items such as output, quality, cost, or time. Case after case shows successful application of the ROI Methodology in programs on such topics as team building, executive development, communications, and empowerment. Additional examples of successful ROI applications can be found in compliance programs in areas such as diversity, prevention of sexual harassment, and policy implementation.

Any type of program or process can be evaluated at the ROI level. Problems may surface when ROI is calculated for programs that should not be evaluated at this level. The ROI Methodology should be reserved for programs that are expensive, that address operational problems or issues related to strategic objectives, or that attract the interest of management because increased accountability is desired.

ROI Is Only for Manufacturing and Service Organizations

Although initial studies on ROI appeared in the manufacturing sector, the service sector quickly picked up the ROI process as a useful tool. After that, use of the ROI Methodology migrated to the nonprofit sector, and organizations such as hospitals and health care firms began endorsing and using the process. Next, ROI evaluation moved through the government sector around the world, and now, educational institutions are beginning to use the ROI Methodology. Several educational institutions use ROI evaluation to measure the impact of their formal degree programs and less-structured continuing education programs and community outreach programs.

It Is Not Always Possible to Isolate the Effects of a Program

Distinguishing the effects of a program from the effects of factors outside the program is always achievable when using the ROI Methodology. There are many ways to isolate the influence of a program, and at least one method will work in any given situation.

The challenge is selecting an appropriate isolation method for the resources and accuracy needed in a particular situation. This myth probably stems from unsuccessful attempts at using a control group arrangement—a classic way to isolate the effect of a process, program, or initiative. In practice, a control group approach does not work in a majority of situations, causing some researchers to abandon the issue of isolating program effects. In reality, many other techniques provide accurate, reliable, and valid methods for isolating the effects of a program.

Measurement of On-the-Job Activities Is Impossible Because Post-Program Control of Participants Is Impossible

This myth is fading as organizations face the reality of implementing workplace solutions to key problems and realize the importance of measuring on-the-job results. Although the program staff does not have direct control of what happens in the workplace, it can influence the process. A new program must be considered within the context of the workplace; the program is owned by the organization, even though individuals and groups involved in the program may have objectives that extend beyond work. Thus, program objectives focus on application and business impact data used in the ROI analysis. Ideally, partnership between key managers produces the objectives that drive the program. In effect, a program or project is a process with partnerships and a common framework to drive business results—not just classroom activity.

ROI Is Appropriate Only for Large Organizations

While it is true that large organizations with enormous budgets have the most interest in ROI, smaller organizations can also use the process, particularly when it is simplified and built into their programs. Organizations with as few as fifty employees have successfully applied the ROI Methodology, using it as a tool for increasing accountability and employee involvement.

The ROI Methodology Has No Standards

An important problem facing measurement and evaluation is a lack of standardization or consistency. Frequently asked questions include "What is a good ROI?" "What should be included in the cost so that I can compare my data with other data?" and "When should specific data be included in the ROI value instead of being left as an intangible benefit?" While these questions are not easily answered, some help is on the way. Standards for the ROI Methodology—the Guiding Principles—have been developed, and more details are also being developed. Also under development is a database that will share thousands of studies so that best practices, patterns, trends, and standards are readily available. For more information on these issues, visit www.roiinstitute.net.

Final Thoughts

The ROI Methodology is not for every organization, individual, or program. Use of the ROI Methodology represents a tremendous paradigm shift as organizations attempt to bring more accountability and results to a variety of programs and processes. The ROI Methodology brings a results-based approach and is client-focused, requiring much contact, communication, dialogue, and agreement with the client group. Key issues must be addressed in ROI calculations, and those issues are explored in this chapter. Cautions and myths about the ROI process are also discussed. The next chapter explains how to use the ROI Methodology to forecast a program's ROI.

5

ROI Forecasting

Sometimes, confusion arises about when evaluating ROI is appropriate. The traditional approach, described in this series, is to base ROI calculations strictly on business impact data obtained after the program has been implemented. In this approach, business performance measures (Level 4 data) are easily converted to a monetary value, which is necessary for an ROI calculation. This chapter shows that ROI calculations are possible in a variety of time frames, using a variety of data. Pre-program ROI forecasts are possible, as well as forecasts with reaction data (Level 1), learning data (Level 2), and application data (Level 3).

The Trade-Offs of Forecasting

ROI can be developed at different times, using different levels of data. Unfortunately, however, the ease, convenience, and low cost of capturing a forecasted ROI create trade-offs in accuracy and credibility. As Figure 5.1 illustrates, ROI can be evaluated at five distinct time intervals during the life cycle of a program. The relationships between credibility, accuracy, cost, and difficulty are also shown in the figure.

Here are descriptions of the five time intervals:

1. A pre-program forecast can be developed, using estimates of the impact of the program. This approach lacks credibility and

Figure 5.1. ROI Forecasts at Different Times and Levels

ROI with:	Data Collection Timing	Credibility	Accuracy	Cost to Develop	Difficulty
1. Pre-program data	Before program	Not very credible	Not very accurate	Inexpensive	Not difficult
2. Reaction and planned action data	During program	↓	↓	↓	↓
3. Learning data	During program				
4. Application and implementation data	After program				
5. Business impact data	After program	Very credible	Very accurate	Expensive	Very difficult

accuracy, but it is also the least expensive and least difficult ROI to calculate. There is value in developing the ROI on a pre-program basis. This will be discussed in the next section.

2. Reaction data can be extended in order to anticipate the impact of a program, including the ROI. In this case, participants anticipate the chain of impact as a program is applied and implemented and then influences specific business measures. While the accuracy and credibility are usually greater than those of the pre-program forecast, this approach still lacks the credibility and accuracy desired in most situations.

3. For some programs, learning data can be used to forecast the actual ROI. This approach is applicable only when formal testing shows a relationship between acquiring certain skills or knowledge and subsequent business performance. When this correlation is available (it is usually developed to validate the test that documents learning), test data can be used to forecast subsequent performance. The performance can then be converted to monetary impact, and the ROI can be developed. This technique has limited potential as an evaluation tool because only a few predictive validation studies have been developed.

4. In some situations, when actual use of skills is critical, the application and implementation of those skills or knowledge can be converted to a value, using employee compensation as a basis. This is particularly helpful in situations in which competencies are being developed and values are placed on improving competencies, even if there is no immediate increase in pay.

5. Finally, the ROI can be developed from business impact data converted directly to monetary values and compared with the costs of the program. This post-program evaluation is the basis for the other ROI calculations in this book and has been the principal approach used in previous chapters. It is the preferred approach, but because of the pressures outlined earlier, it is critical to examine ROI calculations in other time frames.

This chapter will discuss pre-program evaluation and the ROI calculations based on reactions in detail. ROI calculations developed from learning and application data will be discussed more briefly. Examples will illustrate the process.

Pre-Program ROI Forecasting

Perhaps one of the most useful steps in convincing a sponsor that an expense is appropriate is to forecast the ROI for the program. The process is similar to post-program analysis, except that the extent of the impact must be estimated along with the forecasted cost.

Basic Model

Figure 5.2 shows the basic model for capturing the data necessary for a pre-program forecast; this model is a modified version of the post-program ROI process model presented in *ROI Fundamentals*, the first book in this series. In the pre-program forecast, the program outcomes are estimated before program implementation rather than collected after program implementation. Data collection is kept simple, relying on interviews, focus groups, or surveys of experts. Tapping into benchmarking studies or locating previous studies may also be helpful.

Beginning at the reaction level, anticipated or estimated reactions are captured. Next, the anticipated learning is developed, followed by the anticipated application and implementation data. Here, the estimates focus on what must be accomplished in order for the program to be successful. These items may be based on the objectives at each of these levels. Finally, the impact data are estimated by experts. These experts may include subject matter experts, the program supplier, or potential participants in the program. In this model, the levels build on each other. Estimating data at Levels 1, 2, and 3 enhances the quality of the estimated data at Level 4 (impact), which is needed for the analysis.

Figure 5.2. Pre-Program Forecasting Model

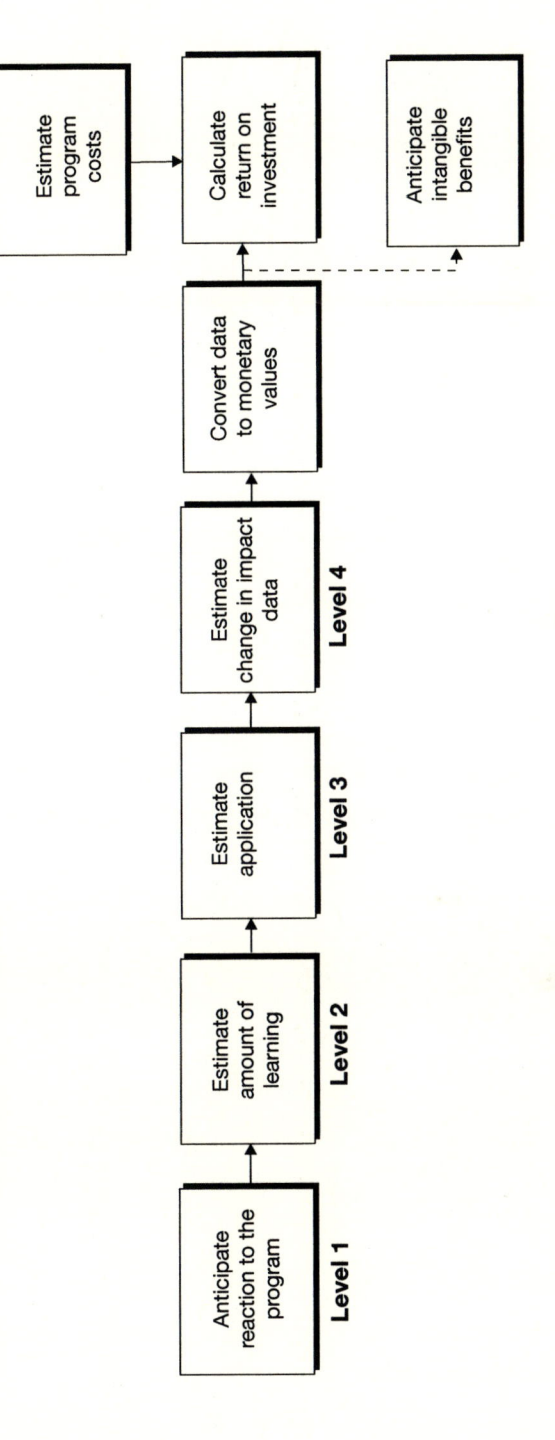

```
[Anticipate reaction    [Estimate amount    [Estimate            [Estimate change    [Convert data to
 to the program]   →     of learning]   →    application]   →    in impact data]  →  monetary values]
  Level 1                 Level 2             Level 3             Level 4                   │
                                                                                            ↓
                                                    [Estimate program costs] → [Calculate return on investment]
                                                                                            ⇡ (dashed)
                                                                               [Anticipate intangible benefits]
```

The model shows that there is no need to isolate the effects of a program as in the post-program model. The individual providing the data is asked the following question: "How much will the business impact measure change as a result of the program?" This question ties the change in the measure directly to the program; thus, isolation is not needed. This approach makes the pre-program process of estimating ROI easier than the post-program ROI process, in which isolating program impact is always required.

Converting data to a monetary value is straightforward; a limited number of techniques are available for data conversion. Locating a standard value or finding an expert to make the estimate is a logical choice. Analyzing records and searching databases are less likely alternatives at the forecasting stage. Securing estimates from stakeholders is the technique of last resort.

Estimating the program's costs should be an easy step; costs can easily be anticipated on the basis of previous or similar programs, factoring in reasonable assumptions about the program. To achieve a fully loaded cost profile, include all cost categories.

The anticipated intangibles are merely speculation in forecasting but can be reliable indicators of which measures may be influenced in addition to those included in the ROI calculation. At this point, it is assumed that these measures will not be converted to monetary values.

The formula used to calculate the ROI is the same as that used in post-program analysis. The monetary value from the data conversion, minus the estimated program cost, is included as the numerator, and the estimated cost of the program is inserted as the denominator. The projected benefit-cost analysis can be developed along with the ROI.

Steps for Forecasting ROI

Eighteen detailed steps are necessary to develop a credible pre-program ROI forecast, using expert input:

1. *Understand the situation.* Individuals providing input to the forecast and conducting the forecast must understand the present situation very well. Naturally, knowledge of the situation is a major requirement to consider when selecting experts.

2. *Predict the present.* A program is sometimes initiated because a particular business impact measure is not doing well. However, such measures often lag the present situation; they may be based on data that are several months old, especially if they are based on dynamic influences that can change dramatically and quickly. It may be beneficial to estimate the current value of the measure, based on assumptions and current trends. Market share data, for example, are often several months old. Trending market share data and examining other influences driving market share can help organizations understand the current situation. Although this appears to be a lot of work, it is not a new responsibility for most of the experts, who are often concerned about the present situation.

3. *Observe warnings.* Closely tied to predicting the present is making sure that warning signs are observed. Red flags signal that something is going against the measure in question, causing it to go in an undesired direction or otherwise not move as it should. These warning signs often raise concerns that lead to programs; they are early warnings that things may get worse. Consequently, it is important that they be factored into the situation as forecasts are made.

4. *Describe the new process, project, program, or solution.* The program must be completely and clearly described to the experts so that they fully understand the mechanics of what is to be implemented. The description should include the scope of the program, the individuals involved, time factors, and whatever else is necessary to express the magnitude of the program.

5. *Develop specific objectives.* These objectives should mirror the levels of evaluation and should include reaction objectives,

learning objectives, application objectives, and impact objectives. Although these may be difficult to develop, they are developed as part of the up-front analysis described in *ROI Fundamentals*, book one of this series. Objectives provide clear direction toward the program's end. The cascading levels of evaluation represent the anticipated chain of impact that will occur as the program is implemented.

6. *Estimate what participants will think about the program.* In this step, the experts try to understand participants' reactions. Will participants support the program? How will they support it? What may cause participants to become unsupportive? The response is important because a negative reaction can cause a program to fail.

7. *Estimate what participants will learn.* To some extent, every program will involve learning, and the experts must estimate what learning will occur. Using the learning objectives, the experts define what the participants will learn, identifying specific knowledge, skills, and information the participants must acquire or enhance during the program.

8. *Anticipate what participants should accomplish in the program.* Building on the application objectives, the experts identify what will be accomplished as the program is implemented successfully. This step details specific actions, tasks, and processes that will be taken by the participants. Steps 6, 7, and 8 provide important information on participants' anticipated reactions, learning, and application of learning that serves as the basis for the next step: estimating improvement in business impact data.

9. *Estimate the improvement in business impact data.* This is a critical step in that the data generated are needed for the financial forecast. The experts provide an estimate—in either absolute numbers or percentages—of the monetary change in the business impact measure (ΔP). While accuracy is important, it is also important to remember that a forecast is no more than an

estimate based on the best data available at a given time; this is why the next step is included.

10. *Apply the confidence estimate.* Because the estimate given in the previous step is not very accurate, an error adjustment is needed. Therefore, a confidence estimate is placed on the value identified in step 9. The experts are asked to indicate the confidence they have in the data they have provided. The confidence level is expressed as a percentage; 0 indicates "no confidence," and 100 indicates "certainty." The confidence level becomes a discount factor in the analysis.

11. *Convert the business impact data to monetary values.* Using one or more of the methods described in *Data Conversion*, book four in this series, the data are converted to monetary values. One value in particular, designated by the letter V, is calculated. If the impact measure represents a desired improvement—for example, in productivity—V represents the monetary gain obtained by attaining one more unit of the measure. If the impact measure is one that the organization is trying to reduce—for example, downtime, mistakes, or complaints—V is the cost that the organization incurs as a result of one incident. For example, the cost of one instance of voluntary employee turnover may be 1.5 times the employee's annual pay.

12. *Calculate the estimated annual impact of each measure.* The estimated annual impact is the predicted improvement directly related to the program in the year after implementation. In formula form, this value is expressed as follows:

$$\Delta I = (\Delta P \times V) \times 12$$

where

ΔI = annual change in monetary value
ΔP = annual change in performance on the impact measure
V = the value of one unit of improvement in the impact measure

If the measure is weekly or monthly, it must be converted to an annual amount. For example, if three lost-time accidents will be prevented each month, the three is multiplied by twelve; the number of accidents that will be prevented annually total thirty-six. If it were three per week and employees worked forty-eight weeks during a year, the value of change in performance would be multiplied by forty-eight for a total of 144 lost-time accidents prevented.

13. *Factor additional years into the analysis for programs that will have a significant useful life beyond the first year.* For these programs, the factor should reflect a diminished benefit in subsequent years. The client or sponsor of the program should provide some indication of the amount of the reduction and the values of performance measures that are desired in the second, third, and successive years. It is important to be conservative by using the smallest numbers possible.

14. *Estimate the fully loaded program cost.* Use all the cost categories described in this book, and denote the value with the letter C when including it in the ROI equation. Include all direct and indirect costs in the calculation.

15. *Calculate the forecast ROI.* Use the total projected benefits and the estimated costs in the standard ROI formula. Calculate the forecast ROI as follows:

$$\text{ROI }(\%) = \frac{\Delta I - C}{C} \times 100$$

16. *Use sensitivity analysis to develop several potential ROI values with different levels of improvement* (ΔP). When more than one measure is changing, the analysis may take the form of a spreadsheet that shows various output scenarios and the subsequent ROI forecasts. Identify the break-even point.

17. *Identify potential intangible benefits.* Anticipate intangible benefits, using input from those most knowledgeable about the situation. Their assumptions will be based on their experience

with similar programs. Remember, intangible benefits are benefits that are not converted to monetary values but that possess value nonetheless.

18. *Communicate the ROI projection and anticipated intangibles with caution.* The target audience must clearly understand that the forecast is based on several assumptions (which should be clearly defined) and that although the values are the best possible estimates, they may include a degree of error.

Following these steps will enable an individual to forecast ROI.

Sources of Expert Input

Several sources of expert input are available for estimating improvement in impact data when a program is implemented. Ideally, experience with similar programs in the organization will inform the estimates made by experts. Experts may include

- Clients or sponsors
- Members of a project team
- Prospective participants
- Subject matter experts
- External experts
- Advocates (individuals who can champion the program)
- Finance and accounting staff
- Analysts (if involved with the program)
- Executives or managers
- Customers

These sources provide an array of possibilities for assistance in estimating the value of an improvement. Because error is part of the process, ask for a confidence measure when using estimates from any source.

With the experts clearly identified, three major steps must be addressed before developing the ROI: input must be gathered from the experts, the data must be converted to monetary values, and costs must be estimated.

Securing Input

First, data must be collected from the individuals whom you have recruited as experts. If the number of individuals is small (for example, if one person from each of the appropriate expert groups is involved), a short interview with each expert may suffice. During interviews, it is critical to avoid bias and to ask clear, succinct questions that are not leading. Questions should be framed in a balanced way in order to capture what may not occur as well as what may occur. If groups are involved, using focus groups may be suitable. For large numbers of people, surveys or questionnaires may be appropriate.

When the groups are diverse and scattered, the Delphi technique may be appropriate. This technique, originally developed by the Rand Corporation in the 1950s, has been used in forecasting and decision making in a variety of disciplines. The Delphi technique was originally devised to help experts achieve better forecasts than they might obtain through traditional group meetings by allowing individuals access to the group without in-person contact. The essential features of a Delphi procedure are anonymity, continual iteration, controlled feedback to participants, and a physical summary of responses. Anonymity is achieved by means of a questionnaire that allows group members to express their opinions and judgments privately. Between all iterations of the questionnaire, the facilitator informs the participants of the opinions of their anonymous colleagues. Typically, this feedback is presented as a simple statistical summary, using mean or median values. The facilitator takes the statistical average in the final round to be the group's judgment (Armstrong, 2001).

In some cases, benchmarking data may be available and can be considered as a source of input for the process of estimating ROI. Previous studies may provide essential input to the process as well. Perhaps an extensive search of databases, using a variety of search engines, will provide useful information that will help in making predictions. The important point is to understand, as much as possible, what may occur as a result of the program.

Conversion to Money

The measures forecast by the experts must be converted to monetary values for one, two, three, or more years, depending on the nature and scope of the program. Standard values are likely to be available for many of these measures. Considering their importance, someone has probably placed monetary values on them. If not, experts are often available to convert the data to monetary values. Otherwise, existing records or databases may be appropriate sources of conversion factors. Another option is to ask stakeholders—perhaps some of the experts listed earlier—to provide the monetary values for the forecast. This step is the only means of showing the money that will be made from the program. *Data Conversion*, book four in this series, covers these techniques in detail.

Estimating Program Costs

Program cost estimates should be based on the most reliable information available and should include the typical categories outlined earlier in this book. The estimates can be based on costs of previous programs. Although the costs are unknown, this task is often relatively easy because of its similarity to budgeting, a process with routine procedures and policies that most practitioners are familiar with. Dividing costs into categories representing the functional processes of the program provides additional insight into program costs. Areas often not given enough attention include analysis, assessment, evaluation, and reporting. If these elements are not properly addressed, much of the value of the program may be missed.

Once the costs and monetary benefits have been estimated, the ROI forecast can be made, using the calculations presented earlier.

Case Study: Retail Merchandise Company—Part A: Pre-Program ROI Forecasting

Considering a case study in which different forecasting issues are explored is instructive. Throughout the rest of this chapter, parts of this case study that are relevant to various sections will be explored.

Situation

Retail Merchandise Company (RMC) is a national chain of 420 stores, located in most major U.S. markets. RMC sells small household items, gifts of all types, electronics, and jewelry, as well as personal accessories. It does not sell clothes or major appliances. RMC executives had been concerned about slow sales growth and were experimenting with several programs designed to boost sales. One concern focused on interaction with customers. Sales associates were not actively involved in the sales process; they usually waited for a customer to make a purchasing decision and then processed the sale. Several store managers had analyzed the situation to determine whether more communication with customers would boost sales. The analysis revealed that the use of very simple techniques to probe for a customer's needs and then guide him or her to a purchase should boost sales in each store.

The senior executives asked the training and development staff to consider implementing a very simple program to teach customer interaction skills to a small group of sales associates. The management team asked the staff to forecast the impact and ROI of the proposed program. If the program's forecast showed an increase in sales and represented a significant payoff for RMC, it would be pilot-tested in a small number of stores.

Proposed Solution

The training and development staff conducted a brief initial needs assessment and identified five simple skills that would need to be covered in the program. Their analysis revealed that the sales associates did not have these skills or were very uncomfortable with using them. The staff selected a program called Interactive Selling Skills that included a significant amount of skill practice. The first part of the program would consist of two days of training, during which the participants would have an opportunity to practice each of the skills with a classmate. After three weeks of on-the-job application of their new skills, the participants would have a final day of training that included a discussion of problems, issues, barriers, and concerns about using the skills. The program, an existing product from an external training supplier, would be taught by the staff of the training supplier for a predetermined facilitation fee. A pre-program forecast was a consideration.

The training and development manager contacted the experts listed in Table 5.1, who provided estimates of the sales increase that would be attributed to the proposed program in three months. Each expert was provided with a description of the program, the skills that would be taught, and the need that it would fill. Each estimate was a best guess based on the person's experience and perspective. Table 5.1 shows their estimates and the calculated ROI for each estimate.

Certain experts have more credibility than others, depending on the target audience perspective. The sales associates don't have a clear understanding of the program. They see no value in the program because they see it as nothing but additional work for them. They may be concerned that customers do not want this additional help and they may also be concerned that this program will mean extra work for them in the future. The vendor sees the most value in the program, but then again, it is the vendor's program. The finance staff is conservative, and the marketing analyst is conservative as well.

Table 5.1. Sales Increase Estimates

Source of Expert Input	Estimated Improvement (Δ)	ROI Forecast
Sales associates	0%	−100%
Department managers	5	−30
Store managers	10	33
Senior executive (sponsor)	15	110
Analyst (needs assessment)	12	95
Vendor (program supplier)	25	350
Marketing analyst	4	−40
Finance staff	2	−80
Benchmarking data	9	22

While the estimates provide the best guess, in collecting these data it is important to also understand the basis on which these individuals arrived at their conclusions. Asking them specifically how they arrived at their estimates would be helpful in assessing their credibility. By adjusting for their confidence in the estimates, a more conservative (and credible) forecast can be developed. In addition, perhaps a credibility ranking for each individual's input from the individual or group who collected the data would be helpful.

Presenting pre-program forecast data to senior mangers presents some challenges due to the variance between estimates. Also pre-program forecasts are often much more generous than the actual ROI of a program. A pre-program forecast should be presented as a matrix, much the way it is shown in Table 5.1.

The break-even point should be calculated to show the management team how much sales need to increase to achieve a break-even scenario.

The person presenting the data (program manager or coordinator) is not included on the list of experts. Although this person might know the potential impact of this program, his or her credibility and potential bias are issues. Also, if the presenter has a recommendation, that will be the number that the group remembers.

ROI Forecast with a Pilot Program

Although the steps presented earlier in this chapter provide a process for estimating the ROI when a pilot program is not conducted, the more favorable approach is to develop a small-scale pilot program and calculate the ROI based on post-program data. This scenario involves the following steps:

1. As in the previous process, develop Level 1, 2, 3, and 4 objectives.
2. Initiate a simple pilot program, without bells and whistles, on a small sample. This strategy keeps the cost extremely low without sacrificing the fundamentals of the program.
3. Fully implement the program with one or more of the typical groups of individuals who can benefit from it. This will require that participants engage in any information sessions as well as apply the information acquired from those sessions.
4. Calculate the ROI, using the ROI model for post-program analysis (the ROI Methodology that is discussed throughout this series).
5. Finally, decide whether to implement the program throughout the organization, given the results of the pilot program.

Post-program evaluation of a pilot program provides much more accurate information on which to base decisions about full implementation of the program. In a pilot program, data can be developed on all six types of measures outlined in this series.

ROI Forecast with Reaction Data

When reaction data include planned applications of the program, these important data can ultimately be used to forecast ROI. By asking how participants plan to use the program and the results that they expect to achieve, more valuable evaluation information

Exhibit 5.1. Important Questions to Ask on Feedback Questionnaires

Planned Improvements

As a result of this program, what specific actions will you attempt as you apply what you have learned?

_____
_____
_____

Please indicate what specific measures, outcomes, or projects will change as a result of your actions.

_____
_____
_____

As a result of the anticipated changes in the measures listed above, please estimate (in monetary values) the benefits to your organization over a period of one year._____

What is the basis of this estimate?

_____
_____
_____

What confidence, expressed as a percentage, can you put in your estimate? (0% = No Confidence; 100% = Certainty)
_____%

---

can be collected. The questions presented in Exhibit 5.1 illustrate how data are collected with an end-of-program questionnaire. Participants are asked to state specifically how they plan to use the program material and the results that they expect to achieve. They are asked to convert their accomplishments to an annual monetary value and show the basis for the estimate. Participants can moderate their responses with a confidence estimate, which makes the data more credible and allows participants to reflect their uncertainty about the process.

When data are tabulated, the confidence level is multiplied by the annual monetary value, which yields a conservative estimate for use in the data analysis. For example, if a participant estimated that the monetary impact of a program will be $10,000 but is only 50 percent confident, a value of $5,000 is used in the calculations.

To develop a summary of the expected benefits, several steps are taken. First, any data that are incomplete, unusable, extreme, or unrealistic are discarded. This practice follows Guiding Principle 8: "Avoid use of extreme items and unsupported claims when calculating ROI."

Next, an adjustment is made for the confidence estimate, as previously described. Individual data items are then totaled.

Following the confidence adjustment, as an optional exercise, the total value is adjusted again by a factor that reflects the subjectivity of the process and the possibility that participants will not achieve the results they anticipate. In many programs, the participants are very enthusiastic about what they have learned and may be overly optimistic about expected accomplishments. This factor adjusts for participants' overestimation. The adjustment factor can be developed with input from management or established by the staff. In one organization, the benefits are multiplied by 50 percent to develop an even more conservative number to use in the ROI equation.

Finally, the ROI is calculated, using the net program benefits divided by the program costs. This value, in essence, becomes the expected return on investment, after the two adjustments for accuracy and subjectivity.

A word of caution is in order when Level 1 ROI data are used to estimate ROI. These calculations are subjective and may not reflect the extent to which participants will actually apply what they have learned to achieve results. A variety of influences in the work environment can enhance or inhibit participants' attainment of performance goals. Having high expectations at the end of a program is no guarantee that those expectations will be met. Disappointments are documented regularly in programs throughout the world and are reported in research findings (Kaufman, 2002).

While this process is subjective and possibly unreliable, it does have some usefulness. First, if evaluation must stop at this level, this approach provides more insight into the value of a program than data from typical reaction questionnaires. Managers usually find estimated ROI data more useful than a report stating, "40 percent of participants rated the program above average." Unfortunately, a high percentage of evaluations stop at this first level of evaluation. The majority of programs do not enjoy rigorous evaluations at Levels 3 and 4. Reporting Level 1 ROI data is a more useful indication of the potential impact of a program than the alternative of reporting attitudes and feelings about the program.

Second, ROI forecast data can form a basis for comparison of different presentations of the same program. If one version of the program forecasts an ROI of 300 percent, whereas another projects 30 percent, it appears that the first program may have been more effective than the other one. The participants in the first program have more confidence in their planned application of the program material.

Third, collecting data for the ROI estimate brings increased attention to program outcomes. Participants leave the program with an understanding that specific behavior change is expected, and this knowledge produces results for the organization. The issue becomes very clear to participants as they anticipate results and convert them to monetary values. Even if their projected improvement is ignored, the exercise is productive because of the important message that has been sent to participants. It helps to change mindsets about the value, impact, and importance of the program.

Fourth, if a follow-up is planned in order to pinpoint postprogram results, the data collected in the Level 1 evaluation can be very helpful for comparison. For example, in a selling program for Wachovia Bank, the results after the program were compared with the forecast results. Such comparison builds the credibility of a forecasting method. End-of-program data collection also helps participants plan the implementation of what they have learned.

Fifth, the data can be used to secure support for follow-up. For example, most executives, when they see ROI forecast data, will quickly say that they don't believe these data, perhaps with good reason. The best way to see whether the results will materialize is to conduct a follow-up. This is an excellent way to secure support for follow-up when support is absent. Essentially, the data are leveraged to build that support.

The use of Level 1 ROI is increasing; organizations are basing a larger part of their ROI calculations on Level 1 data. Although such estimates may be very subjective, they do add value, particularly when they are part of a comprehensive evaluation system.

Case Study: Retail Merchandise Company—Part B: Level 1 ROI Forecasting

The Retail Merchandise Company implemented a new program called Interactive Selling Skills on a pilot basis in order to improve sales performance. In all, forty-eight sales associates were involved (three groups of sixteen). Sales growth is always a critical issue at RMC and usually commands much management attention. The program focused on initiating simple dialogue with customers, assisting them, and guiding them to a purchase decision. Program participants were expected to improve sales within three months after attending the program. At the end of the three-day program, participants completed a comprehensive reaction questionnaire that asked about specific action items planned as a result of the program and the expected sales increase that could be attributed to the use of skills. In addition, participants were asked to explain the basis for their estimates and place a confidence level on them. The first group of participants provided the data shown in Table 5.2.

After receiving the data, the first step is to analyze the data, using the Guiding Principles as a guide to help determine how to manage

Table 5.2. Data from Participants in Interactive Selling Skills Program

Participant Number	Sales Increase Estimate	Basis	Confidence Level
1	25%	Sales	90%
2	20	2 sales per day	80
3	30	Sales increase	70
4	40	3 sales daily	60
5	30	4 sales each day	95
6	100	More sales	100
7	30	3 more sales	80
8	50	4 sales	75
9	10	1 more sale	30
10	22	2 new sales	80
11	25	Sales	90
12	15	2 sales each day	70
13	0	No increase	60
14	100	Many new sales	95
15	50	Additional sales	50
16	Unlimited	More sales and satisfaction	100

responses. A first step is to look for the error adjustment—have participants adjusted data for confidence? Then toss out extreme or unrealistic data.

On the face of it, these data may not seem very reliable. They came from people who are estimating, perhaps in an optimistic way, the sales increase that they expect to achieve. These participants are excited. They see opportunity and value in the new skills that they have acquired. However, the data can be used in a variety of ways. For example, the process of gathering these data focuses participants on results. It requires that they think more about results and not solely about the learning activity. Also, by gathering these data, the program owner can provide the client with a level of comfort that something will change as a result of the program, a greater level than can be offered from data acquired using a typical Level 1 questionnaire. Finally, a program owner wanting to implement a full-blown ROI study can use these data to pique the interest of the client in hopes of gaining funding necessary to conduct the study, as the following material explains.

ROI Forecast with Learning Data

Testing for changes in skills and knowledge is a very common technique for evaluating learning in programs (Level 2 evaluation). In many situations, participants are required to demonstrate their knowledge or skills at the end of a program, and their performance is expressed as a numerical value. When this type of test is developed and used, it must be reliable and valid. A reliable test is one that is stable over time, yielding consistent results. A valid test is one that measures what it purports to measure. A test should reflect the content of the program, and successful mastery of program content should be related to improved job performance. As a result, there should be a strong relationship between test scores and subsequent on-the-job performance. The strength of this relationship, expressed as a correlation coefficient, is a measure of test validity. Figure 5.3 illustrates a perfect correlation between test scores and job performance.

Figure 5.3. Relationship Between Test Scores and Job Performance

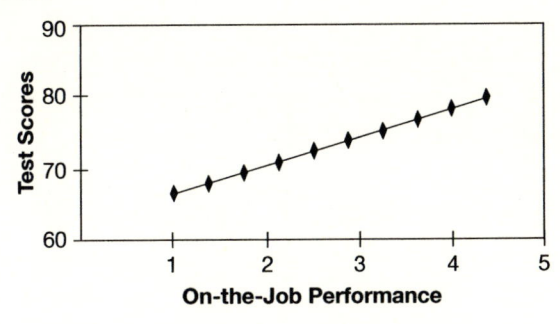

This testing situation provides an excellent opportunity for an ROI calculation with Level 2 data. If there is a statistically significant relationship between test scores and on-the-job performance and the performance can be converted to monetary units, then it is possible to use test scores to estimate the ROI from the program, using the following steps:

- Ensure that the program content reflects the desired on-the-job performance.
- Develop an end-of-program test that reflects program content.
- Establish a statistical relationship between the test data and the output performance of participants.
- Predict performance levels of each participant, using their test scores.
- Convert the performance data to monetary values.
- Compare the net predicted value of the program with program costs.

Case Study: Retail Merchandise Company—Part C: Level 2 ROI Forecasting

When RMC implemented the Interactive Selling Skills program, the program coordinator developed a test in order to predict sales performance based on participants' mastery of the knowledge and skills taught in the program. At the end of the program, participants took the comprehensive test. As part of the test, participants analyzed customer service and sales situations and decided on specific actions. To validate the test, RMC calculated the correlations between test scores and associates' sales performance. The correlation was strong and statistically significant, enabling the program coordinators to use test scores to predict the sales increase for each

Figure 5.4. Correlation Between RMC Test Scores and On-the-Job Sales Increases

[Scatter plot: Test Scores (y-axis, 60–90) vs. On-the-Job Sales Increase (x-axis, 5%–25%), with Average Score line at ~74 intersecting ~14%.]

participant. As a quick way of calculating the estimated return from a program, RMC estimates the output level for each participant, converts the output data to monetary values, and then combines them in order to calculate the estimated ROI. Figure 5.4 shows the correlation.

For the first group of forty-eight participants, the average score on the post-program test was 74, predicting an average sales increase of 14 percent. The average sales per week per associate at the beginning of the program was $9,698. The profit margin was 2 percent, and the cost of the program was $687 per person. A forty-eight-week annual work period was considered.

The ROI is forecast as follows: a 14% sales increase on $9,698 amounts to $1,357. A profit margin of 2 percent means that $27.14 is the profit on the sales increase. However, forty-eight people were involved in the program, so the average profit should be multiplied by forty-eight. Also, the sales measure is a weekly figure, so it should be multiplied by forty-eight weeks in order to yield an annual figure. So the total monetary value is $27.14 × 48 × 48, which equals $62,530. This is the total monetary value of the predicted performance improvement. When this is divided by the cost of the program, or $32,976 ($687 × 48), the BCR is 1:1.9. The forecast predicts that for every dollar invested, $1.90 in benefits will be returned. This translates into a forecast ROI of 90 percent.

This number may not be reliable because it is based on history and does not necessarily indicate what will occur in the future. However, it does provide an indicator of potential program success. This sort of information is useful. In reality, testing relationships such as the one used here may not be known.

Cautions

Again, when end-of-program questionnaires are used, some cautions are in order. The final number is a forecast of the ROI and not the actual value. Although participants acquired skills and knowledge from the program, there is no guarantee that they will apply the techniques and processes successfully and that the desired results will be achieved. This process assumes that the current group of participants has the same relationship to output performance as previous groups. It ignores a variety of environmental influences, which could alter the situation entirely. Finally, the process requires calculating the initial correlation coefficient, which would be difficult to do for most tests.

Advantages

Although this approach develops an estimate based on historical relationships, it can be useful in a comprehensive evaluation strategy because it has several advantages. First, if post-program evaluations (Level 4) are not planned, this process will yield more information about the projected value of the program than would be obtained from raw test scores. This process yields an expected ROI based on the historical relationships involved. Second, because the process develops individual ROI measurements and communicates them to participants, it has the potential to reinforce desired behaviors. It communicates to participants that increased sales and market share are expected as a result of their application of what they learned in the program. Third, this process is likely to have considerable credibility with management and may preclude expensive follow-ups and post-program monitoring. If the relationship on which it is based is statistically sound, the estimate should have credibility with the target audience.

ROI Forecast with Application Data

In almost every program, participants are expected to change their on-the-job behaviors by applying the materials or implementing the program. On-the-job application is critical to program success. Although use of the targeted skills on the job is no guarantee that results will follow, it is an underlying assumption of most programs that if the knowledge and skills are applied, then results will follow. Some of the most prestigious learning organizations, such as Motorola University, base their ultimate evaluation on this assumption. A few organizations take this process a step further by measuring the value of on-the-job behavior change and calculating the ROI. In these situations, estimates are taken from individual participants, their supervisors, the management group, or experts in the field. This process, then, is a forecast of impact, based on changes in behavior on the job immediately after the program. The following steps are used to evaluate the ROI:

1. Specify competencies required in the target job.
2. Indicate what percentage of the job consists of the competencies covered in the program.
3. Determine the monetary value of competencies, using the values of salaries and employee benefits of the participants.
4. Compute the worth of pre-program and post-program skill levels.
5. Subtract post-program values from pre-program values.
6. Compare the net added benefits with the program costs.

This process is described in Chapter Three, where it is called *utility analysis*. It attempts to place a value on the improvement of an individual. Utility analysis examines the behavior change and assigns monetary value based on the salary of the individual; however, it ignores the consequences of the improvement (that is, business impact). Utility analysis is referred to as a Level 3 ROI forecast because it converts changes in behavior to monetary values, using the salaries of the participants as a base.

Case Study: Retail Merchandise Company—Part D: Level 3 ROI Forecasting

RMC implemented the Interactive Selling Skills program, which focused on five basic competencies:

- Identifying customers' needs
- Listening and reacting to customers
- Profiling the user of the product in the electronics department
- Providing excellent customer service
- Recommending specific products

The managers of the sales associates indicated that these five competencies accounted for 55 percent of the sales associate job. In the group that was evaluated, the average annual salary (plus benefits) was $17,332. Multiplying this figure by the amount of job success accounted for by the five competencies (55 percent) yielded a dollar value of $9,533 per participant. If a person were to perform successfully in these competencies for one year, the value to RMC would be $9,533.

Managers rated the associates' skills on each of the competencies on a scale of 1 to 10 before the program was conducted. The average level of skills required to be successful was determined to be 6.32. The average skill rating prior to the program was 4.12, which represented 65 percent of the 6.32. (That is, participants were performing at 65 percent of the level required to be successful in the competencies.) After the program, the skill rating was 6.24, 99 percent of the level needed to be successful.

Dollar values were assigned to the skill levels, based on the participants' salaries. Performance at the required level was worth $9,533. Thus, when they were at a proficiency level of 65 percent, the sales associates were performing at a contribution value of $6,196. Six weeks after the program, the proficiency level of the sales associates reached 99 percent, representing a contribution of $9,438. The difference in these values ($3,242) represented the gain per participant attributable to the program. The program cost $687 per participant.

The BCR is

$$\text{BCR} = \frac{\$3,242}{\$687} = 4.72$$

For every dollar invested, $4.72 is returned. This translates into a 372 percent ROI. This figure is very high.

The ROI figure lacks some credibility because it does not reflect what participants actually do with the skills. Also, the competencies are not available for analysis. However, this approach could be an important alternative for programs that are difficult to forecast because impact data are not readily available.

This program would be best evaluated at Level 4, using actual data collected at the impact level after program implementation. However, for leadership programs in which the impact data may take a variety of forms, this may be a valid approach.

Advantages

Although this process is subjective, it has several useful advantages. First, if there are no plans to track the measurable business impact of a program (Level 4), this approach represents a credible substitute. In many programs—particularly skill-building and competency programs—identifying tangible changes on the job may be difficult. As a result, alternative approaches to determining the worth of a program are needed. Second, this method (utility analysis) has been developed in the literature, so there are several models that can be used. Third, this approach results in data that are usually credible with the top management group if they understand how they were developed and the assumptions behind them. An important point is that the data on the changes in competence level came from the managers, who rated their direct reports, which increases the level of credibility. In this case, the numbers were large enough to make the process statistically significant.

Guidelines for Forecasting

Given the many different time frames for forecasting that are outlined in this chapter, a few guidelines may help you sort through the forecasting possibilities within your organization. These guidelines are based on experience in forecasting a variety of programs (Bowers, 1997).

If You Must Forecast, Forecast Frequently

Forecasting is a process that is both an art and a science, and it needs to be pursued regularly in order to build comfort, experience, and history with the process. Also, those who use the data need to see forecasts frequently in order to integrate forecasting into the evaluation mix.

Consider Forecasting an Essential Evaluation Tool

The first chapter of this book ended with a list of reasons why forecasting ROI is important. The concept is growing in use, and ROI forecasts are being demanded by many organizations. ROI forecasting can be an effective and useful tool when used properly and employed in conjunction with other types of evaluation data. Some organizations have targets for the use of forecasting (for example, if a program exceeds a certain cost, a pre-program forecast will be required). Other organizations target a certain number of programs for a forecast based on reaction data and use the forecasts in the manner described in this chapter. Still other organizations specify some low-level targets for forecasting at Levels 2 and 3. The important point is that you plan for the forecasts and let them be a part of the evaluation mix that is used regularly.

Forecast Different Types of Data

Although most of this chapter focuses on how to develop a forecast using the standard ROI formula, it is helpful to forecast other types of data. A usable, helpful forecast will include predictions about reaction and planned action, the extent of learning, and the extent of application and implementation. Also, the intangible data can be forecast. These types of data are important in anticipating movements and shifts, based on the planned program. Forecasting many types of data is not only helpful in developing the overall forecast but important in understanding the total anticipated impact of the program.

Secure Input from Those Who Know the Process Best

As forecasts are developed, it is essential to gather input from the individuals who best understand the dynamics of the workplace and the measures being influenced by the program. Sometimes, program participants or their immediate managers are the best source. In other situations, a variety of analysts are aware of the major influences in the workplace and the dynamics of those changes. Go to the experts. It will increase the accuracy of your forecast as well as the credibility of the final results.

Understand That Long-Term Forecasts Will Usually Be Inaccurate

Forecasting works much better in a short time frame. For most short-term scenarios, a better grasp of the influences that might drive the measure is possible. When you are working on a long-term basis, a variety of unforeseen new influences can enter the process and drastically change the impact measures. If a long-term forecast is needed, it should be updated regularly as part of a continuously improving process.

Expect Forecasts to Be Biased

Forecasts consist of data coming from those who have an interest in the issue. Some will want the forecast to be optimistic; others will have a pessimistic view. Almost all input is biased in one way or another. Every attempt should be made to minimize the bias, adjust for the bias, and adjust for the uncertainty in the process. Still, your audience will need to recognize that despite your best efforts to eliminate bias, a forecast is a biased prediction.

Commit to the Hard Work of Serious Forecasting

The value of forecasting often depends on the amount of effort put into the process. High-stakes programs need to take a serious approach, collecting all possible data, examining different scenarios, and making the best prediction possible. In these situations, mathematical tools can be valuable aids.

Routinely Review the Success of Forecasting

As forecasts are made, it is imperative that you revisit the forecast with actual post-program data to check the accuracy and the success of the forecast. Performing such reviews on a regular basis aids in the continuous improvement of forecasting processes. Sources may prove to be more credible or less credible, and specific inputs may be more biased or less biased. Some analyses may be more appropriate than others. Constant improvement of the methods and approaches for forecasting within the organization is critical to success.

Be Aware That Assumptions Are the Most Serious Errors in Forecasting

Of all the variables that enter into the forecasting process, the ones with the greatest potential for error are the assumptions made by the individual providing the forecast. Assumptions must be clearly understood and communicated. When multiple inputs are involved, each forecaster should use the same set of assumptions, if possible.

Keep in Mind That Decision Making Is the Purpose of Forecasting

The most important use of forecasting is providing information and input for decision makers. Forecasting is a tool for those who are trying to make decisions about a program. It is not a process for maximizing the output or minimizing any particular variable. It is not a process for dramatically changing the way in which programs are implemented. It is a process for providing data for decisions; that's the greatest utility of forecasting.

Final Thoughts

This chapter illustrates that ROI forecasts can be developed at different points in the life cycle of a program. Although most practitioners and researchers use application and impact data for ROI calculations, there are situations in which Level 3 and Level 4 data are not available or evaluations at those levels are not planned or attempted. ROI forecasts that are developed before a program is implemented can be useful to management and staff, focusing attention on the potential economic impact of a program. Forecasts based on reaction data or learning data are also possible.

Be aware that ROI forecasts may result in a false sense of accuracy. On one hand, as would be expected, pre-program ROI forecasts are the lowest in credibility and accuracy but have the advantage of being inexpensive and relatively easy to conduct. On the other hand, ROI forecasts using Level 3 data are highest in credibility and accuracy but are more expensive and difficult to develop.

Although ROI calculations based on impact (Level 4) data are preferred, ROI forecasts based on other types of data are an important part of a comprehensive and systematic evaluation process. Integrating forecasts into the evaluation routine usually means that targets for different types of ROI forecasts should be established.

References

Armstrong, S. *Principles of Forecasting: A Handbook for Researchers and Practitioners*. Boston: Kluwer, 2001.

Bowers, D. *Forecasting for Control and Profit*. Menlo Park, Calif.: Crisp Publications, 1997.

Kaufman, R. "Resolving the (Often-Deserved) Attacks on Training." *Performance Improvement*, 2002, 41(6), pp. 5–6.

Index

A
Accountability
  journey to increased, 81
  trend toward increased, 13–14, 52
Acquisition costs, 33
Annualized values, 58–59
Anthony, R., 71
Application data
  Retail Merchandise Company case study on, 130–132
  ROI forecasting with, 129–130

B
Benchmarking
  limitations of, 15
  program costs, 2–5
Benefit-cost ratio (BCR), 59–60, 76, 77
Bernthal, P., 80
Bowers, D., 132
Byham, B., 80

C
Cascio, W., 80
Coordinator expenses, 34
Cost accumulation, 42–43
Cost classification matrix, 40–42
Cost Estimating Worksheet, 44–46
Cost estimation
  cost accumulation used for, 42–43
  cost classification matrix for, 40–42
  process and worksheet for, 43–46
Cost forecasting, 6
Cost reporting, 38–40
Cost Worksheet, 47
Costs
  calculating fully loaded, 23–26
  employee benefits, 30
  as essential to ROI Methodology, 1
  estimating, 40–46
  reasons for developing, 2–7
  See also Program costs

D
Data
  ROI forecast using application, 129–132
  ROI forecast using learning, 125–129
  ROI forecast using reaction, 119–125
Delivery/implementation costs, 33–36
Designing/development costs, 31–33
Discounted cash flow, 76–78

E
Economic value added (EVA), 82
Efficiency improvement, 6
Employee benefits costs, 30

Index

Evaluation
  costs of program, 36
  drivers of, 51
  of program cost-effectiveness, 5–7
  ROI as ultimate level of, 8–9
  See also ROI evaluations
Evidence-based management, 14–15

F
Facilitator expenses, 34
Facilities costs, 34–35
Fact-based management, 14–15
Fair Labor Standards Act (FLSA), 22–23
Federal Information Agency (FIA) case study, 46–53, 54
Financial terminology
  definitions as critical, 57–58
  misuse of, 73
  three different ROI ratios, 72–73
Forecasting ROI. *See* ROI forecasting

G
Global Financial Services case study, 66–67

H
Healthcare, Inc. case study, 67–68
Horngren, C., 72
Human resources costs, 3–4
Hunter, J., 79

I
Implementation/delivery costs, 33–36
Internal rate of return (IRR), 78

L
Learning data
  Retail Merchandise Company case study using, 126–129
  ROI forecast with, 125–129

M
Management
  evidence based or fact-based, 14–15
  new business focus of, 14
Metro Transit Authority case study, 68–69
Midwest Electric case study, 69–71
Monitoring costs, benefits of, 2–7

N
Needs assessment/analysis, 30–31
Negative ROI, 87–89
Nickson, D., 12

O
O'Byrne, S., 82
Overhead costs, 36–38

P
Participant expenses, 34
Payback period, 76, 77
Pearlman, K., 79
Pfeffer, J., 15
Pilot program ROI forecasting, 119
Positioning ROI evaluation
  choosing the right formula, 71–73
  determining ROI targets, 75
  developing ROI objectives, 73–75
Pre-program ROI forecasting
  basic model for, 106–108
  conversion to money for, 115
  estimating program costs for, 115–116
  Retail Merchandise Company (RMC) case study on, 116–118
  securing input used in, 114–115
  sources of expert input used in, 113–114
  steps for, 108–113
Profit center
  relationship of ROI evaluation levels to, 81–82
  using strategy of, 80–83
Program costs
  accumulation and estimation of, 40–46
  benchmarking, 2–5
  benefits of monitoring, 6–7
  categories of, 30–38

Index   139

cost classification matrix for, 40–42
employee benefits factor of, 30
evaluating cost-effectiveness, 5–7
Federal Information Agency (FIA) case study of, 46–53, 54
increase of total, 13
pressures to disclose all, 21–23
program cycle context of, 28–29
prorated versus direct, 29
reporting, 38–40
ROI forecasting of, 16–17
sources of, 27–28
See also Costs
Program failures, 12–13
Programs
  materials and fees of, 35–36
  post-program comparisons of, 17–18
  ROI forecast as compliance by, 18

R
Reaction data
  Retail Merchandise Company case study using, 123–125
  ROI forecasting with, 119–123
Reece, J., 71
Regional State University (RSU), 48
Retail Merchandise Company (RMC) case study
  as pre-program ROI forecasting example, 116–118
  as ROI calculation example, 62–66
  as ROI forecasting with application data example, 130–132
  as ROI forecasting with learning data example, 126–129
  as ROI forecasting with reaction data example, 123–125
  See also ROI calculation case studies
Risk forecasting, 17
ROA (return on anticipation), 72–73
ROA (return on assets), 72

ROCE (return on capital employed), 72
ROCE (return on client expectations), 73
ROE (return on expectations), 72
ROE (return on owners' equity), 72
ROI calculation case studies
  Federal Information Agency (FIA), 46–53, 54
  Global Financial Services, 66–67
  Healthcare, Inc., 67–68
  Metro Transit Authority, 68–69
  Midwest Electric, 69–71
  See also Retail Merchandise Company (RMC) case study
ROI calculations
  Approach A to, 24–25
  Approach B to, 25
  basic issues in, 57–61
  comparison of BCR, payback period and, 77
  cost categories used in, 30–38
  examples of, 62–71
  fully loaded costs approach to, 23–26
  policies and guidelines for, 26–27
  tracking benefits along with costs, 26
ROI calculation issues
  annualized values, 58–59
  benefit-cost ratio, 59–60
  concerns to observe during evaluation, 91–94
  definitions/terminology of, 57–58, 72–73
  possibility of negative ROI, 87–89
  ROI can be very large, 85–87
  ROI formula, 60–61
  ROI myths as, 94–101
  validity and credibility of, 89–91
ROI evaluations
  cautions to observe during, 91–94
  chain of impact driving, 74
  defining value and consistency of, 11–12
  executive appetite for, 16

ROI evaluations (*Continued*)
   forces driving increased demand for, 12–16
   forecasting, 16–18
   importance of, 7–12
   positioning, 71–75
   reporting program costs, 38–46
   tabulating program costs, 1–7
   See also Evaluation
ROI forecasting
   with application data, 129–132
   benefits of, 16–18
   at different times and levels, 104
   guidelines for, 132–135
   with learning data, 125–129
   with pilot program, 119
   pre-program, 106–118
   with reaction data, 119–125
   trade-offs of, 103–106
ROI formula, 60–61
ROI Institute, 22
ROI Methodology
   benefits of using, 101
   data addressing value captured by, 12
   distinguishing between profit center strategy and, 80–83
   evaluation as ultimate level of, 8–9
   financial terminology used with, 57–58, 72–73
   myths regarding, 94–101
   problems and barriers revealed by, 87
ROI targets, 75

S
Schmidt, F., 79
"Show me" generation, 10–11
Siddons, S., 12
Sutton, R., 15

T
Technological support costs, 33

U
Uncertainty forecasting, 17
Utility analysis, 78–80

V
Value
   annualized, 58–59
   determination of, 9
   economic value added (EVA), 82
   factors that contribute to high ROI, 85–87
   the new definition of, 11–12

Y
Young, S., 82

About the Authors

Jack J. Phillips, Ph.D., a world-renowned expert on accountability, measurement, and evaluation, provides consulting services for Fortune 500 companies and major global organizations. The author or editor of more than fifty books, Phillips conducts workshops and makes conference presentations throughout the world.

His expertise in measurement and evaluation is based on more than twenty-seven years of corporate experience in the aerospace, textile, metals, construction materials, and banking industries. Phillips has served as training and development manager at two Fortune 500 firms, as senior human resources officer at two firms, as president of a regional bank, and as management professor at a major state university. This background led Phillips to develop the ROI Methodology, a revolutionary process that provides bottom-line figures and accountability for all types of learning, performance improvement, human resources, technology, and public policy programs.

Phillips regularly consults with clients in manufacturing, service, and government organizations in forty-four countries in North and South America, Europe, Africa, Australia, and Asia.

Books most recently authored by Phillips include *Show Me the Money: How to Determine ROI in People, Projects, and Programs* (Berrett-Koehler, 2007); *The Value of Learning* (Pfeiffer, 2007); *How to Build a Successful Consulting Practice* (McGraw-Hill,

2006); *Investing in Your Company's Human Capital: Strategies to Avoid Spending Too Much or Too Little* (Amacom, 2005); *Proving the Value of HR: How and Why to Measure ROI* (Society for Human Resource Management, 2005); *The Leadership Scorecard* (Butterworth-Heinemann, 2004); *Managing Employee Retention* (Butterworth-Heinemann, 2003); *Return on Investment in Training and Performance Improvement Programs*, 2nd edition (Butterworth-Heinemann, 2003); *The Project Management Scorecard* (Butterworth-Heinemann, 2002); *How to Measure Training Results* (McGraw-Hill, 2002); *The Human Resources Scorecard: Measuring the Return on Investment* (Butterworth-Heinemann, 2001); *The Consultant's Scorecard* (McGraw-Hill, 2000); and *Performance Analysis and Consulting* (ASTD, 2000). Phillips served as series editor for the In Action casebook series of the American Society for Training and Development (ASTD), an ambitious publishing project featuring thirty titles. He currently serves as series editor for Butterworth-Heinemann's Improving Human Performance series and for Pfeiffer's new Measurement and Evaluation series.

Phillips has received several awards for his books and his work. The Society for Human Resource Management presented him with an award for one of his books and honored a Phillips ROI study with its highest award for creativity. ASTD gave him its highest award, Distinguished Contribution to Workplace Learning and Development. *Meeting News* named Phillips one of the twenty-five most influential people in the meetings and events industry, based on his work on ROI within the industry.

Phillips holds undergraduate degrees in electrical engineering, physics, and mathematics; a master's degree in decision sciences from Georgia State University; and a Ph.D. degree in human resources management from the University of Alabama.

Jack Phillips has served on the boards of several private businesses—including two NASDAQ companies—and several associations, including ASTD, and nonprofit organizations. He is

chairman of the ROI Institute, Inc., and can be reached at (205) 678-8101, or by e-mail at jack@roiinstitute.net.

Lizette Zúñiga, Ph.D., is an independent senior consultant with ROI Institute. With more than fifteen years of professional experience, she has expertise in leadership and team development, conflict resolution, diversity training, organizational culture assessment, merger integration, strategic planning, program evaluation, ROI, survey design, and needs assessment.

Zúñiga has served as both an internal and an external consultant for Fortune 500 companies. Formerly with First Data Corporation, she led the corporate university's team in assessment and measurement efforts. She executed a university dashboard, linking strategic business objectives to organizational development initiatives as well as critical success factors and key measures. She executed impact studies showing the value of learning and development efforts. In her current capacity as a performance consultant, she assists organizations by conducting various types of assessments and surveys, including organizational culture assessment, needs assessment, and leadership competency assessment. She also assesses the business impact of organizational development interventions and facilitates leadership and team development activities. The impact studies she has conducted address such areas as e-learning, leadership development, sales performance, organizational change interventions, mergers and acquisitions, call center simulation, career development, and use of technology.

Zúñiga's academic contribution is extensive. She has served as an adjunct professor for a major university, teaching adult learning theory and practice and presentation skills, and she currently facilitates a three-day certification course in measuring and evaluating learning and a two-day certification course in ROI for ASTD. She also serves as an online instructor for the University Alliance ROI certification course and is an associate with the ROI Institute. She holds a master's degree in psychology with a concentration in cross-cultural psychology and psychometry from Georgia State University and a Ph.D. degree in leadership and human resource development (HRD) from Barry University. She is certified in Myers-Briggs typology and in ROI evaluation. She has also contributed to the HRD literature by publishing several articles on ROI and program evaluation.

Pfeiffer Publications Guide

This guide is designed to familiarize you with the various types of Pfeiffer publications. The formats section describes the various types of products that we publish; the methodologies section describes the many different ways that content might be provided within a product. We also provide a list of the topic areas in which we publish.

FORMATS

In addition to its extensive book-publishing program, Pfeiffer offers content in an array of formats, from fieldbooks for the practitioner to complete, ready-to-use training packages that support group learning.

FIELDBOOK Designed to provide information and guidance to practitioners in the midst of action. Most fieldbooks are companions to another, sometimes earlier, work, from which its ideas are derived; the fieldbook makes practical what was theoretical in the original text. Fieldbooks can certainly be read from cover to cover. More likely, though, you'll find yourself bouncing around following a particular theme, or dipping in as the mood, and the situation, dictate.

HANDBOOK A contributed volume of work on a single topic, comprising an eclectic mix of ideas, case studies, and best practices sourced by practitioners and experts in the field.

An editor or team of editors usually is appointed to seek out contributors and to evaluate content for relevance to the topic. Think of a handbook not as a ready-to-eat meal, but as a cookbook of ingredients that enables you to create the most fitting experience for the occasion.

RESOURCE Materials designed to support group learning. They come in many forms: a complete, ready-to-use exercise (such as a game); a comprehensive resource on one topic (such as conflict management) containing a variety of methods and approaches; or a collection of like-minded activities (such as icebreakers) on multiple subjects and situations.

TRAINING PACKAGE An entire, ready-to-use learning program that focuses on a particular topic or skill. All packages comprise a guide for the facilitator/trainer and a workbook for the participants. Some packages are supported with additional media—such as video—or learning aids, instruments, or other devices to help participants understand concepts or practice and develop skills.

- *Facilitator/trainer's guide* Contains an introduction to the program, advice on how to organize and facilitate the learning event, and step-by-step instructor notes. The guide also contains copies of presentation materials—handouts, presentations, and overhead designs, for example—used in the program.
- *Participant's workbook* Contains exercises and reading materials that support the learning goal and serves as a valuable reference and support guide for participants in the weeks and months that follow the learning event. Typically, each participant will require his or her own workbook.

ELECTRONIC CD-ROMs and web-based products transform static Pfeiffer content into dynamic, interactive experiences. Designed to take advantage of the searchability, automation, and ease-of-use that technology provides, our e-products bring convenience and immediate accessibility to your workspace.

METHODOLOGIES

CASE STUDY A presentation, in narrative form, of an actual event that has occurred inside an organization. Case studies are not prescriptive, nor are they used to prove a point; they are designed to develop critical analysis and decision-making skills. A case study has a specific time frame, specifies a sequence of events, is narrative in structure, and contains a plot structure—an issue (what should be/have been done?). Use case studies when the goal is to enable participants to apply previously learned theories to the circumstances in the case, decide what is pertinent, identify the real issues, decide what should have been done, and develop a plan of action.

ENERGIZER A short activity that develops readiness for the next session or learning event. Energizers are most commonly used after a break or lunch to

stimulate or refocus the group. Many involve some form of physical activity, so they are a useful way to counter post-lunch lethargy. Other uses include transitioning from one topic to another, where "mental" distancing is important.

EXPERIENTIAL LEARNING ACTIVITY (ELA) A facilitator-led intervention that moves participants through the learning cycle from experience to application (also known as a Structured Experience). ELAs are carefully thought-out designs in which there is a definite learning purpose and intended outcome. Each step—everything that participants do during the activity—facilitates the accomplishment of the stated goal. Each ELA includes complete instructions for facilitating the intervention and a clear statement of goals, suggested group size and timing, materials required, an explanation of the process, and, where appropriate, possible variations to the activity. (For more detail on Experiential Learning Activities, see the Introduction to the *Reference Guide to Handbooks and Annuals*, 1999 edition, Pfeiffer, San Francisco.)

GAME A group activity that has the purpose of fostering team spirit and togetherness in addition to the achievement of a pre-stated goal. Usually contrived—undertaking a desert expedition, for example—this type of learning method offers an engaging means for participants to demonstrate and practice business and interpersonal skills. Games are effective for team building and personal development mainly because the goal is subordinate to the process—the means through which participants reach decisions, collaborate, communicate, and generate trust and understanding. Games often engage teams in "friendly" competition.

ICEBREAKER A (usually) short activity designed to help participants overcome initial anxiety in a training session and/or to acquaint the participants with one another. An icebreaker can be a fun activity or can be tied to specific topics or training goals. While a useful tool in itself, the icebreaker comes into its own in situations where tension or resistance exists within a group.

INSTRUMENT A device used to assess, appraise, evaluate, describe, classify, and summarize various aspects of human behavior. The term used to describe an instrument depends primarily on its format and purpose. These terms include survey, questionnaire, inventory, diagnostic, survey, and poll. Some uses of instruments include providing instrumental feedback to group

members, studying here-and-now processes or functioning within a group, manipulating group composition, and evaluating outcomes of training and other interventions.

Instruments are popular in the training and HR field because, in general, more growth can occur if an individual is provided with a method for focusing specifically on his or her own behavior. Instruments also are used to obtain information that will serve as a basis for change and to assist in workforce planning efforts.

Paper-and-pencil tests still dominate the instrument landscape with a typical package comprising a facilitator's guide, which offers advice on administering the instrument and interpreting the collected data, and an initial set of instruments. Additional instruments are available separately. Pfeiffer, though, is investing heavily in e-instruments. Electronic instrumentation provides effortless distribution and, for larger groups particularly, offers advantages over paper-and-pencil tests in the time it takes to analyze data and provide feedback.

LECTURETTE A short talk that provides an explanation of a principle, model, or process that is pertinent to the participants' current learning needs. A lecturette is intended to establish a common language bond between the trainer and the participants by providing a mutual frame of reference. Use a lecturette as an introduction to a group activity or event, as an interjection during an event, or as a handout.

MODEL A graphic depiction of a system or process and the relationship among its elements. Models provide a frame of reference and something more tangible, and more easily remembered, than a verbal explanation. They also give participants something to "go on," enabling them to track their own progress as they experience the dynamics, processes, and relationships being depicted in the model.

ROLE PLAY A technique in which people assume a role in a situation/scenario: a customer service rep in an angry-customer exchange, for example. The way in which the role is approached is then discussed and feedback is offered. The role play is often repeated using a different approach and/or incorporating changes made based on feedback received. In other words, role playing is a spontaneous interaction involving realistic behavior under artificial (and safe) conditions.

SIMULATION A methodology for understanding the interrelationships among components of a system or process. Simulations differ from games in that they test or use a model that depicts or mirrors some aspect of reality in form, if not necessarily in content. Learning occurs by studying the effects of change on one or more factors of the model. Simulations are commonly used to test hypotheses about what happens in a system—often referred to as "what if?" analysis—or to examine best-case/worst-case scenarios.

THEORY A presentation of an idea from a conjectural perspective. Theories are useful because they encourage us to examine behavior and phenomena through a different lens.

TOPICS

The twin goals of providing effective and practical solutions for workforce training and organization development and meeting the educational needs of training and human resource professionals shape Pfeiffer's publishing program. Core topics include the following:

- Leadership & Management
- Communication & Presentation
- Coaching & Mentoring
- Training & Development
- E-Learning
- Teams & Collaboration
- OD & Strategic Planning
- Human Resources
- Consulting

What will you find on pfeiffer.com?

- The best in workplace performance solutions for training and HR professionals
- Downloadable training tools, exercises, and content
- Web-exclusive offers
- Training tips, articles, and news
- Seamless on-line ordering
- Author guidelines, information on becoming a Pfeiffer Affiliate, and much more

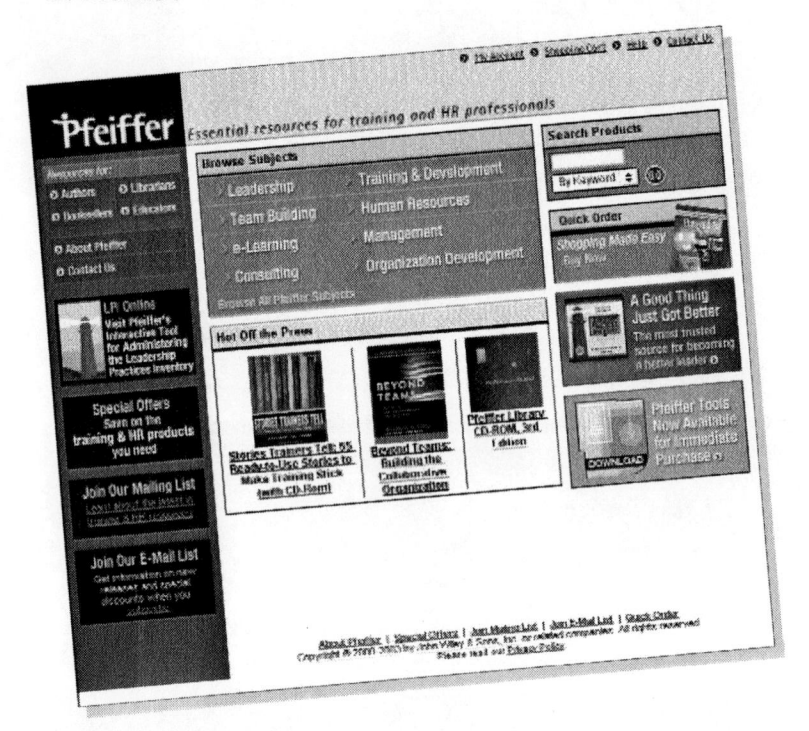

Discover more at www.pfeiffer.com

Measurement and Evaluation Series

Series Editors
Patricia Pulliam Phillips, Ph.D., and Jack J. Phillips, Ph.D.

A six-book set that provides a step-by-step system for planning, measuring, calculating, and communicating evaluation and Return-on-Investment for training and development, featuring:

- Detailed templates
- Complete plans
- Ready-to-use tools
- Real-world case examples

The M&E Series features:

1. *ROI Fundamentals: Why and When to Measure ROI*
   (978-0-7879-8716-9)
2. *Data Collection: Planning For and Collecting All Types of Data*
   (978-0-7879-8718-3)
3. *Isolation of Results: Defining the Impact of the Program*
   (978-0-7879-8719-0)
4. *Data Conversion: Calculating the Monetary Benefits*
   (978-0-7879-8720-6)
5. *Costs and ROI: Evaluating at the Ultimate Level*
   (978-0-7879-8721-3)
6. *Communication and Implementation: Sustaining the Practice*
   (978-0-7879-8722-0)

Plus, the *ROI in Action Casebook* (978-0-7879-8717-6) covers all the major workplace learning and performance applications, including Leadership Development, Sales Training, Performance Improvement, Technical Skills Training, Information Technology Training, Orientation and OJT, and Supervisor Training.

The **ROI Methodology** is a comprehensive measurement and evaluation process that collects six types of measures: Reaction, Satisfaction, and Planned Action; Learning; Application and Implementation; Business Impact; Return on Investment; and Intangible Measures. The process provides a step-by-step system for evaluation and planning, data collection, data analysis, and reporting. It is appropriate for the measurement and evaluation of *all* kinds of performance improvement programs and activities, including training and development, learning, human resources, coaching, meetings and events, consulting, and project management.

Special Offer from the ROI Institute

Send for your own ROI Process Model, an indispensable tool for implementing and presenting ROI in your organization. The ROI Institute is offering an exclusive gift to readers of The Measurement and Evaluation Series. This 11" x 25" multicolor foldout shows the ROI Methodology flow model and the key issues surrounding the implementation of the ROI Methodology. This easy-to-understand overview of the ROI Methodology has proven invaluable to countless professionals when implementing the ROI Methodology. Please return this page or e-mail your information to the address below to receive your free foldout (a $6.00 value). Please check your area(s) of interest in ROI.

Please send me the ROI Process Model described in the book. I am interested in learning more about the following ROI materials and services:

- ☐ Workshops and briefing on ROI
- ☐ Books and support materials on ROI
- ☐ Certification in the ROI Methodology
- ☐ ROI software
- ☐ ROI consulting services
- ☐ ROI Network information
- ☐ ROI benchmarking
- ☐ ROI research

Name _____
Title _____
Organization _____
Address _____
Phone _____
E-mail Address _____

Functional area of interest:

- ☐ Learning and Development/Performance Improvement
- ☐ Human Resources/Human Capital
- ☐ Public Relations/Community Affairs/Government Relations
- ☐ Consulting
- ☐ Sales/Marketing
- ☐ Technology/IT Systems
- ☐ Project Management Solutions
- ☐ Quality/Six Sigma
- ☐ Operations/Methods/Engineering
- ☐ Research and Development/Innovations
- ☐ Finance/Compliance
- ☐ Logistics/Distribution/Supply Chain
- ☐ Public Policy Initiatives
- ☐ Social Programs
- ☐ Other (Please Specify) _____

Organizational Level

- ☐ executive
- ☐ student
- ☐ management
- ☐ evaluator
- ☐ consultant
- ☐ researcher
- ☐ specialist

Return this form or contact The ROI Institute
P.O. Box 380637
Birmingham, AL 35238-0637

Or e-mail information to info@roiinstitute.net
Please allow four to six weeks for delivery.